International Law and Chemical, Biological, Radio-Nuclear (CBRN) Events

International Law and Chemical, Biological, Radio-Nuclear (CBRN) Events

Towards an All-Hazards Approach

Edited by

Andrea de Guttry
Micaela Frulli
Federico Casolari
Ludovica Poli

BRILL
NIJHOFF

LEIDEN | BOSTON

This volume was funded by DIRPOLIS Istituto Scuola Superiore Sant'Anna. 2) Dipartimento di Scienze Giuridiche – Alma Mater Studiorum Università degli Studi di Bologna. 3) Dipartimento di Scienze Giuridiche – Università degli Studi di Firenze. 4) Dipartimento di Giurisprudenza – Università degli Studi di Torino

The Library of Congress Cataloging-in-Publication Data is available online at https://catalog.loc.gov

Typeface for the Latin, Greek, and Cyrillic scripts: "Brill". See and download: brill.com/brill-typeface.

ISBN 978-90-04-50798-2 (hardback)
ISBN 978-90-04-50799-9 (e-book)

This book is printed on acid-free paper and produced in a sustainable manner.

Contents

PART 2
Prevention, Preparedness, Response and Recovery in the Case of CBRN Events

Preface

Events and threats involving the release of Chemical, Biological and Radio-Nuclear (CBRN) substances, as well as the threat of malicious use of Explosives, are among the most fearsome risks in contemporary times. Despite not being a new phenomenon, CBRN risks attracted renewed attention following the 2001 anthrax letters case, which occurred only a few weeks after 9/11. Concern over potential CBRN terrorism was also heightened following the terrorist attacks in Paris (2015) and Brussels (2016). Post-9/11 CBRN events include the use of fentanyl by Russian authorities in the 2002 Moscow Theatre hostage crisis and the recent nerve agent poisoning cases in the UK (2018) and in Russia (2020). But CBRN threats and events may also include the use of banned weapons, both by State and non-State actors, as occurred in Syria; the use of CBRN agents for smaller-scale crimes; industrial accidents involving release of CBRN agents into the environment; and natural disasters or other calamities – such as the spread of COVID-19 in 2020 and the ensuing global pandemic.

Despite the increasing relevance of such events and threats, the level of attention paid to developing a common understanding of both the severity and scale of the full range of CBRN risks and how to address them is still limited; indeed, an agreed definition of what constitutes a CBRN event is still far from being crystalised in relevant international instruments. Also, limited attention has been devoted so far to mapping obligations stemming from the wide range of applicable norms of international law. In this respect, while it is evident that traditional areas such as International Humanitarian Law (IHL, limiting the use of CBRN weapons during armed conflicts) and Arms Control and Disarmament Law (ACDL, restricting their development, possession and transfer) play a significant role in shaping relevant obligations, the contribution given by other strands of international law – namely International Disaster Law, Counter-Terrorism Law, International Criminal Law, International Environmental Law, Human Rights Law, and, as made apparent by the COVID-19 crisis, International Health Law – cannot be ignored. Such a highly complex and fragmented legal framework makes it more difficult to clearly identify relevant obligations and may discourage the adoption of cross-cutting approaches. However, an analysis carried out only in the light of a limited selection of areas of international law risks offering an oversimplified picture of the corresponding legal landscape.

The lack of a holistic attitude towards CBRN threats and events in the international law literature is also due to the consolidated and rigid approach of States and International Organisations (IOs). Notwithstanding the diversity of CBRN agents and events, States and IOs have traditionally used – and are still using – the CBRN label mainly when addressing security issues – or even more narrowly, counter-terrorism issues – whereas the CBRN categorisation is very rarely employed, for instance, when addressing the consequences of natural disasters and public health emergencies. An illustrative example of such an attitude is represented by UN Security Council Resolution 1373 (2001) – the first resolution to refer to CBRN agents, although not under this acronym – where the emphasis is put on the connection between international terrorism and the illegal movement of nuclear, chemical, biological and other potentially deadly materials. The UN's response to the Ebola outbreak of 2014 – with the Security Council qualifying the 'unprecedented extent of the Ebola outbreak in Africa' as a 'threat to international peace and security' (UNSC Res. 2177 of 18 September 2014) – may also be considered a manifestation of such a trend. Even admitting that such a 'securitarian' approach may help to achieve more effective results in CBRN scenarios, it clearly risks downgrading other needs which are duly taken into consideration in other strands of international law (starting from the need to protect human rights and fundamental freedoms).

Against this background, the present volume aims at assessing the current legal framework governing CBRN risks and events and envisaging how this framework might be further developed and better implemented. In particular, filling the above-mentioned gaps, the volume intends to develop a consistent definition of CBRN events, adopting an 'all-hazards' approach, covering both the intentional and accidental release of CBRN substances. Moreover, it seeks to identify in a systematic and comprehensive way all existing obligations, both in times of war and in times of peace. In this respect, the decision has been made to map relevant obligations according to the four phases of the emergency management cycle: namely, prevention (*ie* measures aimed at reducing the risk of a CBRN event), preparedness (eg measures aimed at developing response capabilities should a CBRN emergency occur), response (eg standards and best practices to adopt in order to adequately respond and minimise the risks) and recovery (eg duties to ensure a timely recovery from a CBRN event).

The analysis carried out in this volume is structured into five complementary parts. Part 1 sets the general scene: it firstly identifies a working definition of CBRN events that may be adapted according to the all-hazards approach adopted in the volume; then it investigates the role that different actors may play and develops a taxonomy of the general obligations to prevent, prepare for, respond to and recover from CBRN emergency situations.

Moving from this general framework, Part 2 zooms in to identify specific prevention, preparedness, response and recovery obligations incumbent on

States and other relevant actors in relation to different CBRN scenarios. In particular, the corresponding chapters investigate the state of the art related to CBRN terrorism, industrial and nuclear accidents, and natural disasters (including epidemic outbreaks).

In Part 3, the focus is on CBRN weapons. Here, the existing obligations under IHL and ACDL are carefully examined, together with obligations concerning nuclear disarmament and testing, transfer of CBRN weapons, and existing mechanisms elaborated to ensure their enforcement by States.

Following the analysis of sectoral contexts where specific CBRN obligations may be identified, Part 4 considers some horizontal issues that are recurring more and more in the legal discourse surrounding CBRN events. Here, the interplay with Human Rights Law (HRL) is explored in depth with the aim of identifying both legitimate restrictions to human rights and positive obligations under HRL in the context of CBRN events. The interaction with International Environmental Law and the increasing (and problematic) role of private actors and new technologies are also taken into consideration.

Part 5 examines enforcement mechanisms and remedies. The analysis includes consideration of international criminal law obligations and also the international law framework imposing criminal repression at municipal level of CBRN-related violations that do not amount to international crimes. The part is completed by a study of the IHL and HRL obligations concerning access to remedies for the victims of CBRN events.

Significantly, the analysis carried out in the volume combines the study of general international law and universal instruments with consideration of the cooperation established in specific fora and IOs. A particular emphasis, in this respect, is placed on the solutions elaborated by the European Union (EU). This is not only due to the well-known authority EU law enjoys *vis-à-vis* the municipal law of the Member States, leading in turn to the emergence of harmonised solutions at supranational level. Also relevant is the fact that the law of the European Union has led to the introduction of a plethora of tools which may contribute to minimising CBRN risks (also in the context of the reaction to the COVID-19 pandemic), thus representing a (possible) benchmark for other frameworks of cooperation. In light of the foregoing, and considering the systematic approach the volume adopts in dealing with the different domains of international law, the choice has been made to incorporate the analysis of relevant EU instruments into the above-mentioned parts of the volume, instead of isolating it in a self-contained section.

The volume closes with a concluding chapter where Andrea Gioia, in light of the preceding analyses, offers a broad assessment of the current state of international obligations related to CBRN events.

This volume is one of the outcomes of the project 'International legal obligations related to Prevention, Preparedness, Response and Recovery from CBRN events and status of their implementation in Italy – CBRN-Italy' (ref. no. 20175M8L32), which has been funded by the Italian Ministry of University and Research as a Research Project of National Relevance. The CBRN-Italy project has been carried out since 2019 by the Scuola Superiore Sant'Anna (which is also the lead partner of the Project), the University of Bologna, the University of Florence and the University of Turin. It involves more than 30 researchers (also from other Italian universities), investigating and mapping the legal obligations related to CBRN events and assessing the adequacy of the Italian legal and operative frameworks. This volume traces its origin to a number of events organised (in person and online) within the framework of the CBRN-Italy project to discuss the findings of research activities carried out by contributors with national and international practitioners and subject matter experts, and to the subsequent scholarly dialogue established under the project. We hope that the decision to publish this volume in Open Access format will further support the strengthening of studies and reflections on CBRN risks.

The editors express their gratitude to all those have contributed to the volume, COVID-19 pandemic notwithstanding, to the members of the Advisory Board of the project for their precious suggestions, and to all participants who, while not appearing in the volume, took part in the events and discussions that have made it possible. We are deeply grateful to Andrea Gioia, who agreed to write the conclusions to this volume. Many thanks also go to Silvia Venier for her invaluable support in all stages of the production process of the volume, to Enrico Tinti for the preparation of the analytical index, and to Anthony Wenton for the language revision. The editors of this volume are greatly indebted to BRILL for their enthusiastic support for this editorial project.

Pisa, Bologna, Florence, Turin, December 2021
Andrea de Guttry
Federico Casolari
Micaela Frulli
Ludovica Poli

Acknowledgments

This book is the outcome of research carried out in the scope of the project 'International legal obligations related to Prevention, Preparedness, Response and Recovery from CBRN events and status of their implementation in Italy (CBRN-ITALY)', funded by the Italian Ministry of Education, University and Research under the PRIN Programme (Progetti di Rilevante Interesse Nazionale), Grant Agreement n° 20175M8L32.

Notes on Contributors

Alessandro Mario Amoroso
is PhD fellow in Human Rights and Global Politics at the Scuola Superiore Sant'Anna in Pisa (Italy). He has been a Legal Adviser with the International Committee of the Red Cross and a Programme Officer with the Security and Law Programme at the Geneva Centre for Security Policy. His fields of research are international humanitarian law, human rights, international criminal law, and international law on the use of force. He holds an LLM from the Geneva Academy of International Humanitarian Law and Human Rights and a Law degree from the University of Naples Federico II.

Chiara Tea Antoniazzi
is Post-doctoral Fellow in International Law at the Scuola Superiore Sant'Anna in Pisa (Italy). She holds a Master of Laws and a PhD in International Studies from the University of Trento and spent research periods at the Netherlands Institute of Human Rights (Utrecht, the Netherlands) and at the Raoul Wallenberg Institute of Human Rights and Humanitarian Law (Lund, Sweden). She has investigated various aspects of the promotion and protection of human rights at the regional and international levels; currently, her research focuses on the interrelations between climate change and international law.

Christine Bakker
is currently a Visiting Lecturer at the Scuola Superiore Sant'Anna in Pisa (Italy) and a Visiting Research Fellow at the British Institute of International and Comparative Law in London (UK). She holds a PhD in public international law from the European University Institute (EUI) in Florence (Italy). Previously, she worked at the European Commission (DG Development), as Research Fellow (EUI), Adjunct Professor (LUISS, Rome), Visiting Lecturer (University Rome-3), and undertook consultancies for international organisations. She has published widely on human rights, children's rights, international environmental law and climate change, including I. Alogna, C. Bakker, J.P. Gauci (eds.), "Climate Change Litigation: Global Perspectives" (Brill/Nijhoff, 2021).

Marco Balboni
is Full Professor of International Law at the University of Bologna, where he is also Director of Organisational Unit of the Department of Political and Social Sciences, Forlì Campus. His research interests include, among others,

international refugee law and EU migration law, international and EU non-discrimination law and the role of the EU in promoting and protecting human rights worldwide. Among other activities, he is member of the Editorial board of Diritto, Immigrazione, Cittadinanza, co-director of the University of Bologna's multidisciplinary research network on gender studies Almagender – IRT and has been senior legal adviser for the EU Fundamental Rights Agency.

Martina Buscemi
is Assistant Professor of International Law at the University of Milan. She has published several articles and book chapters on different topics of international law, a monograph on the remedies available for human rights violations committed by the United Nations, and she is co-editor of the book "Legal Sources in Business and Human Rights. Evolving Dynamics in International and European Law", published in 2020 with Brill. She worked at the University of Florence and has been a Visiting Research Fellow at the Max Planck Institute for Comparative Public Law and International Law and at Kobe University.

Francesca Capone
is Assistant Professor (tenure track position) of Public International Law at the Scuola Superiore Sant'Anna in Pisa (Italy). She holds a Joint PhD Degree from the Scuola Superiore Sant'Anna and Tilburg University. In 2012–2013 she worked as a research fellow at the British Institute of International and Comparative Law in London. She has been a visiting fellow and guest lecturer at several academic institutions, and she has undertaken research on a wide range of topics, encompassing the law of remedies, climate change law, the law of State responsibility, the legal framework governing the response to CBRN events and the main issues connected to international law and terrorism.

Federico Casolari
is Associate Professor of EU Law at the University of Bologna. He is Deputy Head of the Department of Legal Studies and member of the University Senate of the University of Bologna. He has over 10 years of international experience in the area of international and EU disaster law. He is one of the editors of the "Routledge Handbook on Human Rights and Disasters" (2018) and member of the Editorial Committee of the "Yearbook of International Disaster Law".

Elena Corcione
is Post-doc Research Fellow in International Law at the University of Gastronomic Sciences in Pollenzo (Bra, Italy). Previously, she has been Post-doc researcher in International Law at the University of Turin and at the Institute

for the International Legal Studies of the Italian National Research Council. She has a PhD from the University of Turin. Her research interests and main publications focus on international law of treaties, international human rights law, international environmental law and business and human rights. She is member of the Italian Society of International Law and the Global Business and Human Rights Scholars Association.

Annalisa Creta
PhD, is a Research Fellow in Public International Law at the Scuola Superiore Sant'Anna in Pisa (Italy), where she focuses on issues related to civilian crisis management. Her main interests lie in Human Rights Law, the International Law on the Use of Force, Collective Security Law and International Disaster Response Law, and she is the author of several publications on the above topics.

Andrea de Guttry
is Full Professor of Public International Law at the Scuola Superiore Sant'Anna in Pisa (Italy). In the period 2005–2020, he has been Deputy Rector in charge of the Master Programmes and of its life-long learning activities. He has over 25 years of international experience in researching and training in the area of disaster management. He has been a Visiting Professor in several Universities worldwide and is one of the editors of the book "International Disaster Response Law", published in 2012 with ASSER/Springer Verlag.

Costanza Di Francesco Maesa
is a Post-Doc Researcher in International Law at the University of Florence. She holds a Double Doctoral diploma in European Law between the University of Bologna and the University of Strasbourg. She has been a post-Doctoral researcher in European Law at the University of Torino and a visiting Fellow in several European Universities. She participated in several European projects. Her research encompasses International and European Environmental law, human rights law, with a focus on data protection, the regulation of new technologies and the adoption of adequate accountability mechanisms in the EU.

Sophie Domaine
is a PhD student in Public International Law at the University of Turin. She holds a Licence en Droit from Université Paris V – Descartes, a Law degree from the University of Turin and a LLM in Environmental Law from Queen Mary University of London. She is a member of the Italian Society of International Law.

Alice Farina
is a student of Master Degree in International Security Studies, offered by the Scuola Superiore Sant'Anna in Pisa and the University of Trento. She has graduated from Maastricht University in European Studies.

Gian Maria Farnelli
PhD, is Senior researcher in international law at the Department of Legal Studies, University of Bologna. He has been research assistant for arbitrators and counsel in inter-State and investor-State disputes. His publications address issues of the law of the sea, investment law, environmental law, State immunity and the law of international adjudication. He is Editorial Assistant of the online journal Questions of International Law and secretary of the Book series "La ricerca del diritto nella comunità internazionale" (Editoriale scientifica).

Federico Ferri
is Research Fellow in EU Law at the University of Bologna, where he also served as Adjunct Professor of EU Internal Market legislation. He holds a PhD in European Law from the University of Bologna and Droit Public from the University of Strasbourg. Over last years he published multiple works about, inter alia, EU environmental law. He cooperates with academic institutions, public bodies, companies and the editorial boards of law reviews. He participates in many national, European and international research networks and projects.

Micaela Frulli
is Full Professor of International Law at the University of Florence, Department of Legal Studies. She was Marie Curie Fellow at the European University Institute in 2010. Her areas of interest include international criminal law, the law of immunities, the use of force in international law; she published extensively in national and international law journals and collected volumes. She is one of the Managing Editors of the journal *Questions of International Law* (http://www.qil-qdi.org/). She is member of the International Law Association, of the European Society of International Law and of the Italian Society of International Law.

Andrea Gioia
is Full Professor of International Law at the University of Modena and Reggio Emilia. After a Law Degree from the University of Pisa, he obtained a Doctorate in International Law from "La Sapienza" University. He was Researcher at the

University of Trento and Associate Professor at the University of Trieste and at the University of Modena. He also worked as expert for the Italian Ministry of Foreign Affairs and as Scientific Adviser to the International Expert Group on Nuclear Liability of the International Atomic Energy Agency (IAEA). From 2010 to 2021, he was on leave from his university and served as Senior Legal Officer at the IAEA.

Laura Magi
is Associate Professor of International Law at the University of Florence, Law Department where she teaches International Law and International Law and Global Challenges. She holds the 'Alberigo Gentili' PhD at the University of Padua and was Max Weber Fellow at the European University Institute in Florence. In 2010 she won the "SIDI Prize" for the best article written by a young International Law scholar. Her research interests include conflicts of norms and jurisdictions, human rights law and international responsibility.

Diego Mauri
is Post-Doc Researcher in International Law at the University of Florence. He holds a PhD in "Human Rights: Evolution, Protection and Limits" from the University of Palermo. He currently teaches at the Master Program "International Relations and European Studies" at the School of Political Sciences "Cesare Alfieri" and at the LLM in "Leadership and Strategic Analysis" in collaboration with the Italian Air Force ("Istituto di Scienze Militare Aeronautiche").

Federica Montanaro
is student of the Master on International Security Studies offered by the Scuola Superiore San'Anna in Pisa and University of Trento. She graduated at LUISS University in Rome, in Politics Philosophy and Economics. She spent a semester at the University Torcuato Di Tella in Buenos Aires, approaching the field of Latin American Studies.

Giulia Perrone
is PhD Fellow in Public International Law at the University of Turin where she is currently studying the impact of scientific progress on international human rights obligations. Her main research interests include biolaw, international human rights law and humanitarian law. She holds a Law Degree from LUISS University and an LLM in International Human Rights and Humanitarian Law from the University of Essex.

Ludovica Poli
is Associate Professor of International Law at the Department of Law of the University of Turin, where she teaches Public International Law and Human Rights Law. Her main field of research is human rights law, although she also explores other fields, including humanitarian law, international criminal law, and the law of international organizations. Her publications cover issues such as the role of regional organizations in peace and security maintenance; the responsibility to protect and humanitarian intervention; women rights, gender and sex crimes in international law; the impact of developments in medical science on fundamental rights and the intersection between human rights protection and bioethics.

Luca Poltronieri Rossetti
is Post-doctoral Researcher in international law at the Scuola Superiore Sant'Annas in Pisa (Italy). He holds a PhD in European and Comparative Legal Studies (international law track) from the University of Trento. His research mainly focuses on international criminal justice, law and procedure. He has interned with the Extraordinary Chambers in the Courts of Cambodia and he has been visiting scholar at the Amsterdam Center for International Law.

Stefano Saluzzo
is Assistant Professor of International Law at the Università del Piemonte Orientale in Alessandria (Italy). He has been visiting lecturer at the Brussels School of International Studies of the Kent University and visiting researcher at the Max Planck Institute for International Procedural Law in Luxembourg. He is also the author of various publications in the field of international humanitarian law, EU external relations and international economic law.

Emanuele Sommario
is Associate Professor of International Law at the Scuola Superiore Sant'Anna in Pisa (Italy). He has been co-responsible of a state-financed research project on International Disaster Law (2013–2016) and is the coordinator of the Jean Monnet Module on European and International Human Rights Standards in Disaster Settings (2021–2023). He is one of the editors of the "Routledge Handbook on Human Rights and Disasters" (2018) and is a member of the editorial board of the "Yearbook of International Disaster Law" (Brill).

Andrea Spagnolo
is Associate Professor of International Law in the Law Department of the University of Turin, where he teaches International Law, International Humanitarian Law and is Director of the International Human Rights Legal Clinic. He has a PhD in International Law from the University of Milan. He has held visiting positions at various universities and research centers. He is the author of a book on the attribution of conduct in the context of European Union peacekeeping operations and of several publications on the responsibility of international organizations, international migration law, peacekeeping, international humanitarian law and human rights. He was member of the Board of the Italian Society of International and European Union Law (2018–2021) and is member of the Faculty of the Center for Defense Higher Studies.

Silvia Venier
is Postdoctoral Fellow in International Law at the Scuola Superiore Sant'Anna in Pisa (Italy). She holds a PhD from the same University and spent research periods at the Essex University Human Rights Centre and at the Centre for Disaster Research of the Copenhagen University. She has published in peer review journals and contributed to edited volumes on topics related to positive obligations under human rights law to protect against emergency situations, international law governing epidemic outbreaks, the right to information and early warning in disaster settings.

Luisa Vierucci
is an expert specialised in International Humanitarian Law, International Human Rights Law and International Criminal Law. She is the author of the monograph on "Gli accordi fra governo e gruppi armati di opposizione nel diritto internazionale" (Editoriale Scientifica, 2013) and a member of the Italian Red Cross Committee of Experts on International Humanitarian Law.

Susanna Villani
is Postdoctoral researcher in EU law at the Department of Political and Social Sciences of the University of Bologna. She is Adjunct Professor for the course of EU Internal Market and International Trade Law at the Forlì Campus of the University of Bologna. In 2018, she got the PhD in EU law at the University of Bologna in co-tutorship with the National Distance Education University (UNED) in Madrid. Winner of the 2019 edition of the "Riccardo Monaco" SIDI award.

Annamaria Viterbo
is Associate Professor of International Law at the Department of Law of the University of Torino and a Law Fellow at the Collegio Carlo Alberto. Formerly a member of the Italian bar, she obtained a PhD in International Economic Law from Bocconi University of Milan. After a Legal Internship at the ECB, she was Jean Monnet Fellow at the Robert Schuman Center for Advanced Studies of the European University Institute and Visiting Scholar at the International Monetary Fund Legal Department. Her research primarily concerns international economic law, with a particular focus on international economic and financial organizations, sovereign debt and EU law of the Economic and Monetary Union.

PART 1

Setting the Scene: Defining CBRN Events, Actors and General Obligations in the Different Phases

CHAPTER 1

The Challenge of Outlining the CBRN Definitional Framework

Micaela Frulli

1 CBRN Events: A Rapidly Evolving Definitional Framework?

Since the early years of the 21st century, incidents related to chemical, biological, radiological, and nuclear agents have been referred to as CBRN threats or events. However, there is no universally accepted definition of a CBRN threat or event, and States, international organisations (IOs) and non-State actors have given their own definitions and designed their own strategies to face such threats. At times, the abbreviation CBRNE is also used, to take into account the use of explosives (E) and improvised explosive devices (IEDs) in terrorist attacks. Although a CBRN legal framework has been established in the context of some IOs, there seems to be a general lack of coordination among the different actors involved, even at the initial stage of identifying the most relevant challenges and including them under a CBRN categorisation.

CBRN threats and events may include the use of chemical, biological, radiological and nuclear weapons, both by State and non-State actors (including terrorist movements); the use of CBRN agents for smaller-scale crimes; industrial accidents involving the release of CBRN agents into the environment; natural disasters or other calamities – such as the spread of COVID-19 in 2020 and the ensuing world pandemic.[1] However, notwithstanding the diversity of CBRN agents and events, States and IOs have traditionally used the CBRN label mainly when addressing security issues – or even more narrowly in a counter-terrorism perspective – whereas, the CBRN categorisation is very rarely employed when addressing natural disasters and public health emergencies. A telling example of the predominant view is UN Security Council resolution 1373 (2001) – the first resolution to refer to CBRN agents (although not under this acronym) – where the emphasis was placed on the connection between international terrorism and the illegal movement of nuclear, chemical, biological

1 Hence, the role of private actors such as multinational enterprises is also relevant, see ch 2 by Di Francesco Maesa.

and other potentially deadly materials.[2] Again in a counter-terrorism perspective, the UN Security Council adopted resolution 1540 (2004), where it affirmed that the proliferation of CBRN weapons and their means of delivery, and the illicit trafficking of related materials, constitute a threat to international peace and security.[3] The acronym was not used in either of these resolutions, but we can see that the CBRN concept was starting to take shape and progress in the direction of setting obligations for States to counter the proliferation and smuggling of weapons of mass destruction, with the specific objective of preventing terrorist acts.[4] Indeed, within the counter-terrorism context, various measures were adopted by the UN Security Council in the following years.[5]

On the other hand, no express references to CBRN threats are found if one looks at the UN framework for disaster relief or, more generally, to the area commonly labelled as disaster risk reduction (DRR). The Sendai Framework for Disaster Risk Reduction 2015–2030 not only does not explicitly refer to CBRN threats, but it excludes armed conflicts and it is mainly focused on natural disasters. Hence, the urgent call by the UN Secretary-General's Special Representative for Disaster Risk Reduction, Mami Mizutori, for the disaster management agencies to include biological hazards and health emergencies as a top priority when developing their preparedness and response capacities.[6] The debate is ongoing on the need for a paradigm shift towards an all-hazards

2 'The Security Council [...] Notes with concern the close *connection between international terrorism* and transnational organized crime, illicit drugs, money-laundering, illegal arms trafficking, *and illegal movement of nuclear, chemical, biological and other potentially deadly materials*, and in this regard emphasizes the need to enhance coordination of efforts on national, subregional, regional and international levels in order to strengthen a global response to this serious challenge and threat to international security', UN Doc. S/RES/1373 (28 September 2001) (emphasis added).

3 'Gravely concerned by the threat of illicit trafficking in nuclear, chemical, or biological weapons and their means of delivery, and related materials, which adds a new dimension to the issue of proliferation of such weapons and also poses a threat to international peace and security', UN Doc. S/RES/1540 (28 April 2004).

4 See also, for another example, the CBRN glossary, adopted by the European Commission Directorate-General Home Affairs Directorate A: Internal security Unit A.1: Crisis management – Terrorism, available at <http://encircle-cbrn.eu/wp-content/uploads/2021/04/cbrn_glossary_en.pdf> (all links were last accessed on 20 May 2021). For the EU response to CBRN events, see ch 10 by Villani, ch 15 by Balboni, ch 19 by Ferri.

5 Addressing CBRN events from a counter-terrorism perspective is indeed a crucial topic to be addressed. Obligations related to prevention, preparedness, response and recovery in the event of CBRN terrorism, including those stemming from UNSC resolutions are analysed in depth in Part II, Section 2.1, ch 7 by Poltronieri Rossetti, ch 8 by de Guttry, ch 9 by Perrone.

6 UNDRR Press Release, 12 March 2020, *UNDRR urges disaster management agencies to prioritize biological hazards*, at <https://www.undrr.org/news/undrr-urges-disaster-management-agencies-prioritize-biological-hazards>. See Part II, Section 2.3: Prevention, preparedness,

approach and for a transition from managing disasters to managing risks, as the development of the Global Risk Assessment Framework (GRAF) concept clearly shows.[7]

2 CBRN Definitional Framework: A Mandatory Shift towards an All-Hazards Approach

In light of this rapidly evolving scenario, fast-tracked by the COVID-19 global pandemic, a broad interpretation of the CBRN category is called for, with a view to including a variety of different events; that is to say, an all-hazards approach must be made mandatory.[8] One of the basic assumptions underlying this volume is that most of the rules emerging in disaster law (both related to man-made and natural disasters) and documents drafted by IOs in this context – although not referring explicitly nor exclusively to CBRN threats – could also be applied to all kind of incidents related to CBRN agents. The CBRN label may still be very useful in the way it has been developed until now – *ie* referred to mainly for its security and counter-terrorism dimensions – but at the same time it has to be construed as applicable to a category of events and threats that is becoming broader in scope.

---

response and recovery in the event of naturally occurring CBRN events, including epidemic outbreaks.

7 'We need a transition from managing disasters to managing risk. *We need to shift from managing "conventional" hazards to engineering an improved understanding of the dynamic interactions with systemic risks*. We need to explore the facilitation of a "new system of relations" that allows future theories and solutions to emerge that are "wider in scope, more accurate in prediction, and solve more problems [...] We recognize that using the same ways of understanding risk that we have always used has made us ill-equipped to manage the challenges we face. A clear example of this is the COVID-19 global emergency', Marc Gordon, Scott Williams, 'Shifting the paradigm: introducing the Global Risk Assessment Framework (GRAF)' UNDRR, 17 April 2020 (emphasis added), available at <https://www.preventionweb.net/news/view/71352>. For the GRAF concept note (September 2018) prepared by a Group of Expert selected by UNISDR (United Nations Office for Disaster Risk Reduction), see <https://www.preventionweb.net/files/globalplatform/5cd89ca4c27b3GRAF_Concept_Note_2018_FINAL.pdf>. See also the *ILC Draft Articles on the Protection of Persons in the Event of Disasters* (2016).

8 In the most recent Report of the UN Secretary General on the Implementation of the Sendai Framework, it is significantly stated that: 'The Sendai Framework presents a paradigm for understanding and managing systemic risk under which the prevailing focus on natural hazards is expanded to include human-made, technological, environmental and biological hazards', UNGA, 'Implementation of the Sendai Framework for Disaster Risk Reduction 2015–2030', Report of the Secretary General, UN Doc. A/75/226 (23 July 2020), para 6.

Against the background of this unavoidable paradigm shift, it is timely and appropriate to investigate whether there is room for a better coordination of international efforts to prevent, prepare, respond to and recover from CBRN threats and events, highlighting the points of connection among the different legal frameworks (or lack thereof) or, more precisely, the points of connection among the different sets of obligations that have emerged and strategies that have developed up until now to prepare and react to different kinds of risks posed by disasters or hazardous events.[9]

To give a significant example: there is a strong point of contact between public health and security issues, as the Ebola outbreak of 2014 clearly demonstrated.[10] The COVID-19 pandemic has already precipitated exceptional humanitarian crises,[11] which may require unprecedented coordination among States in terms of a security or peace maintenance response. The UNSC could not initially adopt a resolution, due to the high tension between the US and China and the US refusal to allow any reference to the World Health Organization.[12] On 3 April 2020, the UN General Assembly adopted a resolution titled 'Global solidarity to fight the coronavirus disease 2019 (COVID-19)'.[13]

9 See Part II, where a comprehensive research approach is adopted.

10 With resolution 2177, the SC determined that the Ebola outbreak in West Africa was a threat to international peace and security (UN Doc S/RES/2177 (2015) determined that: 'the unprecedented extent of the Ebola outbreak in Africa constitutes a threat to international peace and security'.) and recommended that States take a number of steps to help bring the disease under control. Despite the difference between the Ebola outbreak and more 'traditional' threats to the peace, 130 States co-sponsored resolution 2177 and were keen to consider the spread of the disease as a threat to the peace. Anna Hood identifies five categories of explanations that States gave for supporting the resolution, the most interesting one seems to be that of human security broadly interpreted, see A Hood, 'Ebola: A Threat to the Parameters of a Threat to the Peace?' (2015) 16 *Melbourne Journal of International Law*.

11 See 'COVID-19 and Deadly Conflict', *International crisis group*, at <https://www.crisisgroup.org/pandemics_public_health_deadly_conflict>.

12 A Franco-Tunisian draft resolution failed to get adopted in April, *International Rescue Committee*, Press Release, *UN Security Council fails to support global cease-fire*, see <https://www.rescue.org/press-release/un-security-council-fails-support-global-ceasefire-shows-no-response-covid-19>.

13 Here the GA notes 'with great concern the threat to human health, safety and well-being caused by the coronavirus disease 2019 (COVID-19) pandemic, which continues to spread globally'. It then 'reaffirms the central role of the United Nations system in the global response to the coronavirus disease 2019 (COVID-19) pandemic' and it calls for 'intensified international cooperation to contain, mitigate and defeat the pandemic, including by exchanging information, scientific knowledge and best practices and by applying the relevant guidelines recommended by the World Health Organization' UN Doc. A/RES/74/270, 3 April 2020, available at <https://undocs.org/en/A/RES/74/270>.

At the same time, the SG called the attention of the UNSC to a variety of challenges to peace and stability caused by the pandemic.[14] However, due to the lack of agreement among the P5, it was not until 1 July 2020 that the UNSC adopted resolution 2352 where, for the first time, it called for a general ceasefire and humanitarian pause in armed conflicts across the globe.[15]

In sum, COVID-19 and any similar kind of threat fall firmly into the category of CBRN events as understood today. This does not mean that all such events – including the current pandemic – must be inevitably securitised or addressed through a security lens or by using the 'war' metaphor.[16] On the contrary, one of the objectives of this book is precisely to analyse the multitude of potential legal frameworks and the different sets of obligations related to CBRN events – from international health regulations to human rights law, from disarmament and IHL (including the use of CBRN weapons) to environmental law – and to explore their possible interactions.

In light of the above, it is important to adopt, as a common analytical framework, the phases of the disaster management cycle: prevention, preparedness, response and recovery.[17] This framework is a useful instrument for mapping international obligations in various fields and their implementation by States at different moments, as well as for highlighting the merits and pitfalls of legal tools that may be used with regard to CBRN events. The four phases may be briefly described as follows:

---

14 See the General remarks of the Secretary General before the Security Council, 9 April 2020 <https://www.un.org/sg/en/content/sg/statement/2020-04-09/secretary-generals-remarks-the-security-council-the-covid-19-pandemic-delivered>.

15 UN Doc. S/RES/2352 (2020). E Pobjie, 'Covid-19 as a threat to international peace and security: The role of the UN Security Council in addressing the pandemic', *EJILTalk!*, 27 July 2020 <https://www.ejiltalk.org/covid-19-as-a-threat-to-international-peace-and-security-the-role-of-the-un-security-council-in-addressing-the-pandemic/>.

16 Some observers warned about the perils of securitising COVID-19, see C Connolly 'War and the Coronavirus Pandemic', *Third World Approaches to International Law Review, Reflections* #15/2020, 9 April 2020; E Cusato, Beyond War Talk: Laying Bare the Structural Violence of the Pandemic, *EJIL Talk!*, 3 May 2020 <https://www.ejiltalk.org/beyond-war-talk-laying-bare-the-structural-violence-of-the-pandemic/>.

17 For a more detailed description of the phases, see the working paper by S Venier, 'CBRN emergency management cycle: working definitions', available on the Project CBRN_Italy website at <http://www.cbrn-italy.it/en/task-12-phases-cbrn-emergency-management-cycle>; see also ch 3 by Venier, who notes that there is some confusion about the exact boundaries between key concepts related to the emergency management cycle, including the phases of prevention, mitigation and preparedness; see also remarks on definitions in ch 4 by de Guttry and ch 5 by Bakker.

1) Prevention includes those 'activities and measures to avoid existing and new disaster risks' and measures aimed at 'lessening or minimizing of the adverse impacts of a hazardous event' (mitigation) if a disaster occurs anyway.[18] Prevention is crucial to avoiding CBRN events and it includes risks and vulnerabilities assessments.
2) Preparedness, in the DRR terminology, is defined as the knowledge and capacities developed by governments, professional response and recovery organisations, communities and individuals to effectively anticipate, respond to and recover from the impacts of likely, imminent or current disasters. Regarding CBRN events, preparedness is also connected to risk assessments and to capacity building in the form of early-warning systems and procedures that can be quickly implemented in case of need.
3) Response refers to 'actions taken directly before, during or immediately after a disaster in order to save lives, reduce health impacts, ensure public safety and meet the basic subsistence needs of the people affected'. To give an example connected to the COVID-19 pandemic, response activities may include public health measures such as isolation and quarantine.
4) Recovery concerns 'the restoring or improving of livelihoods and health, as well as economic, physical, social, cultural and environmental assets, systems and activities, of a disaster affected community or society, aligning with the principles of sustainable development and "build back better", to avoid or reduce future disaster risk'. With respect to recovery after a CBRN event, it is crucial that victims are provided with adequate and long-term support.

Even a brief description clearly shows that the four phases are not isolated compartments. They are instead to be considered as communicating vessels, so that measures and tools devised for one of the phases may be useful for the others.

18 See Section V, Recommendations of the open-ended intergovernmental expert working group on terminology relating to disaster risk reduction (DRR updated terminology), included in Report of the open-ended intergovernmental expert working group on indicators and terminology relating to disaster risk reduction, 1 December 2016, UN Doc. A/71/644. The recommendations were endorsed by the UNGA Resolution 71/276, UN Doc. A/RES/71/276, 2 February 2017. All the definitions reported in this paragraph are contained in this Report, at 21–22, see <https://www.preventionweb.net/files/50683_oiewgreportenglish.pdf>.

3 An Overview of the CBRN Events Covered in This Book

In light of the above, the CBRN events covered in this book include small- and large-scale, slow and rapid onset, natural and man-made incidents and disasters caused by a CBRN agent.

3.1 *Chemical Threats/Agents*

Chemical threats/events include, in the first place, the weaponisation of various kinds of gas, their use during armed conflicts and their use (including by non-State/terrorist actors) also in times of peace. Notwithstanding various norms prohibiting chemical weapons, they have been repeatedly used, as widely reported, in various conflicts both by States and non-State actors.[19] Chemical weapons have also been used in terrorist attacks causing small or large-scale casualties and spreading panic. Relevant examples include cases dating back to the 1990s. For instance, the use of sarin gas in Japan in June 1994 and again in March 1995 caused great shock and dramatically showed how chemical agents could be employed against helpless citizens.[20]

Over the years, terrorist networks such as Al-Qaeda and ISIL – besides their involvement in armed conflicts and their use of chemical weapons in that context – have been suspected of planning chemical attacks in European cities.[21] Therefore, it is unsurprising that concerns over chemical agents are most frequently expressed in the context of threats from terrorism.[22]

Cases where chemical agents were used to carry out assassinations or assassination attempts are also to be taken into consideration. The VX nerve agent was used to kill North Korean leader Kim Jong Un's half-brother, Kim Jong

19 See for instance A M Amoroso, *The Douma Chemical attack*, Factsheet available on the Project CBRN Italy website at <http://www.cbrn-italy.it/sites/default/files/Factsheet_Douma%20chemical%20attack.pdf>. For an assessment, including the threat of environmental damage, see Part III of this book.

20 See A Vitale, *Tokyo subway sarin attack*, Factsheet available on the Project CBRN Italy website at <http://www.cbrn-italy.it/sites/default/files/factsheet_tokyo%20subway%20sarin%20attack.pdf>. On the adoption of the chemical weapons convention, see ch 23 by Poli.

21 For example, D Bamber, C Hastings, and R Syal, 'Bin Laden British Cell Planned Gas Attack on European Parliament', *The Daily Telegraph* (*London*), 16 September 2001.

22 See Part II, Section 2.1: Prevention, preparedness, response and recovery in the event of CBRN terrorism. It is also appropriate to investigate whether the strategies developed from a counter-terrorism perspective could be adapted to other threats. See for instance the EU shift towards an all-hazards approach; on EU efforts: ch 6 by Casolari, ch 10 by S Villani, ch 15 by Balboni, ch 19 by Ferri.

Nam, at Kuala Lumpur International Airport in Malaysia in 2017.[23] Toxic chemical agents were used in the UK in 2018 in attacks against three-individuals, Mr Sergej Skripal, Ms Yulia Skripal and Mr Nicholas Bailey.[24] The consequences of this kind of use of toxic chemicals in public spaces can extend well beyond the direct target and could potentially affect a large number of victims.

Chemical threats/events also include the accidental release of toxic agents, such as from a chemical plant or a pipeline. The most serious chemical accident ever recorded is the Bhopal disaster that occurred in 1984 in India, where more than 3,000 people died after a highly toxic gas was released from a Union Carbide Pesticides Factory.[25] Very serious industrial accidents had already occurred in Europe, such as the Flixborough accident in 1974[26] and the Seveso disaster in 1976.[27] In addition, the transportation and storage of chemical agents may also cause very serious accidents, like the one that occurred on 4 August 2020 at the port of Beirut when a large amount of ammonium nitrate stored in a warehouse exploded causing more than 2,000 deaths, hundreds of injuries and leaving 300,000 homeless.[28] With respect to accidental chemical events, this book will investigate the role of private actors in detail.[29] Lastly, it is also important to note that natural disasters, such as earthquakes or volcanic eruptions, can also release chemical substances.

---

23 R Latiff, E Chow, *Chemical weapon VX nerve agent killed North Korean leader's half brother: Malaysian Police*, Reuters, 24 February 2017, at <https://www.reuters.com/article/us-northkorea-malaysia-kim/chemical-weapon-vx-nerve-agent-killed-north-korean-leaders-half-brother-malaysian-police-idUSKBN16303Z>.

24 UN Press release, 14 March 2018, available at <https://www.un.org/press/en/2018/sc13247.doc.htm>.

25 Indian officials estimate that the gas leak left nearly 3,000 people dead and 50,000 people permanently disabled and that 15,000 people died subsequently from exposure to the poisonous gas (Unofficial estimates range up to 7,000–8,000 initial deaths, and 15,000–20,000 subsequent deaths), see <https://www.business-humanrights.org/en/union-carbidedow-lawsuit-re-bhopal>.

26 M Dunton, 'Flixborough, 1 June 1974', *The National Archives, Records and Research*, 20 May 2014, available at <https://blog.nationalarchives.gov.uk/flixborough-1-june-1974/>.

27 See M Frulli, D Mauri, *The Seveso disaster*, Factsheet available on the Project CBRN Italy website at <http://www.cbrn-italy.it/sites/default/files/Factsheet_Seveso%20disaster.pdf>.

28 See 'Beirut explosion: What we know so far', BBC News, 11 August 2020, at <https://www.bbc.com/news/world-middle-east-53668493>.

29 See ch 2 by Di Francesco Maesa, ch 30 by Corcione. More in general, see Part II, Section 2.2. Prevention, preparedness, response and recovery in the event of CBRN industrial accidents.

3.2 *Biological Threats/Events*

Biological agents may also be weaponised in a variety of different ways. They may be used as weapons delivered through bombs and missiles, or delivered indirectly through the contamination of water and food. History is full of attempts at using diseases in biological warfare.[30] The 1925 Geneva Protocol was the first explicit ban on the use of biological agents as weapons of war.[31] In spite of the ban, several countries began biological warfare research programmes during World War II. The most prominent one was the Japanese programme, led by the notorious 'Unit 731', located in Manchuria (1932–1945).[32] Negotiations to prohibit biological weapons became part of the international agenda with the creation of the United Nations. The result was the 1972 Biological Weapons Convention (BWC), which prohibited possession of any biological or toxin weapons,[33] although without establishing a monitoring mechanism.[34]

Besides the use of biological weapons by States, both in armed conflicts and outside that context, the issue of bioterrorism has emerged.[35] Al Qaeda allegedly started a biological weapons programme in the late 1990s, in Afghanistan, but there is no evidence that it ever acquired any biological agents. These activities were disrupted by the US Operation Enduring Freedom and the programme was never put back together.[36] Other radical jihadist groups

---

30 E M Eitzen Jr, E T Takafuji, 'Historical overview of biological warfare', in F Sidell, E T Takafuji, D R Franz (eds.) *Medical Aspects of Chemical and Biological Warfare* (Borden Institute, Walter Reed Army Medical Center, 1997), 415–423.

31 J R Walker, 'The 1925 Geneva Protocol: Export Controls, Britain, Poland and Why the Protocol Came to Include "Bacteriological" Warfare', *Harvard Sussex Program Occasional Paper* 05 (2016).

32 P Williams, D Wallace, *Unit 731: Japan's Secret Biological Warfare in World War II* (Free Press 1989); S Harris, 'The Japanese biological warfare programme', in E Geissler, J van Courtland Moon (eds.), *Biological and Toxin Weapons: Research, Development, and Use from the Middle Ages to 1945* (OUP 1999), 127.

33 See ch 23 by Poli.

34 On monitoring mechanisms, see ch 26 by Buscemi.

35 W R Clark, 'Bioterrorism Beginnings: The Rajneesh Cult, Oregon, 1985', in OUP Blog, 5 October 2009, at <https://blog.oup.com/2009/10/bioterrorism-beginnings/>.

36 M Leitenberg, *Assessing the Biological Weapons and Bioterrorism Threat* (University of Michigan 2005); R Mowatt- Larssen, '*Al Qaeda Weapons of Mass Destruction Threat: Hype or Reality?*' *Belfer Center for Science and International Affairs, Harvard Kennedy School*, January 2010, available at <https://www.belfercenter.org/sites/default/files/legacy/files/al-qaeda-wmd-threat.pdf>.

also expressed interest in BW but eventually focused on capabilities easier to acquire such as chemical weapons.[37]

On the other hand, the COVID-19 pandemic clearly shows that infectious diseases can spread on a worldwide basis with very little time to react and with very serious and long-lasting detrimental effects on global health. The category of Global Catastrophic Biological Risks (GCBR) applies to risks involving biological agents – whether naturally emerging or re-emerging, deliberately created and released, or laboratory-engineered and escaped – that could lead to sudden, extraordinary, widespread disaster beyond the collective capability of national and international organisations and the private sector to control.[38] Actually, when comparing the hypothetical nature of intentional attacks with biological weapons/agents with the death toll of the current pandemic (and with the number of victims dying each year from preventable infections), one might question how reasonable it is for States and IOs to allocate vast resources and efforts to preparations for a remote and speculative human-inflicted disaster instead of investing in the management of GCBR events.[39]

3.3 *Radio-Nuclear Threats/Events*

Radio-nuclear agents may also be weaponised for potential use in the context of armed conflicts and/or in the context of terrorist attacks. An example of a radiological threat is the use of radiological dispersal devices (RDDs also called dirty bombs) that disperse radioactive substances used for medical or industrial applications, which are relatively easy to obtain, by attaching them to explosive devices.[40] The efforts to negotiate a radiological weapons

37 S Hummel, 'The Islamic State and WMD: Assessing the Future Threat', *CTC Sentinel* 9, no. 1 (January 2016), 18–22.

38 Global Catastrophic Biological Risks (GCBRs) are biological risks of unprecedented scale that have the potential to cause such significant damage to human civilisation that they undermine its long-term potential. Uncontrolled, the impact of a global catastrophic biological event would cause tremendous loss of life; societal instability; prolonged damage to governments and economies; damage to international relationships; and would threaten global security, see the *Nuclear threat Initiative website* at <https://www.nti.org/about/projects/global-catastrophic-biological-risks/>. See E Cameron, 'Emerging and Converging Global Catastrophic Biological Risks' (2017) 15 *Health security*.

39 On naturally occurring CBRN events, including epidemic outbreaks, see Part II, Section 2.3 of this book.

40 A radioactive 'dirty bomb' or radiological dispersal device (RDD), made by combining radioactive material with conventional explosives to spread it, would not cause catastrophic levels of death and injury on the scale of a nuclear weapon detonation. A dirty bomb explosion could cause significant short- and long-term health problems for those in the area and could leave billions of dollars in damage due to the costs of evacuation, relocation and clean-up. Buildings would have to be demolished and debris removed. Access

convention failed, whereas, as far as nuclear weapons and threats are concerned there has been a long series of treaties aiming at heading towards nuclear disarmament and a ban on nuclear testing.[41]

Radio-nuclear accidents may range from isolated cases of accidental contamination or over-exposure of a few persons (for instance medical professionals) to major catastrophes with global dimensions, like Chernobyl and Fukushima. The disposal of radio-nuclear waste is also capable of causing a CBRN event.

In 1990, the IAEA and the Nuclear Energy Agency of the Organisation for Economic Co-operation and Development (OECD/NEA) developed a scale of gravity: the International Nuclear and Radiological Event Scale (INES). The scale was originally intended to classify events at nuclear power plants but was gradually extended to be applied to events occurring at all installations associated with the civil nuclear industry. It has since been extended and adapted to indicate the gravity of all events associated with the use, storage and transport of radioactive material and radiation sources.[42] There are already several ongoing attempts at drawing up complete lists of radio-nuclear events.[43]

4 Concluding Remarks

The main purpose of this very preliminary and non-exhaustive overview of CBRN events and threats is to highlight the gradual enlargement of the CBRN concept/paradigm and the ensuing need to adopt an all-hazards approach in the investigation of the response of the international community to such threats and in the identification of existing obligations and of the most relevant current challenges. This book is indeed an attempt at addressing crucial

to a contaminated area could be limited for years, until the site is cleaned well enough to meet environmental standards for protecting the public against harmful gamma rays that could penetrate human skin and potentially cause cellular damage.

41 See ch 23 by Poli.

42 The International Nuclear and Radiological Event Scale (INES) is a tool for communicating the safety significance of nuclear and radiological events to the public. Member States use INES on a voluntary basis to rate and communicate events that occur within their territory. It is not a notification or reporting system to be used in emergency response, see <https://www.iaea.org/resources/databases/international-nuclear-and-radiological-event-scale>.

43 See for instance the lists of relevant incidents available, respectively, at <http://www.johnstonsarchive.net/nuclear/radevents/index.html> and in the database of *The Guardian* at <https://www.theguardian.com/news/datablog/2011/mar/14/nuclear-power-plant-accidents-list-rank#data>.

questions such as: Is there any added value in applying strategies adopted in other sectors to CBRN events and to CBRN risk-management? Are the strategies that have been explicitly developed so far to respond to CBRN events useful for dealing with other emergencies such as natural disasters or pandemic outbreaks? This far-reaching approach also explains why a number of horizontal issues are tackled and why a section on responsibilities, enforcement mechanisms and remedies is included.[44]

As COVID-19 found the international community largely unprepared, it seems important not to act as the proverbial generals fighting the last war, by preparing responses applicable only to the threats of yesterday.

Bibliography

Cameron E, 'Emerging and Converging Global Catastrophic Biological Risks' (2017) 15 Health security 337.

Connolly C, 'War and the Coronavirus Pandemic', *Third World Approaches to International Law Review, Reflections* #15/2020, 9 April 2020.

Cusato E, Beyond War Talk: Laying Bare the Structural Violence of the Pandemic, *EJIL Talk!*, 3 May 2020.

Geissler E and van Courtland Moon J (eds.), *Biological and Toxin Weapons: Research, Development, and Use from the Middle Ages to 1945* (OUP 1999).

Hood A, 'Ebola: A Threat to the Parameters of a Threat to the Peace?' (2015) 16 Melbourne Journal of International Law 29.

Leitenberg M, *Assessing the Biological Weapons and Bioterrorism Threat* (University of Michigan 2005).

Pobjie E, 'Covid-19 as a threat to international peace and security: The role of the UN Security Council in addressing the pandemic', *EJILTalk!*, 27 July 2020.

44 See Part IV and Part V of this book.

CHAPTER 2

Main Forms of Interaction between the Key Actors in CBRN Protection: What Way Forward?

Costanza Di Francesco Maesa

1 Introduction

This chapter provides an overview of the role and the main forms of interaction between the actors involved in CBRN protection at the international, regional and domestic levels. The first section gives an overview of the roles played by the main actors involved in CBRN protection, such as international and regional organisations; States; and non-State actors, namely private corporations, non-governmental organisations (NGOs), local communities, academia and the media. A reflection on the different types of interactions between the key actors in CBRN protection (in terms of 'cooperation', 'coordination' and 'collaboration') is then provided in the second section. Finally, the concluding remarks offer some proposals for the creation of more effective forms of inter-organisational partnering between the different actors involved in CBRN protection.

2 Key Actors in CBRN Protection

Managing CBRN events[1] is a complex and dynamic process, which calls for the coordinated action of many different actors, such as States; public authorities; internationals organisations; and non-State actors, such as businesses and non-governmental organisations (NGOs), affected local communities, civil society, the media and academia. In this section, we give a brief overview of the role played by the different actors involved in CBRN protection.[2]

1 See ch 1 by Frulli.

2 We do not analyse thoroughly the role played by those actors. For an in-depth analysis see the chapters of part 2, 3 and 4 of the book.

According to the Sendai Framework for Disaster Risk Reduction (SFDRR), States have the 'overall responsibility for reducing disaster risk'.[3] They, therefore, bear the primary duty to provide 'disaster relief and assistance', to 'ensure the direction, control, coordination and supervision' of the activities performed on their territory and to protect the persons on their territory,[4] while relevant stakeholders have an important role in providing support to States by sharing their knowledge, experience and resources. In particular, the main tasks of community-based organisations, volunteers and civil society, that ensure the participation of vulnerable groups,[5] are to collaborate with public institutions; to engage in the implementation of local, national, regional and global plans and strategies; to provide pragmatic guidance on the implementation of 'normative frameworks, standards and plans for disaster risk reduction'; and to support 'public awareness, a culture of prevention and education on disaster risk'.[6] The role of these actors is, thus, really important in the preparedness and response phases, where the sharing of knowledge and capacities between governments, NGOs and local communities play an essential role in anticipating, responding to and recovering from the impacts of likely, imminent or current disasters.[7]

NGOs, in particular, play a crucial role in disaster settings, since they are closer than government to the affected communities; as a consequence, if States are lacking resources on their own, they may rely on them to provide essential services or to provide assistance to the victims of disasters.[8] In these situations, States have the duty to oversee and supervise NGOs and they can be

3 Sendai Framework for Disaster Risk Reduction 2015–2030 (SFDRR), (2015) UN Doc A/CONF.224/L.2. para 35.

4 UNGA Resolution 46/182 'Strengthening of the coordination of humanitarian emergency assistance of the United Nations' (1991) A/RES/46/182; Inter-Agency Standing Committee (2011), 'Operational Guidelines on the protection of persons in situations of natural disasters' <www.ifrc.org/docs/idrl/I922EN.pdf>.

5 On the procedural and substantive aspects related to the remedies that can be claimed by individuals or groups of victims, see ch 34 by Capone.

6 SFDRR (n 3) para 36(a).

7 UN Secretary-General note, 'Report of the open-ended intergovernmental expert working group on indicators and terminology relating to disaster risk reduction' (2016) A/71/644.

8 K Tierney, 'Disaster governance: social, political, and economic dimensions', (2012) Annual Review of Environment and Resources, 1 (37) 341–363; Y Osa, 'The growing role of NGOs in disaster relief and humanitarian assistance in East Asia', in R Sukma and J Gannon (eds), *A Growing Force: Civil Society's Role in Asian Regional Security* (Brookings Institution Press 2013) 66–89; S Jones, K Oven, B Manyena. and K Aryal, 'Governance struggles and policy processes in disaster risk reduction: a case study from Nepal', (2014) Geoforum (57) 78–90; L Lane and M Hesselman, 'Governing disasters: embracing human rights law and governance in a multi-level, multi-actor disaster governance landscape', (2017) Governance and Politics 2(5) 93–104.

held responsible if they do not perform correctly their oversight and supervision functions.

Recent studies on private companies' contributions to disaster governance found that businesses are also actively engaged in the humanitarian response.[9] Usually the role of private companies in disaster risk management consists both, on the one hand, in commercial activity, *ie* when corporate actors are paid for the products or services they offer or when some disaster-related services are subcontracted to them by State and non-State actors, and, on the other hand, in non-commercial activities, *ie* when private companies stipulate a partnership with NGOs to deliver services or when they make philanthropic donations.[10] Sometimes, public-private partnerships (PPPs) are made between States and private companies to restore heavily damaged critical infrastructure and to make available again essential services, such as water supply, electricity or healthcare.[11] The role of private actors, such as NGOs and private companies is, thus, crucial in CBRN management, when the States' capacities to respond to the disaster event are overwhelmed, even if only temporarily, or when States are not able to act as first responders.[12] However, a detailed analysis of the role and obligations incumbent upon private actors in CBRN protection is provided in other chapters of the book.[13]

International and regional organisations, such as the United Nations (UN), NATO, the European Union (EU), the Organization for Security and Co-operation in Europe (OSCE) and the World Health Organization (WHO), also play an essential role in CBRN protection, as is discussed in Section two of the present chapter and analysed in depth in other parts of the book.[14] Furthermore, human rights supervisory bodies play an important role in defining the international human rights law obligations applicable to CBRN

9 A Telesetsky, 'Beyond voluntary corporate social responsibility: corporate human rights obligations to prevent disasters and to provide temporary emergency relief' (2015) Vanderbilt Journal of Transnational Law 48 1003–1027; S Silingardi, 'Responses by private corporations', in S Breau and K Samuel (eds), *Research Handbook on Disasters and International Law* (Edward Elgar, Cheltenham 2016) 225–249.

10 Global Public Policy Institute, 'Business engagement in humanitarian response and disaster risk management' (2015).

11 Thanks to PPPs, public and private actors work together to minimise the negative consequences of disasters and to ensure the protection of public interests and human rights. F Demiroz and N Kapucu, 'Cross-sector partnerships in managing disasters: experiences from the United States', in T Izumi R and Shaw (eds), *Disaster Management and Private Sectors: Challenges and Potentials* (Springer 2015) 169–186.

12 Osa (n 8); Jones et al (n 8); Lane and Hesselman (n 8).

13 See ch 30 by Corcione and ch 27 by Venier.

14 See part 2 and 3 of the book.

events and in promoting and protecting human rights, such as the rights to life, health, food, water access, education, private and family life, housing, physical security and access to information.[15]

Other important actors in CBRN protection are mass media and social media, which play an essential role in risk awareness and crisis communication.[16] In particular, media play a crucial role in correctly informing the general public on the way to best conserve their own safety in the event of a large-scale CBRN emergency.[17] The duty of media workers in the context of CBRN events does not only consist in communicating true and precise information, but also in verifying that the information communicated to the public does not interfere with any investigative procedure and does not violate the fundamental rights of the victims of the disaster.[18] Considering the importance of the task, some authors have suggested that it would be better if the task of informing the population were 'performed by a dedicated department or press office'.[19] In their view, such an office would ensure a central coordination of interviews and would reduce confusion and inconsistency in the information distributed to the population.[20] In this regard, the 'UNICRI Journalism and Public Information Programme on New Threats' and the UNICRI 'Reporting and Communicating on CBRN Risks Programme' have precisely the objective

15 Inter-Agency Standing Committee (n 4); The Sphere Project, 'Humanitarian charter and minimum standards in humanitarian response' (2011) < https://www.unhcr.org/50b491b09.pdf>; M Hesselman, 'Establishing a full 'cycle of protection' for disaster victims: preparedness, response and recovery according to regional and international human rights supervisory bodies', (2013) Tilburg Law Review 18 (2) 106–132; D Cubie and M Hesselman, 'Accountability for the human rights implications of natural disasters: a proposal for systemic international oversight', (2015) Netherlands Quarterly of Human Rights 33(1) 9–41. See ch 28 by Sommario, ch 27 by Venier, ch 29 by Antoniazzi.

16 On the relationships between information, media and the COVID-19 pandemic, see UNICRI Report, 'Stop the virus of disinformation, the risk of malicious use of social media during COVID-19 and the technology options to fight it' (November 2020) <http://unicri.it/sites/default/files/2021-01/misuse_sm_0.pdf>.

17 G J Rubin, A K Chowdhury and R Amlôt, 'How to communicate with the public about chemical, biological, radiological, or nuclear terrorism: A systematic review of the literature', (2012) Biosecurity and Bioterrorism: Biodefense Strategy, Practice, and Science 10(4) 383–395; F Benolli, M Guidotti and F Bisogni, 'The CBRN Threat. Perspective of an Interagency Response', in G Jacobs et al (eds), *International Security Management* (Springer Nature 2021) 429, 429–445; A Ruggiero and M Vos, 'Communication Challenges in CBRN Terrorism Crises: Expert Perceptions', (2015) Journal of Contingencies and Crisis Management 23(3).

18 UNGA Resolution 74/306 (11 September 2020) A/RES/74/306.

19 Benolli, Guidotti and Bisogni (n 17).

20 Federal Emergency Management Agency (FEMA), 'Effective communication independent study', Washington: (2010) FEMA 242A. Benolli, Guidotti and Bisogni (n 17).

of enhancing the capabilities of journalists and other media workers to report and communicate CBRN risks of any origin.[21]

Equally, academia and research centres play a fundamental role in increasing risk awareness and preventing CBRN events from occurring. An example in this sense is represented by the risk that a virus leaks from a research laboratory, as shown by the doubts which arose in the context of the COVID-19 pandemic.[22] In this regard, it is extremely important that research centres and scientific laboratories adopt specific safety and security rules able to prevent the risk that viruses may be released into the environment. Furthermore, academia can also play an essential role in communicating precise information and seeking solutions to prevent and mitigate the effects of CBRN events.[23]

3 Interactions of the Key Actors in CBRN Protection

As we have seen in the previous section, a plethora of different actors at the international, regional and national levels are involved in the CBRN management cycle. Clear cooperation, coordination and collaboration mechanisms between the numerous actors involved in the CBRN management cycle are therefore essential to ensure the effective and efficient management of CBRN events. However, and despite the existing umbrella principle of cooperation governing the relations and interactions of the legal subjects of international law,[24] there are no universally and internationally accepted definitions of the terms 'cooperation', 'coordination' and 'collaboration' with regard to CBRN

21 See <http://www.unicri.it/journalism-and-public-information-programme-new-threats>.

22 It is still not clear what is the origin of the COVID-19 virus, even if Peter Ben Embarek, the head of the World Health Organization (WHO) mission, said it was 'extremely unlikely' that the virus leaked from a laboratory in the city of Wuhan (<https://www.bbc.com/news/world-asia-china-55996728>). However, this could be an opportunity to reflect more on the safety and security measures adopted in scientific laboratories. In this regard, see <https://thebulletin.org/2020/05/natural-spillover-or-research-lab-leak-why-a-credible-investigation-in-needed-to-determine-the-origin-of-the-coronavirus-pandemic/>.

23 An example is represented by the Joint Security and Resilience Centre (JSaRC). See T Thompson, 'The Practical Realities of Security Management in a Changing World', in G Jacobs et al (eds), *International Security Management* (Springer 2021) 449–462.

24 As provided by Article 1 of the UN Charter, the very goal of the UN is to achieve international cooperation to address international issues. To do so, and as set out in Article 58 of the Charter, the UN coordinates the policies and activities of its specialised agencies. At the European level, the Treaty on the Functioning of the European Union (TFEU) contains in its Title VI, provisions dealing with the EU's relations with international organisations and third countries and union delegations. Article 220 TFEU thus specifically provides that the EU shall maintain appropriate relations with international organisations, and,

events, despite the large number of instruments available at the international, regional and bilateral levels that enshrine provisions on international cooperation in case of disasters.

One of those instruments is Article 7 of the Draft Articles on the Protection of Persons in the Event of Disasters, adopted by the International Law Commission (ILC),[25] which states that 'States shall, as appropriate, cooperate among themselves, with the United Nations, with the components of the Red Cross and Red Crescent Movement, and with other assisting actors'. In the Draft Articles, the term 'coordination' is interestingly referred to as an element included in the notion of 'cooperation'.[26] It should be recalled, however, that the duty to cooperate, despite being described as a well-established and overarching principle of international law,[27] still fuels heated discussions as per its material scope, nature and concrete implementation.[28]

Similarly, the SFDRR, which mainly refers to natural disasters, affirms throughout the text that cooperation is essential to ensure effective protection against disaster situations.[29] In the guiding principles, it also refers to coordination mechanisms, requiring 'a clear articulation of responsibilities across public and private stakeholders, including business and academia'[30] and it

---

in particular, with the United Nations and its specialised agencies, the Council of Europe, the OSCE and the OECD.

25 ILC, 'Draft Articles on the Protection of Persons in Event of Disasters' (2016) II(2) UNYBILC, para 48. With UNGA Res 73/209 (2018), the General Assembly brought to the attention of States the recommendation by the ILC that a convention should be elaborated on the basis of the Draft Articles. It, therefore, decided to include in the provisional agenda of its seventy-fifth session (2020) an item entitled 'Protection of persons in the event of disasters'.

26 ILC (n 24), art. 8, which literally states: '[*c*]*ooperation* in the response to disasters *includes* humanitarian assistance, *coordination of international relief actions and communications*, and making available relief personnel, equipment and goods, and scientific, medical and technical resources' (emphasis added). See also Article 10 of the Draft Articles.

27 ILC, Commentaries, 'Draft Articles on the Protection of Persons in Event of Disasters' (2016) II(2) UNYBILC, para 49.

28 G Bartolini, T Natoli and A Riccardi, Report of the Expert Meeting on the ILC's Draft Articles on the Protection of Persons in the Event of Disasters, (2015) International Law and Disasters Working Papers Series 03 37–40.

29 SFDRR (n 3) para 19(a)(b), paras 1(d), 8, 19(l), 25(c) and Section VI. The SFDRR's principles are drawn on the basis of the principles contained in the UN World Conference on Natural Disaster Reduction, 'Yokohama Strategy for a Safer World: Guidelines for Natural Disaster Prevention, Preparedness and Mitigation, and Plan for Action', (1994) UN A/CONF.172/9, and its Plan of Action, and the Hyogo Framework for Action 2005–2015: Building the Resilience of Nations and Communities to Disasters (2006) UN A/CONF.206/6.

30 SFDRR (n 3) para 19(e)(f).

underlines that it is important to establish government coordination forums composed of relevant stakeholders at the national and local levels, *ie* national and local platforms for disaster risk reduction and designated national contact points.[31] Both the terms 'cooperation' and 'coordination' are used in the same sentence, without any explanation on their possible different meanings and the consequent different implications of these two forms of partnering activities in the preparedness, response and recovery phases.[32] Even the necessity to 'foster *collaboration* across global and regional mechanisms and institutions for the implementation and coherence of instruments and tools relevant to disaster risk reduction'[33] and to 'promote and support *collaboration* among relevant public and private stakeholders to enhance the resilience of business to disasters' (emphasis added)[34] is mentioned in the SFDRR without any further explanation of the meaning of the term. The terms 'cooperation', 'coordination' and 'collaboration' are, thus, used interchangeably in the text, without any definition explaining the differences between them. Similarly, a clear articulation of responsibilities of the actors involved in the partnering activities is not provided in the text.

Those findings are similar in the context of the international documents adopted by the UN. Among them, Resolution 1540(2004)[35] encourages States to take effective measures to prevent the proliferation of nuclear, chemical, or biological weapons by promoting international *cooperation*[36] and enhancing '*coordination* of efforts on national, sub-regional, regional and international levels' (emphasis added).[37] The 'Plan of Action' annexed to the UN Global Counter-Terrorism Strategy of 2006[38] reaffirms that, among the measures necessary to prevent and combat terrorism, cooperation[39] and inter-agency coordination[40] mechanisms have a significant role. Even in those cases, the

31 SFDRR (n 3) paras 27(g) and 48.

32 SFDRR (n 3) para 33(i), which states the importance of promoting 'the *cooperation* of diverse institutions, multiple authorities and related stakeholders at all levels, including affected communities and business, in view of the complex and costly nature of post-disaster reconstruction, under the *coordination* of national authorities' (emphasis added).

33 SFDRR (n 3) para 28(a).

34 SFDRR (n 3) para 31(i).

35 UNSC Res 1540 (28 April 2004) UN Doc S/RES/1540 has been reiterated and extended by Res 1673(2006), Res 1810(2008) and Res 1977(2011).

36 UNSG, Message on the Tenth Anniversary of the adoption of Security Council Resolution 1540(2004) (28 April 2014).

37 UNSC (n 32) para 3(c), Preamble.

38 UNGA (20 September 2006) A/RES/60/288.

39 UNGA (n 35) Preamble, para 3 of the first part, para II, No. 2, 3, 4, 5, 8, 13, para III, No. 1, 4.

40 UNGA (n 35), Preamble, para II, No. 5, 12(a), No. 17, para III, No. 5.

term 'coordination' is used together with the term 'cooperation', with no distinction between the two terms having been made, nor any further explanation having been provided. The absence of clear definitions in the field of inter-agency cooperation on CBRN events has been confirmed also by the findings of a very interesting project,[41] which found out that, in the chemical field, there is no 'coordinated system for the classification of an event and of the ensuing emergency [..] among agencies that would intervene in case of an attack with chemical weapons'.[42] According to the authors of the project, to fill this gap, a coordinated system for the classification of an event in the chemical field should be developed.

To promote cooperation and coordination even further, specific bodies have also been established. Among them, a specific Committee, called 'Committee 1540', which functions as a subsidiary body of the Security Council, has been established to monitor the implementation of the 1540(2004) Resolution's dispositions.[43] Committee 1540, together with the UN Office for Disarmament Affairs (UNODA), is responsible for promoting cooperation between international, regional and sub-regional organisations and other entities, such as the WHO and the Atomic Energy Agency, and to share lessons and experiences with them. UNODA also promotes partnerships with civil society, the private sector and industry to meet the objectives of Resolution 1540(2004).

In the context of the UN Global Counter-Terrorism Strategy, the UN Office of Counter-Terrorism (UNOCT), through its Inter-Agency Working Group on Preventing and Responding to WMD Terrorist Attacks,[44] is working together with the International Atomic Energy Agency (IAEA), the OPCW, the World Health Organization (WHO), the UNODA and other relevant organisations to enhance cooperation and promote coordination mechanisms. Furthermore, the UN Counter-Terrorism Implementation Task Force (CTITF) was established by the Secretary General in 2005, and within it the UN Counter-Terrorism Centre (UNCCT), whose budgetary funding is important for promoting international counter-terrorism cooperation and assisting Member States in their

41 UN Office of Counter-Terrorism (UNOCT), 'Ensuring Effective Interagency Interoperability and Coordinated Communication in Case of Chemical and/or Biological Attacks', (2017) Project of the Counter-Terrorism Implementation Task Force Working Group on Preventing and Responding to Weapons of Mass Destruction Attacks (2015–2019).

42 Ibid, point 12, p 12.

43 UNSC (n 32) para 4.

44 Since 2015 UNOCT, through a project on 'Ensuring Effective Inter-Agency Interoperability and Coordinated Communication in Case of Chemical and/or Biological Attacks' implemented by the UN Counter-Terrorism Centre (UNCCT), has particularly attempted to strengthen cooperation among relevant organisations and agencies.

efforts to implement the UN Global Counter-Terrorism Strategy, was set up in 2011.

In the context of transboundary cooperation in case of nuclear and radiological emergencies originating from the civilian use of related materials, the Convention on Assistance in Case of a Nuclear Accident or Radiological Emergency[45] sets out an international framework for cooperation among States Parties.[46] According to the Convention, the IAEA shall facilitate prompt assistance and give support in the event of nuclear accidents or radiological emergencies.[47] The IAEA has a particularly important role as the focal point for coordination:[48] it collects and disseminates information, supports efforts, assists States Parties to the Convention, maintains liaisons with relevant international organisations and provides its available services.[49] Apart from the IAEA, also the G8 Nuclear Safety and Security Group (G8-NSSG)[50] promotes cooperation among the G8 leaders and other States with regard to nuclear safety and security, and works in close cooperation with already existing multilateral organisations.[51]

However, the proliferation of actors responsible for coordinating the efforts to prevent the proliferation of nuclear, chemical, or biological weapons, to counter-terrorism, or to minimise the consequences of nuclear accidents and radiological emergencies has not been accompanied by a clearer definition of the responsibilities and duties of the different actors involved.

Similar findings can be derived from an overview of the legal instruments adopted at the regional level. Nowadays, many regional instruments[52] and

45 Convention on Assistance in Case of a Nuclear Accident or Radiological Emergency (1986) IAEA-INFCIRC/336.

46 See also the Convention on the Safety of Spent Fuel Management and on the Safety of Radioactive Waste Management (1997), art 1(I).

47 Each State Party shall notify the IAEA and the other States Parties which authorities are competent and which points of contact are authorised to make and receive requests, or accept offers of assistance. Convention (n 42), art 1.

48 The IAEA serves as the focal point for coordination also in relation to the Convention on Early Notification of a Nuclear Accident (1986), art 7ff.

49 Convention (n 42) art 5.

50 The Nuclear Safety and Security Group (NSSG) established at Kananaskis Summit and responsible to Leaders, provides technically informed strategic policy advice on issues that could impact safety and security in the peaceful uses of nuclear energy.

51 J Alger, 'A Guide to Global Nuclear Governance: Safety, Security and Non-proliferation, in Nuclear Energy Futures' (2008).

52 For an overview of the regional agreements dealing with disaster assistance and including provisions on prevention, see the 'Sixth report on the protection of persons in the event of disasters' (2013) UN Doc A/CN.4/662 33. See ch 11 by Creta, ch 6.

bilateral agreements[53] on disaster management contain provisions on cooperation, coordination and collaboration in case of CBRN events and, more generally, disasters. Some examples are the political commitments of the Organization for Security and Co-operation in Europe (OSCE)[54] and the legal framework against CBRN risks adopted at the European level.[55] Even in that case, a brief overview of the EU instruments adopted to manage CBRN risks shows that the terms 'cooperation' and 'coordination' are used indistinctly. It also shows that the creation of specific EU bodies responsible for coordinating the efforts to manage CBRN risks has not been accompanied by a clearer definition of the responsibilities and duties incumbent upon the different actors involved, at the European and national levels, in CBRN protection.

Another form of inter-organisational partnering in disaster risk management are public-private partnerships (PPPs) between public and private actors. In case of PPPs, public and private actors work together to minimise the effects of CBRN events and both the private and the public actors have their responsibilities and duties to perform.[56] A clear division of responsibilities between public and private actors involved in the PPPs is, thus, really important. However, no 'hard law' agreements have been adopted up to now to regulate the issue. Only 'soft law' instruments, such as the disaster response guidelines 'for Establishing Effective Collaboration between Mobile Network Operators and Government Agencies'[57] or the 'Guiding Principles for

53 See eg the Agreement between the Government of the Hellenic Republic and the Government of the Russian Federation on Cooperation in the Field of Prevention and Response to Natural and Man-Made Disasters (2000); Agreement between the Government of the French Republic and the Government of Malaysia on Cooperation in the Field of Disaster Prevention and Management and Civil Security (1998).

54 See particularly the Helsinki Final Act, an agreement signed by 35 Nations that concluded the Conference on Security and Co-operation in Europe, held in Helsinki, Finland, and the following OSCE political commitments, among which the 21st OSCE Ministerial Council, Decision No. 6/14 on the Enhancing Disaster Risk Reduction (5 December 2014) MC.DEC/6/14 ('2014 Basel Ministerial Council Decision on Enhancing Disaster Risk Reduction'). Among others, see the 2003 OSCE Strategy Document for the Economic and Environmental Dimension, Strategy document for the 11th OSCE Ministerial Council in Maastricht (1–2 December 2003) MC(11).JOUR/2 and the 2007 Madrid Declaration on Environment and Security, 15th OSCE Ministerial Council (29–30 November 2007) MC.DOC/4/07.

55 The role of the EU in the protection against CBRN risks is deeply analysed elsewhere in the book. See ch 6 by Casolari, ch 14 by Ferri, ch 15 by Balboni, ch 19 by Ferri.

56 Public-Private-Partnership in Infrastructure Resource Centre (World Bank Group) 'Government objectives: benefits and risks of PPPs' (2016) <https://ppp.worldbank.org/public-private-partnership/overview/ppp-objectives#benefits>.

57 The document has been drafted by the telecom organisation GSMA in 2012.

Public-Private Collaboration for Humanitarian Action',[58] have been adopted. According to the latter, humanitarian and private parties should adhere to the professional standards and codes of conduct developed by the humanitarian community to provide quality assistance. PPPs could, thus, be a way of increasing the accountability of the private sector for violations of human rights if a CBRN event occurs. However, most of these documents are not transposed into hard law agreements; as a result, it is not possible to clearly define the legal accountability of the actors taking part in them.[59]

The foregoing brief overview of the main instruments adopted at the international and regional levels has shown that the three different forms of inter-organisational partnering activities, *ie* cooperation, coordination and collaboration, are often referred to interchangeably. To shed light on the meaning of these concepts, in the next part of the chapter, we, thus, try to conceptualise them on the basis of the studies of authors who have specifically investigated the matter.

3.1 *Definition of the Main Forms of Interactions of the Key Actors in CBRN Protection*

The first form of inter-organisational activity, *ie* cooperation, has been defined as a 'short-term, often informal and voluntary relationship between organisations or parts of an organisation that are characterised by low levels of intensity and risk'.[60] The main features of cooperation, according to this definition, are, thus, short-term, limited and low level connections between organisations. Work towards a common mission and avoidance of programme duplication are the main reasons to cooperate with other organisations during an emergency.[61] In general, the disaster management system, based on

58 UN-OCHA and World Economic Forum 'Guiding Principles for Public-Private Collaboration for Humanitarian Action', (2007).

59 S Silingardi (n 9).

60 E C Martin, 'The Four Cs of Disaster Partnering: Communication, Cooperation, Coordination and Collaboration', Disasters Journal (2014); K Brown and R Keast, 'Citizen-government engagement: Community connection through networked arrangements', (2003) Asian Journal of Public Administration 25(1) 107–131; BA Cigler, 'Multi-Organizational, Multisector and Multicommunity Organizations: Setting the Research Agenda', in MP Mandell (ed) *Getting Results Through Collaboration: Networks and Network Structures for Public Policy and Management* (Quorum Books 2001) 71–85; A Najam, 'The four-C's of third sector-government relations', (2000) Nonprofit Management and Leadership, 10(4) 375–397.

61 N Kapucu 'Interagency communication networks during emergencies: Boundary spanners in multiagency coordination', (2006) The American Review of Public Administration 36(2) 207–225.

cooperation, is increasingly substituting the disaster response system, characterised by a strict military forces' control. Nowadays, civilian and military personnel collaborate thanks to the leadership and coordination role taken by dedicated offices or bodies, such as the UN-OCHA (Office for the Coordination of Humanitarian Affairs), which has the task of taking the leadership role and coordinating the activities of the actors involved in the response phase of disasters of large dimension.[62]

As regards the concept of coordination, it is defined as the working together of organisations in the context of disasters.[63] The characteristic feature of coordination is, therefore, the alignment of the actions of different organisations in order to achieve a shared goal.[64] In practice, it consists of different stages in a process of strict coordination between different organisations, which starts with the sharing of information and resources and may culminate in the creation of a shared vocabulary, procedures and standard operational systems that guide the way the actors involved work together in the CBRN emergency management cycle.[65] In that regard, some studies found that authority, hierarchical organisation and stricter rules in some cases may improve

62 R C Kent, 'The United Nations' humanitarian pillar: Refocusing the UN's disaster and emergency roles and responsibilities', (2004) Disasters 28(2) 216–233; R Dynes, 'Community emergency planning: False assumptions and inappropriate analogies.', (1994) International Journal of Mass Emergencies and Disasters 12(9) 141–158.

63 W Ammann, 'Developing a multi-organisational strategy for managing emergencies and disasters', (2008) Journal of Business Continuity and Emergency Planning 2(4) 390–403; T E Drabek, 'Managing the emergency response', (1985) Public Administration Review 45(s1) 85–92; R Keast and M P Mandell, 'The collaborative push: Pushing beyond rhetoric and gaining evidence', (2011) Manuscript presented at the 15th Annual Conference of the International Research Society for Public Management. Dublin, Ireland; JC Morris, ED Morris and DM Jones, 'Reaching for the philosopher's stone: Contingent coordination and the military's response to Hurricane Katrina' (2007) Public Administration Review 67(1) 94–106; KJ Tierney, 'Emergency medical preparedness and response in disasters: The need for interorganisational coordination' (1985) 45(1) 77–84.

64 L K Comfort, 'Crisis management in hindsight: Cognition, communication, coordination, and control', (2007) Public Administration Review 67(s1) 189–197; TE Drabek and DA McEntire, 'Emergent phenomena and multiorganizational coordination in disasters: Lessons from the research literature', (2002) International Journal of Mass Emergencies and Disasters 20(2) 197–224.

65 S Moore, E Eng and M Daniel, 'International NGOs and the role of network centrality in humanitarian aid operations: A case study of coordination during the 2000 Mozambique floods', (2003) Disasters 27(4) 305–318; M Stephenson, 'Making humanitarian relief networks more effective: Operational coordination, trust and sense making', (2005) Disasters 29(4) 337–350.

coordination.[66] However, at the same time, in disaster settings organisations very often face unique and contingent problems that are not exactly repeated in every disaster situation and need specific and contingent responses not foreseeable in advance.[67]

Finally, collaboration has been defined as a 'long-term relationship between organisations, characterised by high levels of interdependency and high risk, which requires significant power symmetry'.[68] As in the case of coordination, collaboration is described as a process composed of different stages, extending from informal activities to formalised relationships, which may also consist in contractual arrangements.[69] It is particularly important to collaborate in disaster situations because of the limited amount of resources and the difficulty for a single organisation to manage the situation alone.[70] However, for collaboration to be effective, it is necessary to find a balance between the need to control the situation through authority and leadership powers and the necessity to give all the actors involved the same voice and respect the differences of the organisations involved.[71] Collaboration requires a higher embeddedness between organisations than cooperation or coordination, and may even create situations of shared risk and responsibility between collaborators: understanding each other's constraints is thus essential to have an effective collaboration.[72]

---

66 C Hood, 'The Art of the State: Culture, Rhetoric and Public Management' (OUP 1998); D F Kettl, 'Contingent coordination: Practical and theoretical puzzles for homeland security', (2003) The American Review of Public Administration 33(3) 253–277.

67 An example of a system of coordination is represented by the National Management System (NIMS) in the United States. See <https://www.fema.gov/emergency-managers/nims>; W L Waugh and G Streib 'Collaboration and leadership for effective emergency management', (2006) Public Administration Review 66(s1) 131–140.

68 E C. Martin (n 57); B A Cigler (n 120); R Keast and M P Mandell (n 123); JM Coston, 'A model and typology of government-NGO relationships', (1998) Nonprofit and Voluntary Sector Quarterly 27(3) 358–382; A Najam (n 57).

69 I M Nolte and S Boenigk, 'A study of ad hoc network performance in disaster response', (2013) Nonprofit and Voluntary Sector Quarterly 42(1) 148–173; G Simo and A Bies 'The role of nonprofits in disaster response: An expanded model of cross-sector collaboration' (2007) Public Administration Review 67(1) 125–142.

70 W L Waugh and G Streib (n 64).

71 In this respect, cultural understanding and a common language are important facts to facilitate collaboration. Ibid.

72 Comfort (n 61); C Huxham and S Vangen, 'Managing to Collaborate: The Theory and Practice of Collaborative Advantage' (Routledge 2005); N Kapucu, 'Public-nonprofit partnerships for collective action in dynamic contexts of emergencies', (2006) Public Administration 84(1) 205–220.

From the foregoing analysis, we deduce that each form of inter-organisational partnership has its own specificities and implies correlative duties for the actors involved. It is, thus, important to design a legal framework which considers the differences between them and consequently regulates the different responsibilities and duties of all the actors involved in the CBRN emergency management cycle, or, alternatively, to include clearer definitions in the ILC's Draft Articles on the Protection of Persons in the Event of Disasters. That would be an effective way of better defining the responsibilities of the private actors involved in CBRN management and to make every actor accountable for the tasks and activities they performed. That would also help to give an additional protection to the fundamental rights of the persons affected by the disaster. If that is not the case, the risk of duplication of efforts in disaster emergency situations is real, as well as the risk that an effective coordinated approach will not be followed.

4 Concluding Remarks

The present chapter proposed an overview of relevant actors in the governance of CBRN risks and of the forms of 'cooperation', 'coordination' and 'collaboration' between them. In this regard, from the foregoing analysis we deduced that the three types of inter-organisational partnering activities, 'cooperation', 'coordination' and 'collaboration', referred to in the international and regional documents regulating the issue are often referred to interchangeably, without any further explanation of their meaning. However, by conceptualising and defining these terms we found that each form of inter-organisational partnership has its own specificities and implies correlative duties for the actors involved.

In addition, the proliferation of actors at the international, regional and national levels has not been accompanied by a clear division of responsibilities between the actors involved, nor by a coordinated system of control and coordinated supervision. This implies that, in case of misconduct or coordination problems, it may be difficult to ascertain who is accountable. A recent example is given by the approach adopted in the current COVID-19 pandemic.

During the COVID-19 pandemic, the importance of cooperating at the international level was immediately perceived as crucial. International cooperation has therefore been strongly encouraged and international acts have been adopted to this purpose.[73] In particular, coordination, cooperation

73 UNGA Res. 74/270 (Apr. 2, 2020) U.N. Doc. A/RES/74/270; and at the European level, see more information at <https://ec.europa.eu/international-partnerships/topics/eu

and collaboration at all levels of governance was advocated as crucial by the WHO,[74] and the UN.[75] To this end, on the 4th February 2020, 'The United Nations Crisis Management Team' was activated, chaired by WHO, to implement global strategies and provide support to States.[76] At the regional level, WHO Regional Directors coordinate with the UN Development Coordination Office Regional Directors on planning and information sharing. At the national level, it is the Crisis Management Team (CMT) which coordinates with the UN country team in 136 countries 'to facilitate joint action by entities of the UN system and international agencies in support of Member States'.[77] Furthermore, in March 2020, the WHO COVID-19 Partners Platform was launched,[78] in which consenting national authorities, UN country teams and partners collaborate on the COVID-19 response in real-time. Even in this case, no definition of the terms 'cooperation', 'coordination' or 'collaboration' has been provided, and the proliferation of multiple actors at the international, regional and national levels has not been accompanied by a clear division of responsibilities between the actors involved, nor by a coordinated system of control and coordinated supervision. As a result, in case of misconduct or coordination problems, it could be difficult to ascertain who is accountable.

A possible solution to solve the problem, or at least improve the current situation, is to design a binding and coherent legal framework which considers the differences between the terms 'cooperation', 'coordination' and 'collaboration'

-global-response-covid-19_en>. On this issue, see A De Guttry, 'Is the International Community Ready for the Next Pandemic Wave? A Legal Analysis of the Preparedness Rules Codified in Universal Instruments and of their Impact in the Light of the COVID-19 Experience', (2020) Global Jurist 20(3), published online on the 25th of July 2020.

74 See the Res (2020) on the response to coronavirus disease (COVID-19), WHA73.1, A73/CONF./1 Rev.1, paras PP4, PP17, PP19; WHO Executive Board, Special session on the COVID-19 response, 'Update implementation of resolution' on the COVID-19 response, Interim report by the Director-General, (2020) WHA73.1, EBSS/5/2.

75 UNGA Resolution 75/4, Special session of the General Assembly in response to the coronavirus disease (COVID-19) pandemic (9 November 2020) A/RES/75/4; UNGA Resolution 74/306, Comprehensive and coordinated response to the coronavirus disease (COVID-19) pandemic (15 September 2020) A/RES/74/306; UN Comprehensive Response to COVID-19: Saving Lives, Protecting Societies, Recovering Better (June 2020); UN Security Council Press Release, Amid COVID-19 Pandemic, Coordinated, Conflict-Sensitive Responses Crucial to Sustaining Peace, Secretary-General Tells Security Council (August 2020) SC/14275.

76 Among the initiatives implemented by the Crisis Management Team there are the UN framework for the immediate socio-economic response to COVID-19 (2020); COVID-19 Global Humanitarian Response Plan (2020); WHO's Strategic Preparedness and Response Plan, Geneva, World Health Organization (2020); the United Nations COVID-19 Supply Chain System: requesting and receiving supplies, WHO (2020).

77 WHO Executive Board (n 71).

78 For more information, <https://covid19partnersplatform.who.int/en/>.

and consequently regulates the different responsibilities and duties of all the actors involved in the CBRN emergency management cycle. If this is not possible, alternatively, a possible solution could be to draft recommendations, a policy document or to include clearer definitions in the ILC's 'Draft Articles on the Protection of Persons in the Event of Disasters'. That would be an effective way of better defining the responsibilities of the private actors involved in CBRN management and to make every actor accountable for the tasks and activities they performed. It would also help to give an additional protection to the fundamental rights of the persons affected by CBRN events. The inter-organisational model for an effective inter-agency response would, thus, be well defined and clear with regard to the terms used and the duties of the different actors involved.

Bibliography

Ammann W, 'Developing a multi-organisational strategy for managing emergencies and disasters' (2008) Journal of Business Continuity and Emergency Planning 2(4) 390.

Benolli F, Guidotti M and Bisogni F, 'The CBRN Threat. Perspective of an Interagency Response', in G Jacobs et al (eds), *International Security Management* (Springer Nature 2021) 429.

Brown K and Keast R, 'Citizen-government engagement: Community connection through networked arrangements' (2003) Asian Journal of Public Administration 25(1) 107.

Cigler BA, 'Multi-Organizational, Multisector and Multicommunity Organizations: Setting the Research Agenda', in M P Mandell (ed) *Getting Results Through Collaboration: Networks and Network Structures for Public Policy and Management* (Quorum Books 2001) 71.

Comfort LK, 'Crisis management in hindsight: Cognition, communication, coordination, and control' (2007) Public Administration Review 67(s1) 189.

Coston JM, 'A model and typology of government-NGO relationships' (1998) Nonprofit and Voluntary Sector Quarterly 27(3) 358.

Cubie D and Hesselman M, 'Accountability for the human rights implications of natural disasters: a proposal for systemic international oversight' (2015) Netherlands Quarterly of Human Rights 33(1) 9.

Demiroz F and Kapucu N, 'Cross-sector partnerships in managing disasters: experiences from the United States', in T Izumi R and Shaw (eds), *Disaster Management and Private Sectors: Challenges and Potentials* (Springer 2015) 169.

Drabek TE, 'Managing the emergency response' (1985) Public Administration Review 45(s1) 85.

Drabek TE and McEntire DA, 'Emergent phenomena and multiorganizational coordination in disasters: Lessons from the research literature' (2002) International Journal of Mass Emergencies and Disasters 20(2) 197.

Dynes R, 'Community emergency planning: False assumptions and inappropriate analogies' (1994) International Journal of Mass Emergencies and Disasters 12(9) 141.

Hesselman M, 'Establishing a full 'cycle of protection' for disaster victims: preparedness, response and recovery according to regional and international human rights supervisory bodies' (2013) Tilburg Law Review 18 (2) 106.

Hood C, *The Art of the State: Culture, Rhetoric and Public Management* (OUP 1998).

Huxham C and Vangen S, *Managing to Collaborate: The Theory and Practice of Collaborative Advantage* (Routledge 2005).

Jones S, Oven K, Manyena B and Aryal K, 'Governance struggles and policy processes in disaster risk reduction: a case study from Nepal' (2014) Geoforum (57) 78.

Kapucu N, 'Interagency communication networks during emergencies: Boundary spanners in multiagency coordination' (2006) The American Review of Public Administration 36(2) 207.

Kapucu N, 'Public-nonprofit partnerships for collective action in dynamic contexts of emergencies' (2006) Public Administration 84(1) 205.

Keast R and Mandell MP, 'The collaborative push: Pushing beyond rhetoric and gaining evidence' (2011) Manuscript presented at the 15th Annual Conference of the International Research Society for Public Management. Dublin, Ireland.

Kent RC, 'The United Nations' humanitarian pillar: Refocusing the UN's disaster and emergency roles and responsibilities' (2004) Disasters 28(2) 216.

Kettl DF, 'Contingent coordination: Practical and theoretical puzzles for homeland security' (2003) The American Review of Public Administration 33(3) 253.

Lane L and Hesselman M, 'Governing disasters: embracing human rights law and governance in a multi-level, multi-actor disaster governance landscape' (2017) Governance and Politics 2(5) 93.

Martin EC, 'The Four Cs of Disaster Partnering: Communication, Cooperation, Coordination and Collaboration', Disasters Journal (2014).

Moore S, Eng E and Daniel M, 'International NGOs and the role of network centrality in humanitarian aid operations: A case study of coordination during the 2000 Mozambique floods' (2003) Disasters 27(4) 305.

Morris JC, Morris ED and Jones DM, 'Reaching for the philosopher's stone: Contingent coordination and the military's response to Hurricane Katrina' (2007) Public Administration Review 67(1) 94.

Najam A, 'The four-C's of third sector-government relations' (2000) Nonprofit Management and Leadership, 10(4) 375.

Nolte IM and Boenigk S, 'A study of ad hoc network performance in disaster response' (2013) Nonprofit and Voluntary Sector Quarterly 42(1) 148.

Osa Y, 'The growing role of NGOs in disaster relief and humanitarian assistance in East Asia', in R Sukma and J Gannon (eds), *A Growing Force: Civil Society's Role in Asian Regional Security* (Brookings Institution Press 2013) 66.

Rubin GJ, Chowdhury AK and Amlôt R, 'How to communicate with the public about chemical, biological, radiological, or nuclear terrorism: A systematic review of the literature' (2012) Biosecurity and Bioterrorism: Biodefense Strategy, Practice, and Science 10(4) 383.

Ruggiero A and Vos M, 'Communication Challenges in CBRN Terrorism Crises: Expert Perceptions' (2015) Journal of Contingencies and Crisis Management 23(3).

Silingardi S, 'Responses by private corporations', in S Breau and K Samuel (eds), *Research Handbook on Disasters and International Law* (Edward Elgar, Cheltenham 2016) 225.

Simo G and Bies A, 'The role of nonprofits in disaster response: An expanded model of cross-sector collaboration' (2007) Public Administration Review 67(1) 125.

Stephenson M, 'Making humanitarian relief networks more effective: Operational coordination, trust and sense making' (2005) Disasters 29(4) 337.

Telesetsky A, 'Beyond voluntary corporate social responsibility: corporate human rights obligations to prevent disasters and to provide temporary emergency relief' (2015) Vanderbilt Journal of Transnational Law 48 1003.

Thompson T, 'The Practical Realities of Security Management in a Changing World', in G Jacobs et al(eds), *International Security Management* (Springer 2021) 449.

Tierney K, 'Disaster governance: social, political, and economic dimensions' (2012) Annual Review of Environment and Resources, 1 (37) 341.

Tierney KJ, 'Emergency medical preparedness and response in disasters: The need for interorganisational coordination' (1985) 45(1) 77.

CHAPTER 3

International Obligations to Prevent CBRN Emergency Situations

Silvia Venier

1 Introduction

This chapter discusses obligations of general scope (applicable to all types of emergency situations regardless of their origin[1]) that are relevant to the prevention phase, *ie* to those activities and measures that are aimed at completely avoiding existing or new disaster risks or at least at minimising the likelihood of their occurrence.[2] It seeks to present an overview of the principle of prevention in international law and to discuss the interplay with other relevant principles (second section); to identify the legal sources of emergency prevention obligations (third)[3] and to clarify their content (fourth). As far as CBRN events are concerned, prevention measures highly depend on the specific circumstances that need to be avoided. Prevention measures applicable to malicious events include, for example, non-proliferation, counterterrorism and intelligence gathering, while prevention measures related to CBRN events in general refer, for instance, to the identification and mapping of different hazards; the identification of gaps emerging in all policy areas relevant to CBRN protection; and the adoption of measures to enhance the clarity and strength of legal and policy instruments aimed at minimising existing and new CBRN risks. This chapter focuses on prevention of CBRN events in general.[4]

1 Prevention obligations related to specific risks are discussed in other chapters in this volume, *ie* ch 7 by Poltronieri Rossetti, ch 11 by Creta, ch 16 by Venier and Part 3 on CBRN weapons.

2 The risk of an emergency is usually determined based on the likelihood and potential magnitude of a (natural or man-made) hazard combined with the level of vulnerability of the community that may potentially be impacted and its capacity to cope. As understood in the present volume, prevention measures aim at minimising the likelihood and magnitude of the hazard, while those measures aimed at either reducing vulnerabilities or at strengthening the capacity to cope are understood as 'preparedness' measures (see ch 1 by Frulli).

3 In order not to overlap with Part 4, this chapter only briefly touches upon International Human Rights Law (IHRL) and International Environmental Law (IEL) and it does not cover prevention obligations under European Union law in order not to overlap with chapters dealing with the regional perspective.

4 Malicious events are covered in ch 7 by Poltronieri Rossetti and in Part 3 on CBRN weapons.

DOI:10.1163/9789004507999_004

Prevention is discussed here as one of the four phases of emergency management, but some confusion still exists over the definitions of relevant terms. Among the recent clarification efforts, the glossary accompanying the Sendai Framework suggests that 'mitigation' refers to 'the lessening or minimizing of the adverse impacts of a hazardous event',[5] while prevention is said to refer to 'activities and measures to avoid existing and new disaster risks'.[6] However, the proposed examples of measures for the implementation of each concept are to some extent overlapping.[7] Interestingly, the glossary emphasises that prevention measures can be taken 'during or after a hazardous event or disaster to prevent secondary hazards or their consequences, such as measures to prevent the contamination of water',[8] pointing out that it is the function of a given measure, rather than its timing, that classifies it as a measure aimed at preventing a hazardous event. The glossary also suggests that prevention is linked with preparedness, since the latter should be 'based on a sound analysis of disaster risks'.[9] It can thus be concluded that prevention focuses on reducing the risk of a given event (by, first of all, identifying and assessing it), while preparedness refers to adopting measures aimed at minimising the potential impacts should the event occur. That said, some measures may support both prevention and preparedness functions, and thus the potential for the two terms to overlap must be acknowledged.

2 An Overview of Prevention Obligations in International Law

Under international law, prevention obligations are usually understood as 'best efforts obligations, requiring States to take all reasonable or necessary measures to prevent a given event from occurring, but without warranting that the

5 UNGA, 'Report of the open-ended intergovernmental expert working group on indicators and terminology relating to disaster risk reduction' (1 December 2016) UN Doc. A/71/644 (DRR updated terminology) 20. The Recommendations were endorsed by UNGA Res 71/276 (2 February 2017) UN Doc A/RES/71/276.

6 DRR updated terminology (n 5) 21.

7 Examples of mitigation measures proposed by the DRR terminology include 'engineering techniques and hazard resistant construction as well as improved environmental and social policies and public awareness' (ibid 20); examples of prevention measures include 'dams or embankments that eliminate flood risks, land use regulations that do not permit any settlement in high risk zones, seismic engineering designs that ensure the survival and function of a critical building in any likely earthquake and immunization against vaccine preventable diseases' (ibid 21).

8 Ibid.

9 Ibid.

event will not occur'[10] and are thus obligations to act in a certain way which can be breached by negligent acts or omissions.[11] The content of prevention duties is usually linked to the concept of due diligence, which emerged in the 1870s,[12] developed in particular after the 1950s along with new threats generated by highly dangerous activities that resulted in new standards of care,[13] and is now 'on the rise in all fields of International Law'.[14] The exact parameters of due diligence are difficult to pin down due to their flexible and open-ended nature:[15] the degree of diligence required varies depending on different factors, including the degree of risk and the importance of the interest requiring protection, as well as subjective considerations related to the knowledge and capabilities of the actor responsible for such protection. The requirements also differ over time, since the standards are not static but rather reflect new developments and understandings.[16] As indicated by the International Court of Justice (ICJ) in the *Bosnia and Herzegovina v Serbia and Montenegro Genocide* case, due diligence calls for an assessment *in concreto*.[17]

Prevention obligations arise in different international legal contexts.[18] They first emerged in the field of International Environmental Law (IEL), as applicable to hazardous activities carrying the risk of transboundary damage.[19] Prevention of transboundary harm was enshrined in the Stockholm

10 International Law Commission (ILC), 'Draft Articles on Responsibility of States for internationally wrongful acts, with commentaries' (2001) II(2) UNYBILC, Commentary to Draft Article 14(3) para 14.

11 R Barnidge, 'The due diligence principle in International Law' (2006) 8(1) ICLR 95–96.

12 *Alabama Claims Arbitration* (1872) 1 Moore Intl Arbitrations 495.

13 J Kulesza, *Due Diligence in International Law* (Brill 2016) 4.

14 H Krieger and A Peters, 'Due Diligence and Structural Change in the International Legal Order', in H Krieger and A Peters and L Kreuzer (eds), *Due Diligence in the International Legal Order* (OUP 2020) 351.

15 Due diligence is described as 'a variable concept' in eg International Tribunal for the Law of the Sea (ITLOS), 'Responsibilities and obligations of States sponsoring persons and entities with respect to activities in the Area' (Advisory Opinion of 1 February 2011) ITLOS Rep 2011, 117.

16 ILC, 'Draft Articles on prevention of transboundary harm from hazardous activities' (2001) II(2) UNYBILC, Commentary to Draft Article 3, 154.

17 *Application of the Convention on the Prevention and Punishment of the Crime of Genocide* (*Bosnia and Herzegovina v Serbia and Montenegro*) (*Genocide case*) (Judgment of 26 February 2007) ICJ Reports 2007, para 430.

18 G Hafner and I Buffard, 'Obligations of prevention and the precautionary principle' in J Crawford and others, *The law of international responsibility* (OUP 2010).

19 For an overview of the principle of prevention under IEL, see N De Sadeleer, *Environmental Principles: From Political Slogans to Legal Rules* (OUP 2002) ch 2.

and Rio Declarations[20] and found application in numerous international treaties dealing with, for example, marine pollution,[21] climate change,[22] hazardous waste,[23] biological diversity,[24] and desertification.[25] Having been discussed for the first time in the *Trail Smelter* decision in 1938,[26] this principle crystallised through the practice of international tribunals which provided clarifications on its evolving contours.[27] With reference to environmental protection, the ICJ noted that prevention is particularly required 'on account of the often-irreversible character of damage to the environment and of the limitations inherent in the very mechanism of reparation of this type of damage'.[28] In view of these characteristics (*ie* the potential to cause disasters), the principle of prevention is usually complemented by the precautionary principle in situations of scientific uncertainty.[29] According to the ILC Draft Articles on Prevention of Transboundary Harm, appropriate prevention measures include the following:

1) the adoption and implementation of national legislation incorporating 'accepted international standards', which will constitute 'a necessary reference point to determine whether measures adopted are suitable';[30]
2) the identification, in the first place, of the activities which involve significant risks;

20 UN Conference on the Human Environment, Declaration of the UN Conference on the Human Environment (1972), Principle 21; UN Conference on Environment and Development, Rio Declaration on Environment and Development (1992), Principle 2.

21 International Convention for the Prevention of Pollution of the Sea by Oil (1954) art 3; Convention on the Prevention of Marine Pollution by Dumping of Wastes and Other Matter (1972); Convention for the Prevention of Marine Pollution by Dumping from Ships and Aircraft (1972); International Convention for the Prevention of Pollution from Ships (1973).

22 UN Framework Convention on Climate Change (1992) art 3. On the link between climate change and disaster risk reduction, see 'Bali Action Plan' (2007) UN Doc FCCC/CP/2007/6/Add.1, Decision 1/C13, para 1(c)(iii).

23 Basel Convention on the Control of Transboundary Movements of Hazardous Wastes and their Disposal (1989) art 4(2).

24 Convention on Biological Diversity (1992) art 14.

25 UN Convention to Combat Desertification in Those Countries Experiencing Serious Drought and/or Desertification, Particularly in Africa (1994) art 3.

26 *Trail Smelter* (1938) Arbitration Tribunal 33 AJIL 182.

27 This included the customary international law character of the duty to carry out environmental impact assessments, as found in *Case concerning Pulp Mills on the River Uruguay* (*Argentina v Uruguay*) (*Pulp Mills*) (2010) ICJ Reports 14, para 204.

28 *Gabcíkovo–Nagymaros Project* (1997) ICJ Reports 7, para 140.

29 *Pulp Mills*, Separate Opinion by Judge Cançado Trindade, para 61. See also Hafner and Buffard (n 18) 526–531.

30 ILC (n 16) 153.

3) the formulation of relevant policies 'expressed in legislation and administrative regulations and implemented through various enforcement mechanisms';[31]
4) the 'establishment of suitable monitoring mechanisms'.[32]

International cooperation is also envisaged in Draft Articles 4 (cooperation in prevention activities), 8 (timely notification of the risk to the potentially affected State), 9 (consultation on preventive measures) and 12 (continuous exchange of information related to the activity under scrutiny).

Prevention obligations are enshrined in the United Nations (UN) Charter, as the very purpose of the UN is to maintain international peace and security by taking 'effective collective measures for the *prevention* and removal of threats to the peace'.[33] Under the UN system, significant attention is thus given to conflict prevention and prevention of the most serious atrocities.[34] Indeed, the UN Secretary-General recently stated in his 'Report on the prevention of genocide' that the UN should 'change the culture of reaction to one of prevention and be prepared to invest the necessary resources'.[35] The report identifies three main avenues for implementing prevention measures: development of adequate national capacities (eg through the adoption and implementation of adequate legal frameworks); participation in cooperation activities (eg through States' membership in regional and sub-regional initiatives); and development of mechanisms for early detection of threats.[36] As far as the duty to prevent mass atrocities is concerned, the above-mentioned *Genocide* judgment confirmed some elements of the duty to prevent[37] but it generally 'missed a historic opportunity to give the international community some guidance on the content of the positive obligations to prevent the occurrence of what constitutes the gravest of crimes against humanity'.[38]

---

31 Ibid 154.

32 Ibid 156. See *Pulp Mills* (n 27) para 197.

33 Charter of the United Nations (1945) art 1(1) (emphasis added).

34 See eg the Convention on the Prevention and Punishment of the Crime of Genocide (1948) art 1; Convention against Torture and Other Cruel, Inhuman or Degrading Treatment or Punishment (1984) art 2. For an account of the duty to prevent genocide at the UN level, see J Heieck, *A duty to prevent genocide. Due diligence obligations among the P5* (Edward Elgar 2018).

35 UNGA Report of the Secretary General, 'Report on the prevention of genocide' (2019) UN Doc A/HRC/41/24, 3.

36 Ibid 4.

37 *Genocide case* (n 17) para 432.

38 A Gattini, 'Breach of the Obligation to Prevent and Reparation Thereof in the ICJ's Genocide Judgment', 18(4) EJIL (2007) 173.

Further clarifications on the contours of the duty to prevent are offered by other areas of international law, including, in particular, due diligence obligations under International Human Rights Law (IHRL).[39] As noted by some scholars, the principle of prevention has recently started to be discussed in the area of International Disaster Law (IDL), an emerging area which is in the process of consolidation.[40] The next section provides an overview of prevention duties as enshrined in international legal instruments within the IDL field.

3 Sources of Prevention Obligations as Applicable to Emergency Situations

As recognised by the ILC, an important legal foundation for the duty to reduce the risk of disasters – along with IHRL and IEL – is 'the widespread practice of States reflecting their commitment to reduce the risk of disasters'[41] as shown by the inclusion of relevant provisions in multilateral, regional, bilateral treaties[42] and by legislation and policy instruments adopted at the national level.[43]

The Convention and Statute establishing an International Relief Union, adopted in 1927, included among its objectives to 'encourage the study of preventive measures against disasters'.[44] Following this, however, for quite some time emergency prevention was addressed only within the environmental sector or by soft law instruments adopted in the field of Disaster Risk Reduction (DRR, discussed below). It was not until very recently that emergency prevention was included in two multilateral treaties outside the environmental

39 See eg Inter-American Court of Human Rights (IACtHR), *Velasquez Rodriguez v Honduras* (1988) IACtHR ser C No. 4 (174–175); European Court of Human Rights (ECtHR), *Öneryildiz v. Turkey* (2005) 41 EHHR 20 (93); *Budayeva and others v Russia* (2014) 59 EHRR 2 (152). For a discussion of positive obligations under IHRL see ch 27 by Venier.

40 B Nicoletti, 'The Prevention of Natural and Man-Made Disasters: What Duties for States?' in A de Guttry, M Gestri and G Venturini (eds) *International Disaster Response Law* (Springer 2012) 179; M Sossai, 'States' failure to take preventive action as a human rights issue' in F Zorzi Giustiniani and others (eds), *Routledge Handbook of Human Rights and Disasters* (Routledge 2018) 123; E Sommario, 'One law to bind them all: International Law and disaster resilience' in A Harwig and M Simoncini (eds), *Law and the Management of Disasters: The Challenge of Resilience* (Routledge 2016) 247.

41 ILC, 'Report of the International Law Commission, Protection of Persons in Event of Disasters' (2016) UN Doc A/71/10, Commentary to Draft Article 9 para 5.

42 Ibid.

43 Ibid para 6.

44 Convention and Statute establishing an International Relief Union (1927) art 2(2).

sector, namely the Framework Convention on Civil Defence Assistance, which requires Member States 'to explore all possibilities for cooperation in the area of prevention, forecasting [...]',[45] and the Tampere Convention, which expressly made disaster 'prediction and mitigation' a priority, obliging States and other actors, *inter alia*, 'to facilitate the use of telecommunication resources for disaster *mitigation*' (emphasis added), to cooperate by sharing information and technologies and to reduce any barriers to the use of telecommunications in this field.[46]

Particularly relevant to the CBRN field is the Convention on Nuclear Safety (CNS) which is entirely devoted to promoting nuclear safety in order to prevent nuclear disasters.[47] The Convention applies to 'any land-based civil nuclear power plant' (Article 2(i)) and imposes various prevention obligations, including to 'ensure that all reasonably practicable improvements are made as a matter of urgency to upgrade the safety of the nuclear installation' (Article 6); to establish national safety requirements, a system for licensing, a system of inspections, and to ensure the enforcement of applicable regulations (Article 7); to ensure the safety of installations in relation to their siting (Article 17), design and construction (Article 18) and operation (Article 19). States are not bound by any specific technical benchmarks as those proposed by the IAEA are non-binding safety standards; however, States must submit reports on their implementation of the Convention, which are peer reviewed (Article 5 on Reporting) based on the idea that this process will result in harmonising standards at the global level. Scholars have commented on several weaknesses of the CNS provisions,[48] which were recently confirmed by the Fukushima disaster.[49] In terms of protection against industrial accidents

45 Framework Convention on Civil Defence Assistance (2000) art 4.

46 Tampere Convention on the Provision of Telecommunication Resources for Disaster Mitigation and Relief Operations (1998) art 3 and art 9.

47 Convention on Nuclear Safety (1994); See ILC, 'Sixth report on the protection of persons in the event of disasters' (2013) UN Doc A/CN.4/662 33. See ch 11 by Creta.

48 See eg E Benz, 'Lessons from Fukushima: Strengthening the International Regulations of Nuclear Energy' (2013) 37(3) Wm. & Mary Envtl. L. & Pol'y Rev.

49 As emphasised by eg the Japanese Independent Commission, in terms of risk assessment, Fukushima highlighted the need to take into account the worst-case scenarios, to tailor risk assessments to site-specific hazards and to regularly update these assessments; in terms of safety standards and monitoring, the disaster highlighted the importance of having an independent nuclear regulatory authority at the domestic level and mandatory safety standards at the international level. The National Diet of Japan, 'The official report of the Fukushima Nuclear Accident Independent Investigative Commission. Executive Summary' (The National Diet of Japan, 2012); A Cavoski, 'Revisiting the Convention on Nuclear Safety: Lessons Learned from the Fukushima Accident' (2013) 3 AsianJIntL 365.

more generally, the International Labour Organization (ILO) Prevention Convention ensures the protection of workers against the risk of major industrial accidents.[50]

Nowadays, a wide variety of regional instruments[51] and bilateral agreements[52] on emergency management include provisions on prevention duties. For instance, the UN Economic Commission for Europe (UNECE) Convention on the Transboundary Effects of Industrial Accidents, which applies to 'any activity involving hazardous substances' (Article 1(a)),[53] imposes obligations on States Parties to take 'appropriate legislative, administrative and financial measures' (Article 3) and to cooperate to implement their prevention obligations (Article 6). Examples of relevant ad hoc measures include identifying hazardous activities and performing risk assessments; setting specific safety objectives; adopting legislative provisions and guidelines; applying 'the most appropriate technology in order to prevent industrial accidents'; and educating and training all persons engaged in hazardous activities, to ensure that safety regulations are implemented internally and that adequate monitoring mechanisms (including on-site inspections) are in place. Pursuant to Article 9(2), the public shall be given the opportunity to participate in decision making about hazardous installations.

Looking at other regional actors, since the adoption of the Helsinki Final Act in 1975, the Organization for Security and Cooperation in Europe (OSCE) recognises the importance of cooperation in DRR activities.[54] The cornerstone of OSCE efforts in this field is the Basel Ministerial Decision on Enhancing Disaster Risk Reduction, adopted in 2014,[55] which encourages Participating States to adopt an integrated DRR strategy; to exchange relevant technologies and know-how; to incorporate local knowledge and to raise risk awareness at the local level; and to strengthen the exchange of knowledge and experience among States. In Asia and the Pacific, the ASEAN Agreement on Disaster

50 ILO Convention concerning the Prevention of Major Industrial Accidents (1993).

51 For an overview of regional agreements, see ILC (n 41) 35ff; for the EU, see ch 14 by Ferri.

52 See eg the Agreement between the Government of the Hellenic Republic and the Government of the Russian Federation on Cooperation in the Field of Prevention and Response to Natural and Man-Made Disasters (2000); Agreement between the Government of the French Republic and the Government of Malaysia on Cooperation in the Field of Disaster Prevention and Management and Civil Security (1998) preambular para 4.

53 Convention on the Transboundary Effects of Industrial Accidents (1992) art X.

54 For an overview, see <https://www.osce.org/oceea/disaster-risk-reduction> (all links were last accessed on 3 December 2021).

55 21st OSCE Ministerial Council, Decision No. 6/14 on Enhancing Disaster Risk Reduction (5 December 2014).

Management and Emergency Response contains three categories of DRR obligations, namely risk identification and monitoring (Article 5), prevention and mitigation (Article 6), and disaster preparedness (Article 7).[56] As far as the first two are concerned, States Parties are under the obligations to identify all disaster risks within their territory and to assign disaster risk levels to each potential hazard according to agreed criteria, as well as to identify, prevent and reduce risks arising from hazards by adopting adequate frameworks, allocating necessary resources, promoting public awareness and education, and promoting and utilising indigenous knowledge and practice.

Resolutions of the UN General Assembly (UNGA) have long recognised the crucial role of disaster prevention.[57] Since the late 1980s, UNGA Resolutions have been critical to establishing and supporting what is nowadays known as DRR, and they remain the key vehicle for clarifying the contours of the duty to prevent disasters at the international level.[58] In the first DRR strategy, the Yokohama Strategy (1995–2005), States were called upon to develop a 'global culture of prevention as an essential component of an integrated approach to disaster reduction', by focusing on education and training in disaster prevention; improving awareness in vulnerable communities; improving risk assessments and warnings; implementing effective national legislation and administrative action; and improving coordination and cooperation at the international and regional levels.[59] The Hyogo Framework (2005–2015),[60] which built upon the lessons learned in the previous decade, identified four priorities for action devoted to prevention (with a fifth dedicated to preparedness), namely to ensure that DRR is a priority at the national level; to identify, assess and monitor disaster risks; to use knowledge, innovation and education to build a culture of knowledge; and to reduce the underlying risk factors.

Nowadays, three out of four priorities of the Sendai Framework (2015–2030)[61] focus on disaster prevention, namely understanding disaster risk,

56 ASEAN Agreement on Disaster Management and Emergency Response (2005).

57 Recently, UNGA Res 243 (23 December 2014) UN Doc A/RES/69/243, op para 44 (urging States to prioritise risk management and shift towards an anticipatory approach to humanitarian crises); for a compilation of the UN Resolutions on disaster prevention up to 2009, see OCHA, 'Compilation of United Nations Resolutions on Humanitarian Assistance' (2009), s 7, 69ff.

58 See UNGA Res 236 (22 December 1989) UN Doc A/RES/44/236.

59 UN World Conference on Natural Disaster Reduction, 'Yokohama Strategy for a Safer World: Guidelines for Natural Disaster Prevention, Preparedness and Mitigation, and Plan for Action' (1994) UN Doc A/CONF.172/9.

60 Hyogo Framework for Action 2005–2015: Building the Resilience of Nations and Communities to Disasters (2006) UN Doc A/CONF.206/6.

61 Sendai Framework for Disaster Risk Reduction 2015–2030 (2015) UN Doc A/CONF.224/L.2.

strengthening disaster risk governance and investing in DRR. The Sendai Framework emphasises that disaster risk should be understood 'in all its dimensions of vulnerability, capacity, exposure of persons and assets, hazard characteristics and the environment' (para 23). National authorities are called upon to promote the collection, systematic evaluation, periodical update and dissemination of disaster risk information to all potentially interested groups, and to promote dialogue among scientific and technical communities. At the regional and global levels, international disaster risk maps should be developed and effective regional and global campaigns should be promoted as instruments for public awareness and education. Recommendations for strengthening DRR include mainstreaming it into all policies and sectors and improving coordination; promoting mechanisms for disaster risk transfer and insurance; risk-sharing and retention; and financial protection. Regional DRR strategies have also been defined that propose priorities for actions similar to the ones of the Sendai Framework.[62]

4 Clarifying the Content of the Obligation to Prevent Emergency Situations

The lack of a comprehensive instrument covering protection against disasters at the international level, along with the difficulties in delimiting the contours of prevention due to its flexible and evolving character, do not allow an easy identification of the exact content of emergency prevention duties under international law. Nevertheless, from the previous analysis some key obligations emerge: (i) the duty to adopt adequate legal and regulatory frameworks and implement ad hoc risk mitigation measures targeted at specific risks; (ii) the duty to perform risk assessment, mitigation and awareness activities; and (c) the duty to cooperate in prevention activities with other States and in international and regional fora.[63] These prevention duties have been confirmed under the

---

62 Examples include the European Roadmap for Disaster Risk Reduction (2015–2030), <https://www.preventionweb.net/files/48721_efdrrroadmap20152020anditsactions20.pdf>; Africa Regional Strategy for Disaster Risk Reduction (2004), <https://www.preventionweb.net/files/4038_africaregionalstrategy1.pdf>; APEC Framework on Disaster Risk Reduction (2015–2030), <http://mddb.apec.org/Documents/2015/SOM/CSOM/15_csom_002.pdf>.

63 Similarly, Nicoletti (n 40) found that emergency prevention is realised through the duties to assess the risk, to cooperate in prevention activities and to warn. Interestingly, Sossai has emphasised that the duty to prevent contains not only obligations of conduct but also obligations of result, which include the duty to adopt adequate administrative, legal and institutional frameworks. See Sossai (n 40) 123.

ILC Draft Articles on the Protection of Persons in the Event of Disasters. Draft Article 9 establishes the basic obligation to reduce the risk of disasters by taking certain measures (including through legislation and regulation) and provides an indicative list of the most prominent types of contemporary DRR efforts, including the conduct of risk assessments, the collection and dissemination of risk and past loss information, and the installation and operation of early warning systems.[64]

Looking at the adoption of adequate legal and regulatory frameworks and of ad hoc risk mitigation measures, legislation is generally recognised as being the most effective way to facilitate the taking of DRR measures at the domestic level and should be understood 'in broad terms to cover as many manifestations of law as possible'.[65] It may be asked what a legal, policy and administrative framework would need to address to be 'adequate' in these contexts. The International Federation of the Red Cross and Red Crescent Societies (IFRC) 'Handbook on Law and Disaster Risk Reduction' provides some indications on this[66] and some examples of national implementation have also emerged.[67] The IFRC has also developed a ten point checklist on law and DRR,[68] which refers to the need for a law dedicated to DRR establishing clear roles and responsibilities and allocating adequate resources; mainstreaming DRR in other sectors; the promotion of education, training and awareness-raising on DRR; the inclusion of multiple actors in decisions and activities with particular attention devoted to gender issues and vulnerable groups; and the establishment of monitoring mechanisms. Generally speaking, there is an increased recognition that in elaborating DRR frameworks States must engage with

64 At the 4th session of the Global Platform for Disaster Risk Reduction, held in Geneva in 2013, it was affirmed that 'there is a growing recognition that the prevention and reduction of disaster risk is a legal obligation, encompassing risk assessments, the establishment of early warning systems, and the right to access risk information'. UNISDR, 'Proceedings of the Fourth Session of the Global Platform for Disaster Risk Reduction. Chair's Summary' (UNISDR 2013) 13. Note that early warning is not discussed in this chapter as it is usually understood as a preparedness measure.

65 ILC (n 41) Commentary to Draft Art 9, para 12.

66 IFRC and UNDP, 'The Handbook on Law and Disaster Risk Reduction' (IFRC and UNDP 2015).

67 National Implementation Reports are available on the Disaster Law Programme Website at https://www.ifrc.org/en/what-we-do/disaster-law/research-tools-and-publications/disaster-law-publications/. A detailed report is IFRC and UNDP, 'Implementing the Law on Disaster Management in Cambodia. Developing subsidiary Legislation' (2017) <https://www.ifrc.org/docs/IDRL/Cambodia%20DM%20Subsidiary%20Legislation%20Report%20LR.PDF>.

68 IFRC and UNDP, 'The Checklist on Law and Disaster Risk Reduction' (IFRC and UNDP 2015).

key stakeholders and with the public at large. One of the guiding principles of the Sendai Framework affirms that DRR requires an 'all-of-society engagement and partnership' as well as 'inclusive, accessible and non-discriminatory participation, paying particular attention to the most vulnerable groups'.[69] In their concluding observations, UN HR monitoring bodies have indeed started to encourage States to collect the views of the most vulnerable groups while developing DRR frameworks.[70]

Regional HR Courts have provided some further guidance on what a legal and administrative framework has to cover to be considered adequate. For instance, the European Court of Human Rights (ECtHR) clarified that, in the context of dangerous industrial activities, regulations must at least govern the 'licensing, setting up, operation, security and supervision of such activities', while also emphasising more general requirements, such as ensuring the public's right to information and providing appropriate procedures for identifying any shortcomings in the processes concerned and any errors committed by those responsible at different levels.[71]

International organisations (IOs) and other actors offer legislative assistance to Member States on the domestic implementation of international obligations. For instance, the 1540 Committee established pursuant to Security Council Resolution 1540 on CBRN terrorism, has developed a matrix covering key prevention measures to be included in domestic legislation, such as the ratification of international and regional arms control and disarmament treaties; the adoption of laws that prohibit and penalise the conduct mentioned in SC Resolution 1540; and the availability of mechanisms to account for, govern the export of and secure dangerous material.[72] Legislative assistance is also provided by the Organisation for the Prohibition of Chemical Weapons (OPCW), which has published a 'National Legislation Implementation Kit' arranged according to the provisions of the Chemical Weapons Convention,[73] and by the IAEA, which has recently strengthened its efforts to support States in adopting adequate legislation in the nuclear sector through the publication of the 'Handbook on Nuclear Law'.[74]

---

69 Sendai Framework (n 61) para 19(d).

70 E Sommario and S Venier, 'Human Rights Law and Disaster Risk Reduction' (2018) 49 QIL Zoom-in <http://www.qil-qdi.org/human-rights-law-disaster-risk-reduction/> See also ch 27 by Venier.

71 *Öneryildiz* (n 39) para 90.

72 1540 Committee, 'Matrix Template', <http://www.un.org/en/sc/1540/national-implementation/1540-matrices/matrix-template.shtml>.

73 OPCW, 'National Legislation. Implementation Kit for the Chemical Weapons Convention. 'Initial measures'' (OPCW 2012).

74 IAEA, 'Handbook on Nuclear Law – Implementing Legislation' (IAEA 2010).

Moving on to the duty to perform risk assessments, this 'is about generating knowledge concerning hazards, exposure and vulnerabilities as well as disaster risk trends' and 'it is the first step towards any sensible measure to reduce the risk of disasters'.[75] As discussed in the second section above, the requirement of risk assessment has particularly developed within IEL and has been incorporated in various forms in many international agreements related to the protection of the environment, and is now part of customary international (environmental) law.[76] The modalities to conduct the assessment are normally left to national legislation. Appendix II of the Environmental Impact Assessment (EIA) Convention is an exception since it lists nine items as determining the content of the EIA, including a description of the proposed activity and of alternatives; a description of the potential environmental impact and the mitigation measures taken; an identification of gaps and uncertainties encountered when compiling the EIA; as well as an outline of the monitoring mechanisms in place.

In relation to nuclear accidents, key requirements for risk assessments have emerged from the Fukushima disaster, such as the need for assessments to take into account the worst-case scenarios, to be regularly updated, and to be carried out by an independent authority.[77] It is common understanding that knowledge of the risk should be gained through both specific and multi-hazard risk assessments that also consider cascading effects and that assessments should be discussed with interested parties and the population potentially affected. Section V of the Sendai Framework on the role of non-State stakeholders puts emphasis on involving civil society; ensuring participation of vulnerable groups; engaging with the academic and technological communities to support the assessment of risks and transfer of knowledge; and engaging with the media. Furthermore, UN HR monitoring bodies have recommended that the data collected on disaster loss should be disaggregated by sex, income and disability.[78] Once the risk has been assessed, a key activity is to enhance awareness among the potentially affected population (not discussed here since it generally refers to preparedness).

Turning our attention to the last obligation, *ie* the duty to cooperate, relevant instruments at the international, regional and bilateral levels contain provisions on international cooperation in disaster prevention,[79] to which the

75 ILC (n 41) Commentary to Draft Art 9, para 20.

76 See eg Convention on Environmental Impact Assessment in a Transboundary Context (1991); see also the treaties included in ILC (n 16) fn 900.

77 Japanese Independent Commission (n 49).

78 Sommario and Venier (n 70).

79 These are presented in ILC (n 41) 27ff.

ILC's Draft Article 7 is also devoted as it covers cooperation both on prevention and response. As recognised by the Sendai Framework, cooperation is indispensable for ensuring effective protection, as it complements the primary duty of the authorities of the affected State to take care of the population under its jurisdiction.[80] The forms of cooperation on disaster prevention may vary a lot, but at the very least they shall include the exchange of information on disaster risks and on the prevention (and preparedness) measures adopted to mitigate these risks at the domestic level, as well as the training of experts on disaster prevention and prediction.[81]

International cooperation should also aim at establishing harmonised measures for those hazards that are likely to have transboundary implications, such as in the case of nuclear accidents. In these cases, the divergence between the prevention and preparedness frameworks adopted by neighbouring States may become a matter of concern as they create uncertainty and confusion. A study conducted by the Dutch Safety Board, for instance, has discussed this issue in depth in the nuclear sector, assessing the degree of cooperation between authorities in Belgium, the Netherlands and Germany, and identifying several gaps that should be addressed, with respect to coordination of licensing procedures, supervision of nuclear power plants and establishment of similar crisis management procedures.[82]

5 Concluding Remarks

The present chapter has provided an overview of the sources and content of the obligations to prevent emergency situations under international law. The concept of prevention is usually implemented through obligations of conduct, the scope of which depends on the seriousness of the risk and its likely transboundary character, as well as on the responsible State's knowledge and capacity to act. The legal foundations of the duty to reduce the risk of disasters are obligations enshrined in different legal contexts, in particular under IHRL, IEL, IDL and domestic legislation. Although the primary responsibility to take

80 Sendai Framework (n 61) guiding principle 19(a).

81 See eg France-Italy, Convention in the Area of the Prediction and Prevention of Major Risks and on Mutual Assistance in the Event of Natural or Man-Made Disasters (1992) art 1.

82 Dutch Safety Authority (DSA), 'Cooperation on Nuclear Safety' (DSA 2018). No international agreement seems to have been adopted among the three States on these issues until now.

action to reduce the risk of disasters rests on public authorities, a variety of stakeholders are involved in disaster prevention activities. Of particular note is the increasingly important role of IOs, and of soft law instruments adopted under their auspices, in clarifying the content of the duty to prevent.

Despite the difficulties in clearly delimiting its content, the chapter has proposed three types of corollary duties, namely the duty to adopt adequate legal and regulatory frameworks and ad hoc risk mitigation measures; to perform risk assessment and mitigation activities; and to cooperate in prevention activities with other States and in international and regional fora. Further clarifications on the exact requirements of these obligations are generally provided by soft law instruments adopted within the DRR field, as well as recommendations and guidance documents created by IOs and other actors, including UN HR monitoring authorities. The level of implementation that has been achieved in relation to the prevention obligations outlined in this chapter, and the effectiveness of relevant enforcement mechanisms, are assessed in the chapters dealing with prevention of specific CBRN risks and with specific fields of law such as IHRL and IEL.

Bibliography

Barnidge R, 'The due diligence principle in International Law' (2006) 8(1) ICLR 81.

Benz E, 'Lessons from Fukushima: Strengthening the International Regulations of Nuclear Energy' (2013) 37(3) Wm. & Mary Envtl. L. & Pol'y Rev 845.

Cavoski A, 'Revisiting the Convention on Nuclear Safety: Lessons Learned from the Fukushima Accident' (2013) 3 AsianJIntL 365.

De Sadeleer N, *Environmental Principles: From Political Slogans to Legal Rules* (OUP 2002).

Gattini A, 'Breach of the Obligation to Prevent and Reparation Thereof in the ICJ's Genocide Judgment', 18(4) EJIL (2007) 695.

Hafner G and Buffard I, 'Obligations of prevention and the precautionary principle' in J Crawford and others, *The law of international responsibility* (OUP 2010).

Heieck J, *A duty to prevent genocide. Due diligence obligations among the P5* (Edward Elgar 2018).

Krieger H, Peters A and Kreuzer L (eds), *Due Diligence in the International Legal Order* (OUP 2020).

Kulesza J, *Due Diligence in International Law* (Brill 2016).

Nicoletti B, 'The Prevention of Natural and Man-Made Disasters: What Duties for States?' in A de Guttry, M Gestri and G Venturini (eds) *International Disaster Response Law* (Springer 2012).

Sommario E and Venier S, 'Human Rights Law and Disaster Risk Reduction' (2018) 49 QIL Zoom-in 29.

Sommario E, 'One law to bind them all: International Law and disaster resilience' in A Harwig and M Simoncini (eds), *Law and the Management of Disasters: The Challenge of Resilience* (Routledge 2016).

Sossai M, 'States' failure to take preventive action as a human rights issue' in F Zorzi Giustiniani and others (eds), *Routledge Handbook of Human Rights and Disasters* (Routledge 2018).

CHAPTER 4

Rules of General Scope in Order to Be Prepared to Deal with CBRN Emergency Situations

Andrea de Guttry

1 Introduction

CBRN events are very often unpredictable but also almost inevitable: taking into account the tremendous damage they can cause, States must establish adequate mitigation measures to minimise the consequences of these events.

This chapter investigates the general preparedness measures which States and, where applicable, international organisations (IOs) are expected to adopt. The analysis is devoted to the relevant rules, including hard and soft law, which regulate disaster governance at the universal, regional[1] and bilateral levels. However, it has to be underlined that preparedness obligations are rooted not only in the specific treaties analysed in the next paragraphs but also in rules aimed at protecting fundamental human rights,[2] the environment[3] and even in an autonomous rule of customary international law. According to the International Law Commission (ILC), '[e]ach State shall reduce the risk of disasters by taking appropriate measures, including through legislation and regulations, to prevent, mitigate, and prepare for disasters'.[4] This rule draws, according to the ILC, 'on principles emanating from international human rights law [...] and from a number of international environmental law principles, including the "due diligence" principle',[5] and it is based on a 'widespread

1 The EU rules will not be examined here, as they will be analysed in ch 10 by Villani in this volume.

2 See ch 27 by Venier in this volume.

3 See ch 29 by Antoniazzi in this volume.

4 ILC, 'Draft articles on the protection of persons in the event of disasters' (26 May 2016) UNGA, 'Report of the International Law Commission, Protection of Persons in Event of Disasters' (2016) UN Doc A/71/10, para 9. The ILC further states that the word 'shall' signifies 'the existence of the international legal obligation to act in the manner described in the paragraph and is the most succinct way to convey the sense of that legal obligation', see ibid, Commentary to Article 9, para 9.

5 Ibid para 4. On the 'due diligence' principle, see more in R Pisillo Mazzeschi, *Due diligence e responsabilità internazionale degli Stati*, (Giuffrè 1989), R Pisillo Mazzeschi, 'The Due Diligence Rule and the Nature of the International Responsibility of States' (1992) 35 German

 | DOI:10.1163/9789004507999_005

practice of States reflecting their commitment to reduce the risk of disasters'[6] and recognition that this commitment has been incorporated by States into their national policies and legal frameworks.[7]

Preparedness obligations specific only to given CBRN events, such as terrorist actions, industrial incidents or natural events such as pandemics are not examined in this contribution as they form the core of other chapters in this volume.

2 Terminological Clarification: The Notion of 'Preparedness' for CBRN Events

In Chapter 1, specific definitions of the different phases of a CBRN event were provided. However, considering the close interconnections between prevention, preparedness and response actions – and given that the borders between these three phases tend to be thin, making overlapping almost inevitable – it is worthwhile to isolate a few key features of the concept of preparedness. In general terms, this concept refers to the measures that must be adopted to enable the competent authorities to effectively deal with CBRN-related events and mitigate the consequences of such events. Preparedness was more precisely defined in 2016 in a Report to the UN General Assembly as:

> The knowledge and capacities developed by governments, response and recovery organizations, communities and individuals to effectively anticipate, respond to and recover from the impacts of likely, imminent or current disasters.[8]

Preparedness measures inevitably involve a wide range of activities to be performed by different actors, such as States, IOs, individuals (who are to be trained on how to behave in emergency situations), civil society and community leaders, and public agencies.

Yearbook of International Law, R Provost (ed.), *State Responsibility in International Law* (Routledge 2002) and J Kulesza, *Due Diligence in International Law* (Brill 2016) 4.

6 ILC (n 4) Commentary to Draft Article 9, para 5.

7 Ibid para 6.

8 UNGA, 'Report of the open-ended intergovernmental expert working group on indicators and terminology relating to disaster risk reduction' (1 December 2016) UN Doc A/71/644.

3 Preparedness Rules in International Instruments: At the Universal Level

The concept of preparedness likely first emerged during the preparatory works of the Convention Establishing the International Relief Union (IRU) in 1926,[9] although it did not appear in the final text. After this experience, a new trend emerged: issues related to disaster prevention, preparedness and management were regulated in separate treaties, each dedicated to one specific issue, such as the transport of goods by sea[10] or air,[11] customs,[12] health regulations,[13] international cooperation,[14] human rights,[15] waste management,[16] protection of the safety and security of international personnel involved in emergency operations,[17] safeguarding of the environment,[18] telecommunications[19] and so on. Many of these sectoral agreements are entirely dedicated to preparedness measures,[20] while others simply contain one or more preparedness rules.

---

9 The draft text of the IRU, submitted to the League of Nations States on 14 December 1925, expressly mentioned in art 2, para 4 that the IRU should have been tasked to adopt, if necessary 'measures based upon principles of preparedness and insurance': <https://biblio-archive.unog.ch/Dateien/CouncilMSD/C-2-M-2-1926-II_EN.pdf>. All links were last accessed in May 2021.

10 For an example, see the London Convention on Facilitation of International Maritime Traffic (1965), of which Section F is devoted to Natural Disaster Relief Work.

11 See letter C of ch 8 of International Standards and Recommended Practices, Facilitation, Annex 9 of the Convention on International Civil Aviation (1997).

12 For an example, see the Customs Convention on the Temporary Importation of Professional Equipment (1961), the International Convention on the Simplification and Harmonization of Customs Procedures (Kyoto Convention, 1973), the Revised Kyoto Convention (2000).

13 WHO, International Health Regulations, (2005) Second Edition: <http://whqlibdoc.who.int/publications/2008/9789241580410_eng.pdf>.

14 Although the activation of the international cooperation mechanism is typically related to the response phase (see more on this in ch 5 by Bakker in this volume), the codified rules which regulate international cooperation are to be considered as preparedness measures as they allow, should cooperation be requested, a swift response.

15 See ch 28 by Sommario in this volume.

16 Basel Convention on the Control of Transboundary Movement of Hazardous Wastes and their Disposal (1989).

17 See the Optional Protocol of the Convention on the Safety of United Nations and Associated Personnel (2005).

18 See ch 29 by Antoniazzi in this volume.

19 For an example, see the Tampere Convention on the Provision of Telecommunication Resources for Disaster Mitigation and Relief Operations (1998).

20 For example, treaties specifically devoted to regulating the modalities of requesting international support to face a given disaster or aimed at regulating the transport of emergency goods in advance.

Sometimes their application is restricted to a specific environment (marine,[21] atmosphere[22]). Over the last three decades, States, IOs, NGOs, the scientific community and the International Federation of Red Cross and Red Crescent Societies (IFRC) have also promoted the adoption of soft law instruments on specific issues related to preparedness activities to better deal with potential man-made or natural disasters involving the release of CBRN substances.[23] These soft law instruments – together with numerous additional political activities, carried out in different emergency-related contexts during recent decades[24] – have contributed to raising awareness and creating a sense of urgency in the UN family about the need for a more strategic approach to dealing with disasters. It is within this context that the UN General Assembly adopted the landmark Resolution 46/182 'Strengthening of the coordination of humanitarian emergency assistance of the United Nations', which established the framework within which international disaster relief activities are undertaken. Although Resolution 46/182 already contained several references to preparedness measures, these were further developed in successive UNGA Resolutions which significantly broadened the concept to include new issues, such as the link between prevention, preparedness, disaster risk reduction and capacity building;[25] the need to take into account the specific necessities of the affected population and to give appropriate consideration to, *inter alia*,

21 Ch XI-2 of the International Convention for the Safety of Life at Sea (SOLAS; 1974) regulates a significant number of preparedness obligations incumbent on the ship owner. Even more detailed rules were introduced in the 2002 International Ship and Port Facility Security (ISPS) Code.

22 For an example, see art 10 of the Agreement Governing the Activities of States on the Moon and other Celestial Bodies (1979): G Oberst, 'Protecting Satellites From Space Terrorism', Satellite Magazine (March 2009): <https://www.hoganlovells.com/~/media/hogan-lovells/pdf/publication/viasatellitemarch2009gerryoberst_pdf>.

23 For an example, see the IFRC Declaration of Principles for International Humanitarian Relief to the Civilian Population in Disaster Situations (1969), the Customs Council Recommendation to Expedite the Forwarding of Relief Consignments (1970), the Turku Declaration of Minimum Humanitarian Standards (1990), the Measures to Expedite Relief adopted by both the ICRC and ECOSOC (1997).

24 For an example, see the Resolution of the Inter-Parliamentary Union on International Cooperation for the Prevention and Management of Transborder Natural Disasters (2003): <http://www.ipu.org/conf-e/108-2.htm> in which the IPU 'Encourages the international community to co-operate more closely in mitigating the adverse effects of transborder natural disasters through improved preparedness ...'.

25 UNGA Res 69/243 (23 December 2014) UN Doc A/RES 69/243, op para 39.

gender,[26] age and disability;[27] the importance of consistently utilising early warning systems[28] and more space-based and ground-based remote-sensing technologies;[29] the urgent need to differentiate between disasters occurring in rural and urban areas when designing and implementing preparedness strategies;[30] and the importance of international cooperation and multilateralism as an expression of partnership and solidarity among all individuals, communities, States, and regional and international organisations, in all stages of disaster management.[31]

The adoption by the World Conference on Disaster Reduction of the 'Hyogo Framework for Action 2005–2015: Building the resilience of nations and communities to disasters'[32] and its successor, the 2015 'Sendai Framework', represent two more key UN achievements. One of the Sendai Framework priorities is dedicated to enhancing disaster preparedness, and specific measures are proposed to achieve this.

To address the challenges identified in the implementation of the Sendai Framework, in 2017, the UN adopted the 'Plan of Action on Disaster Risk Reduction: Towards a Risk-informed and Integrated Approach to Sustainable Development',[33] which emphasises the role and the priorities of the UN in supporting preparedness measures both at the international and local levels. This Plan is perfectly in keeping with the 2030 Agenda for Sustainable Development adopted by the UN General Assembly in September 2015.[34]

---

26 Ibid para 34, stressing the importance of the full and equal participation of women in decision-making and of gender mainstreaming in developing and implementing disaster preparedness.

27 Ibid para 36.

28 UNGA Res 54/233 (25 February 2000) UN Doc A/RES/54/233, para 4.

29 UNGA Res 69/243 (n 25) para 28.

30 UNGA Res 231 (21 December 2012) UN Doc A/RES/67/231, para 20.

31 UNGA Res 75/27 (7 December 2020) UN Doc A/RES 75/27.

32 <http://www.preventionweb.net/english/professional/publications/v.php?id=1037&pid:3&pif:3>.

33 <https://www.preventionweb.net/files/49076_unplanofaction.pdf>.

34 Sustainable Development Goal 3, devoted to the need to ensure 'healthy lives and promote well-being for all at all ages', indicates the strengthening of the capacity of all countries, in particular developing countries, 'for early warning, risk reduction and management of national and global health risks' as one of the targets to be achieved by 2030: <https://sdgs.un.org/goals/goal3>.

Likewise, UNESCO,[35] UNICRI[36] and the IFRC[37] have also adopted soft law instruments focusing on preparedness measures in specific areas.

3.1 *At the Regional Level: In Europe*

Given that preparedness measures are highly context-specific, *ie* they need to be tailored to the specific culture and situation to be effective, the development of such measures at the regional level is particularly valuable. The analysis starts with the European continent (with the exception of the EU-specific measures, to which a chapter of this book is devoted)[38] before shifting to the other regions of the world. This allows a comparative picture to be developed of interesting lessons learned from the various continents.

In 1987, the Committee of Ministers of the Council of Europe (CoE) adopted Resolution (87) creating the EUR-OPA Major Hazards Agreement.[39] Through this Agreement, a series of Medium Term Plans have been adopted, including most recently, the 'Medium Term Plan 2016–2020',[40] which codifies several recommendations and suggestions on how public authorities can contribute to promoting a healthy perception (rather than fear) of potential risks among the wider public.[41] Within the OSCE (the geographical limits of which go beyond the European continent), attention to disaster preparedness and management emerged much later, and only in 2014 were Participating States invited 'to develop, co-ordinate and implement, where appropriate, disaster risk reduction measures with climate change adaptation and mitigation

---

35 H Stovel, *Risk Preparedness: A Management Manual for World Cultural Heritage* (ICCROM 1998) <https://www.iccrom.org/sites/default/files/ICCROM_17_RiskPreparedness_en.pdf>.

36 The United Nations Interregional Crime and Justice Research Institute launched the CBRN Risk Mitigation and Security Governance Programme to encourage States to adopt a comprehensive CBRN approach to preparedness measures: <http://www.unicri.it/topics/cbrn/>. Subsequently, UNICRI further developed 'CBRN Security Governance indicators' (<http://www.unicri.it/topics/cbrn/security_governance/>) to help national leaders to check whether their preparedness measures are operating effectively.

37 IFRC, 'Guidelines for the domestic facilitation and regulation of international disaster relief and initial recovery assistance' (2007) 30IC/07/R04 <https://www.icrc.org/en/doc/assets/files/red-cross-crescent-movement/31st-international-conference/idrl-guidelines-en.pdf>.

38 See ch 6 by Casolari in this volume.

39 Participation in this group is open to Member States of the Council of Europe, the European Commission or any other interested State. Currently, there are 26 Member States: <http://www.coe.int/T/DG4/MajorHazards/Default_en.asp>.

40 <https://www.coe.int/en/web/europarisks/statutory-meetings>.

41 Action Plan, pt II.

plans at all appropriate levels'.[42] Since then, the Office of the Co-ordinator of OSCE Economic and Environmental Activities (OCEEA) has been tasked with assisting the Participating States – upon their request and where appropriate – in implementing 'increased preparedness for cross-border implications of disasters', 'raising disaster risk awareness at the local level, and [promoting] community-based and gender/age/disability-sensitive disaster risk reduction'.[43] While these activities testify to an increasing awareness of the importance of preparedness activities,[44] it is important to note that the OSCE preparedness measures are drafted in a rather vague manner.

Although its geographical scope is, once again, wider than the European continent, NATO has been actively involved in promoting both preparedness structures and policies. The NATO Combined Joint CBRN Defence Task Force is trained and equipped to deal with CBRN events and/or attacks involving hazardous material, which affect NATO populations, territory or forces, including civilian crisis situations such as natural disasters and industrial accidents.[45] As far as NATO policies are concerned, the document 'Commitment to Enhance Resilience', adopted during the 2016 North Atlantic Council in Warsaw,[46] emphasised that 'resilience is an essential basis for credible deterrence and defence and effective fulfilment of the Alliance's core tasks'.[47] In this context,

42 For an example, see the OSCE Madrid Declaration on Environment and Security (2007) and OSCE Ministerial Council, Decision No. 6/14, Enhancing Disaster Risk Reduction (5 December 2014) MC.DEC/6/14 <https://www.osce.org/files/f/documents/8/6/130406.pdf>.

43 Ibid.

44 For an example, see the OSCE 'Good Practices Guide on Non Nuclear Critical Energy Infrastructure Protection from Terrorist Attacks Focusing on Threats Emanating from Cyberspace' <https://www.osce.org/files/f/documents/4/b/103500.pdf>.

45 <https://www.nato.int/cps/en/natohq/topics_49156.htm>. According to NATO sources, the Battalion 'played a key planning role during the 2004 Summer Olympics in Greece, and the 2004 Istanbul Summit, where it supported CBRN-related contingency operations'. Ibid.

46 *Warsaw Summit Communiqué Issued by the Heads of State and Government participating in the meeting of the North Atlantic Council in Warsaw 8–9 July 2016*, <https://www.nato.int/cps/en/natohq/official_texts_133180.htm>.

47 These measures are aimed at guaranteeing the continuity of government and critical government services, energy supplies, resilient food and water resources, and integrity of civil communications and transportation systems, <https://www.nato.int/cps/en/natohq/topics_49158.htm>. In 2020, NATO was expected to present a report on the state of civil preparedness, assessing if and to what extent the 2016 Resilience Commitments have been implemented and/or require updating in the face of new challenges, particularly in the fields of transport and energy. Due to the COVID-19 pandemic, the finalisation of the report has been postponed, <https://www.nato.int/cps/en/natohq/opinions_174772.htm?selectedLocale=en>.

the word 'resilience' is used instead of integration to denote the concept of preparedness.[48] Moreover, NATO has been very active in the preparation of soft law instruments.[49]

In other European areas, such as the Nordic, Central European, Baltic, Arctic and Black Sea regions, attention has been mainly focused on two points: codification of mutual emergency assistance agreements to facilitate the delivery of international assistance in case of incidents,[50] and codification of agreements devoted specifically to preparedness measures.[51]

3.2 *In the African Continent*

The first African Regional Strategy for Disaster Risk Reduction (hereafter the 'African Strategy') was developed by the African Union in 2003.[52] It included various preparedness actions, such as identifying and assessing disaster risks, increasing public awareness of disaster risk reduction and improving the governance of disaster risk reduction institutions. Several Programmes of Action (PoAs) for the Implementation of the African Strategy were subsequently approved: the most recent was adopted in 2017 and covers the period from 2015–2030.[53] Three aspects of this PoA deserve special mention: first

48 The preference shown for the term 'resilience' is most probably due to the fact that this principle is anchored in art 3 of the Alliance's founding treaty.

49 For an example, see NATO, 'NATO guidance on Improving Resilience of National and Cross-Border Energy Networks', 'NATO guidance for Incidents Involving Mass Casualties', the 'Non-Binding Guidelines and Minimum Standards for CBRN First Responders' (2014), <https://www.nato.int/nato_static_fl2014/assets/pdf/pdf_2016_08/20160802_140801-cep-first-responders-CBRN-, ng.pdf>.

50 In the eastern part of the European continent, an impressive pro-activism – especially by the Commonwealth of Independent States – in the area of preparedness has developed over recent decades, with a specific focus on preparing Member States to request/receive international support and assistance in case of natural or man-made disaster.

51 For an example, see the Agreement Among the Governments of the Participating States of the Black Sea Economic Cooperation on Collaboration in Emergency Assistance and Emergency Response to Natural and Man-made Disasters (1998), the Nordic Public Health Preparedness Agreement (2002) and the Agreement Between the Governments in the Barents Euro-Arctic Region on Cooperation Within the Field of Emergency Prevention, Preparedness and Response (2008).

52 African Union and others, 'Disaster Risk Reduction for Sustainable Development in Africa, Africa Regional Strategy for Disaster Risk Reduction' (2004), <https://www.preventionweb.net/files/4038_africaregionalstrategy1.pdf>.

53 Decision of the African Union Executive Council at its 30th Ordinary Session, January 2017 [EX.CL/Dec.943 (XXX)], endorsing the Programme of Action for the Implementation of the Sendai Framework for Disaster Risk Reduction 2015–2030 in Africa, <https://www.preventionweb.net/files/49455_poaforsendaiimplementationinafrica.pdf>.

of all, it includes a matrix of specific activities to be carried out at the continental, regional, national and sub-national/local levels and has a special section devoted to preparedness activities.[54] Secondly, the PoA introduces a new monitoring and reporting system with the aim of increasing effective implementation.[55] Finally, the PoA identifies key stakeholders at various levels and describes the roles and tasks assigned to each of them. This last point is extremely important in order to avoid overlapping responsibilities (which might risk exacerbating inter-institutional tensions) and to increase the accountability of the different actors involved.

The path undertaken by the African Union (AU) has also been, in large part, followed by sub-regional organisations, which sometimes focus on specific aspects.[56] The Economic Community of West African States (ECOWAS), for example, adopted an innovative document in 2020 which devotes special attention to gender issues: the 'ECOWAS Disaster Risk Reduction Gender Strategy and Action Plan 2020–2030'.[57] This ECOWAS decision should be praised and used as a model, not only within the African continent but globally, for its consideration of the definition and implementation of specific gender-sensitive preparedness activities.

3.3 *In the Americas*

In the American continent, which, due to its geography and morphology, is prone to major natural disasters, the Organization of American States (OAS) and its members have focused mostly on outlining international responses as a preparedness measure. In this context, although it has been ratified by only

54 The matrix identifies specific preparedness goals to be achieved at the continental level ('Effectively coordinate preparedness and integrate preparedness measures for effective response'), the regional level ('Establish and strengthen multi-hazard early warning systems and regional mechanisms for early action and response'), the national level ('Establish and strengthen emergency preparedness, response and recovery support and coordination mechanisms, capacities and facilities, including coordination centres') and at the sub-national/local level ('Establish and Strengthen multidisciplinary local disaster risk management mechanisms').

55 See more in D van Niekerk, C Coetzee, L Nemakonde, 'Implementing the Sendai Framework in Africa: Progress against the Targets (2015–2018)' (2020) 11 International Journal of Disaster Risk Science, 179–189.

56 On the activities of the several African regional organisations in the areas under scrutiny, refer to N Wasonga Orago 'Africa and MENA Region (2018)' 1(1) *Yearbook of International Disaster Law Online*, <https://brill.com/view/journals/yido/1/1/article-p326_326.xml?language=en>.

57 <https://www.gfdrr.org/sites/default/files/publication/ECOWAS%20GSAP_EN_Final.pdf>.

six States so far,[58] the 1991 Inter-American Convention to Facilitate Disaster Assistance introduced several innovations and has influenced subsequent international practice, especially within the continent. A decade later, during the 2001 Third Summit of the Americas, the parties not only confirmed their commitment to continue implementing policies that enhance their ability 'to prevent, mitigate and respond to the consequences of natural disasters',[59] but also adopted an ambitious Plan of Action in which States are required to adopt several preparedness measures.[60] Sub-regional agreements aimed at reinforcing international cooperation were adopted in the Caribbean region,[61] Central America[62] and the Andean region.[63]

3.4 *In Asia*

One of the main achievements in this region, thus far, was the creation, in 1998, of the Asian Disaster Reduction Centre, located in Kobe, Hyogo Prefecture, Japan.[64] A few years later, the Association of South-East Asian Nations (ASEAN) finalised the 2005 Agreement on Disaster Management and Emergency Response, in order to provide 'effective mechanisms to achieve substantial reduction of disaster losses in lives and in the social, economic and environmental assets of the Parties'.[65] The agreement provides detailed disaster preparedness obligations incumbent upon Member States and contains a notable innovation, namely the establishment of the ASEAN Standby Arrangements for Disaster Relief and Emergency Response (Article 9). On a voluntary basis, each party earmarks assets and resources available for disaster

58 The treaty has been ratified by only six States so far, see <http://www.oas.org/juridico/english/Sigs/a-54.html>.

59 See the Declaration of Quebec City, <http://www.summit-americas.org/iii_summit/iii_summit_dec_en.pdf>.

60 Plan of Action adopted during the III Summit of the Americas, <http://www.summit-americas.org/iii_summit/iii_summit_poa_en.pdf>.

61 See the Agreement establishing the Caribbean Disaster Emergency Response Agency (1991) and the Agreement for Regional Cooperation on Natural Disasters (1999).

62 For an example, see the Coordination Centre for Natural Disaster Prevention in Central America.

63 See the Comité Andino para la Prevención y Atención de Desastres (2002) and the Protocolo Adicional al Acuerdo Marco sobre Medio Ambiente del MERCOSUR en Materia de Cooperación y Asistencia Frente a Emergencias Ambientales (2004), which also contains very precise rules governing the disaster preparedness phase, see <http://www.comunidadandina.org/StaticFiles/DocOf/DEC529.pdf>.

64 Its mission is to enhance the disaster resilience of member countries, build safe communities, and create a society where sustainable development is possible. See more at <http://www.adrc.asia/aboutus/index.html>.

65 Art 2 of the 2005 Agreement.

relief and emergency response, such as search and rescue teams, military and civilian assets, emergency stockpiles of disaster relief items, and so forth. An online inventory has been created: it gives the focal points of the ASEAN Committee on Disaster Management (ACDM) rapid access to all the necessary information and provides a clear picture of available resources – an excellent example of a preparedness measure.

The South Asian Association for Regional Cooperation (SAARC), which groups together several States in the region,[66] approved the Agreement on Rapid Response to Natural Disasters in 2001,[67] requiring States to jointly or individually develop 'strategies and contingency/response plans to reduce losses from disasters';[68] to organise periodic mock drills to test their preparedness measures; and to earmark assets and capacities to be used in future disaster management operations.[69] Similar agreements have been adopted within the framework of the Shanghai Cooperation Organisation (SCO),[70] while the Gulf Cooperation Council has decided to create a Disaster Centre.[71]

3.5 *In the Rest of the World*

Considering the particular situation of the Arctic region and the increasing effects exerted on it by human activities, an Emergency Prevention, Preparedness and Response (EPPR) Working Group was established in 1991, under the auspices of the Arctic Council, with the goal of ensuring adequate emergency responses.[72] At the opposite end of the world, the 1991 Protocol on Environmental Protection to the Antarctic Treaty[73] seems much more focused on the prevention and response phases to the neglect of preparedness obligations.

66 Afghanistan, Bangladesh, Bhutan, India, Maldives, Nepal, Pakistan and Sri Lanka are the Member States of SAARC.

67 <https://www.preventionweb.net/files/61014_254.pdf>.

68 Art V of the Treaty.

69 Art VI of the Treaty. For appropriate management of these events, the SAARC Disaster Management Centre (SDMC) is operating in New Delhi.

70 Agreement on Disaster Relief Mutual Assistance between the Governments of the Member States of the Shanghai Cooperation Organization (2005): according to art 1, the agreement is applicable should there be an event causing the dispersion of CBRN substances: <http://eng.sectsco.org/documents/>.

71 <https://www.gcc-sg.org>.

72 The WG has two tasks: to develop an international instrument on Arctic marine oil pollution preparedness and response and to develop a set of recommendations or best practices in the area of prevention of marine oil pollution. More information can be found at <https://eppr.org/>.

73 <https://treaties.un.org/doc/Publication/UNTS/Volume%202941/volume-2941-A-5778.pdf>.

More relevant to the topic under discussion here, are the activities promoted by the associations of island States: the Pacific island countries have adopted a list of voluntary preparedness actions in the 'Framework for Resilient Development in the Pacific. An Integrated Approach to Address Climate Change and Disaster Risk Management, 2017–2030'.[74] Additionally, the Alliance of Small Islands has been actively involved in the promotion of national policies aimed at fostering resilience in all its dimensions and supporting the development of 'Climate smart resilient islands', which can be considered a preparedness measure to better face disasters.[75]

Finally, the role played by the G7/G8 needs to be commented on. Preparedness measures were addressed for the first time in the Annexes to the 2015 Final Declaration of the G7 meeting.[76] One year later, at the Ise-Shima Summit, the G7 leaders emphasised their commitment to taking concrete actions to advance global health, especially by strengthening 'prevention and preparedness against public health emergencies'.[77] Additional documents devoted specifically to preparedness measures for the current COVID-19 pandemic are examined in Chapter 17.

3.6 *At the Bilateral Level*

In order to fulfil obligations to protect the basic human rights of the affected population, and being well aware that the magnitude of man-made or natural disasters requires the support and cooperation of other partners, many States have concluded bilateral agreements that refer to serious incidents[78] or natural or man-made events of a certain gravity (which would undoubtedly apply to an event provoking the release of CBRN substances). Although in most cases these bilateral treaties have been signed between neighbouring States, in several instances they have been concluded between States far away from each other. In such cases, the treaties are often instrumental

74 <http://tep-a.org/wp-content/uploads/2017/05/FRDP_2016_finalResilient_Dev_pacific.pdf>.

75 For more details, see the letter by the Chair of AOSIS to the UNSG on 8 August 2019 on the occasion of the UN Climate Action Summit 2019, <https://www.aosis.org/wp-content/uploads/2019/09/SIDS-Package-Letter-from-AOSIS-Chair-to-UNSG.pdf>.

76 Annex to the G7 Leaders' Declaration, Schloss Elmau, Germany, 8 June 2015.

77 In the Biarritz 2019 G7 Declaration dedicated to 'Tackling Fragilities and Preventing Crises in Developing Countries', special attention was devoted to fragile and conflict-prone States and the importance of 'promoting greater investments in prevention, resilience, preparedness and early action, building early warning-early action mechanisms'.

78 Art 2 of the Agreement Between the Republic of Austria and the Republic of Croatia on Mutual Assistance in the Event of Disasters or Serious Accidents (2004). <http://disasterlaw.sssup.it/wp-content/uploads/2014/10/Agreement-Austria-Croatia-2006.pdf>.

in reinforcing the capacity of one State to deal with major disasters through capacity-building initiatives sponsored and promoted by the partner State.[79] Many of these treaties regulate not only international assistance, but they also make specific reference to other preparedness obligations incumbent on States.[80] Some bilateral conventions are devoted to regulating only specific areas of cooperation,[81] while others have been stipulated between a State and IOs (regional or global).[82]

4 Summing up: The Content of Preparedness Obligations

The investigation carried out in the previous paragraphs highlights that there are numerous international rules (at the universal, regional and even bilateral levels) dedicated to preparedness activities for serious incidents (such as those causing the release of CBRN substances) of any origin that might occur in the foreseeable future. According to these rules, States and IOs (where relevant) are required to:

a) ensure the acquisition, use and sharing of accurate data and other information, including sex- and age-disaggregated data and data on vulnerable groups, in order to fully assess risks and facilitate more focused preparedness;
b) strengthen effective multi-hazard early warning systems, for both sudden- and slow-onset hazards, and strengthen the use of science and technology to inform risk management, hazard/disaster preparedness and policy development;

79 For an example, see the MoU between Italy and Venezuela on bilateral cooperation in civil protection issues (2007).

80 In several bilateral treaties, there are rules devoted to reinforcing the level of preparedness of the parties through exchanging information, developing research programmes, and organising specialised courses and emergency operation drills. See, for example, the Protocol of Intentions between the USA Federal Emergency Management Agency and the Ministry of Defence of the Republic of Bulgaria on Cooperation on Natural and Man-made Technological Emergency Prevention and Response (2000).

81 For examples, see the Air Agreement on Humanitarian, Emergency, AirTaxi and Ambulance Flights Between Italy and Spain (1984) and the Agreement between the Governments of the Republic of Kazakhstan, the Kyrgyz Republic and the Republic of Uzbekistan on Co-operation and Interaction in the Field of Research on Earthquakes and Forecasting of Seismic Danger (1995).

82 For an example, see the Scientific Co-operation Agreement on Co-operation in Hydro-Meteorological Monitoring, Natural Disaster Prevention and Early Warning Between Italy and the Caribbean Community (2006).

c) promote the resilience of new and existing critical infrastructure, including water, transportation and telecommunications infrastructure; educational facilities; and hospitals and other health facilities to ensure that they remain safe, effective and operational during and after disasters to provide life-saving and essential services;
d) adopt sound preparedness plans in conjunction with interested communities that include clear provisions on the chain of command in case a CBRN event occurs; rules on the potential activation of international cooperation mechanisms; procedures to regularly update the preparedness plans;[83] and dedicated financial contributions for their implementation;[84]
e) have a proper and well-functioning health system, which has the necessary equipment and stands ready to be activated;
f) establish a contingency stockpile of emergency relief items;
g) improve coordination among relevant UN bodies and cooperation with governments of affected countries, as well as regional and other relevant organisations, with the aim of maximising the effectiveness of preparedness measures; reducing the impact of natural disasters; and facilitating the delivery of international assistance, particularly to developing countries;[85]
h) promote regular disaster preparedness, response and recovery exercises, such as evacuation drills, training and the establishment of area-based support systems, with a view to ensuring rapid and effective responses to disasters and related displacement, including access to safe shelter, essential food and non-food relief supplies as per local needs;
i) ensure information flows are planned well in advance and have clear guidance on who is entitled to issue official updates about the event and its consequences.

In addition to these general rules on preparedness measures for any CBRN event, States must also fulfil preparedness obligations for specific types of CBRN events (such as terrorism, industrial incidents, pandemics). These latter rules are examined in Chapters 16, 17 and 18.

The analysis of the preparedness rules allows us to draw a few conclusions: first of all, it appears that those drafted at the universal level are comprehensive and they cover almost all the relevant aspects, without significant gaps. This is strong evidence that awareness about the importance of CBRN preparedness

83 UNGA Resolution 65/133 (15 December 2010) UN Doc A/RES/65/133, para 11.
84 UNGA/RES/69/243 (n 25).
85 UNGA Resolution 59/212 (3 March 2005) UN Doc A/RES/59/212, para 7.

measures has significantly increased in the international community over recent decades, at least as far as the codification of the rules is concerned.

A second aspect which emerges is the limited codification of specific CBRN preparedness rules at the regional level. This might be explained by the fact that the universal rules are generally perceived as sufficient. Only a very limited number of regional organisations (especially NATO and, albeit to a more limited extent, ECOWAS) have devoted significant efforts to upgrading and updating their preparedness capacities to deal with CBRN events. The proactive preparedness attitude of NATO and ECOWAS might be explained by the military background of NATO and the specific attention to regional security issues of ECOWAS.

A third emerging issue is the lack of distinction between prevention and preparedness measures on one side and preparedness and response measures on the other. However, dividing the management of a CBRN event into phases is crucial in order to better identify what has to be done and who is responsible for the different activities to be carried out. The lack of distinction between different phases might also cause a risk of confusing overlaps; thus, a comprehensive and well-structured approach to the different phases of an event involving the release of CBRN substances is of fundamental importance.

5 Preliminary Assessment of the Degree of Implementation of the International Preparedness Rules within States' Domestic Legal Orders and Concluding Remarks

To implement all these measures, States (and sometimes relevant IOs) not only have a heavy workload but also significant costs. With a few exceptions,[86] there is very limited information available regarding the degree of effective domestication of the generic international preparedness measures listed above. A few States have implemented most of the general preparedness measures in their domestic systems, creating ad hoc institutions or publishing manuals and guidelines on how to manage a CBRN event[87] and adopting

86 For example, the status of the implementation of UNSC Resolution 1540 (28 April 2004) UN Doc S/RES/1540 is regularly monitored by the Resolution Committee, which is tasked to report on the resolution's implementation to the Security Council: see <https://www.un.org/en/sc/1540/comprehensive-and-annual-reviews/2021-comprehensive-review.shtml>.

87 Public Health England, 'Chemical, biological, radiological and nuclear incidents: clinical management and health protection' (2018) and 'Chemical, biological, radiological and

national CBRN strategies.[88] However, in most cases, States have not been very active in implementing the preparedness measures,[89] with the most popular justification for the failure to fulfil these obligations[90] being a lack of financial resources. While this argument is well founded in the case of vulnerable States or States affected by a conflict or international sanctions,[91] it is less convincing for countries with reasonably comprehensive and robust health systems. In fact, it has been calculated that 'financing improved preparedness might cost less than $1 per person per year, not a huge sum compared to the scale of the risks to human lives and livelihoods'.[92] Nonetheless, in a few – mainly Western – countries, guaranteeing sustained commitment to financing preparedness measures often proves to be extremely difficult 'since the mark of success is that nothing happens, and there will always be multiple competing

nuclear incidents: clinical action cards', <https://www.gov.uk/government/publications/chemical-biological-radiological-and-nuclear-incidents-recognise-and-respond>.

88 For an example, see the Chemical, Biological, Radiological, Nuclear and Explosives Resilience Action Plan for Canada, 2011: <https://www.publicsafety.gc.ca/cnt/rsrcs/pblctns/rslnc-ctn-pln/rslnc-ctn-pln-eng.pdf>. This document includes a significant number of preparedness actions which the Government of Canada undertakes to implement. See also the Emergency Management Strategy for Canada, Toward a Resilient 2030: <https://www.publicsafety.gc.ca/cnt/rsrcs/pblctns/mrgncy-mngmnt-strtgy/mrgncy-mngmnt-strtgy-en.pdf>.

89 This is also confirmed by a recent study carried out at the request of the European Parliament: EP, Directorate General for Internal Policies, Policy Department for Citizens' Rights and Constitutional Affairs, 'Member States' Preparedness for CBRN Threat Study' (2018), <https://www.statewatch.org/news/2018/may/ep-study-cbrn-threats-ms-preparedness-5-18.pdf>.

90 According to another line of thinking, the poor performance of various States can be explained by the influence of external elements on their attitude, such as 'perceived risk, disaster preparedness knowledge, prior disaster experiences, and certain sociodemographic characteristics such as gender, age, education, and family income': E Y Chan, J Y Ho 'Urban community disaster and emergency health risk perceptions and preparedness', in R Shaw, K Shiwaku, T Izumi (eds.) *Science and Technology in Disaster Risk Reduction in Asia* (Elsevier 2018). See also S Appleby-Arnold, N Brockdorff, I Jakovljev, S Zdravković, 'Applying cultural values to encourage disaster preparedness: Lessons from a low-hazard country' (2018) 31 International Journal of Disaster Risk Reduction, 37–44.

91 In a recent study on the impact of economic sanctions on preparedness measures, the authors demonstrated that, due to their high costs, preparedness measures may be among the first to suffer from economic sanctions: E V McLean and T Whang 'Economic Sanctions and Government Spending Adjustments: The Case of Disaster Preparedness?' (2019) British Journal of Political Science, First View, 1.

92 World Bank, International Working Group on Financing Preparedness, 'From Panic and Neglect to Investing in Health Security: Financing Pandemic Preparedness at a National Level' (2017), <https://documents.worldbank.org/en/publication/documents-reports/documentdetail/979591495652724770/from-panic-and-neglect-to-investing-in-health-security-financing-pandemic-preparedness-at-a-national-level>.

priorities'.[93] This dilemma was addressed in a well-known European Court of Human Rights judgment, which stated in clear terms that 'an impossible or disproportionate burden must not be imposed on the authorities without consideration being given, in particular, to the operational choices which they must make in terms of priorities and resources'.[94] Borrowing a concept widely used in the jurisprudence of international human rights courts, States enjoy a 'margin of appreciation' in determining which preparedness measures must come first and which will have to be implemented later.[95] The exercise of this discretionary power is, however, always subject to the control of the relevant courts should there be a dispute as to whether a State respected its preparedness obligations.[96]

To face the worldwide problem of scarcity of financial resources to implement preparedness measures, international financial institutions have undertaken specific initiatives. For example, the World Bank launched the Global Facility for Disaster Reduction and Recovery (GFDRR), a global partnership that helps developing countries better understand and reduce their vulnerability to natural hazards and climate change.[97] Additionally, the EU has generously supported several national projects around the world to increase preparedness for the serious risks associated with disasters and especially CBRN events.[98]

---

93 Ibid.

94 European Court of Human Rights (ECtHR), *Budayeva and others v Russia* (2014) 59 EHRR 2, para 135.

95 When it comes to choosing the measures to be adopted by the States, the ECtHR has consistently held that 'where the State is required to take positive measures, the choice of means is in principle a matter that falls within the Contracting State's margin of appreciation. There are different avenues to ensure Convention rights, and even if the State has failed to apply one particular measure provided by domestic law, it may still fulfil its positive duty by other means': ECtHR, *Kolyadenko and Others v Russia*, App. nos. 17423/05 et al., para 220.

96 In *Budayeva* (n 95) para 136, the ECtHR stated that 'In assessing whether the respondent State had complied with the positive obligation, the Court must consider [...] the domestic decision-making process, including the appropriate investigations and studies, and the complexity of the issue, especially where conflicting Convention interests are involved'.

97 GFDRR is a grant-funding mechanism managed by the World Bank that supports disaster risk management projects worldwide <https://www.gfdrr.org/en/global-facility-disaster-reduction-and-recovery)>.

98 See more on these EU programmes in ch 10 by Villani in this volume.

In general terms, as revealed by several recent studies,[99] the degree of implementation of preparedness rules at the national level is far from ideal and the delays are not always due to the high costs of the required measures. The full implementation of the international preparedness rules at national level is an essential condition for minimising the consequences of any CBRN event, and there is an urgent need to identify new tools to improve the current situation. It might be useful to introduce more detailed targets to be achieved within a specific time period:[100] this would help the individual States to better coordinate and synchronise the implementation phase. It is also of utmost importance to design more sophisticated and convincing monitoring mechanisms.[101] Compared with other thematic areas, such as human rights, in which effective monitoring and enforcement mechanisms have significantly increased respect for the relevant rules, the current monitoring mechanisms devoted to preparedness measures are woefully insufficient (if not non-existent) with very limited exceptions.[102] This is a problematic issue which deserves to receive more attention in the near future: any new treaty (universal or regional) dealing with preparedness obligations should always incorporate a strong and sophisticated monitoring and implementation verification mechanism. The credibility and effectiveness of the relevant rules would enormously benefit from this innovation.

This survey of the general preparedness obligations codified in international treaties (universal, regional and bilateral), as well as in soft law instruments,

---

99 See, for example, the data regularly provided in the Global Health Security Index, <https://www.ghsindex.org/>.

100 The approach of the Sendai Framework of identifying seven global targets to achieve is an important step as this makes it easier to track global progress towards achieving the goal of the Sendai Framework itself.

101 It is not by chance that one of the expected key results of the 'UN Plan of Action on Disaster Risk Reduction for Resilience: Towards a Risk-informed and Integrated Approach to Sustainable Development' is that the 'UN system and related organizations [will] have supported countries in monitoring the implementation of the Sendai Framework, ensuring coherence with the monitoring frameworks of the Sustainable Development Goals, the Paris Agreement, the New Urban Agenda and other international frameworks'.

102 For example, the sophisticated and innovative monitoring mechanism introduced in the treaties regulating preparedness measures in the health sector: see ch 17 by de Guttry in this volume. An interesting example of a monitoring system for preparedness obligations is foreseen in the OPCW Convention, where States are required to provide the Secretariat with information about the various means of protection available against chemical weapons. The annual 'Report of the OPCW on the Implementation of the Convention on the Prohibition of the Development, Production, Stockpiling and Use of Chemical Weapons and on their Destruction'.

has demonstrated that there are currently many (potentially too many) diverse sources regulating similar State obligations. Although this situation is preferable to the opposite (no rules at all), it highlights the extraordinary importance of closer relations and more effective forms of cooperation among the different actors involved in the production of these rules. While acknowledging the strenuous efforts of the UN to encourage closer coordination of all relevant international actors involved in disaster management, it is the opinion of the present author that more could and should be done. In many regional treaties, there are interesting and promising commitments to reinforce cooperation with other relevant actors: nice words codified into the various treaties now need to be transformed into concrete measures which will achieve real cooperation and synergy among the actors involved in both the definition and monitoring of preparedness measures. Further delays cannot be justified considering current risks and the lessons learned from various disasters in which CBRN substances have been released.

Bibliography

Appleby-Arnold S, Brockdorff N, Jakovljev I, Zdravković S 'Applying cultural values to encourage disaster preparedness: Lessons from a low-hazard country' (2018) 31 International Journal of Disaster Risk Reduction, 37.

Chan E Y, Ho J Y 'Urban community disaster and emergency health risk perceptions and preparedness', in R Shaw, K Shiwaku, T Izumi (eds.) *Science and Technology in Disaster Risk Reduction in Asia* (Elsevier 2018), 95.

Kulesza J, *Due Diligence in International Law* (Brill 2016).

McLean E V and Whang T, 'Economic Sanctions and Government Spending Adjustments: The Case of Disaster Preparedness?' (2019) British Journal of Political Science, First View, 394.

Oberst G, 'Protecting Satellites from Space Terrorism', Satellite Magazine (March 2009).

Pisillo Mazzeschi R, *Due diligence e responsabilità internazionale degli Stati* (Giuffrè 1989).

Pisillo Mazzeschi R, 'The Due Diligence Rule and the Nature of the International Responsibility of States', (1992) 35 German Yearbook of International Law, 9.

Stove H, *Risk Preparedness: A Management Manual for World Cultural Heritage* (ICCROM 1992).

Trapp R, 'Art. X Assistance and Protection against Chemical Weapons', in W Krutzsch, E Myjer, R Trapp (eds.), *The Chemical Weapons Convention: A Commentary, Part Three, Articles of the Chemical Weapons Convention* (OUP 2014), 331.

van Niekerk D, Coetzee C, Nemakonde L 'Implementing the Sendai Framework in Africa: Progress against the Targets (2015–2018)', (2020) 11 International Journal of Disaster Risk Science, 179.

Wasonga Orago N, 'Africa and MENA Region (2018)', (2018) 1 Yearbook of International Disaster Law Online, 326.

World Bank, International Working Group on Financing Preparedness, *From Panic and Neglect to Investing in Health Security: Financing Pandemic Preparedness at a National Level* (Washington 2017).

CHAPTER 5

General Obligations to Respond to and Recover from CBRN Emergency Situations

Christine Bakker

1 Introduction

When responding to emergency situations including CBRN events, the international community acknowledges the need for international cooperation, coordination, and assistance. International support is often also required in the aftermath of a CBRN (or other) emergency, as the affected communities recover from its social, economic, and other impacts. This chapter examines international obligations and standards of a general scope, included in universal, regional[1] and bilateral instruments related to the response and recovery phases of CBRN emergencies, from an 'all-hazards perspective'.[2] Therefore, this chapter analyses the obligations and guidance included in both legally binding instruments and in 'soft-law' instruments, such as resolutions and guidelines, for response and recovery actions that are applicable to any CBRN event, whether resulting from man-made or from natural causes. The response and recovery rules that exclusively apply to specific CBRN events, such as terrorism, industrial accidents and naturally occurring events, including pandemics, are discussed elsewhere in this volume.[3] The analysis focuses on the obligations and standards applicable to States, and, where appropriate, to international organisations and non-State actors.

The chapter first recalls the definitions of key terms used in this contribution (Section 2). It subsequently identifies the main sources of general obligations to respond to and recover from CBRN emergencies, adopted at the universal and regional levels, as well as considering some examples of bilateral agreements (Section 3). The chapter then identifies the main categories of response and recovery obligations and the available enforcement mechanisms

1 European Union instruments are not addressed, since they are the subject of separate contributions in this volume: ch 6 by Casolari, ch 10 by Villani, ch 15 by Balboni, ch 19 by Ferri.

2 See ch 1 by Frulli in this volume.

3 On response and recovery obligations related to CBRN terrorism, see ch 9 by Perrone; on CBRN industrial accidents, see ch 13 by Bakker and Montanaro; and on naturally occurring CBRN events, see ch 18 by Bakker and Farina in this volume.

 | DOI:10.1163/9789004507999_006

(Section 4), before concluding with some remarks on the strengths and weaknesses of the overall regulatory framework for disaster response and recovery.

2 'Setting the Stage': Terminology

This chapter adopts the definitions of 'response' and 'recovery' laid down in the Report of the open-ended intergovernmental expert working group on indicators and terminology relating to disaster risk reduction, endorsed by the UN General Assembly in 2016.[4] Therefore, 'response' is understood as:

> Actions taken directly before, during or immediately after a disaster in order to save lives, reduce health impacts, ensure public safety and meet the basic subsistence needs of the people affected.[5]

The actions adopted in the response phase mainly focus on the period during and immediately after a disaster. Actions taken 'directly before' a disaster only fall within the scope of 'response' when they are adopted immediately before a disaster because it has been forecasted as about to occur. Otherwise, actions taken directly before the occurrence of an event are generally considered to be part of the preparedness phase.[6] This chapter will therefore not consider obligations related to the 'development' of response capacities, nor to the adoption of legislation, guidelines or policies, which relate to the preparation of the response, and therefore belong to disaster 'preparedness.'

Turning to the recovery phase of the disaster management cycle, the analysis applies the following definition of 'recovery':

> The restoring or improving of livelihoods and health, as well as economic, physical, social, cultural and environmental assets, systems and activities, of a disaster- affected community or society, aligning with the principles of sustainable development and "build back better", to avoid or reduce future disaster risk.[7]

---

4 UNGA 'Report of the open-ended intergovernmental expert working group on indicators and terminology relating to disaster risk reduction' (1 December 2016) UN Doc A/71/644 (hereafter 'Report of the open-ended WG') The Recommendations were endorsed by UNGA Res 71/276 (2 February 2017) UN Doc A/RES/71/276. See also ch 1 by Frulli in this volume.

5 Ibid 22.

6 See ch 4 by de Guttry in this volume.

7 Report of the open-ended WG (n 4) 21.

Therefore, the focus in this phase is on the period starting immediately after the disaster. Depending on the nature and severity of the disaster, the recovery phase can have a varied duration. In this analysis, 'rehabilitation' and 'reconstruction' are also considered as part of the recovery phase. In the report of the open-ended working group, 'rehabilitation' is defined with a focus on short-term measures, as '(t)he restoration of basic services and facilities for the functioning of a community or a society affected by a disaster',[8] whereas 'reconstruction' refers to 'the medium- and long-term rebuilding and sustainable restoration of resilient critical infrastructures, services, housing, facilities and livelihoods required for the full functioning of a community or a society affected by a disaster'.[9]

The reasons for adopting such a broad interpretation of 'recovery' are, firstly, that the three abovementioned post-disaster phases (recovery, rehabilitation, and reconstruction) pursue the same ultimate objective, namely, to avoid or reduce future disaster risk. Secondly, by doing so, the recovery phase then 'closes the loop' of the disaster management cycle by connecting it again with the 'prevention phase'.[10]

Regarding the terms 'affected' and 'assisting States', the definitions included in the International Law Commission's Draft Articles on the Protection of Persons in the Event of Disasters[11] are used, according to which an 'affected State' is understood as 'a State in whose territory, or in territory under whose jurisdiction or control, a disaster takes place'.[12] On the other hand, the term 'assisting State' refers to 'a State providing assistance to an affected State with its consent'.[13]

3 Response and Recovery Obligations of a General Scope in Legal and 'Soft-Law' Instruments

This section examines how international law, as well as soft-law instruments adopted at the universal (3.1), regional (3.2) and bilateral (3.3) levels, have

8 Ibid 22.

9 Ibid 21.

10 D A Farber 'International Law and the Disaster Cycle' in D Caron, M J Kelly, A Telesetsky (eds), *The International Law of Disaster Relief* (CUP 2014) 19.

11 ILC Draft Articles on the protection of persons in the event of disasters, Report of the International Law Commission, Sixty-eighth session (2016) A/71/10 (hereafter 'ILC Draft Articles').

12 Ibid art 3(b).

13 Ibid art 3(c).

prescribed what States and, where applicable, international organisations (IOs) and non-State actors are required or recommended to do in the response and recovery phases of any disaster, including all CBRN events. In this context, reference will also be made to the ILC Draft Articles and to the commentaries thereto,[14] since these are based on an authoritative analysis of existing instruments and customary international law. Whereas to date, they are not legally binding, the Draft Articles can be considered as a 'soft-law' instrument, providing guidance for States and other actors.

3.1 *Obligations Deriving from Universal Instruments*

Considering the devastating, often long-term, impact of disasters, including CBRN events, on people, societies, and the environment, the ways in which States and other actors respond to such events is guided by several bodies of international law. The relevant obligations of States and IOs included in human rights law, international humanitarian law, international environmental law, and international arms control law are discussed elsewhere in this volume.[15] Therefore, this chapter will focus on the obligations deriving from International Disaster Law (3.1.2). However, first, some general principles of international law will be discussed which provide the 'contours' of the international normative framework on disaster relief.

3.1.1 General Principles of International Law

In the first place, the principle of cooperation should be mentioned, which, according to the ILC, 'is indispensable for the protection of persons in the event of disasters'.[16] It is enshrined in Article 1(3) of the United Nations (UN) Charter as one of the main purposes of the UN. Moreover, Article 55 elaborates on the purposes of cooperation, which include the promotion of 'solutions of international economic, social, health, and related problems'.[17] Article 56 provides that, for the achievement of these purposes, '(a)ll Members pledge themselves to take joint and separate action in cooperation with the Organization'.[18] The principle of cooperation is closely related to the concept of solidarity which, as confirmed by the ILC, constitutes 'a fundamental value

---

14 Ibid.

15 On human rights law, see ch 27 by Venier and ch 28 by Sommario; on international environmental law, see ch 29 by Antoniazzi; on international arms control law, see ch 23 by Poli and ch 24 by Spagnolo; on obligations deriving from IHL related to CBRN weapons, see ch 21 by Mauri, and ch 22 by Saluzzo in this volume.

16 ILC Draft Articles (n 11), Commentary to Article 7 (Duty to cooperate) 36.

17 UN Charter, art 55(b).

18 UN Charter, art 56.

in international relations'[19] and a 'key concept underlying the topic' of disaster management.[20] However, the exact content of this principle, is still debated.[21] The same is true for international cooperation, which generally refers to 'voluntary, co-ordinated action of two or more States which takes place under a legal regime and serves a specific objective.'[22] However, the question to what extent the principle of cooperation implies any legal obligations for States, has not been conclusively resolved. Do third States have an international obligation to offer and to provide assistance to a State affected by a disaster? And does an affected State have a legal obligation to request or to accept external assistance for disaster response and recovery? These questions are directly related to another fundamental principle of international law: the principle of sovereignty.

Affirmed by the UN Charter in its Article 2, the principle of sovereignty is a cornerstone of international law.[23] The ILC Draft Articles also stress this principle, and reaffirm the primary role of the affected State in the provision of disaster relief assistance.[24] In particular, disaster assistance by third States, international organisations or Non-Governmental Organisations (NGOs) can only be provided if the affected State has given its prior consent.[25] Indeed, 'the territorial State's sovereignty also implies the competence on the one hand to establish the regulatory and legal framework governing international assistance',[26] which is part of the preparedness phase, 'and on the other hand to coordinate and monitor it',[27] which, instead, belongs to the response phase. Similarly, the sovereign powers of the affected State, including its primary responsibility to take care of its own population, and the responsibility to coordinate external assistance, also apply to the recovery phase. These sovereign competences are generally considered to fall within the domestic sphere of each State, in which other States cannot intervene based on Article 2(7) of the UN Charter. Indeed, the proposal of the International Commission for Intervention and State Sovereignty (ICSS) to extend the doctrine of the international communities' 'Responsibility to Protect (R2P)' also to the situation in

19 ILC Draft Articles (n 11) preambular para 4.

20 Ibid Commentary on preambular para 4, para 49(4).

21 F Zorzi Giustiniani, *International Law in Disaster Scenarios Applicable Rules and Principles* (Springer 2020) 93–104.

22 Ibid 95.

23 J Crawford, *Brownlie's Principles of International Law* (OUP 2019, 9th edn) ch 20.

24 ILC Draft Articles (n 11) final preambular para.

25 E Tokunaga 'Evolution of International Disaster Response Law: Toward Codification and Progressive Development of the Law' in Caron a.o. (n 10) 46–66; Zorzi Giustiniani (n 21) 74.

26 Zorzi Giustiniani (n 21) 57, 60.

27 Ibid.

which a State is 'unable or unwilling' to protect its own population in the event of an overwhelming natural or environmental catastrophe and the affected State does not call for assistance, was not accepted by the UN General Assembly.[28] As summarised by Eburn et al., '(i)t is the sovereign right of states to offer only that assistance that they wish to offer. There is no universal obligation imposed by international law that requires states to seek or make assistance available'.[29] At the same time, with the adoption of several resolutions of the UN General Assembly on the coordination of humanitarian emergency assistance, in particular UNGA Resolution 46/82,[30] the international community has explicitly recognised that a balance must be found between the urgency of providing humanitarian relief to victims of disasters and emergency situations on the one hand, and the sovereignty and primary role of the affected States on the other. In this regard, the ILC Draft Articles state that '(t)o the extent that a disaster manifestly exceeds its national response capacity, the affected State has the duty to seek assistance from, as appropriate, other States, the United Nations, and other potential assisting actors'.[31]

3.1.2 International Disaster Law

International Disaster Law (IDL) has developed as a special regime of international law over several decades. Numerous regulatory instruments and guidelines have been adopted at international and regional levels, often addressing a certain type of disaster or a specific disaster-related issue, which has resulted in a complex patchwork of norms, and to uncertainty in the delivery of disaster response in practice.[32] In recent years, several initiatives have been undertaken to improve this situation, including through the work of the

---

28 See M Eburn, A E Collins, and K da Costa, 'Recognising Limits of International Law in Disaster Risk Reduction as Problem and Solution' in K L H Samuel, M Aronsson-Storrier, K Nakjavani Bookmiller, *The Cambridge Handbook of Disaster Risk Reduction and International Law* (CUP 2019) 118. As part of the 'R2P', a competence for the international community to act, under certain conditions, when the territorial State is unable or unwilling to protect its own population was, however, accepted for war crimes, crimes against humanity and genocide, see UNGA, Resolution 60/1, 2005 World Summit Outcome (24 October 2005) A/RES/60/1.

29 Eburn a.o. (n 28) 119.

30 UNGA Resolution 46/82 (19 December 1991). Previous resolutions affirming this recognition are UNGA Res A/ 43/131 (1998) and A/45/100 (1990).

31 ILC Draft Articles (n 11) art 11.

32 IFRC, 'World Disasters Report 2020: Come Heat or High Water'; M Kelly 'Introduction' in Caron a.o. (n 10) 1.

ILC on the Draft Articles,[33] and the adoption of the comprehensive Sendai Framework by the UN General Assembly in 2015.[34]

The Sendai Framework builds on its predecessors, the Hyogo Framework for Action 2005–2015[35] and the Yokohama Strategy and Plan of Action for a Safer World,[36] while adopting an innovative approach, according to which disaster prevention and reduction should be fully integrated into all phases of disaster management. The focus of the Sendai Framework is predominantly on fostering preparedness[37] and only a few recommendations specifically concern response actions as such.[38] However, the Framework also recommends actions to be adopted in the aftermath of a disaster:

> (d)isasters have demonstrated that the recovery, rehabilitation and reconstruction phase, which needs to be prepared ahead of a disaster, is a critical opportunity to "Build Back Better", including through integrating disaster risk reduction into development measures, making nations and communities resilient to disasters.[39]

To achieve this, the Framework recommends measures to be adopted at the national and local levels, such as 'promot[ing] the resilience of new and existing critical infrastructure [...] to ensure that they remain safe, effective and operational during and after disasters in order to provide live-saving and essential services'[40] and 'ensur[ing] the continuity of operations and planning, including social and economic recovery, and the provision of basic services in the post-disaster phase'.[41] States are also recommended to promote cooperation between institutions, authorities and stakeholders, under the coordination of national authorities.[42] The Sendai Framework thus confirms the primary role of the affected State, whose consent is required for the mobilisation of external

33 ILC Draft Articles (n 11).

34 UNGA Res A/RES/69/283, Sendai Framework for Disaster Risk Reduction 2015–2030 (23 June 2015) (hereafter 'Sendai Framework').

35 Hyogo Framework for Action 2005–2015: Building the Resilience of Nations and Communities to Disasters (2006) UN Doc A/CONF.206/6.

36 UN World Conference on Natural Disaster Reduction, 'Yokohama Strategy for a Safer World: Guidelines for Natural Disaster Prevention, Preparedness and Mitigation, and Plan for Action', (1994) UN Doc A/CONF.172/9.

37 See ch 4 by de Guttry in this volume.

38 Sendai Framework (n 34) para 34.

39 Ibid para 32.

40 Ibid para 33(c).

41 Ibid para 33(g).

42 Ibid para 33(i).

assistance, and who is responsible for the coordination of all cooperation activities. Nevertheless, it also makes recommendations for the involvement of all stakeholders, including civil society (with specific reference to women, children, persons with disabilities, older people, indigenous peoples and migrants), private investors, academia and scientific research institutions, as well as business, private sector financial institutions, and philanthropic foundations.[43] Although the Sendai Framework is not legally binding, it provides comprehensive, authoritative guidance for disaster risk reduction across the globe and for a wide range of actors.

With the subsequent adoption of the revised UN Plan of Action on Disaster Risk Reduction for Resilience,[44] the UN committed itself to ensuring that the implementation of the Sendai Framework contributes to an integrated approach to the achievement of the 2030 Agenda for Sustainable Development.[45] Similarly, for individual States, the integration of disaster response and recovery actions into sectoral policies is explicitly foreseen in the targets adopted for the realisation of the Sustainable Development Goals (SDGs),[46] including those related to SDG 9 (building resilient infrastructure) and SDG 3 (ensuring healthy lives and well-being for everyone).

Another source providing detailed guidance for States, are the Guidelines for the Domestic Facilitation and Regulation of International Disaster Relief and Initial Recovery Assistance (2007), developed by the International Federation of Red Cross and Red Crescent Societies (IFRC). These guidelines were adopted by the States Parties to the Geneva Conventions and the International Red Cross and Red Crescent Movement, and their implementation has been encouraged by the UN General Assembly.[47] They contain recommendations for affected States, assisting States and humanitarian organisations and cover, *inter alia*, early warning, initiation and termination of international disaster relief and initial recovery assistance, and legal facilities for entry and operations.

In addition to these 'soft-law' instruments of a general scope, other international instruments (both binding and non-binding) address more specific

43 Ibid paras 35, 36.

44 UN Plan of Action on Disaster Risk Reduction for Resilience: Towards a Risk Informed and Integrated Approach to Sustainable Development (2017) <https://www.preventionweb.net/publications/view/49076>.

45 UN General Assembly, Transforming our world: the 2030 Agenda for Sustainable Development (21 October 2015), A/RES/70/1.

46 Ibid.

47 Eg UN General Assembly Resolution 72/133 of 11 December 2017 on Strengthening of the coordination of emergency humanitarian assistance of the United Nations.

aspects of disaster response. For example, the duty of States to protect disaster relief personnel is laid down in the Optional Protocol to the 1994 UN Convention on the Safety of UN and Associated Personnel.[48] This Protocol requires States to ensure the safety and security of UN and associated personnel engaged in UN operations, including for the purpose of delivering emergency humanitarian assistance. Such a 'duty of care' also derives from the affected States' positive human rights obligations to protect, *inter alia*, the rights to life and to health of all persons within their jurisdiction, including both domestic and foreign disaster relief personnel.[49] Moreover, the International Committee of the Red Cross (ICRC) has issued a document providing detailed guidance on self-protection of emergency personnel engaged in CBRN response.[50]

Another issue is the use of military and civil defence assets (MCDA), comprising personnel, equipment, supplies and services, in disaster response. The Guidelines on the Use of Foreign Military and Civil Defence Assets in Disaster Relief (Oslo Guidelines) were initially adopted in 1994 by a group of 14 States from various regions, IOs and NGOs, and revised in 2007. The Oslo Guidelines provide guidance for affected States and UN agencies that use *foreign* MCDA in disaster relief; for assisting States that offer such assets; and for transit States, through which MCDA assets need to pass to reach the disaster-affected area. The guidelines, formulated in cooperation with UNOCHA,[51] cover issues such as Status of Forces Agreements; the responsibility of the host State for providing adequate security for foreign MCDA support; coordination of relief actions; and operational standards. Complementary guidance was adopted in 2003 on the use of MCDA to support UN humanitarian activities.[52]

Moreover, States Parties to the 1998 Tampere Convention on the Provision of Telecommunication Resources for Disaster Mitigation and Relief Operations have committed themselves to facilitate the provision of prompt telecommunications assistance to mitigate the impact of a disaster, by, *inter alia*, waiving regulatory barriers such as licensing requirements to use allocated frequencies and restrictions on the import of telecommunications equipment. Furthermore, the 1999 Revised Kyoto Convention on the Simplification and Harmonization of Customs Procedures, adopted by the World Customs

48 Optional Protocol to the UN Convention on the Safety of UN and Associated Personnel (2005).

49 See also ch 27 by Venier in this volume.

50 ICRC, 'Chemical, Biological, Radiological and Nuclear Response: Introductory Guidance' (2014). See also the NATO guidelines discussed in Section 3.2.

51 United Nations Office for the Coordination of Humanitarian Affairs.

52 Guidelines on the Use of Military and Civil Defence Assets to Support United Nations Humanitarian Activities in Complex Emergencies (2003).

Organization, contains obligatory rules for States Parties concerning, *inter alia*, transparency and predictability of customs actions; standardisation and simplification of goods declarations and supporting documents; simplified procedures for authorised persons; and coordinated interventions with other border agencies.

All these international instruments are implemented within the overall UN framework for humanitarian assistance. Although the first efforts regarding emergency assistance date back to 1971, UN General Assembly Resolution 46/182 of 1991 'designed the blueprint for today's international humanitarian system'.[53] Resolution 46/182 focuses on the coordination of humanitarian assistance in complex emergencies and natural disasters. Since then, numerous resolutions and guidelines have been adopted in the UN context,[54] culminating in the UNGA's adoption of the SDGs and the Sendai Framework.

3.2 *Obligations Deriving from Regional Instruments*

At the regional level, the most comprehensive guidance on response to CBRN events is provided by two sets of guidelines adopted by the North Atlantic Treaty Organization (NATO).[55] Firstly, the NATO/ Euro-Atlantic Partnership Council Guidelines on International Assistance in the Event of a CBRN Incident or Natural Disaster,[56] offer detailed operational guidance for preparedness and response actions of both 'requesting' and 'assisting' nations. These non-binding guidelines address, *inter alia*, the assessment by the requesting nation of whether international assistance is required and, if so, how to make a formal request for international assistance; equipment, goods, and transport related issues; and recommended modalities for facilitating the activities of assisting personnel and the quality of assistance.

53 See <https://www.unocha.org/story/resolution-46182-which-created-humanitarian-system-turns-twenty-five>.

54 Eg UNGA Resolution 57/150, Strengthening the effectiveness and coordination of international urban search and rescue assistance. See further: <https://www.undrr.org/about-undrr/history>.

55 NATO is included among the regional organisations because of the geographical concentration of its Member States in Europe, together with the United States.

56 NATO/Euro-Atlantic Partnership Council, Checklist and Non-Binding Guidelines for the Request, Reception and Provision of International Assistance in the Event of a CBRN Incident or Natural Disaster, EAPC(SCEPC)N(2009)0016, MULTI REF (25 May 2009) <https://www.nato.int/eadrcc/docs/checklist_eng.pdf>.

Secondly, the NATO Guidelines for First Responders to a CBRN Incident[57] are designed to improve multi-agency interoperability in first response to CBRN incidents. The guidelines set out detailed steps for both CBRN preparedness and response, regarding (1) information gathering, assessment and dissemination, (2) scene management, (3) saving and protecting life, and (4) additional/specialist support. For each of these fields, the guidelines recommend procedures, capabilities, and equipment.

Other regional instruments that address response and recovery to all types of disasters include the following:[58]

At the European level,[59] the Council of Europe's 1987 European and Mediterranean Major Hazards Agreement (EUR-OPA) created the inter-governmental Co-operation Group for the Prevention of, Protection Against, and Organisation of Relief in Major Natural and Technological Disasters.[60] Although it focuses on disaster prevention and preparedness, initiatives related to post-disaster recovery are also implemented, including training in psychological post-trauma support for victims. Other instruments have been concluded in European sub-regional contexts, such as an agreement concluded among Participating States of the Black Sea Economic Cooperation (BSEC) group[61] in Central Europe, setting out obligations for, *inter alia*, the delivery of disaster assistance without discrimination, coordination, and the expedition of customs procedures.

Moreover, the United Nations Economic Commission for Europe (UNECE) adopted the Convention on the Protection and Use of Transboundary Watercourses and International Lakes,[62] which calls on aid requesting States to reduce border-crossing formalities, waive assisting State liability and assume costs. In 2018, UNECE published, together with the UN Office for Disaster Risk

---

57 NATO Guidelines for First Responders to a CBRN Incident, updated on 1 August 2014 <https://www.nato.int/nato_static_fl2014/assets/pdf/pdf_2016_08/20160802_140801-cep-first-responders-CBRN-eng.pdf>.

58 For a more complete overview of instruments for disaster management, see International Federation of Red Cross and Red Crescent Societies (IFRC), 'Law and legal issues in international disaster response: a desk study' (Geneva, 2007), <https://www.ifrc.org/PageFiles/41194/113600-idrl-deskstudy-en.pdf>.

59 However, European Union instruments are discussed elsewhere in this volume (n 1).

60 See <https://rm.coe.int/draft-medium-term-plan-2021-2025/16809f9f54>.

61 Agreement of the Governments of the Participating States of the Black Sea Economic Cooperation (BSEC) on Collaboration in Emergency Assistance and Emergency Response to Natural and Man-Made Disasters (1998), and its Additional Protocol (2005).

62 UNECE Convention on the Protection and Use of Transboundary Watercourses and International Lakes (1992).

Reduction (UNDRR), an implementation guide for addressing water-related disasters and transboundary cooperation, providing recommendations for communities on how to integrate disaster risk management with climate change adaptation, including in the response and recovery phases.[63]

In Africa, the 2004 Africa Regional Strategy for Disaster Risk Reduction, adopted by the African Union (AU) together with the New Partnership for Africa's Development (NEPAD), facilitates inter-State cooperation, integrating disaster risk reduction into sustainable development and poverty-eradication actions. Another example is the Action Plan of the Economic Community of West African States (ECOWAS) for the Implementation of the Central Africa Gender Responsive Regional Strategy for Risk Prevention, Disaster Management and Climate Change Adaptation, adopted in 2015, and revised in 2020. This Action Plan aims to contribute to the objectives of the Sendai Framework, focusing on the empowerment and participation of women, including in disaster response and recovery.[64]

Turning to the Americas and the Caribbean, the Inter-American Convention to Facilitate Disaster Relief[65] sets out modalities for the request and provision of disaster relief assistance, and response measures to be taken by affected and assisting States. However, this convention has been ratified by only six States and has never been implemented. Furthermore, in 2003, the OAS Member States adopted the Inter-American Strategic Plan for Policy on Vulnerability Reduction, Risk Management and Disaster Response (IASP), which seeks, *inter alia*, to improve emergency preparedness and response, and to 'make economic and social infrastructure more resilient for sustainable development and hemispheric security'.[66] Several sub-regional agreements on disaster risk reduction assistance and cooperation have also been concluded, including agreements by the Caribbean Community (CARICOM),[67] and by the Association of Caribbean States (ASC).[68]

Finally, in Asia, several instruments have been adopted in the context of the Association of Southeast Asian Nations (ASEAN), including the ASEAN Agreement on Disaster Management and Emergency Response (2005), which

63 UNECE-UNISDR, Words into Action Guidelines: An implementation guide for addressing water-related disasters and transboundary cooperation (2018).

64 See <https://www.gfdrr.org/sites/default/files/publication/ECOWAS%20GSAP_EN_Final.pdf>.

65 Inter-American Convention on Disaster Relief (1991).

66 Ibid.

67 Agreement Establishing the Caribbean Disaster Emergency Response Agency (1991).

68 Agreement between Member States and Associate Members of the Association of Caribbean States for Regional Cooperation on Natural Disasters (1999).

sets out modalities for reducing the number of lives lost and the amount of damage caused to social, economic, and environmental assets, as a result of disasters, as well as ways for increasing regional and international cooperation in this regard. Additional sub-regional agreements were agreed by the South Asian Association for Regional Cooperation (SAARC), the Asia-Pacific Economic Cooperation (APEC) forum, the Pacific Islands Forum (PIF), and by a number of bodies in the Middle East, including the League of Arab States.[69] While the large majority of these regional instruments cover international cooperation for disaster response, only limited attention is given to post-disaster recovery. However, a more integrated approach to disaster management is gradually being introduced in regional cooperation, in accordance with the Sendai Framework.

3.3 *Obligations Deriving from Bilateral Agreements*

Besides these international and regional instruments, many bilateral agreements on disaster response have been concluded among States across the globe. As reported by the IFRC, of the bilateral treaties starting in the 1970s and 1990s, a 'substantial proportion were mutual assistance agreements, particularly between European states'.[70] Other agreements have been concluded between States across different regions.[71] Common trends in bilateral cooperation agreements include modalities for the management of emergency teams and the minimalisation of frontier-crossing formalities on the part of the requesting State (waiving or expediting visa or work permit requirements, and waiving of duties and taxes on relief goods and equipment). These agreements also 'commonly require receiving states to waive any claims against assisting states for any damage their operations might cause and to assume liability for third-party claims other than international torts or gross negligence'.[72] Furthermore, arrangements are generally included regarding the responsibility for the costs of the operation and for the physical protection of assisting personnel, goods, and equipment.

---

69 See IFRC (n 58), 69–70, 78–79.

70 IFRC (n 58) 80. Eg Agreement between Sweden and Norway concerning the Improvement of Rescue Services in Frontier Areas (1974), Agreement between Austria and the Czech Republic on Mutual Assistance in the Event of Disasters or Serious Accidents (1998).

71 Eg Memorandum of Understanding Between the USA and Ukraine on Cooperation in Natural and Man-Made Technological Emergency Prevention and Response (2000) and the Agreement between Switzerland and the Philippines on Cooperation in the Event of Natural Disaster or Major Emergencies of 2001.

72 IFRC (n 58) 81.

Many States have concluded bilateral agreements with several others, both within the same region and beyond. For example, Croatia has ratified eight bilateral agreements on protection and rescue with neighbouring and other European States,[73] and the EU.[74] After the severe earthquake that struck central Croatia on 29 December 2020 and which affected an estimated 120,000 people, several EU Member States (many of which had also concluded bilateral cooperation agreements with Croatia) offered immediate assistance, mobilised in a coordinated response effort by the EU Civil Protection Mechanism. India, for its part, has concluded bilateral agreements on disaster relief cooperation with some European States[75] and also with the Russian Federation, Tajikistan, Japan, and Indonesia.[76] In the aftermath of the 2004 Tsunami in the Indian Ocean, in which an estimated 230,000 people lost their lives across five countries, most of these States provided disaster relief assistance to India and the other affected States, contributing to a massive global mobilisation of funds and technical assistance. While Japan assisted the relief operations in the Indian Bay of Bengal by sending troops, helicopters, and naval vessels, India simultaneously supported, *inter alia*, Sri Lanka and Indonesia with relief operations,[77] including rescue and medical teams. India also provided support to Japan after the Fukushima disaster in 2011, and typhoon Hagibis in 2019. Moreover, bilateral disaster relief is often mobilised by national development cooperation agencies, such as the United States Agency for International Development (USAID)[78] or the Japanese International Cooperation Agency (JICA),[79] independently of the existence of specific bilateral cooperation agreements with the affected State(s).

73 Hungary (1997), Slovenia (1997), Bosnia and Herzegovina (2001), Slovakia (2003), Poland (2003), Austria (2004), France (2007), and Montenegro (2008).

74 See <https://ec.europa.eu/echo/files/civil_protection/vademecum/hr/2-hr-1.html>.

75 Switzerland, Germany.

76 Indian Ministry of Home Affairs, 'International Cooperation on Disaster Management', 18 December 2018, <https://pib.gov.in/PressReleasePage.aspx?PRID=1556471>.

77 See <https://www.eastasiaforum.org/2019/11/23/improving-india-japan-disaster-response-after-typhoon-hagibis/>.

78 USAID deployed a Disaster-Assistance Response Team to respond to back-to-back hurricanes in Central America in November 2020, see <https://www.usaid.gov/news-information/press-releases/nov-18-2020-usaid-deploys-disaster-assistance-response-team-response-hurricanes>.

79 In 2020, Japan dispatched several disaster relief expert teams to Mauritius after a severe oil spill from a Japanese bulk carrier on the Mauritian coast, See <https://www.jica.go.jp/english/news/press/2020/202010230.html>.

4 Main Categories of Response and Recovery Obligations

As the preceding overview shows, many normative instruments include obligations or recommendations related to the response and recovery phases of disaster management. Despite differences in their scope (international, regional, or bilateral), their focus (general or specific) and their nature (hard-law or soft-law), nevertheless, some main categories of obligations/recommendations can be distinguished. These will be summarised below, distinguishing between, on the one hand, the response and recovery phases and, on the other hand, between affected States, assisting States, and other actors (4.1–4.2). It will also be demonstrated that despite the proliferation of rules for disaster response and recovery, only limited possibilities exist for their legal enforcement (4.3).

4.1 *Categories of Obligations Concerning the Response Phase*

4.1.1 Affected States

The main clusters of obligations and recommendations addressed to affected States are related to six aspects of disaster response: (i) information and notification, (ii) operational response activities, (iii) requesting and giving consent to external assistance, (iv) coordination of domestic external assistance, (v) facilitating entry of external personnel, goods, and equipment, and (vi) protection of relief personnel, goods, and equipment ('duty of care').

Regarding (i) information and notification, affected States must ensure the timely notification of the population, including vulnerable groups, of potential risks associated with a forecasted disaster. They also have an obligation to ensure the timely notification of neighbouring and third States of potential cross-border risks of such a disaster. Concerning operational response activities (ii), including evacuation, medical care, and emergency action to secure physical infrastructure, affected States must ensure timely, adequate, and effective assistance to those affected by the disaster within their own territory or under their jurisdiction. This includes giving priority to disaster relief in public spending; using all available means, including military resources when appropriate; making available the necessary medical, technical, and scientific resources, as well as telecommunication facilities; and providing basic services, including food, water, and shelter. Affected States must ensure delivery of relief assistance in a non-discriminatory manner, as well as direct participation of victims at all stages, and must address specific needs of vulnerable groups.

While all applicable instruments recommend that affected States request and accept external assistance (by giving their consent) (iii), at present, this does not constitute a legally binding obligation for all affected States in all emergencies. However, positive human rights obligations have been interpreted by authoritative bodies to imply such an obligation in situations where national response capacities are insufficient.[80] Based on the principle of sovereignty, IDL instruments reaffirm the primary role of affected States in the coordination of all disaster relief actions, whether provided by domestic or foreign first responders, civil protection staff or military personnel (iv). They can request assistance from IOs or humanitarian NGOs to support such coordination.

With a view to facilitating the entry of external personnel, goods, and equipment (v), affected States are either recommended or (if foreseen in specific binding international, regional, or bilateral instruments) obliged to waive or expedite visas and temporary work permits, to recognise professional certificates of external assistance personnel, and to waive customs and other duties for the import of goods and equipment for disaster relief. Finally, affected States are required – based on human rights law and specific conventions, supported by non-binding international guidelines – to adopt all necessary measures to protect the safety and security of both domestic and external relief personnel, and the goods and equipment used in disaster relief operations (vi).

The implementation of these obligations in national legislation varies greatly among States. For example, the Sri Lanka Disaster Management Act of 2005, adopted after the 2004 Tsunami, provides for the establishment of specialised institutions for disaster management and the preparation of disaster management plans.[81] In its 2017 report on compliance with the targets of the Sendai Framework, Sri Lanka replied, *inter alia*, that not all people in areas prone to disasters have access to early warning information.[82] While the National Disaster Management Plan (2013–2017) provides details on, *inter alia*, notifying the population and coordinating response activities, it does not provide any guidance on requesting external assistance or facilitating the entry of external personnel and equipment.

On the other hand, the regulatory framework on disaster management in Canada is an example of far-reaching national implementation of the international obligations and guidelines. Based on the Emergency Management Act,[83] the Emergency Management Framework for Canada provides overall guidance

80 See ch 27 by Venier in this volume.

81 Sri Lanka Disaster Management Act, No. 13 (13 May 2005) <https://www.preventionweb.net/files/22112_15417srilankadisastermanagementactn.pdf>.

82 See <https://www.preventionweb.net/files/53159_srilankalka.pdf>.

83 Emergency Management Act, S.C. 2007, c.15 (22 June 2007).

for all parties involved in disaster risk management, and 'underscores the linkages between climate change and emergency management, and the need for all areas of society to work together to enhance resilience'.[84] Moreover, the Emergency Management Strategy for Canada – Towards a Resilient 2030 offers additional guidelines and describes the sharing of responsibilities among federal, provincial and territorial (FTP) governments, and other stakeholders, including 'Indigenous peoples, municipalities, communities, volunteer and non-governmental organizations, the private sector, critical infrastructure owners and operators, academia, and volunteers'.[85]

4.1.2 Assisting States

The main response obligations and recommendations for assisting States, concern (i) offering and providing external assistance, (ii) complying with the coordination by the affected State during operational response activities, and (iii) providing protection for disaster relief personnel, including MCDA, sent abroad. As mentioned above (Section 4.1.1), offering and providing external assistance to an affected State is strongly recommended across instruments, but there is no generalised legal obligation for States to offer such assistance in all circumstances. Assisting States must comply with the affected State's coordination of response actions, as well as with their extraterritorial obligations under human rights law – also reaffirmed in IDL instruments – including non-discrimination, addressing specific needs of vulnerable groups, and ensuring victim participation.[86] Furthermore, assisting States also have a complementary 'duty of care' to protect the relief personnel (both civilian and military) who are sent abroad by ensuring, *inter alia*, that they are adequately equipped for their tasks and, in the case of MCDA, that an adequate SOFA is concluded with the affected State.

In many States, external assistance for disaster response and recovery falls within the responsibilities of the Ministries for foreign affairs and/or development cooperation and is the subject of specific regulatory frameworks and policies. For example, in Australia, the Department of Foreign Affairs and Trade (DFAT) is responsible for external disaster assistance, and the 'Humanitarian Strategy'[87] articulates how DFAT will respond to humanitarian crises. In line

84 See <https://www.publicsafety.gc.ca/cnt/rsrcs/pblctns/2017-mrgnc-mngmnt-frmwrk/2017-mrgnc-mngmnt-frmwrk-en.pdf> p 3.

85 See <https://www.publicsafety.gc.ca/cnt/rsrcs/pblctns/mrgncy-mngmnt-strtgy/mrgncy-mngmnt-strtgy-en.pdf>.

86 See also ch 27 by Venier in this volume.

87 DFAT Humanitarian Strategy (2016) <https://www.dfat.gov.au/sites/default/files/dfat-humanitarian-strategy.pdf>.

with international standards, this strategy is underpinned by guiding principles, which include:

> putting affected people at the centre of planning and delivery of humanitarian assistance; promoting internationally agreed principles of humanity, impartiality, neutrality, and independence; promoting respect for and compliance with international law; doing no harm and adopting conflict sensitive approaches; supplementing – not substituting – national and local efforts.[88]

4.1.3 International Organisations (IOs) and NGOs

Obligations for IOs related to disaster response are sometimes included in specific conventions adopted in the context of that organisation.[89] They generally require the IO to offer and, if accepted by the affected State, to provide external assistance, and to comply with the coordination carried out by that same State. IOs must also comply with general human rights standards, including non-discrimination and the inclusion of vulnerable groups, and are recommended to follow international guidance on, for example, the use of MCDA and the protection of relief personnel. Moreover, while it is quite rare for international or regional instruments to impose legally binding disaster obligations on NGOs, several non-binding instruments of IDL, including the Sendai Framework, provide detailed guidance on the involvement of NGOs in disaster response and recovery actions.

4.2 *Categories of Obligations Concerning the Recovery Phase*

Regarding the recovery phase, the main obligations are related to two overarching objectives of post-disaster recovery, as confirmed in instruments adopted in recent years.[90] While the affected States have the primary responsibility for their implementation, assisting States and IOs are expected to align their external assistance with these objectives. Firstly, States are expected to integrate disaster recovery action into a broader disaster risk management strategy, in accordance with the 'building back better' approach. Secondly, States and IOs should integrate disaster recovery action with actions for sustainable development and climate change adaptation. Therefore, States and

---

88 Ibid, p. 2.

89 Eg conventions adopted by the IAEA, WHO, see ch 13 by Bakker and Montanaro, and ch 18 by Bakker and Farina in this volume.

90 In particular, the 2015 Sendai Framework, the 2015 SDGs, and the 2015 Paris Agreement on Climate Change.

IOs are strongly recommended to ensure policy coherence between the three above-mentioned 'agendas' in the planning and implementation stages of disaster recovery actions. To this end, an affected State should ensure adequate coordination of all types of external assistance that it receives, including assistance received through bilateral, regional and multilateral development cooperation, and climate financing. Finally, IOs and NGOs should contribute to the realisation of these overarching objectives, to the extent that this is foreseen in specific conventions, or in their own statutes or policies. Many IOs and NGOs have adopted strategies and policies that translate these objectives into concrete guidelines, both for their own activities and for States.[91]

4.3 *Enforcement Mechanisms*

When considering the plurality of rules and guidance adopted with respect to disaster response and recovery, including CBRN events, the question arises whether, and how, compliance with these rules can be enforced. Since IDL instruments are, for the most part, not legally binding, no specific avenues exist to hold States or other actors legally accountable for their failure to adequately implement the relevant international norms. However, three points should be considered in this regard. Firstly, obligations of States included in legally binding instruments belonging to other bodies of international law (human rights law, international environmental law, international humanitarian law, disarmament law, nuclear safety law), which are also relevant for disaster response and recovery, are, at least in part, subject to specific enforcement mechanisms, which are discussed elsewhere in this volume.[92]

Secondly, some of the legally binding instruments analysed in this chapter do provide for specific mechanisms for ensuring compliance. For example, the UNECE Convention on the Protection and Use of Transboundary Watercourses and International Lakes provides for consultations among States, regular review meetings of the Parties, and dispute settlement either through negotiation, submission to the International Court of Justice (ICJ), or arbitration.[93]

---

91 Eg UNDRR, 'Integrating Disaster Risk Reduction and Climate Change Adaptation in the UN Sustainable Development Cooperation Framework' (2020) <https://www.undrr.org/publication/integrating-disaster-risk-reduction-and-climate-change-adaptation-un-sustainable>; UNCICEF, 'UNICEF and Disaster Reduction'; UNDP, 'Disaster and Climate Risk Governance in UNDP' (2017); IFRC, 'From crisis to Recovery' <https://www.ifrc.org/en/what-we-do/disaster-management/from-crisis-to-recovery/>.

92 Supra (n 15).

93 UNECE Convention (n 62) arts 10, 17, 22.

Specific dispute settlement mechanisms are also foreseen in the Tampere Convention,[94] and in the Revised Kyoto Convention.[95]

Finally, even though no legal enforcement mechanisms exist for most IDL instruments, nevertheless, some modalities have been created for monitoring States' compliance with the agreed rules. In particular, the Sendai Framework provides for a regular review of progress on its implementation, coordinated by the United Nations Office for Disaster Risk Reduction (UNDRR), based on reporting by States and web-based monitoring systems using specific targets and indicators.[96] At the regional level, the monitoring of compliance with disaster management agreements varies from one region to another, but it is generally ensured through consultation and review, rather than legal enforcement mechanisms.

5 Concluding Remarks

The international normative framework for disaster response and recovery comprises a myriad of rules and standards with various strengths and weaknesses. On the positive side, substantial efforts have been made in recent years to streamline international instruments, and to integrate different, but complementary 'agendas', in particular between disaster risk reduction, sustainable development and climate change adaptation. In this regard, comprehensive strategies adopted at the international level, such as the Sendai Framework, have also had a significant impact on regional and national policies. Indeed, in many States, disaster management strategies have progressively been reoriented to achieve such an integrated approach. Besides the comprehensive DRR strategies of Australia and Canada, as mentioned above (Section 4), similar approaches integrating DRR, climate action and sustainable development, have also been adopted in, *inter alia*, Germany[97] and Singapore.[98]

However, important limitations on integration persist, due to, *inter alia*, differences in the legal nature (binding v non-binding) of the relevant instruments; a lack of effective enforcement mechanisms; and insufficient

94 1998 Tampere Convention on the Provision of Telecommunication Resources for Disaster Mitigation and Relief Operations, art 11.

95 Revised Kyoto Convention on the Simplification and Harmonization of Customs Procedures (1999) art 14.

96 Sendai Framework (n 34), paras 48(c), 50.

97 See <https://www.bmz.de/en/issues/naturkatastrophen/deutsche_politik/index.html>.

98 UNDRR, 'Disaster Risk Reduction Singapore: Status Report 2020'.

coordination of the implementation of norms adopted in different areas (human rights, environmental law, climate change law, health law, disaster law) and at different levels (international, regional, sub-regional). For example, a study published by the UN Food and Agricultural Organization in 2019, examined governance challenges for implementing an integrated approach to DRR and climate change adaptation in agricultural sectors. It concluded that several issues still hamper such an integrated approach, including a 'strong response-oriented (rather than prevention-oriented) attitude towards disasters within government'; 'the absence of clear leadership, and incentives for convergence [...] within government bodies in charge of the two domains'; 'insufficient clarity on roles and responsibilities between state and sub-national governments'; and 'lack of participation and influence of local stakeholders and the concerned communities in identifying priority problems, providing information on conditions and potential solutions based on community knowledge and experience, and in planning and implementing processes.'[99]

There is still much work to be done to 'untangle' and clarify the existing patchwork of norms, and to overcome the practical challenges for their implementation. Hopefully, this book will help to respond to this urgent need.

Acknowledgement

The author wishes to thank Alice Farina and Federica Montanaro for their excellent research assistance for this contribution.

Bibliography

Caron D, Kelly M J and Telesetsky A (eds), *The International Law of Disaster Relief* (CUP 2014).

Crawford J, *Brownlie's Principles of International Law* (OUP 2019, 9th edn).

De Guttry A, Gestri M and Venturini G (eds), *International Disaster Response Law* (TMC Asser 2012).

Easthope L, *The Recovery Myth: Plans and Situated Realities of Post-Disaster Response* (Springer/Palgrave MacMillan 2018).

99 FAO, 'Governance challenges for disaster risk reduction and climate change adaptation convergence in agriculture: Guidance for analysis' <http://www.fao.org/policy-support/tools-and-publications/resources-details/en/c/1206461/>.

Eburn M, Collins A E, and da Costa K, 'Recognising Limits of International Law in Disaster Risk Reduction as Problem and Solution' in Samuel K L H a.o., *The Cambridge Handbook of Disaster Risk Reduction and International Law* (CUP 2019).

Farber D A, 'International Law and the Disaster Cycle' in Caron a.o. (eds), *The International Law of Disaster Relief* (CUP 2014).

Kelly M, 'Introduction' in Caron a.o. *The International Law of Disaster Relief* (CUP 2014).

Lyster R, *Climate Justice and Disaster Law* (CUP 2015).

Samuel K L H, Aronsson-Storrier M, Nakjavani Bookmiller K, *The Cambridge Handbook of Disaster Risk Reduction and International Law* (CUP 2019).

Tokunaga E, 'Evolution of International Disaster Response Law: Toward Codification and Progressive Development of the Law' in Caron a.o. *The International Law of Disaster Relief* (CUP 2014).

Zorzi Giustiniani F, *International Law in Disaster Scenarios Applicable Rules and Principles* (Springer 2020).

CHAPTER 6

Regional Perspective: Distribution of Powers and Cooperation Patterns under EU Law as Applicable to CBRN Protection

Federico Casolari

1 Introduction

The management cycle applicable to CBRN events is, in certain critical respects, incompatible with the multilevel allocation of competences and powers which characterises the fundamental architecture of the European Union (EU).[1] Exactly as in the case of the EU legal provisions dealing with natural and man-made disasters in general,[2] it is not possible to identify a unitary legal framework applicable at the supranational level for CBRN event prevention, preparedness, response and recovery. Relevant provisions are spread out across the EU Treaties and legislation,[3] covering different aspects and distinct stages of the management cycle. Moreover, CBRN events are not explicitly mentioned in EU primary law: EU Treaties only mention possible CBRN-related events, such as 'armed aggression' (Article 42(7) TEU), 'disasters' (Article 3(2)(g) TEU and Articles 107(2)(b), 196, 214, 222 TFEU), 'terrorist attacks/threats/activities' (Articles 75, 83 and 222 TFEU), and 'exceptional occurrences' (Articles 107(2)(b) and 122 TFEU). Also relevant is that the Treaties recognise the primacy of the Member States' prerogative powers over their essential functions, including the exclusive competence of the Member States in maintaining law and order and safeguarding national security (Article 4(2) TEU). As is apparent, all these features risk downsizing the EU role and undermining supranational cooperation on CBRN matters.

Against this background, this chapter seeks to provide a general survey of the cooperation instruments elaborated at supranational level to maximise

1 S Garben, I Govaere (eds), *The Division of Competences between the EU and the Member States – Reflections on the Past, the Present and the Future* (Hart 2017).

2 M Gestri, 'EU Disaster Response Law: Principles and Instruments', in A de Guttry et al (eds), *International Disaster Response Law* (TMC Asser Press 2012).

3 For a general survey, see Eurojust, *CBRN-E Handbook* (June 2017) <https://op.europa.eu/en/publication-detail/-/publication/9c70e7ce-8c65-11e7-b5c6-01aa75ed71a1> (all links were last accessed 5 June 2021).

DOI:10.1163/9789004507999_007

the joint efforts of the EU and the Member States in the area of CBRN protection. The ultimate goal is to identify general trends and approaches in the allocation of competences and powers between the Union and the Member States in the CBRN domain and to detect critical points that could be relevant in the analysis of the different EU sectoral policies dealing with that domain.[4]

The analysis has been divided into three sections. Section 2 sheds light on the prerogative powers retained by Member States with regard to public order and national security, assessing to what extent those prerogative powers can affect the effectiveness of the EU's action in the CBRN domain. Section 3 is a mapping exercise: it identifies the major forms of cooperation elaborated in the CBRN domain at supranational level and considers their possible influence on Member States' action. Section 4 focuses on two meaningful EU primary law provisions – namely Articles 42(7) TEU and 222 TFEU – that are quite illustrative of the delicate balancing act involving the EU and the Member States with respect to protection from CBRN events.

2 Member States' Prerogatives under Article 4(2) TEU

In approaching the cooperation framework that the Union and Member States have elaborated on CBRN matters, it is particularly apt to start off by considering the role played by the so-called 'national identities clause'. Enshrined in Article 4(2) TEU, the clause imposes upon the Union a general obligation to respect the essential functions of the Member States, as well as their exclusive competence in protecting public order and national security.[5] One could therefore conclude that only Member States may act in such domains. In other words, a straight-forward, first reading of the clause could be interpreted as excluding any possibility for the Union to interfere with matters over which the Member States exercise sovereign prerogative powers; thus, significantly limiting the Union's capacity to manage CBRN matters. It is indeed evident that some CBRN matters are strictly intertwined with the security policies of the Member States while, in other cases (in particular when related to natural

4 Such analysis is carried out by other chapters in this volume, *ie* ch 10 by Villani, ch 14 and ch 19 by Ferri and ch 33 by Farnelli. These chapters do not deal with the cooperation framework concerning radiological and nuclear substances which is mainly carried out within Euratom. The latter cooperation is analysed by Balboni in ch 15.

5 Cf. B Guastaferro, 'Sincere Cooperation and Respect for National Identities', in R Schütze, T Tridimas (eds) *Oxford Principles of European Union Law – The European Union Legal Order*, vol. I (OUP 2018); G Di Federico, *L'identità nazionale degli Stati membri nel diritto dell'Unione europea* (Editoriale Scientifica 2017).

events), they involve the maintenance of public order – a circumstance that can be named here as 'the CBRN-security nexus'.

Yet, on closer inspection, a different interpretation of the clause is possible. In particular, if one considers the attitude shown by the European Court of Justice (ECJ) towards Members States' reserved powers, the conclusion may be reached that those powers do not exclude *per se* the possibility for the Union to exercise its influence in the corresponding domain. The doctrine elaborated by Luxembourg judges – also known as the 'framing of powers' doctrine – imposes a general obligation upon the Member States to exercise their prerogative powers *having due regard to EU law*.[6] In practice, besides the need to respect, in any case, the fundamental values upon which the Union is based (Article 2 TEU),[7] the national identities clause must be read in conjunction with the other principles governing the interaction between the Union and the Member States, which are enshrined in Article 4 TEU. In particular, it is the principle of sincere cooperation (Article 4(3) TEU) that ensures that national identities do not amount to general reservations to the effectiveness of EU law.[8] The strengthening of the loyalty duties of the Member States – especially the abstention duties flowing from the loyalty clause enshrined in Article 4(3) TEU – contributed to blurring the divide between EU and Member State prerogatives, leading in turn to a more flexible understanding of the principle of conferral, mentioned in Article 4(1) TEU.[9]

Numerous are the areas where such an approach has been affirmed in the case law of the ECJ: loss and acquisition of nationality,[10] social security,[11] organisation of education systems,[12] organisation of justice,[13] and direct taxation.[14]

---

6 Case C-457/18 *Slovenia v Croatia* ECLI:EU:C:2019:1067, Opinion of AG Pikamäe, para 138. Cf. L Azoulai, 'The 'Retained Powers' Formula in the Case Law of the European Court of Justice: EU Law as Total Law?' (2011) 4 European Journal of Legal Studies 192; B de Witte, 'Exclusive Member States Competences – Is There Such a Thing?', in S Garben, I Govaere (n 1); L Boucon, 'EU Law and Retained Powers of Member States', in L Azoulai (ed) *The Question of Competence in the European Union* (OUP 2014).

7 See, for instance, Case C-502/19 *Oriol Junqueras Vies* ECLI:EU:C:2019:1115, where the Court recognised that MEPs' immunities, which help to give concrete form to the value of democracy referred to in Article 2 TEU, shall prevail over the reaction put in place by a Member State (Spain) to preserve its territorial integrity against a secession bid.

8 Guastaferro (n 5); G Di Federico (n 5) 149; F Casolari, *Leale cooperazione tra Stati membri e Unione europea* (Editoriale Scientifica 2020) 207.

9 Casolari (n 8) 88.

10 Case C-369/90 *Micheletti* [1992] ECR I-4239, para 10.

11 Case C-647/13 *Melchior* ECLI:EU:C:2015:54, para 21.

12 Joined Cases C-11/06 and C-12/06 *Morgan and Bucher* [2007] I-9161, para 24.

13 Case C-619/18 *Commission v Poland* ECLI:EU:C:2019:531, para 52.

14 Case C-279/93 *Schumacker* [1995] I-225, paras 21–24.

Quite significantly, the Court has also recognised its relevance with regard to the maintenance of public order and the safeguarding of internal security.[15] In particular, the Court of Justice has stated that the recognition by EU primary law of Member States' prerogatives in situations which may affect law and order or public security cannot lead to the conclusion that 'the Treaty contains an inherent general exception excluding all measures taken for reasons of law and order or public security from the scope of European Union law'.[16]

3 Supranational Cooperation Schemes

Having clarified the extent to which Member States' prerogatives and retained powers may influence EU action on CBRN events, it is now time to identify the major supranational CBRN cooperation schemes that have been elaborated so far. The analysis will start by considering binding measures that impose uniform or harmonised rules and obligations upon the Member States (3.1). This will be followed by consideration of mechanisms that support or facilitate action by the Member States themselves (3.2). The survey will conclude with a reference to the role that non-binding acts adopted by EU institutions may play in the CBRN domain (3.3).

3.1 *Cooperation through Harmonisation: From the Protection of the Internal Market to the Fight against Terrorism*

A first form of cooperation elaborated at supranational level aims at establishing harmonised procedures and rules among Member States for dealing with specific CBRN substances. On the one hand, this cooperation promotes a high level of human health and the protection of the environment from risks posed by CBRN substances. On the other hand, it ensures the proper functioning and integrity of the internal market and the related freedom of movement of goods. The need to preserve this freedom, which represents one of the fundamental pillars upon which the internal market is based, explains why cooperation in this area is quite strong, as well as the mandatory nature of the Member States' related duties. Indeed, even though the EU's competence related to the functioning of the internal market is shared in nature, the preemption exercised by the Union in triggering that competence gives the former a (temporary) exclusive power, preventing Member States from legislating

15 Case C-265/95 *Commission v France* [1997] I-6959, paras 33–35.

16 Joined Cases C-715/17, C-718/17 and C-719/17 *Commission v Poland, Hungary and Czech Republic* ECLI:EU:C:2020:257, para 143.

in the same areas. This strengthens the supranational cooperation and minimises the risks of differentiations and 'race to the bottom' effects of the relevant legal framework.

Particularly illustrative of such a trend is the REACH Regulation, a veritable milestone of environmental and health protection at EU level, which concerns the registration, evaluation, authorisation and restriction of chemicals.[17] The REACH Regulation was adopted on the basis of Article 114 TFEU – the most important legal basis for the establishment and functioning of the EU internal market[18] – and its 141 articles and 17 annexes require Member States to comprehensively align their legislation on chemical substances and follow uniform procedures for collecting and assessing information on the properties and hazards of those substances, thus leading to a common playing field for their internal market.[19]

The same logic informs the Regulation on classification, labelling and packaging of substances and mixtures (CLP Regulation),[20] which is based on the United Nations' Globally Harmonized System (GHS) and grounded on Article 114 TFEU, and the Regulation concerning the export and import of hazardous chemicals, also known as the Prior Informed Consent (PIC) Regulation.[21] Although the PIC Regulation was adopted on a different legal basis – *ie* Article 192(1) TFEU together with Article 207 TFEU – it also introduces a uniform normative framework, by establishing an import and export regime for these substances among the Member States and by placing common obligations on companies wishing to export chemicals to non-EU countries. The link with the common commercial policy (Article 207 TFEU), a domain covered by an exclusive competence of the Union, explains why, like in the case of the REACH and CLP Regulations, the PIC Regulation imposes a strict cooperation framework upon the Member States.[22]

17 Regulation (EC) 1907/2006 of 18 December 2006 concerning the Registration, Evaluation, Authorisation and Restriction of Chemicals (REACH) [2006] OJ L396/1.

18 M Kellerbauer, 'Article 114 TFEU', in M Kellerbauer et al (eds), *The EU Treaties and the Charter of Fundamental Rights* (OUP 2019).

19 For a detailed analysis of the REACH Regulation, see L Bergkamp (ed), *The European Union REACH Regulation for chemicals: Law and practice* (OUP 2013).

20 Regulation (EC) 1272/2008 of 16 December 2008 on classification, labelling and packaging of substances and mixtures [2008] OJ L353/1.

21 Regulation (EU) 649/2012 of 4 July 2012 concerning the export and import of hazardous chemicals [2012] OJ L201/60.

22 This is also the case with Regulation (EC) 428/2009 on a supranational regime for the control of exports, transfer, brokering and transit of dual-use items. See also ch 25 by Viterbo, in this volume.

Actually, cooperation mechanisms by means of harmonising measures have also been adopted in the CBRN domain within the framework of other sectoral policies of the Union. By relying on the main legal basis for EU environmental measures, that is, Article 192(1) TFEU, legislative frameworks have been developed concerning the handling[23] and shipment of waste,[24] as well as the control of major-accident hazards involving dangerous substances.[25] With a view to ensuring a high level of protection for human health and the environment throughout the Union in a consistent and effective manner, these instruments introduce harmonised procedures to be implemented by Member States. Likewise, in the context of the EU transport policy (Article 100 TFEU), a common vessel traffic monitoring and information system and common requirements concerning the transport of dangerous or polluting goods have been adopted,[26] while the so-called 'flexibility clause' (Article 352 TFEU) has been triggered to develop the first European procedures for the identification and designation of European critical infrastructures and the assessment of the need to improve their protection.[27]

Also in these cases, in line with what we have seen with regard to the internal market legislation on CBRN matters, the shared nature of relevant EU competences implies a pre-emption requiring Member States not to legislate in the same domains (unless the Union decides to cease exercising its competence). However, this does not mean that Member States are completely prevented from acting unilaterally. Not only do States have the possibility to invoke the CBRN-security nexus, thus exercising their own prerogatives to maintain public order and national security, but they may also enjoy – unlike the cooperation mechanisms on chemicals – a larger discretion in adopting implementing measures. The latter circumstance is due to the (rather) limited degree of harmonisation pursued by the great majority of these further pieces of legislation. This is the case, for instance, with the European critical infrastructure (ECI) Directive which represents, according to the legislature, 'a first step-by-step approach to identify and designate ECIs [...] As such this Directive should be reviewed with a view to assessing its impact [...] and

23 Directive 2008/98/EC of 19 November 2008 on waste [2008] OJ L312/3.

24 Regulation (EC) 1013/2006 of 14 June 2006 on shipments of waste [2006] OJ L190/1.

25 Directive 2012/18/EU of 4 July 2012 on the control of major-accident hazards involving dangerous substances [2012] OJ L197/1.

26 Directive 2002/59/EC of 27 June 2002 establishing a Community vessel traffic monitoring and information system [2002] OJ L208/10.

27 Council Directive 2008/114/EC of 8 December 2008 on the identification and designation of European critical infrastructures and the assessment of the need to improve their protection [2008] OJ L345/75.

extending its scope of application' (Recital 5). A similar reasoning applies to Directive (EU) 2017/541 on combating terrorism: based on Article 83(1) TFEU, the Directive establishes 'minimum rules' on the definition of terror-related criminal offences and sanctions, and for the protection of, support of and assistance to, victims of terrorism (Article 1).

3.2 *Cooperation through Assistance and Coordination. The Union Civil Protection Mechanism and the Framework Concerning Serious Cross-Border Threats to Health*

A different cooperation scheme consists of mechanisms put in place by the Union to assist, support and coordinate Member States in facing CBRN-related scenarios. Unlike the cooperation instruments discussed in the previous subsection, these mechanisms are not intended to impose any obligation on the Member States to align their laws and regulations with EU standards. On the contrary, they are based on the weakest form of competence the EU may exercise, that is, the supporting and coordinating competence. Pursuant to Article 2(5) TFEU, the exercise of such a competence does not produce any pre-emptive effect and shall not entail harmonisation of Member States' legislation. Yet, weakness does not necessarily mean uselessness. Indeed, if one considers the two major pieces of legislation adopted so far by the Union under supporting competences related to CBRN matters, namely Decision No 1082/2013/EU on serious cross-border threats to health and Decision No 1313/2013/EU on a Union Civil Protection Mechanism (UCPM), it is evident how relevant such cooperation established at supranational level may become.[28] The functioning of these two instruments is extensively illustrated in another chapter.[29] Here, it suffices to mention that they have contributed to establishing an integrated platform of cooperation for managing calamitous events. But even more importantly, this result has essentially been achieved *without imposing any specific duties upon the States*. More precisely, by means of conditionality mechanisms (which are mainly based on the financial assistance of the Union), the two instruments have led to a *voluntary harmonisation* among the Member States, facilitating the prevention, preparedness and response to disasters.

As for the UCPM, this has been realised by encouraging the pre-commitment of national resources for emergency response (the European Civil Protection Pool) in disaster scenarios, by supporting the Member States' prevention and preparedness efforts and, more recently, by creating a European last-resort

28 The two Decisions have been adopted on the basis of Articles 168 and 196 TFEU, respectively.

29 See ch 19 by Ferri in this volume.

reserve of additional capacities (the 'rescEU' reserve) that are acquired, rented or leased by Member States thanks to the financial support of the European Commission.

Decision 1082/2013/EU has introduced a variety of measures concerning the monitoring, early warning, and combating of serious cross-border threats to health, in order to coordinate and complement national policies. Of particular relevance for present purposes is the procedure for the joint procurement of medical countermeasures. This initiative arose because of the H1N1 flu pandemic of 2009, which highlighted weaknesses in the abilities of Member States to access and purchase pandemic vaccines and medications – weaknesses that have been further highlighted in the context of the COVID-19 pandemic. Quite significantly, the Joint Procurement Mechanism is based on a Joint Procurement Agreement (JPA) providing for *voluntary cooperation* which enables participating Member States to jointly purchase medical countermeasures. In the context of the COVID-19 crisis, Member States have decided to include the ongoing negotiations under the JPA in a fast-track procurement procedure supported by the Emergency support facility established by Regulation (EU) 2016/369.[30]

Without adopting the top-down logic that characterises the cooperation schemes based on the approximation of Member States' laws and regulations, both Decisions have nonetheless contributed to putting all Member States on a level playing field in managing disaster scenarios. However, in the wake of the COVID-19 pandemic, both the Union and the Member States have called for a significant revision of the voluntary schemes of cooperation in this field, so as to strengthen the cooperation and fill the existing gaps. In both cases, the decision has been taken to reshape the mechanisms in a stronger way. In 2020, the European Commission adopted two proposals for reframing the UCPM and the Cross-border health threats Decisions. As for the UCPM, its revision aims at strengthening the system, which is understood to be excessively based on Member States' voluntary resources, a situation that may undermine the capacity to intervene when, as in the case of COVID-19, all, or most, Member States are impacted by the same emergency (or threat) simultaneously.[31] Concerning the Cross-border health threats Decision, the European Commission has proposed strengthening the framework of

30 Council Regulation (EU) 2020/521 of 14 April 2020 activating the Emergency support under Regulation (EU) 2016/369, and amending its provisions taking into account the COVID-19 outbreak [2020] OJ L117/3.

31 Doc. COM(2020) 220 final, 2 June 2020. The Commission's proposal has been adopted in May 2021: Regulation (EU) 2021/836 of 20 May 2021 amending Decision No 1313/2013 [2021] OJ L185/1.

preparedness and response to threats by creating a single legislative mechanism, which should pave the way for the establishment of a European Health Union.[32] Additionally, both the Joint Procurement Mechanism and the Union's guidance on the adoption of common measures at EU level should be further enhanced by the new mechanism.

It is true that the planned revisions are likely to help reinforce the supranational management of calamitous events (including CBRN-related events). That said, given the limited competences the Union may exercise in the domains of health and civil protection, it is doubtful that such revisions could legitimate a further strengthening of supranational prerogative powers without a substantive shift in the understanding of those competences. It must not be forgotten that criticisms of the 'soft' nature of EU prerogative powers have already been raised regarding the existing mechanisms.[33] It follows that a clearer (and more legally sound) solution, leading to a significant enhancement of EU prerogative powers in those areas, should ideally imply a change to the current allocation of competences between the Member States and the Union through Treaty revision.

3.3 *Cooperating Softly ...*

This brings us to consider another way of establishing cooperation schemes on CBRN matters: the possibility of introducing common arrangements by means of EU soft law instruments.[34] The instrument, *par excellence*, for this is the action plan. In particular, building upon previous plans, in 2017, the European Commission adopted a new action plan to enhance preparedness against chemical, biological, radiological and nuclear security risks.[35] Adopting an all-hazards approach, the plan includes a series of actions that should be implemented at supranational and national level to improve the overall capacity to manage CBRN risks and events. Viewed from this perspective, the action plan defines objectives and timetables for developing specific policies, which may be invoked to justify the adoption of specific pieces of legislation, and which shape the background against which the existing legislation should be understood and interpreted.

While action plans may be the 'gold standard', it is impossible to ignore that a range of soft law instruments have gained terrific momentum in the

32 Cf. doc. COM(2020) 727 final, 11 November 2020.

33 F Casolari, 'Europe (2018)' (2019) 1 Yearbook of International Disaster Law 346.

34 Interestingly, as stressed in other chapters in this volume, this seems to be a general trend concerning the international law framework applicable to the CBRN domain.

35 Doc. COM(2017) 610 final, 18 October 2017.

context of the reaction to the COVID-19 pandemic. In fact, since March 2020, the EU institutions (in particular, the EU Commission) have been adopting non-binding instruments – such as guidelines and recommendations – with a view to establishing coordination mechanisms among the Member States that facilitate joined-up responses to the pandemic.[36] Particularly illustrative of the rationale behind such an approach is the Joint European Roadmap towards lifting COVID-19 containment measures.[37] Adopted on 15 April 2020, the Roadmap constitutes a joint effort by the European Commission and the European Council where the two institutions urge the establishment of a common framework among the Member States in order to prevent unilateral decisions from undermining the integrated nature of the internal market, as well as the common response put in place to fight against a cross-border threat to public health.[38] All in all, the Roadmap echoes the ECJ's reasoning for elaborating the 'frame of powers doctrine':[39] Member States' loyalty duties towards the Union require a supranational coordination (including in cases where national prerogatives may be relevant) and impose abstention obligations when unilateral action risks jeopardising the EU's objectives. Significantly, the Roadmap clarifies that the coordination of relevant measures shall take place in the context of the Integrated Political Crisis Response (ICPR), a set of arrangements established to respond at Union political level to crises having a wide-ranging impact or political significance, which should be used by the Council in the event of the invocation of the solidarity clause enshrined in Article 222 TFEU.[40]

Such an approach has both advantages and disadvantages. Supporters might claim that a soft-law approach will ensure more rapid, flexible and effective management, even in cases where the allocation of competences between the EU and the Member States is not completely clear. Detractors claim that the downside of such a flexible approach is that it may become too flexible, thus raising doubts as to its legitimacy and transparency and preventing the possibility to establish a permanent platform of cooperation among EU

36 See AM Pacces, M Weimer, 'From Diversity to Coordination: A European Approach to COVID-19' (2020) European Journal of Risk Regulation 283; O Stefan, 'COVID-19 Soft Law: Voluminous, Effective, Legitimate? A Research Agenda' (2020) 5 European Papers. European Forum 663.

37 Available at <https://ec.europa.eu/info/sites/info/files/communication_-_a_european_roadmap_to_lifting_coronavirus_containment_measures_0.pdf>.

38 Ibid, 5–6.

39 Above, sect 2.

40 Below, sect 4.

actors and Member States.[41] Notwithstanding the fact that ECJ case law has helped to clarify the possible legal effects of EU soft-law instruments, though not excluding the possibility of assessing their validity in light of EU primary law,[42] it is evident that the informality characterising such instruments risks undermining the notion of a 'Union based on the rule of law', that is, the fundamental condition that both the EU and the Member States must respect the constitutional framework established by EU primary law.[43]

4 In Search of the Right Balance: Article 42(7) TEU and Article 222 TFEU

There is one last form of possible cooperation among the Union and the Member States in the CBRN domain that deserves to be mentioned. It arises out of the possibilities offered by the so-called mutual assistance and solidarity clauses. Both clauses are intended to represent *a last resort mechanism* that may be triggered by a State in need, provided that all national and supranational tools available did not give an effective response.

Enshrined in Article 42(7) TEU, the mutual assistance clause requires Member States to aid and assist 'by all the means in their power' other EU States that are the victim of armed aggression. The clause thus introduces legal obligations upon Member States. However, Article 42(7) TEU, in line with the national identities clause, also highlights the need to respect 'the specific character of the security and defence policy' of Member States, as well as their commitments under the NATO umbrella. Moreover, no further elements are given for assessing the appropriateness of Member States' assistance. Also relevant is that the clause excludes any institutional involvement of the EU machinery. In sum, the clause allows for significant flexibility in its implementation, and it is mainly framed as an intergovernmental instrument triggering a horizontal cooperation among Member States.[44]

---

41 G Di Federico, 'Stuck in the middle with you … wondering what it is I should do. Some considerations on EU's response to COVID-19' (2020) 7 Eurojus.it 60, 77–78; M Eliantonio, O Stefan, 'The Elusive Legitimacy of EU Soft Law: An Analysis of Consultation and Participation in the Process of Adopting COVID-19 Soft Law in the EU' (2021) 12 European Journal of Risk Regulation 159.

42 Cf. Case C-501/18 *BT v Balgarska Narodna Banka* ECLI:EU:C:2021:249.

43 Case 294/83 *Parti écologiste 'Les Verts' v European Parliament* [1986] 1339, para 23.

44 T Ramopoulos, 'Article 42 TEU', in M Kellerbauer et al (n 18) 281–282.

Conceived as one of the political responses to the terrorist attack in Madrid (2004) and the floods in Central Europe (2002), the solidarity clause, which is enshrined in Article 222 TFEU, requires the Union and the Member States to act jointly if a Member State is a victim of a terrorist attack or the victim of a natural or man-made disaster.[45] Therefore, this clause also introduces substantive obligations for Member States. That said, there are, however, important differences between the two clauses. First, the events allowing a State to trigger Article 222 TFEU can hardly be covered by Article 42(7) TEU. Secondly, Article 222 TFEU is firmly rooted in the institutional framework of the Union. As this chapter has already anticipated, the EU ICPR provides the platform upon which decisions concerning the management of relevant crises are based. Furthermore, unlike the mutual assistance clause, the solidarity clause is covered by the jurisdiction of the ECJ, thus opening the possibility for judicial scrutiny of the behaviour of relevant actors. A third element which deserves to be mentioned is related to the duty bearers under the two clauses: whilst Article 42(7) TEU only mentions Member States' obligations, Article 222 TFEU also provides for solidarity duties upon the Union, leading to the introduction of a vertical cooperation with the EU States.

In light of the foregoing, it may be concluded that while the mutual assistance clause reflects in its entirety the intergovernmental nature of defence policy, also recognising a reinforced role to the margin of appreciation Member States may play in that field, the solidarity clause tries to carry out a balance between the prerogatives of Member States – pursuant to Declaration No 37 on Article 222 TFEU the latter keep the right to choose the most appropriate means to comply with their solidarity obligations towards the Member State concerned – and the need to put flesh on the bones of European solidarity through the institutionalisation of the procedures and enforcement mechanisms. In this light, and considering the foregoing considerations concerning the other forms of cooperation mechanisms (and the possible impact of the CBRN-security nexus), it is not surprising that the solidarity clause has never been triggered so far. On the contrary, following the terrorist attacks of 13 November 2015 in Paris, France decided to invoke Article 42(7) TEU, despite the lack of reference to terrorism in the Treaty provision, thus developing an informal bilateral discussion with other Member States.[46]

45 For a general analysis of the clause, see M Gestri (n 2), S. Villani, *The Concept of Solidarity within EU Disaster Law. A legal assessment* (Bononia University Press, 2021) 199.

46 NIM Nowáky, 'The invocation of the European Union's Mutual Assistance Clause: A Call for Enforced Solidarity' (2017) 22 European Foreign Affairs Review 357.

5 Concluding Remarks

This chapter has analysed the cooperation frameworks the EU and the Member States have elaborated to manage the CBRN matter. In this respect, the following conclusions may be drawn. As in the case of EU disaster law, the legal framework concerning CBRN matters is highly fragmented and largely dependent on a flexible allocation of competences between the Union and the Member States. Such a flexibility is caused by different factors. First, the CBRN-security nexus may play a relevant role in giving Member States the possibility to exercise a margin of appreciation in implementing EU law. This chapter has argued, in line with the ECJ's case law, that the possibility for Member States to rely on their retained powers in maintaining public order and national security is inversely proportional to the intensity of EU competences. In other words, the more EU law is capable of affecting municipal law – as in the case of the EU approximation measures related to CBRN products – the more Member States will have difficulties in invoking derogations from the supranational legal framework. Secondly, flexibility may depend on the specific features of the EU competences at stake. In particular, we have seen that the coordinating and supporting competences in the domains of health and civil protection have led to the development of cooperation platforms which heavily rely on States' will. Thirdly, flexibility may be a consequence of the emergency scenario which the Union and the Member States are facing. In this respect, the flexible approach largely consists of recourse to soft-law instruments establishing cooperation frameworks at the intersection of EU and Member States' competences. The reaction to the COVID-19 pandemic is a clear illustration of this growing attitude.

Undoubtedly, a flexible approach may present some advantages that help to ensure a quick and tailor-made action; also, it becomes evident from the foregoing that it is generally easier for Member States to accept soft or informal cooperation mechanisms than hard solutions – their reluctance to make full use of the solidarity clause is nothing but an example of that trend. However, flexibility is not unproblematic. On the one hand, it prevents the Union and the Member States from developing stable solutions; on the other, it risks undermining respect for the EU rule of law, a risk which is already visible in other emergency-related scenarios (such as the economic and financial crises and the so-called 'refugee crisis') where a similar approach has been developed.[47]

47 C Kilpatrick, 'On the Rule of Law and Economic Emergency: The Degradation of Basic Legal Values in Europe's Bailouts' (2015) 35 Oxford Journal of Legal Studies 325; F Casolari, 'The 'unbearable' lightness of soft law: on the European Union's recourse to informal

It is thus essential for EU institutions and Member States to take a resolute course of action to ensure a strengthening of the supranational capacity to manage CBRN matters (and, more generally, disaster scenarios). A first possibility, in this respect, could be a reconsideration of the existing legal bases, promoting the extension of their possible scope – such a maximalist approach is already visible in the use of Article 207 TFEU in the context of the EU common commercial policy.[48] Even more importantly, lessons learned from the COVID-19 pandemic should lead the Union and the Member States to go the extra mile in an effort to agree on a revision of EU primary law that may really contribute to improving resilience at supranational level.[49]

Bibliography

Azoulai L, 'The 'Retained Powers' Formula in the Case Law of the European Court of Justice: EU Law as Total Law?' (2011) 4 European Journal of Legal Studies 192.

Bergkamp L (ed), *The European Union REACH Regulation for chemicals: Law and practice* (OUP 2013).

Boucon L, 'EU Law and Retained Powers of Member States', in L Azoulai (ed), *The Question of Competence in the European Union* (OUP 2014).

Casolari F, 'Europe (2018)' (2019) 1 *Yearbook of International Disaster Law* 346.

Casolari F, 'The 'unbearable' lightness of soft law: on the European Union's recourse to informal instruments in the fight against irregular migration', in F Ippolito et al (eds), *Bilateral Relations in the Mediterranean. Prospects for Migration Issues* (Edward Elgar Publishing 2020).

Casolari F, *Leale cooperazione tra Stati membri e Unione europea* (Editoriale Scientifica 2020).

Di Federico G, 'Stuck in the middle with you … wondering what it is I should do. Some considerations on EU's response to COVID-19' (2020) 7 Eurojus.it 60.

Di Federico G, *L'identità nazionale degli Stati membri nel diritto dell'Unione europea* (Editoriale Scientifica 2017).

instruments in the fight against irregular migration', in F Ippolito et al (eds), *Bilateral Relations in the Mediterranean. Prospects for Migration Issues* (Edward Elgar Publishing 2020).

48 G Kübek, 'Redefining the boundaries of the Common Commercial Policy and the ERTA doctrine' (2018) 55 Common Market Law Review 883.

49 Cf. *Joint Declaration on the Conference on the Future of Europe. Engaging with Citizens for Democracy – Building a More Resilient Europe* (10 March 2021) <https://ec.europa.eu/info/sites/info/files/en_-_joint_declaration_on_the_conference_on_the_future_of_europe.pdf>.

Eliantonio M, Stefan O, 'The Elusive Legitimacy of EU Soft Law: An Analysis of Consultation and Participation in the Process of Adopting COVID-19 Soft Law in the EU' (2021) 12 European Journal of Risk Regulation 159.

Garben S, Govaere I (eds), *The Division of Competences between the EU and the Member States – Reflections on the Past, the Present and the Future* (Hart 2017).

Gestri M, 'EU Disaster Response Law: Principles and Instruments', in A de Guttry et al (eds), *International Disaster Response Law* (TMC Asser Press 2012).

Guastaferro B, 'Sincere Cooperation and Respect for National Identities', in R Schütze, T Tridimas (eds), *Oxford Principles of European Union Law – The European Union Legal Order*, vol. I (OUP 2018).

Kellerbauer M et al (eds), *The EU Treaties and the Charter of Fundamental Rights* (OUP 2019).

Kilpatrick C, 'On the Rule of Law and Economic Emergency: The Degradation of Basic Legal Values in Europe's Bailouts' (2015) 35 Oxford Journal of Legal Studies 325.

Kübek G, 'Redefining the boundaries of the Common Commercial Policy and the ERTA doctrine' (2018) 55 Common Market Law Review 883.

Nowáky NIM, 'The invocation of the European Union's Mutual Assistance Clause: A Call for Enforced Solidarity' (2017) 22 European Foreign Affairs Review 357.

Pacces AM, Weimer M, 'From Diversity to Coordination: A European Approach to COVID-19' (2020) European Journal of Risk Regulation 283.

Stefan O, 'COVID-19 Soft Law: Voluminous, Effective, Legitimate? A Research Agenda' (2020) 5 European Papers. European Forum 663.

Villani S, *The Concept of Solidarity within EU Disaster Law. A legal assessment* (Bononia University Press, 2021).

PART 2

Prevention, Preparedness, Response and Recovery in the Case of CBRN Events

CHAPTER 7

States' Obligations to Prevent CBRN Terrorism under Treaty Law and United Nations Security Council Resolutions

Luca Poltronieri Rossetti

1 Introduction

The international legal framework on CBRN threats has traditionally been developed based on a predominantly State-centred approach,[1] under the assumption that States are the subjects more likely to possess the capacity to obtain, develop and deploy CBRN weapons.[2] However, following high-profile episodes of attempted and successful CBRN terrorist attacks,[3] the unveiling of highly organised and powerful terrorist organisations forced States and international organisations to refocus their anti-terrorism and arms control efforts to address the risk of acts of CBRN terrorism by non-State actors (NSAs).[4] While this risk is relatively small compared to that of conventional, non-CBRN terrorist attacks, the possibility of acquisition and use of CBRN weapons by terrorist groups cannot be easily ruled out,[5] and has required States to intensify

1 Particularly in older treaties, the focus of disarmament obligations is on the conduct of States vis-à-vis other States. See eg Treaty on the Non-Proliferation of Nuclear Weapons (1968) (NPT) arts 2, 3. See M Asada, 'Security Council Resolution 1540 to Combat WMD Terrorism: Effectiveness and Legitimacy in International Legislation' (2008) 13 JC&SL 305–306.

2 Ibid. For a long time the probability of nuclear terrorism has been considered relatively low. See CJ Mark, T Taylor, E Eyster, W Maraman and J Wechler, 'Can Terrorists Build Nuclear Weapons' in P Leventhal and Y Alexander (eds), *Preventing Nuclear Terrorism, The Report and Papers of the International Task Force on Prevention of Nuclear Terrorism* (Lexington Books 1987) 60.

3 The mid-90s terrorist attacks carried out in Japan by the Aum Shinrikyo and the case of anthrax letters in the USA were a turning point with regard to States' attitudes towards chemical and biological attacks.

4 This has become particularly evident since the adoption of UNSC Res 1373 (28 September 2001) UN Doc S/RES/1373 and of UNSC Res 1540 (28 April 2004) UN Doc S/RES/1540.

5 On the probability of nuclear terrorism, see CC Joyner and AI Parkhouse, 'Nuclear Terrorism in a Globalizing World: Assessing the Threat and the Emerging Management Regime' (2009) 45 StanJIntlL 214. The reported use of chemical weapons in Syria shows that both States and non-State actors might be willing to deploy them.

cooperation efforts to foster prevention and preparedness.[6] In this connection, the pertinent treaty-based regime has been integrated by UN-imposed obligations, as well as by regional instruments.[7]

This chapter, taking into account the different components of prevention as defined in earlier chapters, attempts to identify the specific content of States' obligations to prevent CBRN terrorism resulting from the interplay between treaty law and UN Security Council resolutions. The contribution seeks to categorise prevention obligations according to their object and function; to analyse the normative relations between treaty law and UNSC resolutions; and briefly discusses the issue of implementation and enforcement of prevention obligations by States.

2 CBRN Terrorist Threats: The Challenge of Dealing with Non-State Actors

As a result of the State-centric character of the legal framework relating to CBRN weapons and materials,[8] the pertinent treaties create predominantly inter-State and institutionalised regimes of cooperation, mutual assistance and information,[9] and mechanisms of inspection and control to ensure the physical protection of CBRN materials and weapons.[10] This approach rests on the assumption that these threats, considering the inherent technical and

6 For an analysis of generic and specific preparedness obligations, see chs 4 and 8 by de Guttry. It should be noted that, due to the uncertainty on the exact delimitation between the concepts of prevention and preparedness, it is difficult to draw a clear-cut distinction between obligations pertaining to the former and to the latter. Therefore, some of the pertinent international norms can be examined from both perspectives.

7 On regional perspectives, particularly in the European context, see chs 6 by Casolari, 10 by Villani, 14 by Ferri, and 15 by Balboni.

8 Non-proliferation treaties originally focused on preventing the 'horizontal proliferation' of nuclear weapons and on the destruction of chemical and biological weapons possessed by States. See RJ Mathews, 'WMD Arms Control Agreements in the Post-September 11 Security Environment: Part of the Counter-Terrorism Toolbox' (2007) 8 Melbourne Journal of International Law 294.

9 Regimes of cooperation exist under all major non-proliferation and anti-terrorism treaties, and have been reinforced under the UNSC's legal framework. See paras 3.1 and 3.2 in this contribution.

10 This is the case with the Convention on the Prohibition of the Development, Production, Stockpiling and Use of Chemical Weapons and on their Destruction (1993) (CWC), particularly under Part IV(A) of the Verification Annex. With regard to physical protection, the most important legal instrument is the Convention on the Physical Protection of Nuclear Materials (1979) (CPPNM).

organisational obstacles, are more likely to come from States, which might directly acquire from other States CBRN weapons (or parts of them), or the materials and know-how to develop them. Nevertheless, experience has shown that NSAs might be willing to obtain or develop these kinds of weapons in order to use (or threaten to use) them in furtherance of their criminal purposes.[11] Moreover, the globalisation of trade, technological and scientific advancements, and the increasingly easy access to information, have opened new possibilities to criminal organisations, making it imperative to adapt the existing instruments to new challenges.[12] At the same time, when considering the multifaceted terrorist phenomenon, the pertinent sectoral conventions – with notable exceptions in the field of nuclear terrorism[13] – have mainly focused on conventional forms of terrorist attack, only more recently devoting specific attention to the CBRN threat, under the influence of UNSC resolutions.[14]

Against this backdrop, the non-State character of terrorist actors that might be inclined to use CBRN weapons poses serious challenges to the identification of the scope and content of States' obligations to prevent such acts, as well as to their implementation and enforcement.[15]

3 The Different Categories of Prevention Obligations

In attempting a classification of States' obligations to prevent CBRN terrorism, it is useful to distinguish between different categories of obligations according

11 On the reasons for terrorist groups to consider the acquisition and use of CBRN weapons, see J Revill, 'Past as Prologue: The Risk of Adoption of Chemical and Biological Weapons by Non-State Actors in the EU' (2017) 8 European Journal of Risk Regulation 629; SE Meulenbelt and MS Nieuwenhuizen, '"Non-State actors" pursuit of CBRN weapons: From motivation to potential humanitarian consequences' (2015) 97 IRRC 835–839.

12 Ibid 843–847; Joyner and Parkhouse (n 5) 206–208, 211–212.

13 CPPNM (n 10) art 7(1)(e)(ii), in particular as modified by the Amendment (2005) (CPPNM Amendment); International Convention for the Suppression of Acts of Nuclear Terrorism (2005) (ICSANT); International Convention for the Suppression of Terrorist Bombings (1997) (ICSTB).

14 Instruments such as the Convention for the Suppression of Unlawful Acts Against the Safety of Maritime Navigation (1988) (SUA Convention) have been updated to take into account CBRN terrorism. See Protocol to the SUA Convention (2005) (2005 SUA Protocol) art 3*bis*. See also Convention on the Suppression of Unlawful Acts Relating to International Civil Aviation (2010) (Beijing Convention) art 1(1)(g)–(i).

15 In other words, it is necessary to establish if and to what extent provisions that do not directly tackle CBRN terrorism can nevertheless be the source of prevention obligations applicable to this threat.

to their function and object. In this regard, prevention obligations incumbent on States can relate to:

a) The legal regime on CBRN weapons (or parts thereof), materials and related equipment that might be used for terrorist purposes. These obligations serve prevention purposes because they prohibit, limit or otherwise strictly regulate State conduct that might increase the probability of NSAs acquiring or developing CBRN weapons that could be used in terrorist attacks. Therefore, the main function of this set of obligations, from the point of view of prevention, is to reduce the risk of such weapons or materials falling into the wrong hands.[16] A related subset of obligations, lying at the boundary between prevention and preparedness, concerns duties of cooperation, mutual assistance and sharing of information in relation to CBRN disasters, which apply also to the consequences of terrorist actions.[17]

b) The conduct of individuals and legal entities characterised as terrorism under international law, in particular when involving CBRN weapons or materials. These obligations concern the duty to criminalise, investigate, prosecute and punish (or extradite) the alleged perpetrators of acts prohibited by international instruments on terrorism.[18] This duty is frequently coupled with obligations of technical, administrative and judicial cooperation among States to prevent and counter such acts.[19] This regime, thanks especially to UNSC resolutions, has gradually extended to the countering of underlying conduct, such as financing and other forms of support to terrorist organisations.[20] These obligations serve prevention purposes because they oblige States to set up appropriate legislative, administrative, financial and judicial mechanisms that create a hostile environment for the commission of acts of terrorism, thus helping to prevent, deter and eventually punish their commission.[21]

---

16 This is in line with the understanding of prevention as explained in chs 1 by Frulli and 3 by Venier.

17 For instance, duties of early warning and cooperation based on disaster law instruments, although mainly relevant to the preparedness and response phase, might contribute to the prevention of CBRN terrorism. See n 36.

18 CPPNM (n 10) art 7; ICSANT (n 13) arts 2, 5, 6; ICSTB (n 13) arts 2, 5; SUA Convention (n 14) arts 3(2), 3*bis*, 5*bis* (as amended by the 2005 SUA Protocol); Beijing Convention (n 14) arts 1(1)–(3), 3; International Convention for the Suppression of the Financing of Terrorism (1999) (CFT) arts 2, 4, 5, 8.

19 CPPNM (n 10) arts 5, 8; ICSANT (n 13) arts 7, 8, 18; ICSTB (n 13) art 15; SUA Convention (n 14) arts 8, 8*bis* (as amended by the 2005 SUA Protocol); Beijing Convention (n 14) art 17; CFT (n 18) arts 12, 18.

20 UNSC Res 1373 (n 4) op paras 1–3; UNSC Res 1540 (n 4) op paras 1–3.

21 On duties of criminalisation, see ch 33 by Amoroso.

To summarise, the identification of the precise content of obligations to prevent acts of CBRN terrorism requires, on the one hand, ascertaining the degree of concurrent applicability of non-proliferation and anti-terrorism obligations to this specific threat and, on the other hand, an assessment of the functional relations between obligations stemming from treaties and obligations stemming from UNSC resolutions.[22]

3.1 *Prevention Obligations Deriving from Non-Proliferation and Physical Protection Regimes*

The first set of prevention obligations concerns the legal regime applicable to CBRN weapons and materials that might be turned into weapons. By subjecting such objects – and State conduct in relation to them – to severely restrictive regulation, these provisions aim at reducing or eliminating the risk of acquisition, development and use of CBRN materials for non-peaceful purposes by both States and NSAs.

Beginning with analysis of older international instruments, it can be argued that treaties mainly aimed at regulating State conduct in relation to nuclear weapons, such as the Treaty on the Non-Proliferation of Nuclear Weapons (NPT), are the source of obligations that can contribute to the prevention of any misuse or diversion of such weapons, including for terrorist purposes. This is the case with respect to the obligations incumbent on nuclear States not to transfer nuclear weapons or assist, encourage, or induce a non-nuclear State to manufacture, acquire or control such weapons;[23] and the symmetric obligations imposed on non-nuclear States.[24] In addition, States Parties, under the supervision of the IAEA, undertake to accept certain standards of protection and safety in relation to peaceful nuclear activities and facilities 'with a view to *preventing* diversion of nuclear energy from peaceful uses to nuclear weapons or other nuclear explosive devices'.[25] An even more sophisticated and institutionalised regime, which includes a verification mechanism designed to identify stockpiles for the purposes of destruction, is provided under the Chemical Weapons Convention (CWC).[26] Article 1 of the CWC establishes that States are prevented not only from using chemical weapons, but

22 On this issue, see Asada (n 1) 315–317.

23 NPT (n 1) art 1. For an in-depth analysis of States' obligations on nuclear disarmament and testing, see ch 24 by Spagnolo.

24 NPT (n 1) art 2.

25 Ibid arts 3 and 5 (emphasis added). These obligations can serve prevention purposes in relation to nuclear terrorism, since their implementation strengthens the protection of nuclear materials that might be diverted from peaceful uses also by NSAs.

26 CWC Verification Annex (n 10). See also ch 23 by Poli.

also from developing, producing, otherwise acquiring, stockpiling or retaining chemical weapons, or transferring such weapons to *anyone*, and from assisting, encouraging or inducing *anyone* to engage in any activity that is prohibited for States Parties.[27] The expression 'anyone' certainly encompasses both States and non-State actors, making the prohibition relevant also for the prevention of terrorism. Despite a more limited scope and a less structured oversight system, the Biological Weapons Convention (BWC) contains similar provisions.[28] It is evident from the letter, object and purpose of these provisions that States' obligations to prevent the proliferation of CBRN weapons, as authoritatively clarified by the relevant treaty bodies, extend to State conduct vis-à-vis NSAs and to the conduct of NSAs themselves.[29] Moreover, in the case of chemical and biological weapons, the provision of regimes for their destruction ensures – if properly implemented – the elimination of the risk of use for terrorist purposes.

International cooperation to stop the proliferation of CBRN weapons and materials has been reinforced through the Convention on the Physical Protection of Nuclear Materials (CPPNM), which contributes to the prevention of terrorism by imposing obligations on States concerning the international transportation of nuclear materials.[30] The Convention creates a physical protection regime for nuclear materials as a prerequisite for their export, import and transit on the territory of States Parties.[31] The CPPNM also creates a system of information sharing, technical cooperation and mutual assistance. This protective infrastructure was significantly enhanced in 2005 through an amendment, which has extended the application of some of the Convention's provisions to situations other than the international transportation of nuclear

27 CWC (n 10) art 1(1)(a) and (d) (emphasis added).

28 Convention on the Prohibition of the Development, Production and Stockpiling of Bacteriological (Biological) and Toxin Weapons and on their Destruction (1972) (BWC) arts 1–4.

29 See IAEA (Board of Governors) 'Nuclear Security Plan 2018–2021' (14 September 2017) GC(61)/24, 1 referring to the Agency's role in this field as established in the plans adopted in 2002, 2005, 2009 and 2013; OPCW (Executive Council) 'Decision: Addressing the Threat Posed by the Use of Chemical Weapons by Non-State Actors' (13 October 2017) EC-86/DEC.9, 1–4 focusing on States' obligations to prevent and punish the use of chemical weapons by NSAS; BWC (Conference of the States Parties) 'Final Document of the 4th Review Conference of the States Parties to the BWC' (25 November–6 December 1996) BWC/CONF.IV/9, 17, according to which 'The States Parties recognize the need to ensure [...] the effective fulfilment of their obligations under the Convention in order, inter alia, to exclude use of biological and toxin weapons in terrorist or criminal activity'.

30 CPPNM (n 10) arts 3, 4.

31 For an in-depth analysis of this regime, see ch 25 by Viterbo.

materials.[32] The content of the obligation of physical protection is clarified by reference to 12 fundamental principles, some of which fall squarely under the concept of prevention.[33] These provisions must be read together with those of the Convention on Nuclear Safety, which creates a web of similar prevention obligations relating to civil nuclear activities.[34] Although non-binding, the recommendations formulated by the IAEA complement these provisions on the technical aspects of protection of nuclear and radioactive materials.[35] Also disaster management treaties contain provisions that might be applicable to disasters caused by acts of CBRN terrorism, especially in relation to early warning or notification of accidents or the provision of mutual technical assistance in the prevention of disasters.[36] Despite the fact that most of the aforementioned provisions do not refer directly to terrorist threats, taken together and read in light of the extensive interpretations put forward by the specialised international organisations and agencies, they are instrumental to giving substance to the obligation to prevent acts of CBRN terrorism, under all three general understandings of prevention for the purposes of this study.[37]

This layer of conventional obligations is further reinforced by UNSC Resolution 1540 (2004), which tackles the issue of CBRN terrorism and NSAs' access to CBRN materials. More specifically, the Resolution imposes upon all States the obligation to adopt and enforce effective measures to ensure the safety and physical protection of CBRN materials; to establish controls on the movement, transportation and import-export of these materials in order to prevent their proliferation; as well as a general duty to refrain 'from providing any form of support to non-State actors that attempt to develop, acquire,

32 CPPNM (n 10) art 2 as amended which applies also to the domestic context.

33 See the reference to an adequate 'Legislative and Regulatory Framework' (Principle C); the identification of a 'Competent Authority' for implementation (Principle D); risk assessment based on the level of 'Threat' (Principle G) and a 'Graded Approach' to physical protection (Principle H).

34 Convention on Nuclear Safety (1994) arts 7, 14, 17–19.

35 See eg IAEA, 'Code of Conduct on the Safety and Security of Radioactive Sources' (January 2004) IAEA/CODEOC/2004, and the two related documents IAEA, 'Guidance on the Import and Export of Radioactive Sources' (March 2005) IAEA/CODEOC/IMP-EXP/2005 and IAEA, 'Guidance on the Management of Disused Radioactive Sources' (April 2018) IAEA/CODEOC/MGT-DRS/2018.

36 Convention on Early Notification of a Nuclear Accident (1986) arts 1–3; Convention on Assistance in the Case of a Nuclear Accident or Radiological Emergency (1986) arts 1–4.

37 As described in ch 3 by Venier, prevention consists of three main aspects, namely the adoption of adequate legal and regulatory frameworks; the duty to perform risk assessments; and the duty to cooperate to reduce the risk of adverse events.

manufacture, possess, transport, transfer or use nuclear, chemical or biological weapons and their means of delivery'.[38]

3.2 *Prevention Obligations Concerning the Conduct of Individuals and Entities in Relation to CBRN Terrorist Activities*

The second set of prevention obligations stems from treaties and UNSC resolutions that impose a duty on States to criminalise and prosecute terrorist conduct that might involve CBRN materials or weapons, and conduct that contributes to financing, preparing, facilitating or organising terrorist acts. By requesting States to modify their legal systems and to cooperate to effectively proscribe, investigate, prosecute and punish these acts – including some underlying activities far removed from an actual terrorist attack – these obligations contribute to preventing CBRN terrorist acts through the deterrent function of criminal law and other forms of administrative, civil and financial control. While the exact content of the duty to criminalise and prosecute CBRN-related unlawful conduct is analysed elsewhere in this volume,[39] it is appropriate to mention here its most relevant aspects in relation to prevention, without delving into the jurisdictional and cooperation regime.[40]

The most densely regulated area in this regard is that of nuclear terrorism. Article 7 of the CPPNM imposes several duties of criminalisation, requiring States to criminalise actions undertaken without lawful authority, involving the receipt, possession, use, transfer, alteration, disposal or dispersal of nuclear material likely to cause death or serious injury to persons or damage to property;[41] theft, robbery, embezzlement or fraudulent obtaining of nuclear material;[42] demands for nuclear material by threat or use of force or intimidation;[43] and – most importantly – threats to commit such offences '*in order to compel a natural or legal person, international organization or State to do or to refrain from doing any act*'.[44] The 2005 Amendment to the CPPNM adds a duty to criminalise nuclear smuggling as a stand-alone offence, and reinforces

---

38 UNSC Res 1540 (n 4) op para 1.

39 See ch 32 by Vierucci and ch 33 by Amoroso.

40 On the jurisdictional regime of anti-terrorism treaties, see R Kolb, 'The Exercise of Criminal Jurisdiction over International Terrorists' in A Bianchi (ed), *Enforcing International Law Norms Against Terrorism* (Hart Publishing 2004). On issues of extradition, see MA Newton, 'Terrorist crimes and the *aut dedere aut judicare* obligation' in L van den Herik and N Schrijver (eds), *Counter-Terrorism Strategies in a Fragmented International Legal Order: Meeting the Challenges* (CUP 2013).

41 CPPNM (n 10) art 7(1)(a).

42 Ibid art 7(1)(b)–(c).

43 Ibid art 7(1)(d).

44 Ibid art 7(1)(e) (emphasis added).

States' obligations in the field of cooperation and sharing of information in case of threats of nuclear sabotage.[45] Pervasive obligations functional to the prevention of nuclear terrorism are also imposed under Article 2 of the International Convention for the Suppression of Acts of Nuclear Terrorism (ICSANT). In particular, Article 2(1)(b)(iii) expressly contemplates the criminalisation of the use (or threat of use) of radioactive material or devices, and of the use or damage of a nuclear facility in a manner which releases or risks the release of radioactive material in connection with a terrorist intent. The International Convention for the Suppression of Terrorist Bombings (ICSTB) specifically tackles the use of CBRN explosives or lethal devices, and includes an explicit reference to offences 'intended or calculated to provoke *a state of terror* in the general public or in a group of persons or particular persons'.[46] The preventive scope of the Convention is limited by the fact that it only imposes the criminalisation of offences that are either completed or, at least, attempted, but excludes planning and preparatory acts.[47] Nevertheless, Article 15 of the Convention imposes a general duty of inter-State cooperation to prevent and counter terrorist bombings, including through the sharing of information and transfer of technology.[48]

The survey of this category of prevention obligations would not be complete without reference to the sectoral treaties dealing with the safety of maritime navigation, fixed platforms located on the continental shelf and civil aviation. The 2005 SUA Protocol reinforces the criminalisation of acts against the safety of navigation by referring to various types of conduct, both of individuals and legal entities, including the use (or threat of use) of CBRN weapons, as well as the transportation on ships of CBRN weapons or 'equipment, materials or software or related technology that significantly contributes to the design, manufacture or delivery of a BCN weapon, with the intention that it will be used for such purpose'.[49] Analogous provisions are contained in the 2005 Protocol to the Protocol for the Suppression of Unlawful Acts against

45 CPPNM (n 10) art 7(1)(d) as amended regarding smuggling, defined as an 'act which constitutes the carrying, sending, or moving of nuclear material into or out of a State without lawful authority'; and letter (e) as regards sabotage of nuclear facilities. See also art 5(3) in relation to duties of cooperation in the case of a credible threat of sabotage.

46 ICSTB (n 13) art 5 (emphasis added).

47 Obviously, States are not prevented from criminalising preparatory acts, such as a criminal agreement to use CBRN weapons.

48 ICSTB (n 13) art 15.

49 SUA as amended by the 2005 SUA Protocol (n 14) arts 3(2), 3*bis*(1)(b)(iv).

the Safety of Fixed Platforms located on the Continental Shelf[50] and in the 2010 Beijing Convention on the Safety of Civil Aviation.[51]

With specific regard to chemical and biological weapons, criminalisation provisions capable of covering their use for terrorist purposes are contained both in the CWC and in the BWC.[52] The Treaty on the Prohibition Nuclear Weapons (TPNW), which entered into force on 22 January 2021 and is ratified by some 50 States,[53] mimics these provisions with regard to nuclear weapons, establishing that States Parties shall take 'all appropriate legal, administrative and other measures, including the imposition of penal sanctions, to prevent and suppress any activity prohibited to a State Party under this Treaty *undertaken by persons* or on territory under its jurisdiction or control'.[54]

While it is true that criminalisation of various forms of CBRN-related conduct might well contribute to the prevention of acts of CBRN terrorism through deterrence, it has been pointed out that effective prevention requires that States act much earlier, such as at the stage of design and preparation of terrorist acts, and that they effectively counter the financing of terrorist activities.[55] This is the area most deeply influenced by the 'legislative' activity of the UNSC in recent years.[56]

UNSC Resolution 1373 sets a number of general obligations to prevent terrorism, in relation to the financing of terrorist organisations; the provision of any form of support to terrorists; the provision of early warning to other States through the exchange of information; the denial of safe haven; the criminalisation and prosecution of various kinds of conduct related to

50 Protocol of 2005 to the Protocol for the Suppression of Unlawful Acts against the Safety of Fixed Platforms Located on the Continental Shelf (2005) arts 2*bis*, 2*ter*.

51 Beijing Convention (n 14) art 1(1)(g)–(i).

52 CWC (n 10) art 7(1)(a)–(c); BWC (n 28) art 4.

53 Treaty on the Prohibition of Nuclear Weapons (2007) (TPNW).

54 Ibid art 5(2) (emphasis added).

55 Mathews (n 8) 306 speaks of a '"pre-September 11" and "post-September 11"' approach. Asada (n 1) 313 stresses the importance of prevention and the limits of investigation and punishment, which only intervene after the threat has materialised.

56 The adoption of Resolutions 1373 and 1540 sparked doctrinal debate with regard to the power of the UNSC to 'legislate' for the international community. A very critical view was expressed by DH Joyner, 'Non-Proliferation Law and the United Nations System: Resolution 1540 and the Limits of the Power of the Security Council' (2007) 20(2) LJIL 489. On the same topic, see also O Bosch and P van Ham (eds), *Global Non-Proliferation and Counter-Terrorism: The Impact of UNSCR 1540* (Brookings Institution Press 2007); S Talmon, 'The Security Council as World Legislature' (2005) 99(1) AJIL 188–190. In earlier literature, the UNSC's power to impose on States both specific and general prevention measures had been recognised by C Tomuschat, 'Obligations Arising for States without or against Their Will' (1993) 241 Recueil des Cours de l'Académie de Droit International 345.

terrorist acts; and the limitation of free movement of terrorists.[57] This resolution, while being concerned with the terrorist phenomenon in general, makes a specific reference to the potential use of CBRN materials and the related challenges.[58] The UNSC's call on States to strengthen cooperation and to ratify the International Convention for the Suppression of Financing of Terrorism (CFT) greatly contributed to the entry into force of this instrument.[59] Article 2 of the CFT clarifies what constitutes financing of terrorism for the purposes of the Convention, partly by reference to the terrorist conduct defined in the sectoral treaties listed in the annex, and clarifies the different modes of liability (including attempt, participation as accomplice, organising or directing others to commit an offence, intentionally contributing to its commission by a group of people).[60] The Convention, similarly to Resolution 1373, then goes on to establish obligations placed at the uncertain boundary between prevention and preparedness, when it imposes on States the duty to enact appropriate criminal legislation and to cooperate in preventing financing by 'taking all practicable measures' (such as freezing of funds) to counter the preparation of such offences.[61]

UNSC Resolution 1540 (2004) marked a significant development in the UNSC's approach to the fight against CBRN terrorism, by fully acknowledging this global phenomenon and by addressing States' obligations vis-à-vis NSAS. It established, *inter alia*, that States 'shall refrain from providing any form of support to non-State actors that attempt to develop, acquire, manufacture, possess, transport, transfer or use nuclear, chemical or biological weapons and their means of delivery';[62] that they 'shall adopt and enforce appropriate effective laws which prohibit any non-State actor to manufacture, acquire, possess, develop, transport, transfer or use nuclear, chemical or biological weapons [...] *in particular for terrorist purposes*';[63] and that all States are called upon to 'take cooperative action to *prevent* illicit trafficking in nuclear, chemical or biological weapons, their means of delivery, and related materials'.[64] This was coupled

57 UNSC Res 1373 (n 4) op paras 1–3.
58 Ibid op para 4.
59 At the time of the 9/11 attacks only four States had ratified it (Botswana, Sri Lanka, United Kingdom, Uzbekistan). After the adoption of Resolution 1373, ratifications quickly rose to the required 22 necessary for the entry into force.
60 CFT (n 18) art 2. The range of types of conduct and modes of liability that fall under the duty of criminalisation and prosecution significantly expands the anticipatory use of criminal law.
61 Ibid art 18.
62 UNSC Res 1540 (n 4) op para 1.
63 Ibid op para 2 (emphasis added).
64 Ibid op para 10 (emphasis added).

with a call on States to fully implement their obligations under the existing multilateral treaties and with the institution of a Committee to supervise compliance with the Resolution.[65] This course of action, also in light of the lack of adequate implementation and reporting by some States, was reaffirmed by the UNSC in Resolution 2325 (2016).[66]

To summarise, the common traits of this set of prevention obligations are: a) The duty of criminalisation of CBRN-related terrorist conduct under both principal and accessory forms of liability, which extends to certain preparatory conduct. The determination of penalties is left to States, provided that they are appropriate, proportionate to the gravity of the conduct and realise the required prevention objectives; b) The imposition upon States, even beyond the material scope of the duties of criminalisation, of obligations to cooperate in the prevention of CBRN-related terrorist conduct; c) The trend towards an ever-increasing anticipation of prevention activities, including the punishability of conduct removed in time and space from an actual CBRN terrorist attack but instrumental to increasing the risk of it occurring, with particular emphasis on financing.

4 The Impact of the UN-Derived Legal Regime on Treaty Obligations and the Issue of National Implementation and Enforcement

A second distinction between different kinds of prevention obligations relates to their source. While treaties can only create obligations for the States Parties, posing insurmountable challenges to the effectiveness of prevention obligations in situations involving non-parties, UNSC resolutions adopted under Chapter VII of the Charter are binding upon all States Parties to the organisation, and are capable of reducing – at least in theory – the risk of discrepancies among national legal systems and the existence of safe havens for terrorist activities. In this connection, treaty obligations, some of which already enjoyed a quasi-universal character, have been reinforced and further expanded by UNSC resolutions, in a clear attempt to 'universalise' them and urge States to

65 Ibid op para 4.

66 UNSC Res 2325 (15 December 2016) UN Doc S/RES/2325 op paras 3–4. On the status of implementation and enforcement, see Chair of the Security Council Committee established pursuant to Resolution 1540 (2004), 'Letter dated 9 December 2016 from the Chair of the Security Council Committee established pursuant to resolution 1540 (2004) addressed to the President of the Security Council', containing the 'Report of the Security Council Committee established pursuant to resolution 1540' (2016) S/2016/1038 (2016 Report) paras 25–35.

comply under the concurrent authority of the two sets of sources. The impact of these resolutions on both existing and emerging treaties must be briefly examined.

To begin with, the pertinent UNSC resolutions contain safeguard clauses, according to which none of the obligations set out by the resolutions should be interpreted as conflicting with existing obligations incumbent on States based on treaties already in force.[67]

With regard to the relationship between UNSC resolutions and existing or emerging treaty regimes, in some cases, the UNSC's intervention attempted to fill gaps in the conventional regimes, or to reinforce them by providing a more uniform legal framework. Moreover, the adoption of resolutions under Chapter VII allowed the UNSC to 'universalise' obligations already in existence for some (but not all) States under treaty law, or to create new general obligations of a latitude hardly attainable through sectoral treaties. Sometimes the resolutions of the UNSC have made binding upon States obligations already envisaged by treaties not yet in force, such as in the case of Resolution 1373, which imposed on States obligations almost identical to those contained in the 1999 FTC.[68] UNSC resolutions, with their calls for cooperation in the prevention of terrorism and proliferation, have also sought to incentivise States to become parties to existing treaties, to amend treaties in order to take into account the CBRN threat, or to negotiate the conclusion of new treaties, and have contributed to their entry into force.[69]

The effects of UNSC resolutions are also felt in relation to the implementation and enforcement of underlying treaty obligations. For instance, the creation of an oversight mechanism under Resolution 1540 and the work of the Committee have increased international supervision in relation to both the obligations created by the Resolution and by treaties. This is because the ratification and implementation of treaties can itself constitute a form of implementation of UNSC-imposed obligations, particularly under the heading of the obligation to cooperate in order to prevent terrorism and CBRN proliferation.[70] This is clearly demonstrated by the States' and Committee's

67 See eg UNSC Res 1540 (n 4) op para 5; UNSC Res 2325 (n 66) preambular para 3.

68 A quick comparison of the two texts clearly shows this. See also M Happold, 'Security Council Resolution 1373 and the Constitution of the United Nations' (2003) 16(3) LJIL 594.

69 The influence of UNSC resolutions on the adoption and ratification of instruments such as the 2005 Amendment to CPPNM, the Protocol to the SUA Convention, the Beijing Convention, and the TPNW is particularly evident.

70 This is implicit in the Resolution's call for the ratification, implementation and enforcement of existing treaties.

reporting practice.[71] At the same time, the practice of the Committee has been significant in providing assistance to States at the implementation stage, thanks to the sharing of technical expertise and best practices, and to the coordination with other specialised institutions and agencies (such as the IAEA and OPCW).[72]

The focus on implementation and enforcement is evident from the wording of the resolutions, which makes it clear that the prevention of CBRN terrorism can only be effective through diligent fulfilment by States of their obligations, in close cooperation with each other and the relevant international organisations and technical bodies. On this crucial point, it should be noted that, despite the activity of the Committee, many States have yet to fully implement their obligations or have poor track records as regards actual enforcement of national prevention measures.[73] Some States have offered limited cooperation with the supervisory body, something which prompted the Council to recall the role of the Committee and the importance of States' reporting and compliance in Resolution 2325 (2016).[74]

5 Concluding Remarks

This contribution has attempted to provide a categorisation of States' universal or quasi-universal obligations to prevent CBRN terrorism, which are disseminated across various fields of international law and legal instruments. This categorisation was based on a functional analysis of the object and purpose of

---

71 See eg the 2016 Report (n 66) paras 54–55 and Annex VII titled 'Adherence by States to non-proliferation-related treaties, conventions, protocols and other instruments relevant to Security Council resolution 1540 (2004) as at 24 April 2016', which shows the close connection between the implementation of treaty obligations and UN-imposed obligations.

72 The 1540 Committee has in various ways provided assistance to States in the design of implementation measures, in connection with specialised international agencies. See 2016 Report (n 66) paras 180–189 for a summary of the activities of assistance and international cooperation fostered by the Committee. See also Annex XIX for the list and content of requests for assistance. With regard to obligations relating to the financing of terrorism, see Counter-Terrorism Committee Executive Directorate, 'Technical Guide to the Implementation of Security Council Resolution 1373 and other relevant resolutions' (2017) UN Doc S/2017/716.

73 See 2016 Report (n 66) paras 25–35. The 2021 comprehensive review was postponed due to the Covid-19 pandemic. See also 'Review on the implementation of resolution 1540 (2004) for 2020' (2020) S/AC.44/2020/OC.84 paras 9–10.

74 UNSC Res 2325 (n 66) preambular paras 8–10, op paras 3–4. In particular, some States have delayed the presentation of (or have yet to present) their first report under Resolution 1540.

different sets of obligations incumbent on States, which contribute to realising discrete but interconnected aspects of prevention.

The analysis carried out in the previous paragraphs revealed the sheer complexity of the universal legal framework on the prevention of CBRN terrorism, which is further increased by the interaction with regional, subregional and bilateral instruments, as well as by an increasingly dense web of soft law initiatives.[75] Despite the UNSC's attempts to build a unifying framework of general and specific obligations in support of the underlying treaty regime, fragmentation and lack of coordination still persist, with negative consequences on the effectiveness of prevention.

Finally, it has been underlined that only through full implementation and enforcement of prevention obligations at the national and regional level, under the supervision of and in close dialogue with the relevant international organisations and technical bodies, is it possible to realise an effective prevention-preparedness-response cycle capable of reducing the risk of CBRN acts of terrorism and of minimising their consequences. Experience shows that the pursuit of this objective requires a constant process of adaptation of the legal framework to meet the ever-changing challenges to the security of the international community, of which CBRN terrorism constitutes a prominent example.

Bibliography

Asada M, 'Security Council Resolution 1540 to Combat WMD Terrorism: Effectiveness and Legitimacy in International Legislation' (2008) 13 JC&SL 303.

Bosch O and van Ham P (eds), *Global Non-Proliferation and Counter-Terrorism: The Impact of UNSCR 1540* (Brookings Institution Press 2007).

Happold M, 'Security Council Resolution 1373 and the Constitution of the United Nations' (2003) 16(3) LJIL 593.

Joyner CC and Parkhouse AI, 'Nuclear Terrorism in a Globalizing World: Assessing the Threat and the Emerging Management Regime' (2009) 45 StanJIntlL 203.

75 Non-binding initiatives are abundant in the area of CBRN materials and weapons. Examples include the Proliferation Security Initiatives; the Global Initiative to Combat Nuclear Terrorism; the EU CBRN Centres of Excellence Initiative; the IAEA NSSC-Network; the NATO Joint CBRN Defence COE. In late 2020, INTERPOL and the UNCTC launched a joint initiative to produce a Global Threat Study on Non-State Actors and Their CBRNE Materials. See <https://www.interpol.int/en/News-and-Events/News/2020/INTERPOL-and-UN-launch-initiative-on-CBRNE-terror-threats> (all links were last accessed on 25 November 2021).

Joyner DH, 'Non-Proliferation Law and the United Nations System: Resolution 1540 and the Limits of the Power of the Security Council' (2007) 20(2) LJIL 489.

Kolb R, 'The Exercise of Criminal Jurisdiction over International Terrorists' in A Bianchi (ed), *Enforcing International Law Norms Against Terrorism* (Hart Publishing 2004) 227.

Mark CJ, Taylor T, Eyster E, Maraman W and Wechler J, 'Can Terrorists Build Nuclear Weapons' in P Leventhal and Y Alexander (eds), *Preventing Nuclear Terrorism, The Report and Papers of the International Task Force on Prevention of Nuclear Terrorism* (Lexington Books 1987) 55.

Mathews RJ, 'WMD Arms Control Agreements in the Post-September 11 Security Environment: Part of the Counter-Terrorism Toolbox' (2007) 8 Melbourne Journal of International Law 292.

Meulenbelt SE and Nieuwenhuizen MS, 'Non-State actors' pursuit of CBRN weapons: From motivation to potential humanitarian consequences' (2015) 97 IRRC 831.

Newton MA, 'Terrorist crimes and the *aut dedere aut judicare* obligation' in L van den Herik and N Schrijver (eds), *Counter-Terrorism Strategies in a Fragmented International Legal Order: Meeting the Challenges* (CUP 2013) 68.

Revill J, 'Past as Prologue: The Risk of Adoption of Chemical and Biological Weapons by Non-State Actors in the EU' (2017) 8 European Journal of Risk Regulation 626.

Talmon S, 'The Security Council as World Legislature' (2005) 99(1) AJIL 175.

Tomuschat C, 'Obligations Arising for States without or against Their Will' (1993) 241 Recueil des Cours de l'Académie de Droit International 344.

CHAPTER 8

Preparedness Rules Applicable to CBRN Terrorism

Andrea de Guttry

1 Introduction

Many international studies,[1] criminal investigations,[2] and intelligence reports from international organisations (IOs)[3] and national institutions[4] have reached the conclusion that, for a multiplicity of reasons,[5] there is an increas-

1 According to E Dinu, 'Assessing CBRN terrorism threats', in S Fei, I Anthony (eds), *Reassessing CBRN Threats in a Changing Global Environment* (SIPRI 2019), the threat posed by CBRN terrorism 'is still considered relevant, driven by political, ideological, social, economic and technological factors. Although threats should not be unnecessarily exaggerated, attack could plausibly be conducted with CBRN means targeting random civilians or selected individuals because of their political or ideological significance', p. 13. See also K Ivanova and T Sandler, 'CBRN Attack Perpetrators: An Empirical Study'(2007) 3(49) Foreign Policy Analysis, 273.

2 Europol, *Terrorism Situation and Trend Report* (*TE-SAT*) *2017*, p 16: <www.europol.europa.eu/sites/default/files/documents/tesat2017.pdf>. All links were last accessed in May 2021.

3 Vladimir Voronkov, Under-Secretary-General of the UN Office for Counter-Terrorism, stated recently that 'Over the years, terrorists have tested new ways and means to acquire and use more dangerous weapons [....] including weapons incorporating CBRN materials [...] Recent events such as the use of chemical weapons on civilians by terrorist groups during the terrific war that started in Syria in 2011 have shown us that this is indeed a very real threat'. United Nations Office for Counter-Terrorism, *Ensuring Effective Interagency Operability and Coordination in Case of Chemical and/or Biological Attacks,* (UN 2017). In a recent study by E Nexon and C Wachte, commissioned by the European Parliament and titled '*EU preparedness against CBRN weapons*', reference is made to 'repeated chemical attacks by both State and non-state actors in the context of the Syrian conflict (since 2012), allegations about a North Korean offensive chemical programme and the assassination of the North Korean leader's half-brother with VX nerve agent (2017), the Salisbury Novichok poisonings likely perpetrated by individuals affiliated to a State security service, as well as the disruption of two ricin terror plots in Germany and France (2018)': <https://www.europarl.europa.eu/RegData/etudes/STUD/2019/603875/EXPO_STU(2019)603875_EN.pdf>.

4 According to the CIA, Al-Qaeda and several associated extremist groups 'have a wide variety of potential agents and delivery means to choose from for CBRN attacks': CIA, *Terrorist CBRN: Material and Effects,* <https://www.cia.gov/library/reports/general-reports-1/CBRN_threat_wo.pdf>.

5 These are the reasons identified by E Dinu, n 1, '1. Sophisticated CBRN agents are potentially highly lethal while being silent killers, and therefore harder to detect and contain; 2. Any attack using CBRN material would attract attention and receive prime-time coverage in the mass media; 3. CBRN attacks would most certainly provoke terror and panic among civilians;

ing risk that terrorist groups might make use of CBRN material to carry out attacks in the near future, or target installations containing CBRN material. To reduce the risk of these events, which could be extremely deadly and cause widespread damage, it is essential all over the world to adopt, test and continuously update not only prevention procedures[6] but also specific preparedness measures. While there is no guarantee that these measures will succeed, even if fully implemented, they can minimise and mitigate the consequences of such malicious events.[7] Furthermore, as no State has the capacity to deal with the consequences of a serious CBRN terrorist event on its own, reinforced international cooperation is not only desirable but necessary.

This chapter investigates the content of international obligations and soft law instruments related to preparedness measures, which States and, where applicable, International Organisations are expected to adopt and implement to face potential CBRN terrorism activities. Therefore, the chapter is mostly devoted to careful examination of relevant international treaties at the universal and regional levels, as well as UN Resolutions and soft law instruments. The closing paragraph is devoted to a preliminary assessment of the effective impact of these measures and the degree to which they are implemented at the national level.

The definition of 'preparedness' is that already adopted in Chapter 4, according to which, in general terms, a state of preparedness is 'the product of a combination of planning, allocation of resources, training, exercising, and organizing to build, sustain, and improve operational capabilities based on risk assessments'.[8] This chapter will not examine the generic preparedness obligations which States are supposed to implement to face any kind of potential CBRN event (including malicious events caused by terrorists), as these were already examined in Chapter 4.

---

4. CBRN materials have the potential to inflict serious consequences and collateral economic damage (e.g. by contaminating the environment and affecting animal and human health); 5. CBRN materials offer the means to blackmail governments or at least pressure them; and 6. Possession and use of CBRN means would place the perpetrator in a position of perceived power vis-à-vis national authorities (at least temporarily)'.

6 See ch 7 by Poltronieri Rossetti in this volume.

7 A very interesting and comprehensive analysis of the drivers of violent extremism (which often then transforms into terrorist activities) is offered in the 24 December 2015 Report of the Secretary General of the UN, 'Plan of Action to Prevent Violent Extremism' (UN doc A/70/674).

8 Ibid p 42.

2 Preparedness Obligations Regulated in International Instruments

2.1 *At the Universal Level*

In Chapter 4, the conclusion was reached, on the basis of a detailed analysis of international treaties, that States and IOs must adopt a wide array of generic preparedness measures to deal with any kind of CBRN event.[9] The following paragraphs investigate preparedness measures dealing specifically and exclusively with CBRN terrorist activities. While in the past such rules have been rare,[10] more recently they have attracted increasing interest, especially at the regional level. However, this recent trend is far from uniform, and there are still several relevant conventions devoted to terrorism that do not contain any reference to preparedness measures.[11]

The first universal agreement to codify preparedness obligations related to potential terrorist activities was the Convention for the Suppression of Unlawful Seizure of Aircraft (1970). According to Article 9 of this Convention, whenever a person on board an aircraft in flight unlawfully – by force or threat or any other form of intimidation (which might include the threat to use CBRN substances) – seizes or attempts to exercise control of that aircraft, contracting States 'shall take all appropriate measures to restore control of the aircraft to its lawful commander or to preserve his control of the aircraft'.[12] While the rule seems to be relevant mostly in the 'response' phase of a CBRN terrorist event, it is mentioned here because it implies that States must adopt all relevant measures to be prepared to confront this kind of criminal act, using whatever policy is deemed appropriate (that is, to negotiate or to use force). The importance of the adoption of these measures was reiterated by the

9 See ch 4 by de Guttry.

10 One of the exceptions that is worth remembering is represented by P K Ray, *Disaster Preparedness Against Accidents or Terrorist Attack (Chemical, Biological, Radiological)*, (New Age International Limited Publisher 2006).

11 For example, the well-known and relevant Convention on the Physical Protection of Nuclear Material (1980; renamed after the 2005 Amendment as the Convention on the Physical Protection of Nuclear Material and Nuclear Facilities) does not contain any reference to preparedness obligations. This is also the case of several other relevant international treaties, such as the Convention on the Suppression of Unlawful Acts Relating to International Civil Aviation (2010), the Montreal Convention for the Suppression of Unlawful Acts Against the Safety of Civil Aviation (1971), and the Montreal Protocol for the Suppression of Unlawful Acts of Violence at Airports Serving International Civil Aviation (1988).

12 N M Poulantzas, 'The Hague Convention for the Suppression of Unlawful Seizure of Aircraft (December 16, 1970)', NILR, (1971)18 (1), pp 25–75. See also J F Murphy, *Punishing International Terrorists: The Legal Framework for Policy Initiatives*, (Rowm and Allanheld 1985).

International Civil Aviation Organization in the 2017 Global Aviation Security Plan,[13] which enumerated five key priorities, almost all of which are in the realm of preparedness.[14]

Moreover, the International Convention Against the Taking of Hostages (1979) contains a relevant rule related to preparedness obligations. Although this Convention does not directly refer to terrorism in its title, the Preamble makes the connections between hostage-taking and terrorism very explicit.[15] Thus, the Convention is applicable whenever, for example, a terrorist group takes hostages and then threatens to use CBRN substances if forceful attempts are made to free them, or such a group uses hostages as a bargaining chip to access CBRN materials. Article 3 requires the State in whose territory the hostage is held to 'take all measures it considers appropriate to ease the situation of the hostage, in particular, to secure his release and, after his release, to facilitate, when relevant, his departure'. Although drafted in a very generic manner, this rule requires States to be prepared to manage a possible hostage-taking situation in an appropriate manner. Once again, this obligation mainly refers to the response phase, but it can clearly be interpreted as also implying that States must adopt proper preparedness measures in advance, in order to be ready to face a hostage-taking situation.

In the International Convention for the Suppression of the Financing of Terrorism (1999),[16] a few more preparedness obligations were codified in order to guarantee greater transparency and to improve the monitoring of financial transactions and flows. To this end, States Parties are expected to take all practicable measures for the identification of unusual or suspicious dealings suspected of stemming from a criminal activity.[17] Introducing specific rules in the domestic legal system can qualify as a preparedness measure, while the actual use of the same rules is part of the response phase.[18]

---

13 <https://www.icao.int/Security/Documents/GLOBAL%20AVIATION%20SECURITY%20PLAN%20EN.pdf>.

14 The five priorities are to a) enhance risk awareness and response, b) develop security culture and human capability, c) improve technological resources and foster innovation, d) improve oversight and quality assurance and e) increase cooperation and support.

15 It is reaffirmed that it is urgently necessary to develop international cooperation between States 'in devising and adopting effective measures for the prevention, prosecution and punishment of all acts of taking of hostages as manifestations of international terrorism'.

16 The Convention was adopted by UNGA Resolution 54/109 (9 December 1999), UN Doc A/Res (54/109).

17 Art 18, para 1, letter b.

18 See N Angelet, 'Vers un renforcement de la prévention et de la répression du terrorisme par des moyens financiers et économiques' in K Bannelier, T Christakis, O Corten and B Delcourt (eds), *Le droit international face au terrorisme*, (Pedone 2002), 219–238;

While the risk of terrorists (mis)using the financial system is high, there is also a menace that terrorist groups could use nuclear material. This concern was at the core of The Hague Nuclear Security Summit (2015). A communiqué adopted on 25 March 2015[19] reaffirmed 'the need to maintain effective emergency preparedness, response and mitigation capabilities in a manner that addresses both nuclear security and nuclear safety'.[20] Making further reference to this communiqué, on 14 December 2016, a group of States coordinated by South Korea[21] presented the Joint Statement on Supporting Nuclear and Radiological Terrorism Preparedness and Response Capabilities,[22] which contains a comprehensive list of what needs to be included in nuclear terrorism preparedness and response capabilities.[23]Additional relevant treaty obligations codified in conventions devoted to CBRN weapons are further examined in Part 3 of this book.

The UN has obviously played a relevant role in this context, focusing on several terrorism-related issues,[24] including prevention, punishment of terrorists and international cooperation. However, only in the more recent UNSC Resolution 2341 (2017), on threats to international peace and security caused by terrorist acts, was there wide agreement on the importance of preparedness measures that entail multiple streams of efforts, such as 'planning; public information and warning; operational coordination; [...] cybersecurity; physical protective measures; risk management for protection programmes and

I Bantekas, 'The International Law of Terrorist Financing', (2003) 97 AJIL, 315–333; R Lavalle, 'The International Convention for the Suppression of the Financing of Terrorism', (2000) 60 ZaöRV 491–510.

19 The main goal of the Nuclear Security Summit Initiative is 'to address the threat of nuclear terrorism by minimizing and securing weapons-usable civilian nuclear materials, enhancing international cooperation to prevent the illicit acquisition of nuclear material by non-state actors such as terrorist groups and smugglers, and taking steps to strengthen the global nuclear security system': <https://www.armscontrol.org/factsheets/NuclearSecuritySummit>.

20 <https://2009-2017.state.gov/documents/organization/237002.pdf>.

21 The Joint Statement has been endorsed by 24 States, including the USA.

22 A Joint Statement on Supporting Nuclear and Radiological Terrorism Preparedness and Response Capabilities, IAEA INFCIRC/90414, December 2016: <https://www.iaea.org/sites/default/files/publications/documents/infcircs/2016/infcirc904.pdf>.

23 The capabilities are grouped under the following headings: National Policies and Plans; Technical Expertise and Capabilities; Public Communications and Education; Sustainment of Capabilities; International Coordination and Assistance Mechanism.

24 As far as CBRN-related activities are concerned, the Security Council has specifically addressed the threat of WMD/CBRN terrorism in Resolutions 1373 (28 September 2001), UN Doc S/Res/1373 and 1540 (28 April 2004), UN Doc S/RES/1540, which focused on prevention and repression; surprisingly, no reference is found regarding preparedness obligations.

activities'. Member States are therefore urged to adopt the necessary preparedness measures, as well as to promote 'better interoperability in security and consequence management'.[25] In addition, the UN General Assembly has devoted several resolutions to this issue.[26] For example, the 2006 Resolution on the UN Global Counter-Terrorism Strategy[27] enumerates several preparedness measures which States are required to introduce at the national level. The status of implementation of these measures is at the core of the Annual Review of the UN Global Counter-Terrorism Strategy. Recently,[28] the GA directed attention to the preparedness measure related to potential terrorist attacks against critical infrastructure that could significantly disrupt the functioning of government and the private sector alike, as well as cause knock-on effects. In light of this risk, Member States have been invited to consider the 'growing importance of protecting critical infrastructure from terrorist attacks and of fostering comprehensive preparedness for such attacks, including through public-private partnership, as appropriate'.[29] In another Resolution, adopted in December 2020, the UNGA encouraged Member States 'to participate, on a voluntary basis, in the Incident and Trafficking Database programme of the International Atomic Energy Agency'.[30] This is a voluntary mechanism for the international exchange of information on incidents of illicit trafficking and other unauthorised activities and events involving nuclear and other radioactive material, aimed at supporting the Participating States to be better prepared to deal with radioactive and nuclear material that may have fallen out of regulatory control.

The UN Counter-Terrorism Implementation Task Force Working Group on the Protection of Critical Infrastructure including Vulnerable Targets, Internet and Tourism Security developed a Compendium of good practices for

25 Para 2 of the UNSC Resolution 2341(2017), UN doc/S/Res/2341. During the discussion of this resolution, the Acting President of the Security Council underlined that this resolution was a decisive step 'towards global preparedness for terrorist attacks': UN Doc S/PV.7882 (13 February 2017), 3.

26 For an example, see UNGA Resolution 46/51 (9 December 1991), UN Doc A/RES/46/51; and the 2005 World Summit Outcome, particularly its section on terrorism (UNGA Resolution 60/1 (24 October 2005: UN Doc A/RES/60/1).

27 The United Nations Global Counter-Terrorism Strategy, UNGA Resolution 60/288 (8 September 2006), UN Doc A/RES/60/288.

28 UNGA Resolution 72/288 (2 July 2018), UN Doc A/RES/72/284.

29 Member States are also encouraged to consider developing or further improving their strategies for 'reducing risks to critical infrastructure from terrorist attacks, which should include, inter alia, [...] taking preparedness measures, including effective responses to such attacks'. Ibid para 42.

30 UNGA Resolution 75/70 (20 December 2020), A/RES/775/70.

the protection of critical infrastructure against terrorist attacks (with noteworthy indicators, standards, risk assessment measures, recommendations and good practices).[31] Finally, in 2008, the International Atomic Energy Agency released a reference manual that details how to prevent, detect and respond to an incident of nuclear terrorism.[32]

Great attention has also been devoted to preparedness measures related to potential terrorist activities at the regional level. In the following paragraphs, attention will be focused on the relevant activities carried out in the different regional settings.

2.2 *At the Regional Level*

This section is devoted to the specific measures adopted within the European continent (with the exception of the activities carried out by the EU),[33] in Africa, in the Americas, and in Asia and the rest of the world. This overview will provide a comparative picture of the measures adopted and the valuable lessons learned in the different regional contexts.

2.2.1 In Europe

Notwithstanding the fact that, since 1990, the Council of Europe has carried out numerous activities in the areas of terrorism prevention and response,[34] it was not until 2005 that preparedness measures were introduced in the Convention on the Prevention of Terrorism.[35] The situation within the OSCE is very similar: a first, timid reference to preparedness measures was codified in the 2001 OSCE Council Decision No. 1, Combating Terrorism, to which the

31 <https://www.un.org/counterterrorism/sites/www.un.org.counterterrorism/files/eng_compendium-cip-final-version-120618.pdf>.

32 <https://www-pub.iaea.org/MTCD/publications/PDF/pub1309_web.pdf>.

33 The EU measures are analysed in ch 10 by Villani.

34 We refer, for example, to the Convention on Laundering, Search, Seizure and Confiscation of the Proceeds from Crime to Include the Financing of Terrorism (1990); the Convention on Laundering, Search, Seizure and Confiscation of the Proceeds from Crime (1999); and the Convention on Laundering, Search, Seizure and Confiscation of the Proceeds from Crime and on the Financing of Terrorism (2005). All these conventions are mostly focused on prevention and repression of terrorism.

35 Art 3, para 2 of this treaty requires States to take such measures 'as may be necessary to improve and develop the cooperation among national authorities with a view to preventing terrorist offences and their negative effects by, inter alia: […] c) enhancing training and coordination plans for civil emergencies'.

Plan of Action for Combating Terrorism was annexed.[36] Specific preparedness rules were introduced in the 2002 OSCE Charter on Preventing and Combating Terrorism[37] and in the 2007 OSCE Decision No. 6/07 Protecting Critical Energy Infrastructure from Terrorist Attacks.[38]

Unlike the Council of Europe and the OSCE, NATO has a much more solid record of paying attention to preparedness measures. As an example, at the 2016 Warsaw NATO Summit, Allied leaders issued a communiqué stressing their willingness to cooperate to 'prevent, mitigate, and respond effectively to terrorist attacks, including through our efforts to project stability'.[39] Making specific reference to CBRN events, the NATO leaders restated their firm commitment to ensure that the organisation:

> continues to be both strategically and operationally prepared with policies, plans, and capabilities to counter a wide range of state and non-state Chemical, Biological, Radiological, and Nuclear (CBRN) threats, based on NATO's Comprehensive Strategic-Level Policy for Preventing the Proliferation of WMD and Defending Against CBRN.[40]

The NATO communiqué also clarifies the specific goals of the preparedness measures. These include continuity of government and critical government services, energy supplies, resilient food and water resources, civil communications systems and civil transportation systems. The definition of specific goals to be achieved, standards to be respected and procedures to be enforced boosts the implementation of the necessary preparedness measures and favours more standardised and homogeneous approaches. As such, this structured approach to preparedness measures should serve as a reference point for

36 <https://www.osce.org/mc/22645?download=true>. Participating States are required to offer adequate training opportunities to the personnel of domestic financial institutions 'in counterterrorism areas inter alia on monitoring of financial flows and on prevention of money laundering'. Para 25.

37 According to para 28 of the Charter on Preventing and Combating Terrorism (2002), the OSCE Participating States 'Will make every effort to minimize those dangers through national efforts and through strengthening and enhancing the existing multilateral instruments in the fields of arms control, disarmament and non-proliferation'.

38 <https://www.osce.org/files/f/documents/4/5/29482.pdf>.

39 Warsaw Summit Communiqué Issued by the Heads of State and Government participating in the meeting of the North Atlantic Council in Warsaw (8–9 July 2016), para 8: <https://www.nato.int/cps/en/natohq/official_texts_133169.htm?selectedLocale=en>. See more in ch 10 by Villani.

40 Ibid para 74.

other relevant international and domestic actors. Additionally, NATO has contributed to the promotion of soft law by approving procedural guidelines for strategic, operational and tactical planners responsible for CBRN preparedness and response. Among these, the following two deserve special attention: the 2009 Non-Binding Guidelines for Enhanced Civil-Military Cooperation to Deal with the Consequences of Large-Scale CBRN Events Associated with Terrorist Attacks[41] and the Non-Binding Guidelines and Minimum Standards for CBRN First Responders.[42]

The Eastern part of the European continent has also been impressively proactive in adopting measures aimed at preparing Member States to request/receive international support and assistance in case of terrorist events (especially if they involve CBRN material). This vigour is clearly reflected in the numerous treaties signed within the Commonwealth of Independent States[43] that regulate how mutual assistance will be conducted in the event of a terrorist event.[44]

Finally, brief reference is made to the relevant activities carried out in Southern Europe, where the countries of the Euro-Mediterranean partnership – guided by the principles and objectives of the Barcelona Declaration[45] – have adopted the Euro-Mediterranean Code of Conduct on Countering Terrorism, declaring their commitment to 'be prepared to minimise the consequences of attacks', 'share experience on managing the consequences of terrorist attacks and build contacts as appropriate'.[46]

41 <https://www.securityresearch-cou.eu/sites/default/files/PO%282019%2900054%20-%20Non%20Binding%20Guidelines%20on%20Civil-Military%20Cooperation%20in%20CBRN%20Defence.pdf>.

42 <https://www.nato.int/nato_static_fl2014/assets/pdf/pdf_2016_08/20160802_140801-cep-first-responders-CBRN-, ng.pdf>.

43 See, for example, the Treaty on Cooperation Among the States Members of the Commonwealth of Independent States in Combating Terrorism (1999): <https://treaties.un.org/doc/db/Terrorism/csi-english.pdf>.

44 See also the protocol approving regulations on the procedure for organising and conducting joint counter-terrorism Activities in the Territories of States Members of the Commonwealth of Independent States (2002): <https://read.un-ilibrary.org/international-law-and-justice/international-instruments-related-to-the-prevention-and-suppression-of-international-terrorism_652e7898-en>.

45 Barcelona Declaration, adopted at the Euro-Mediterranean Conference (27–28/11/95): <http://www.eeas.europa.eu/archives/docs/euromed/docs/bd_en.pdf>.

46 The Code of Conduct on Countering Terrorism was agreed at the Euro-Mediterranean Conference (27 and 28 November 2005): <http://www.eeas.europa.eu/archives/docs/euromed/summit1105/terrorism_en.pdf>.

2.2.2 In the African Continent

In the African continent, the issue of preparedness has received special attention due to the involvement of relevant regional organisations in matters related to terrorism. For example, in the Organisation of African Unity (OAU) Convention on the Prevention and Combating of Terrorism (1999), the States Parties decided to 'co-operate among themselves, where possible, in providing any available technical assistance in drawing up programmes or organizing, where necessary and for the benefit of their personnel, joint training courses involving one or several States Parties in the area of control of terrorist acts, in order to improve their scientific, technical and operational capacities'.[47] In the Plan of Action of the African Union High-Level Inter-Governmental Meeting on the Prevention and Combating of Terrorism (2002),[48] a few additional preparedness obligations were introduced, including requirements for Member States to 'provide regular training to immigration officials with regard to the profiling of travellers and the verification of the authenticity of documents'[49] and to:

> establish or develop anti-terrorist units and provide them with access to specific equipment and the requisite training to enhance the efficiency of their counter-terrorism units, particularly in matters of intervention, protection and detection.

In the Protocol to the OAU Convention on the Prevention and Combating of Terrorism (2004), there is an innovative reference to the need for preparedness measures adopted by States to always be consistent with the States' human rights obligations.[50] This important link was also codified in the 2005 Resolution on the Protection of Human Rights and the Rule of Law in the Fight Against Terrorism, adopted by the African Commission on Human and Peoples' Rights.[51]

Within the African continent, many sub-regional agreements have introduced additional preparedness measures. The measures adopted by the Economic Community of West African States (ECOWAS) can rightfully be

47 Art 5, para 6 of the 1999 Treaty.

48 <http://www.peaceau.org/uploads/au-anti-terrorism-plan-of-action.pdf>.

49 Ibid para 11, letter i.

50 The Parties committed themselves to 'take all necessary measures to protect the fundamental human rights of their populations against all acts of terrorism'.

51 ACHPR/Res.88 (XXXVIII) 05: <https://www.achpr.org/sessions/resolutions?id=222>. States are required to 'Fully comply with their obligations under the African Charter on Human and Peoples' Rights and other international human rights treaties'.

considered some of the most innovative worldwide. After codifying several sub-regional treaties dealing with terrorism,[52] in 2013, ECOWAS adopted the innovative Political Declaration and Common Position Against Terrorism,[53] to which the ECOWAS Counter-Terrorism Strategy is annexed. This is a detailed document built upon three pillars: prevent, pursue and reconstruct.[54] Specific preparedness measures are spelled out in Pillar 2.[55] To ensure speedy implementation, ECOWAS adopted a counter-terrorism implementation plan, which lists specific actions to be undertaken by Member States.[56]

2.2.3 In the Americas

Compared to other regions, the progress of the North and South American continents concerning preparedness measures clearly lags behind. Although the Organization of American States (OAS) has traditionally played an important role in the fight against terrorism,[57] the OAS Member States only expressed their clear commitment to strengthening 'the capacity of our states to promote citizen security and to respond effectively to insecurity, crime, and violence, by adapting their legal framework, structures, operational procedures, and management mechanisms, as necessary' in 2008 in the document entitled 'Commitment to Public Security in the Americas'.[58]

---

52 The following are the key sub-regional treaties adopted within ECOWAS and dealing with terrorism: ECOWAS Convention on Small Arms and Light Weapons, Their Ammunition and Other Related Materials (2006); Protocol Relating to the Establishment of an ECOWAS Bureau of Intelligence and Investigation on Criminal Matters (2006); ECOWAS Convention on Extradition; and 1992 ECOWAS Convention on Mutual Judicial Assistance in Criminal Matters (1994).

53 <https://www.ecowas.int/wp-content/uploads/2019/05/POLITICAL-DECLARATION-ENG.pdf>.

54 Ibid, para 20.

55 In Pillar 2 of the ECOWAS Strategy, there is a list of preparedness measures that States are required to implement.

56 <https://www.ecowas.int/wp-content/uploads/2019/05/IMPLEMENTATION-PLAN-CT.pdf>.

57 In 1999, the OAS General Assembly decided to establish the Inter-American Committee against Terrorism (Resolution AG/RES.1650 (XXIX-O/99)). See more on CICTE at <http://www.oas.org/en/sms/cicte/default.asp>.

58 The document was adopted at the First Meeting of the Ministers Responsible for Public Security in the Americas (7 and 8 October 2008): <https://www.oas.org/en/media_center/press_release.asp?sCodigo=S-040/15>. See also M B Lloyd, *Transnational Crimes in the Americas: Law, Policy and Institutions*, (Anthem Press 2018).

2.2.4 In Asia and the Rest of the World

In Asia, a leading role in the fight against terrorism has been played by the Association of Southeast Asian Nations (ASEAN), which adopted a specific Convention on Counter Terrorism in 2007.[59] Article VI of this Convention requires States to strengthen their 'capability and readiness to deal with chemical, biological, radiological, nuclear (CBRN) terrorism, cyber terrorism and any new forms of terrorism'.[60] Preparedness measures received additional and more detailed attention in the ASEAN Plan of Action in Combating Transnational Crime (2016–2025).[61]

While the Organisation of Islamic Cooperation (OIC) has thus far shown limited interest in preparedness measures related to terrorism,[62] the Shanghai Cooperation Organisation (SCO) has a proven record of interest in the area. Four relevant treaties have been adopted by the SCO to regulate specific aspects of terrorist activities which might involve CBRN material.[63] The first reference to preparedness measures can be found in the Agreement on Regional Anti-Terrorist Structure Between the Member States (2002) in which a regional anti-terrorist structure is created to assist Member States

---

59 See more on the ACCT: M Borelli, 'ASEAN Counter-terrorism Weaknesses', (2017) 9(9) Counter Terrorist Trends and Analyses, pp 14–20, S Tan and H Nasu, 'Asean and The Development of Counter-Terrorism Law and Policy in Southeast Asia', (2016) 39(3) University of New South Wales Law Journal, pp 1291–1238.

60 A thought-provoking and comprehensive overview of the measures adopted within ASEAN to prevent terrorist attacks and to increase preparedness levels is to be found in R Yasir and R Tiara, 'The Implementation of the ASEAN Convention on Counter Terrorism in Preventing Terrorism for ASEAN Countries': <https://www.researchgate.net/publication/338479485_The_Implementation_of_the_ASEAN_Convention_on_Counter_Terrorism_in_Preventing_Terrorism_for_ASEAN_Countries/citation/download>.

61 <https://asean.org/wp-content/uploads/2012/05/ASEAN-Plan-of-Action-in-Combating-TC_Adopted-by-11th-AMMTC-on-20Sept17.pdf>.

62 Art 4 of the OIC Convention on Combating International Terrorism (1999) states that 'Contracting States shall cooperate within the scope of their capabilities to provide available technical assistance for preparing programmes or holding joint training sessions with one or more Contracting States if the need arises for personnel required in the field of combating terrorism in order to improve their scientific and practical potential and upgrade their performance standards'. In the Arab Convention for the Suppression of Terrorism (1998), adopted within the Arab League, there is a similar reference to preparedness measures: <https://www.refworld.org/pdfid/3de5e4984.pdf>.

63 The Shanghai Convention on Combating Terrorism, Separatism and Extremism (2001), the Agreement on Regional Anti-Terrorist Structure Between the Member States of the Shanghai Cooperation Organisation (2002), the Convention Against terrorism (2009) and the Agreement on Cooperation in Combating Crime Between the Governments of the Member States of the Shanghai Cooperation Organisation (2010).

'in preparing and conducting anti-terrorist command and staff and battle exercises at the request of concerned parties'. In this specific case, the preparedness obligations are incumbent on the newly created structure and not on the Member States.

Other regional treaties in the same area do not contain any specific reference to preparedness measures, being mostly focused on prevention, punishment and extradition issues, as well as the financing of terrorist groups.[64]

3 Summing up: The Content of the Key Preparedness Measures Related to CBRN Terrorist Events that Are Regulated in International Instruments

The investigation carried out in the previous paragraphs allows us to now sum up the main preparedness measures related to CBRN terrorist events, which States are required to implement. To be better prepared to deal with future CBRN terrorist events, States are expected to adopt relevant measures which will allow them:

- to guarantee continuity of government and critical government services, energy supplies, resilient food and water resources and civil communications systems;
- to quickly request and receive international assistance;
- to deal with specific activities, such as those involving the seizure of an aircraft or the detention of hostages with the threat of using CBRN substances;
- to investigate and respond to any terrorist attack involving CBRN substances, especially those against critical infrastructure, means of public transportation and critical energy infrastructure;
- to immediately detect attempts to illegally import/export CBRN substances, as well as individual precursor elements that can be used to make CBRN substances;
- to protect sensitive sites (civil and military) which contain or use CBRN substances (nuclear plants, chemical production factories, etc.);
- to increase the resilience capacity of populations and institutions at all levels;
- to regularly organise training activities and exercises to prevent misuse of the financial system for financing terrorism and to prevent the use of fake travel documents;

64 See, for example, the Additional Protocol to the South Asian Association for Regional Co-operation Regional Convention on Suppression of Terrorism (2004).

- to have a well-prepared communication strategy which allows a wider audience affected by the terrorist event to be to correctly informed, and to prevent, as much as possible, the spread of fake news;
- to use, if appropriate, military assets to face terrorist activities involving CBRN substances.

While universal instruments and institutions have traditionally been the primary promoters of these measures, regional organisations have been less active. Considering that the relevant universal rules are comprehensive and rather detailed, regional organisations have, in most cases, limited themselves to reiterating rules already codified, without any significant added value. Only NATO and ECOWAS have opted for a far more dynamic role in defining preparedness rules in order to enable a better mitigation of the terrorist risk by their Member States. The uniquely dynamic attitude of these two organisations is partly explained by their military/strongly security-oriented nature.

4 Concluding Remarks and Preliminary Assessment of the Impact of the International Obligations and of the Soft Law Instruments Related to Preparedness Activities

This chapter has demonstrated the increasing attention States and IOs are paying to preparedness measures specifically aimed at potential CBRN terrorist events. This attention is largely due to the concern that terrorist groups might use CBRN materials in their activities in the near future. States are therefore required to implement not only the generic preparedness rules applicable to any CBRN event, as described in Chapter 4, but also the specific measures related to CBRN terrorist events investigated in this chapter.

The increasing number of preparedness rules codified in treaties and in soft law instruments is undoubtedly an important achievement. States now face the challenge of fully and quickly implementing these measures at the domestic level. Recent studies[65] and reports on the degree of domestication of these measures have reached the conclusion that these preparedness measures are far from being fully implemented. The justifications States use for their delays are usually based on the costs of the preparedness activities and the difficulty of justifying the necessary investment, especially in countries facing other challenges or in which significant terrorist activities have not (yet) occurred.

65 For example, see the European Parliament, Directorate General for Internal Policies, Policy Department for Citizens' Rights and Constitutional Affairs, 'Terrorism: Member States' Preparedness for CBRN Threats Study': <https://www.statewatch.org/news/2018/may/ep-study-cbrn-threats-ms-preparedness-5-18.pdf>.

However, the decision of a few States to create national ad hoc institutions[66] or to adopt national CBRN strategies and plans to deal with potential terrorist activities[67] deserves recognition. Additionally, it is envisaged that future treaties on CBRN terrorism will give greater attention to developing more systematic, credible and effective independent monitoring mechanisms which, together with increased technical and financial backing, could represent a stimulus and a valuable support to States in the timely implementation of their international preparedness obligations. The current delays in the national implementation of the terrorism-specific preparedness measures strongly justify this new approach.

The failure to fully implement preparedness activities at the national level (the level at which most of the measures must inevitably be implemented), makes international cooperation even more important as a tool to stimulate States to fully implement their international obligations. Thus, all efforts carried out in this regard and the numerous treaties regulating the details of such cooperation are encouraging and need to be praised, strongly supported and broadened.

Finally, in the case of CBRN terrorist activities, the use of military assets can represent a fundamental tool for both the prevention and the response phase.[68] To facilitate the use of these assets in a non-war context, several administrative and organisational measures need to be orchestrated: as mentioned in Chapter 4, these measures can be qualified as preparedness activities. Their adoption is a new and valuable tool to prepare States to handle potential CBRN terrorist events.

Bibliography

Angelet N, 'Vers un renforcement de la prévention et de la répression du terrorisme par des moyens financiers et économiques' in K Bannelier, T Christakis, O Corten and B Delcourt (eds), *Le droit international face au terrorisme* (Pedone 2002).

Bantekas I, 'The International Law of Terrorist Financing' (2003) 97 AJIL 315.

66 For example, see the Centre for Emergency Preparedness and Response in the United Kingdom's Health Protection Agency: <http://www.istc.int/en/institute/13473>.

67 For example, see the 2011 Chemical, Biological, Radiological, Nuclear and Explosives Resilience Strategy for Canada (<https://www.publicsafety.gc.ca/cnt/rsrcs/pblctns/rslnc-strtg/index-en.aspx>) and the subsequent Chemical, Biological, Radiological, Nuclear and Explosives Resilience Action Plan for Canada, which is an integral part of the strategy (<https://www.publicsafety.gc.ca/cnt/rsrcs/pblctns/rslnc-ctn-pln/index-en.aspx>).

68 This specific aspect emerges also in the EP Study, EU Preparedness Against CBRN Weapons, cit. in n 3.

Borelli M, 'ASEAN Counter-terrorism Weaknesses' (2017) 9(9) Counter Terrorist Trends and Analyses 14.

CIA, 'Terrorist CBRN: Material and Effects' <https://www.cia.gov/library/reports/general-reports-1/CBRN_threat_wo.pdf>.

Dinu E, 'Assessing CBRN terrorism threats' in S Fei, I Anthony (eds), *Reassessing CBRN Threats in a Changing Global Environment* (SIPRI 2019).

European Parliament, Directorate General for Internal Policies, Policy Department For Citizens' Rights and Constitutional Affairs, 'Terrorism: Member States' Preparedness for CBRN Threats Study' <https://www.statewatch.org/news/2018/may/ep-study-cbrn-threats-ms-preparedness-5-18.pdf>.

Europol, 'Terrorism Situation and Trend report (TE-SAT) 2017' <www.europol.europa.eu/sites/default/files/documents/tesat2017.pdf>.

Ivanova K and Sandler T, 'CBRN Attack Perpetrators: An Empirical Study' (2007) 3(4) Foreign Policy Analysis 273.

Lambert J, *Terrorism and Hostages in International Law: A Commentary on the Hostages Convention 1979* (Grotius 1990).

Lavalle R, 'The International Convention for the Suppression of the Financing of Terrorism' (2000) 60 ZaöRV 491.

Lloyd M B, *Transnational Crimes in the Americas: Law, Policy and Institutions* (Anthem Press 2018).

Murphy J F, *Punishing International Terrorists: The Legal Framework for Policy Initiatives* (Rowm and Allanheld 1985).

Poulantzas N M, 'The Hague Convention for the Suppression of Unlawful Seizure of Aircraft (December 16, 1970)' (1971) 18(1) NILR 25.

Ray P K, *Disaster Preparedness Against Accidents or Terrorist Attack (Chemical, Biological, Radiological)* (New Age International Limited Publisher 2006).

Saul B, 'International Convention Against The Taking Of Hostages', United Nations Audiovisual Library of International Law <https://legal.un.org/avl/pdf/ha/icath/icath_e.pdf>.

Tan S and Nasu H, 'Asean and the Development of Counter-Terrorism Law and Policy in Southeast Asia' (2016) 39(3) University of New South Wales Law Journal 1291.

Yasir R and Tiara R, 'The Implementation of the ASEAN Convention on Counter Terrorism in Preventing Terrorism for ASEAN Countries' <https://www.researchgate.net/publication/338479485_The_Implementation_of_the_ASEAN_Convention_on_Counter_Terrorism_in_Preventing_Terrorism_for_ASEAN_Countries/citation/download>.

CHAPTER 9

Response and Recovery in the Event of CBRN Terrorism

Giulia Perrone

1 Introduction

The present chapter examines the strengths and limitations of the international legal framework applicable to the response and recovery phases that follow CBRN terrorist activities and that are not regulated by humanitarian law or other branches of international law, including human rights law.[1]

To this end, Section 2 and Section 3 respectively review universal obligations concerning response and recovery that stem from international treaties and United Nations (UN) resolutions, also considering the most relevant non-binding guidelines for inter-agency cooperation and the activity of national first responders. Section 4 discusses the gaps and shortcomings in monitoring, sanctioning and implementation. Section 5 concerns bilateral and multilateral agreements, while Section 6 analyses the regional framework concerning CBRN terrorism response and recovery, namely the North Atlantic Treaty Organization (NATO), African, American, Asian and European (with the exclusion of European Union[2]) contexts. Section 7 concludes the chapter.

The main finding is that, although the proliferation of international legal instruments against CBRN terrorism reveals a significant commitment to counter the phenomenon, the plurality of legal tools and the lack of effective monitoring and sanctioning mechanisms hinder the effectiveness of such a framework.

2 Response to CBRN Terrorism: The International Legal Framework

A review of the international legal instruments concerning CBRN terrorism reveals that the response phase primarily requires States to investigate the

1 International obligations of more general scope to respond to and recover from CBRN emergency situations are discussed in ch 5 by Bakker.

2 On the EU, see ch 10 by Villani.

facts and ensure that perpetrators are brought to justice.[3] Complementary measures are also required, including the provision of mutual assistance, both legal and operational, and the exchange of information beyond national borders. The present section reads international treaties together with soft law instruments with the aim of discussing the strengths and weaknesses of the international legal framework regulating States' response to CBRN terrorism.

Resolution 1540 is the starting point of the present inquiry. It was adopted in 2001 by the UN Security Council (SC) under Chapter VII of the UN Charter. As with UNSC Resolution 1373 (2001), Resolution 1540 represents an example of the UN Security Council acting in a quasi-legislative capacity and imposing on all States the obligation to undertake internal legal reforms to include counter-terrorism measures. Beyond recognising the proliferation of nuclear, chemical and biological weapons as a threat to international peace and security, Resolution 1540 connects this threat with the risk that non-State actors may acquire, develop, traffic or use weapons of mass destruction (WMD). Whilst the existing multilateral regime on non-proliferation and disarmament was originally aimed at dealing only with States,[4] Resolution 1540 requires all UN Member States, independently from their participation in international treaties, to establish and enforce (upon completion of a fair trial) appropriate criminal and civil penalties applicable to non-State actors for acts connected with the preparation and perpetration of CBRN terrorist attacks. To adopt such measures, it is mandatory for all States to criminalise terrorism-related offences under their national law and to investigate the relevant facts when terrorist events occur.

Although technological innovations, such as the use of satellites for gathering intelligence, have progressively enhanced the possibility of cross-border surveillance and investigation, their effectiveness is not *per se* sufficient to adequately respond to CBRN terrorism, especially when this requires international cooperation. Both the investigation of facts and the prosecution of perpetrators can be seriously hindered by significant differences in the national contexts, including with regard to the level of available resources, national legislation, the use of special investigation techniques and the admissibility problems of certain types of evidence before national courts. In this regard, Resolution 1540 requires States to offer adequate assistance, both legal and operational, to other States which lack legal and regulatory infrastructure, implementation

3 Jurisdiction and the principle of *aut dedere aut judicare* are discussed in ch 33 by Amoroso.

4 Treaty on the Non-Proliferation of Nuclear Weapons (NPT, 1968); Biological and Toxin Weapons Convention (BWC, 1972); Chemical Weapons Convention (CWC, 1993).

experience and/or resources for the investigation and prosecution, among others, of CBRN terrorist events.

Relevant provisions can also be found in the UN international treaties specifically dealing with CBRN terrorism, according to which States are required to criminalise certain offences, investigate the facts and ensure that the offenders are brought to justice.[5] Complementary to the obligations to investigate and prosecute, is the mandate to exchange accurate and verified information. Indeed, States are required to inform 'without delay' other States and 'where appropriate' international organisations about the commission of one or more of the offences made punishable by the Convention.[6] Moreover, States shall afford mutual assistance, both legal and operational, including in criminal or extradition proceedings.[7]

In addition to binding instruments, the response phase is also addressed in a set of soft law instruments and initiatives, including the Proliferation Security Initiative, the Global Initiative to Combat Nuclear Terrorism, the Nuclear Security Summits and the G8 Global Partnership Against the Spread of WMD. On 17 December 2020, INTERPOL and the United Nations Counter-Terrorism Centre (UNCCT) of the United Nations Office of Counter-Terrorism (UNOCT) launched a joint initiative aimed at enhancing national responses to crimes committed by non-State actors and involving CBRNE (explosive) materials. More broadly, in 2006, the UN General Assembly adopted by consensus the Global Counter-Terrorism Strategy, the main policy framework for international action against terrorism within the UN system. The Strategy condemns terrorism in all its forms – including with the use of CBRN weapons – and it provides States with guidance on the most effective measures to combat the phenomenon. Although general in its scope, the document also specifically covers the response phase of CBRN attacks by calling on States to cooperate with one another in order to 'find, deny safe haven and bring to justice, on the basis of the principle of extradite or prosecute, any person who supports, facilitates, participates or attempts to participate in the financing, planning,

5 Convention on the physical protection of nuclear material (CPPNM, 1968) art 3; International convention for the suppression of acts of nuclear terrorism (ICSANT, as amended in 2005) art 5; International convention for the suppression of terrorist bombings (Terrorist bombings convention, 1997) art 4; Protocol to the Convention for the Suppression of Unlawful Acts against the Safety of Maritime Navigation (2005) art 5; Protocol to the Protocol to the Convention for the suppression of unlawful acts against the safety of fixed platforms located on the continental shelf (SUA protocol, 2005) arts 2 bis and 2 ter; Convention for the suppression of unlawful acts relating to international civil aviation (Beijing convention, 2010) art 3.

6 ICSANT art 7(1)(b).

7 CCPNM art 13; ICSANT art 14; Terrorist Bombing Convention art 10; SUA Convention art 8 bis and art 12; Beijing Convention art 17.

preparation or perpetration of terrorist acts or provides safe havens'.[8] To this end, the Strategy stresses the need to maximise the exchange of relevant information and to afford mutual assistance for timely investigation and prosecution in the aftermath of CBRN terrorist acts.

3 Recovery from CBRN Terrorism: The International Legal Framework

Strongly connected with States' response to CBRN terrorism and of utmost importance for its consequences, is the recovery phase. The international legal framework dealing with recovery, however, is fragmented, incomplete and inconsistent.

In the aftermath of a terrorism-related offence, a few UN treaties require States to locate, render harmless and recover any CBRN materials unlawfully taken and/or used, including through international cooperation.[9] Arguably, however, the attention paid to the recovery phase is not adequate to the complexity of terrorist events. This can be confirmed on the basis of two considerations: first, both the UN conventions and Resolution 1540 are silent on the treatment of the victims of terrorism; second, the prosecution of perpetrators is incomplete if considered independently from the rehabilitation and reintegration of the wrongdoers. The present section briefly addresses both these issues.

In its Resolution 73/305 (2019), the UN General Assembly calls on States to strengthen international cooperation to respect the dignity and legal rights of victims of terrorism, including the right to be considered for witness protection measures. The Resolution emphasises that all victims should have their status, rights and protection recognised, regardless of the identification, apprehension, prosecution or conviction of the perpetrators; also, they should be properly involved in the development of criminal justice strategies against terrorism, including those concerning the prosecution, rehabilitation and reintegration of the offenders.[10] While all the victims, experts and witnesses must receive proper assistance, special protection is to be granted to those who give testimony in criminal proceedings, their relatives and other persons

8 UNGA Res 60/288 (20 September 2006) 5.

9 Amendment to the CPPNM (2005) art 2A(1)(b) and art 5(1)(b); ICSANT (2005) art 2 and art 5; Beijing Convention (2010) art 16(2).

10 UNGA Res 305 (2 July 2019) UN Doc A/RES/73/305, para 4 and 6.

close to them. This is what emerges from, among others, the UN Convention against Transnational Organized Crime (art 25) and the UN Convention against Corruption (art 32) which require States Parties to protect the identity, physical integrity and safety of such persons with adequate measures, including by entering into agreements or arrangements with other States for their relocation.

However, the absence of an agreed definition of 'victims of terrorism' in international law gives rise to a variety of different understandings and legal consequences at the national level.[11] While it is of primary importance that individuals who are entitled to hold the status and receive support as victims are clearly identifiable for the purpose of domestic legislation, the wide variety of laws, policies and procedures is not consistent with the transnational nature of terrorism. Indeed, the harmonisation of national systems has become of paramount importance for the transnational protection of the victims, which also includes facilitating the victims' participation in trial proceedings, access to information, rehabilitation and compensation.[12]

Turning to the second consideration – that is, the insufficient attention paid to the rehabilitation and reintegration of perpetrators in the recovery process – the UNSC Resolutions 2178 (2014) and 2396 (2017) are particularly relevant. They address, *inter alia*, the cross-border movements of Foreign Terrorist Fighters (FTFs) and call for comprehensive and tailored prosecution, rehabilitation and reintegration strategies for those involved in terrorist activities. The issue was specifically addressed by the participants in the 2020 UN Virtual Counter-Terrorism Week, who emphasised that rehabilitation and reintegration are long-term processes that should begin during detention and continue afterwards. They require a multisectoral approach, including skills development, psychosocial care and economic reintegration.

11 The UNGA 'Declaration of Basic Principles of Justice for Victims of Crime and Abuse of Power' (1985) provides the soft law basis for the international standards concerning the treatment of victims and it is designed to assist governments and the international community in their efforts to secure justice and assistance for victims of crime. Although it does not specifically refer to CBRN terrorism, it could nevertheless be considered a valid guiding instrument for national legislation dealing with CBRN terrorist events.

12 The 'Madrid Memorandum on Good Practices for Assistance to Victims of Terrorism Immediately after the Attack and in Criminal Proceedings' (2012) provides good practices that can help identify international standards in the establishment of victim-support mechanisms. For a human rights perspective, see 'Report of the Special Rapporteur on the promotion and protection of human rights and fundamental freedoms while countering terrorism' (4 June 2012) UN Doc A/HRC/20/14; see also ch 27 by Venier, ch 34 by Capone, ch 5 by Bakker.

4 Monitoring, Sanctioning and Implementation Gaps

Despite the proliferation of international legal instruments dealing with CBRN terrorism, national implementation is far from ideal. Both the UN treaty system and Resolution 1540 contain significant gaps in their monitoring and sanctioning mechanisms, leading to implementation shortfalls at the national level.

On the one hand, UN agencies widely promote the ratification of international conventions dealing with CBRN terrorism;[13] on the other hand, however, the UN framework does not offer any effective tool for measuring States' progress in the implementation of international obligations, nor does it provide for any sanctions in the event of non-compliance. As a result, in the absence of any indicators, benchmarks or penalties, States are given broad discretion in the fulfilment of their duties, with the advancement of their counter-terrorism measures left uncertain and their violations of international obligations never dealt with.

The effectiveness of the '1540 system' is also controversial. Since the very adoption of Resolution 1540, governments have lamented a 'legitimacy deficit' due to the imposition of general and legally binding obligations on 193 Member States without their explicit consent. Indeed, with the 15 Members of the UNSC relying on Chapter VII of the UN Charter, Resolution 1540 has been perceived as a departure from the consensual nature of international law, especially because it shares multiple features with any general disarmament treaty but lacked the negotiation processes prior to its final adoption. The necessity to overcome criticisms and facilitate implementation has led the '1540 Committee' – a body created as a Special Political Mission under the Sanctions and Monitoring cluster – to adopt a voluntary and cooperative approach, thus refraining from any investigative and sanctioning measures.[14]

13 For example, based on the 2018 UNODC Report 'Supporting legal responses and criminal justice capacity to prevent and counter terrorism', between 2003 and 2018, UNODC has provided legislative services that have led to the review and drafting of 172 pieces of national counter-terrorism legislation; also, according to the Report of the Secretary General on the 'Activities of the United Nations system in implementing the United Nations Global Counter-Terrorism Strategy' (20 April 2018) UN Doc A/72/840: 'Since January 2016, it has contributed to 40 additional ratifications by Member States of the international conventions and protocols related to terrorism, assisted in revising or drafting more than 35 pieces of legislation and trained more than 8,000 criminal justice officials through more than 400 workshops'.

14 Broadly on the '1540 Committee': S Shirazyan, 'Building A Universal Counter-Proliferation Regime: The Institutional Limits of United Nations Security Council Resolution 1540' 18, Journal of National Security Law and Policy (2019) 150, 162.

While the political strategy has favoured a general acceptance of Resolution 1540, it has not contributed to the achievement of its effective implementation.

The monitoring mechanism identified to overcome the initial inconsistencies in States' reporting – the 1540 matrix – has proved to be effective solely for the quantitative analysis of national measures. Indeed, it allows for the translation of primary data into standard templates with no further investigation on the information provided.

Based on the information recorded in the 1540 matrices, the latest report of the 1540 Committee (2016) shows an overall increase of approximately 7% in the quantity of measures adopted pursuant to Resolution 1540, compared to 2011.[15] What the report does not clarify is the type and effectiveness of the measures adopted. The absence of any substantive assessment gives the monitoring process a mere formal dimension, leaving space for obsolete or false information in States' reports. Syria is a case in point, with its reports repeatedly declaring the non-possession of chemical weapons,[16] later contradicted by the confirmation of their use by the IS and the Syrian government.[17]

Problems also arise with regard to the match-making role of the Committee between assistance seekers and providers. According to the available data, only nine States that are registered as assistance providers (out of 47) have responded to legal or technical assistance requests; also, specific needs are rarely met, including those concerning the adoption of legislative measures to respond to and recover from terrorist acts.[18]

Although not exhaustive,[19] the present section suggests that the existing gaps in monitoring and enforcing the implementation of international

15 UNSC, 'Letter dated 9 December 2016 from the Chair of the Security Council Committee established pursuant to resolution 1540 (2004) addressed to the President of the Security Council' (9 December 2016) UN Doc S/2016/1038, para 28.

16 UNSC 1540 Committee, 'Note verbale dated 14 October 2004 from the Permanent Mission of the Syrian Arab Republic to the United Nations addressed to the Chairman of the Committee' (24 November 2004) UN Doc S/AC.44/2004/(02)/70; 'Note verbale dated 7 November 2005 from the Permanent Mission of the Syrian Arab Republic to the United Nations addressed to the Chairman of the Committee' (10 November 2005) UN Doc S/AC.44/2004/(02)/70/Add.3.

17 OPCW, 'Report of the OPCW Fact-Finding Mission in Syria Regarding an Alleged Incident in Khan Shaykhun, Syrian Arab Republic April 2017' (29 June 2017) UN Doc S/1510/2017.

18 UNSC 1540 Committee, '2016 Comprehensive Review Background Paper for the Formal Open Consultations by the 1540 Committee' (2016) 8, <http://www.un.org/en/sc/1540/documents/CR-June-Consultation-Background-Paper.pdf> (all links were last accessed on 30 November 2021).

19 The implementation of the NPT, BWC and CWC is also problematic. See J Tucker, 'Bridging the Gaps: Achieving the Potential of the Nonproliferation Treaties to Combat Nuclear, Biological, and Chemical Terrorism' 83(2/3) Die Friedens-Warte (2008) 81, 103.

obligations adversely affect the impact of the international legal framework dealing with the consequences of CBRN terrorism.

5 Response and Recovery in Bilateral and Multilateral Agreements

Obligations to respond to and recover from CBRN terrorism stem also from a multitude of bilateral and multilateral agreements stipulated between two or more States (either within the same region or not) or between States and international organisations. Some of these agreements regulate criminal justice cooperation, some provide a basis for the relocation of witnesses or other persons under protection and several others govern the sharing of terrorism-related information for the effective investigation of facts beyond national borders.[20] Other response and recovery obligations are also expressly mentioned, including emergency response and training programmes.[21]

6 Response and Recovery: The Regional Legal Framework and Its Implementation

The present section provides an overview of the main regional instruments relevant to CBRN terrorism response and recovery. To this end, the analysis focuses on NATO, the African region, the Americas, the Asian region and the European region (with the exclusion of the European Union[22]).

6.1 *NATO*

Two soft-law instruments are particularly important for the response and recovery phases, namely the 2014 'Guidelines for First Responders to a CBRN Incident' and the 2019 'Non-binding Guidelines for Enhanced Civil-Military Cooperation to Deal with the Consequences of Large-Scale CBRN Events

20 For example, on 31 August 2020, a Memorandum of Agreement (MoA) was signed by ICAO and the UN Office of Counter-Terrorism (UNOCT) aimed at facilitating criminal investigations into terrorist offenses through the collection and analysis of Advance Passenger Information and Passenger Name Record data. See also: Accordo tra il Governo della Repubblica italiana e il Governo della Repubblica d'Austria in materia di cooperazione di polizia (L. 209/2016); Agreement on the cooperation in the area of witness protection (Republic of Austria, Republic of Bulgaria, Republic of Croatia, Czech Republic, Hungary, Romania, Slovak Republic, Republic of Slovenia, 11 October 2012).

21 For example: Memorandum of understanding between the Italian public security department and the Sudanese national police (3 October 2016).

22 On the EU, see ch 10 by Villani.

Associated with Terrorist Attacks' (2019). While the former clarifies the actions required by all first responders in the immediate aftermath of CBRN incidents, the latter provides detailed guidance on how to coordinate civil-military operations in the event of CBRN terrorism. Indeed, military capabilities include specialised competences and training concerning the medical treatment of CBRN casualties, detection of nonconventional weapons and decontamination. When civil authorities are overwhelmed, military resources can significantly contribute to a successful response.

However, command and control operations during a CBRN incident require the highest coordination between civil and military authorities, that is, the mutual understanding of roles and resources, including via a comprehensive legal review and joint training courses. While such measures seem to belong to the preparedness phase, they allow for the use of military assets when civil responders lack capacity.

6.2 *The African Region*

At the regional level, three instruments adopted by regional organisations require States Parties to criminalise terrorism-related offences, investigate the relevant facts, prosecute perpetrators and provide victims with adequate assistance. They are the Arab League Convention on the Suppression of Terrorism (1998); the Organisation of the Islamic Conference (OIC) Convention on Combating International Terrorism (1999) (today an instrument of the Organisation of Islamic Cooperation); and the Organisation of African Unity (OAU) Convention on the Prevention and Combating of Terrorism (1999) (today an instrument of the African Union, AU). While the first two treaties are silent about any implementation monitoring mechanisms, the OAU Convention has been integrated with an additional protocol, adopted in 2004, which requires States Parties to regularly report to the AU's Peace and Security Council (PSC) on the measures taken to combat terrorism.[23] Moreover, the AU has developed an 'African Model Anti-Terrorism Law' as a soft law instrument aimed at providing a blueprint for domestic legislation, including with regard to terrorist offences involving CBRN materials.[24]

At sub-regional level, further legal instruments relevant to the response and recovery phases have been adopted by the Southern African Development Community (SADC) and the Economic Community of West African States (ECOWAS). Both the SADC 'Declaration on Terrorism' (2002) and the ECOWAS

23 As of 30 November 2021, the Protocol has been ratified by 21 of the 55 AU Member States, <www.au.int>.

24 African Union, 'African Model Anti-Terrorism Law' (2011) para XXXIX.

'Political Declaration and Common Position against Terrorism' (2013) task States Parties with condemning terrorism-related offences and ensuring that offenders are brought to justice. To this end, they emphasise the need for inter-State cooperation on the sharing of relevant information and the harmonisation of prosecution mechanisms. Unlike the SADC, ECOWAS expressly calls on Member States to criminalise terrorist offences, including with the provision of severe penalties for perpetrators of such acts, and adopts a Counter-Terrorism Strategy and Implementation Plan based on three Pillars: Prevent, Pursue and Repair. The latter two Pillars are particularly relevant to States' response and recovery because they respectively concern the need to strengthen national legislation so as to incorporate all criminal justice aspects of counter-terrorism, and the reconstruction of the society through the recovery and rehabilitation of the victims of terrorism and their families.

6.3 *The Asian Region*

There are four regional and sub-regional instruments that are relevant to CBRN terrorism response and recovery: the Shanghai Convention on Combating Terrorism, Separatism and Extremism (2001) by the Shanghai Cooperation Organisation (SCO); the Mutual Legal Assistance Treaty (MLAT, 2004) by the Association of Southeast Asian Nations (ASEAN); the ASEAN Convention on Counter Terrorism (ACCT, 2007); and the Convention on Suppression of Terrorism (1987) by the South Asian Association for Regional Cooperation (SAARC) with its Additional Protocol (2004).

All of these instruments require States Parties to suppress identified offences connected with terrorism – including those involving CBRN materials – prosecute perpetrators, afford mutual assistance and cooperate in the sharing of information. In addition to the obligations concerning States' response to CBRN terrorism, the ACCT is the only one that focuses on some recovery measures to be adopted by the Parties, namely the sharing of best practices on rehabilitative programmes, including, where appropriate, the social reintegration of the wrongdoers. A reference to the victims of terrorism can be found in the ASEAN Comprehensive Plan of Action on Counter Terrorism (2009), a soft law instrument aimed, among other objectives, at developing and adopting standard operating procedures for the protection of civilians in the event of a terrorist attack, including by providing those affected with adequate support.

However, similarly to other treaties, the ACCT presents at least two weaknesses that hinder its implementation.[25] First, the lack of enforcement

25 H Nasu, R McLaughlin, D Rothwell, S Sang Tan, 'Counter-Terrorism In The Legal Authority of ASEAN as a Security Institution' (Cambridge University Press 2019) 78.

mechanisms, which poses the risk of its provisions remaining dead letter. Second, an overly cautious approach to the exchange of information due to national sensitivities.[26] Arguably, the low level of integration and mutual trust makes ASEAN Member States reluctant to share intelligence at the regional level.[27] Nevertheless, governments tend to conclude bilateral agreements involving a swift exchange of information between the Parties in order to ensure adequate intervention in the aftermath of any terrorist attacks.[28]

6.4 *The Inter-American Region*

The main legal instrument dealing with terrorist events is the Inter-American Convention Against Terrorism, adopted in 2002 by the Organization of American States (OAS). The treaty requires States Parties to ratify, among other treaties, the CPPNM and the Terrorist Bombing Convention, and to adopt domestic legislation that criminalises and punishes the offences identified therein. To this end, the Convention obliges States Parties to cooperate in the exchange of information and to afford one another the greatest measure of expeditious mutual legal assistance with respect to the investigation of facts and the prosecution of the offenders. In 1999, the OAS created the Inter-American Committee against Terrorism (CICTE), the only regional body tasked with the promotion and development of coordinated strategies to combat terrorism and its evolving nature, including through the implementation of Resolution 1540 (2004), once adopted. Ten years later, it launched the Inter-American Network on Counter-Terrorism, a project aimed at enhancing the timely exchange of operational information to respond to attacks and manage their consequences. Insufficient attention, however, is paid to the recovery measures to be adopted in the aftermath of terrorist events.

At sub-regional level, a common strategy to counter terrorism was adopted in 2018 within the Caribbean Community (CARICOM). Unlike the OAS framework, the CARICOM strategy includes recovery measures, including the necessity to provide victims with adequate support and the importance of developing rehabilitation and reintegration processes for the offenders. In

26 Ibid.

27 An initiative worth mentioning is 'Our Eyes', a regional intelligence sharing alliance launched in Bali in 2018. It involves the collection, processing and presentation of strategic information on terrorism through the ASEAN Direct Communication Infrastructure. The initiative aims at coordinating ASEAN's responses against ongoing threats, including CBRN attacks.

28 For example, the Australian-funded Jakarta Centre for Law Enforcement Cooperation (JCLEC) has served as a platform for multilateral intelligence cooperation and collaboration.

order to monitor its implementation, the strategy develops success indicators linked to the actions suggested in the plan and a timeframe for measuring States' progress in the achievement of identified goals.

6.5 *The European Region (with the Exclusion of the European Union)*

In the aftermath of the 9/11 attacks, the threat of large-scale terrorism involving the use of CBRN weapons led the Council of Europe (CoE) to invite Member States to ratify and implement international treaties against CBRN terrorism, including with the development of emergency intervention and public health relief plans in the event of bioterrorism.[29] With the aim to incorporate 'fragmented legal texts together',[30] the CoE also adopted the Convention on the Prevention of Terrorism (2005) which, despite its title, contains some provisions that are also relevant to the response and recovery phases. Indeed, in addition to the criminalisation of terrorist offences, States Parties are required to investigate the facts, prosecute perpetrators and punish the wrongdoers with 'effective, proportionate and dissuasive'[31] sanctions. The obligation to cooperate in the exchange of information and in criminal investigations is also emphasised in the Additional Protocol to the Convention (2015) which explicitly includes the exchange of 'any available relevant information concerning persons travelling abroad for the purpose of terrorism'.[32]

As far as recovery is concerned, the Convention requires the Parties to adopt domestic measures to protect and support the victims and their families, including with financial assistance, compensation, psychological support and effective access to criminal procedures (art 13). Guidance on victims' protection is also provided by the CoE soft law 'Guidelines on Human Rights and the Fight against Terrorism' (Guideline No XVII) and the additional 'Guidelines on the protection of victims of terrorism' (Principle No 1). Rules specifically concerning witness protection are also in place, as those who 'stand up for truth and justice must be guaranteed reliable and durable protection, in particular legal and psychological support and robust physical protection before, during and after the trial' (CoE Res 2038 (2015)). They are included in the Criminal Law Convention on Corruption; the CoE Convention on Action against Trafficking in Human Beings; the Second Additional Protocol to the European Convention on Mutual Assistance in Criminal Matters; and Committee of Ministers Recommendations No R(97)13 concerning intimidation of witnesses and the

29 CoE Res 1367 (2 March 2004).
30 CoE Rec 1644 (29 January 2004).
31 CoE Convention on the Prevention of Terrorism (2005).
32 Additional Protocol to the CoE Convention on the Prevention of Terrorism (2015) art 7.

rights of the defence, Rec(2001)11 concerning the fight against organised crime, and Rec(2005)9 on the protection of witnesses and collaborators with justice.

More generally, the CoE Committee on Counter-Terrorism (CDCT) has also developed the Counter-Terrorism Strategy 2018–2022.[33] Based on the three Pillars 'Prevention, Prosecution and Protection', the Strategy assists States with non-binding guidelines concerning, among other issues, the conduct of investigations into terrorist offences, the prosecution of the offenders and the provision of adequate compensation and assistance to the victims of terrorism and their families.

7 Concluding Remarks

The analysis of the international legal framework reveals a plurality of instruments, either binding or non-binding on States, dealing with the short- and long-term consequences of CBRN terrorist offences. The proliferation of tools shows great commitment at the international level to counter CBRN terrorism. However, it also carries the risk of resulting in a broad and complex picture wherein all required efforts remain dead letter.

A first finding that emerges from this chapter is the difference in clarity between the definition of international obligations concerning the response phase and the recovery one.

Indeed, in order to respond to CBRN terrorist events, States are required to investigate the facts and ensure that perpetrators are brought to justice. To this end, States must criminalise terrorist offences at the national level, including with the provision of sanctions that are adequate to the severity of such acts. Also, States are required to cooperate in the exchange of information, in the conduct of criminal proceedings and to afford mutual assistance both at the legal and operational level.

On the contrary, the framework concerning the recovery from CRBN terrorism is not consistent, as different instruments provide different views. Arguably, this phase can be considered as involving three interconnected steps: the recovery of CBRN materials unlawfully taken and/or used; the assistance for the victims; and the rehabilitation of the wrongdoers.

In addition to the confusion stemming from the plurality of instruments and views, domestic implementation is also problematic.

33 CoE Counter-Terrorism Strategy 2018–2022, activity 3.3.

Despite the efforts towards the adoption of a comprehensive convention on international terrorism,[34] the implementation of the existing framework is far from being effective. Resolution 1540 is paradigmatic in this regard. Indeed, the overall 30,632 domestic measures recorded in 2016 – with an increase of approximately 7% compared to 2011 – have been commended by the 1540 Committee as an indicator of great success. However, the lack of any substantial assessment excludes the existence of a qualitative analysis of such measures, leaving space for obsolete or false information in States' reporting, as already happened in the case of Syria.

In conclusion, while the proliferation of international instruments against CBRN terrorism reveals a general commitment to respond to the phenomenon and recover from its manifestations, the confusing plurality of legal tools and the gaps in their implementation hinder the effectiveness of such a framework.

Bibliography

Nasu H, McLaughlin R, Rothwell D, Sang Tan S, 'Counter-Terrorism In The Legal Authority of ASEAN as a Security Institution' (Cambridge University Press 2019) 78.

OPCW, 'Report of the OPCW Fact-Finding Mission in Syria Regarding an Alleged Incident in Khan Shaykhun, Syrian Arab Republic April 2017' (29 June 2017) UN Doc S/1510/2017.

Shirazyan S, 'Building A Universal Counter-Proliferation Regime: The Institutional Limits of United Nations Security Council Resolution 1540' 18, Journal of National Security Law and Policy (2019) 150.

Tucker J, 'Bridging the Gaps: Achieving the Potential of the Nonproliferation Treaties to Combat Nuclear, Biological, and Chemical Terrorism' 83(2/3) Die Friedens-Warte (2008) 81.

UN Secretary General 'Activities of the United Nations system in implementing the United Nations Global Counter-Terrorism Strategy' (20 April 2018) UN Doc A/72/840.

UN Special Rapporteur on the promotion and protection of human rights and fundamental freedoms while countering terrorism (4 June 2012) UN Doc A/HRC/20/14.

UNODC 'Supporting legal responses and criminal justice capacity to prevent and counter terrorism' (2018).

UNSC 1540 Committee, '2016 Comprehensive Review Background Paper for the Formal Open Consultations by the 1540 Committee' (2016).

34 See UNGA Res 51/210 (16 January 1997) UN Doc A/RES/51/210 and UNGA Res 71/151 (20 December 2016) UN Doc A/RES/71/151.

UNSC 1540 Committee, 'Note verbale dated 14 October 2004 from the Permanent Mission of the Syrian Arab Republic to the United Nations addressed to the Chairman of the Committee' (24 November 2004) UN Doc S/AC.44/2004/(02)/70.

UNSC 1540 Committee, 'Note verbale dated 7 November 2005 from the Permanent Mission of the Syrian Arab Republic to the United Nations addressed to the Chairman of the Committee' (10 November 2005) UN Doc S/AC.44/2004/(02)/70/Add.3.

UNSC, 'Letter dated 9 December 2016 from the Chair of the Security Council Committee established pursuant to resolution 1540 (2004) addressed to the President of the Security Council' (9 December 2016) UN Doc S/2016/1038.

CHAPTER 10

Regional Perspective: CBRN Terrorism-Related Obligations under European Union Law

Susanna Villani

1 Introduction

The fight against terrorism has traditionally been perceived as a domestic security concern, but the terrorist attacks in the US and the EU in the early 2000s were the trigger for a new and unprecedented climate of cooperation between the EU Member States and the EU institutions in that field. The general reticence to abandon control over terrorist threats at national level gave way to an increased desire for a common strategy for overcoming the weaknesses in national and supranational emergency preparation and response. Such an enhanced political focus on terrorism also made it possible to accelerate decision-making processes on specific dimensions of intervention, including law enforcement and judicial cooperation, intelligence cooperation, border controls and the adoption of measures for combating the financing of terrorism.[1] The EU as a whole has thus acquired an increasingly important role as an actor in counter-terrorism practices based on the four strategic 'pillars' covering prevention, preparedness, response and recovery to be built alongside the Member States' action.

1 A selection of relevant contributions would include: M den Boer and J Monar, 'Keynote Article: 11 September and the Challenge of Global Terrorism to the EU as a Security Actor' (2002) 40(4) JComMarSt 11; D Keohane, *The EU and Counter-Terrorism* (CER 2005); D Spence (ed), *The European Union and Terrorism* (John Harper 2007); R Bossong, 'The Action Plan on Combating Terrorism: A Flawed Instrument of EU Security Governance' (2008) 46(1) JComMarSt 27; M O'Neill, *The Evolving EU Counter-terrorism Legal Framework* (Routledge 2011); J Argomaniz, *The EU and Counter-Terrorism: Politics, Polity and Policies After 9/11* (Taylor & Francis Group 2011); C Eckes, 'The Legal Framework of the European Union's Counter-Terrorist Policies: Full of Good Intentions?' in C Eckes and T Konstadinides (eds), *Crime within the Area of Freedom, Security and Justice: A European Public Order* (CUP 2011) 127; C Murphy, 'EU Counter-terrorism Law: What Kind of Exemplar of Transnational Law?' (2019) 21 CYELS 217.

Against this backdrop, the threats posed by CBRN material have progressively become an integral part of the EU counter-terrorism strategy.[2] As early as 2010, the Internal Security Strategy[3] put forward a shared agenda for Member States, the EU institutions, and agencies like Europol, as well as civil society and local authorities, envisaging the implementation of measures against CBRN risks as a priority. The terrorist attacks that occurred in Europe from 2015 onwards, as well as sporadic events like the toxic chemical attack in Salisbury in 2018, have confirmed the need to consciously introduce the nexus between CBRN and security, be the threat posed by States or non-State actors. Even though terrorists have tended to use commercial or homemade explosives, CBRN agents such as sarin, ricin or anthrax also represent a serious threat, especially when acquired through illicit trafficking that may be difficult to detect. Although 2019 saw a downward trend in terrorist attacks, the threat remains high and terrorist groups are progressively developing the knowledge and capacity to weaponise CBRN materials.[4] The intention to carry out terrorist attacks using this kind of material also continues to appear on terrorist online forums and social media, via cloud-based instant messaging services promoting and explaining the use of biological weapons.[5] The fact that terrorist groups are developing the knowledge and capacity to acquire and use CBRN materials represents an 'evolving threat' for the EU. Since it is increasingly real both inside and outside the EU, multiple actions and strategies in the realm of the CBRN management cycle have been adopted, with attention not only to the phase of response but also to those of prevention, preparedness and recovery. In July 2020, the European Commission renewed the EU Security Union Strategy,[6] which focuses on priority areas ranging from combating terrorism and organised crime, to preventing and detecting hybrid threats and increasing the resilience of critical infrastructure, to promoting cybersecurity and fostering research and innovation. The strategy also calls for major cooperation and

2 C Kaunert and S Léonard, 'The European Union's response to the CBRN terrorist threat: A multiple streams approach' (2019) 65(3) Politique européenne 148.

3 Communication from the Commission to the European Parliament and the Council, The EU Internal Security Strategy in Action: Five steps towards a more secure Europe, COM(2010) 673 final.

4 Europol, European Union Terrorism Situation and Trend Report (2020).

5 Ibid 21.

6 Communication from the Commission to the European Parliament, the European Council, the Council, the European Economic and Social Committee and the Committee of the Regions on the EU Security Union Strategy, COM(2020) 605 final.

coordination at EU level, especially when terrorism acquires a cross-border and sectoral dimension, like that concerning CBRN-related threats.[7]

The following sections describe the EU's approach to CBRN threats linked to terrorist acts, beginning with an overview of the EU's competences in the field of terrorism and of the EU's general strategy in this domain. The core of the chapter will be an exploration of the possibilities for developing specific obligations of prevention, preparedness, response and recovery for the EU Member States by proposing potential scenarios in light of the soft strategy encapsulated in the EU CBRN Action Plans. Finally, a description of the initiatives of international cooperation, as evidence of the close link between the internal and the external dimension of security, will be provided. Some concluding remarks will then follow.

2 The 'Soft' Strategy against CBRN Threats at EU Level as a Mirror of the Division of Competences in the Field of Terrorism

The Lisbon revision introduced specific provisions for EU action in the area of counter-terrorism, thereby widening the EU's competences and upholding the institutional framework.[8] In particular, Article 83 TFEU lists terrorism among the serious crimes with a cross-border dimension, thus allowing the possibility to establish common minimum rules. However, the Union's competence is not aimed at a full harmonisation of issues like the fight against terrorism. From an EU constitutional point of view, this is also confirmed by the so-called 'national identity clause' enshrined in Article 4(2) TEU, which states that 'national security remains the sole responsibility of each Member State'[9] and by Article 72 TFEU, which recognises national prerogatives over maintaining law and order and safeguarding internal security.[10] Hence, the area of combating terrorism does not form an ordinary shared competence, but rather one in which the joint action depends heavily on the willingness of Member States that remain the principal actors in this domain. In this equilibrium of competences, Article 222 TFEU deserves particular mention as it

7 M Martellini and A Malizia (eds), *Cyber and Chemical, Biological, Radiological, Nuclear, Explosives Challenges* (Springer 2017).

8 C Eckes (n 1) 127.

9 G Di Federico, *L'identità Nazionale degli Stati Membri nel Diritto dell'Unione Europea. Natura e portata dell'art. 4, par. 2, TUE* (Editoriale Scientifica 2017).

10 For detailed insights, ch 6, para 3 by Casolari.

imposes specific obligations of cooperation and solidarity upon the Union and the Member States in case of emergency. However, notwithstanding its potential, the 'solidarity clause' still remains underdeveloped.[11]

The limited margin of manoeuvre of the EU, determined by the division of competences with the Member States as well as the fact that no primary law provision deals specifically with CBRN-related threats, is clearly reflected in the soft instruments the EU has adopted over the years.

2.1 *The Elaboration of an EU 'Soft' Strategy against CBRN Threats*

The first political and programmatic strategy intended to guarantee closer cooperation and coordination on CBRN-related aspects was proposed at the European Council meeting held in Ghent in 2001.[12] Highlighting the fight against CBRN terrorism as an important area for EU action, alongside the five priorities of the Anti-terrorism Roadmap,[13] the Heads of State and Government urged the Commission and the Council 'to prepare a programme to improve cooperation between the Member States on the evaluation of risks, alerts and intervention, the storage of such means, and in the field of research'.[14] Following these indications, they adopted a joint programme to improve cooperation in the EU for preventing and limiting the consequences of CBRN terrorist threats,[15] which was subsequently revised and widened by the Council and Commission's Solidarity Programme,[16] following the 2004 attacks in Madrid. Moreover, tackling terrorists' access to weapons and explosives, ranging from components for homemade explosives to CBRN material, was also seen as a key action under the EU Strategy Against Proliferation of Weapons of

11 M Gestri, 'La clausola di solidarietà europea in caso di attacchi terroristici e calamità (art. 222 TFUE)', *Studi in onore di Luigi Costato* (Jovane 2014) 537.

12 European Council, Declaration by the Heads of State or Government of the European Union and the President of the Commission, Follow-Up to the September 11 Attacks and the Fight Against Terrorism, Doc. SN 4296/2/01.

13 European Council, Anti-terrorism Roadmap (2001) Doc. SN 4019/01. The roadmap included specific priorities of the EU counter-terrorism policy, namely police and judicial cooperation, international legal instruments, measures against the financing of terrorism, air security, and the coordination of the EU's global action.

14 Doc. SN 4296/2/01 (n 12), point 4.

15 Council of the European Union, Adoption of the programme to improve cooperation in the European Union for preventing and limiting the consequences of chemical, biological, radiological or nuclear terrorist threats, Doc. 14627/02.

16 Council of the European Union, EU Solidarity Programme on the consequences of terrorist threats and attacks (revised/widened CBRN Programme): Adoption, Doc. 15480/04.

Mass Destruction (WMD)[17] and the 2005 EU Counter-Terrorism Strategy.[18] In 2007, the Green Paper on bio-preparedness launched a consultation process on how to improve the EU's preparedness and response to biological threats of both non-terrorist and terrorist origin.[19] This process was given additional impetus by the 2007 Council Conclusions on addressing CBRN Risks and on Bio-preparedness.[20] On the basis of a Commission Communication,[21] in 2009, the Council formally adopted an EU CBRN Action Plan,[22] which represented the first political commitment based on a roadmap of intentions for reducing the threat of and damage from CBRN incidents of accidental, natural and intentional origin. The Action Plan identified and detailed the three areas of intervention that make up the CBRN risk management cycle, and stressed that these areas are to be read according to an all-hazards approach that respects the primary responsibility of the Member States and is 'guided by the principle of solidarity'.[23] The 124 different fields of action financially supported through existing Community programmes and instruments were listed in Annex I of the Action Plan. In addition, the recommendations included the monitoring of industrial use of high-risk chemicals, the identification of facilities having biological agents, and the improvement of security checks of personnel handling chemical or biological agents.[24] The Action Plan was

17 Council of the European Union, Fight against the proliferation of weapons of mass destruction – EU strategy against proliferation of Weapons of Mass Destruction, Doc. 15708/03. For an overview of the tools adopted until 2018, see Annex II to the Annual Progress Report on the Implementation of the European Union Strategy Against the Proliferation of Weapons of Mass Destruction (2018), Doc. 7909/19, Add. See, K Zwolski, 'Unrecognized and Unwelcome? The Role of the EU in Preventing the Proliferation of CBRN Weapons, Materials and Knowledge' (2011) 12 Perspectives on European Politics and Society 477.

18 The strategy underlines the importance of working 'with partners and international organisations on [...] non-proliferation of CBRN materials [...], as well as [providing] technical assistance on protective security to priority third countries'. See, Council of the European Union, The European Union Counter-terrorism Strategy, Doc. 14469/4/05, point 11.

19 Green Paper on bio-preparedness, COM(2007) 399 final.

20 Council Conclusions of 6 December 2007 on addressing Chemical, Biological, Radiological and Nuclear Risks and on Bio-preparedness, Doc. 16589/07.

21 Communication from the Commission to the European Parliament and the Council on Strengthening Chemical, Biological, Radiological and Nuclear Security in the European Union – an EU CBRN Action Plan, Doc. 11480/09.

22 Council of the European Union, Council Conclusions on strengthening chemical, biological, radiological and nuclear (CBRN) security in the European Union – An EU CBRN Action Plan: Adoption, Doc. 15505/1/09 REV 1.

23 Ibid Annex I, 9.

24 See ch 14 by Ferri.

intended to be implemented by EU bodies, such as the European Commission, the EEAS and Europol; Member States' public authorities; and other relevant stakeholders, such as the private sector, the health care sector, and academic institutions. The CBRN Advisory Group was established to coordinate the work, alongside subgroups for coordinating issues related to chemical, biological, radiological and nuclear security, respectively.

In May 2012, the European Commission issued the first 'Progress Report on the Implementation of the EU CBRN Action Plan',[25] identifying both achievements and shortcomings. As well as a better understanding of the nature of these threats generally, the report acknowledged that progress had been made on increasing information sharing by means of a CBRN Glossary and inclusion of CBRN incidents in the European Bomb Data System. In addition to these achievements, the report listed projects that had been implemented at local, national, EU and international level, based on assessment of the relevant risks. These efforts included establishing the European network of specialised CBRN law enforcement units;[26] setting up the Early Warning System (EWS) for law enforcement authorities for incidents related to high risk CBRN materials; as well as creating a dedicated EU training infrastructure, the European Nuclear Security Training Centre (EUSECTRA). In addition, following the outcomes of the 2012 conference 'Strategic EU-level CBRN-E Conference: A New EU-CBRNE Agenda',[27] which underlined the need for a flexible approach encompassing also the explosive (E) materials,[28] the scope of the Action Plan was informally widened, thus paving the way to the adoption of a new EU CBRN-E Agenda.[29]

25 European Commission, Progress Report on the Implementation of the EU CBRN action plan, May 2012 (public version).

26 Council conclusions on the creation of a European network of specialised CBRN law enforcement units 3096th Justice and Home Affairs Council meeting Luxembourg, Doc. 10338/11.

27 The Conference was organised in order to discuss the preliminary achievements of the Action Plan on Enhancing the Security of Explosives adopted in 2008 that was essentially aimed at preventing the use of explosive devices by terrorists.

28 Council of the European Union, An Action Plan on Enhancing the Security of Explosives, Doc. 8109/08. After the Paris attacks, another Action Plan against illicit trafficking in and use of firearms and explosives was adopted (Communication from the Commission to the European Parliament, the European Council, the Council, Implementing the European Agenda on Security: EU action plan against illicit trafficking in and use of firearms and explosives, COM(2015) 624 final). Regulation (EU) 2019/1148 of the European Parliament and the Council on the marketing and use of explosives precursors (OJ L 186, 11.7.2019) was adopted in 2019 and started to be applied from 1 February 2021.

29 Council of the European Union, Draft Council Conclusions on the new CBRNE agenda – Adoption, Doc. 16980/12. R Roffey, 'The EU as an Actor in CBRNE Crisis: A General

As for the financing terms, the EU Instrument for Stability 2014–2020[30] funded a number of measures to promote CBRN security practices, strengthen effective control of illicit CBRN trafficking, and enforce export control on dual-use goods.[31] Furthermore, the Commission introduced a new and comprehensive approach for elaborating a strategy[32] to deter future CBRN-E risks at EU level, paving the way for the adoption of a specific Action Plan to enhance preparedness against CBRN security risks.[33] More than in the previous documents, the 2017 Communication elaborating this specific Action Plan included prominent references to the use of CBRN materials by terrorist groups as an 'evolving threat' for the EU and thus the necessity to focus on shared preparedness strategies. In order to effectively counter such a threat, four priorities were identified: 1) reducing the accessibility of CBRN materials; 2) ensuring a more robust preparedness for and response to CBRN security incidents; 3) building stronger internal-external links in CBRN security with the key regional and international EU partners; and 4) enhancing the knowledge of CBRN-related risks. Each of these objectives was then related to specific commitments, actions and deliverables to be performed in a well-defined timeframe both by civil and military assets as set out, *inter alia*, in Article 222 TFEU. Indeed, while civil protection forces are extremely relevant, using armed forces permits a comprehensive capability-based planning approach thanks to a staff that undergoes regular CBRN training. Military capabilities include specialised competencies, namely medical expertise regarding the treatment of chemical or biological casualties, detection and identification of nonconventional warfare agents, and decontamination. Accordingly, in comparison to the first CBRN Action Plan, the 2017 Action Plan seems not only to be more detailed in terms of envisaged actions but also to channel the outputs in a more structured

Picture', in D O'Mathúna and I de Miguel Beriain (eds), *Ethics and Law for Chemical, Biological, Radiological, Nuclear & Explosive Crises* (Springer 2019) 23.

30 Regulation (EU) No 230/2014 of the European Parliament and the Council of 11 March 2014 establishing an Instrument for Stability, OJ L 77/1 of 15.3.2014.

31 In this regard, particularly noteworthy was the adoption of Council Regulation (EC) No 428/2009 of 5 May 2009 setting up a Community regime for the control of exports, transfer, brokering and transit of dual-use items, OJ L 134 of 29.5.2009.

32 Communication from the Commission to the European Parliament, the Council, the European Economic and Social Committee and the Committee of the Regions on a new EU approach to the detection and mitigation of CBRN-E risks, COM(2014) 247 final.

33 Communication from the Commission to the European Parliament, the Council, the European Economic and Social Committee and the Committee of the Regions, Action Plan to enhance preparedness against chemical, biological, radiological and nuclear security risks, COM/2017/0610 final.

way thereby contributing to reinforcing the common framework for Member States' cooperative interventions that, up to that time, were not as brilliant as expected.[34]

3 Searching for Obligations in the CBRN-Related Terrorist Threats Domain

The EU Action Plans, as well as the various instruments of operational cooperation mentioned above, do not have legal force but just a programmatic character. Indeed, while demonstrating an intention to enhance both 'horizontal' coordination among Member States and 'vertical' coordination between the EU and Member States at all phases of the CBRN risk management cycle, they do not establish specific obligations either for the EU institutions or for the Member States. However, this does not automatically mean that an EU legal framework for countering CBRN terrorism is absent. As a matter of fact, on the basis of Article 83 TFEU, in 2017, the EU adopted the noteworthy Directive on combating terrorism[35] which, as well as reinforcing the legal framework, covers conduct related to terrorism more comprehensively by including not only the 'classical' terrorist tactics but also an explicit reference to the use of CBRN devices.[36] Hence, the adoption of soft law instruments represents the natural complement to the binding acts adopted at EU level, thus allowing the development of a comprehensive strategy of cooperation while respecting the division of competences. Moreover, the content of these instruments may serve to further integrate the CBRN domain within the obligations enshrined in the main secondary law instruments in the field of terrorism. Nonetheless, it must be noted that the lack of a specific set of obligations limits the opportunity to have clear-cut distinctions between the obligations to be applied to the different phases of the CBRN risk management cycle.

---

34 S N Chatfield, *Member States' Preparedness for CBRN Threats*, 2018.

35 Directive (EU) 2017/541 of the European Parliament and of the Council of 15 March 2017 on combating terrorism and replacing Council Framework Decision 2002/475/JHA and amending Council Decision 2005/671/JHA, OJ L 88 of 31.3.2017.

36 Ibid art 3, paras (1)(f) and (g): '(f) manufacture, possession, acquisition, transport, supply or use of explosives or weapons, including chemical, biological, radiological or nuclear weapons, as well as research into, and development of, chemical, biological, radiological or nuclear weapon; (g) release of dangerous substances, or causing fires, floods or explosions, the effect of which is to endanger human life'.

3.1 *Obligations of Prevention against CBRN Threats*

The main focus of the activities included in the Action Plan 2010–2015 was on the 'prevention' phase, concentrated on the security of CBRN materials and facilities; development of a high-security culture among staff; identification of suspicious transactions and behaviours; improvement of the security of transport; information exchange; import and export regimes; and strengthening of cooperation on the security of nuclear materials.[37] As a supplement to pure prevention, the 'detection' phase (which often may overlap with preparedness) concerns the capacity to effectively detect CBRN materials by referring to common minimum detection standards; establishing trialling, testing and certification schemes for CBRN detection; and improving the exchange of good practices for ensuring an appropriate response to an incident.

Looking at the obligations of prevention, it is firstly worth exploring Directive 2017/541 on combating terrorism, which, as mentioned, also applies to CBRN-related terrorist threats. The Directive imposes a duty on Member States to take measures to ensure that the provision of instructions on the making or use of explosives, firearms or other weapons or noxious or hazardous substances is punishable as a criminal offence when committed intentionally.[38] Indeed, the classification of activities that must be prevented as criminal acts in the domestic legal systems and the provision of appropriate penalties is a necessary precondition for the elaboration of preventive measures.[39] More broadly, besides being relevant within the criminal law domain, criminalising and punishing these offences also allows the Member States to fully comply with their obligations related to the chemical field. Indeed, following the 2018 Salisbury attacks, as requested by the European Council,[40] the Commission focused especially on chemical threats by stepping up its actions against

37 For insights on the management of nuclear devices, see ch 15 by Balboni.

38 Ibid arts 5–8. On specific duties of criminalisation, see ch 32 by Vierucci and ch 33 by Amoroso. As reported also by Poltronieri Rossetti (ch 7), the application of obligations of deterrence can be extended to the prevention phase in the field of CBRN terrorism.

39 On 30 September 2020, the Commission adopted a Report assessing the measures taken by the Member States. The assessment concludes that the transposition of the Directive has led to a substantive strengthening of the Member States' criminal justice approach to terrorism, but also that the inclusion of certain types of CBRN weapons, such as radiological and nuclear weapons, is missing. See, Report from the Commission to the European Parliament and the Council based on Article 29(1) of Directive (EU) 2017/541 of the European Parliament and of the Council of 15 March 2017 on combating terrorism and replacing Council Framework Decision 2002/475/JHA and amending Council Decision 2005/671/JHA, COM(2020) 619 final.

40 European Council Conclusions, 18 October 2018, para 8; European Council conclusions, 22 March 2018, para 11.

CBRN threats and its collaboration with Member States and developing a common list of chemical substances of concern. The Commission also launched a dialogue with the private sector to explore possibilities for reducing the accessibility to terrorists of chemical substances which can be processed or combined with other substances for chemical attacks. Additionally, in the wake of the Chemical Weapons Convention, the Foreign Affairs Council adopted Regulation 2018/1542[41] and Decision (CFSP) 2018/1544 concerning restrictive measures against the proliferation and use of chemical weapons.[42] In particular, the latter requires the States to take the necessary measures to prevent the entry into, or transit through, their territories of natural persons responsible for or involved in the use of chemical weapons, including any toxic chemicals. Again, the explicit criminalisation of this conduct within the national legal order would contribute to the implementation of this requirement by the Member States, according to a preventive approach.

Ensuring the criminalisation of conduct involving the use of CBRN material not only helps to deter potential attacks but also to set a benchmark for cooperation in the information exchange between national authorities and with the EU agencies. As a matter of fact, prevention measures are essentially based on information exchange between the competent national authorities, as established in Council Framework Decision 2006/960/JHA,[43] Decision 2008/615/JHA (Prüm Decision),[44] and Decision 2005/671/JHA.[45] This set of legislation imposes an obligation upon Member States to share information, calling for the creation of national contact points for the exchange of information resulting from criminal investigations of terrorist offences, including CBRN-related ones. The information, while respecting the essential security interests of the Member States, shall be sent by the national authorities to Europol and has to

41 Council Regulation (EU) 2018/1542 of 15 October 2018 concerning restrictive measures against the proliferation and use of chemical weapons, OJ L 259/12 of 16.10.2018.

42 Consolidated text: Council Decision (CFSP) 2018/1544 of 15 October 2018 concerning restrictive measures against the proliferation and use of chemical weapons, OJ L 259 of 16.10.2018.

43 Council Framework Decision 2006/960/JHA of 18 December 2006 on simplifying the exchange of information and intelligence between law enforcement authorities of the Member States of the European Union, OJ L 386/89 of 29.12.2006.

44 Council Decision 2008/615/JHA of 23 June 2008 on the stepping up of cross-border cooperation, particularly in combating terrorism and cross-border crime, OJ L 210/1 of 6.8.2008.

45 Council Decision 2005/671/JHA of 20 September 2005 on the exchange of information and cooperation concerning terrorist offences, OJ L 253/22 of 29.9.2005.

contain some specific details, including details on 'the threat posed by the possession of weapons of mass destruction'.[46]

Finally, according to Article 21 of the Directive on combating terrorism, the Member States are asked to take the necessary measures to ensure the prompt removal of online content constituting a public provocation to commit a terrorist offence. Following on from this provision, in 2018, the Commission proposed the adoption of a Regulation to introduce prevention measures not only against the online dissemination of material inciting terrorism but also material used for recruitment or training purposes.[47] The proposal enshrines specific duties of care on hosting service providers concerning the removal of terrorist content or disabling of access to it. In addition, it includes an obligation for the Member States to monitor the implementation of the Regulation. Furthermore, the Member States must inform, coordinate and cooperate with each other and, where appropriate, with relevant Union bodies such as Europol, to ensure co-ordination with regards to issuing removal orders (orders compelling hosting service providers to remove content) and referrals (which require hosting service providers to expeditiously assess content for possible removal).[48] As for the CBRN field, the content of the proposed act could be easily interpreted as including an obligation upon the service providers to remove online content concerning the fabrication and use of CBRN material for terrorist purposes and upon the States to collect information about these activities to be shared with the other Member States.

3.2 *Obligations of Preparedness against CBRN Threats*

The adoption of the 2017 Action Plan on preparedness makes it evident that there is an increasing interest in cooperating on this specific phase that is essentially based on monitoring, early warning, detection capabilities and surveillance actions. The main action included in the Action Plan was intended to better control the illicit entry of high risk CBRN materials and to optimise the ability to detect such materials at internal level. As a result, alongside the development of minimum detection and sampling standards set by the European Committee for Standardisation (CEN), the strengthening of risk-based customs controls to intercept dangerous CBRN materials at the border has been put at the centre of this specific action, even though the border with prevention may appear blurry. Finally, to further improve coordination and knowledge

46 Ibid art 2.

47 Commission proposal for Regulation to prevent the dissemination of terrorist content online, COM (2018) 640 final.

48 Ibid art 13.

concerning CBRN risks at EU level, the main proposal has been to establish an EU CBRN security network pooling together the efforts of all the CBRN actors at strategic and operational level. It is anticipated that the network will rely on an advisory group bringing together all the CBRN coordinators of the Member States, a support network composed of existing CBRN centres across the EU and a CBRN hub in the European Counter-Terrorism Centre at Europol.

These relevant initiatives of cooperation and coordination are, however, matched with very few obligations. Most of them can be derived from Decision 1082/2013/EU on serious cross-border threats to health,[49] which is also mentioned in Council Decision 2014/415/EU on the implementation of the solidarity clause.[50] Indeed, Decision 1082/2013/EU represents a decisive legislative development with regard to the biological area since it has not only set up provisions to strengthen preparedness and response planning in the EU but has also formalised the role of the Health Security Committee (HSC) established on the basis of the Presidency Conclusions on bioterrorism.[51] Given the Decision's broad material scope of application, notably covering threats of biological and chemical origin, as well as threats of 'unknown origin', this instrument is relevant also when dealing with preparedness against CBRN threats linked to terrorist conduct, even though it is mainly applicable to non-intentional events. In this regard, Member States and the Commission have an obligation to consult with each other within the HSC in order to share best practice and experience on preparedness, as well as promote the interoperability of national preparedness planning. To meet this obligation, every three years Member States must provide the Commission with an update on the latest situation at national level.[52] Moreover, Member States must inform the Commission in a timely manner of the main aspects of any revisions they make to their preparedness planning at national level, with particular focus on cross-border dimensions of revisions.[53] For its part, the Commission must adopt templates to be used by the Member States when sending the

49 Decision No 1082/2013/EU of the European Parliament and of the Council of 22 October 2013 on serious cross-border threats to health and repealing Decision No 2119/98/EC, OJ 293/1 of 5.11.2013. As extensively reported by Ferri (ch 19), the Commission has recently proposed replacing Decision 2013/1082 with a Regulation. See, Proposal for a Regulation of the European Parliament and of the Council on serious cross-border threats to health and repealing Decision No 1082/2013, COM(2020) 727 final. For further details on the content of Decision 1082/2013, see ch 19 by Ferri.

50 Council Decision 2014/415/EU of 24 June 2014 on the arrangements for the implementation by the Union of the solidarity clause, OJ L 192/53 of 1.7.2014.

51 Presidency Conclusions on bioterrorism, Doc. 13826/01.

52 Decision No 1082/2013/EU (n 49), art 4(2).

53 Decision No 1082/2013/EU (n 49), art 4(3).

information and make them available to the members of the HSC.[54] Over recent years, cooperation within the HSC has led to an improvement in cross-sectoral training activities, with the involvement of various stakeholders, as well as the creation of a CBRN detection pool. Moreover, Member States have been encouraged to commit new CBRN capacities to the European Emergency Response Capacity (EERC), especially the EU Medical Corps for dealing with biological threats, within the framework of the EU Civil Protection Mechanism.[55] The EU Civil Protection Mechanism represents another practical and effective way for implementing a cooperative approach and is dealt with by Ferri in Chapter 19 of this book.

3.3 *Obligations of Response against CBRN Threats*

The EU legal framework on response to CBRN hazards is composed of different instruments setting out modalities for responding to emergency situations when they potentially pose a serious cross-border threat to health and when public health measures taken to counter that threat are insufficient to ensure a high level of protection of human health.[56] The response framework covers interventions from the period immediately before the occurrence of the CBRN event through to the response to and recovery from the incident.

Moving on to more specific terms, Article 9 of Decision 1082/2013 sets an obligation for the national authorities of the Member States to submit an alert notification through the Early Warning and Response System (EWRS) in the event of a serious cross-border threat to health in order to ensure that the other States and the Commission are duly informed in a timely manner.[57] The national authorities are also required to communicate through the EWRS

54 The template to be used by the Member States when providing the information on their preparedness and response planning in relation to serious cross border threats to health is included in Commission Implementing Decision 2014/504/EU of 25 July 2014 implementing Decision No 1082/2013/EU of the European Parliament and of the Council with regard to the template for providing the information on preparedness and response planning in relation to serious cross-border threats to health, OJ L 223/25 of 29.7.2014. According to the Report on the implementation of Decision 1082/2013/EU, made available on 7 December 2015, as of 23 October 2015, 26 EU Member States and one EEA country provided the requested information. Since then, however, no other reports have been issued and only a workshop on the state of play of preparedness on serious cross-border threats to health in the EU was organised in 2018.

55 For analysis of the civil protection tools in the context of CBRN, see ch 19 by Ferri.

56 Decision No 1082/2013/EU (n 49), Preamble, point 9.

57 From 5 November 2013 until 4 September 2015, a total of 168 messages were posted with 354 comments. Of the remaining messages, 90 were alert notifications and 78 were information messages. See, EU Monitor, Explanatory Memorandum to COM(2015) 617.

any available relevant information that may be useful for the coordination of the response, including some details that are particularly applicable also to CBRN threats: (a) the type and origin of the agent; (b) the date and place of the incident or outbreak; (c) means of transmission or dissemination; (d) toxicological data; (e) detection and confirmation methods; (f) measures other than public health measures that have been implemented or are intended to be taken at the national level.[58] It must be noted, however, that the obligation to issue an alert notification only applies in extreme situations: the notification is required only where the scale and severity of the threat concerned are or could become so significant that they affect or could affect more than one Member State and require or could require a coordinated response at the Union level.[59]

Where an alert has been notified, Member States have an obligation to consult each other within the HSC and in liaison with the Commission with a view to coordinating the national responses, as well as the risk and crisis communication to the public and to healthcare professionals. Then, the Commission shall adopt the procedures necessary for the uniform implementation of the required information exchange, consultation and coordination (Article 11). Such a basic obligation is further reinforced by the specific obligation of mutual assistance which requires other Member States' competent authorities to provide assistance to a State affected by one of the serious events outlined in Council Decision 2008/615/JHA, in compliance with the affected State's consent and its national law. The measures of response to be adopted include not only the notification of the serious situation and the coordination of the measures but also the dispatching of officers, specialists and advisers and supplying equipment, at the request of the Member State within whose

58 The provision also refers to the Commission's obligation to make available to the Member States' national authorities, through the EWRS, any information that may be useful for coordinating the response, including information transmitted through rapid alert and information systems established under other provisions, including the Common Emergency Communication and Information System (CECIS), a web-based alert and notification application enabling a real-time exchange of information. The specific obligations concerning the early exchange of information in the event of a radiological and nuclear emergency are discussed in ch 15 by Balboni.

59 Decision No 1082/2013/EU (n 49), Preamble, point 16. While not mentioned by Decision 1082/2013, the general procedure of notification should also take into account the content of Regulation 178/2002, requiring the Member States to notify the Commission of a direct or indirect risk to human health deriving from food or feed under a rapid alert system primarily addressed to the European Food Safety Authority. See, Regulation (EC) No 178/2002 of the European Parliament and of the Council of 28 January 2002 laying down the general principles and requirements of food law, establishing the European Food Safety Authority and laying down procedures in matters of food safety, OJ L 31/1 of 1.2.2002, art 50.

territory the situation has arisen.[60] To link the response phase to the process of criminalisation, thus closing the circle of emergency management, it deserves to be mentioned that, according to Decision (CFSP) 2018/154, the Council may impose sanctions on persons in the form of banning travel to the EU and freezing their assets, and on entities in the form of freezing assets, where they are directly or indirectly involved in the use and proliferation of chemical weapons.[61] Pursuant to this Decision and in light of the fact that under the Chemical Weapons Convention any poisoning of an individual through the use of a nerve agent is considered a use of chemical weapons,[62] following the assassination attempt on Alexei Navalny, the Council adopted restrictive measures against six persons and one entity.[63]

Going beyond the response phase and towards the recovery one, Title V of Directive 2017/541/EU introduces a set of obligations of recovery for the Member States *vis-à-vis* the victims of terrorism.[64] According to Article 24, the Member States shall ensure the provision of support services addressing victims' specific needs, including (a) emotional and psychological support; (b) provision of advice and information on any relevant legal, practical or financial matters, including facilitating the exercise of the right to information; (c) assistance with compensation claims for victims of terrorism, under the national law of the Member State concerned. Moreover, Article 24, para 4, stresses that the specialist support services are to be provided immediately

60 Council Decision 2008/615/JHA (n 44), art 18.

61 Decision (CFSP) 2018/154 (n 42), art 2. On 12 October 2020, the Council decided to extend the regime allowing the EU to impose restrictive measures on persons and entities involved in the development and use of chemical weapons by one year, until 16 October 2021.

62 For the position of the EU institutions, see European Parliament resolution of 17 September 2020 on the situation in Russia: the poisoning of Alexei Navalny (2020/2777(RSP)), 17 September 2020; Outcome Document 11598/20 of the 3774th Council meeting Foreign Affairs, Brussels, 12 October 2020.

63 Council Decision (CFSP) 2020/1482 of 14 October 2020 amending Decision (CFSP) 2018/1544 concerning restrictive measures against the proliferation and use of chemical weapons, OJ L 341 of 15.10.2020.

64 According to art 2, para 1, of Directive 2012/29/EU, 'victim' means: (i) a natural person who has suffered harm, including physical, mental or emotional harm or economic loss which was directly caused by a criminal offence; (ii) family members of a person whose death was directly caused by a criminal offence and who have suffered harm as a result of that person's death. See, Directive 2012/29/EU of the European Parliament and of the Council of 25 October 2012 establishing minimum standards on the rights, support and protection of victims of crime, and replacing Council Framework Decision 2001/220/JHA, OJ L 315/57 of 14.11.2012.

after an attack and for as long as necessary.[65] This is a significant aspect in the case of CBRN attacks where, unlike with the use of conventional weapons, the effects may not be immediately manifest, and a long term follow up and treatment might be necessary. Finally, Member States are required to adopt measures to protect victims of terrorism and their family members (Article 25), as well as to guarantee that the victims of terrorism resident in another Member State are informed about the support services and compensation schemes available in the Member State where the terrorist offence was committed (Article 26).

4 Instruments of External Cooperation in the CBRN Domain

The investigation of the EU legal framework concerning CBRN threats related to terrorism cannot be complete without an overview of the external dimension.[66] In the CBRN domain, the demand of enhanced cooperation with third countries and strategic partners requires paying special attention to the NATO framework and the EU Global CBRN Centres of Excellence.[67]

In 2010, NATO's New Strategic Concept[68] recognised the threat posed by terrorists' capacity to use modern technologies, including CBRN assets. In order not to compete with NATO in the EU's own capacity-building initiatives and to avoid duplication of efforts, common and coordinated efforts to counter hybrid threats have been defined. During the EU-NATO summit held in Warsaw in 2016,[69] the parties decided to boost the ability to counter hybrid threats and considered a series of proposals on the implementation of measures in this regard, especially in the preparedness phase. The main proposals comprised

65 For comments, J Maliszewska-Nienartowicz, 'A New Chapter in the EU Counterterrorism Policy? The Main Changes Introduced by the Directive 2017/541 on Combating Terrorism' (2017) 37 PolishYIL 185.

66 Comprehensive Assessment of EU Security Policy, accompanying the document: Communication from the Commission to the European Parliament, the European Council and the Council – Ninth progress report towards an effective and genuine Security Union, COM(2017) 407 final.

67 J Sabol et al, 'Current Activities of the European Union in Fighting CBRN Terrorism Worldwide', in S Apikyan and D Diamond (eds), *Nuclear Threats and Security Challenges* (Springer 2015) 157.

68 Strategic Concept for the Defence and Security of the Members of the North Atlantic Treaty Organization, Adopted by Heads of State and Government at the NATO Summit in Lisbon 19–20 November 2010, 11. See also ch 8 by de Guttry.

69 Joint Declaration by the President of the European Council, the President of the European Commission, and the Secretary General of the North Atlantic Treaty Organization.

the strengthening of staff-to-staff cooperation on civil preparedness, including risk assessments, medical evacuation, mass casualty incidents, and population movement, as well as harmonising practice and procedures, and exploring the inclusion of EU staff in the NATO Resilience Advisory Support Teams and of NATO staff in relevant EU advisory prevention and preparedness missions.

Following the Warsaw Joint Declaration, eight EU Member States and the US established the European Centre of Excellence for Countering Hybrid Threats (Hybrid CoE).[70] The Memorandum of Understanding (MoU)[71] created this hub of expertise to support individual and collective efforts to enhance civil-military capabilities, resilience, and preparedness to counter hybrid threats. This is in line with the broader idea of including CBRN threats under the umbrella of hybrid threats posed by States and non-State actors, recognised by the Commission and the High Representative.[72] The Hybrid CoE is intended to be a platform for sharing best practices, building capability and testing new ideas on defence against hybrid threats, as well as to act as a neutral facilitator between the EU and NATO through strategic, scenario-based discussions and exercises. However, as expressly stressed in Section 15 of the MoU, no rights and obligations for the Parties are established and so the Hybrid CoE only represents a formal instrument of cooperation at supranational level.

Besides this forum, the EU has established a Centre of Excellence specifically dedicated to the improvement of cooperation with third countries in the CBRN domain. The origins of the so-called CBRN CoE initiative can be found in the Instrument for Stability and it now fits within the Instrument contributing to Stability and Peace (IcSP).[73] Pursuant to Article 5, para 18(b) of the IcSP Regulation, it contributes to CBRN risk mitigation and capacity building measures in partner countries and allows the EU to fund CoE projects covering accidental, natural and intentional risks. In a broader perspective, such a program is aligned with the EU's commitments as a responsible global actor, not only with respect to the promotion of 'stronger multilateral cooperation'[74]

70 For comments, E Nexon and C Wachtel, *EU preparedness against CBRN weapons*, European Parliament Study, 2019.

71 Memorandum of Understanding on the European Centre of Excellence for countering hybrid threats, 11 April 2017.

72 Joint Communication of the European Commission and the High Representative for Foreign Affairs and Security Policy to the European Parliament, the European Council and the Council, Increasing resilience and bolstering capabilities to address hybrid threats, JOIN(2018) 16 final.

73 Regulation (EU) No 230/2014 of the European Parliament and of the Council of 11 March 2014 establishing an instrument contributing to stability and peace, OJ L 77/1 of 15.3.2014.

74 Art 21(h), TEU.

for addressing global peace and security challenges but also with respect to the assistance of 'populations, countries and regions confronting natural or man-made disasters'.[75]

The methodology of the CoE is based on a soft nature in terms of institutionalisation and is built on the national systems developed by the partner countries themselves which participate on a voluntary basis. At the moment, the regional Centres cover 62 countries in eight regions and are facilitated by a Regional Secretariat. From an operational point of view, the initiative is taken forward jointly by the EEAS, DG Development and Cooperation – EuropeAid, and the Joint Research Centre, while its implementation is supported by the United Nations Interregional Crime and Justice Research Institute. All the projects implemented are intended to deal with the individual phases of the CBRN risk management cycle and they may be adapted to cover any geographical area or type of CBRN risk.

According to the last report issued by the Court of Auditors,[76] the CoE initiative has contributed to mitigating CBRN threats, but many challenges remain, especially from the EU side, which has not properly and fully implemented the Court's previous recommendations.[77] In particular, the EU delegations' limited involvement in promoting the initiative does not sufficiently guarantee the long-term, robust cooperation that results in the elaboration of effective national action plans. Moreover, from the partner countries' side, their interaction, with the EU and with each other, concerning CBRN risk mitigation capacities is limited by the irregular organisation of meetings and discussions on guidelines, best practices and lessons learned. In light of the suggestions made by the Court of Auditors, one could expect to see further development of cooperative regional projects, thus creating a constant political and operational dialogue on new priorities and targets with other third countries.

5 Concluding Remarks

The present chapter has presented an overview of the evolution of the approach at EU level towards CBRN threats in the field of counter-terrorism. While the letter represents a national domain, the concept of cooperation

75 Art 21 (g), TEU.

76 European Court of Auditors, 'The EU Chemical, Biological, Radiological and Nuclear Centres of Excellence: more progress needed', 2018.

77 European Court of Auditors, 'Can the EU's Centres of Excellence initiative contribute effectively to mitigating chemical, biological, radiological and nuclear risks from outside the EU?', 2014.

among the Member States and the Union has steadily expanded, thereby becoming the broader 'container' for a variety of specific legal obligations. In particular, the CBRN Action Plans have introduced an all-hazards approach, major coordination and information sharing mechanisms, capacity building, joint exercises, and sharing of best practices by the Member States, with the support of the EU institutions. Over the years, a dense coordinating network with third countries and NATO partners has also been established, demonstrating how the internal dimension of protection and preparedness must be complemented by the external one. Alongside soft mechanisms of intervention, essentially based on the willingness of the participating Member States and thus not backed by strong enforcement measures, primary law has helped to extend the scope of action at EU level in this domain by justifying the adoption of secondary law acts. However, a specific act dealing with CBRN terrorism is still lacking and the main obligations upon the Member States on this issue are derived from various other instruments that were mainly developed for addressing other policy issues, especially cross-border health threats, but that also contain measures relevant to tackling the CBRN terrorist threat. It is also interesting to note that, while the CBRN Action Plans are intended to develop instruments of prevention, preparedness and response that may apply to any potential event, including events of a wholly internal character, the essential prerequisite for imposing obligations upon the Member States is precisely the cross-border nature of the threat. In any case, except for the duty to punish terror-related offences in domestic law, the other obligations can be classified as obligations of cooperative conduct aimed at establishing a more coordinated framework in accordance with the principle of loyal cooperation. Ultimately, since it is challenging to obtain detailed and transparent information on the effective implementation of the envisaged mechanisms by States and on their respect for the related obligations because of the national security concerns at stake, the more viable choice seems to be to rely on the cooperative attitude of the States rather than on well-structured and imposed monitoring instruments.

Bibliography

Argomaniz J, *The EU and Counter-Terrorism: Politics, Polity and Policies After 9/11* (Taylor & Francis Group 2011).

Bakardjieva Engelbrekt A, Michalski A (eds), *The European Union: Facing the Challenge of Multiple Security Threats* (Edward Elgar 2018).

Bossong R, 'The Action Plan on Combating Terrorism: A Flawed Instrument of EU Security Governance' (2008) 46/1 JComMarSt 27.

Chatfield SN, *Member States' Preparedness for CBRN Threats*, April 2018.

Di Federico G, *L'identità Nazionale degli Stati Membri nel Diritto dell'Unione Europea. Natura e Portata dell'art. 4, par. 2, TUE* (Editoriale Scientifica 2017).

Eckes C, 'The Legal Framework of the European Union's Counter-Terrorist Policies: Full of Good Intentions?', in C Eckes, T Konstadinides (eds), *Crime within the Area of Freedom, Security and Justice: A European Public Order* (Cambridge University Press 2011) 127.

Gestri M, 'La clausola di solidarietà europea in caso di attacchi terroristici e calamità (art. 222 TFUE)', Studi in onore di Luigi Costato (Jovane 2014) 537.

Kaunert C, Léonard S, 'The European Union's response to the CBRN terrorist threat: A multiple streams approach' (2019) 65(3) Politique européenne 148.

Keohane D, *The EU and Counter-Terrorism* (CER 2005).

Maliszewska-Nienartowicz J, 'A New Chapter in the EU Counterterrorism Policy? The Main Changes Introduced by the Directive 2017/541 on Combating Terrorism' (2017) 37 PolishYIL 185.

Malizia A, D'Arienzo M (eds), *Enhancing CBRNE Safety & Security: Proceedings of the SICC 2017 Conference: Science as the first countermeasure for CBRNE and Cyber threats* (Springer 2018).

Monar J, 'Keynote Article: 11 September and the Challenge of Global Terrorism to the EU as a Security Actor' (2002) 40(4) JComMarSt 11.

Murphy C, 'EU Counter-terrorism Law: What Kind of Exemplar of Transnational Law?' (2019) 21 CYELS 217.

Nexon E, Wachtel C, *EU preparedness against CBRN weapons*, European Parliament Study 2019.

O'Neill M, *The Evolving EU Counter-terrorism Legal Framework* (Routledge 2011).

Roffey R, 'The EU as an Actor in CBRNE Crisis: A General Picture', in D O'Mathúna, I de Miguel Beriain (eds), *Ethics and Law for Chemical, Biological, Radiological, Nuclear & Explosive Crises* (Springer 2019).

Sabol J, Šesták B, Polívka L, Mroz K, 'Current Activities of the European Union in Fighting CBRN Terrorism Worldwide', in S Apikyan, D Diamond (eds), *Nuclear Threats and Security Challenges* (Springer 2015) 157.

Spence D (ed), *The European Union and Terrorism* (John Harper 2007).

Zwolski K, 'Unrecognized and Unwelcome? The Role of the EU in Preventing the Proliferation of CBRN Weapons, Materials and Knowledge' (2011) 12(4) Perspectives on European Politics and Society 477.

CHAPTER 11

International Obligations to Prevent CBRN Industrial and Nuclear Accidents

Annalisa Creta

1 Introduction

The set of rules establishing the duty to prevent CBRN events interconnects with those obligations setting standards aimed at preventing industrial and nuclear accidents, in particular, when those events release into the environment hazardous chemical, biological, radiological or nuclear substances, originating from out of date or poorly maintained technological or industrial conditions, dangerous procedures, infrastructure failures, specific human activities, or natural events, with serious adverse effects on human beings and the environment.[1] Examples of CBRN events in this regard can result from industrial accidents involving fires or explosions; chemical spills at a chemical plant or storage facility; an accident at a nuclear power plant; accidents during transport of CBRN agents for industrial purposes; or natural disasters, such as an earthquake, tsunami or floods, leading to damage of an industrial plant or storage facility.[2] In many countries, industrial hazards are further amplified by ageing or abandoned installations and by 'insufficient institutional and legal capacities to deal with technological risk reduction'.[3] The toxic gas release in Bophal, India in 1984; the disaster at the Chernobyl nuclear power plant in Ukraine in 1986; the Buncefield fire in the United Kingdom in 2005; the Deepwater Horizon oil spill in the Gulf of Mexico in 2010; the 2015 Bento Rodriguez and the 2019 Brumadinho dam disasters in Brazil; the liquified petroleum gas accident in Ghana in 2017; the chemical explosion at the Beirut port in August 2020, constitute only the most famous accidents that have caused casualties, injuries, major environmental pollution and economic

1 UNDRR, 'Global Assessment Report on Disaster Risk Reduction' (UNDRR 2019) 119 (GAR 2019).

2 UNGA, 'Report of the open-ended intergovernmental expert working group on indicators and terminology relating to disaster risk reduction' (1 December 2016) UN Doc. A/71/644 (DRR updated terminology) 21. The Recommendations were endorsed by UNGA Res 71/276 (2 February 2017) UN Doc A/RES/71/276.

3 UNDRR (n 1) 119.

© ANNALISA CRETA, 2022 | DOI:10.1163/9789004507999_012

losses. Serious technological accidents have also been caused by natural events, such as landslides, hurricanes, high winds, tsunamis, lightning, cold/hot temperature, floods, heavy rains etc, of which an illustrative example is the complex disaster that struck East Japan in 2011, involving the Fukushima Daiichi nuclear power plant.

What is the normative framework for preventing such serious accidents? What is the content of such obligations? This contribution constitutes a 'zoom in' on this precise category of CBRN-induced disasters of non-malicious origin. After an overview of legal instruments focused on preventing such situations, the role of international organisations in this endeavour will also be scoped out. Some emerging trends and challenges will be identified.

2 Definition of the Problem

2.1 *Terminological Clarifications*

The present analysis focuses *rationae materiae* on the prevention of CBRN industrial and nuclear accidents.

The concept of prevention refers to 'activities and measures to avoid existing and new disaster risks'.[4] As specified by the Open-ended intergovernmental Expert Working Group on indicators and terminology relating to disaster risk reduction, '[w]hile certain disaster risks cannot be eliminated, prevention aims at reducing vulnerability and exposure in such contexts where, as a result, the risk of disaster is removed.'[5]

A legal definition of what an 'industrial accident' is, can be found in Article 1 (a) (i) and (ii) of the 1992 Convention on the Transboundary Effects of Industrial Accidents,[6] which specifies that:

> 'Industrial accident' means an event resulting from an uncontrolled development in the course of any activity involving hazardous substances either: (i) In an installation, for example during manufacture, use, storage, handling, or disposal; or (ii) During transportation in so far as it is covered by paragraph 2 (d) of Article 2.

4 DRR updated terminology (n 2), 21. For a thorough analysis of the definition of prevention and of the duty to prevent emergency situations in international law refer to ch 3 by Venier.

5 Ibid.

6 Convention on the Transboundary Effects of Industrial Accidents (1992). (TEIA Convention). *Infra.*

Several soft law instruments contain further clarifications on the meaning of term as it relates to the material scope of the present analysis. The 2003 OECD Guiding Principles on Chemical Accidents Preparedness, Prevention and Response specify that 'chemical accident' means 'any unplanned event involving hazardous substances that causes or is liable to cause harm to health, the environment or property, such as loss of containment of hazardous substances, explosions, and fires'.[7]

A descriptive definition of 'nuclear accident' is contained in the 2018 IAEA Safety Glossary, which considers a 'nuclear accident' as:

> [a]ny accident involving facilities or activities from which a release of radioactive material occurs or is likely to occur and which has resulted or may result in an international significant transboundary release that could be of radiological safety significance for another State.[8]

An explanation of what a 'technological hazard' is, is given by the open-ended intergovernmental expert working group on indicators and terminology relating to disaster risk reduction.[9] This umbrella definition encompasses both chemical, industrial, nuclear/radiological accidents:

> Technological hazards originate from technological or industrial conditions, dangerous procedures, infrastructure failures or specific human activities. Examples include industrial pollution,[10] nuclear radiation, toxic wastes, dam failures, transport accidents, factory explosions, fires and chemical spills. Technological hazards also may arise directly as a result of the impacts of a natural hazard event.

---

7 OECD, 'Guiding Principles on Chemical Accidents Preparedness, Prevention and Response' (2003), Annex I. (OECD Guiding Principles). Annex I of the TEIA Convention contains a list of hazardous substances and their threshold quantities.

8 IAEA, 'IAEA Safety Glossary: 2018 Edition', (IAEA, 2019), 12. The document also specifies that such definition is derived from the statement of the scope of application in Article 1 of the Convention on Early Notification of a Nuclear Accident. This Convention has a limited scope of application, and 'it is unreasonable to consider a nuclear accident to be only an accident that results or may result in an international significant transboundary release.' Ibid.

9 DRR updated terminology (n 2) 19.

10 As per the scope of this and the ensuing chapters dealing with 'industrial accidents', industrial pollution is relevant for the purposes of our analysis if strictly linked to an event falling within the definition of 'industrial accident' and therefore clustered as a 'sudden-onset' event. 'Slow-onset' events fall outside the scope of this contribution. See also on this aspect, ch 27 by Sommario and ch 30 by Corcione.

Hence, when referring to industrial accidents in this chapter, we will discuss events originating from the above technological hazards: industrial, chemical, nuclear/radiological. Incidents originating from biological hazards are not dealt with here as they do not fall within the above definitions.[11]

3 Prevention of Industrial and Nuclear Accidents

This section focuses on the analysis of the content of the obligations to prevent industrial and nuclear accidents contained in specific normative instruments by providing an overview of the relevant prevention provisions through a three-pronged approach: instruments dealing in a direct way with industrial accidents; instruments focusing on specific hazardous substances; and instruments specifically dealing with nuclear accidents. Furthermore, the section will zoom in on bilateral, subregional and regional treaties.[12]

3.1 *Instruments Directly Relating to the Prevention of Industrial Accidents*

Only two international conventions focus specifically on industrial accidents: the Convention on the Transboundary Effects of Industrial Accidents[13] of 1992 and the Prevention of Major Industrial Accidents Convention (No. 174) of 1993.[14]

The scope of the TEIA Convention is, *inter alia*, to prevent accidents involving hazardous activities (including the production, use, storage, management or disposal of hazardous substances) that may have transboundary effects.[15]

11 Indeed, 'biological hazards are of organic origin or conveyed by biological vectors, including pathogenic microorganisms, toxins and bioactive substances. Examples are bacteria, viruses or parasites, as well as venomous wildlife and insects, poisonous plants and mosquitoes carrying disease-causing agents.' DRR updated terminology (n 2) 19. On this see, *inter alia*, ch 30 by Corcione.

12 The normative work carried out at the EU level is examined in ch 14 by Ferri and 15 by Balboni.

13 TEIA Convention (n 6). The Convention has been in force since the year 2000 and, at the time of writing, the instrument has 41 ratifications. Its geographical scope of application, as one can discern from its parties encompasses an area that stretches from Canada and the United States of America in the West to the Russian Federation and Central Asia in the East.

14 Prevention of Major Industrial Accidents Convention (No. 174) (1993) (Convention No. 174).

15 As per its art 2, the Convention does not apply to nuclear accidents or radiological emergencies; accidents at military installations; dam failures, with the exception of the effects of industrial accidents caused by such failures; land-based transport accidents, except for

Article 3 indicates that, to implement the Convention, the parties shall take appropriate legislative, regulatory, administrative and financial measures for, *inter alia*, the prevention of industrial accidents.

The Convention is currently the only instrument within the United Nations system to set out industrial safety requirements and to regulate relations between States to prevent industrial accidents of a transboundary nature by identifying potentially hazardous activities; requiring targeted preventive, preparedness and response measures;[16] and providing a governance mechanism for regional cooperation[17] to address transboundary disaster risk reduction.

Provisions containing preventive obligations require parties to focus on how to anticipate the risk of industrial accidents and regulate such risks. Article 6 refers to the adoption of 'appropriate measures for the prevention of industrial accidents, including measures to induce action by operators to reduce the risk of industrial accidents.' Annex IV contains a list of 'effective measures', that, *inter alia*, encompass: adoption of a legislative and regulatory framework for the prevention of accidents; collection of relevant data and risk analysis; development of risk reduction measures; application of the most appropriate technology; appropriate education and training of all those engaged in hazardous activities on-site; and monitoring and auditing of hazardous activities and inspections.

A key step in preventing an industrial accident consists in the identification of hazardous activities within the territory of a State Party. Annex I specifies the criteria for such identification. Articles 4 and 9 impose the duty to make information on hazardous activities available to the public and other potentially affected countries. Inter-State cooperation is necessary to reduce the transboundary impact of an industrial accident in case of occurrence.

Article 6 also requires that operators of any hazardous activity carry out an analysis and evaluation of the activity based on benchmarks detailed in Annex V. The hazard analysis includes a study of the technical specifications of the installation and its production processes; the identification of the

emergency response to such accidents, and transportation on the site of the hazardous activity; accidental release of genetically modified organisms; accidents caused by activities in the marine environment, including seabed exploration or exploitation; and spills of oil or other harmful substances at sea.

16 See ch 12 by Domaine and 13 by Bakker.

17 This is the Conference of the Parties (CoP) that has, *inter alia*, the task of reviewing the implementation of the Convention and advising countries on issues concerning prevention, preparedness and response to industrial accidents with transboundary consequences. The CoP is assisted by two working groups, respectively on implementation and on development. *Infra*.

potential hazards; and an assessment of the probability of those identified hazards occurring, based on lessons learned from previous experiences of accidents at similar industrial installations.

Several guidelines have been also produced under the auspices of the Convention for assisting States Parties in meeting their prevention obligations. These contribute to clarifying the content of such prevention obligations.[18]

The Prevention of Major Industrial Accidents Convention (No. 174) and its accompanying Prevention of Major Industrial Accidents Recommendation (No. 181)[19] – adopted within the framework of the ILO – provide for precautionary measures to avoid[20] or minimise the consequences of industrial disasters due to chemicals and other hazardous substances. Overall, the legal instrument provides for the development of a 'coherent national policy concerning the protection of workers, the public and the environment'[21] and measures involving central and local government; employers and workers; and bodies, such as the police, fire and medical authorities, concerned with emergency planning. Recommendation No. 181 supplements the provisions of the Convention, including the international exchange of information, urging multinational enterprises to develop common prevention measures for all their undertakings, and calling for the establishment of compensation schemes for workers harmed by industrial accidents. It also provides guidance on the implementation of national policies on major industrial accidents.[22]

The Convention establishes the obligation for the national competent authority to create a 'system for the identification of major hazard installations', following consultations with the most representative organisations of

18 UNECE, 'Amending the Guidelines to facilitate the identification of hazardous activities for the purposes of the Convention', ECE/CP.TEIA/38/Add.1, Decision 2018/1, <https://unece.org/DAM/env/documents/2019/TEIA/ENG_Guidelines_to_facilitate_the_identification_of_hazardous_activities_for_the_purposes_of_the_UNECE_Industrial_Accidents_Convention__Location_Criteria_.pdf>; 'Safety guidelines and good practices for Tailings Management Facilities', ECE/CP.TEIA/26, <https://unece.org/DAM/env/documents/2014/TEIA/Publications/1326665_ECE_TMF_Publication.pdf>; 'Safety Guidelines and Good Practices for Pipelines', ECE/CP.TEIA/27, <https://unece.org/fileadmin/DAM/env/documents/2015/TEIA/publications/Pipelines-Layout-WEB.pdf>; 'Checklist System for Safety Reports', 2012, <https://unece.org/fileadmin/DAM/env/teia/doc/Annex%201%20Checklist%20System%20for%20Safety%20Reports%20in%20English.pdf>. All links were last accessed on 30 May 2021.

19 Prevention of Major Industrial Accidents Recommendation (No. 181) (1993).

20 Convention No. 174 (n 14) art 1.

21 Ibid art 4.

22 An ILO Code of Practice – Major Industrial Accidents was adopted in 1991, prior to Convention No. 174, and aims at providing guidance for setting up an administrative, legal and technical system for the control of major hazard installations.

employers and workers and other interested parties who may be affected.[23] In respect of the major hazard installations identified, Article 9 requires employers to establish and maintain a system of major hazard control, requiring a number of preventive actions. A comprehensive siting policy 'arranging for the appropriate separation of proposed major hazard installations from working and residential areas and public facilities, and appropriate measures for existing installations' shall also be adopted by national competent authorities. Among the preventive measures, the Convention also establishes the obligation to provide appropriate education and training of all persons engaged in hazardous on-site activities and of those involved in the related inspection, investigation and assessment activities.[24]

3.2 *Instruments Focusing on Specific Hazardous Substances*

The ILO Chemicals Convention No. 170[25] and Chemicals Recommendation No. 177[26] address hazards relating to chemicals. They are both general in scope and relate to all such hazards. The Convention provides for a comprehensive national framework for the safe use of chemicals at work, including the formulation, implementation and periodic review of a coherent national policy. It does not prohibit the use of certain substances but prioritises prevention and only allows protective measures as a last resort if risks cannot be prevented, eliminated or minimised. Article 4 obliges ratifying States, in close consultation with the most representative organisations of employers and workers, to formulate, implement and periodically review a coherent policy on safety in the use of chemicals at work. The instrument also establishes detailed prevention-related responsibilities for employers, including to assess chemical hazards at worksites and adopt measures to limit the exposure of workers to hazardous chemicals; ensure an environmentally sound disposal of chemical waste; and constantly inform and train workers on chemical risks in the workplace.[27]

The Recommendation concerning Chemical Accident Prevention, Preparedness and Response[28] adopted by the OECD Council on 15 January 2004, calls for the establishment or strengthening by States of national programmes

23 Convention No. 174, (n 14), art 5 (1). The concept of major hazard refers to an industrial activity requiring controls over and above those applied in normal factory operations, for protecting both workers and the population living and working in the surrounding areas.

24 Ibid, art 17–20.

25 Chemicals Convention, (No. 170), (1990).

26 Chemicals Recommendation (No. 177), (1990).

27 Convention No. 170 (n 25), art. 6–13.

28 OECD, 'Recommendation of the Council concerning Chemical Accident Prevention, Preparedness and Response', OECD/LEGAL/0319.

for the prevention of, preparedness for, and response to accidents involving hazardous substances and to take into account the OECD Guiding Principles[29] and the OECD Guidance on Safety Performance Indicators.[30] The OECD Guiding Principles constitute a very detailed guidance tool on how to implement in practice the obligation to prevent chemical accidents, translating into concrete measures the responsibilities of several actors in each and every phase of an enterprise: from design and construction, through operation and maintenance, to decommissioning, closure and/or demolition. The Part on prevention is the longest of the Guiding Principles: it spells out, in Chapter 1, some general principles, stressing that prevention is the concern of a wide range of different parties. Chapters 2–4 give more specific information on the roles and responsibilities of industry, public authorities, and the public and other stakeholders, respectively. The OECD Guidance on Safety Performance Indicators is a companion to the Guiding Principles, assisting stakeholders in establishing programmes for assessing their own performance related to the prevention of, preparedness for, and response to chemical accidents.

It is also necessary to briefly mention here three international treaties concluded under the auspices of UNEP that deal with the production and use of certain hazardous chemicals, their trade, sharing of information and responsibilities; and the management and disposal of those substances when they become waste. The Basel Convention on the Control of Transboundary Movement of Hazardous Wastes and their Disposal (1989),[31] the Rotterdam Convention on the Prior Informed Consent Procedure for Certain Hazardous Chemicals and Pesticides in International Trade (1998),[32] and the Stockholm Convention on Persistent Organic Pollutants (2001)[33] are three multilateral environmental agreements with the common objective of protecting human health and the environment from hazardous chemicals and waste. The prescriptions contained in the above instruments constitute *per se* additional measures to prevent industrial accidents, since they focus on regulating aspects related to specific hazardous substances that could potentially contribute to triggering such accidents.

29 OECD Guiding Principles (n 7).

30 OECD, 'Guidance on Safety Performance Indicators', (2003).

31 Basel Convention on the Control of Transboundary Movement of Hazardous Wastes and their Disposal (1989).

32 Rotterdam Convention on Prior Informed Consent Procedure for Certain Hazardous Chemicals and Pesticides in International Trade (1998).

33 Stockholm Convention on Persistent Organic Pollutants (2001).

3.3 *The Obligation to Prevent Nuclear Accidents in International Law: Nuclear Safety*

The 1986 Chernobyl nuclear accident was the catalyst for the development of international nuclear law and the conclusion of binding instruments increasingly focusing on nuclear safety and emergency preparedness and response. International law regulates the issue of nuclear accidents through a three-pronged perspective: nuclear safety and security; emergency preparedness and response; and liability for nuclear damage.[34] Our analysis will only focus on the first perspective and solely on those nuclear safety norms aimed at preventing nuclear accidents of a non-malicious origin.[35] Nuclear safety relates to all those measures aimed at preventing an accident with radiological consequences and at mitigating such consequences should they occur.[36] In this endeavour, two conventions focusing on the prevention of nuclear accidents are in force: the 1994 Convention on Nuclear Safety and the 1997 Joint Convention on the Safety of Spent Fuel management and on the Safety of Radioactive Waste Management.[37]

One of the objectives of the Convention on Nuclear Safety is 'to prevent accidents with radiological consequences and to mitigate such consequences should they occur'.[38] Its scope encompasses the safety of 'nuclear installations' defined as any land-based civil nuclear power plant under a contracting party's jurisdiction, including such storage, handling and treatment facilities for radioactive materials as are on the same site and are directly related to the operation of the nuclear power plant.[39]

The core substantive prevention obligations are contained in Articles 4 to 19 and encompass the adoption and implementation of a legislative and

---

34 A Gioia, 'Nuclear Accidents and International Law', in A de Guttry, M Gestri and G Venturini (eds), *International Disaster Response Law* (Springer 2012), 86.

35 Nuclear security legal instruments are excluded from the analysis since they are the focus of other chapters in this volume.

36 Convention on Nuclear Safety (1994), *Preamble.*

37 Joint Convention on the Safety of Spent Fuel management and on the Safety of Radioactive Waste Management (1997), (Joint Convention).

38 Convention on Nuclear Safety, (n 36) art 1.

39 Ibid, art 2 i). That of nuclear installations is a narrow definition. A nuclear plant ceases to be so – thus falling outside the scope of the Convention – when 'all nuclear fuel elements have been removed permanently from the reactor core and have been stored safely in accordance with approved procedures, and a decommissioning programme has been agreed to by the regulatory body.' Ibid.

regulatory framework;[40] the designation of a regulatory body;[41] technical safety obligations related to the siting,[42] design, construction[43] and operation[44] of nuclear installations; the availability of adequate financial and human resources; and the assessment and verification of safety, quality assurance and emergency preparedness.[45] Under Article 9, parties have, moreover, the obligation to ensure that 'prime responsibility for the safety of a nuclear installation rests with the holder of the relevant license' and to 'take appropriate steps to ensure that each license holder meets its responsibility'.

The focus of the Joint Convention is on safety in respect of two separate but interconnected matters: spent fuel management – eg all activities that relate to the handling or storage of spent fuel, excluding off-site transportation – and radioactive waste management, which implies all activities, including decommissioning activities, that relate to the handling, pre-treatment, treatment, conditioning, storage, or disposal of radioactive waste, excluding off-site transportation.[46] The instrument contains a set of substantive obligations to prevent accidents with radiological consequences during any stage of spent fuel or radioactive waste management that reproduces the scheme already codified in the Nuclear Safety Convention and encompasses, in Chapter 4, the adoption and implementation of a legislative and regulatory framework; a regulatory body; responsibilities of the licence holder; requirements related

40 Ibid, art 7. The legislative and regulatory framework shall provide for the establishment of applicable national safety requirements and regulations; a system of licensing with regard to nuclear installations and the prohibition of the operation of a nuclear installation without a licence; a system of regulatory inspection and assessment of nuclear installations to ascertain compliance with applicable regulations and the terms of licences; the enforcement of applicable regulations and of the terms of licences, including suspension, modification or revocation.

41 Ibid, art 8. The regulatory body should be separate from any other body or organisation 'concerned with the promotion or utilization of nuclear energy'.

42 Ibid, art 17. Arts 17–19 establish specific obligations relating to the safety of installations covering all the steps to undertake during the entire cycle of the installation of a nuclear plant (from the decision on the site to its full operativity). Of particular relevance is the obligation to consult neighbouring States Parties in case they are affected by the installation and to provide the necessary information to allow them to evaluate the likely safety impact of the site on their own territory (art 17 (iii)).

43 Ibid, art 18.

44 Ibid, art 19.

45 Ibid, arts 10 and 16.

46 Joint Convention (n 37), art 2 i) and o). Art 3 clarifies that the scope of the convention is on spent fuel resulting from the operation of civilian nuclear reactors and radioactive waste deriving from civilian applications.

to human and financial resources; quality assurance; and operational radiation protection. Chapters 2 and 3 establish parallel sets of specific measures governing the safety of spent fuel management and the safety of radioactive waste management that contemplate specific obligations related to the siting, design and construction, and operation of facilities. Article 27 contains a provision related to transboundary movements and the obligation to take appropriate steps to ensure that such movements are undertaken in compliance with the provisions of the Convention and other relevant international law norms.

Both conventions have a soft law foundation. Their main feature is that of being 'incentive conventions'[47] that establish general nuclear safety requirements in conjunction with a non-coercive procedural mechanism – in peer review format – to ensure the realisation of basic conventional safety objectives. In this regard, soft law instruments play a key role in detailing the content of such objectives and the measures to adopt and implement to achieve them. The codes of conduct, recommendations and guidelines drawn up by expert groups of international nuclear organisations, particularly the IAEA,[48] Euratom and the NEA, and subsequently approved by the governing bodies of those organisations, provide the supplementary sources that give content to prevention obligations and contribute to implementation of national regulations by ensuring a certain level of standardisation.[49]

3.4 *Regional, Sub-regional and Bilateral Instruments*

Except for the European Union, which has adopted a series of directives and regulations relevant to the prevention of industrial accidents,[50] and the UNECE that has hosted the negotiations of the TEIA Convention, only in a very few other instances have regional organisations specifically addressed the issue. The OSCE and the Council of Europe have addressed industrial accidents but only in general terms and not as part of standard-setting efforts in this area.

---

47 A Stanič, 'EU Law on Nuclear Safety', Journal of Energy & Natural Resources Law, 2010, 28(1), 148. See, in this regard, the Preamble to the CNS (viii) which states that the instrument 'entails a commitment to the application of fundamental safety principles for nuclear installations rather than of detailed safety standards and that there are internationally formulated safety guidelines which are updated from time to time and so can provide guidance[...]'. The Joint Convention is more specific in this regard and its Preamble at (xiv) even lists some soft law standards.

48 A full account of those standards can be found at: <https://www.iaea.org/resources/safety-standards/>.

49 V Lamm, 'Reflections on the development of international nuclear law', NLB, No. 99 Vol. 2017/1, (OECD 2017), 31–44.

50 *Infra*, ch 14 by Ferri.

Under the aegis of the OSCE, in 1989, at the meeting on the Protection of the Environment of the (then) CSCE in Sofia, Member States recognised the importance of establishing regional or sub regional mechanisms for response, assistance, and exchange of information in environmental emergencies, with a predominant focus on industrial accidents. Participating States also stressed the need to prevent and control the transboundary effects of industrial accidents and recommended 'consultation and exchange of information on the prevention and control of industrial accidents and their transboundary effects'.[51] In the OSCE Ministerial Declaration on the 20th Anniversary of the Disaster at the Chernobyl Nuclear Power Plant, Participating States stressed 'how important it is for the international community to develop and apply commonly agreed policies and strategies to ensure that appropriate arrangements are in place for the prevention of, and response to, technological accidents and their consequences for human beings and the environment'.[52]

Within the Council of Europe, in 1987, the Committee of Ministers adopted a resolution for setting up a co-operation group for the prevention of, protection against, and organisation of relief in major natural and technological disasters, with the objective to make a multidisciplinary study on cooperation methods, *inter alia*, on prevention of technological disasters.[53]

As for other regional organisations, aspects related to the prevention of industrial accidents have been dealt with under the larger umbrella of disaster risk reduction.[54]

---

51 CSCE, 'Report on Conclusions and Recommendations of the Meeting on the Protection of the Environment of the Conference on Security and Co-operation in Europe', (1990). Part I of the report includes recommendations on the prevention and control of the transboundary effects of industrial accidents.

52 OSCE, 'Ministerial Declaration on the 20th Anniversary of the Disaster at the Chernobyl Nuclear Power Plant (MC DOC/3/05)', (2005).

53 Council of Europe, 'Resolution (87)2 Setting up a co-operation group for the prevention of, protection against, and organization of relief in major natural and technological disasters, adopted by the Committee of Ministers on 20 March 1987', (1987). This led to the creation of the EUR-OPA Major Hazards Agreement, a platform for cooperation in the field of major natural and technological disasters between Europe and the South of the Mediterranean. The agreement is open and now includes 24 Member States of the Council of Europe, Lebanon and Morocco.

54 See ch 3 by Venier. In this regard, see as examples: ASEAN, Agreement on Disaster Management and Emergency Response, (2005); African Union, 'Decision of the African Union Executive Council at its 30th Ordinary Session, January 2017 [EX.CL/Dec.943 (XXX)], endorsing the Programme of Action for the Implementation of the Sendai Framework for Disaster Risk Reduction 2015–2030 in Africa', (2017); African Union/NEPAD, 'Africa Regional Strategy for Disaster Risk Reduction', (2004).

At the bilateral and sub-regional level, the obligation to prevent industrial accidents is embedded in treaties more generally focusing on inter-State cooperation in the field of disaster prevention, preparedness and response. Indeed, obligations related to the prevention of industrial accidents contained therein focus on cooperation among the contracting parties in several areas that encompass the exchange of information on emergency management and transfer of technology in relation to, *inter alia*, effective disaster prevention; lessons learned, including from technology-related emergencies; national laws and regulations in this field; the dangers and consequences of disasters and serious accidents that could spread to the territory of the other contracting States; and related measuring data. Such collaboration also focuses on the implementation of common research and training programmes and the exchange of experts and specialists in the field of industrial and technological risk prevention and risk assessment.[55]

Among those treaties, those focusing on 'assistance' in case of natural and/or technological disasters usually include a specific provision entitled 'other forms of cooperation' in which the above elements are contained. Other conventions focus instead precisely on cooperation in the field of 'forecast and prevention of natural and technological disasters' and, besides listing the areas for such joint efforts, usually provide for the establishment of mechanisms for joint consultation in this regard.[56]

At the regional and sub-regional level, several treaties are in force that relate to cooperation, *inter alia*, in the field of accident prevention, which also includes industrial and nuclear accidents. Examples are the agreements concluded within the framework of the Community of Independent States on interaction in the field of prevention and reduction of consequences of

55 See eg the following instruments: Agreement between Estonia and Finland on cooperation in the field of emergency prevention, preparedness and response (34/2015); Bilateral rescue service cooperation agreement between Finland and Russia on cooperation for the prevention of accidents and their consequences (51 and 52/1996); Cooperation Agreement on The Forecast, Prevention and Mitigation of Natural and Technological Disasters Among the Government of the Republic of Austria, the Government of the Republic of Croatia, the Government of the Republic of Hungary, the Government of the Republic of Italy, the Government of the Republic of Poland, the Government of the Republic of Slovenia (1992).

56 See eg, France and Switzerland Agreement on mutual assistance in the event of disasters or serious accidents (1987); Netherlands and Belgium Convention on mutual assistance in combating disasters and accidents (1984); Convenzione tra la Repubblica Italiana e la Confederazione Svizzera sulla cooperazione nel campo della previsione e prevenzione dei rischi maggiori e dell'assistenza reciproca in caso di catastrofi naturali o dovute all'attività dell'uomo (1995).

natural and technological disasters and in the field of prevention and elimination of emergencies,[57] that establish an obligation to cooperate for the prevention of emergency situations. On the same lines are the NORDRED agreement between Denmark, Finland, Norway, Sweden and Iceland on cooperation across State frontiers to prevent or limit damage to persons or property or to the environment in the event of accidents[58] and the Agreement between the governments in the Barents Euro-Arctic region on cooperation within the field of emergency prevention, preparedness and response.[59] The Framework Convention on the Protection and Sustainable Development of the Carpathians, establishes that the parties 'shall promote cleaner production technologies, in order to adequately prevent, respond to and remediate industrial accidents and their consequences, as well as to preserve human health and mountain ecosystems'.[60]

3.5 *The Elements of the Duty to Prevent Industrial Accidents*

Legal provisions addressing the prevention of industrial and nuclear accidents mostly provide for courses of action.[61] The duty to prevent such accidents includes procedural and substantive obligations; internal and external, vertical and horizontal obligations; obligations triggering responsibilities for private actors and other stakeholders; and obligations related to environmental protection and to the responsibilities owed to future generations.

3.5.1 Substantive and Procedural Obligations

Procedural obligations include (a) information exchange and notification; (b) facilitation of public participation in decision-making; (c) access to

57 Intergovernmental agreement on interaction in the field of the prevention and reduction of consequences of natural and technological disasters (1993); Agreement on the control of transboundary movements of hazardous and other wastes (1996); Agreement on cooperation of the Member States of the Commonwealth of Independent States in the field of prevention and elimination of emergencies (2015).

58 NORDRED agreement between Denmark, Finland, Norway, Sweden and Iceland on cooperation across State frontiers to prevent or limit damage to persons or property or to the environment in the case of accidents, (1992).

59 Agreement between the governments in the Barents Euro-Arctic region on cooperation within the field of emergency prevention, preparedness and response, (2008). Parties to this treaty are Sweden, Russia, Norway and Finland.

60 Framework Convention on the Protection and Sustainable Development of the Carpathians (2003), art 10 (1).

61 In this regard see: L A Duvic-Paoli, 'Prevention in International Environmental Law and the Anticipation of Risk(s): A Multifaceted Norm' in M Ambrus, R Rayfuse, W Werner, *Imagining the Future: Conceptions of Risk and the Regulation of Uncertainty in International Law* (2017), 141–160.

remedies for harm; (d) appropriate education and training of all persons engaged in hazardous activities. Substantive duties encompass (a) to adopt and implement a legal framework; (b) to establish procedures for the identification of hazardous activities including a licensing or authorisation system; (c) the framing of a system of regulatory inspections, evaluation of risks, and systematic safety assessments; (d) the establishment of policies on the siting of hazardous activities; (e) obligations relating to transboundary harm.[62]

3.5.2 Internal and External, Vertical and Horizontal Obligations

A different type of obligations for States can also be identified. A first level of obligations relates to internal duties, focusing on how each State should act nationally to prevent industrial accidents, also in consideration of the effects on citizens and the need to ensure their rights are guaranteed (vertical obligations).[63] A second level entails external and horizontal duties, namely obligations of each State *vis-à-vis* another or other States. The latter include the obligations to set up an industrial accident notification system; to exchange relevant information to, *inter alia*, prevent accidents; to exchange relevant technology; and to identify points of contact for industrial accidents.

3.5.3 Responsibilities of the Private Sector and Other Relevant Actors

A series of responsibilities for preventing industrial and nuclear accidents fall upon actors other than the State, namely the 'industry', the 'workers' and the 'licence holders'.[64] In general, businesses have a duty to develop an operational safety culture in their facilities. It is the industry that materially has to identify and assess hazardous risks, and enact specific measures to prevent and mitigate their impact. Another obligation relates to the duty to communicate information about the risks created by their activities. Such duties are recurrent in all the relevant treaties. As to specific duties of workers, reference must be made to Convention Nos. 170 and 174[65] where specific duties to comply and cooperate fall upon workers' representatives and employees themselves. The conventions on nuclear-related aspects recognise the key role played by licence holders in nuclear safety and establish the obligation

62 Such classification reflects the main prescriptions indicated in the 2001 ILC Draft Articles on Prevention of Transboundary Harm. See its Article 3 and the related Commentary. ILC, 'Draft Articles on prevention of transboundary harm from hazardous activities' (2001) II(2) UNYBILC.

63 On this aspect, refer to ch 27 by Venier.

64 For a detailed account on these aspects, refer to ch 30 by Corcione.

65 Convention No. 170 (n 25), art 17; Convention No. 174 (n 14), art 20 and 21.

upon contracting parties to ensure that 'prime responsibility'[66] for the safety of a nuclear installation and of spent fuel or radioactive waste management rests with licence holders and to take appropriate steps for those actors to meet such responsibilities.[67] This entails that public authorities bear an 'overall responsibility' that is distinct from the 'prime responsibility' of operators and encompasses the obligation to establish a control framework consisting of binding requirements, that also include provisions for monitoring and enforcement,[68] and for ensuring that licence holders or the industry more generally meet their responsibility.

3.5.4 Obligations Relating to Environmental Protection and to Future Generations

The obligation to prevent industrial accidents is directly linked to environmental protection.[69] The TEIA Convention applies to the prevention of, preparedness for and response to industrial accidents capable of causing transboundary effects, where 'effects' are defined as, *inter alia*, adverse consequences caused by an industrial accident on flora and fauna, soil, water, air and landscape.[70] Its Preamble also makes reference to the special importance, in the interest of present and future generations, of protecting human beings and the environment against the effects of industrial accidents.[71] The Convention on Nuclear Safety recalls environmental protection and one of its objectives is 'to establish and maintain effective defences in nuclear installations against potential radiological hazards in order to protect individuals, society and the environment from harmful effects of ionizing radiation from

66 Convention on Nuclear Safety (n 36), art 9.

67 Of course, the ultimate responsibility rests with the Contracting Party which has jurisdiction over the nuclear plant or spent fuel or over the radioactive waste.

68 A control framework, as explained in the OECD Guiding Principles, should consist of 'binding requirements (set out in, for example, laws and regulations). In addition, public authorities should make sure that standards, codes and guidance are developed (such as codes of practice and quality assurance guides). These materials should be designed to enable each interested party to determine whether the appropriate safety objectives are being met.' Moreover, such legislative framework should also include provisions for monitoring the safety of hazardous installations during all phases of their life cycle (eg through review programmes or a system of inspections). OECD Guiding Principles (n 7), 67 and 73.

69 In this regard, also refer to HRC, 'Report of the Independent Expert on the issue of human rights obligations relating to the enjoyment of a safe, clean, healthy and sustainable environment, John H. Knox', A/HRC/25/53 (2013).

70 TEIA Convention, (n 6), art 2 (1) 1 c).

71 Ibid, art 3 (1) and Preamble.

such installations'.[72] Also, Article 1 of the Joint Convention lists one of the purposes of the treaty as ensuring 'that during all stages of spent fuel and radioactive waste management there are effective defenses against potential hazards so that individuals, society and the environment are protected from harmful effects of ionizing radiation, now and in the future'.[73]

3.6 *Monitoring and Enforcement Mechanisms*

International conventions focusing specifically on the prevention of industrial and nuclear accidents, namely the TEIA Convention, Convention No. 174, the Convention on Nuclear Safety and the Joint Convention, all provide for a system of review of States Parties' implementation of the obligations enshrined in the treaties.

In the case of the UNECE and IAEA instruments, the monitoring mechanism is founded on peer review. The TEIA Convention's CoP[74] is, *inter alia*, tasked to review the implementation of the treaty through a system of regular reporting by the parties. Each report is reviewed by the Working Group on Implementation, which is also tasked with engaging in an active dialogue with the parties when it 'becomes aware of possible difficulties in the implementation of the Convention, to understand the situation in these countries more accurately and to provide advice and make recommendations on the implementation of the Convention, share good practices and draw attention to existing guidance and tools'.[75] The Working Group is mandated also to 'monitor the progress of assistance activities within the programme of work under the Convention and, if no progress is made in the implementation of the Convention, request the countries benefitting from such activities to provide an explanation'.[76] Sensitive information provided in the national implementation reports is kept confidential and only shared between States Parties.

The Convention on Nuclear Safety and the Joint Convention[77] both establish a peer review system and review meetings to evaluate the extent of the implementation of treaty provisions, thus providing for a cooperative peer

72 Convention on Nuclear Safety (n 36), art 1 (ii).

73 Joint Convention (n 37), art 1.

74 Ibid, art 18.

75 UNECE, 'Report of the Conference of the Parties on its ninth meeting. Addendum Decisions and other outcomes adopted at the ninth meeting', *Terms of Reference of the Working Group on Implementation* ECE/CP.TEIA/32/Add.1, 19 April 2017, 10 para 4 (d).

76 Ibid, para 4 (i).

77 Convention on Nuclear Safety (n 36), artt. 20–28; Joint Convention (n 37) , arts 29–37.

review mechanism.[78] These two conventions are an example of multilateral treaties that have 'increasingly de-emphasised coercive application/enforcement measures for the sake of a facilitative, co-operative approach'.[79] This undoubtedly has positive effects on the process of deepening the substantial aspects related to the implementation of obligations of conduct, through interactive dialogue among relevant actors. However, it remains to be ascertained the extent to which such a process has implications on the effective national enactment of international prevention obligations. The monitoring of compliance with the provisions of Convention No. 174 is ensured by the system used for supervising the application of all International Labour Standards, based primarily on information provided by governments in their reports on the application of conventions they have ratified. Such reporting is required in accordance with Article 22 of the ILO Constitution and must include observations made by employers' and workers' organisations.[80] There is also a complaint procedure for governments and ILO delegates to examine allegations that the provisions of a ratified convention are not effectively being observed in any one of the Member countries, which may include the establishment of a Commission of Inquiry. If a State refuses to comply with recommendations made by a Commission of Inquiry, the Governing Body can take measures to secure compliance under Article 33 of the ILO Constitution.

These monitoring mechanisms have developed practices and procedures that have proved effective in scrutinising the extent to which States have met their obligations under the relevant treaties to which they are a party and in encouraging further implementation. The process of preparing national reports is not only an international obligation but also an opportunity for the reporting State to assess what it has achieved and what more it needs to do to prevent industrial and nuclear accidents. The procedure is not adversarial, and the aim is to engage in a constructive dialogue to assist the State in its efforts to implement the treaty as fully and effectively as possible.

---

78 For a comment on this mechanism, see: C Stoiber, 'International Convention on Nuclear Safety: National Reporting as the Key to Effective Implementation,' in N Horbach (ed), *Contemporary Developments in Nuclear energy law: Harmonizing Legislation in CEES/NIS*, (1999), 100.

79 G Handl, 'The IAEA Nuclear Safety Conventions: An Example of Successful "Treaty Management?"', NLB, No. 72, (OECD 2003), 10.

80 Reports are first examined in closed meetings by a Committee of Experts on the Application of Conventions and Recommendations (CEACR). Committee reports are then considered at the annual session of the International Labour Conference by a tripartite Conference Committee on the Application of Conventions and Recommendations.

The Working Group on implementation of the TEIA Convention, in its ninth report of November 2020, expressed overall satisfaction with the enactment at national level of provisions in the area of prevention of industrial accidents.[81] However, in recalling that the prevention is strongly linked with the identification and notification of hazardous activities, it encouraged all parties and committed countries to continue their efforts to improve preventive measures in a transboundary context by strengthening their risk assessment and prevention measures for industrial accidents triggered by natural disasters; by developing policies, strategies and measures for the prevention of accidents involving hazardous activities; and by developing and/or strengthening notification and consultation mechanisms.[82]

4 Building the Capacities to Prevent Accidents: The Role of IOs

International organisations provide guidance and tools to assist countries in meeting the obligations of the international instruments they have ratified. This is done through technical assistance and capacity building programmes; the adoption of soft law instruments, guidelines and codes of conduct; specific compliance review processes; systems of visits and onsite inspections; facilitating the identification and sharing of good practices and lessons learned by States; providing technological know-how; and establishing cooperation programmes.[83] Relevant agencies also gather in inter-agency coordination forums to collaboratively tackle issues related to industrial and chemical, radiological and nuclear accidents. An Inter-Agency Coordination Group on Industrial and Chemical Accidents was set up in 2013[84] and the Inter-Agency

81 UNECE, 'Ninth report on the implementation of the Convention (2016–2018) Report by the Working Group on Implementation', ECE/CP.TEIA/2020/5 25 September 2020, para 27. 31 In the ninth reporting period, 31 reports by parties and one committed country were examined.

82 UNECE, 'Updated draft decision on strengthening the implementation of the Convention Submitted by the Working Group on Implementation,' ECE/CP.TEIA/2020/L.2 20 November 2020, paras 7–12.

83 Inter-Agency Coordination Group for Industrial and Chemical Accidents, 'International efforts for industrial and chemical accidents prevention, preparedness and response', (2017) <https://circabc.europa.eu/d/d/workspace/SpacesStore/1a754cca-365d-4d43-ab47-f0d9de110d34/Inter-Agency%20Coodination%20Group%20-%20brochure.pdf>.

84 It is composed of the following entities: UNECE, ILO, UNDRR, UNEP, OPWC, OECD, WHO, JRC, EOCS, UNITAR.

Committee on Radiological and Nuclear Emergencies (IACRNE) was established in September 1986 in the aftermath of the Chernobyl accident.[85]

The Flexible Framework for Addressing Chemical Accident Prevention and Preparedness (CAPP) methodology, developed by UNEP, is a guidance tool for national governments – in particular emerging and developing economies – to strengthen their national policies and legislative frameworks, with the objective of preventing accidents or minimising their environmental, social and economic impacts through the development and implementation of an appropriate chemical accident prevention and preparedness programme.[86] A twin action at the local level is the Awareness and Preparedness for Emergencies at Local Level (APELL), a modular, flexible methodological international tool that UNEP has developed for preventing accidents and, in case of their occurrence, minimising their impacts.

The OECD's specific Programme on Chemical Accidents, managed by the Working Group on Chemical Accidents, has the twofold task to foster the sharing of experiences amongst governments and other stakeholders and to recommend policy options for enhancing the prevention of, preparedness for and response to chemical accidents.[87] Through this programme, the Working Group has also been focusing on issues such as Natech; changes in ownership of hazardous facilities; upgrading or decommissioning of ageing installations; and new approaches to inspections.

On nuclear safety, the OECD Nuclear Energy Agency (NEA) assists States in maintaining and further developing, through international cooperation, the scientific, technological and legal bases required for a safe, environmentally sound and economical use of nuclear energy for peaceful purposes. After the Fukushima Daiichi nuclear power plant accident, the Agency has also been

85 The IAEA provides the secretariat for the IACRNE which is composed also of the following other members: FAO, UNOCHA, WHO, WMO, the EC and the OECD-Nuclear Energy Agency (NEA).

86 UNEP, 'A Flexible Framework Initiative for Addressing Chemical Accident Prevention and Preparedness, An Implementation Support Package', (2012).

87 The issue of chemical accident prevention, preparedness and response took on a level of urgency and political importance with the massive accident in Bhopal, India. At the OECD Environment Committee that met at Ministerial Level in June 1985, the OECD Governments declared that 'they will ensure the existence of appropriate measures to control potentially hazardous installations, including measures to prevent accidents.' These discussions resulted in the creation of a chemical accidents programme, a forum for participating stakeholders to share experiences on accidents and to learn from each other's challenges and progress.

actively engaged in the identification of lessons learned and setting priorities for their implementation.[88]

UNECE carries out the secretariat functions for the TEIA Convention that brings countries together to standardise approaches to industrial accident prevention, response, and the minimisation of their possible effects. Within this framework, it facilitates the drafting and adoption of guidelines and other policy documents that provide guidance on the adoption and implementation of adequate measures compliant with the prescriptions of the Convention. Through the Cooperation and Assistance Programme established by the CoP in 2004, UNECE carries out capacity building programmes for countries experiencing difficulties in complying with the instrument's provisions,[89] and also for States wishing to join the Convention but facing difficulties in aligning their national legislation with its requirements.[90] Such activities are aimed at supporting targeted countries to improve their institutional structures, governance and coordination mechanisms, and to revise and further develop adequate legislative frameworks for industrial accident prevention, preparedness and response; as well as working with national authorities and operators to upgrade their knowledge and skills in this realm.

5 Challenges to Prevention. Some Concluding Remarks

Governments have the primary responsibility for preventing industrial and nuclear accidents, which entails, as has emerged from the above investigation, procedural and substantive duties, internal and external obligations, and an overall duty of prevention for the purposes of protecting the environment and future generations. It is through action at the national level that international obligations are transformed into meaningful measures. But challenges to prevention exist that undermine the legal framework and existing (and needed) capacities for a meaningful implementation of such normative provisions.

88 NEA, 'The Fukushima Daiichi Nuclear Power Plant Accident: OECD/NEA Nuclear Safety Response and Lessons Learnt', (2013); NEA/CNRA/R(2014)1, 'Working Group on Operating Experience [Wgoe] Report on Fukushima Daiichi NPP Precursor Events', (2014).

89 ECE/CP.TEIA/39, 'Implementation Guide for Central Asia on the UNECE Convention on the Transboundary Effects of Industrial Accidents', (2019).

90 ECE/CP.TEIA/2008/5, 'Strategic approach for the Assistance Programme, Note by the Bureau of the Conference of the Parties and the Working Group on Implementation', 2 September 2008.

5.1 *Normative Challenges*

The normative framework establishing the obligations to prevent industrial and nuclear accidents is scattered in a constellation of international conventions that, though focusing on different aspects of the issue at stake, follow the same coherent scheme based on a core set of underlying duties.

Soft law plays an important guidance role for the interpretation and implementation of those obligations. In some cases, soft law instruments are directly recalled as a reference in the text of binding treaties or are adopted in the aftermath of the entry into force of a treaty to provide guidance on its implementation, taking into account also technological developments. The approach of using non-binding instruments in this field has great advantages, in view of their flexibility and adaptation to new technological developments.

Though scattered in different hard and soft law instruments, existing norms provide for a comprehensive set of tools to prevent accidents. However, such a framework falls short when it is necessary to address and adapt quickly and comprehensively to new challenges. For example, 'disaster risk reduction frameworks have not yet really addressed the issue of technological risks in general and Natech in particular'.[91] While several international organisations[92] have launched initiatives to address Natech risk management, especially after Fukushima, data granularity as it relates to Natech accidents and deficiencies in existing safety legislation make it very difficult to measure progress in the adaptation of the obligation to prevent industrial accidents to such kinds of events.[93]

5.2 *Implementation Challenges*

Recent experience from major accidents has also shown that the existence of an adequate legislative framework is not sufficient for the prevention of accidents on its own but needs necessarily to be integrated with additional initiatives and a coherent system for learning from the past. This entails the continuous refinement and re-assessment of preventive measures to avoid complacency and to use lessons learned from accidents to reinforce such

91 E Krausmann, S Girgin, A Necci, 'Natural Hazard impacts on industry and critical infrastructure: Natech risk drivers and risk management performance indicators', International Journal of Disaster Risk Reduction, 40 (2019), 1.

92 Such as the OECD's Natech Project that culminated in a Natech addendum to the OECD Guiding Principles (n 7). Another example is represented by the work of the United Nations Office for Disaster Risk reduction that prepared the 'Words in Action Guidelines for National Disaster Risk Assessment and for Man-made/Technological Hazards'.

93 E Krausmann, S Girgin, A Necci, (n 91), *passim*.

measures.[94] This requires paying attention to aspects related to the management, operation, and control of hazardous installations, from their conception to their decommissioning/demolition. In order to do so, the prevention of accidents should not only be a legal obligation but also a political priority to be addressed in an integrated manner: at the community, municipal, regional and national levels and globally; as well as coordinating approaches across borders. Second, it is also to be recalled that assessing the risk of an industrial accident is at the very core of prevention. In this endeavour, a multidisciplinary and cross-sectoral approach must be adopted to assess the risk, since the risk of industrial accident can be highly variable and dependent on many influencing factors. The Sendai Framework[95] calls for this shift in methodology through its four priorities and systems-based approaches to risk management. The Sendai Framework constitutes a policy instrument that provides guidance for designing risk reduction systems[96] in a multi-hazard, multi-stakeholder and multidisciplinary way.

As recalled by the Director General of the Nuclear Energy Agency, 'ensuring safety is a process that evolves as we learn through research and the evaluation of operating experience and operating capacities'[97] as are and should be the measures conceived to prevent industrial accidents.

Bibliography

African Union/NEPAD, 'Africa Regional Strategy for Disaster Risk Reduction', (2004).

CSCE, 'Report on Conclusions and Recommendations of the Meeting on the Protection of the Environment of the Conference on Security and Co-operation in Europe', (1990).

Duvic-Paoli L A, 'Prevention in International Environmental Law and the Anticipation of Risk(s): A Multifaceted Norm' in Ambrus M, Rayfuse R, Werner W, *Imagining the Future: Conceptions of Risk and the Regulation of Uncertainty in International Law* (OUP 2017).

94 OECD, 'Towards an All-Hazards Approach to Emergency Preparedness and Response', NEA No. 7308, (OECD 2018).

95 Sendai Framework for Disaster Risk Reduction 2015–2030, (2015) UN Doc A/CONF.224/L.2., 14–20.

96 See, in this regard, M H Wood, L Fabbri, 'Challenges and opportunities for assessing global progress in reducing chemical accident risks', Progress in Disaster Science 4 (2019).

97 OECD, 'Five Years after the Fukushima Daiichi Accident: Nuclear Safety Improvements and Lessons Learnt', NEA No. 7284, (OECD 2016), 4.

ECE/CP.TEIA/39, 'Implementation Guide for Central Asia on the UNECE Convention on the Transboundary Effects of Industrial Accidents', (2019).

Gioia A, 'Nuclear Accidents and International Law', in de Guttry A, Gestri M and Venturini G (eds), *International Disaster Response Law* (Springer 2012).

Handl G, 'The IAEA Nuclear Safety Conventions: An Example of Successful "Treaty Management?"', NLB, No. 72, (OECD Paris 2003).

HRC, 'Report of the Independent Expert on the issue of human rights obligations relating to the enjoyment of a safe, clean, healthy and sustainable environment, John H. Knox', A/HRC/25/53, 30 December 2013 (2013).

IAEA, 'IAEA Safety Glossary: 2018 Edition', (IAEA Vienna 2019).

Krausmann E, Girgin S, Necci A, 'Natural Hazard impacts on industry and critical infrastructure: Natech risk drivers and risk management performance indicators', International Journal of Disaster Risk Reduction 40 (2019) 10.1016/j.ijdrr.2019.101163.

Lamm V, 'Reflections on the development of international nuclear law', NLB, No. 99 Vol. 2017/1, (OECD Paris 2017).

NEA, 'The Fukushima Daiichi Nuclear Power Plant Accident: OECD/NEA Nuclear Safety Response and Lessons Learnt', (OECD Paris 2013).

NEA/CNRA/R(2014)1, 'Working Group on Operating Experience Report on Fukushima Daiichi NPP Precursor Events', (OECD Paris 2014).

OECD, 'Guiding Principles on Chemical Accidents Preparedness, Prevention and Response', (OECD Paris 2003), Annex I.

OECD, 'Five Years after the Fukushima Daiichi Accident: Nuclear Safety Improvements and Lessons Learnt', NEA No. 7284, (OECD Paris 2016).

OECD, 'Towards an All-Hazards Approach to Emergency Preparedness and Response', NEA No. 7308, (OECD Paris 2018).

Stanič A, 'EU Law on Nuclear Safety', Journal of Energy & Natural Resources Law, Vol. 28, No. 1, 2010.

Stoiber C, 'International Convention on Nuclear Safety: National Reporting as the Key to Effective Implementation,' in Horbach N (ed), *Contemporary Developments in Nuclear energy law: Harmonizing Legislation in CEES/NIS*, (Kluwer Law International 1999).

UNDRR, 'Global Assessment Report on Disaster Risk Reduction', Geneva, (UNDRR, 2019).

UNECE, 'Checklist System for Safety Reports', (United Nations Geneva 2012).

UNECE, 'Report of the Conference of the Parties on its ninth meeting. Addendum Decisions and other outcomes adopted at the ninth meeting', *Terms of Reference of the Working Group on Implementation* ECE/CP.TEIA/32/Add.1, 19 April 2017.

UNECE, 'Ninth report on the implementation of the Convention (2016–2018) Report by the Working Group on Implementation', ECE/CP.TEIA/2020/5, 25 September 2020.

UNEP, 'A Flexible Framework Initiative for Addressing Chemical Accident Prevention and Preparedness, An Implementation Support Package', (2012).

UNGA 'Report of the open-ended intergovernmental expert working group on indicators and terminology relating to disaster risk reduction', UN Doc. A/71/644, 1 December 2016, (2016).

Wood M H, Fabbri L, 'Challenges and opportunities for assessing global progress in reducing chemical accident risks', Progress in Disaster Science 4 (2019). DOI:10.1016/j.pdisas.2019.100044.

CHAPTER 12

Preparedness Obligations Related to CBRN Industrial Accidents

Sophie Domaine

1 Introduction

No matter how stringent prevention measures are,[1] industrial accidents may occur; thus, the international community, the States and the population affected must be prepared to deal with their consequences. Indeed, industrial operations involve substances that do not usually represent a great threat to our health or our environment, but that are nevertheless potentially hazardous. Even the safest plant is never totally risk-free. Preparing for CBRN emergencies is an extremely complex undertaking, which involves a high number of governmental authorities and private actors, at the national, regional, and local level. Moreover, when an incident has potential transboundary impacts, it becomes a matter of international concern and, therefore, international measures – universal, regional, or bilateral – are required.[2]

This chapter will examine preparedness obligations specifically related to CBRN industrial accidents contained in international treaties, regional instruments, and bilateral agreements (second section).[3] When discussing preparedness obligations at universal level, the analysis will be twofold: first, obligations enshrined in multilateral treaties specifically dealing with industrial accidents; then, obligations included in international instruments concerning radionuclear hazards. A review of soft law instruments adopted by international organisations (IOs) relevant to the field will also be conducted (third section). Finally, an attempt to assess current developments in the implementation of preparedness measures for industrial accidents and to reflect on potential improvements will be made (fourth section).

1 See ch 11 by Creta.
2 IAEA, 'Handbook on Nuclear Law – Implementing Legislation' (IAEA 2010) 79.
3 Preparedness obligations for CBRN accidents under EU law will be covered in ch 14 by Ferri.

2 Preparedness Obligations in International Treaties, Regional Instruments, and Bilateral Agreements

Emergency preparedness is defined as '[t]he knowledge and capacities developed by governments, professional response and recovery organizations, communities and individuals to effectively anticipate, respond to, and recover from, the impacts of likely, imminent or current hazard events or conditions'.[4] An industrial accident, on the other hand, is 'an event resulting from an uncontrolled development in the course of any activity involving hazardous substances either [...] [i]n an installation [...] or [...] [d]uring transportation'.[5] As in the previous chapter, the industrial accidents examined will be sudden-onset-events originating from the following technological hazards: industrial, chemical, and radionuclear.

The adoption of multilateral treaties regarding preparedness and emergency assistance obligations was considered unattainable throughout the 1960s and 1970s.[6] But then the Chernobyl disaster occurred in 1986 and international agreements on emergency preparedness, whose approval had been discussed at length without result, were promptly adopted.[7] This section will review the preparedness obligations related to CBRN industrial accidents at different levels: universal, regional, and bilateral. The first subsection will analyse preparedness obligations contained in multilateral treaties which specifically deal with industrial accidents; then, international instruments concerning radionuclear hazards will be discussed.

2.1 *Instruments Directly Dealing with Industrial Accidents*

The most important agreement in the field is the Convention on the Transboundary Effects of Industrial Accidents (TEIA Convention).[8] Obligations regarding preparedness measures are set out in Article 8. The parties must take all appropriate measures to establish and maintain adequate emergency preparedness for industrial accidents and to mitigate transboundary effects of

4 UNISDR, 'UNISDIR Terminology on Disaster Risk Reduction' (May 2009), <https://www.undrr.org/publication/2009-unisdr-terminology-disaster-risk-reduction> (all links were last accessed on 30 May 2021). See ch 4 by De Guttry.

5 Convention on the Transboundary Effects of Industrial Accidents (1992) art 1.

6 J Rautenbach, W Tonhauser and A Wetherall, 'Overview of the International Legal Framework Governing the Safe and Peaceful Uses of Nuclear Energy – Some Practical Steps' in *International Nuclear Law in the Post-Chernobyl Period* (OECD/NEA 2006) 9.

7 S Kuş, 'International nuclear law in the 25 years between Chernobyl and Fukushima and beyond ...' (2011) 87(1) NLB 7, 9.

8 Convention on the Transboundary Effects of Industrial Accidents (1992).

such accidents. The contingency plans outlined by each party must be shared with all the others and reviewed regularly. The party of origin shall ensure the preparation and implementation of on-site contingency plans for hazardous activities, whereas, each State Party shall guarantee the preparation and implementation of off-site contingency plans, covering measures to be taken within its territory to prevent and minimise transboundary effects. In the case of several States being affected by a hazardous operation, parties are expected to make their plans mutually compatible and, where appropriate, even draw up joint off-site contingency plans to facilitate the adoption of adequate response measures.[9]

Emergency preparedness measures that Contracting States might adopt are included in Annex VII to the Convention. All contingency plans must include the actions necessary to localise emergencies and to prevent or minimise their transboundary effects. They shall also incorporate arrangements for warning people when they need to evacuate, and they should give on-site personnel and rescue forces details of technical and organisational procedures for responding in the event of an industrial accident.

Moreover, according to Article 9, the parties have to ensure that adequate information is given to the public in the areas capable of being affected by an industrial accident arising from a hazardous activity.[10] Each member of the Convention, through the channel deemed appropriate, must transmit to the population the elements contained in Annex VIII, namely, among others: the name of the company carrying out the hazardous activity; an explanation, in simple terms, of the hazardous activity, including the common names or the generic names or the general danger classification of the substances and preparations which are involved and their risks; general information resulting from an environmental impact assessment, if available; general information relating to the nature of an industrial accident that could possibly occur, including its potential effects on the population and the environment; and adequate information on how the affected population will be warned and kept informed in the event of an industrial accident. The public concerned – both in the State of origin and in the potentially affected State – must also be guaranteed an opportunity to participate in relevant procedures to express their views and concerns on preparedness measures. In accordance with each party's national legal system, natural or legal persons who are being adversely affected by the transboundary effects of an industrial accident in the territory of a party must have access to administrative and judicial proceedings, including the

9 Ibid art 8.1, 8.2 and 8.3.

10 Ibid Annex VIII 'Information to the public pursuant to Article 9'.

possibility of starting a legal action and of appealing a decision affecting their rights.[11]

The only other multilateral treaty focussing specifically on industrial accidents is the Prevention of Major Industrial Accidents Convention.[12] Even though its core focus is prevention, this Convention includes some provisions concerning preparedness. According to Article 9, the employer must establish and maintain a documented system of major hazard control, including the preparation of effective site emergency plans and procedures, with periodic testing and evaluation of their effectiveness resulting in relevant revisions. The employer shall also inform the authorities responsible for the preparation of off-site emergency plans about site emergency procedures and potential accidents originating from the installation.[13] In compliance with Part IV on 'off-site emergency preparedness', the competent authorities, taking into account the information provided by the employer, must ensure that emergency plans and procedures containing provisions for the protection of the public and the environment outside the site of each major hazard installation are established, updated and coordinated with the relevant actors.[14] In particular, said authorities have to ensure that information on safety measures and the correct behaviour to adopt in the event of a major accident is disseminated to members of the public without their having to request it; that warning is given as soon as possible in the event of an accident of this type; and that where a major accident could have transboundary effects, this information is provided to the States concerned, in order to guarantee cooperation and coordination.[15]

Besides these two specifically targeted conventions, international preparedness obligations related to CBRN industrial accidents at the universal level are to be found in the 2005 International Health Regulations (IHR).[16] The purpose and scope of the IHR are to prevent, protect against, control and provide a public health response to the international spread of diseases.[17] There is no explicit mention of emergency preparedness measures in relation to industrial accidents in the IHR; however, in the Preamble,[18] a reference to the resolution

---

11 Ibid art 9.3.

12 ILO Prevention of Major Industrial Accidents Convention (No. 174) (1993). It only has 18 ratifications. See more in ch 11 by Creta.

13 Ibid art 9(d).

14 Ibid art 15.

15 Ibid art 16.

16 International Health Regulations (2005). IHR are largely discussed in section 2.3 of this volume, which concerns epidemic outbreaks.

17 IHR art 2.

18 Ibid recital III.

adopted in 2002 by the World Health Assembly (WHA) is made, recalling the need to revise and update the IHR taking into account the global public health response to accidental dissemination of biological or chemical agents or radionuclear material.[19] Indeed, the release of this type of material following an industrial accident would constitute a threat to the integrity of public health systems. For these reasons, the WHA urges Member States to ensure that national disease-surveillance plans, complementary to global ones, are put in place and that collaboration and mutual support is guaranteed to enhance national capacity in the fields of epidemiology, laboratory diagnoses, toxicology, and case management. Hence, IHR articles concerning 'Information and public health response'[20] must now be read in light of the 2002 WHA resolution, implying that States – bearing in mind that CBRN incidents can affect global public health – must develop, strengthen and maintain the capacity to detect those events.

2.2 *Instruments Concerning Radionuclear Incidents*

Following the Chernobyl nuclear plant accident, two international conventions, based on existing non-legally binding guidelines, were adopted by the international community, under the auspices of the International Atomic Energy Agency (IAEA):[21] the Convention on Early Notification of a Nuclear Accident (Early Notification Convention) and the Convention on Assistance in the Case of a Nuclear Accident or Radiological Emergency (Assistance Convention).[22] With regard to preparedness, according to the Assistance Convention, States must notify the IAEA of the experts, equipment, and materials they can make available to provide assistance in the event of such an accident or emergency. The IAEA may also assist a State Party in the preparation

19 WHA, 'Resolution on global public health response to natural occurrence, accidental release or deliberate use of biological and chemical agents or radionuclear material that affect health' (18 May 2002) UN Doc A55/VR/9. No international treaty regarding biological industrial accidents is in force: these are hardly ever addressed as a separate issue but considered in the broader context of CBRN events. Moreover, they fall outside the definition of technological hazards leading to industrial accidents. See on this aspect ch 11 and ch 30 by Corcione.

20 IHR art 5, 6, 7 and 13.

21 Kuş (n 7) 9 citing IAEA, 'Guidelines for Mutual Emergency Assistance Arrangements in Connection with a Nuclear Accident or Radiological Emergency' (January 1984) INFCIRC/310; IAEA, 'Guidelines on Reportable Events, Integrated Planning and Information Exchange in Transboundary Release of Radioactive Materials' (January 1985) INFCIRC/321.

22 Convention on Early Notification of a Nuclear Accident (1986). Convention on Assistance in the Case of a Nuclear Accident or Radiological Emergency (1986). See ch 13 by Bakker and Montanaro for response to CBRN industrial accidents.

of emergency plans and appropriate legislation to deal with potential nuclear accidents; in the development of proper training programmes for personnel to deal with radiological emergencies; and in the promotion of suitable radiation monitoring programmes, procedures and standards.[23] Article 5(1)(g) of the Early Notification Convention requires parties to provide the States concerned and the IAEA with information related to the off-site protective measures taken or planned. As with the Assistance Convention, one of the most significant features of the Early Notification Convention is the role assigned to the IAEA.[24] Indeed, according to Article 8, the Agency is required, upon request, to assist a State without nuclear installations itself but bordering a State with an active nuclear programme – which is not party to the convention – to develop an appropriate radiation monitoring system.[25]

These two conventions represent the cornerstones of the international emergency preparedness (and response) framework applicable to radionuclear accidents;[26] still, their texts do not mention the notion of 'preparedness' directly. This was introduced in the Convention on Nuclear Safety (CNS),[27] adopted in 1994, which finally includes a provision on emergency preparedness. The general aim of the CNS is that Contracting Parties operating land-based civil nuclear power plants maintain a high level of safety by establishing, and subscribing to, fundamental safety principles. The parties' common interest in achieving higher levels of safety is developed and promoted through regular meetings. For this reason, an innovative and dynamic element was introduced: parties must submit reports on the implementation of their obligations for 'peer review' at meetings, that are normally held at IAEA headquarters in Vienna. The CNS specifically addresses emergency preparedness in Article 16 which requires the installation State to ensure that 'on-site and off-site emergency plans [...] are routinely tested for nuclear installations and cover the activities to be carried out in the event of an emergency'.[28] Each Contracting

23 Assistance Convention art 5(b) i, ii and iv.

24 A Gioia, 'Nuclear Accidents and International Law' in A de Guttry, M Gestri, G Venturini (eds), *International Disaster Response Law* (Springer 2012) 97.

25 Early Notification Convention art 8.

26 G Handl, 'Nuclear Off-site Emergency Preparedness and Response: Some International Legal Aspects' in JL Black-Branch, D Fleck (eds), *Nuclear Non-Proliferation in International Law – Volume III, Legal Aspects of the Use of Nuclear Energy for Peaceful Purposes* (Springer 2016) 317.

27 Convention on Nuclear Safety (1994). The CNS has currently 90 Contracting Parties, including all States with operating nuclear power plants. See O Jankowitsch-Prevor, 'The Convention on Nuclear Safety' in *International Nuclear Law in the Post-Chernobyl Period* (OECD/NEA 2006) 155ff.

28 CNS art 16.1.

Party is also obliged to 'take the appropriate steps to ensure that, insofar as they are likely to be affected by a radiological emergency, its own population and the competent authorities of the States in the vicinity of the nuclear installation are provided with appropriate information for emergency planning and response'.[29] Likewise, Contracting Parties which do not have a nuclear plant on their territory but are likely to be affected in the event of a radiological emergency at an installation in the vicinity are required to prepare and develop emergency plans for their territory.[30] Once preparedness obligations and good practices are enshrined at the international level, it is the responsibility of each Member State and its competent authorities to provide for emergency preparedness regulations and to ensure, more generally, the application of the highest standards of nuclear safety at the national level.[31]

The international emergency preparedness and response (EPR) framework[32] not only consists of international legal instruments but also of IAEA safety standards and operational arrangements.[33] Besides its role as leading organisation for the negotiation of international nuclear safety treaties, the IAEA's primary statutory mandate is, in fact, to 'establish or adopt, in consultation and, where appropriate, in collaboration with the competent organs of the UN and with the specialised agencies concerned, standards of safety for protection of health and minimisation of danger to life and property [...] and to provide for the application of these standards to its own operations'.[34] These technical norms are the core of preparedness measures for nuclear and radiological accidents. Although assessing the legal value of the Agency standards goes beyond the scope of this chapter, it is important to underline briefly that, even if they do not have binding force on Member States, they have more force than mere acts of 'soft law' and, indeed, produce highly significant normative effects.[35] Indeed, the purpose of these Safety Standards is that they should be applied as binding technical norms through incorporation into domestic or international law.[36]

---

29 Ibid art 16.2.

30 Ibid art 16.3.

31 IAEA, 'Action Plan on Nuclear Safety' (13 September 2011) <https://www.iaea.org/sites/default/files/actionplanns.pdf>.

32 Nuclear safety and security in Europe will be discussed in ch 15 by Balboni.

33 See, for this categorisation, IAEA, 'Operations Manual for Incident and Emergency Communication' (2019) EPR-IEComm, 1.

34 Statute of the International Atomic Energy Agency (1956) art III.A.6.

35 Handl (n 26) 322.

36 O Jankowitsch-Prevor, 'The Normative Role of the International Atomic Energy Agency, Legal Basis and Legal Sources' in *International Nuclear Law: History, Evolution and Outlook*

The IAEA Safety Standards are divided, hierarchically, into Safety Fundamentals, Safety Requirements and Safety Guides.[37] The General Safety Requirements on Preparedness and Response for a Nuclear or Radiological Emergency[38] establish the conditions for ensuring an adequate level of preparedness and response for all types of nuclear or radiological emergency. These 26 Safety Requirements are formulated to be of use to governments, emergency response organisations, other authorities at the local, regional, and national levels, as well as to relevant international organisations.

The IAEA published three Safety Guides on the issue of preparedness. According to Article 5(a) of the Assistance Convention, the Agency must disseminate to States Parties information concerning methodologies, techniques and research data relating to emergency response. The Safety Guide on Arrangements for Preparedness for a Nuclear or Radiological Emergency is, thus, aimed at providing guidance on preparedness for nuclear or radiological emergency, describing appropriate responses to a range of potential emergency scenarios, and delivering background information on past experiences.[39] The General Safety Guide on Criteria for Use in Preparedness and Response for a Nuclear or Radiological Emergency contains a set of generic measurements – expressed in terms of radiation dose – that facilitate decision-making concerning preparedness and response actions.[40] This publication also offers simple language explanations of these criteria for public officials and the population. The latest General Safety Guide published by the IAEA is the Arrangements for Public Communication in Preparedness and Response for a Nuclear or Radiological Emergency.[41] The Guide focusses on communication with the public and media and on the coordination of the official information in preparation for a radionuclear emergency. It supports Member States by outlining, beforehand, the processes needed to provide useful, timely, truthful, consistent, clear, and appropriate information to the public and by explaining how to respond to rumours and requests from the population and from the media.

(OECD/NEA 2010) 22. Handl (n 26) 322 refers to a "Normative Pull' of EPR-Related Safety Standards'.

37 IAEA, 'Long term structure of the IAEA Safety Standards and current status' (May 2021) 4, <http://www-ns.iaea.org/committees/files/CSS/205/status.pdf>. There are no Safety Fundamentals concerning preparedness.

38 IAEA, 'Safety Standards Series No. GSR Part 7' (2015).

39 IAEA, 'Safety Standards Series No. GS-G-2.1' (2007).

40 IAEA, 'Safety Standards Series No. GSG-2' (2011).

41 IAEA, 'Safety Standards Series No. GSG-14' (2020).

The framework on preparedness for nuclear emergency is undoubtedly complex:[42] the IAEA Safety Standards series complement the conventions on Assistance and Early Notification and the CNS. States might find it challenging to implement all these rules domestically;[43] for this reason, international institutional assistance is necessary and operational arrangements have been developed. Indeed, to clarify the interactions between various international organisations during a radionuclear emergency, a Joint Radiation Emergency Management Plan of the International Organizations (JPLAN) was established.[44] The Agency also releases and updates an Operations Manual for Incident and Emergency Communication,[45] in order to provide technical guidance on preparedness measures and information exchange between IAEA Member States, Assistance and Early Notification Conventions' Contracting Parties and concerned IOs.

2.3 *Regional, Subregional, and Bilateral Treaties*

The TEIA Convention covers all types of industrial accidents, except for nuclear accidents or radiological emergencies.[46] The latter sector is regulated at the universal level within the IAEA framework. As for the European Union, a series of acts relevant to industrial accident prevention have been implemented[47] and nuclear safety and security in Europe has its own regulatory framework.[48] Nonetheless, before the adoption of the Assistance and the Early Notification Conventions – and even before the Chernobyl disaster – four Northern European countries had already signed a multilateral agreement on mutual assistance, under the auspices of the IAEA. The Nordic Mutual

42 Criticisms stating that the IAEA EPR requirements are too numerous and detailed, thus, practically impeding States from complying with them, are common; see: Handl (n 26) 324 citing ENCO, 'Review of Current Off-site Nuclear Emergency Preparedness and Response Arrangements in EU Member States and Neighbouring Countries' (December2013)<https://op.europa.eu/it/publication-detail/-/publication/e6f9c4fb-8720-44e7-8ae5-331da3b1bfb8>.

43 Handl (n 26) 320.

44 IAEA, 'Joint Radiation Emergency Management Plan of the International Organizations' (2017) EPR-JPLAN, <https://www.iaea.org/publications/11163/joint-radiation-emergency-management-plan-of-the-international-organizations>.

45 IAEA, 'Operations Manual for Incident and Emergency Communication' (2019) EPR-IEComm, <https://www.iaea.org/publications/8939/operations-manual-for-incident-and-emergency-communication>.

46 TEIA Convention art 2.2.

47 See ch 14 by Ferri.

48 See ch 15 by Balboni.

Emergency Assistance Agreement in connection with Radiation Accidents[49] was adopted in 1963 by Denmark, Finland, Norway, and Sweden – and the IAEA – to create a sub-regional space of cooperation in the event of an incident involving damage from ionising radiation. The aim of the Agreement is to establish in advance the terms for requesting and providing assistance between Contracting States and the IAEA in case of emergency. The special functions of the Agency, which can be consulted only upon request of a party, are described in Article II and include giving advice on the measures to be taken, assisting Member States that are not parties to said agreement, and coordinating the provision of assistance. Although still primitive, these norms are an initial example of cross-border cooperation related to preparedness for radiological emergencies, representing a sort of foundation for the two 1986 Conventions.

The Eastern part of the European continent has been very active in promoting legal instruments for increased cooperation in disaster management, focussing both on assistance and preparedness.[50] With regard to the topic of this chapter, it is worth mentioning the various bilateral treaties that the Russian Federation concluded with several States, mainly from Eastern Europe, regarding cooperation in the sphere of the prevention of industrial accidents, catastrophes, natural disasters, and the mitigation of their consequences, in the years following the dissolution of the Soviet Union.[51] Even though the focus of these treaties is prevention, measures regarding preparedness and mutual assistance in case of industrial accidents are included. In general, in each agreement, parties are required to cooperate, to exchange information and to provide assistance for the mitigation of the effects of these accidents. Such cooperation activities encompass, *inter alia*, the exchange of information and technology between specialists and scientists of the two parties; the planning of joint conferences, seminars, workshops, and training; and the co-development and implementation of research projects, publications, reports and case studies.[52]

49 Nordic Mutual Emergency Assistance Agreement in connection with Radiation Accidents (1964).

50 As illustrated in ch 4 by De Guttry.

51 Russia signed this type of agreement with Kazakhstan, Bulgaria, Moldova, Mongolia, Armenia, Ukraine, Portugal, Greece, and Slovenia. See, eg, Agreement between the Russian Federation and the Republic of Armenia on cooperation in the sphere of prevention of industrial accidents, natural disasters and liquidation of the consequences thereof (1996).

52 Ibid art 3.

3 The Role of Soft Law Instruments

Apart from the international obligations illustrated thus far, the area of emergency preparedness for CBRN industrial accidents is characterised by the existence of a large number of soft law instruments. There are many IOs working in the field, which regularly adopt technical guidelines, reports, and recommendations of best practices. This section will briefly analyse the role of some fundamental IOs dealing with CBRN – the WHO, UNEP and the OECD – focussing on the relevance of soft law instruments for preparedness measures related to industrial accidents.

In the context of the UN system, the topic of preparedness for chemical industrial accidents has been addressed by different agencies and offices. Even though the programmes elaborated by these UN organisms are of a soft law nature – therefore not legally binding for Member States – they nevertheless have a strategic role in promoting technical guidelines and best practices, which are eventually incorporated in national rules. The focus of these instruments is the creation of networks, since effective action to ensure preparedness for industrial accidents requires coordinated efforts of multiple stakeholders at the local and national levels, such as government bodies, industry, workers, and community groups.

Through the International Programme on Chemical Safety (IPCS),[53] the WHO is attempting to establish a sound scientific basis for the management of chemicals and the strengthening of States' capabilities on chemical safety.[54] Chemical safety covers all chemicals, natural and manufactured, and the full range of exposure situations, including industrial accidents. In 2017, the Seventieth WHA approved the Road Map to Enhance Health Sector Engagement[55] within the Strategic Approach to International Chemicals Management (SAICM) policy framework.[56] In the context of the Chemicals Road Map, the WHO Global Chemicals and Health Network was instituted,[57] with links to existing subregional, regional, and international networks, aimed at facilitating its health sector implementation. Under the IPCS, the WHO

53 WHO Executive Board, 'Resolution on the International Programme on Chemical Safety' (18 January 1984) UN Doc EB73/Conf. Paper No. 3 Rev. 1.

54 Hereby the link with the 2002 WHA resolution. *Supra*.

55 WHA, Resolution on 'The role of the health sector in the Strategic Approach to International Chemicals Management towards the 2020 goal and beyond' (28 May 2016) UN Doc WHA69.4. For the Chemicals Road Map: <https://www.who.int/publications/i/item/WHO-FWC-PHE-EPE-17.03>.

56 See <www.saicm.org/>.

57 See <https://www.who.int/groups/global-chemicals-and-health-network/about>.

Chemical Risk Assessment Network was also established,[58] with the objectives, among others, of providing a forum for scientific and technical exchange; facilitating and contributing to capacity building; promoting best practices and the harmonisation of methodologies; and assisting institutions in the identification of research needs and with the promotion of the application of new science in risk assessment. The WHO also convenes international conferences and regional meetings to strengthen the networks cooperation and facilitates emergency responses.[59] Guidance and training materials to reinforce preparedness for chemical emergencies have also been published.[60]

Under the umbrella of the United Nations Environmental Programme (UNEP),[61] the Awareness and Preparedness for Emergencies at Local Level (APELL) programme has been implemented in more than 30 countries since 1988, to raise awareness about hazards and risks, improve preparedness planning and prepare coordinated emergency plans.[62] Within the context of the Sendai Framework for Disaster Risk Reduction,[63] in 2015, UNEP launched the APELL Handbook,[64] aimed at promoting a resilient and responsible community and at raising awareness about technological or natural hazards and measures for preparedness and emergency response. The APELL methodology is based on five elements: (i) engaging stakeholders; (ii) understanding hazards and risks; (iii) preparedness planning; (iv) implementing, disseminating, and testing; and (v) maintaining APELL. Furthermore, through the Flexible

---

58 See <https://www.who.int/groups/chemical-risk-assessment-network>.

59 Preparedness and response (ch 13) are inevitably intertwined.

60 See, *inter alia*, WHO, 'Communicating risk in public health emergencies: a WHO guideline for emergency risk communication (ERC) policy and practice' (2017), <https://www.who.int/publications/i/item/9789241550208>.

61 UNEP was founded in 1972 following the Stockholm Conference on the Human Environment: see UNGA, 'Report of the United Nations Conference on Human Environment' (5–16 June 197) UN Doc A/CONF.48/14/REV.1.

62 See <https://www.unep.org/explore-topics/disasters-conflicts/what-we-do/preparedness-and-response/awareness-and-preparedness>.

63 UNDRR, Sendai Framework for Disaster Risk Reduction 2015–2030 (2015), <https://www.undrr.org/publication/sendai-framework-disaster-risk-reduction-2015-2030>. The Sendai Framework covers not only natural but also technological hazards, an advancement from its predecessor, the Hyogo Framework for Action 2005–2015. Among technological risks are chemical and industrial, as well as radiological, nuclear, biological and Natech hazards. See UNDRR, 'Global assessment report on disaster risk reduction 2019' (2019) xv, <https://www.undrr.org/publication/global-assessment-report-disaster-risk-reduction-2019>.

64 UNEP, *APELL Handbook: A process for improving community awareness and preparedness for technological hazards and environmental emergencies*, Second edition (2015), <https://www.preventionweb.net/publications/view/45469>.

Framework for addressing Chemical Accident Prevention and Preparedness (CAPP),[65] UNEP works to promote chemical accident preparedness in emerging economies and developing countries that need support to address these increased risks. The goal of this Framework is to support national governments in the implementation of an appropriate CAPP programme. These programmes include the collection of laws, regulations, policies, guidance, and other instruments established by a State to address the various aspects of CAPP. A set of guidelines, in collaboration with the Inter-Organization Programme for the Sound Management of Chemicals (IOMC)[66] and pursuant to the SAICM policy, were released: the Flexible Framework for Addressing Chemical Accident Prevention and Preparedness guidance[67] and the Implementation-support package.[68] The experiences regarding the development of CAPP programmes were also encapsulated in a report on Case studies of implementation,[69] with the objective of disseminating the results and lessons learned from national projects, as well as presenting new recommendations.[70]

Under the umbrella of the OECD,[71] the Nuclear Energy Agency (NEA), an intergovernmental agency bringing together countries in a non-political forum, was established with the aim to 'further the development of the production and uses of nuclear energy [...] for peaceful purposes by the participating countries, through co-operation [...] and a harmonization of measures taken at the national level'.[72] The NEA does not play an operational role in case of

65 See <https://www.unenvironment.org/pt-br/node/653>.

66 The IOMC was established in 1995, following recommendations made by the 1992 UN Conference on Environment and Development to strengthen co-operation and increase international coordination in the field of chemical safety. The participating organisations are FAO, ILO, UNEP, UNIDO, UNITAR, WHO, and OECD. The World Bank and UNDP are observers.

67 UNEP, *A Flexible Framework for addressing chemical accident prevention and preparedness. A guidance document* (2010).

68 UNEP, *A Flexible Framework for addressing chemical accident prevention and preparedness, An Implementation Support Package* (2012).

69 UNEP, *Chemical Accident Prevention and Preparedness, Case studies of implementation* (2015).

70 A review of the efforts and joint activities of the IOs involved in preparedness for industrial accidents can be found in the report of the Inter-Agency Coordination Group, an informal forum that brings together institutions working on the prevention of, preparedness for and response to industrial and chemical accidents: Inter-Agency Coordination Group for Industrial and Chemical Accidents, *International efforts for industrial and chemical accidents prevention, preparedness and response* (2017), <https://www.preventionweb.net/publication/international-efforts-industrial-and-chemical-accidents-prevention-preparedness-and>.

71 Convention on the Organisation for Economic Co-operation and Development (1960).

72 Statute of the OECD Nuclear Energy Agency (1995) art 1.

nuclear emergencies, but it is actively involved in efforts to improve the international management of radionuclear accident emergency preparedness through the preparation and conduct of the International Nuclear Emergency Exercise (INEX) series.[73] These exercises, carried out by the NEA Working Party on Nuclear Emergency Matters (WPNEM),[74] are aimed at testing and proving the effectiveness of existing international nuclear emergency response plans and procedures. The WPNEM works to identify needs in preparedness for the early and intermediate phases of a radionuclear emergency, including accidents, in coordination with Member States and other international organisations. From the evaluation of the INEX exercises series, the WPNEM has drawn lessons and knowledge which provided a substantial and unbiased basis for the development of subsequent strategies and recommendations for enhancing emergency preparedness systems nationally and internationally, with a particular focus on decision-making, international communication, and information exchange.

The OECD also adopted a series of Guiding Principles for Chemical Accidents, Prevention, Preparedness and Response.[75] These Principles constitute a – non-binding – guidance for public authorities, industry, non-governmental organisations, as well as members of the public potentially affected in the event of an accident. They apply to all hazardous installations, and they address issues related to the preparation for accidents through emergency planning, land-use strategy, and communication with the public.[76]

4 Current Developments in the Implementation of Preparedness Measures for CBRN Industrial Accidents

The present chapter has provided an overview of the sources and content of preparedness obligations related to CBRN industrial accidents under international law. The effectiveness of their implementation varies largely depending on the sector.

---

73 See <https://www.oecd-nea.org/jcms/pl_27015/international-nuclear-emergency-exercises-inex>.

74 Further information at <https://www.oecd-nea.org/jcms/pl_26861/working-party-on-nuclear-emergency-matters-wpnem>.

75 OECD, 'OECD Guiding Principles for Chemical Accident Prevention, Preparedness and Response Guidance for Industry (including Management and Labour), Public Authorities, Communities, and other Stakeholders', Second edition (OECD Environment, Health and Safety Publications, Series on Chemical Accidents No. 10 2003).

76 Ibid pt B: Emergency Preparedness/Mitigation, 85–110.

Nuclear accidents – fortunately – rarely occur, but, as the 2011 Fukushima incident reminded us, they can happen, and the international community – as well as national and local authorities – must be prepared to deal with them. While the effects of the Japanese nuclear catastrophe were milder than the ones stemming from the Chernobyl disaster, undoubtedly thanks to the nuclear safety regime developed internationally, Fukushima nevertheless demonstrated that much work still needs to be done. No matter how strong a national EPR framework is, a country cannot cope with a nuclear catastrophe alone: preparedness action at the local level is not enough. Although emergency planning is a matter of exclusive domestic jurisdiction, the Fukushima accident made clear that international coordination of preparedness measures should be strengthened, at least in the case of neighbouring States, which should share cross-border technical expertise and mutual trust.[77] Also, revising and improving off-site emergency preparedness capabilities at the global level was deemed crucial.

Nonetheless, the international legally binding framework has not been subject to amendments in response.[78] However, the same year, 2011, the IAEA issued the Action Plan on Nuclear Safety to strengthen nuclear safety, including by reinforcing measures regarding emergency preparedness, through the full cooperation and participation of Member States and the involvement of many stakeholders.[79] Member States are now obliged to conduct a regular review of their national emergency preparedness arrangements and

77 At present, joint decisions between neighbouring States on how to harmonise communication procedures prior to and during an emergency do not exist, notwithstanding the potential transnational nature of a nuclear crisis. Discussions on cooperation between the Netherlands, Belgium and Germany concerning the nuclear power plants in the border areas are emerging. See Dutch Safety Board, 'Cooperation on nuclear safety, An investigation into the cooperation between the Netherlands, Belgium and Germany concerning the nuclear power plants in the border areas' (January 2018), <https://www.onderzoeksraad.nl/en/page/4341/cooperation-on-nuclear-safety>.

78 Following the Fukushima accident, the Contracting Parties to the CNS decided to hold a dedicated meeting in 2012, where the Action Plan was issued. Other dedicated meetings took place, where proposals for amendments to the CNS were discussed; however, the parties eventually agreed, in 2015, on a mere political declaration (IAEA, 'Vienna Declaration on Nuclear Safety' (9 February 2015) IAEA Doc. CNS/DC/2015/2/Rev.1). See SG Burns, 'The impact of the major nuclear power plant accidents on the international legal framework for nuclear power' (2018) 101(1) NLB 7, 21–27; E Durand-Poudret, 'Towards a new international framework for nuclear safety: Developments from Fukushima to Vienna' (2015) 95(1) NLB 27; PR Johnson, 'The post-Fukushima Daiichi response: The role of the Convention on Nuclear Safety in strengthening the legal framework for nuclear safety' (2013) 91(1) NLB 7.

79 IAEA (n 31).

capabilities, with the IAEA Secretariat providing support and assistance; at the same time, the IAEA Secretariat, the Member States and all relevant international organisations are asked to review the international emergency preparedness arrangements and capabilities.[80] In order to assist with implementing the Action Plan, a report by the IAEA Director General, addressing the causes and consequences of the Fukushima accident and providing a comprehensive understanding of what happened during the accident, was released in 2015,[81] along with five accompanying Technical Volumes, one of which is dedicated to emergency preparedness and response.[82]

The enhancement of nuclear safety, including emergency preparedness and response, remains one of the priorities identified by the IAEA. As stated in the Agency's 2020 Nuclear Safety Review, Member States are increasingly requesting technical assistance and advice to reinforce national and regional emergency preparedness arrangements. Indeed, in 2019 alone, the Agency held 40 emergency preparedness and response training events at the regional and interregional level and 15 at the national level, with participants from 133 Member States.[83] Hence, among the Agency's priorities for 2020 and beyond, related to preparedness, there is the improvement of the IAEA Safety Standards, using the lessons acquired from the Fukushima accident, and the provision of continuous support to Member States to develop their capacity building programmes, through education and training, international conferences, peer reviews, knowledge networks, and relevant workshops.[84]

As for industrial accidents in general, the parties at the 2020 TEIA Convention meeting[85] concluded that emergency preparedness obligations deriving from the Convention are largely at an acceptable level, even though testing, updating, and reviewing emergency plans in cooperation with neighbouring countries continue to be challenging for many States. Thus, when the parties adopted the subsequent decision on strengthening implementation,

80 Ibid 3.

81 IAEA, 'The Fukushima Daiichi Accident, Report by the Director General' (2015) IAEA Doc. GC(59)/14.

82 IAEA, 'The Fukushima Daiichi Accident, Technical Volume 3/5, Emergency Preparedness and Response' (2015) <https://www.iaea.org/publications/10962/the-fukushima-daiichi-accident>.

83 IAEA, 'Nuclear Safety Review 2020' (September 2020) IAEA Doc. GC(64)/INF/3, 4–5.

84 Ibid 5–6.

85 UN Economic Commission for Europe, Conference of the Parties to the TEIA Convention, 'Ninth report on the implementation of the Convention (2016–2018)' (25 September 2020) ECE/CP.TEIA/2020/5.

they committed themselves to make further progress towards reinforcing and developing joint or harmonised emergency plans.[86]

Nonetheless, the production and use of chemicals continue to grow worldwide, particularly in developing countries, and too many industrial accidents involving chemicals still occur. Their consequences may be less severe than they used to be,[87] but the frequency with which they happen remains a concern.[88] Among the causes – direct or indirect – of these accidents are the non-compliance of companies with emergency preparedness regulations; the negligence of authorities in supervising companies' business operations, in implementing relevant laws and in conducting safety inspections;[89] and the failure of on-site and off-site emergency plans and measures related to risk communication.[90] Ultimately, when sound chemical safety is not ensured, the risk of industrial accidents occurring is significant. Even though preparedness measures related to industrial accidents involving chemicals are outlined on the international plane – albeit mainly by means of soft law – their implementation at the national level is not always effective. Indeed, since the recommendations concerning chemical safety coming from the UN and the OECD are not binding, there is no obligation for the States to implement them. Moreover, even when national legislation is enacted, it is not always easy to ensure that the rules are respected by the companies operating in the State's territory. Just as with nuclear safety, a harmonised global vision regarding preparedness obligations – possibly by means of a targeted binding instrument – could be the right tool to halt the harmful effects of improperly managed chemicals.

---

86 Economic Commission for Europe, Conference of the Parties to the TEIA Convention, 'Updated draft decision on strengthening the implementation of the Convention' (20 November 2020) ECE/CP.TEIA/2020/L.2, paras 13–14.

87 See, eg, the 1984 Bhopal disaster where a major gas leak accident took place.

88 Examples are the 2015 Tianjin explosions and the 2020 Vizag gas leak. See 'Tianjin explosion: China sets final death toll at 173, ending search for survivors' The Guardian (12 September 2015) <https://www.theguardian.com/world/2015/sep/12/tianjin-explosion-china-sets-final-death-toll-at-173-ending-search-for-survivors> and 'LG Polymers: Was negligence behind India's deadly gas leak?' BBC News (24 May 2020) <https://www.bbc.com/news/world-asia-india-52723762#:~:text=People%20who%20live%20close%20to,May%20to%20a%20pungent%20smell.&text=a%20toxic%20compound-,The%20cause%20of%20the%20deaths%20was%20inhalation%20of%20vapours%20of,had%20leaked%20from%20the%20factory>.

89 A Xia, 'Tianjin explosions' in G Davies, J Goldkorn and L Tomba (eds), *China Story Yearbook 2015 Pollution* (ANU Press 2015), 208–209.

90 DS Bisht, 'Vizag gas leak: Curtain calls on the accountability of LG Polymers' Down ToEarth (10 July 2020) <https://www.downtoearth.org.in/news/pollution/vizag-gas-leak-curtain-calls-on-the-accountability-of-lg-polymers-72222#:~:text=Gross%20negligence%20by%20LG%20Polymers,2020%2C%20said%20a%20government%20report>.

Bibliography

Burns SG, 'The impact of the major nuclear power plant accidents on the international legal framework for nuclear power' (2018) 101(1) NLB 7 21.

Durand-Poudret E, 'Towards a new international framework for nuclear safety: Developments from Fukushima to Vienna' (2015) 95(1) NLB 27.

Gioia A, 'Nuclear Accidents and International Law' in A de Guttry, M Gestri, G Venturini (eds), *International Disaster Response Law* (Springer 2012).

Handl G, 'Nuclear Off-site Emergency Preparedness and Response: Some International Legal Aspects' in JL Black-Branch, D Fleck (eds), *Nuclear Non-Proliferation in International Law – Volume III, Legal Aspects of the Use of Nuclear Energy for Peaceful Purposes* (Springer 2016).

Inter-Agency Coordination Group for Industrial and Chemical Accidents, *International efforts for industrial and chemical accidents prevention, preparedness and response* (2017).

Jankowitsch-Prevor O, 'The Convention on Nuclear Safety' in *International Nuclear Law in the Post-Chernobyl Period* (OECD/NEA 2006).

Jankowitsch-Prevor O, 'The Normative Role of the International Atomic Energy Agency, Legal Basis and Legal Sources' in *International Nuclear Law: History, Evolution and Outlook* (OECD/NEA 2010).

Johnson PR, 'The post-Fukushima Daiichi response: The role of the Convention on Nuclear Safety in strengthening the legal framework for nuclear safety' (2013) 91(1) NLB 7.

Kuş S, 'International nuclear law in the 25 years between Chernobyl and Fukushima and beyond ...' (2011) 87(1) NLB 7.

Rautenbach J, Tonhauser W and Wetherall A, 'Overview of the International Legal Framework Governing the Safe and Peaceful Uses of Nuclear Energy – Some Practical Steps' in *International Nuclear Law in the Post-Chernobyl Period* (OECD/NEA 2006).

UNEP, *A Flexible Framework for addressing chemical accident prevention and preparedness. A guidance document* (2010).

UNEP, *A Flexible Framework for addressing chemical accident prevention and preparedness, An Implementation Support Package* (2012).

UNEP, *APELL Handbook: A process for improving community awareness and preparedness for technological hazards and environmental emergencies*, Second edition (2015).

UNEP, *Chemical Accident Prevention and Preparedness, Case studies of implementation* (2015).

Xia A, 'Tianjin explosions' in G Davies, J Goldkorn and L Tomba (eds), *China Story Yearbook 2015 Pollution* (ANU Press 2015).

CHAPTER 13

Response and Recovery in the Event of CBRN Industrial Accidents

Christine Bakker and Federica Montanaro

1 Introduction

In recent decades, several disasters occurred, involving the release of CBRN agents due to industrial accidents, including the 1984 Bhopal disaster in India, where more than 3,000 people died after a highly toxic chemical gas was released from a Union Carbide Pesticides Factory, and the nuclear catastrophe of Chernobyl (Ukraine, 1986). CBRN industrial accidents can also be triggered by natural disasters, such as the major accident that occurred at the Japanese Fukushima Daiichi Nuclear Power Plant in 2011, caused by the Tōhoku earthquake and tsunami. In the aftermath of these severe CBRN accidents, the increased sense of urgency within the international community to ensure a more adequate prevention, preparedness, and response to such emergencies, has led to the adoption of new legal instruments and guidelines, and to the adjustment of existing ones.

This chapter will examine the specific obligations of States – and, where appropriate, those of international organisations (IOs) and private actors – related to the response and recovery from CBRN industrial accidents. The chapter considers, in Section 2, the response and recovery obligations included in binding and 'soft-law' instruments adopted at the universal and regional levels. However, the chapter will not discuss the relevant rules adopted by the European Union, which are examined elsewhere in this volume.[1] After some preliminary remarks (2.1.), the chapter discusses the rules and guidance related to industrial accidents involving all 'hazardous activities' (2.2.), those related to industrial accidents involving chemical and biological substances (2.3.), and those adopted for such incidents involving radiological and nuclear agents (2.4.). For each type of industrial accident, the existing specific regulatory instruments and guidelines will be identified, and the main types of obligations of States included in these instruments will be mentioned. The chapter will also consider whether any particular enforcement mechanisms have been

1 See ch 14 by Ferri in this volume.

created to ensure compliance with these provisions. Based on this analysis, the chapter will discuss some of the main challenges for the implementation of the specific international rules on the response and recovery phases after CBRN industrial accidents at the national level (Section 3). One of the main challenges that emerges, is that, while the existing international instruments applicable to CBRN industrial accidents provide quite specific guidance related to response measures, recommendations related to the recovery from such accidents are rather limited.

2 Specific Response and Recovery Obligations in International Instruments

2.1 *Preliminary Remarks*

The management of industrial accidents presents highly specific challenges for States, especially since the management of such events is 'hybrid' in nature. Indeed, while governments have the ultimate responsibility for the health, welfare and safety of their resident population and environment,[2] industrial plants are often owned by private corporations, which therefore play a key role in the whole emergency management cycle. Most importantly, States have clearly defined obligations to ensure that both public and private actors, who are responsible for the management of hazardous activities involving CBRN substances, adopt all the necessary response measures to minimise the consequences of such accidents. Such obligations include an appropriate communication structure, a clear and hierarchical decision-making procedure, and a duty to cooperate among the private and public sectors.[3]

The definition of 'industrial accidents' adopted in this chapter is taken from the Convention on the Transboundary Effects of Industrial Accidents (TEIA) concluded by the United Nations Economic Commission for Europe (UNECE).[4] However, while 'hazardous substances' in the UNECE definition refers to any substance 'involving risk or danger, especially to somebody's

2 International Federation of the Red Cross (IFRC), 'Introduction to the Guidelines for the Domestic Facilitation and Regulation of International Disaster Relief and Initial Recovery Assistance' (2011).

3 International Atomic Energy Agency (IAEA), 'Human and Organizational Factors in Nuclear Safety in the Light of the Accident at the Fukushima Daiichi Nuclear Power Plant' (2014).

4 United Nations Economic Commission for Europe (UNECE), 'Convention on the Transboundary Effects of Industrial Accidents' (1992) (hereafter: 'UNECE TEIA Convention'), art 1(a)(i). and (ii): '"Industrial accident" means an event resulting from an uncontrolled development in the course of any activity involving hazardous substances either: (i) In an installation, for example during manufacture, use, storage, handling, or disposal; or (ii) During transportation in so far as it is covered by paragraph 2 (d) of Article 2'. This latter

health or safety',[5] this chapter only considers the CBRN subset of such hazardous substances.

Two further preliminary remarks should be made. Firstly, no unified normative framework exists that regulates the response to CBRN industrial accidents. Therefore, specific norms and obligations need to be inferred from several legal and soft-law instruments. The guidance provided for disaster response and recovery in international instruments of a general scope, in particular, the Sendai Framework for Disaster Reduction[6] and the WHO's International Health Regulations, and in regional instruments on disaster management,[7] also applies to CBRN industrial accidents. These instruments are discussed elsewhere in this volume and will not be addressed in this chapter.[8] Moreover, the chapter will not discuss the content of bilateral agreements that have been concluded between States to provide mutual assistance in the event of industrial accidents, because such agreements generally have a broader scope, encompassing all types of disasters.[9] However, some examples of bilateral agreements that specifically focus on CBRN industrial accidents will be mentioned.[10]

Secondly, due to the specificity and potential health dangers involved in the response to CBRN industrial accidents, difficulties may arise, which were not foreseen in the prepared 'response plans'.[11] As will be shown below, this requires a constant adjustment of the applicable legal frameworks and of their implementation modalities.

2.2 *Rules Related to Industrial Accidents Involving All 'Hazardous Activities'*

At the international level, the International Labour Organization (ILO) Convention on the Prevention of Major Industrial Accidents[12] not only provides guidance on the 'prevention' of such accidents but also on the limitation of their consequences, which falls within the scope of 'response' actions. This Convention applies to 'major hazard installations' but not to nuclear

provision refers to 'Land-based transport accidents with the exception of: (i) Emergency response to such accidents; (ii) Transportation on the site of the hazardous activity.'

5 UNECE TEIA Convention (n 4) art 1(b).

6 Sendai Framework for Disaster Reduction (2015).

7 UNECE TEIA Convention (n 4) art 1(b).

8 See ch 5 by Bakker, and ch 18 by Bakker and Farina in this volume.

9 See ch 5 by Bakker in this volume.

10 See below, Section 2.4.

11 See below, Section 3. See also V Cozzani, 'Industrial accidents triggered by flood events: Analysis of past accidents', Journal of Hazardous Materials (2010).

12 ILO Convention No. 174 (1993) and its Recommendation (1993).

installations and plants processing radioactive substances.[13] Obligations concerning the 'limitation of consequences' of industrial accidents include the obligations on employers to inform the competent authorities as soon as an accident occurs; to report to the competent authorities, within a fixed timeframe after a major accident, on the causes of the accident, its immediate on-site consequences, and any action taken to mitigate its effects; and to make recommendations to prevent recurrence.[14] With regard to enforcement, the ILO Constitution provides, besides regular reporting by States, for two grievance procedures,[15] under which ILO constituents can file a 'representation' or 'complaint' concerning the non-compliance of any ILO Member State with an ILO Convention. The ILO Governing Body can then decide to set up an ad hoc tripartite committee or a high-level commission of inquiry to examine the case, which will make recommendations to the State concerned.[16] While Article 26 (complaints of non-observance) has never been activated in relation to an industrial accident, the situation is different for Article 24 (representations of non-observance of conventions). For example, this procedure was activated following the February 2006 explosion – and the subsequent release of a high quantity of methane gas – in the coalmine Unit 8 in Pasta de Conchos, in the State of Coahuila, Mexico, resulting in the death of 65 mine workers. Eight trade unions and workers' organisations complained about serious shortcomings in the manner in which the Mexican Government had monitored compliance with health and safety measures, working conditions and preventative measures, *inter alia*, through the national inspection services. Following the report of the tripartite Committee set up for this representation, the ILO Governing Body made specific recommendations for improvements and prevention of future incidents.[17]

At the regional level, an important instrument in this field is the abovementioned UNECE TEIA Convention.[18] It mainly focuses on the European

13 ILO Convention (n 12) art 1(3)(a). A 'hazardous substance' is defined as 'a substance or mixture of substances which by virtue of chemical, physical or toxicological properties, either singly or in combination, constitutes a hazard.' (art 3(a), ILO Convention No. 174.

14 Ibid articles 13, 14.

15 Constitution of the International Labour Organization (1919), art 24, art 26.

16 See also ch 11 by Creta in this volume.

17 ILO, 'Representation (article 24) – Mexico – C150, C155, C170' (2009). For further information, see <https://www.ilo.org/dyn/normlex/en/f?p=1000:50010:::NO:50010:P50010_ARTICLE_NO:24>.

18 UNECE TEIA Convention (n 4).

context, but some of its parties are non-European States.[19] The Convention aims to protect the environment and people against the effects of industrial accidents, and applies to both man-made and naturally-induced (eg through earthquakes, tsunamis, floods) industrial accidents capable of causing transboundary effects.[20] Its applicability extends to accidents involving hazardous substances, as mentioned above.[21] However, it does not apply to nuclear accidents and radiological emergencies, nor to the accidental release of genetically modified organisms.[22] In particular, it provides that, in the event of an industrial accident, or imminent threat thereof, 'the Parties concerned shall ensure that the effects are assessed – where appropriate, jointly for the purpose of taking adequate response measures.'[23] Moreover, it requires that the parties concerned shall endeavour to coordinate their response measures. Finally, the Convention confers to the affected States the right to ask for assistance from other parties,[24] and requires them to cooperate to facilitate such assistance.[25] Compliance with the Convention is monitored through regular reporting by States to the Conference of States Parties, and the review of these reports by a Working Group on Implementation, which can also make recommendations for improvements.[26]

Moreover, many regional organisations have adopted agreements for cooperation in the event of disasters, broadly defined.[27] These agreements often also refer to cooperation in the event of hazardous industrial incidents.[28] Similarly, numerous bilateral agreements between States across the globe provide for such cooperation, such as a Memorandum of Understanding between

19 The Convention has been ratified by 41, mostly European States, but also including the Russian Federation and some Central Asian States. However, the USA and Canada have signed but not ratified it.

20 Ibid art 2.

21 See above, section 2.1.

22 UNECE TEIA Convention (n 4), art 2(2)(a) and (g).

23 Ibid art 11.

24 Ibid art 12.

25 Ibid 12(2).

26 UNECE, 'Report of the Conference of the Parties on its ninth meeting. Addendum Decisions and other outcomes adopted at the ninth meeting', *Terms of Reference of the Working Group on Implementation* ECE/CP.TEIA/32/Add.1, 19 April 2017. See also ch 11 by Creta in this volume.

27 See ch 5 by Bakker in this volume.

28 Eg Protocolo Adicional Al Acuerdo Marco Sobre Medio Ambiente Del Mercosur En Materia De Cooperación Y Asistencia Ante Emergencias Ambientales', (2004), Annex para 2.2.

the Russian Federation and the United States, which makes specific reference to industrial accidents.[29] Other mutual assistance agreements exclusively focus on industrial accidents.[30]

2.3 *Rules Related to Industrial Accidents Involving Chemical Substances*

In the absence of a specific legally binding instrument concerning chemical industrial accidents, the main universal instrument that provides specific guidance for the response to such accidents is the Flash Environmental Assessment Tool (FEAT).[31] This non-binding instrument was adopted by the Joint Environmental Unit (JEU) of the UN Environment Programme (UN Environment) and the UN Office for the Coordination of Humanitarian Affairs (OCHA), a partnership that pairs the environmental expertise of UN Environment with the humanitarian response network coordinated by OCHA. This JEU partnership provides assistance to countries requesting support, 'to address the environmental impacts of sudden-onset disasters and accidents by coordinating international preparedness and response activities.'[32] In the first hours after a chemical accident, the JEU can send experts and equipment to the affected area to work together with national authorities 'to conduct rapid assessments, test for the presence of hazardous materials, analyse the possible effects on communities, and assist with the development of response and monitoring strategies.'[33]

At the regional level, the Guiding Principles for Chemical Accidents, Prevention, Preparedness and Response[34] were adopted by the Organisation for Economic Co-operation and Development (OECD). This non-binding instrument offers a comprehensive and detailed overview of, *inter alia*, the

29 'Memorandum of Understanding Between the Government of the Russian Federation and the Government of the United States of America on Cooperation in Natural and Man-Made Technological Emergency Prevention and Response', (1996), art 1. See also ch 11 by Creta in this volume.

30 Eg the Agreement between Greece and Ukraine, on the co-operation in the field of prevention of industrial accidents, natural disasters, and the elimination of their consequences (Law 2950/01, Government Gazette 246A), or an agreement between France and Switzerland <http://www.admin.ch/opc/fr/classified-compilation/19870007/index.html>. All links were last accessed on 27 May 2021.

31 UN Environment and the Office for the Coordination of Humanitarian Affairs (JEU), 'Flash Environmental Assessment Tool (FEAT)' (2017).

32 Inter-Agency Coordination Group for Industrial and Chemical Accidents. 'The International Efforts for Industrial and Chemical Accidents Prevention, Preparedness and Response' (2017).

33 Ibid.

34 OECD, Guiding Principles for Chemical Accidents, Prevention, Preparedness and Response (2003).

response measures that industry, public authorities, communities, and other stakeholders should implement in the aftermath of a chemical accident. After the immediate notification of an accident by the management of the affected industrial facility to the competent authorities, the emergency plan, as developed in accordance with these same guidelines, must be implemented, and adequate and timely communication is a crucial element of the response actions. For instance, '(s)ystems should be activated to warn the members of the public who might be affected by the accident,'[35] external expert assistance should be requested when the on-site response capacities are not sufficient, and hospitals must be alerted.[36] The Guiding Principles also provide guidance for the follow-up of a chemical accident, addressing the assessment of consequences, incident reporting and investigations.[37] However, this instrument does not address the issues associated with recovery following an accident, such as environmental clean-up.[38] Although no specific enforcement mechanisms are foreseen to ensure compliance with these guidelines, both the OECD Working Group on Chemical Accidents, and the Inter-Agency Coordination Group on Chemical Accidents[39] monitor the practice of States in this regard and can recommend improvements.

Two other relevant instruments concern the response to oil pollution at sea. The first is the International Convention on Oil Pollution Preparedness, Response and Cooperation[40] and its Protocol on Preparedness, Response and Co-operation to Pollution Incidents by Hazardous and Noxious Substances,[41] which require States Parties, *inter alia*, to inform other parties of marine discharges of oil or other hazardous or noxious substances that might affect them; to cooperate 'subject to their capabilities and the availability of relevant resources'; and to 'provide advisory services, technical support and equipment', in the event of a serious incident.[42] While the enforcement of these instruments is ensured at the national level, the International Maritime Organization

35 Ibid Part C 'Emergency Response' para 9.

36 Ibid paras 10.10, 10.12.

37 Ibid Part D 'Follow-up to incidents (accidents and near-misses)'.

38 Ibid.

39 An informal forum that brings together international organisations and institutions working on prevention of, preparedness for and response to industrial and chemical accidents. See also ch 11 by Creta in this volume.

40 International Convention on Oil Pollution Preparedness, Response and Cooperation (1990) (hereafter: 'Oil Pollution Convention').

41 Protocol to the International Oil Pollution Convention on Preparedness, Response and Co-operation to Pollution Incidents by Hazardous and Noxious Substances (2000).

42 Oil Pollution Convention (n 40) art 5, art 6; Protocol to this Convention (n 41) art 3, art 5.

plays a coordinating role in, *inter alia*, the established reporting procedures.[43] Secondly, the regional Agreement on Cooperation on Marine Oil Pollution Preparedness and Response in the Arctic (MOSPA)[44] aims to increase cooperation and coordination among Arctic countries in case of oil spill response operations. Moreover, it contains an obligation to provide mutual assistance in case of oil spills exceeding national response capacity.[45] Any disputes concerning the application or interpretation of this Agreement shall be resolved through direct consultations (MOSPA, Article 18).

2.4 *Industrial Accidents Involving Radiological and Nuclear Substances*

The following analysis adopts the definitions of the terms 'nuclear emergencies' and 'radiological emergencies' offered by the International Federation of the Red Cross.[46]

The International Atomic Energy Agency (IAEA) is one of the key actors engaged in the regulation of this field. After the nuclear disaster in Chernobyl, the IAEA General Conference adopted two conventions regarding nuclear accidents, which both include specific response obligations. Firstly, the 1986 Convention on Assistance in the Case of a Nuclear Accident or Radiological Emergency[47] sets out basic rules for the initiation, coordination, and operation of international assistance operations in case of nuclear or radiological events, referring, *inter alia*, to the provision of equipment and personnel. Moreover, the Convention requests the IAEA to provide, at the request of an affected State, several forms of assistance related to, *inter alia*, the identification of the need for external assistance and its coordination, and the provision of direct support for response activities. Secondly, the Convention on Early Notification of a Nuclear Accident[48] sets forth the obligations that a State experiencing any kind of accident involving the dispersion of radiological elements has towards third States Parties that are, or may be affected by such incident.[49] Besides the obligation to notify and inform third parties,[50] there is a general obligation to

43 Ibid art 12.
44 'Agreement on Cooperation on Marine Oil Pollution Preparedness and Response in the Arctic', (2013).
45 Ibid section 1.
46 IFRC (n 2).
47 IAEA Convention on Assistance in the Case of a Nuclear Accident or Radiological Emergency (1986) ('Assistance Convention').
48 IAEA Convention on Early Notification of a Nuclear Accident (1986) ('Early Notification Convention').
49 Ibid art 1.
50 Ibid art 2.

minimise the radiological consequences of the event[51] and an obligation to provide in-depth reports about the event.[52] However, States' 'obligation' of notification only applies to nuclear events listed in the Convention; in case of events that are not listed, States are only 'recommended' to notify.[53]

Moreover, the IAEA, as an international organisation, also has some specific obligations. In particular, the Early Notification Convention stipulates the IAEA's obligations related to the notification of a nuclear event to third States,[54] and to the provision of assistance to States Parties.[55] Similarly, with respect to the response to an accident or emergency, the Assistance Convention determines that the IAEA has obligations related to, *inter alia*, the provision and coordination of assistance to States Parties at their request (art 2), such as to 'make available [...] appropriate resources allocated for the purpose of conducting an initial assessment of the accident or emergency', and to 'offer its good offices to the States Parties and Member States in the event of a nuclear accident or radiological emergency'.[56] The IAEA is generally requested to promote, facilitate and support cooperation between States Parties (art 1(3)), including in the response to a nuclear or radiological incident.

A third Convention was adopted in 1994: the IAEA Convention on Nuclear Safety,[57] which aims to 'prevent accidents with radiological consequences and to mitigate such consequences should they occur'.[58] The necessity to mitigate or minimise the consequences of any accident or malicious act involving a radioactive source is also stated in the IAEA Code of Conduct on the Safety and Security of Radioactive Sources.[59] Furthermore, the Joint Convention on the Safety of Spent Fuel Management and on the Safety of Radioactive Waste Management[60] aims, *inter alia*, 'to prevent accidents with radiological consequences and to mitigate their consequences should they occur during any stage of spent fuel or radioactive waste management.'[61] States Parties must 'take appropriate steps to ensure that [...] in the event that an unplanned or

---

51 Ibid art 3.

52 Ibid art 5.

53 Ibid art 1, art 3.

54 Ibid art 4.

55 Ibid.

56 Assistance Convention (n 47) art 5.

57 IAEA, Convention on Nuclear Safety (1994).

58 Ibid art 1 para iii. See also ch 11 by Creta in this volume.

59 IAEA, Code of Conduct on the Safety and Security of Radioactive Sources (2004) art 5, para iii.

60 Joint Convention on the Safety of Spent Fuel Management and on the Safety of Radioactive Waste Management (1997).

61 Ibid art 1(iii).

uncontrolled release of radioactive materials into the environment occurs, appropriate corrective measures are implemented to control the release and mitigate its effects.'[62]

Regarding the monitoring of States' compliance with these conventions, the situation is as follows. The abovementioned IAEA Assistance Convention, and the Early Notification Convention do not foresee any specific mechanisms to monitor States' compliance with their obligations. However, the IAEA has been entrusted with the task of supporting the implementation of these conventions. Moreover, compliance with the Convention on Nuclear Safety is monitored through a peer review mechanism, involving reporting by all Contracting Parties at regular review meetings.[63] A similar review mechanism exists for monitoring compliance with the Joint Convention on the Safety of Spent Fuel Management and on the Safety of Radioactive Waste Management.[64]

Finally, several regional,[65] and numerous bilateral, agreements have been concluded among States around the world for preventing or minimising injury and damage which may result in the event of a nuclear accident or radiological emergency.[66]

3 Challenges for the Implementation of the International Rules on the Response and Recovery Phases at the National Level – Lessons Learned from Practice

It should be highlighted that the overview of response and recovery obligations outlined in the preceding sections is nuanced on a State-to-State basis because of the generalised[67] practice of adopting reservations to specific provisions in the relevant treaties, which may reduce the effectiveness of emergency

62 Ibid art 24(3).

63 See also A Gioia, 'Nuclear Accidents and International Law', in A de Guttry, M Gestri and G Venturini (eds,), International Disaster Response Law (Springer 2012).

64 Joint Convention (n 60) art 30, art 32.

65 Eg Nordic Mutual Emergency Assistance Agreement in Connection with Radiation Accidents (1963), Asian Nuclear Safety Network (ANSN, 2002).

66 Eg Agreement between Germany and the Russian Federation Concerning Co-operation and Exchange of Information and Experience in the Field of Nuclear Safety and Radiation Protection (2003), Agreement between Romania and Ukraine on Early Notification of Nuclear Accidents and Exchange of Information in the Field of Nuclear and Radiation Safety (2004). For an overview of relevant regional and bilateral agreements concluded up to 1990, see <https://www-pub.iaea.org/MTCD/Publications/PDF/Pub850Web.pdf>. See also ch 11 by Creta and ch 12 by Domaine in this volume.

67 Eg see <https://www.iaea.org/resources/treaties/treaties-under-IAEA-auspices>.

response. For instance, the Convention on Early Notification of a Nuclear Accident[68] is qualified by declarations, reservations or objections adopted by 54 out of 127 States Parties.[69] Similarly, the Convention on Assistance in the Case of a Nuclear Accident or Radiological Emergency[70] is characterised by reservations adopted by 62 out of its 122 parties.[71]

As practice has shown, every incident (apart from being a tragedy) is also a 'testing and learning moment', crucial to understanding the strengths and weaknesses of current response protocols, and to improving them by identifying novel best-practices. The IAEA addresses this 'evolutive-learning rationale' in the outcome of the International Experts Meeting on Human and Organizational Factors in Nuclear Safety in the Light of the Accident at the Fukushima Daiichi Nuclear Power Plant.[72] The report identifies the lessons learned after this accident from a human and organisational factors standpoint, highlighting the need for a re-examination of some of the key elements of emergency response,[73] including the clear definition and communication of the roles and responsibilities of stakeholders and decision-makers. The document recommends a systemic approach to nuclear safety and response, integrating human, technical and organisational factors.[74]

However, as the IFRC's Nuclear and Radiological Emergency Guidelines Preparedness, Response and Recovery[75] state: '(t)he variable circumstances and unique characteristics of an emergency at its onset usually require prompt accommodating adjustments to predefined response plans and underlying assumptions.'[76] This document, therefore, suggests the adoption of a dynamic

68 IAEA (n 48).

69 See <https://www.oecd-nea.org/jcms/pl_29135/convention-on-early-notification-of-a-nuclear-accident-early-notification-convention>.

70 IAEA (n 47).

71 See <https://www.oecd-nea.org/jcms/pl_29131/convention-on-assistance-in-the-case-of-a-nuclear-accident-or-radiological-emergency-convention-on-assistance>.

72 IAEA (n 3).

73 See also Y Takamura, 'Release of Radioactive Substances into the Sea and International Law: The Japanese Experience in the Course of Nuclear Disaster', in D Caron, M J Kelly, A Telesetsky (eds), *The International Law of Disaster Relief* (CUP 2014) 89; M Saghafi Mohammad and B M Ghofrani, 'Accident management support tools in nuclear power plants: A post-Fukushima review' (Progress in Nuclear Energy 2016).

74 Systematic risk management seeks to gain as much information as possible about a potential situation, as far ahead of expected events as possible, then conduct as much mitigation as reasonably practicable, with the aim of removing risk or, where that is not possible, reducing risk as much as reasonably practicable.

75 International Federation of the Red Cross, 'Nuclear and Radiological Emergency Guidelines Preparedness, Response and Recovery' (2015).

76 Ibid p 55.

risk management[77] approach during the response phase, alongside the above-mentioned systematic approach. The Guidelines clarify:

> (w)here controls are in place to make and check decisions as an emergent range of issues unfold, dynamic risk assessment and dynamic risk management are extremely important tools that allow pre-determined (systematic) preparedness to 'fit' the unique challenges of a specific situation and this is an essential aspect of all incidents, emergency and crisis preparedness, response and recovery.[78]

In this context, the role of the industrial facilities themselves is crucial, alongside that of the competent State authorities. The OECD Guiding Principles for Chemical Accident Prevention, Preparedness and Response[79] provide an example of guidance for the management of hazardous facilities in the event of an industrial CBRN accident.[80] The Guidelines also describe the role of other actors in the response phase of an industrial accident, including the public, the media and NGOs.[81] Such an 'inclusive approach' to disaster management, involving all stakeholders, is fully in line with other international instruments, including the Sendai Framework.[82]

Finally, another challenge is represented by the absence of international treaties in force regarding biological industrial accidents.[83] Indeed, the issue of biological industrial accidents is hardly ever addressed as a separate issue. Instead, it is considered in the broader context of CBRN events.[84] In practice, the necessity to apply the general instruments to such specific situations may reduce the effectiveness of States' response capabilities.

77 Ibid. The document defines dynamic risk management as contraposed to the systematic risk management approach. It 'takes the view that every situation is different, and one needs to see the problem in order to fix it as it emerges from possible to actual. The presumption in this case is that the "experience will get us through"'.

78 Ibid 60.

79 OECD Guiding Principles (n 34).

80 See above (section 2.3.), and B Hosseinniaa et al, 'Multi-plant emergency response for tackling major accidents in chemical industrial areas' (Safety Science 2018).

81 Ibid chapter 11.

82 Sendai Framework (n 9).

83 See ch 12 by Domaine in this volume.

84 Eg WHA, 'Resolution on global public health response to natural occurrence, accidental release or deliberate use of biological and chemical agents or radionuclear material that affect health' (18 May 2002) UN Doc A55/VR/9, as illustrated in ch 12 by Domaine in this volume.

4 Concluding Remarks

In this chapter, an overview has been provided of the main international and regional instruments setting out obligations or guidance for States, IOs, and private actors, for the response and recovery phases related to CBRN industrial accidents. The examination has shed some light on the complexities that are associated with the response to CBRN industrial accidents, and on the way in which States, acting through international and regional organisations, have attempted to regulate the response to such events in order to protect people and the environment. Such responses, by States, IOs, industry, and other stakeholders, need to be constantly reviewed and perfected, in accordance with the changing challenges and lessons learned. The analysis has also shown that the specific regulatory instruments and guidelines related to industrial accidents involving CBRN substances generally focus on prevention, preparedness and response, while the guidance provided in these instruments for the recovery from such incidents is relatively scarce. Indeed, as the Inter-Agency Coordination Group for Industrial and Chemical Accidents affirms in its 'Challenges Ahead' report: 'if agencies have strong programmes in relation to the prevention, preparedness and response, the specific cleaning and recovery stages require more work'.

Bibliography

Cozzani V, *Industrial accidents triggered by flood events: Analysis of past accidents* (Journal of Hazardous Materials 2010).

Gioia A, 'Nuclear Accidents and International Law', in A de Guttry, M Gestri and G Venturini (eds,), International Disaster Response Law (Springer 2012).

Hosseinniaa B et al, *Multi-plant emergency response for tackling major accidents in chemical industrial areas* (Safety Science 2018).

Inter-Agency Coordination Group for Industrial and Chemical Accidents. 'The International Efforts for Industrial and Chemical Accidents Prevention, Preparedness and Response' (2017).

International Atomic Energy Agency (IAEA), 'Human and Organizational Factors in Nuclear Safety in the Light of the Accident at the Fukushima Daiichi Nuclear Power Plant' (2014).

Saghafi M and Mohammad Ghofrani B M, *Accident management support tools in nuclear power plants: A post-Fukushima review* (Progress in Nuclear Energy 2016).

Takamura Y, *Release of Radioactive Substances into the Sea and International Law: The Japanese Experience in the Course of Nuclear Disaster* (The International Law of Disaster Relief 2014).

CHAPTER 14

Regional Perspective: Obligations under European Union Law as Applicable to CBRN Industrial Accidents

Federico Ferri

1 Introduction: The Applicable Legal Framework

Obligations related to CBRN industrial accidents can be spotted in several EU secondary law acts. However, the applicable legal framework is rather scattered, in the sense that it is not limited to one single measure specifically designed to regulate this sector. Accordingly, the chapter is structured as follows. First, the main baseline legislative acts are introduced, even if these norms do not directly refer to CBRN scenarios.[1] Then, obligations of prevention, preparedness and response (plus, if any, recovery) are examined.

The core piece of legislation is Directive 2012/18/EU on the control of major-accident hazards involving dangerous substances (Seveso III).[2] The Directive is then to be interpreted as also tackling CBRN industrial accidents,[3] primarily those of a chemical nature.[4] For this reason, Directive 2012/18 completes the EU chemicals legislation[5] which also comprises rules governing the marketing

1 Relevant rules pertaining to the EURATOM regulatory framework will not be analysed here. See ch 15 by Balboni.

2 Directive 2012/18/EU of the European Parliament and of the Council of 4 July 2012 on the control of major-accident hazards involving dangerous substances, amending and subsequently repealing Council Directive 96/82/EC [2012] OJ L197/1.

3 EUROJUST, 'CBRN-E Handbook. Overview of EU and International Legislation Applicable to CBRN (Chemical, Biological, Radiological and Nuclear) Substances and Explosives. Supranational Entities, Systems and Databases Active in the Field of CBRN-E' (June 2017) <https://op.europa.eu/it/publication-detail/-/publication/9c70e7ce-8c65-11e7-b5c6-01aa75ed71a1> 9–10 (all links were last accessed XX Month XXXX).

4 CoU Brief, 'CBRN-E' (Issue 5 March 2019) <https://www.securityresearch-cou.eu/sites/default/files/13th%20CoU%20Brief%20Theme%202%20CBRNE%20v2.pdf> 2.

5 See in particular Regulation (EC) No 1907/2006 of the European Parliament and of the Council of 18 December 2006 concerning the Registration, Evaluation, Authorisation and Restriction of Chemicals (REACH), establishing a European Chemicals Agency, amending Directive 1999/45/EC and repealing Council Regulation (EEC) No 793/93 and Commission Regulation (EC) No 1488/94 as well as Council Directive 76/769/EEC and Commission Directives 91/155/EEC, 93/67/EEC, 93/105/EC and 2000/21/EC [2006] OJ L396/1; Regulation

© FEDERICO FERRI, 2022 | DOI:10.1163/9789004507999_015

and use of specific products, restrictions on the placing on the market and use of certain hazardous substances and preparations, and norms applicable to exports of dangerous substances.

The measure at stake mainly falls within the scope of application of the EU's environmental policy, as its legal basis is Article 192(1) TFEU and its ultimate goal is to bring about a high level of protection, especially in the environmental and health domains. The whole system was also found to be highly coherent with the Union Civil Protection Mechanism.[6]

It must be stressed that this Directive, whose transposition was due by 1 June 2015, amended the legal framework in a sector that the EU started to regulate almost 40 years ago. First, Directive 82/501/EEC (Seveso I)[7] introduced obligations to fulfil in case of major-accident hazards of certain industrial activities. Then, Directive 96/82/EC (Seveso II)[8] – which was passed after the adoption of the United Nations Economic Commission for Europe (UNECE) Convention on the Transboundary Effects of Industrial Accidents[9] – replaced Seveso I and reshaped the previous discipline.[10] Finally, Seveso II was amended by Directive 2003/105/EC[11] and repealed by Directive 2012/18 with

(EC) No 1272/2008 of the European Parliament and of the Council of 16 December 2008 on classification, labelling and packaging of substances and mixtures, amending and repealing Directives 67/548/EEC and 1999/45/EC, and amending Regulation (EC) No 1907/2006 [2008] OJ L353/1; Regulation (EU) No 649/2012 of the European Parliament and of the Council of 4 July 2012 concerning the export and import of hazardous chemicals [2012] OJ L201/60.

6 European Commission, Interim evaluation of the Union Civil Protection Mechanism, 2014–2016: Final Report, August 2017, 72. The Union Civil Protection Mechanism is dealt with *infra* (see ch 19 by Ferri).

7 Council Directive 82/501/EEC of 24 June 1982 on the major-accident hazards of certain industrial activities [1982] OJ L230/1. For more information on the historical background, see J Wettig, S Porter and C Kirchsteiger, 'Major industrial accidents regulation in the European Union' (1999) 12(1) Journal of Loss Prevention in the Process Industries 19–20.

8 Council Directive 96/82/EC of 9 December 1996 on the control of major-accident hazards involving dangerous substances [1997] OJ L10/13. See especially B Pozzo (ed.), *The Implementation of the Seveso Directives in an Enlarged Europe: A Look into the Past and a Challenge for the Future* (Wolters Kluwer 2009).

9 Convention on the Transboundary Effects of Industrial Accidents of the United Nations Economic Commission for Europe (1992).

10 G Boldi, 'La disciplina dei rischi di incidenti industriali', in B Caravita, L Cassetti and A Morrone (eds.), *Diritto dell'ambiente* (Giappichelli 2016) 231, 232ff.

11 Directive 2003/105/EC of the European Parliament and of the Council of 16 December 2003 amending Council Directive 96/82/EC on the control of major-accident hazards involving dangerous substances [2003] OJ L345/97.

effect from 1 June 2015.[12] Chiefly, Seveso III introduced two different classes of establishments, amended the list of dangerous substances, strengthened the requirements for public information (which are, in turn, one of the main pillars of another instrument promoted under the UNECE, namely the 1998 Aarhus Convention).[13]

Directive 2012/18 covers the dangerous substances mentioned in Annex I and it applies to the management cycle of major accidents[14] that can take place in an 'establishment'[15] (Article 3). The scope of Seveso III is limited by some substantial exceptions listed in Article 2(2).[16] The Directive distinguishes between 'lower-tier' and 'upper-tier' establishments, depending on the type and quantity of dangerous substances dealt with in the case concerned.[17] As one can imagine, upper-tier establishments are meant to be potentially more

12 The degree of implementation of Seveso II until 2014 was considered rather positive. See Report from the Commission 'Report on the application in the Member States of Directive 96/82/EC on the control of major-accident hazards involving dangerous substances for the period 2012–2014', COM (2017) 665 final. More details can be found in J Calero et al, 'Analysis and Summary of Member States' Reports on the Implementation of Directive 96/82/EC on the Control of Major Accident Hazards Involving Dangerous Substances. Final Report' (Amec Foster Wheeler and European Commission Directorate-General for Environment, May 2017), <https://op.europa.eu/en/publication-detail/-/publication/26c9aa63-523e-11e7-a5ca-01aa75ed71a1>.

13 Convention on Access to Information, Public Participation in Decision-Making and Access to Justice in Environmental Matters (1998).

14 This expression means 'an occurrence such as a major emission, fire, or explosion resulting from uncontrolled developments in the course of the operation of any establishment covered by this Directive, and leading to serious danger to human health or the environment, immediate or delayed, inside or outside the establishment, and involving one or more dangerous substances'. See ibid art 3(13). Sometimes the Directive also refers to 'near misses': see, for example, ibid Recital 24, art 10(5), art 20(6). However, the EU legislator failed to define this kind of occurrence. Apparently, this expression is used to stimulate the taking of precautionary measures under Seveso III.

15 An establishment is the 'whole location under the control of an operator where dangerous substances are present in one or more installations, including common or related infrastructures or activities'. See ibid art 3(1). The combined provisions of points 1 and 13 of Article 3 allow one to conclude that the concept of 'industrial accident' does not cover export and import activities. This is why further acts like Regulation (EU) 649/2012 (n 5) will not be analysed in the present chapter.

16 These exceptions mainly refer to military establishments, waste landfill sites, transport and exploitation activities.

17 As its predecessor, Directive 2012/18 (n 2) follows a so-called 'two-tier approach'. Basically, for each named substance and for each generic category of substances and preparations, two different qualifying quantities (a lower and an upper value) are mentioned in Annex I, Parts 1 and 2.

dangerous; accordingly, the Directive provides more stringent obligations where these establishments come into play.

Based on the Preamble of Seveso III (Recital 6), the whole legal framework applicable to industrial accidents revolves around the need for operators to take all necessary steps 'to prevent major accidents, to mitigate their consequences and to take recovery measures'. In particular, it rests on a communication system which involves the operator and a national competent authority, which is to be specifically set up or appointed by each Member State.[18] The system also functions to allow Member States to submit timely and accurate information to the European Commission, which retains some important powers under the Directive[19] and is assisted by other bodies as well.[20]

With a view to fostering the enforcement of the obligations prescribed by the Directive, Article 20 provides that Member States shall ensure that the competent authorities organise a system of inspections to be conducted in accordance with relevant criteria. Inspections must be appropriate to the type of establishment concerned and sufficient for a planned and systematic examination of the technical, organisational or managerial systems employed.

Seveso III sets minimum requirements for implementing legislation. In this regard, either the Commission or the Member States benefit from the support offered by the 'Seveso Expert Group', whose core mission is to discuss the implementation issues of Directive 2012/18. Reportedly, so far, the implementation of the Directive has been satisfactory and 'Member States are attempting to ingrain the concepts of major industrial accident prevention and protection within the culture of their countries'.[21] Generally speaking,

18 The rules concerning the obligation to set up or appoint a national competent authority are contained in ibid art 6.

19 Overall, the Commission was considered as a 'super-regulator' in this framework: see A Maniatis, 'Approche De La Directive Seveso III' (2019) 77 Curentul Juridic, The Juridical Current, Le Courant Juridique 13, 17.

20 For example, the Joint Research Centre (JRC), that is to say the European Commission's science and knowledge service, should be mentioned. It supports EU policies with independent scientific evidence throughout the entire policy cycle. As far as industrial accidents are concerned, the activity of the JRC Major Accident Hazards Bureau (MAHB) is of particular importance; chiefly, the MAHB has created the MINERVA portal where one can find relevant information, publications, and tools on control of major chemical hazards (<https://minerva.jrc.ec.europa.eu/en/minerva>).

21 M White, 'High Hazard Operations: Volume 1. SEVESO III: The Regulatory Framework for Major Industrial Accidents in the EU' (Specialty Technical Consultants 2017), <http://www.specialtytechnicalconsultants.com/wp-content/uploads/Regulatory-Framework-for-Industrial-Accidents-in-EU-eBook-Vol-1.pdf> 6.

many Member States managed to incorporate Seveso III requirements into national legislation by the time prescribed by the Directive, even though, also in 2021, the Commission has decided to send letters of formal notice to a few EU countries to seek the improvement of their national rules on prevention of major accidents involving dangerous substances.[22] Apparently, the majority of the implementation concerns highlighted do not relate to horizontal aspects but to technical issues linked to specific substances.[23]

Some relevant provisions on protection against CBRN industrial accidents can also be found in EU secondary law on waste, keeping in mind that the EU has planned to achieve full coherence between the laws implementing waste and chemicals policies.[24] Waste can be covered by CBRN-related initiatives,[25] as shown by some projects delivered on behalf of the EU CBRN Centres of Excellence (CoE) initiative.[26] Attention should be drawn especially to hazardous waste, pursuant to the definition provided by Directive 2008/98/EC establishing the baseline framework on waste.[27] Since Directive 2012/18 does not apply to waste landfill sites[28] – including underground waste storage – it may be useful to refer to some EU legislative acts addressing this subject matter in the context of industrial accidents, namely Directive 2008/98, Directive 1999/31/EC on the landfill of waste,[29] and Directive 2006/21/EC on the management of waste from extractive industries.[30]

At the heart of the legal regime applicable to waste management and CBRN industrial accidents is Article 17 of Directive 2008/98, which establishes, along the lines of Article 13, that Member States 'shall take the necessary action' to ensure that the management of hazardous waste (from the production phase)

---

22 <https://ec.europa.eu/commission/presscorner/detail/en/inf_21_2743>.

23 <https://www.dsb.no/globalassets/dokumenter/farlige-stoffer-npf/industrisikkerhet/questions--answers-seveso-iii-directive-version-2018.pdf> 9ff.

24 Communication from the Commission to the European Parliament, the Council, the European Economic and Social Committee and the Committee of the Regions, On the implementation of the circular economy package: options to address the interface between chemical, product and waste legislation, COM (2018) 32 final, 7.

25 EUROJUST (n 3).

26 See <https://europa.eu/cbrn-risk-mitigation/projects_en>. As for the EU CBRN Centres of Excellence initiative, see ch 10 by Villani.

27 Directive 2008/98/EC of the European Parliament and of the Council of 19 November 2008 on waste and repealing certain Directives [2008] OJ L312/3. See in particular art 3(2) and Annex III.

28 Directive 2012/18 (n 2), art 2(2).

29 Council Directive 1999/31/EC of 26 April 1999 on the landfill of waste [1999] OJ L182/1.

30 Directive 2006/21/EC of the European Parliament and of the Council of 15 March 2006 on the management of waste from extractive industries and amending Directive 2004/35/EC [2006] OJ L102/15.

is carried out 'in conditions providing protection for the environment and human health'. Similarly, Article 8(3)(iii) of Directive 1999/31 simply provides that the landfill shall be operated in such a manner that the necessary measures are taken to prevent accidents and limit their consequences.

Another legislative act that may be relevant in the field of CBRN industrial accidents is Directive 2008/114/EC on European critical infrastructures (ECI Directive).[31] The very goal of this Directive is to contribute to the protection of people *vis à vis* the risks stemming from ECIs. It does not directly address industrial accidents, but it does also tackle this kind of issue since it was adopted to foster protection of critical infrastructures[32] the disruption or destruction of which would have a significant impact of a transboundary nature. Therefore, industrial accidents may certainly fall within the field of application of Directive 2008/114.

Furthermore, even though Article 3(3) states that the sectors to be used for the purposes of implementing the Directive are just energy and transport, at its root is the need to follow an all-hazards approach (Recital 3); and, in any case, Recital 9 confirms that the energy sector may include electricity transmission parts of nuclear power plants. This means that the ECI Directive might also apply in certain CBRN scenarios.

One of the most peculiar aspects of the ECI Directive is that it was adopted by virtue of the 'flexibility clause' enshrined in Article 308 ECT (now Article 352 TFEU). Possibly, this circumstance played a meaningful role in the allocation of powers within the ECI system. Indeed, Recital 6 anticipates that '(t)he primary and ultimate responsibility for protecting ECIs falls on the Member States and the owners/operators of such infrastructures'. So, the powers of the European Commission are quite limited compared to the ones of the Member States.

That said, it should not be forgotten that the EU also committed to cooperate internationally for the achievement of a high level of protection in the field of major industrial accidents, including those amounting to CBRN events.[33]

31 Council Directive 2008/114/EC of 8 December 2008 on the identification and designation of European critical infrastructures and the assessment of the need to improve their protection [2008] OJ L345/75.

32 A critical infrastructure is defined as 'an asset, system or part thereof located in Member States which is essential for the maintenance of vital societal functions, health, safety, security, economic or social well-being of people, and the disruption or destruction of which would have a significant impact in a Member State as a result of the failure to maintain those functions'. See ibid art 2(a).

33 See, inter alia, <https://circabc.europa.eu/d/d/workspace/SpacesStore/1a754cca-365d-4d43-ab47-f0d9de110d34/Inter-Agency%20Coodination%20Group%20-%20brochure.pdf>.

Besides bilateral activities and cooperation with candidate countries, the EU ratified the abovementioned Convention on the Transboundary Effects of Industrial Accidents and participates in all relevant international fora, especially those which aim to contribute to the achievement of the Sustainable Development Goals and the mission of the Sendai Framework for Disaster Risk Reduction.

For example, the EU (alongside its Member States) provides political and financial support to the United Nations Environment Programme (UNEP). In this regard, it is worth mentioning the UNEP Flexible Framework Initiative for Addressing Chemical Accident Prevention and Preparedness.[34] This initiative is not binding, but it may have some influence at supranational level on the development of prevention and preparedness approaches. In particular, it is meant to enable the design of tailor-made programmes for chemical accident prevention and preparedness related to hazardous installations.

Furthermore, due to the intensive cooperation between the EU and the Organization for Economic Co-operation and Development (OECD), another meaningful initiative is the OECD Programme on chemical accidents.[35] The main activities carried out within this programme are aimed at developing common principles and policy guidance on prevention of, preparedness for, and response to chemical accidents, analysing issues of concern (also in order to make recommendations concerning best practices), and facilitating the sharing of information and experience.

Collaboration patterns were also developed by the Council of Europe, which invited the EU to share the knowledge accumulated and urged the European States (including EU Member States) to update applicable legislation on the prevention and limitation of industrial hazards, especially in residential areas, to improve cross-border cooperation.[36]

2 Obligations of Prevention

The main obligations regarding the prevention of CBRN industrial accidents are contained in Directive 2012/18.

34 See, in particular, UNEP, 'A Flexible Framework for Addressing Chemical Accident Prevention and Preparedness. A Guidance Document', 2010, <https://www.eecentre.org/wp-content/uploads/2009/01/UN_Flexible_Framework_WEB_FINAL.pdf>.

35 For further information see <http://www.oecd.org/env/ehs/chemical-accidents/thechemicalaccidentsprogramme.htm>.

36 See for example Council of Europe, Resolution of the Parliamentary Assembly of the 1430 of 18 March 2005.

To start with, the fact that the *ex ante* dimension of the system laid down by this Directive is more pronounced does not go unnoticed. As clarified by Recital 3, Seveso III primarily focuses on the need to prevent major accidents. Indeed, the need to further strengthen the level of protection concerning the prevention of these events was one of the main reasons behind the choice of the EU legislator to repeal Seveso II. So, the *ex ante* dimension of the system laid down by Directive 2012/18 is more pronounced.

However, it is worth clarifying that Seveso III prescribes provisions on the 'control' of certain dangerous accidents. This expression suggests that the Directive puts forward a far-reaching approach, which is not only limited to imposing *ex ante* obligations. Moreover, Article 1 sets forth rules for the prevention of major accidents involving dangerous substances, and the limitation of their consequences for human health and the environment, with the aim to ensure a high level of protection throughout the Union in a consistent and effective manner.

As for prevention obligations under Seveso III, the first one is quite generic and leaves discretionary powers to national competent authorities. On the basis of Article 5, Member States must ensure that the operator is obliged to take all necessary measures to prevent major accidents and to limit the consequences of such events for human health and the environment.

Articles 8 and 10 are the key provisions on the prevention of major-accident hazards involving dangerous substances. They draw, respectively, from Articles 7 and 9 of Directive 96/82 and establish obligations that Member States shall comply with by imposing rules of conduct on the operators. The fulfilment of these obligations shall be attested through documents to be sent to the competent authority and reviewed periodically (at least every five years).[37]

Article 8 provides that operators shall draft a major-accident prevention policy (MAPP). This document basically indicates the operator's overall approach and measures for controlling major-accident hazards and it includes an explanation of the appropriate safety management systems.[38] The MAPP must be implemented 'by appropriate means, structures and by a safety management system proportionate to the major-accident hazards, and the complexity of the organisation or the activities of the establishment'.[39] Needless to say, the

37 These documents must be reviewed also in case of relevant modifications concerning the operator's overall activity; some major examples of situations in which these obligations must be carried out are listed in Decision 2012/18 (n 2), art 11.

38 See also ibid Recital 12.

39 Ibid art 8(5).

proportionality assessment under Article 8 leaves some leeway to the authority tasked with the performance of this evaluation.

The safety management system must be designed in conformity with the principles and requirements established by Annex III to the Directive, which apply in particular to the following areas: organisation and personnel; identification and evaluation of major hazards; operational control; management of change; planning for emergencies; monitoring performance; audit and review.

Article 10 adds that the operators of upper-tier establishments have to produce a safety report. This document is, at least in part, supplementary to the MAPP. Above all, the safety report serves to demonstrate that the operator has identified the major-accident hazards and possible major-accident scenarios and that, against this background, the necessary measures have been taken to prevent such accidents and to limit their consequences for human health and the environment.[40] These measures are not limited to the operation concerned, since the operator has to demonstrate that adequate safety and reliability have been 'taken into account' with reference to anything that is connected with that operation and which is linked to major-accident hazards inside the establishment.

Article 13 of Seveso III prescribes more general obligations on land-use planning for Member States. These obligations are aimed at bringing more added value to the pursuit of the objectives of preventing major accidents and limiting their consequences for human health and the environment. Article 13 obligations mainly amount to control duties for future developments, like new sites, modifications or new developments in the vicinity.[41] For the purpose of aligning land-use or other relevant policies (and the procedures for their implementation) with the Directive, Member States shall also ensure that all the authorities concerned set up appropriate consultation procedures.

Moving to EU secondary law on waste, Directive 2006/21/EC on the management of waste from extractive industries needs to be considered. Directive 1999/31/EC on the landfill of waste fails to provide for rules similar to the ones of the 'Seveso system'. To the contrary, Directive 2006/21 is more detailed.

40 To this end, the safety report shall contain at least the data and information listed in Annex II, which refer to the following aspects: management system and organisation of the establishment (with a view to major-accident prevention); presentation of environment of the establishment; description of the installation; identification and accidental risks analysis and prevention methods; measures of protection and intervention to limit the consequences of a major accident.

41 For example, it is necessary to take into account technical aspects, safety distancing issues, and the particular natural sensitivity or interest of certain areas, as indicated in Directive 2012/18 (n 2), art 13(2).

Above all, it imposes on the Member States the obligation to ensure that major-accident hazards are identified and that each operator, before the start of operations, draws up a major-accident[42] prevention policy for the management of extractive waste and puts into effect a safety management system implementing it. The core provisions are contained in Section 1 of Annex I, whose provisions basically mirror those of Annex III of Directive 2012/18.

Shifting the focus to Directive 2008/114/EC, it seems clear that it was mainly designed to develop an *ex ante* approach, almost entirely centred on prevention measures. As explained by Article 1, the ECI Directive establishes a procedure for the identification and designation of European critical infrastructures in each Member State's territory, and a common approach for assessing the need to improve their protection.

The first part of Article 1 lays down some conditions which anticipate the fulfilment of prevention obligations. Both the identification and designation procedures are primarily run by Member States. The European Commission is entitled to receive information and can assist the Member States where necessary, but only in exceptional circumstances does it have the power to formulate recommendations. The proper functioning of the system put in place by the Directive depends on the efficiency of multilevel communication channels, which are also essential to preventing industrial accidents involving ECIs. As illustrated in Recital 14 '(t)he efficient identification of risks, threats and vulnerabilities in the particular sectors requires communication both between owners/operators of ECIs and the Member States, and between the Member States and the Commission'. Nevertheless, as already anticipated, the key players are the Member States.

To identify ECIs in their territories Member States are required to follow the procedure indicated in Annex III to the Directive. In particular, they must base their overall assessment on the cross-cutting criteria provided by Article 3(2): the potential number of fatalities or injuries, the significance of economic loss and/or degradation of products or services (including potential environmental effects), and the impact on public confidence, physical suffering and disruption of daily life (including the loss of essential services). Article 3(2) clarifies that the precise thresholds set under these criteria (eg putting a figure on the actual number of fatalities or injuries) must be based on the severity of the impact of the disruption or destruction of a particular infrastructure by taking into account its characteristics. Beyond this stipulation, Member States are free to determine precise thresholds on a case-by-case basis. The designation of an ECI (Article 4) is the result of an agreement between at least two Member

42 This expression is defined in Directive 2006/21 (n 30), art 3(16).

States: the one where the ECI is located and one or more other Member States which may be significantly affected by damage to that infrastructure.

The main prevention obligations require the definition of procedures and compliance with reporting duties.

In accordance with Article 5, once an ECI has been designated, the relevant operator security plan (OSP) must be prepared (unless an equivalent already exists). This procedure must identify the critical infrastructure assets of the ECI and the security solutions that already exist or are in the process of being implemented.[43] In every ECI, a Security Liaison Officer, or equivalent, must be appointed and he or she will be the point of contact between the owner/ operator of the ECI and the relevant Member State authority for security related issues (Article 6).

As regards the involvement of the European Commission, Article 7 requires the Member States to conduct a threat assessment in relation to each ECI subsector within the first year following the designation. Member States also have to submit reports to the European Commission every two years, providing summaries of the types of risks, threats and vulnerabilities encountered. In line with the broad logic of the Directive, the reporting obligations incumbent on the Member States are not particularly detailed and the Commission is not entitled to take binding initiatives on the basis of the information received.

3 Obligations of Preparedness

While prevention obligations concerning industrial accidents (also applicable to CBRN scenarios) can be found also outside Directive 2012/18, preparedness obligations are mainly contained in this piece of legislation.

In the framework of Seveso III, the main preparedness provision is Article 12. It refers to the preparation of emergency plans that shall be put into effect in case of major accidents or of an uncontrolled event which by its nature could

43 Under Annex II to Directive 2008/114 (n 31), the OSP procedure also covers a risk analysis based on major threat scenarios, vulnerability of each asset, and potential impact, plus the identification, selection and prioritisation of counter-measures and procedures, which encompass both permanent and graduated security measures. The former type of measures concerns indispensable security investments and means which are relevant to be employed at all times, while graduated security measures can be activated according to varying risk and threat levels. Annex II refers to measures such as: 'technical measures (including installation of detection, access control, protection and prevention means); organisational measures (including procedures for alerts and crisis management); control and verification measures; communication; awareness raising and training; and security of information systems'.

reasonably be expected to lead to a major accident.[44] The obligation applies only where upper-tier establishments are concerned and is completed by Annex IV, which indicates the information to be communicated through the emergency plans.

Pursuant to Article 12(3), the emergency plans are aimed at mitigating the effects of incidents – especially negative consequences on human health and the environment – and at enabling the efficient flow of all relevant information when incidents occur. They also serve to guide the activities to be put in place to secure restoration and clean-up of the environment.

In light of their strategic significance, according to Article 12(6), emergency plans must be periodically reviewed and duly tested (at least every three years). However, review (and test) obligations concerning emergency plans are more detailed than similar obligations established by Articles 8 and 10 with regard to MAPP, safety management systems and safety reports.[45]

There are two categories of emergency plans. First, internal emergency plans to be drawn up by the operators, in consultation with the personnel (and regarding measures applicable) inside the establishment.[46] Second, external emergency plans that may be drawn up by the competent authority[47] based on specific information supplied by the operators and, under certain circumstances, after the public concerned have been allowed to express their opinion.[48]

Both kinds of emergency plans are also required by Article 6 (paragraphs 3 and 4) of Directive 2006/21 on the management of waste from extractive industries, which lays down similar rules to those enshrined in Article 12 of Directive 2012/18.

A peculiar manifestation of the preparedness obligations provided for by Directive 2012/18 is contained in the combined provisions of Article 14 and Annex V. The rules in question basically provide that some crucial information must be made available to the general public or to the public concerned

44 Directive 2012/18 (n 2), art 12(7).

45 See also ibid art 12(6), which clarifies that the review of emergency plans shall be carried out by taking into account 'changes occurring in the establishments concerned or within the emergency services concerned, new technical knowledge, and knowledge concerning the response to major accidents'.

46 Ibid art 12(1)(a) and art 12(4).

47 The competent authority maintains the power to decide that, in view of the information contained in the safety report to be provided by the operator under Article 10, the requirement to produce an external emergency plan can be disregarded; such decision shall simply be duly motivated (ibid art 12(8)).

48 This prerogative must be accorded only when the emergency plans are being established or substantially modified (ibid art 12(5)).

(although the Directive does not specify either which subject must carry out such activity or how to do it). For sure, one of the key functions of Article 14 information is to enable efficient reactions in case of incidents. From this point of view, Article 14(2)(a) is paradigmatic, as it requires that all persons likely to be affected by a major accident involving an upper-tier establishment receive regular, direct, clear, and intelligible 'information on safety measures and requisite behaviour' so that they are prepared in the event of such an accident.

The obligations under Article 14 are of a different nature to the activities of public consultation and participation, which are dictated by Article 15. The scope of the latter (in line with the broad logic of the 1998 Aarhus Convention) is to ensure public consultation and participation in decision-making when a specific new project has been tabled. However, it is fair to assume that the combination of Articles 14 and 15 contributes to the reduction of the gap between risk regulation and risk communication that characterised the early stages of the Seveso legal framework.[49]

4 Obligations of Response

The previous paragraphs have demonstrated that response obligations in the field of CBRN industrial accidents are almost exclusively contained in Directive 2012/18.[50] These obligations have to be respected by the operators and the competent authorities – via national regulations – when a major accident takes place.

The first provision to focus on is Article 16. Here the EU legislator listed the information to be communicated to the competent authority by the operator as soon as it becomes available. The information required mainly refers to: the circumstances of the accident; the dangerous substances involved; the data available for assessing the negative consequences of the accident on human health, the environment and property; and the emergency measures taken by the operator in the immediate post-accident timeframe. In addition, the operator must provide information concerning the steps it plans to take in order to mitigate the effects of the accident and to prevent such an accident from recurring in the future.

---

49 See on this point O Renn, 'Risk Communication at the Community Level: European Lessons from the Seveso Directive' (1989) 39(10) Journal of the Air & Waste Management Association 1301, 1307.

50 Some general obligations are contained also in Directive 2006/21 (n 30), arts 6(4) and 16(3).

The primary function of the information supplied by the operator is to put the competent authority in the best position to take broader-range initiatives, as established by Article 17 (and some of these measures appear to be halfway between the response and recovery phases).[51] In particular, Article 17(a) stipulates that the competent authority, based on all the circumstances that it is aware of, shall take 'any urgent, medium-term and long-term measures which may prove necessary for a full analysis of the technical, organisational and managerial aspects of the accident'. Then, it must take appropriate action to ensure the mitigation of the effects and that any necessary remedial measures are taken; in this respect, Article 17(c) clarifies that these measures are to be put in place by the operator at the request of the competent authority. Lastly, according to Article 17(e), the competent authority must provide the persons likely to be affected with information on the accident which has occurred and, where relevant, with information on all mitigation measures undertaken.

As for the suitability of the measures, the competent authority has considerable discretion to decide which are the most appropriate ones, given that no additional requirements have been established by either the Directive or the Commission's implementing acts.

The synergies developed between the operator and the competent authority are also aimed at allowing the Member State concerned to provide the European Commission with details on the event that has occurred as soon as practicable – and at the latest within one year of the date of the accident – as prescribed by Article 18.[52] Nevertheless, nothing in the text of the Directive seems to suggest that the Commission can impose specific obligations upon the competent authority in order to guide its activities during the response phase.

Bearing the above in mind, it should be added that the provisions establishing response obligations lead, in their turn, to new prevention obligations. For example, within the meaning of Article 16(c)(ii) the operator also has to take measures to prevent any recurrence of an accident like the one that has occurred and, accordingly, these initiatives must be communicated to the competent authority, so that it can make recommendations on future preventive measures, pursuant to Article 17(d). Likewise, the information to be supplied

51 However, even though Recital 6 of Directive 2012/18 (above, Section 1) mentions the recovery phase also when introducing the need to impose (indirect) general obligations on the operators, except for art 17, the provisions contained in the Directive almost never refer to this phase.

52 However, more detailed criteria are set forth in Directive 2012/18 (n 2), Annex VI.

by Member States to the European Commission following a major accident to which Article 18(1) refers are meant to also pursue the prevention of further similar events. In this respect, an essential part of the major accident control cycle is represented by the lessons learned from past accidents.[53]

5 Concluding Remarks

The analysis carried out in this chapter has shown that the EU legal framework applicable to CBRN industrial accidents is rather limited and weak.

The obligations detected are not particularly strict and their scope of application is quite limited. This means that Member States enjoy much room for manoeuvre as regards the power to regulate this domain. Such leeway tends to broaden as security issues gain momentum, since they are subject to the exclusive competence of the Member States by virtue of Article 4(2) TEU. That appears to be the case especially of Directive 2008/114; in fact, as observed by the European Commission, 'because the generality of some of the Directive's provisions left room for different interpretations by Member States, it has only to a limited degree achieved the objective of establishing a common approach to the assessment of the need to improve the protection of ECI'.[54]

There is also a clear imbalance between *ex ante* and *ex post* obligations. It can be argued that while the former set of obligations has been developed, at least to a certain degree, this is not the case for the latter; moreover, when considering *ex ante* obligations, it is undisputed that the prevention phase has been developed more than the one of preparedness. Accordingly, when it comes to response it is necessary to refer to other EU secondary law acts, especially those adopted in the realm of the EU civil protection policy.

In addition, although Seveso III – when compared to the other Directives examined above – seems suitable to govern the issues characterising industrial accidents, the overall legal framework is quite old with regard to the need to properly address evolving CBRN threats and events. This is true especially if one considers the Directive on critical infrastructures. Indeed, two main

53 See also Directive 2012/18 (n 2), art 21(4) and B Weibull, C Fredstrom and M H Wood, 'Learning Lessons from Accidents Key Points and Conclusions for Inspectors of Major Chemical Hazard Sites. A Seveso Inspection Series Publication' (JRC Technical Report, 2020) <https://publications.jrc.ec.europa.eu/repository/bitstream/JRC120014/mjv_report_-_learning_from_incidents_ed_2cf_online_jrc_v2.pdf>.

54 Commission Staff Working Document Evaluation of Council Directive 2008/114 on the Identification and designation of European critical infrastructures and the assessment of the need to improve their protection, SWD(2019)308 final, 33.

aspects have been stressed by the Expert Group on the Control of Major Accident Hazards Involving Dangerous Substances. First, it was suggested that recent developments in the nature of threats require a different approach, meaning that new focus areas should be considered (like cybersecurity, insider threats, hybrid threats, drones); second, Directive 2008/114 should change from an instrument that only identifies critical infrastructures to a tool that also addresses resilience protection.[55]

While waiting for possible amendments, if any, the EU and Member States should strive to develop common guidelines and strategies to be adapted in a flexible way to different national scenarios, at least as far as transboundary negative effects are considered. In this respect, international cooperation will keep playing a major role.

Bibliography

Boldi G, 'La disciplina dei rischi di incidenti industriali', in B Caravita, L Cassetti and A Morrone (eds.), *Diritto dell'ambiente* (Giappichelli 2016) 231.

Maniatis A, 'Approche De La Directive Seveso III' (2019) 77 Curentul Juridic, The Juridical Current, Le Courant Juridique 13.

Pozzo B (ed.), *The Implementation of the Seveso Directives in an Enlarged Europe: A Look into the Past and a Challenge for the Future* (Wolters Kluwer 2009).

Renn O, 'Risk Communication at the Community Level: European Lessons from the Seveso Directive' (1989) 39(10) Journal of the Air & Waste Management Association 1301.

Weibull B, Fredstrom C and Wood M H, 'Learning Lessons from Accidents Key Points and Conclusions for Inspectors of Major Chemical Hazard Sites. A Seveso Inspection Series Publication' (JRC Technical Report, 2020) 1.

Wettig J, Porter S and Kirchsteiger C, 'Major industrial accidents regulation in the European Union' (1999) 12(1) Journal of Loss Prevention in the Process Industries 19.

White M, 'High Hazard Operations: Volume 1. SEVESO III: The Regulatory Framework for Major Industrial Accidents in the EU' (Specialty Technical Consultants 2017) 2.

55 6th Meeting of the Commission Expert Group on the Control of Major Accident Hazards Involving Dangerous Substances, 7 March 2018 (Minutes of 26 March 2018) 2–3.

CHAPTER 15

Nuclear Safety and Security in Europe

Marco Balboni

1 General Framework: The Euratom and European Union Treaties

As a matter of principle, the Euratom Treaty does not provide for a clear competence in the matter of Nuclear Safety and Security (NSS).[1] Euratom's major objective is to promote nuclear industrial development. In light of this objective, the Community is meant to promote research and ensure the dissemination of technical information; establish uniform safety standards to protect the health of workers and of the general public; ensure that these standards are applied; and facilitate and ensure investment, particularly by encouraging new ventures by undertakings.[2]

In this framework, Title 2, Chapter 3 of the Euratom Treaty is entitled 'Health and Safety', but deals exclusively with issues concerning radiation protection for the workers and the general public, setting out the content and limits of the powers of the Community in this field.[3] In particular, Articles 30 and 31 provide for the establishment of basic standards for the protection of the health of workers and the general public against the dangers arising from ionising radiation. Article 30 provides a definition of the basic standards and Article 31 describes the procedure for the adoption and enforcement of those standards. Article 32 provides that the basic standards established according to Article 30 may be revised or supplemented in accordance with the procedure laid down in Article 31, while Article 33 specifies the duties of the Member States in implementing the obligations coming from the European framework and the duties of reporting to the Commission.[4] The last provisions provide

1 The European Atomic Energy Community (EAEC – Euratom) was established in 1957 as one of the then three Communities. While the European Economic Community has evolved into the present European Union and the European Coal and Steel Community has expired (in 2002), Euratom continues to exist without substantial changes to its autonomous personality.

2 See also the competences attributed to the Euratom Supply Agency by the Council Decision establishing Statutes for the Euratom Supply Agency, 2008/114/EC, Euratom (2008) OJ L41 15.

3 D Fouquet, 'Nuclear Policy in the EU from a Legal and Institutional Point-of-View', in Haas R, Mez L, Ajanovic A (eds), *The Technological and Economic Future of Nuclear Power. Energiepolitik und Klimaschutz. Energy Policy and Climate Protection* (Springer VS 2019).

4 Art 33 says that 'Each Member State shall lay down the appropriate provisions, whether by legislation, regulation or administrative action, to ensure compliance with the basic

© MARCO BALBONI, 2022 | DOI:10.1163/9789004507999_016

a legal basis for legislation in the field of surveillance of radioactivity levels, apparently giving an important role to the Commission which reflects the so-called dirigiste imprint given by the drafters to the Euratom Treaty.[5] Not very clear is the external competence of the Community, especially in relation to the competences maintained by the Member States.[6]

It seems clear that Article 30 does not give any competence to Euratom to directly safeguard Nuclear Power stations. As indicated by O' Driscoll:

> [i]t essentially provides for the Community to establish a series of dose limits for exposure of human beings to radiation [...] But it does not provide any competence to Euratom either with respect to possible damage to the natural environment caused by radiation, and perhaps even more remarkably, it provides no Euratom Community competence with respect to the safety of nuclear reactors.[7]

In other words, competences are limited to radiation protection, which focuses on effects of radioactivity on human health, not on nuclear safety as such, which rather focuses on technical aspects of installations. Nuclear safety was not included in the Euratom Treaty as an autonomous competence with an autonomous legal basis.[8]

This framework depends basically on the rationale upon which the Euratom Treaty was initially conceived. Essentially, it is and remains an organisation

---

standards which have been established and shall take the necessary measures with regard to teaching, education and vocational training. The Commission shall make appropriate recommendations for harmonising the provisions applicable in this field in the Member States. To this end, the Member States shall communicate to the Commission the provisions applicable at the date of entry into force of this Treaty and any subsequent draft provisions of the same kind'.

5 Arts 34–39. On these provisions, see below Section 2.

6 Art 101, para 1 Euratom says that 'The Community may, within the limits of its powers and jurisdiction, enter into obligations by concluding agreements or contracts with a third State, an international organisation or a national of a third State'. See also art 29, para 1, according to which 'Where an agreement or contract for the exchange of scientific or industrial information in the nuclear field between a Member State, a person or an undertaking on the one hand, and a third State, an international organisation or a national of a third State on the other, requires, on either part, the signature of a State acting in its sovereign capacity, it shall be concluded by the Commission'.

7 M O'Driscoll, *The European Parliament and the EURATOM Treaty: past, present and future* (European Parliament, Luxembourg, 2002).

8 A Söndersen, *Euratom at the Crossroads* (European University Institute 2014) 283. The present paper owes a lot to this PhD thesis, which offers an extensive analysis of the problems dealt with here.

whose main object is to improve the development of nuclear energy among Member States. Therefore, the Treaty does not fit into the actual internal energy market and its concerns about safety and security. The technology it was established to support is no longer economically competitive. There are now a multitude of possible suppliers which can guarantee security without the risks and internalised burdens associated with nuclear energy production, storage and radioactive waste.

Despite these limits, the Treaty has never been amended so far, even if some Member States have complained about this.[9]

However, thanks to the case law of the Court of Justice, Euratom seems to benefit from a new competence in the field of NSS, which may provide a new rationale for the organisation.

The defining moment for this development lies in the worldwide response to the Chernobyl accident in 1986, which is also the starting point of the Euratom policy in the field of NSS, despite the lack of an autonomous legal basis in the Treaty.

As is well known, in the wake of the accident, four conventions were adopted at the international level under the aegis of the IAEA: the Convention on Early Notification of a Nuclear Accident, the Convention on Assistance in the case of a Nuclear Accident or Radiological Emergency (the two Emergency Conventions), the Convention on Nuclear Safety and the Joint Convention on the Safety of Spent Fuel Management and on the Safety of Radioactive Waste Management.[10] These Conventions form the so-called 'nuclear safety family'.

Shortly after their adoption, Euratom, which had been a negotiator, took steps for acceding, but the problem of competence arose. In particular, the

9 See, for instance, Declaration No. 54 made by the Federal Republic of Germany, Ireland, the Republic of Hungary, the Republic of Austria and the Kingdom of Sweden, annexed to the Final Act of the Intergovernmental Conference which adopted the Treaty of Lisbon (2007), according to which 'Germany, Ireland, Hungary, Austria and Sweden note that the core provisions of the Treaty establishing the European Atomic Energy Community have not been substantially amended since its entry into force and need to be brought up to date. They therefore support the idea of a Conference of the Representatives of the Governments of the Member States, which should be convened as soon as possible': Consolidated Version of the Treaty on the Functioning of the European Union (2012) OJ C326 47.

10 Convention on Early Notification of a Nuclear Accident (1986); Convention on Assistance in the case of a Nuclear Accident or Radiological Emergency (1986); Convention on Nuclear Safety (1994); Joint Convention on the Safety of Spent Fuel Management and on the Safety of Radioactive Waste Management (1997). See A Gioia, 'Nuclear Accidents and International Law', in A De Guttry, M Gestri, G Venturini (eds), *International Disaster Response Law* (T.M.C. Asser Press 2012).

Commission and the Council disagreed on the extent to which Euratom could be bound by the Conventions. With the *Nuclear Safety Case*, settled in 2002, the Commission brought an action before the Court of Justice for partial annulment of the Council Decision approving the accession to the Nuclear Safety Convention, particularly of the attached Declaration adopted on the basis of Article 30(4)(iii) of the Convention, which requires a 'regional integration organization' willing to accede to declare 'what articles of the Convention apply to it, and the extent of its competence in the field covered by those articles'. According to the Commission, the Declaration infringed Community law in that it did not refer to all the competences of the Community in the fields covered by the Convention, particularly in the field of installations safety.[11] In order to ensure the 'practical effect' of the 'Health and Safety' provisions of the Euratom Treaty, the Court of Justice found it was 'not appropriate [...] to draw an artificial distinction between the protection of the general public and the safety of sources of ionizing radiation', or, in other words, distinguish between 'radiation protection' and 'nuclear safety for installations', adding that the development of scientific knowledge requires an integrated approach between radiation protection and nuclear safety. On the basis of these arguments, the Court was able to give a broad interpretation, especially of Articles 32 and 33 of the Euratom Treaty, thereby broadening the competence of Euratom to include also NSS policy.[12]

As is evident, the concrete effect of that case was to give to the Euratom Treaty a new rationale, while the initial one, *ie* the promotion of nuclear industry, appeared already obsolete.

The disagreement between the Council and the Commission on the competence issue resulted in a significant delay in acceding to the four international Conventions on nuclear safety. Despite the role played by Euratom during the negotiations and the specific clause on accession for regional integration organisations, Euratom only acceded to the Conventions years after their adoption, joining the Nuclear Safety Convention in 2000, the Joint Convention in 2005 and the two Emergency Conventions in 2006. Nevertheless, the *Nuclear Safety Case* has been of great importance for ensuring the full participation of the Community in the international conventions mentioned above and for the development of the internal legislation in the field.

---

11 Case C-29/99, *Commission v. Council* (2002) ECR I-11221.

12 Art 32 provides for supplementary measures to the basic standards recalled by art 30, and art 33 recalls the duties of the Member States in implementing Community obligations: see above.

If at the beginning Euratom was probably the only European Community to have competences in the matters of 'Health and Safety' in the nuclear field, even if limited to certain aspects, this is not any more the case. The progressive expansion of its competences has made the EU another important actor in the field.

The EU has no competences in the areas of operational safety of nuclear power plants, management and safe disposal of radioactive waste, storage or disposal facilities, or decommissioning of installations.[13] However, the conferral to the EU of certain general competences may have the effect of including also NSS policy. This is especially true with competences in the environmental field, conferred to the then European Community with the approval of the Single European Act in 1986.[14] Following the conferral of this competence, a number of provisions equally relevant for NSS policy have been adopted on the basis of the EU competences.[15] Clearly, radiation protection and environmental protection are closely linked and this may imply a certain overlap between the two sets of provisions. More generally, most of the competences conferred to the Euratom Community may be included in the more general EU competencies.[16]

This finding rises a number of questions.

First of all, the need to maintain a specific treaty on nuclear matters. This is too large an issue to discuss here. Suffice to say that a merger of the Euratom Treaty into the Treaties establishing the European Union is widely supported.[17]

Second, the relations between the Euratom Treaty and the Treaties concerning the European Union. Article 106a, para 3 of the Euratom Treaty says that 'The provisions of the Treaty on European Union and of the Treaty on the Functioning of the European Union shall not derogate from the provisions of this Treaty'. The 'shall not derogate' clause has often been interpreted as an expression of the principle *lex specialis derogat legi generali*. In the interpretation of the Court of Justice, this seems to imply that whenever the Euratom Treaty is silent, the EU Treaties may apply, especially as far as rules and

13 D Fouquet (n 3) 169.

14 Even if the Community had already intervened in the matter of the environment on the basis of the so-called flexibility clause.

15 Below Section 2.

16 Starting with the establishment of free circulation within the European Market, one of the main objectives of the Euratom Treaty at the beginning, and the relations with third countries: D Fouquet (n 2) 178.

17 A Söndersen (n 8) 33.

principles of a fundamental character are concerned.[18] A case in point is the *Temelín* case concerning Austrian legislation which, in substance, authorised actions for injunction to prevent a potential nuisance caused by an installation situated abroad, while for installations situated in the country only an action for compensation was admitted. In this case, the European Court of Justice (ECJ) declared that the discrimination contained in the Austrian law 'leads to the same outcome as a difference in treatment on grounds of nationality'. This discriminatory treatment 'does come within the scope of application of the EAEC Treaty' and cannot be 'justified on grounds of protecting life, public health, the environment or property rights' because 'the Community legislative framework contributes precisely and essentially towards ensuring such protection'.[19]

However, it remains unclear and open to discussion to what extent EU principles and rules may be transposed into the framework of the Euratom Treaty and caution seems to be appropriate in the matter.[20]

Third, the problem of choosing the correct legal basis for the adoption of the legal acts. This question is particularly crucial, considering the different processes of decision making that characterise the two organisations. Having never been amended, within the Euratom Treaty the role of the European Parliament is purely consultative, while this is not any more the case within the European Union,[21] where the European Parliament usually assumes the role of co-legislator with the Council, as is the case in the field of the environment. In fact, sometimes the European Parliament has challenged the legal basis chosen for the adoption of certain acts relevant to the environmental field, but the Court of Justice has normally dismissed such actions.[22]

With this framework in mind, the following sections consider the relevant legislation. In Section two, the analysis looks at measures of prevention and preparedness, while Section three deals with response and recovery measures.[23]

---

18 See also art 106, para 1 which enumerates a number of Articles of the European Union Treaties which 'shall apply to' the Euratom Treaty.

19 Case C-115/08, *Land Oberösterreich v. ČEZ, Temelín case* (2009) ECR I-10265.

20 One may think, for instance, of the EU rules on competition: A Söndersen (n 8) 408.

21 According to some, it is precisely for this reason that the Member States are unwilling to open a process of amendment of the Treaty. See I Cenevska, 'The European Parliament and the European Atomic and Energy Community: A Legitimacy Crisis?' (2010) 35 ELR 415.

22 Below Section 2, n 41.

23 Although it is not always easy to distinguish between the different kinds of measures mentioned in the text, prevention and preparedness measures tend to precede the event,

2 Measures of Prevention and Preparedness

Measures of prevention and preparedness basically concern three areas: radiation protection, nuclear safety and waste treatment. Measures concerning radiation protection are typically based on Euratom Treaty provisions, while measures concerning nuclear safety and waste treatment have been adopted in order to implement or facilitate the implementation of the international conventions belonging to the so called 'nuclear safety family'.

As said, Title 2, Chapter 3 of the Euratom Treaty, entitled 'Health and Safety', regulates human exposure to artificial ionising radiation (arts 30 to 39). While arts 30 to 33 concern the establishment of basic standards, arts 34 to 39 regulate the surveillance of radioactivity according to those standards.

On the basis of Article 30ff.,[24] adoption of dose standards has usually been done following the line established by the International Commission for Radiological Protection (ICRP). Probably, the most important achievements are the uniform safety standards on radiation protection, enacted after the Chernobyl disaster, and the obligations for new Eastern European Member States to either comply with certain safety standards regarding nuclear installations or to shut down their Soviet-style reactors.[25] In 2013, the basic safety standards (BSS) Directives as revised were replaced by Council Directive 2013/59/Euratom of 5 December 2013, laying down basic safety standards for protection against the dangers arising from exposure to ionising radiation which repealed the previously applicable rules.[26]

As far as the mechanism of surveillance is concerned, Article 35 establishes that the European Commission is entitled to access and scrutinise Member States' facilities which monitor levels of radioactivity, while Article 36 requires that the Commission is periodically informed on the levels of radioactivity in

even if they mainly focus on preparing to deal with it, while response and recovery measures tend to follow: see ch 12 by Domaine.

24 See above Section 1.

25 S Wolf, 'Euratom, the European Court of Justice, and the Limits of Nuclear Integration in Europe', (2001) 12 German Law Journal 1638.

26 Council Directive 2013/59/Euratom of 5 December 2013 laying down basic safety standards for protection against the dangers arising from exposure to ionising radiation, and repealing Directives 89/618/Euratom, 90/641/Euratom, 96/29/Euratom, 97/43/Euratom and 2003/122/Euratom (2013) OJ L13 1. See also Council Directive 2013/51/Euratom of 22 October 2013 laying down requirements for the protection of the health of the general public with regard to radioactive substances in water intended for human consumption (2013) OJ L296 12.

the Member States.[27] Thus, if a Member State were to withhold information in the event of a serious nuclear accident, the Commission could still inform the public in the EU and neighbouring countries. Article 37 obliges Member States to provide information on 'any plan for the disposal of radioactive waste' in order to enable the Commission 'to determine whether the implementation of such plan is liable to result in the radioactive contamination of the water, soil or airspace of another Member State'. The aim is to avoid transboundary contamination, not contamination within a Member State. Finally, Article 38 establishes that:

> in cases of urgency, the Commission shall issue a directive requiring the Member State concerned to take, within a period laid down by the Commission, all necessary measures to prevent infringement of the basic standards and to ensure compliance with regulations. In case of failure to implement these obligations, the Commission or any Member State concerned may forthwith, by way of derogation from Articles 258 and 259 of the Treaty on the Functioning of the European Union, bring the matter before the Court of Justice of the European Union.[28]

The Nuclear Safety Directive transfers major provisions from the International Convention on Nuclear Safety (CNS) of July 1994 and further safety principles into European Euratom legislation.[29] Its basic structure mirrors the Convention, which is essentially designed to protect individuals, society and the environment from harm by establishing and maintaining effective protection against radiological hazards in nuclear installations, even if it does not contain any mandatory provisions for safety control.[30]

The Directive requires Member States to submit certain practices that involve a hazard from ionising radiation to a system of reporting and prior

27 For the acquisition of the information, the Commission relies on the European Community Urgent Radiological Information Exchange.

28 S Wolf (n 25) 1657.

29 Council Directive 2009/71/Euratom of 25 June 2009 establishing a Community framework for the nuclear safety of nuclear installations (2009) OJ L172 18. See Y Pouler and P Krs, 'The Momentum of the European Directive on Nuclear Safety – From the Complexity of Nuclear Safety to Key Messages Addressed to European Citizens' (2010) 85 NLB 5.

30 According to some, the similarity of structure between the Convention and the Directive 'was meant to distinguish clearly between the objectives and the obligations of the Member States'. This, however, has not been fully achieved since there is an 'essential overlap between the scope of application, the definitions and the operational articles': F Dehousse, *The Nuclear Safety Framework in the European Union after Fukushima* (Egmont Paper 73 2014) 17.

authorisation and to ensure protection from radiation for the population in normal circumstances. It further requires the establishment of a 'national legislative, regulatory and organizational framework'. This national framework shall establish responsibilities for the adoption of national safety requirements, a licensing system, the provision of a system of nuclear safety supervision, and enforcement actions. The regulatory authorities should be independent from any person or organisation concerned with the promotion or utilisation of nuclear energy and should be entrusted with the necessary legal powers and human and financial resources. According to the Directive, primary responsibility for nuclear safety rests with the licence holder. The Directive requires arrangements for education and training. It also requires the provision of information to the public, but it leaves flexibility for the Member States in this regard. Information should be made available to the public according to national legislation and international obligations without jeopardising '*other interests*', such as security, recognised in national or international law. Member States are obliged to submit a report to the Commission every three years on the implementation of the Directive. The surveillance of that implementation is based on a system of peer review. In order to avoid duplication with the obligations established by the Conventions, Member States may 'take advantage of the review and the reporting cycles under the Nuclear Safety Convention'.

Member States must arrange for self-assessments of their national framework at least every ten years. The Member States shall also invite an international peer review, the outcome of which should be reported to the Commission and the other Member States. Unlike the Convention, the reports and the outcome are public. The peer review mechanism is defined by the Directive as a 'learning mechanism'.

The above analysis reveals that the Directive establishes a very general framework, leaving wide discretion to the Member States and their internal implementing legislation.

The Fukushima accident in 2011 triggered further developments, without reversing the basic framework.

First of all, the Commission adopted a programme of risk and safety assessments (so-called 'stress tests'). The stress test exercises of all nuclear power plants in the EU started on 1 June 2011, under the auspices of the Commission and the European Nuclear Safety Regulators' Group (ENSREG).[31] The process involves, *inter alia*, pre-assessments (by plant operators), national reports (by the national regulators), peer reviews (evaluation teams consisting of one

31 See <http://www.ensreg.eu/> (all links were last accessed on 20 May 2021).

Commission representative and six ENSREG members), and the publication of both the national reports and the results of the peer reviews.[32]

Secondly, a new Directive amending the previous one was adopted.[33] The Directive came into force in 2014, providing for implementation by the Member States by 2017. The amended Directive essentially reinforces the provisions of the existing Directive. However, common safety standards are not yet in sight.

As far as waste treatment is concerned, the approach of the Nuclear Waste Directive is very similar to the approach adopted by the Nuclear Safety Directive.[34]

The Directive establishes a Community framework for ensuring responsible and safe management of spent fuel and radioactive waste and avoiding undue burdens on future generations. The Directive recalls the Joint Convention and the non-binding IAEA Safety Standards, attributing to each Member State the ultimate responsibility for management of spent fuel and radioactive waste. The national framework must include a system for licensing, control, documentation, enforcement actions, national requirements for public information and participation, and a financing scheme. The Member States are also required to establish an independent regulatory authority. Finally, the Directive establishes a reporting system and a peer review system very similar to those established by the Nuclear Safety Directive. The Directive states that radioactive waste must be disposed of in the country where it was generated, unless there are agreements with other countries,[35] and that storage could be accepted as a temporary solution but not an alternative to disposal.[36]

---

32 For documents and information about the EU nuclear stress tests, see European Commission, <https://ec.europa.eu/commission/presscorner/detail/en/IP_12_1051>.

33 Council Directive 2014/87/Euratom of 8 July 2014 amending Directive 2009/71/Euratom establishing a Community Framework for the nuclear safety of nuclear installations (2014) OJ L219 42.

34 Council Directive 2011/70/Euratom of 19 July 2011 establishing a Community Framework for the Responsible and Safe Management of Spent Fuel and Radioactive Waste (2011) OJ L199 48. See U Blohm-Hieber, 'The Radioactive Waste Directive: A Necessary Step in the Management of Spent Fuel and Radioactive Waste in the European Union' (2011) 88 NLB 21.

35 Exceptions to the principle are submitted to strict rules on shipment and responsibility. See also Council Regulation 1493/93/Euratom of 8 June 1993 on shipments of radioactive substances between Member States (1993) OJ L148 1, and Council Directive 2006/117/Euratom of 20 November 2006 on the supervision and control of shipments of radioactive waste and spent fuel (2006) OJ L337 21.

36 However, Member States continue to take different approaches to the management of radioactive waste and nuclear waste is mainly stored in temporary storage facilities.

In sum, while in the field of radiation protection the Euratom Treaty provides for substantive measures concerning dose limits and a strict mechanism of surveillance, both Directives on nuclear safety and waste treatment simply repeat the content of the International Conventions on the matter. The main difference in respect to the international system lies in the enforcement role of the European Commission, which has at its disposal an infringement procedure mechanism in order to compel the observance of the obligations provided.[37] As far as common safety standards are concerned, these are left to European informal bodies, such as the Western European Nuclear Regulators' Association (WENRA) composed of Regulatory Authorities in the Member States.

Further measures of prevention and preparedness have been adopted on the basis of the EU competences, especially in the field of environment.[38] They concern mainly information and participation rights and are of utmost importance in order to ensure preparedness of the general public. In some cases, there is obvious overlap with similar measures adopted on the basis of the Euratom Treaty.

The EC Directive on the quality of water intended for human consumption also covers radioactive substances.[39] In order to avoid overlaps and on the basis of the principle *lex specialis derogat legi generali*, the Commission proposed a Euratom Directive concerning only radioactive substances.[40] However, this implied a change in the choice of the legal basis with the consequent undermining of the role of the European Parliament which brought an action for annulment of the Directive before the Court of Justice.[41]

---

37 To this author's knowledge, the procedure has been used in few cases and only for failure to transpose the Directive into national law: Case C-434/18, *Commission v. Italy* (2019) OJ C305 25 concerning the failure to notify the European Commission of the national programme for the implementation of the spent fuel and radioactive waste management policy, as required by art 15(4) Council Directive 2011/70/Euratom, and the similar case C-391/18, *Commission v. Republic of Croatia*, (2019) OJ C 280 33.

38 See S Emmerechts, 'Environmental Law and Nuclear Law: A Growing Symbiosis' (2008) 82 NLB 91.

39 Council Directive 1998/83/EC of 3 November 1998 on the quality of water intended for human consumption, OJ 1998 No L330, 5 December 1998, 32.

40 Art 7 of Council Directive 2013/51/Euratom of 22 October 2013 laying down requirements for the protection of the health of the general public with regard to radioactive substances in water intended for human consumption (n 26).

41 Case C-48/14, *European Parliament v. Council of the European Union* (2015) ECR I-91 (action dismissed).

The Directive concerning the Environmental Impact Assessment (EIA) also covers nuclear installations.[42] While the scope of the Directive is broader than the procedure provided by Article 37 Euratom, this last provision provides a much more relevant role for the Commission than the role provided by the Directive.

As is well known, the Aarhus Convention sets up rules for access to information, public participation, and public access to justice in environmental matters.[43] Only the EU signed and acceded to the Convention.[44] However, the Convention has been transposed into the EU legal order either through EU directives, applicable also to nuclear matters, or Euratom directives. Among the first group, the EIA Directive;[45] among the second group, the Nuclear Safety Directive, which includes requirements concerning the provision of information to the public, and the Nuclear Waste Directive, which includes provisions on public participation and access to information.

The same is probably true for the obligations to provide information and, more generally, ensure cooperation between the States Parties, established by the Convention on the Law of the Sea of the United Nations, especially those obligations established by Part XII devoted to 'Protection and preservation of the marine environment', which was approved only by the then European Community as a mixed agreement.[46] As is well known, in the *MOX Plant* case, the Court of Justice decided that it has exclusive jurisdiction over disputes concerning the implementation of the provisions of the Convention by Member States, given that such provisions involve obligations which come

42 Directive 2011/92/EU of the European Parliament and the Council of 13 December 2011 on the assessment of effects of certain public and private projects on the environment (2012) OJ L26 1.

43 Convention on Access to Information, Public Participation in Decision Making and Access to Justice in Environmental Matters (1998).

44 The EU signed the Convention in 1998 and acceded to it in 2005.

45 See also Directive 2003/4/EC of the European Parliament and of the Council of 28 January 2003 on public access to environmental information and repealing Council Directive 90/313/EEC (2003) OJ L41 26; Directive 2003/35/EC of the European Parliament and of the Council of 26 May 2003 providing for public participation in respect of the drawing up of certain plans and programmes relating to the environment and amending with regard to public participation and access to justice Council Directives 85/337/EEC and 96/61/EC (2003) OJ L156 17.

46 Council Decision 98/392/EC of 23 March 1998 concerning the conclusion by the European Community of the United Nations Convention of 10 December 1982 on the Law of the Sea and the Agreement of 28 July 1994 relating to the implementation of Part XI thereof (1998) OJ L179 1.

within the scope of either the then EC Treaty or the Euratom Treaty, with the consequence that the institution of a proceeding before a different jurisdiction would involve a 'manifest risk that the jurisdictional order laid down in the Treaties and, consequently, the autonomy of the Community legal system may be adversely affected'.[47]

3 Measures of Response and Recovery

Response and recovery are ensured by different kind of measures.[48] The most important interventions in this field concern the adoption of emergency measures, while other types of measures remain lacking. For instance, there are no rules on nuclear liability, while international conventions on the matter do exist.[49] A competence in the field of criminal sanctions remains uncertain, even if in the opinion of the Commission an analogy with the *Environment Penalty Case* is possible.[50]

Most of the emergency measures have been adopted as a response to the Chernobyl accident. As already explained, Euratom acceded to the two International Emergency Conventions only in 2006.[51] However, in the meantime, a number of provisions were adopted, either in the field of emergency information (covered by the Early Notification Convention) or in the field of assistance (covered by the Assistance Convention).

The first measures on early information exchange were introduced as early as 1980 with the Euratom BSS Directive. This obliged the Member States to notify any accident involving exposure of the population to the Commission and to neighbouring Member States.[52]

---

47 Case C-459/03, *Commission of the European Communities v. Ireland* (2006) ECR I-4635. As is well known, Ireland tried first to institute the proceeding before an arbitral tribunal established under UNCLOS, which decided to suspend the proceeding pending an evaluation by the Court of Justice.

48 See ch 5 by Bakker.

49 A Söndersen (n 8) 283, 340.

50 Case C-176/03, *Commission v. Council, Environmental Penalty case* (2005) ECR I-7879, with which the Court of Justice decided that, despite the absence of competence, the adoption of European measures in criminal matters was permissible if necessary in order to ensure that the measures adopted in the environmental field are fully effective. See ch 33 by Amoroso.

51 See above Section 1.

52 Art 45(5) of Council Directive 80/836/Euratom of 15 July 1980 amending the Directives laying down the basic safety standards for the health protection of the general public and workers against the dangers of ionizing radiation (1980) L246 1.

As a response to the Chernobyl accident, in 1987, on the basis of Article 31 Euratom, the Council adopted the European Community Urgent Radiological Information Exchange (so called ECURIE system), which is the Community arrangement for the early exchange of information in the event of a radiological emergency,[53] adopted the same day as the Council approved the Early Notification Convention. The ECURIE system is very similar to the mechanism established by the Convention, but the coordinating role is assumed by the European Commission instead of the IAEA. In the event of an accident, the Commission collects and transmits information to the Member States. The Commission is the hub of information through the Joint Research Centre.[54] The Member States must notify the Commission and the Member States potentially affected when they intend to take measures to protect the general public. The system aims to ensure that Member States are promptly informed in order to apply the provisions laid down by the BSS Directives. Thus, there is a close link to the other Directives adopted on the basis of the Health and Safety Euratom provisions. In 2003, Euratom entered into an agreement extending these provisions to neighbouring and candidate States.

Given the fact that Euratom acceded later to the Early Notification Convention and that all Member States are parties to the Convention, a link between the EU system and the IAEA system was necessary. In 1991, an informal cooperation was established between Euratom and the IAEA. This cooperation provides that the system which first receives the information should inform the other one. In addition, Euratom undertook to apply the Convention pending its accession which was, as said, in 2006.

In addition to the ECURIE system, the Directive laying down basic safety standards for protection against the dangers arising from exposure to ionising radiation[55] obliges Member States to provide information to the public concerning planned health protection measures.[56] In the *Gibraltar Submarine Case*, the Court decided that in the case of repair of a nuclear-powered

53 Council Decision 87/600 Euratom of 14 December 1987 on Community arrangements for the early exchange of information in the event of a radiological emergency (1987) OJ L371 76.

54 <https://ec.europa.eu/jrc/en>.

55 Council Directive 2013/59/Euratom of 5 December 2013 laying down basic safety standards for protection against the dangers arising from exposure to ionizing radiation (n 26).

56 Some overlaps may be found with the Rapid Alert System for Food and Feed (RASFF) adopted under the TFUE: Regulation (EC) No 178/2002 of the European Parliament and of the Council of 28 January 2002 laying down general principles and requirements of food law, establishing the European Food Safety Authority and laying down procedures in matters of food safety (2002) OJ L31 1.

submarine, the Directive did not require the State to inform the public about health protection measures.[57]

Also in the field of Emergency Assistance, some measures were adopted before the accession to the International Convention. In 2001, the Council decided to establish a Monitoring and Information Centre (MIC) with the purpose of facilitating cooperation in civil protection assistance.[58] In 2007, a revised mechanism was established in response to the Tsunami accident with the aim of developing a European rapid response capability.[59] Both mechanisms also provide for financial assistance and are not limited to nuclear emergencies, as shown by their legal bases which include the European Union Treaties. In the same vein, worthy of mention are the solidarity clause included in the Lisbon Treaty (art 222);[60] Article 196 TFEU on a European system of civil protection;[61] and Article 122 TFEU on financial assistance to Member States.

Some emergency measures may also be taken in other fields on a case by case basis. For instance, in the wake of the events in Fukushima, the European Commission enacted an emergency measure to protect consumers in the EU from contaminated Japanese food and feed, on the basis of the Regulation laying down the general principles and requirements of food law.[62]

4 Conclusion

From a general point of view, the European supranational framework in the field of Nuclear Safety and Security appears somewhat fragmented and inconsistent. This seems largely due to the manner in which powers and competences have been conferred to the supranational level, previously to the Euratom Community and then to the European Union. Probably as a consequence, acts adopted in the field do not result in a robust and solid system.

57 Case C-65/04, *Commission of the European Communities v. United Kingdom of Great Britain and Northern Ireland, Gibraltar Submarine case* (2006) ECR I-2239.

58 Council Decision 2001/792/EC, Euratom of 23 October 2001 establishing a Community mechanism to facilitate reinforced cooperation in civil protection assistance interventions (2001) OJ L297 7.

59 Council Decision 2007/779/EC, Euratom of 8 November 2007 establishing a Community Civil Protection Mechanism (recast) (2007) OJ L314 9.

60 See ch 6 by Casolari.

61 See ch 14 and ch 19 by Ferri.

62 See art 53 (1) (b)(ii) of Regulation (EC) No 178/2002 of the European Parliament and of the Council of 28 January 2002 laying down the general principles and requirements of food law, establishing the European Food Safety Authority and laying down procedures in matters of food safety (n 56).

While there is some regulation in the field of prevention and preparedness, mainly as a transposition into the European context of the supervision system adopted at the international level by the relevant conventions, there is no adequate system of response and recovery. The most adequate way forward is probably to reconsider the entire framework as soon as possible, starting with the relationship between the Euratom and European Union Treaties.

Bibliography

Blohm-Hieber U, 'The Radioactive Waste Directive: A Necessary Step in the Management of Spent Fuel and Radioactive Waste in the European Union' (2011) 88 NLB 21.

Cenevska I, 'The European Parliament and the European Atomic and Energy Community: A Legitimacy Crisis?' (2010) 35 ELR 415.

Dehousse F, *The Nuclear Safety Framework in the European Union after Fukushima* (Egmont Paper 73 2014).

Emmerechts S, 'Environmental Law and Nuclear Law: A Growing Symbiosis' (2008) 82 NLB 91.

Fouquet D, 'Nuclear Policy in the EU from a Legal and Institutional Point-of-View', in R Haas, L Mez, A Ajanovic (eds), *The Technological and Economic Future of Nuclear Power. Energiepolitik und Klimaschutz. Energy Policy and Climate Protection* (Springer VS 2019).

Gioia A, 'Nuclear Accidents and International Law', in A De Guttry, M Gestri, G Venturini (eds), *International Disaster Response Law* (T.M.C. Asser Press 2012).

O'Driscoll M, *The European Parliament and the EURATOM Treaty: past, present and future* (European Parliament, Luxembourg, 2002).

Pouler Y, Krs P, 'The Momentum of the European Directive on Nuclear Safety – From the Complexity of Nuclear Safety to Key Messages Addressed to European Citizens' (2010) 85 NLB 5.

Söndersen A, *Euratom at the Crossroads* (European University Institute 2014).

Wolf S, 'Euratom, the European Court of Justice, and the Limits of Nuclear Integration in Europe', (2001) 12 German Law Journal 1638.

CHAPTER 16

Prevention Obligations Applicable to Naturally Occurring CBRN Events

Silvia Venier

1 Introduction

Naturally occurring CBRN events refer to emergency situations caused by natural hazards that have the potential to release CBRN substances. The most prominent examples include volcanic eruptions and seismic activities, which may emit dangerous gases, and epidemic outbreaks caused by infectious diseases. While natural phenomena have long been understood as 'acts of God' with very limited room for prevention, in modern times there is growing recognition that even the risks posed by natural hazards can be mitigated and that the magnitude of their impact heavily depends on man-made choices. Laws and regulations have thus a specific role to play in these contexts.[1] A feature that the hazards discussed in this chapter have in common is their low probability but potentially high impact, which poses many challenges for their regulation, due to scientific uncertainties and difficulties in understanding what is actually required to prevent and to be prepared to respond.

This chapter aims to identify whether any obligations to prevent naturally occurring CBRN events exist under international law and to explore their content (section 2); to discuss the implementation of these obligations in light of the lessons learned from past and present emergencies (3); and to draw some conclusions on the status of prevention obligations applicable to naturally occurring CBRN events (4). The chapter focuses on naturally occurring events that have the potential to release CBRN substances on their own, while natural events impacting on CBRN facilities (so-called 'Natech' events, short for Natural Hazards Triggering Technological Disasters) are discussed elsewhere in this volume.[2]

1 KC Lauta, *Disaster Law* (Routledge 2014).

2 See ch 11 by Creta and ch 15 by Balboni, as well as ch 3 by Venier on general prevention obligations.

2 Sources and Content of Prevention Obligations Related to Naturally Occurring CBRN Events

As detailed in Chapter 3, the main duties to prevent emergency situations include the duties to adopt adequate legal and policy frameworks; to adopt ad hoc measures to mitigate specific risks and to perform risk assessments; and to cooperate in prevention activities with other States and International Organisations (IOs). The main sources of these duties are general principles of international law (such as sovereignty, solidarity, due diligence) and rules pertaining to specific branches of international law. This section explores to what extent these obligations can be applied to naturally occurring CBRN events and also whether there are any ad hoc prevention obligations specifically designed for such events.

Adopting adequate legal and policy frameworks and ad hoc hazard mitigation measures and engaging in international cooperation on prevention activities remain the main obligations in terms of prevention also in relation to naturally occurring CBRN events. For instance, with reference to volcanic risks it has been stated that '[i]n many cultures, volcanic risks are perceived to be susceptible to governance with the objective of achieving their effective mitigation and have become the responsibility of the institutions and stakeholders of relevant social communities'.[3] Volcanic risks demand ad hoc prevention measures, including regular monitoring of unrest periods, the movement of tectonic plates and of the volcano's surface, as well as adequate assessment of the likelihood of eruption and the potential consequences. Policy and legal instruments must be informed by the outcomes of risk assessments. Other ad hoc risk mitigation measures may include ensuring that people do not live near the most dangerous areas around the volcano.

Volcano hazard monitoring is recognised as an international Standard And Recommended Practice (SARP) under the terms of Annex 3 on 'Meteorological service for International Air Navigation' to the Convention on International Civil Aviation.[4] Pursuant to Standards 3.5 on 'Volcanic ash advisory centres' and 3.6 on 'State volcano observatories', Member States shall ensure that those centres and observatories have the capacities to monitor significant pre-eruption

---

3 RJ Bretton, J Gottsmann and R Christie, 'The role of Laws within the Governance of Volcanic Risks' (2017) Advs In Volcanology. The same authors clarify that 'volcanic risk governance' includes 'all attempts to manage the three constituent variables of risk including steps to mitigate volcanic hazards (there are very few successful examples of this), reduce the exposure of people, assets etc. and reduce their vulnerability when exposed', ibid 24.

4 Convention on International Civil Aviation (1944). Annex 3 on 'Meteorological service for International Air Navigation' (2007).

and eruption activity and the release of ash into the atmosphere and to report relevant information as quickly as practicable. The World Organization of Volcano Observatories (WOVO),[5] a Commission of the International Association of Volcanology and Chemistry of the Earth's Interior (IAVCEI) provides a network for institutions engaged in volcanic surveillance and 'responsible for warning authorities and the public about hazardous volcanic unrest' (as indicated on the WOVO website). WOVOdat is a comprehensive global dataset on volcanic unrest which allows standardisation of data collection and aims at improving eruption forecasts. This is an example of international cooperation on prevention activities aimed at increasing understanding of natural hazards and assessing associated risks. Interestingly, it has been suggested that in terms of cooperation in understanding volcanic risks, the adoption of the Sendai Framework will result in greater emphasis being placed on 'the importance of not only the collection and interpretation of monitoring data but also the better characterisation of unrest periods'.[6]

One important aspect that is particularly relevant for the present discussion are the health implications of the dangerous gases following a volcanic eruption. The Pan American Health Organization (PAHO) for instance recalls the importance of integrating health considerations into volcanic risk monitoring and suggests that the analysis of volcanic risks and of community vulnerability is one of the few prevention measures available to mitigate volcanic risks to people's health.[7] Some scholars have noted that more studies are needed on both the acute and chronic health effects of volcanic ash and have recommended 'a more systematic approach to multi-disciplinary studies in future eruptions [...] including establishing an archive of ash samples and a website containing health advice for the public, together with scientific and medical study guidelines for volcanologists and health-care workers'.[8]

A recent case brought to the attention of the European Court of Human Rights (ECtHR), declared inadmissible for failure to exhaust domestic remedies, concerned the lack of adequate regulatory frameworks and ad hoc measures to mitigate the risk of eruption of Mount Vesuvius in Italy, one of the most dangerous volcanoes in the world not only for the magnitude of a

---

5 <https://wovo.wovodat.org/index.php> (all links were last accessed on 20 June 2021).

6 RJ Bretton, J Gottsmann and R Christie (n 3) 32.

7 PAHO, 'Guía de preparativos de salud frente a erupciones volcánicas. El sector salud frente al riesgo volcanico' (2005), 50.

8 CJ Horwell and PJ Baxter, 'The respiratory health hazards of volcanic ash: a review for volcanic risk mitigation' (2006) 69 Bull Volcano 1.

potential eruption but also considering the high number of people residing in the areas around the volcano.[9] In its decision, the Court emphasised that the domestic legal framework allows the applicants to bring proceedings to administrative courts, and clarified that evidence was provided by the government on the adoption of risk mitigation measures, including the establishment of a monitoring system that regularly provides seismological data, the adoption of measures to support people to move away from the residential areas close to Vesuvius, as well as preparedness measures, such as the adoption of an emergency evacuation plan that had been updated in light of the outcomes of a simulation exercise carried out in 2006. On the other hand, the applicants complained about the lack of information on the emergency plan and the lack of training.

Turning our attention to infectious diseases, ad hoc measures to prevent their spread generally refer to reducing the risk of spill-over events, *ie* of new viruses jumping from animals to humans, and to immunisation. Looking at spill-over events, scholars have recently suggested that knowing more details about the origin of an outbreak is crucial to putting in place adequate risk mitigation strategies.[10] For instance, with reference to the current pandemic, potential causes that have been identified include the wildlife trade at the Huanan market in Wuhan or an accident during scientific research,[11] so any prevention strategies would need to address these aspects in terms of, for example, restrictions on the wildlife trade or improved safety standards in both field research and laboratories. Scholars have called for an investigative process on the origins of SARS-CoV-2 that should be 'transparent, collaborative, international, and, to the extent possible, devoid of political interest',[12] but it is not clear to what extent finding a definite answer about the origins of

9 *Viviani et autres contre l'Italie*, Requête no 9713/13 (ECtHR 24 Mars 2015). It must be noted that the jurisprudence of national and regional courts can either reinforce existing obligations or clarify what is actually needed to ensure respect for them, and this is particularly the case for legal frameworks applicable to the emergency management field, which are still in the process of consolidation.

10 According to Relman, key details that should (and could) be revealed include: 'a plausible and suitably detailed recent evolutionary history of the virus, the identity and provenance of its most recent ancestors, and surprisingly, the place, time, and mechanism of transmission of the first human infection'. D Relman, 'To stop the next pandemic, we need to unravel the origins of COVID-19', 117(47) PNAS (2020) 2.

11 F Lentzos, 'Natural spillover or research lab leak? Why a credible investigation is needed to determine the origin of the coronavirus pandemic' (2020) Bulletin of the Atomic Scientists.

12 Relman (n 10) p. 2.

the outbreak will be possible, due to both technical difficulties and political hurdles.[13]

As the International Health Regulations (IHR)[14] do not enshrine any requirements on preventing spill-over events (or on investigating their origins: these are the central questions surrounding the 'one health approach'),[15] the source for the current WHO-led investigation is the Resolution adopted in May 2020 by the 73rd World Health Assembly (WHA, with the explicit consent of 140 States and no vocal opposition), which requests the WHO Director General:

> to continue to work [...] to identify the zoonotic source of the virus and the route of introduction to the human population, including the possible role of intermediate hosts, including through efforts such as scientific and collaborative field missions, which will enable *targeted interventions* and *a research agenda to reduce the risk of similar events occurring*, as well as to *provide guidance on how to prevent infection* with severe acute respiratory syndrome coronavirus 2 (SARS-COV2) in animals and humans and *prevent the establishment of new zoonotic reservoirs*, as well as to *reduce further risks of emergence and transmission* of zoonotic diseases.[16]

The WHA thus recently managed to reach wide consensus on the need for an investigation into the origins of the pandemic and on the investigation's purposes and final aims, *ie* to propose targeted interventions, a research agenda and guidelines aimed at reducing the risk of spill-over events in the future.[17] The outcomes of the study will probably also inform the 'impartial, independent and comprehensive evaluation' requested by the same Resolution in order 'to review experience gained and lessons learned from the WHO-coordinated

13 <https://www.nature.com/articles/d41586-020-03165-9>.

14 International Health Regulations (2005).

15 See ch 29 by Antoniazzi.

16 WHA Res 73.1 'COVID-19 response' (2020) para 9(6) (emphasis added).

17 For the time being, the only document publicly available on this investigation are the Terms of Reference for the Chinese part of the study released in July 2020. The studies will aim 'to (i) explore how the circulation of SARS-CoV-2 might have started and (ii) gather evidence from the cluster of cases identified in December 2019 for potential links and clues as to its origin'. The second phase of the investigation will explore more in detail some of the first part's findings, looking at other countries. See WHO, 'WHO-convened Global Study of the Origins of SARS-CoV-2: Terms of References for the China Part' (2020) <https://www.who.int/publications/m/item/who-convened-global-study-of-the-origins-of-sars-cov-2>.

international health response to COVID-19 and to make recommendations to improve capacity for global pandemic *prevention*, preparedness and response'.[18]

Another measure to prevent the spread of infectious diseases is immunisation. From an international law perspective, the main issues here concern enabling global equitable access to vaccines. The WHA Resolution recognised 'the role of extensive immunization against COVID-19 as a global public good for health in preventing, containing and stopping transmission in order to bring the pandemic to an end, once safe, quality, efficacious, effective, accessible and affordable vaccines are available'.[19] The Immunization Agenda 2030 (IA2030), also recently adopted by the WHA,[20] aims at providing 'a long-term strategic framework to guide a dynamic operational phase, responding to changes in country needs and the global context over the next decade'.[21] Since these developments, however, 'the global legal landscape has shifted from a rhetoric of global public goods to a reality largely based on nationalism', considering that wealthy nations secured more than 2 billion doses of potential Covid-19 vaccines using Advance Purchase Agreements (APA).[22] The next few months will tell us more about the extent to which the international community is ready – in terms of political will and technical capacity – to ensure prompt access to vaccines for the entire world population.

Finally, mention must be made of the obligation to prevent the international spread of infectious diseases that lies at the very core of the WHO Constitution (Articles 2 and 21)[23] and of the IHR (Article 2), which provide the basis for a 'stronger and more coordinated collective action' on global disease control.[24] Prevention here refers to minimising the risk of (domestic and) international spread through, for example, the timely detection of

18 WHA Res (n 16) para 10 (emphasis added). UNGA Res A/RES/74/306 (preamble) has welcomed this initiative.

19 WHA Res (n 16) Para 6.

20 WHA Decision WHA73(9) (2020).

21 WHO, 'Immunisation Agenda 2030. A global strategy to leave no one behind' (2020).

22 AL Phelan et al., 'Legal agreements: barriers and enablers to global equitable COVID-19 vaccine access' (2020) 396 The Lancet 800.

23 Among the tasks assigned to the WHO, Article 2 lists '(g) to stimulate and advance work to eradicate epidemic, endemic and other diseases', while Article 21 establishes that the World Health Assembly 'shall have authority to adopt regulations concerning: (a) sanitary and quarantine requirements and other procedures designed to *prevent* the international spread of disease' (emphasis added). Constitution of the World Health Organization (1946).

24 S Negri, 'Communicable disease control', in GL Burci and B Toebes, *Research Handbook on Global Health Law* (Edward Elgar 2018) 268.

suspected cases (surveillance),[25] the timely notification to the WHO and the international community (notification), and prophylaxis.[26] The most important novelties introduced by the revised IHR are exactly the duties to 'develop, strengthen and maintain [...] the capacity to detect, assess, notify and report events' (Article 5(1)) and to promptly notify the WHO (*ie* within 24 hours) of all events within their territories that may constitute a Public Health Emergency of International Concern (PHEIC) (Article 6). The revised IHR confers an enhanced role to the WHO in terms of preventing the international spread of diseases by granting the organisation the authority to declare a PHEIC. The WHO has a specific role to play also in terms of surveillance, and an integrated global alert and response system has been set up relying on around 250 surveillance networks globally, including the Global Outbreak Alert and Response Network (GOARN).[27]

To sum up, with reference to naturally occurring CBRN events, some ad hoc prevention obligations exist but they are limited to the prevention of the international spread of infectious diseases under the terms of the IHR, which are usually understood as mainly covering preparedness and response and have thus not been dealt with in detail in the present chapter. Looking at the other prevention measures, *ie* minimising the risk of spill-over events and immunisation, the interest of the international community has been growing during the current pandemic outbreak. In relation to the prevention of other CBRN natural events, volcanic hazard monitoring is an established standard and recommended practice at the international level under the terms of the International Convention on Civil Aviation. Interesting developments in this field include collaboration activities related to harmonising the methodologies for data collection and risk assessment, for which the Sendai Framework provided the reference policy framework. A crucial gap that has emerged however is the lack of studies on the health effects of volcanic ash, which would need to be integrated into volcanic risk assessments.

25 Surveillance is defined as 'the systematic ongoing collection, collation and analysis of data for public health purposes and the timely dissemination of public health information for assessment and public health response as necessary'. IHR, Article 1 Definitions. From this definition, it is clear that surveillance has an important role to play in terms of risk assessment, which is among the prevention measures identified in the present chapter.

26 The development of surveillance and notification capacities is generally understood as a preparedness measure, to which ch 17 is devoted; the actual use of such capacities is considered to be part of the response phase (see ch 18). The present chapter is limited to discussing to what extent surveillance and notification as required under the IHR can ensure prevention of the international spread of outbreaks.

27 See <https://extranet.who.int/goarn/>.

3 Lessons Learned with Respect to the Prevention of Naturally Occurring CBRN Events

Some lessons learned from past events of naturally occurring CBRN events have offered the opportunity to evaluate the implementation of prevention duties as discussed above.

Some lessons on volcanic risk assessment can be drawn from the 2010 Icelandic Eyjafjallajökull eruption that paralysed the European skies for one week. According to the OECD, this crisis 'highlighted the difficulty of co-ordinating and synthesising scientific input from many different disciplines and institutions and translating these into useful policy advice at very short notice'.[28] Similarly, Alexander discussed the lessons learned from the Eyjafjallajökull eruption and pointed out the need for national and international regulatory bodies to make a more serious effort to evaluate the risks to civil aviation of volcanic eruptions (including catastrophic scenarios and the widest possible range of consequences); to more rigorously define the threshold for safe flying on the basis of evidence-based practice and appropriate meteorological and geological remote sensing; and to broaden the regulation of European airspace to include also natural hazard impacts.[29] Some issues relevant for the protection of health also emerged, such as the need to ensure that different disciplines interact in risk assessment activities and to harmonise data.

Looking at epidemic outbreaks, the PHEICs declared after the entry into force of the IHR highlighted major gaps, especially in terms of prevention of international spread; the poor development of surveillance and response capacities at the domestic level; the lack of compliance by States with the temporary recommendations, without any enforcement mechanism available; the role of the WHO in the PHEIC determination; and the coordination of the international response.[30] The COVID-19 pandemic demonstrated that

28 <https://www.oecd-ilibrary.org/science-and-technology/scientific-advice-for-policy-making_5js33l1jcpwb-en>.

29 D Alexander, 'Volcanic Ash in the Atmosphere and Risks for Civil Aviation: A Study in European Crisis Management' (2013) 4(1) Int. J. Disaster Risk Sci.

30 See WHO Review Committee on the Functioning of the International Health Regulations, 'Implementation of the International Health Regulations. Report of the Review Committee on the Functioning of the International Health Regulations (2005) in relation to Pandemic (H1N1) 2009' (2011) UN Doc. A64/10; 'Report of the Review Committee on the Role of the International Health Regulations (2005) in the Ebola Outbreak and Response' (WHO 2016) A69/21.

surveillance and notification capabilities have improved[31] but also emphasised major shortcomings. The requirement enshrined under Article 6 of the IHR to notify the WHO within 24 hours of the first suspected case of a SARS-like disease (which is key in preventing international spread) was probably breached.[32] Moreover, considering the key elements of any prevention obligation (*ie* knowledge of risk and severity of potential harm), it has to be noted that for many years experts had been warning that the risk of an outbreak with a pandemic potential was very concrete.[33] Despite the fact that the situation in China was dramatically and rapidly worsening, European States were slow in detecting the first cases in their territories and in adopting adequate prevention measures. Furthermore, it may be argued that States had even more demanding obligations to prevent the second waves that arrived in autumn, since they had knowledge that its occurrence was very likely, and they also knew which measures were adequate to limit the spread. Yet, the response was often still inadequate.

Looking at immunisation, during the H1N1 outbreak in 2009, a controversy surrounding vaccine access emerged when news circulated of a conflict of interest between WHO Expert Committee members and the pharmaceutical

31 GL Burci, 'The Outbreak of COVID-19 Coronavirus: are the International Health Regulations fit for purpose?' (EJIL!Talk, 27 February 2020), <https://www.ejiltalk.org/the-outbreak-of-covid-19-coronavirus-are-the-international-health-regulations-fit-for-purpose/>.

32 There is evidence that the first unusual cases of viral pneumonia emerged in late November – early December in Wuhan and that doctors sought to warn colleagues and public health authorities immediately (see <https://www.theguardian.com/world/2020/mar/13/first-covid-19-case-happened-in-november-china-government-records-show-report>; <https://www.thelancet.com/journals/lancet/article/PIIS0140-6736(20)30183-5/fulltext>. The official report provided by the WHO can be found at <https://www.who.int/csr/don/12-january-2020-novel-coronavirus-china/en/>. The official notification to the WHO was made on December 31st, and that same day, the Wuhan Health Commission published a notice confirming that 27 people were suffering from pneumonia of an unknown cause but that there was 'no need to be alarmed' since the disease was 'preventable and controllable'. The official statement by the Wuhan Health Commission was published at <http://wjw.wuhan.gov.cn/front/web/showDetail/2019123108989> but it is no longer available. The need to contain panic is a common concern during the first phases of emergency situations, even if scientific evidence suggests the opposite, *ie* the importance of informing the potentially affected population with clear and complete messages.

33 See <https://www.nationalgeographic.com/science/2020/04/experts-warned-pandemic-decades-ago-why-not-ready-for-coronavirus/>. On preparedness obligations related to epidemic outbreaks, see ch 17 by de Guttry.

industries that produce the vaccines. This news prompted Indonesia's refusal to share influenza samples with the WHO Global Influenza Surveillance and Response System (GISRS), in protest against the inequalities in the distribution of vaccines developed through the GISRS. According to one possible interpretation of the IHR, these samples may constitute 'public health information' about a potential PHEIC and therefore may have to be shared with the WHO. On the other side, the IHR recognises each State's sovereignty to adopt its own health policies. Furthermore, a virus discovered in a nation's territory can be defined as a 'genetic resource' of that nation (which cannot be shared or used without that nation's consent) under the terms of the Convention on Biological Diversity. The Pandemic Influenza Preparedness Framework, adopted in 2011, sought to solve this controversy by identifying international norms with respect to sharing novel influenza viruses with pandemic potential, as well as sharing pandemic vaccines developed from those viruses.[34] Under this framework, WHO intends to distribute pandemic influenza vaccines to countries on the basis of public health risks and needs; however, the COVID-19 pandemic demonstrates that this commitment does not appear to be enough to guide national decisions on vaccine distribution.

4 Concluding Remarks

The present chapter has explored obligations to prevent naturally occurring CBRN events under international law. In addition to the main sources of prevention obligations under general principles of international law and under other branches, ad hoc prevention obligations and international cooperation requirements on prevention activities have been investigated in relation to some examples of natural CBRN hazards, namely volcanic eruptions and infectious diseases.

The adoption of adequate legal and policy frameworks and of ad hoc hazard mitigation measures; the conduct of risk assessments; and international cooperation on prevention activities remain the crucial obligations in terms of prevention also in relation to such events. The legal obligations discussed

34 See Report of the Open-Ended Working Group of Member States on Pandemic Influenza Preparedness: Sharing of Influenza Viruses and Access to Vaccines and Other Benefits, WHO Doc. A64/8 (2011). For a discussion on the dispute, see D Cohen and P Carter, 'WHO and the Pandemic Flu Conspiracies' (2010) British Medical Journal 340; on the new framework, see R Gatter, 'The New Global Framework for Pandemic Influenza Virus and Vaccines Sharing', in IG Cohen, *The Globalisation of Health Care* (OUP 2013).

in the present chapter represent a rather fragmented and weak framework, which is, however, complemented and reinforced by soft law instruments and is expected to be further consolidated by relevant practice.

In relation to volcanic eruptions, the dangerous gases emitted may have important consequences on health and the environment, as well as on infrastructure including civil aviation. In fact, volcanic hazard monitoring is an established standard and recommended practice at the international level under the terms of the International Convention on Civil Aviation. As noted above, interesting developments in this field include collaboration activities related to harmonising the methodologies for data collection and risk assessment, for which the Sendai Framework provided the reference policy framework. However, one important aspect that has been neglected until now are the health implications of the dangerous gases following a volcanic eruption: more studies would be needed in order to integrate health considerations into volcanic hazard monitoring.

Looking at epidemic outbreaks, the evaluation of the international response to COVID-19 will shed light on the main weaknesses of the global health crisis prevention system. The interest of the international community has recently been growing in relation to two key prevention measures, *ie* the prevention of spill-over events and equitable access to immunisation, as demonstrated by the recent wide consensus at the WHA on the need to deepen our understanding of the origins of the outbreak and to propose adequate solutions to minimise the risk of such events in the future. The world is currently facing an unprecedented global health crisis that is having deep societal and economic implications. Complex as it may be to address the question of the extent to which epidemic outbreaks can be prevented, this is exactly the moment when we have the opportunity to devote resources to investigating the efficacy of the prevention requirements enshrined under the international law applicable to infectious diseases.

Bibliography

Alexander D, 'Volcanic Ash in the Atmosphere and Risks for Civil Aviation: A Study in European Crisis Management' (2013) 4(1) Int. J. Disaster Risk Sci 9.

Bretton RJ, Gottsmann J and Christie R, 'The role of Laws within the Governance of Volcanic Risks' (2017) Advs In Volcanology 23.

Cohen D and Carter P, 'WHO and the Pandemic Flu Conspiracies' (2010) British Medical Journal 340.

Gatter R, 'The New Global Framework for Pandemic Influenza Virus and Vaccines Sharing', in IG Cohen (ed), *The Globalisation of Health Care* (OUP 2013).

Horwell CJ and Baxter PJ, 'The respiratory health hazards of volcanic ash: a review for volcanic risk mitigation' (2006) 69 Bull Volcano 1.

Lauta KC, *Disaster Law* (Routledge 2014).

Negri S, 'Communicable disease control', in GL Burci and B Toebes (eds), *Research Handbook on Global Health Law* (Edward Elgar 2018).

Phelan AL et al, 'Legal agreements: barriers and enablers to global equitable COVID-19 vaccine access' (2020) 396 The Lancet 800.

Relman D, 'To stop the next pandemic, we need to unravel the origins of COVID-19', 117(47) PNAS (2020) 29246.

CHAPTER 17

Preparedness Rules Applicable to Naturally Occurring CBRN Incidents with Special Emphasis on Biological Events

Andrea de Guttry

1 Introduction

According to the Global Disaster Alert and Coordination System,[1] in the period between 23–29 April 2021, there were, globally, 11 earthquakes (each with a magnitude higher than 5), two tropical cyclones, two volcanic eruptions and two floods; each of these events, due to their nature and strength, could have caused spillages and/or contaminations. Furthermore, there are ongoing infectious diseases and pandemics,[2] which have been an endemic part of human history,[3] and which will, inevitably, continue to happen in the near future.[4]

1 <https://www.gdacs.org/>.

2 Thus far, the WHO has not provided a clear definition of 'pandemic', although reference is often made to the 'pandemic phase' of infectious diseases. For the purposes of this article, a pandemic is the worldwide spread of a new disease which has a significant impact on the affected societies. On the problems related to the definition of pandemic, see P Doshi, 'The elusive definition of pandemic influenza', (2011) Bulletin of the WHO: <https://www.scielosp.org/article/bwho/2011.v89n7/532-538/en/>. All links were last accessed in May 2021.

3 Over the last 100 years, several pandemics have been registered: the Spanish flu in 1918 (with a death toll of about 40 million), the Asian flu in 1956–1958 (with a death toll of about 2 million), the flu pandemic in 1961 (with a death toll of about 1 million), the HIV/AIDS pandemic in 2005–2012 (with a death toll of about 36 million), and the H1N1 pandemic in 2009–2010 (with a death toll of about 500,000).

4 A recent study stated that a future influenza pandemic 'is inevitable, although it cannot be predicted when it will happen nor how severe it will be': European Centre for Disease Prevention and Control, 'Guide to Revision of National Pandemic Influenza Preparedness Plans. Lessons Learned from the 2009 A (H1N1) Pandemic', (2017) <https://www.ecdc.europa.eu/sites/default/files/documents/Guide-to-pandemic-preparedness-revised.pdf>. Virologists candidly admit that, despite enormous advances in virology and epidemiology, 'many fundamental scientific questions concerning the origins, virulence, and diffusion of influenza remain unanswered': V Smil, *A Complete History of Pandemics, Global Catastrophes and Trends: The Next 50 Years* (The MIT Press, 2008).

The cost associated with all these types of events will, inevitably, increase in years to come.[5]

Given this situation, while prevention remains an essential tool, preparedness measures are crucial in order to have the earliest and most adequate response to any natural CBRN event that may arise.[6] Chapters 2 and 4 have already offered a detailed definition of the notion of preparedness, and this definition continues to be used here. It suffices to note that, according to the WHO,[7] emergency preparedness is defined as 'the knowledge and capacities and organizational systems developed by governments, response and recovery organizations, communities and individuals to effectively anticipate, respond to, and recover from the impacts of likely, imminent, emerging, or current emergencies'.

In this chapter, attention is focused on relevant international preparedness obligations (with the exception of those adopted by the European Union, examined in Chapter 19) applicable only to natural events and mainly to pandemics. In fact, most of the obligations associated with natural CBRN events not linked to pandemics (such as seismic events, volcanic eruptions etc.)[8] are regulated in general agreements dealing with any kind of CBRN event and have, therefore, already been investigated in Chapter 4.

5 The World Bank has estimated that 'the annual global cost of a moderate to severe pandemic would be around US$570 billion, or 0.7 percent of global income': World Bank Group', *'Global Crisis Response Platform'*, (2016): <http://documents.worldbank.org/curated/en/334721474058777148/pdf/WBG-Global-Crisis-Response-Platform-08252016.pdf>. A recent study by the Asian Development Bank estimates the global losses from COVID-19 as 'ranging from $2.0 trillion to $4.1 trillion, equal to 2.3%–4.8% of global GD': Asian Development Bank, 'Asian Development Outlook 2020: What Drives Innovation in Asia? Special Topic: The Impact of the Coronavirus Outbreak – An Update XIV', (2020): <https://www.adb.org/sites/default/files/publication/575626/ado2020.pdf>.

6 During the COVID-19 crisis, the lack of sufficient personal protective equipment, even for healthcare workers, and insufficient coordination among the different actors involved in the response phase, caused serious problems in many countries and affected the quality of the medical response.

7 WHO, A Strategic Framework for Emergency Preparedness, (2017): <https://apps.who.int/iris/bitstream/handle/10665/254883/9789241511827-eng.pdf;jsessionid=9C16566E3601A231C5B27AE39302E5C1?sequence=1>.

8 See more on these events in ch 4 and ch 12.

2 Specific Preparedness Obligations Regulated in International Instruments

Due to the increase in the number of natural disaster events and the more severe consequences attached thereto, preparedness measures have captured growing interest, especially in the field of pandemics.[9] The WHO has played a major role in this development. Initially, the WHO developed soft law instruments such as guidelines, guides and checklists that contributed to increasing awareness of how to be better equipped for future pandemics.[10] Later, preparedness obligations were introduced, mainly through the 2005 International Health Regulations (IHR).[11] Article 13 of the IHR requires each State to 'develop, strengthen and maintain [...] the capacity to respond promptly and effectively to public health risks and public health emergencies of international concern as set out in Annex 1'.[12] This annex defines the core capacity requirements for surveillance and response. States are required to be properly equipped (both in terms of decision-making procedures and physical infrastructures) and to have staff duly trained to be ready a) to detect and report diseases or deaths above expected levels for the particular time and place; and b) to manage the health emergency by providing support through specialised staff, laboratory analysis of samples (domestically or through collaborating centres) and logistical assistance (eg equipment, supplies and transport). In 2011, the 64th World Health Assembly adopted the Pandemic Influenza Preparedness (PIP) Framework for Sharing Influenza Viruses, Vaccines and Other Benefits,[13] which contains several important recommendations with impacts that extend far beyond a given event. States must guarantee to immediately share H5N1 and other influenza viruses with human pandemic potential with the WHO Collaborating Centre on Influenza or the WHO H5 Reference Laboratory.[14] National Influenza Centres and other authorised laboratories must make supplies of non-commercial diagnostic reagents and test kits for identifying and

9 See P Sands, 'The Neglected Dimension of Global Security: A Framework for Countering Infectious Disease Crises', (2016) 13 *New England Journal of Medicine*, 1281.

10 See the following section.

11 The legal basis of the IHR is provided in Articles 21(a) and 22 of the WHO Constitution, which confer upon the World Health Assembly the authority to adopt regulations 'designed to prevent the international spread of diseases'.

12 On the basis of paragraph 1 of Article 13, States may demand an extension of the five-year deadline.

13 WHO, Pandemic Influenza Preparedness Framework for the Sharing of Influenza Viruses and Access to Vaccines and other Benefits (2011): <https://apps.who.int/iris/bitstream/handle/10665/44796/9789241503082_eng.pdf?sequence=1>.

14 Art 5.1.

characterising specimens of influenza available free of charge.[15] Moreover, influenza vaccine manufacturers must be urged to set aside a portion of each production cycle of vaccines for H5N1 and other influenza viruses with human pandemic potential for stockpiling and/or use by developing countries.[16] All these preparedness measures are useful to tackle other types of pandemics as well.[17]

In the same vein, the Convention on the Prohibition of the Development, Production and Stockpiling of Bacteriological (Biological) and Toxin Weapons and on Their Destruction (1972) reinforces international capabilities for mitigation of outbreaks of any disease, not only those provoked by an alleged use of biological or toxin weapons.[18] In December 2014, a list of desired preparedness measures was approved during the meeting of the States Parties to the 1972 Convention. These measures, which must be considered as mere recommendations, include the availability of capable personnel/necessary national resources; national plans; appropriate command, control and coordination of cross-governmental planning and response; and regular training activities to strengthen national capacities.[19] The rising interest in preparedness measures is likewise testified by the WHO's decision to organise regular Meetings of Experts on Assistance, Response and Preparedness.[20]

The UN system has also played a role in this endeavour to reinforce national capacities to face a natural disaster[21] or pandemic. In UN General Assembly

15 Art 6.4.1.

16 Art 10.1. The WHO Director-General has been tasked with seeking, in cooperation with several stakeholders, commitments for contributions to maintain and further develop a stockpile of antiviral medicines and associated equipment for use in containment of outbreaks of H5N1 and other influenza viruses with human pandemic potential and to establish and maintain a stockpile of vaccines and associated equipment, including syringes, needles and applicators: Art 6.9.1.

17 S Negri, 'Communicable disease control', in G L Burci and B Toebes (eds.), *Research Handbook on Global Health Law*, (Elgar Publishing Ltd. 2018).

18 At the Eighth Review Conference, which took place in 2016, the parties stressed that 'national preparedness and capacities also contribute directly to international capabilities for response, investigation and mitigation of outbreaks of disease, including those due to alleged use of biological or toxin weapons': Eighth Review Conference of the States Parties to the Convention on the Prohibition of the Development, Production and Stockpiling of Bacteriological (Biological) and Toxin Weapons and on Their Destruction, BWC/CONF.VIII/4 (Jan. 11, 2017), para 40.

19 Meeting of the State Parties to the Convention on the Prohibition of the Development, Production and Stockpiling of Bacteriological (Biological) and Toxin Weapons and on Their Destruction (BWC), BWC/MSP/2014/5 (Dec. 15, 2014), para 34.

20 The Eighth Review Conference and the 2017 Meeting of States Parties defined the working methods and the task of the Meetings of Experts.

21 See more in ch 4 by de Guttry.

(UNGA) Resolution 60/262 approving the Political Declaration on HIV/AIDS,[22] heads of State and government committed to adopting national plans:

> to increase the capacity of human resources for health to meet the urgent need for the training and retention of a broad range of health workers, including community-based health workers; improve training and management and working conditions, including treatment for health workers; and effectively govern the recruitment, retention and deployment of new and existing health workers.

Making reference to the outbreak of the Ebola virus in the Democratic Republic of Congo, in Resolution 2439 (2018), the SC requested all components of the UN family 'to accelerate their response to the Ebola outbreak, within the overall coordination of WHO, including by supporting the development and implementation of preparedness and operational plans'.[23] A few months later, in a statement issued by the President of the Security Council, Member States and civil society in affected and at-risk countries were requested 'to work urgently with relevant partners to improve their preparedness for preventing, detecting and responding to possible cases, as well as to implement optimal vaccine strategies that have maximum impact on curtailing the outbreak'.[24] Furthermore, the Special Session of the UNGA, which took place on 3–4 December 2020, represented a unique opportunity to address the Covid-19 pandemic and its health, humanitarian and socio-economic impacts around the world. Finally, Resolution 75/27, adopted on 7 December by the UNGA, and proclaiming 27 December as the International Day of Epidemic Preparedness,[25] further testifies to the attention being devoted by the UN to the strategic importance of these measures in dealing with pandemic events.

To be truly effective, these measures must be highly contextualised and tailored to the specific cultural and socio-economic situation in which they are expected to produce their effects. The regional level seems optimal to achieve this, as it allows for tactics to be calibrated to the peculiar features of a specific geo-political area. As highlighted in Chapter 4, European organisations (or regional organisations with mostly European members/participating States)

22 GA Res. 60/262 (15 June 2006), UN Doc A/RES/60/262.

23 SC Res. 2439 (30 Oct. 2018), UN Doc S/RES/2439, para 14. The SC already stressed the fundamental importance of preparedness measures in the previous SC Res. 2177 (18 September 2014), UN Doc S/RES/2177, devoted to the first Ebola outbreak in Liberia and bordering States.

24 S/PRST/2019/6 (2 Aug. 2019).

25 GA Res. 75/27 (7 December 2020), UN Doc A/RES775/27.

have contributed significantly to increasing the attention given to generic preparedness measures (*ie* measures applicable to any kind of disaster, including natural disasters); this might explain why the same organisations (with the exception of the EU) have not adopted many preparedness rules to deal specifically with natural disasters or pandemics. However, for most of these organisations, the COVID-19 pandemic was eye-opening. The case of the OSCE is paradigmatic: in the 1975 Final Act of the Conference on Security and Co-Operation in Europe, the participating States identified research on viral diseases as one of the areas for potential reinforced cooperation. However, not much happened in this direction until the COVID-19 outbreak, when the OSCE suddenly devoted several studies, reports and recommendations to issues related to the ongoing pandemic.[26] Almost the same phenomenon occurred within other regional organisations, such as NATO,[27] the OAS,[28] ASEAN[29] and the African Union.[30] Finally, while most of the bilateral treaties devoted to the management of cooperation in case of disasters are applicable to both man-made and natural disasters (and therefore were analysed in Chapter 4), in a limited number of cases, they regulate specific preparedness measures applicable only to natural disasters.[31]

---

26 Among these, one may recall the specific attention devoted to human rights; elections and the right to vote; the freedom of press and speech; vulnerable groups and national minorities in need of special protection; and the impact of the pandemic on migration and trafficking of human beings. A comprehensive overview of the OSCE activities related to the COVID-19 pandemic is available at <https://www.osce.org/covid19-portal#response>.

27 For an overall picture of NATO activities undertaken to face the COVID-19 pandemic, see: <https://www.nato.int/cps/en/natohq/174592.htm>.

28 The OAS, unlike other regional organisations, decided to launch the Post-COVID-19: OAS Portal for Consultations, Forums and Repository: <https://www.oas.org/ext/en/main/covid-19/RepositoryZZ.

29 <https://asean.org/?static_post=updates-asean-health-sector-efforts-combat-novel-coronavirus-covid-19>.

30 See the 'Africa Joint Continental Strategy for COVID-19', adopted on March 5, 2020: <https://au.int/sites/default/files/documents/38264-doc-africa_joint_continental_strategy for covid-19_outbreak.pdf>. More information on the AU activities related to the COVID-19 pandemic is available at <https://au.int/en/covid19>.

31 See, for example, the Scientific Co-operation Agreement on Co-operation in Hydro-Meteorological Monitoring, Natural Disaster Prevention and Early Warning between Italy and the Caribbean Community (2006) or the Agreement between Italy and the UN Economic Commission for Latin America on Disaster Prevention in Latin America and in the Caribbean (1998), which are aimed at providing financial support to various specific activities in the area of disaster prevention and mitigation.

3 The Relevant Role of Soft Law and Guidelines

Considering the specific nature of preparedness measures and the continuous technological evolution that requires their quick adaptation and revision, more and more international, as well as some national and non-governmental, institutions have promoted non-binding documents (guidelines, resolutions, actions plans, etc.) to increase the level of preparedness of both IOs and States. The so-called soft law instruments generally present several advantages compared to international treaties. The process of adopting these documents is usually less time-consuming than a treaty, and updating them is, in most cases, quick and uncomplicated. These key features make soft law instruments very relevant to the framework under investigation here, especially in light of the rapid and continuous evolution of the biological agents and their mutation capacity. The list of soft law instruments dealing with preparedness measures to face potential natural events that could provoke the release of CBRN substances, or to deal with pandemics, is very long. Those applicable to any kind of natural event were analysed in Chapter 4. Additional soft law instruments specifically dealing with pandemics have been adopted within the WHO:[32] among them, the 'COVID-19 Strategic Preparedness and Response Plan', adopted in February 2020 and updated in January 2021, deserves special attention.[33] This document, aims to guide the public health response to COVID-19 at national and subnational levels, and to update the global strategic priorities in support of this effort. In addition, this document is complemented by the COVID-19 Operational Plan, which sets out updated operational planning guidelines to support country preparedness and response; global and regional support to accelerate equitable access to new COVID-19 tools; research and innovation priorities; as well as key performance indicators for monitoring and evaluation. Other soft law instruments address specific issues related to the type of

32 There are several of these documents, such as WHO, Pandemic Influenza Risk Management, – A WHO Guide to Inform & Harmonize National and International Preparedness and Response (2017): <https://www.who.int/influenza/preparedness/pandemic/influenza_risk_management/en/>; WHO, Summary of Key Information Practical to Countries Experiencing Outbreaks of a (H5N1) and other Subtypes of Avian Influence (2016): <https://www.who.int/influenza/resources/publications/avian_influenza_packagev1/en/)>; WHO, Pandemic Influenza Preparedness and Response, WHO Guidance Document (2009): <https://www.who.int/influenza/resources/documents/pandemic_guidance_04_2009/en/>; WHO, Checklist for Influenza Pandemic Preparedness Planning (2005): <https://www.who.int/csr/resources/publications/influenza/WHO_CDS_CSR_GIP_2005_4/en/>.

33 The COVID-19 Strategic Preparedness and Response Plan 2021 is available at <https://www.who.int/publications/i/item/WHO-WHE-2021.02>.

disaster, the nature of the risk, the location where such events occur, the use of military assets[34] and international assistance. Compared to the general soft law tools devoted to preparedness, investigated in Chapter 4, in the specific area of preparedness, the measures present a few distinctive features: they are more numerous, drafted in a more detailed manner and devoted to a very broad spectrum of thematic issues.

Numerous soft law instruments have also been adopted at the regional level. Good examples are provided by the 'Asia Pacific Strategy for Emerging Diseases and Public Health Emergencies (APSED III): Advancing Implementation of the International Health Regulations'[35] and by the 2019 'Statement by the Heads of the Shanghai Cooperation Organisation Member States on Joint Efforts Against the Threat of Epidemics in the SCO Space'.[36] Finally, between 2014 and 2018, G7 Member States made 55 commitments, including preparedness, related to health emergencies specifically.[37] In the recent declaration adopted in Paris in May 2019, the G7 Health Ministers confirmed their commitment to 'continue to offer assistance to 76 partner countries and regions, building on countries' expertise and existing partnership, for this implementation, in particular to strengthen and maintain core capacities required; and therefore, to help reduce the vulnerability of countries to public health emergencies'.[38]

4 Current Challenges in the Implementation of Preparedness Measures at the National Level

The examination carried out in the previous paragraphs regarding treaties and soft law rules devoted to preparedness measures, evidences that States and IO's

34 During the COVID-19 lockdowns, the role of the armed forces was very visible in many States. The army was used to support the local police in patrolling the streets and protecting specific targets, to provide logistical support to the health system and to produce medicine and personal safety equipment.

35 WHO, Asia Pacific Strategy for Emerging Diseases and Public Health Emergencies (APSED III): Advancing implementation of the International Health Regulations (2005): <https://iris.wpro.who.int/handle/10665.1/13654>.

36 The statement was adopted during the Shanghai Cooperation Organisation Heads of State Council Meeting (Bishkek, 13–14 June 2019) <http://eng.sectsco.org/documents/>.

37 All the documents adopted by the G7, G8 and G20 are available at <http://www.g7g20.utoronto.ca>.

38 G7 Health Ministers Declaration: For an Inclusive, Evidence-Based and Sustainable G7 Action in Global Health (Paris, May 17, 2019): <http://www.g7.utoronto.ca/healthmins/2019-health.html>.

are required and/or encouraged to implement, in addition to those already listed in Chapter 4,[39] the following activities:[40]

- regularly update emergency planning related to natural disasters, including pandemics;[41]
- establish legal and operational frameworks to allow both first responders and law enforcement officers (if needed) to intervene quickly and safely;[42]
- maintain effective disease surveillance and laboratory systems with enough capacity to analyse samples (domestically or through collaborating centres);[43] to detect and report diseases or deaths above expected levels in all areas within the territory of a State;[44] and to report newly emerging diseases that could spread internationally;[45]
- encourage rapid, systematic and timely sharing of H5N1 and other influenza viruses with human pandemic potential with WHO Collaborating Centres on Influenza and WHO H5 Reference Laboratories;[46]
- ensure ongoing global monitoring, risk assessment and the development of safe and effective influenza vaccines, in conformity with the Standard Material Transfer Agreement;[47]
- ensure that the capacities set forth for designated points of entry are developed;[48]

39 See also M Aronsson-Storrier', in K Samuel, M Aronsson-Storrier, K Nakjavani (eds.), *The Cambridge Handbook of Disaster Risk Reduction and International Law*, (Cambridge University Press 2019).

40 Almost all of them are related to pandemics, given that those associated with natural CBRN events – such as seismic events, volcanic eruptions etc. – are mostly regulated in general agreements dealing with any kind of CBRN event and have, therefore, already been described in ch 4 by de Guttry.

41 Annex 1 to the IHR; Meeting of the States Parties to the BWC (n 18); WHO, Regional Office for Europe, 'Key Changes to Pandemic Plans by Member States of the Who European Region Based on Lessons Learned from the 2009 Pandemic' (WHO 2012).

42 Art 44, letter d) of the IHR; Annex 1 to the IHR; WHO, 'Delivering Global Health Security through Sustainable Financing' (WHO 2018).

43 Art 13, para 1 of the IHR; Annex 1 to the IHR.

44 Art 13, para 1, of the IHR; Annex 1 to the IHR.

45 Art 13, para 1, and Art 19, letter c) of the IHR; Annex 1 to the IHR.

46 World Health Assembly, Resolution WHA 60.28 (May 23, 2007); WHO; Pandemic Influenza Preparedness Framework.

47 WHO, Pandemic Influenza Preparedness Framework. The Standard Material Transfer Agreement establishes the rights and obligations of Global Influenza Surveillance and Response System.

48 Art 19, letter a), and arts 20–26 of the IHR; Annex 1 to the IHR.

- maintain the necessary infrastructure to respond to health emergencies[49] and the ability of the health system to expand beyond normal operations to meet a sudden increased demand;[50]
- guarantee the availability, when needed, of enough support from specialised staff and logistical assistance, to be activated through a proper emergency organisation and through the establishment of a more extensive global, public health reserve workforce;[51]
- make available adequate and updated equipment, including, where appropriate, personal protective clothing, decontamination lorries, and so forth;[52]
- adopt clear provisions on the chain of command during a pandemic event;[53]
- deliver adequate training and exercises to prepare and test relevant staff;[54]
- mobilise financial resources to facilitate implementation of IHR obligations and, possibly, the creation of a contingency fund for public health emergencies;[55]
- ensure that designated National IHR Focal Points have the authority, resources, procedures, knowledge and training to communicate with all levels of their governments and on behalf of their governments, as necessary;[56]
- provide coordination and capabilities at the national and regional levels;[57]
- collect and disseminate information on science and technology developments, including new research in areas relevant to the BWC; exchange information about databases and networks and ensure access to such databases and networks.[58]

---

49 Art 13, para 1, of the IHR; Annex 1 to the IHR.

50 WHO, 2013 Checklist and indicators for monitoring progress in the development of IHR core capacities in State parties.

51 Art 13 IHR, Review Committee on the Functioning of the IHR (2005) in Relation to Pandemic (H1N1) 2009.

52 Art 13, para 1, of the IHR; Annex 1 to the IHR.

53 Meeting of the States Parties to the BWC (Dec. 15, 2014) (n 18) WHO, Emergency Response Framework- II Edition (2017): <https://apps.who.int/iris/bitstream/handle/10665/258604/9789241512299-eng.pdf?sequence=1>.

54 G.A. Res. 60/262 (n 21); Meeting of the States Parties to the BWC (Dec. 15, 2014).

55 Art 44, letter c) of the IHR; Annex 1 to the IHR; Review Committee on the Functioning of the IHR (2005) in Relation to Pandemic (H1N1) 2009.

56 WHO Review Committee on Second Extensions for Establishing National Public Health Capacities and on IHR Implementation (2014); Annex 1 to the IHR.

57 Art 13, para 5 and Art 44 of the IHR; Annex 1 to the IHR, WHO, 'Delivering Global Health Security through Sustainable Financing', (WHO 2018).

58 Proposals for the Final Document of the Eighth Review Conference of the Biological and Toxin Weapon Convention, Submitted by the Bolivarian Republic of Venezuela on Behalf of the Group of the Non-Aligned Movement and Other States, <https://www.unog.ch/80256EDD006B8954/(httpAssets)/A6E0EA72D8D9F2BFC1258061

It seems undisputable (particularly in light of the COVID-19 pandemic) that these measures cover almost all the different fields of action and continue to be relevant. Unfortunately, the degree of their national implementation is far from satisfactory, and the situation is often aggravated due to the fragmentation (between the national, regional and local levels) of the responsibilities in the management of health systems, as well as their high costs. In countries with a reasonably comprehensive and robust health system, it has been calculated that 'financing improved preparedness might cost less than $1 per person per year, not a huge sum compared to the scale of the risks to human lives and livelihoods'.[59] Participating in the 2017 Munich Security Conference, Bill Gates underlined the irony 'that the cost of ensuring adequate pandemic preparedness worldwide is estimated at $3.4 billion a year – yet the projected annual loss from a pandemic could run as high as $570 billion'.[60] Although, in light of the experience of the COVID-19 pandemic, this estimate might need to be updated, considering also more general expenses not directly related to the reinforcement of the health sector (for example, transportation systems, re-organisation of the schools etc.). Clearly, the resources that need to be invested to ensure adequate preparedness are significantly less than those needed to recover from a pandemic. Reducing the costs of vaccines,[61] making the acquisition contracts more transparent and facilitating access to international financial instruments to support investments in pandemic preparedness have, therefore, become key priorities for the international community. To achieve these goals, an unprecedented effort has been carried out. Firstly, new ideas and recommendations have been elaborated, especially in the framework of the recently established International Working Group on

007885AE/$file/NAM+GROUP-BWC+-+WORKING+PAPER+VIII+REV+CONF-ISP-ISU-S&T+-FINAL+VERSION.pdf>.

59 International Working Group on Financing Preparedness (2017).

60 <https://www.gatesfoundation.org/Media-Center/Speeches/2017/05/Bill-Gates-Munich-Security-Conference>. According to another study, these figures are different: 'whereas the cost of response and economic loss from a pandemic is estimated to be as much as $60 billion per year, it is estimated that $4.6 billion per year, or 0.65 cents per person, would be enough to address current capacity gaps in epidemic readiness': A Glassman, B Datema and A McClelland, 'Financing Outbreak Preparedness: Where Are We and What Next?' (2018): <https://www.cgdev.org/blog/financing-outbreak-preparedness-where-are-we-and-what-next>.

61 The main aim of the Global Alliance for Vaccines and Immunisation (GAVI), launched in 2000 by the Bill and Melinda Gates Foundation, is precisely to encourage manufacturers to lower vaccine prices for the poorest countries in return for long-term, high-volume and predictable demand from those countries.

Financing Pandemic Preparedness.[62] Secondly, extraordinary work has been carried out to increase awareness of the importance and urgency of mobilising financial resources for 'strengthening preparedness for and prevention of pandemics'.[63] Several tools have been created to support national governments in financing national preparedness plans,[64] including the World Bank's Pandemic Emergency Financing Facility;[65] the Regional Disease Surveillance Systems Enhancement Program;[66] the International Bank for Reconstruction and Development Catastrophe Deferred Drawdown Option;[67] the Global Crisis Response Platform, launched by the World Bank Group;[68] and the new options offered by the International Development Association[69] and by the Coalition for Epidemic Preparedness Innovations.[70] Although various recent

---

62 WHO, 'Delivering Global Health Security through Sustainable Financing', (WHO 2018).

63 G7 Ise-Shima Leaders' Declaration – G7 Ise-Shima Summit, 26–27 May 2016, <http://www.g7.utoronto.ca/summit/2016shima/ise-shima-declaration-en.pdf>. For an analysis of the real implementation of these commitments by the G7 States, see the G7 Research Group at the Munk School of Global Affairs at Trinity College in the University of Toronto, 'Ise-Shimag7 Interim Compliance Report, 29 May 2016 to 19 February 2017' (2017): <http://www.g7.utoronto.ca/evaluations/2016compliance-interim/10-2016-g7-compliance-interim-health.pdf>.

64 See more at P L Osewe, 'Options for financing pandemic preparedness', (2017) 95 *Bulletin of The World Health Organisation*.

65 The PEF is a facility established for the purpose of providing financial support to eligible countries and responding agencies to help prevent a high-severity infectious disease outbreak from becoming a pandemic: The International Bank for Reconstruction and Development, the International Development Band and the World Health Organization, Pandemic Emergency Financing Facility Framework (June 27, 2017). <http://pubdocs.worldbank.org/en/670191509025137260/PEF-Framework.pdf>.

66 One of the specific aims of this programme is to strengthen national and regional cross-sectoral capacity for collaborative disease surveillance and epidemic preparedness in West Africa: <https://projects.worldbank.org/en/projects-operations/project-detail/P154807>.

67 The Development Policy Loan with a Catastrophe Deferred Drawdown Option (Cat DDO) is a contingent financing line that provides immediate liquidity to address shocks related to natural disasters and/or health-related events: <http://pubdocs.worldbank.org/en/526461507314946994/product-note-cat-ddo-ibrd-2018.pdf>.

68 The GCRP should provide scaled up, systematic and better coordinated support for managing and mitigating current and future crises across the spectrum of risks and vulnerabilities: World Bank Group (2016) (n 5), para 10.

69 In 2016, the IDA expressed its commitment 'to support at least 25 IDA countries in developing pandemic preparedness plans': IDA, Towards 2030: Investing in Growth, Resilience and Opportunity, approved by the Executive Directors of IDA on January 12, 2017 (modified on January 31, 2017): <http://documents.worldbank.org/curated/en/348661486654455091/pdf/112728-correct-file-PUBLIC-Rpt-from-EDs-Additions-to-IDA-Resources-2-9-17-For-Disclosure.pdf>.

70 <https://cepi.net/>.

studies have demonstrated that the funds available for preparedness measures continue to be insufficient, too fragmented and often not well known or easy to access by interested States,[71] all these recent efforts are moving in the right direction, albeit slowly.

5 Concluding Remarks

This chapter has identified the preparedness measures that States and IO's are required or recommended to adopt to face potential natural events involving CBRN material and, in particular, to deal with pandemics, in order to reduce the number of potential victims, as well as protect the health of communities[72] and, especially, of the most vulnerable groups. Needless to say, all these measures have to be carried out in full compliance with international law and, more specifically, with international human rights law.[73] The investigation has also highlighted the major challenges confronted in the implementation of these measures which, with only a few laudable exceptions,[74] is far from uniform[75] and satisfactory.[76] To increase the degree of fulfilment of all these

71 P Sands, 'Financing pandemic preparedness: from analysis to recommendations', World Bank Blogs (2017), <https://blogs.worldbank.org/health/financing-pandemic-preparedness-analysis-recommendations>; Glassman, Datema and McClelland (n x).

72 R Gofin, 'Preparedness and response to terrorism: A framework for public health action', (2005) 15 *European Journal of Public Health*, 100. Some of the measures are also meant to prevent serious environmental problems and major issues that might affect societal and governmental stability.

73 Although referring to the response phase, in Res. 74/270 2 April 2020), UN Doc. A/RES/74/270, the UNGA emphasised 'the need for full respect for human rights, and stresses that there is no place for any form of discrimination, racism and xenophobia in the response to the pandemic'.

74 In a few States, ad hoc structures/institutions have been created or tasked to deal with the preparedness issue. For example, in the UK the Centre for Emergency Preparedness and Response has been established within the UK's Health Protection Agency. A List of national influenza pandemic preparedness plans of the EU and EFTA countries is available at <https://www.ecdc.europa.eu/en/seasonal-influenza/preparedness/influenza-pandemic-preparedness-plans>.

75 Discrepancies in the degree of preparedness among States are often correlated to level of development, where 'countries with greater levels of national income have higher levels of national preparedness. 39 low-income countries have the lowest levels of preparedness, while higher-income countries score the highest capacity levels for preparedness': WHO, 'Thematic Paper on the Status of Country Preparedness Capacities. Background Report Commissioned by The Global Preparedness Monitoring Board' (2019): <https://apps.who.int/gpmb/assets/thematic_papers/tr-2.pdf>, p 17.

76 Available data indicate that 'most countries currently have low-to-moderate levels of national preparedness': ibid p 4. Making more specific reference to preparedness to

preparedness measures, several proposals are currently on the table, starting from the suggestion, reiterated in a recent appeal signed on 30 March 2021 by more than 20 world leaders, 'that nations should work together towards a new international treaty for pandemic preparedness and response' which would represent 'a milestone in stepping up pandemic preparedness at the highest political level'.[77] Other proposals recommend the introduction of new monitoring schemes,[78] and the launch of new committees 'to evaluate country capacity to prevent, detect and rapidly respond to public health threats independently of whether they are naturally occurring, deliberate or accidental'.[79] The logic behind these monitoring and evaluation systems is mainly to assess if, and to what extent, the preparedness obligations codified in the various treaties are being adequately implemented by the States in a timely manner. However, more recently, a new mechanism has surfaced that attempts to incentivise States to proactively implement preparedness measures. The WHO's 'Pandemic Influenza Preparedness Framework for the Sharing of Influenza Viruses and Access to Vaccines and Other Benefits' is a good example of this new approach.[80] As reflected in its title, the framework

deal with new pandemics, the 2014 Report of the WHO Review Committee on Second Extensions for Establishing National Public Health Capacities and on IHR Implementation stated that, though progress had been made in many areas, there was still a multitude of unresolved or only partially resolved issues: Report of the Review Committee on Second Extensions for Establishing National Public Health Capacities and on IHR Implementation (n 55).

77 'COVID-19 shows why united action is needed for more robust international health architecture' – Op-ed article by President Charles Michel, WHO Director-General Dr Tedros Adhanom Ghebreyesus and more than 20 world leaders: <https://www.consilium.europa.eu/en/press/press-releases/2021/03/30/pandemic-treaty-op-ed/>.

78 Within the WHO, States Parties and the Director-General were requested to regularly report to the Health Assembly on implementation of the regulations. To support and facilitate the work of Member States in preparing their national reports, the WHO developed a monitoring framework through which States Parties can monitor and evaluate their own implementation of IHR capacities in accordance with the requirements for capacity development outlined in Annex 1 of the IHR: WHO, International Health Regulations (2005) (n x), IHR Monitoring and Evaluation Framework (2018): <https://apps.who.int/iris/bitstream/handle/10665/276651/WHO-WHE-CPI-2018.51-eng.pdf?sequence=1>. These national reports are examined by a review committee appointed by the WHO Director-General.

79 WHO, Joint External Evaluation Tool: International Health Regulations (2005), Second Edition (2018): <https://apps.who.int/iris/bitstream/handle/10665/259961/9789241550222-eng.pdf?sequence=1>. at 8. So far, more than 100 States have undertaken a JEE (the JEE mission reports are available at <https://www.who.int/ihr/procedures/mission-reports/en/>), resulting in the detection of more than 6,000 critical capacity gaps: Glassman, Datema and McClelland (n x).

80 The framework document also introduced an additional oversight mechanism that includes the World Health Assembly, the Director-General and the independent 'Advisory

offers several incentives (such as facilitated access to antiviral stockpiles and to vaccines in the inter-pandemic period, tiered pricing, technology transfer, and sustainable and innovative financing opportunities) to States that fulfil their preparedness obligations. This new modality of encouraging good practices deserves the highest attention,[81] and it will be interesting to see if it increases compliance with preparedness measures in the near future, whether they are codified in international conventions or amount to mere soft law rules. More sophisticated mechanisms favouring the full and timely implementation of preparedness rules represent a fundamental step in the right direction,[82] especially considering that failure to respect an international obligation is a violation of international law. Within Europe, the ECtHR has repeatedly confirmed that States have an obligation to ensure the proper organisation and functioning of their health protection systems,[83] and it has not hesitated to condemn States which knew about dysfunctions in their hospitals but did not undertake necessary measures to redress the situation.[84] Although these conclusions of the Court formally apply only to the specific cases brought to its attention, and refer to the violations of specific hard law rules, they impact the interpretation of the ECHR rules and, thanks to cross-fertilisation among international courts, might even have a wider influence. Therefore, the jurisprudence

---

Group', and it is expected to provide evidence-based reporting, assessment and recommendations regarding the functioning of the framework (Art 27).

81 According to a recent study of the WHO, there are currently 'too few incentives to encourage countries to invest in preparedness, and there has been limited progress in developing innovative financial motivators (e.g. matched funding from donors)': WHO (2019) (n 73).

82 The ongoing discussion within the WHO regarding how to continue to improve the IHR's existing monitoring system presents important evidence of the increasing attention devoted to this crucial aspect. For an example, see WHO, Meeting Report: WHO Technical Review Meeting of the Joint External Evaluation (JEE) Tool and Process, (2017): <https://apps.who.int/iris/bitstream/handle/10665/259206/WHO-WHE-CPI-2017.53-eng.pdf?sequence=1>.

83 The Court has, however, emphasised that the States' substantive positive obligations in this area are limited to a duty to establish an effective regulatory framework compelling hospitals, whether private or public, to adopt appropriate measures for the protection of patients' lives; this might arise where a systemic or structural dysfunction in hospital services results in a patient being deprived of access to life-saving emergency treatment, provided that the authorities knew or ought to have known about that risk and failed to undertake the necessary measures to prevent that risk from materialising, thus putting patients' lives in danger. ECtHR, *Case of Lopes de Sousa Fernandes v. Portugal*, (Application no. 56080/13), Judgment, 19 December 2017.

84 ECtHR, *Case of Lopes de Sousa Fernandes v. Portugal*, (Application no. 56080/13), Judgment, 19 December 2017. See also ECtHR, *Case of Asiye Genc v. Turkey*, (Application No. 24109/07), Judgment, 27 January 2015.

of the European Court might help to significantly stimulate States to act in a more consistent manner in the national implementation of preparedness measures, both those codified in conventions and those emerging from soft law instruments.

The analysis carried out in the preceding sections further revealed that at least some measures have attracted a high level of interest (and therefore numerous rules have been codified), while others have received less attention. Those related to the organisation of international assistance are to be listed in the first category, as there are dozens of universal, regional, sub-regional and even bilateral treaties devoted to regulating the activation of international assistance mechanisms. The plurality of options available to States for requesting international assistance is, as stated by the ILC, perfectly consistent with the discretionary power of the disaster-affected State 'to choose from other States, the United Nations, and other potential assisting actors the assistance that is most appropriate to its specific needs'.[85] The second category (grouping issues which have been neglected so far) includes the preparation of well-planned information flows during an emergency; this is unfortunate, as preparation on how to communicate risks during an extraordinary event is of the utmost importance, given the vital need to ensure public and professional confidence and trust in a crisis.[86]

Finally, to remain relevant and effective, all the preparedness measures need not only to be fully implemented at the national level but also must be constantly reviewed and updated – failure to do so could have devastating impacts on human lives, wreaking havoc on long-term social and economic development. More than ever, as stated in UNGA Resolution 75/27 of December 2020, 'global health crises threaten to overwhelm already overstretched health systems, disrupt global supply chains and cause disproportionate devastation of the livelihoods of people, including women and children, and the economies of the poorest and most vulnerable countries'. Considering the innovative drugs and diagnostics currently available, as well as new early-warning technologies and technical tools, inaction can no longer be justified, whether in legal, political or moral terms.

---

85 Art 11 of the ILC Report.

86 The WHO has been very active in producing relevant guides and handbooks on this specific issue: see, for example, the 2008 WHO Outbreak Communication Planning Guide <https://www.who.int/ihr/elibrary/WHOOutbreakCommsPlanngGuide.pdf> and WHO, 'Effective Media Communications During Public Health Emergencies. A WHO Handbook', (2005): <http://www.who.int/csr/resources/publications/WHO_CDS_2005_31/en/>.

5.1 *Information on This Chapter*

This chapter is a revised and updated version of the article 'Is the International Community Ready for the Next Pandemic Wave? A Legal Analysis of the Preparedness Rules Codified in Universal Instruments and of Their Impact in the Light of the COVID-19 Experience', published by the same author in 20(3) Global Jurist (2020), pp 1–41.

Bibliography

Aronsson-Storrier M, 'Exploring the Foundations: The Principles of Prevention, Mitigation, and Preparedness in International Law', in K Samuel, M Aronsson-Storrier, K Nakjavani (eds.), The *Cambridge Handbook of Disaster Risk Reduction and International Law*, (Cambridge University Press 2019), 52.

Asian Development Bank, Asian Development Bank, 'Asian Development Outlook 2020: What Drives Innovation in Asia? Special Topic: The Impact of the Coronavirus Outbreak – An Update XIV', (2020): <https://www.adb.org/sites/default/files/publication/575626/ado2020.pdf>.

Doshi P, 'The elusive definition of pandemic influenza', Bulletin of the WHO (2011): <https://www.scielosp.org/article/bwho/2011.v89n7/532-538/en/>.

Glassman A, Datema B and McClelland A, 'Financing Outbreak Preparedness: Where Are We and What Next?' (2018): <https://www.cgdev.org/blog/financing-outbreak-preparedness-where-are-we-and-what-next>.

Global Preparedness Monitoring Board, 'A World at Risk: Annual Report on Global Preparedness for Health Emergencies' (2019), <https://apps.who.int/gpmb/assets/annual_report/GPMB_Annual_Report_English.pdf>.

Gofin R, 'Preparedness and response to terrorism: A framework for public health action', (2005) 15 European Journal of Public Health, 100.

International Working Group on Financing Preparedness (2017).

Negri S, 'Communicable disease control', in G L Burci and B Toebes (eds.), *Research Handbook on Global Health Law,* (Elgar Publishing Ltd. 2018), 265.

Osewe P L, 'Options for financing pandemic preparedness', (2017) 95 Bulletin of The World Health Organisation, 794.

Sands P, 'The Neglected Dimension of Global Security: A Framework for Countering Infectious Disease Crises', (2016) 13 New England Journal of Medicine, 1281.

Sands P, 'Financing pandemic preparedness: from analysis to recommendations', World Bank Blogs (2017), <https://blogs.worldbank.org/health/financing-pandemic-preparedness-analysis-recommendations>.

Sands P, 'The first line of defense against outbreaks is to finance pandemic preparedness at a national level', World Bank Blogs (2017): <https://blogs.worldbank.org/

health/first-line-defense-against-outbreaks-finance-pandemic-preparedness -national-level>.

Smil V, *A Complete History of Pandemics, Global Catastrophes and Trends: The Next 50 Years*, (The MIT Press, 2008).

The G7 Research Group at the Munk School of Global Affairs at Trinity College in the University of Toronto, 'Ise-Shimag7 Interim Compliance Report, 29 May 2016 To 19 February 2017' (2017): <http://www.g7.utoronto.ca/evaluations/2016 compliance-interim/10-2016-g7-compliance-interim-health.pdf.

WHO, Asia Pacific Strategy for Emerging Diseases and Public Health Emergencies (APSED III): Advancing implementation of the International Health Regulations (2005): <https://iris.wpro.who.int/handle/10665.1/13654>.

WHO, 'Delivering Global Health Security through Sustainable Financing', (WHO 2018).

WHO, Regional Office for Europe, 'Key Changes to Pandemic Plans by Member States of the WHO European Region Based on Lessons Learned from the 2009 Pandemic' (WHO 2012).

WHO, 'Thematic Paper on the Status of Country Preparedness Capacities. Background Report Commissioned by The Global Preparedness Monitoring Board, (2019): <https://apps.who.int/gpmb/assets/thematic_papers/tr-2.pdf>.

World Bank Group', 'Global Crisis Response Platform', (2016): <http://documents .worldbank.org/curated/en/334721474058771487/pdf/WBG-Global-Crisis-Response -Platform-08252016.pdf>.

CHAPTER 18

Response and Recovery Related to Naturally Occurring CBRN Events: Focusing on Epidemic Outbreaks, including COVID-19

Christine Bakker and Alice Farina

1 Introduction

Besides man-made industrial accidents, terrorist attacks and acts of war, CBRN agents can also be released by naturally occurring events. Such events include natural disasters (eg hurricanes, earthquakes, or floods), which can lead to spillage of CBRN substances into the environment, as occurred during the 2011 Fukushima nuclear accident.[1] Moreover, epidemic outbreaks also constitute naturally generated CBRN incidents, since viruses or illness-causing bacteria fall within the scope of 'biological' agents.[2] Regarding the COVID-19 crisis, the United Nations Security Council (UNSC) underscored in its Resolution 2532 that 'combating this pandemic requires greater national, regional and international cooperation and solidarity, and a coordinated, inclusive, comprehensive and global international response'.[3]

This chapter examines the specific obligations of States – and, where appropriate, those of international organisations (IOs) – related to the response and recovery from naturally occurring CBRN events, with a special focus on epidemic outbreaks, including the COVID-19 pandemic.

The chapter first provides a brief overview of the main international and regional regulatory instruments setting out response and recovery obligations and recommendations related to CBRN events caused by natural disasters, considering both legally binding and 'soft-law' instruments (2.1.). It then examines the specific response and recovery obligations and guidelines included in international and regional instruments related to epidemic outbreaks (2.2.), distinguishing between the rules related to all epidemics; to particular epidemic outbreaks, such as Ebola and HIV/AIDS; and those adopted for the

1 See ch 13 by Bakker, Montanaro in this volume.
2 See ch 1 by Frulli in this volume.
3 UNSC Res 2532 (1 July 2020) UN Doc S/RES/2532.

DOI:10.1163/9789004507999_019

COVID-19 pandemic.[4] The chapter concludes by discussing some of the lessons learned and main challenges identified with respect to the application of the identified rules to the ongoing response to the COVID-19 crisis, also considering whether any specific monitoring or enforcement mechanisms exist to ensure compliance with these rules (Section 3). The analysis shows that the existing regulatory instruments provide detailed guidance for the response to natural disasters and epidemic outbreaks, whereas relatively little attention is paid to the recovery phase.

2 Specific Response and Recovery Obligations and Guidance for Naturally Occurring CBRN Events

2.1 *Response and Recovery Rules Related to CBRN Events Caused by Natural Disasters*

CBRN substances can be released into the environment due to natural disasters, eg when a chemical or nuclear facility, or a waste management site are damaged by an earthquake, flood, tornado, or volcanic eruption. In those situations, several sets of rules apply; on the one hand, those adopted for the management of natural disasters and, on the other hand, the tailored rules applicable to accidents that require specific safeguards, eg for the containment of specified hazardous substances. These latter rules are often contained in '*lex specialis*' and are dealt with elsewhere in this volume.[5] Therefore, in this section, only those instruments that generally apply to natural disasters will be mentioned.

2.1.1 Main Instruments Setting Out Obligations for Responding to Natural Disasters

In the absence of a specific international convention on disaster reduction, the proclamation of the 1990s as the 'International Decade of Natural Disaster Reduction' by UNGA Resolution 42/169,[6] and the adoption of the Yokohama Strategy and Plan of Action,[7] expressed a significant international

4 Since bilateral agreements on mutual disaster relief assistance generally cover all types of disasters, including naturally occurring CBRN events, they are discussed in ch 5 by Bakker in this volume.

5 See ch 16 by Venier (concerning volcanic eruptions) and ch 13 by Bakker and Montanaro (regarding industrial accidents) in this volume.

6 UN Doc A/RES/42/169 (11 December 1987).

7 UN World Conference on Natural Disaster Reduction, 'Yokohama Strategy for a Safer World: Guidelines for Natural Disaster Prevention, Preparedness and Mitigation, and Plan for Action', (1994) UN Doc A/CONF.172/9.

commitment, focusing on the management of natural disasters. In subsequent international 'soft-law' instruments, such as the Hyogo Framework for Action 2005–2015,[8] and the Sendai Framework on Disaster Reduction,[9] this focus was broadened to an 'all-hazards' approach, including man-made disasters.[10] Regarding disaster response, these instruments attach fundamental importance to the coordination of assistance and to international cooperation.

Moreover, the Operational Guidelines on the Protection of Persons in Situations of Natural Disasters of the UN Inter-Agency Standing Committee,[11] provide detailed guidance on how to protect human rights during the response and recovery phases of natural disasters. The Guidelines are primarily addressed to IOs and NGOs. Furthermore, UNGA Resolution 57/150[12] aims at strengthening coordinated international urban search and rescue assistance. Finally, several regional agreements regulate cooperation on natural disasters,[13] and numerous bilateral mutual assistance agreements exist, covering either all types of emergencies[14] or only natural disasters.[15]

2.1.2 Obligations and Guidelines for the Recovery from Natural Disasters

The international instrument that most explicitly refers to post-disaster recovery is the Sendai Framework,[16] which affirms that:

---

8 Hyogo Framework for Action 2005–2015: Building the Resilience of Nations and Communities to Disasters (2006) UN Doc A/CONF.206/6.

9 Sendai Framework on Disaster Reduction (2015).

10 See also ch 4 by de Guttry and ch 5 by Bakker in this volume.

11 IASC, Operational Guidelines on the Protection of Persons in Situations of Natural Disasters (Washington, D.C., Brookings-Bern Project on Internal Displacement, 2011). Created by the UNGA in 1991, the IASC is the highest-level humanitarian coordination forum of the UN system, bringing together the executive heads of 18 UN and non-UN organisations to ensure coherence in their humanitarian action.

12 UNGA Resolution 57/150 (27 February 2003) UN Doc A/Res/57/150, which endorsed the Guidelines of the International Search and Rescue Advisory Group.

13 Emergency Technical Co-operation Agreement between the Pan American Health Organization and the Government of Suriname in Case of a Major Natural Disaster (1983), Agreement Between Member States and Associate Members of the Association of Caribbean States for Regional Cooperation on Natural Disasters (1999).

14 See ch 5 by Bakker in this volume; <https://documents-dds-ny.un.org/doc/UNDOC/GEN/N08/291/20/PDF/N0829120.pdf?OpenElement> (all links were last accessed on 25 June 2021).

15 Eg Agreement between the USA and Mexico on Cooperation in Cases of Natural Disasters (1980), Agreement on Mutual Assistance between Portuguese and Spanish Fire and Emergency Services (1980).

16 Sendai Framework (n 9).

> (d)isasters have demonstrated that the recovery, rehabilitation and reconstruction phase, which needs to be prepared ahead of a disaster, is a critical opportunity to "Build Back Better", including through integrating disaster risk reduction into development measures, making nations and communities resilient to disasters.[17]

To this end, several measures are recommended to States, such as the promotion of resilience of critical infrastructure, including hospitals and other health facilities.[18] States are also recommended to ensure the continuity of social and economic recovery,[19] and to integrate recovery actions with the SDGs and climate change resilience. Moreover, an active involvement of civil society – including women, youth, indigenous people – and other stakeholders, such as the private sector and academia, is promoted, also in the recovery phase of a disaster.[20]

However, in practice, the implementation of Build Back Better recovery strategies is not always straightforward. For example, in a post-hurricane, post-earthquake and cholera-affected Haiti and in a post-earthquake Nepal, the 'history of conflict, weak governance and heavy dependency on external donors and experts mean that focusing on the one triggering event [...] should not be the narrow starting point for a BBB [Build Back Better] strategy'.[21] Similarly, 'where conflict and the failure of governance'[22] were the norm even before the (naturally occurring) event, as in the city of Goma before the volcanic eruption[23] in 2002, Build Back Better represents a rather 'utopian' recovery framework: the local government relies necessarily on donors and (international) agencies.[24]

2.2 *Response and Recovery Rules Related to Epidemic Outbreaks*

While the general obligations and recommendations mentioned above (subsection 2.1.) also apply to epidemics, many instruments have been adopted which set out more specific rules for the management of epidemic outbreaks. These will be examined below, distinguishing between rules applicable to

17 Ibid para 32.
18 Ibid para 33(c).
19 Ibid para 33(g).
20 Ibid para 36.
21 B Winser, '"Build Back Better?" The challenge of Goma and beyond' (2019) International Journal of Disaster Risk Reduction <http://dx.doi.org.10/1016/j.ijdrr.2017.09.027>.
22 Ibid.
23 See also ch 16 by Venier in this volume.
24 Ibid.

all epidemics (2.2.1.), those related to epidemics such as Ebola and HIV/AIDS (2.2.2.) and those specifically pertaining to COVID-19 (2.2.3).

2.2.1 All Epidemic Outbreaks

The World Health Organization (WHO) is the most prominent actor in the field of international health law. The WHO Constitution (WHOC)[25] defines the functions of the organisation, including the task 'to stimulate and advance work to eradicate epidemic, endemic and other diseases'.[26] Based on the WHOC, each Member State has annual reporting obligations on the action taken 'to improve the health of its population'[27] and 'with respect to recommendations made to it by the Organization'.[28] However, the main international instrument applicable to health emergencies is the International Health Regulations (IHR),[29] a treaty adopted by the World Health Assembly (WHA).[30] The IHR sets out several obligations for States: (i) detection and assessment of potential disease 'events';[31] (ii) notification of the WHO of disease events which might constitute a public health emergency of international concern;[32] (iii) information sharing during unexpected or unusual public health events;[33] (iv) timely adoption of health measures;[34] and (v) cooperation with third States and the WHO.[35] Moreover, all States Parties 'shall undertake to cooperate with each other, to the extent possible', including in the response to disease 'events'; the provision or facilitation of technical cooperation and logistical support; and the mobilisation of financial resources.[36]

In this context, reference should also be made to States' duty to cooperate based on Article 2(1) of the International Covenant on Economic, Social and Cultural Rights (ICESCR), in relation to the right to the highest attainable standard of physical and mental health (Article 12, ICESCR). In particular, Article 12(2)(c) provides that 'the steps to be taken by the States Parties to the present Covenant to achieve the full realization of this right shall include

---

25 Constitution of the World Health Organization (2005) (hereafter: 'WHOC').
26 Ibid art 2(g).
27 WHOC art 61.
28 WHOC art 62.
29 International Health Regulations (1951, revised in 2005) (hereafter: 'IHR').
30 The WHO's decision-making body, in which all 194 WHO Member States participate.
31 IHR (n 29) art 6(1). According to art 1(1), '"event" means a manifestation of disease or an occurrence that creates a potential for disease'.
32 Ibid.
33 Ibid art 7.
34 Ibid art 27, art 42.
35 Ibid art 44.
36 Ibid art 44(1).

those necessary for [...] (c) the prevention, treatment, and control of epidemic, endemic, occupational and other diseases'.[37] As argued by Desierto, 'the baseline duty to cooperate under Article 2(1) of the ICESCR in relation to the right to health under Article 12 of the ICESCR is all too clear that cooperation MUST include that which is necessary to prevent, treat, and control epidemics, including global pandemics such as COVID-19'.[38]

At the regional level, various soft-law instruments address cooperation during epidemic outbreaks. For example, the Africa Regional Strategy for Disaster Risk Reduction (ARS-DRR)[39] affirms that in Africa, 'epidemics are the major cause of disasters'.[40] The ARS-DRR Programme of Action[41] recommends actions for integrating disaster reduction into emergency response and recovery activities.[42] Moreover, the Asia Pacific Strategy for Emerging Diseases and Public Health Emergencies,[43] aims to '(s)trengthen rapid and appropriate response to and recovery from emerging diseases and public health emergencies',[44] recommending States, for instance, to support data sharing nationally and internationally.[45] Information sharing and coordination are also central recommendations of the Strategic Framework for the Prevention and Control of Emerging and Epidemic-prone Infectious Diseases in the Eastern Mediterranean Region 2019–2023,[46] supported by the competent WHO Regional Office. WHO Regional Offices in other regions have supported similar strategies, such as the Pan-American Health Organization's Draft Strategic Plan 2020–2025 for Health Emergencies,[47] and the Action Plan to Improve Public Health Preparedness and Response in the WHO European Region

37 International Covenant on Economic, Social and Cultural Rights ('ICESR', 1966). See also ch 16 by Venier in this volume.

38 D Desierto, 'Equitable COVID Vaccine Distribution and Access: Enforcing International Legal Obligations under Economic, Social, and Cultural Rights and the Right to Development' in *EJIL:Talk*, 2 February 2021.

39 African Regional Strategy for Disaster Risk Reduction (2004) (hereafter: 'ARS-DDR').

40 Ibid para 2.1.

41 Programme of Action for the Implementation of the Africa Regional Strategy for Disaster Risk Reduction (2006–2015).

42 Ibid 13.

43 WHO, Asia Pacific Strategy for Emerging Diseases and Public Health Emergencies (2017).

44 Ibid 5.

45 Ibid 23.

46 See <https://applications.emro.who.int/docs/WHOEMCSR293E-eng.pdf?ua=1>.

47 Pan-American Health Organization, <https://www.paho.org/hq/index.php?option=com_docman&view=download&alias=50284-health-emergencies-strategic-plan-2020-25-draft&category_slug=disasters-english-1853&Itemid=270&lang=en>.

2018–2023.[48] Although these strategies focus on preparedness and response, they also cover preparatory actions for effective recovery.[49]

2.2.2 Specific Epidemic Outbreaks, Other Than COVID-19

Over the years, various instruments have been adopted to ensure a coordinated response to specific epidemics, such as the 2003 outbreak of SARS;[50] HIV/AIDS; influenza; and the Ebola outbreaks in West Africa (2014–2016) and the Democratic Republic of Congo (DRC, 2018–2019). Responding to the SARS outbreak, the WHO issued recommendations to stop international spread,[51] including information sharing and international reporting. As affirmed by Mahoney and Le Duc, 'the outbreak was successfully contained within 4 months and represents a good example of how the IHR mechanisms can be successfully applied during coordination of outbreak responses'.[52] Moreover, regarding HIV/AIDS, since 1987, guidelines for preparedness, response and international cooperation have been provided in numerous resolutions of the UNGA[53] and WHO,[54] and in documents published by the Joint UN Programme on HIV/AIDS (UNAIDS).[55]

With a view to strengthening the international response to influenza, in 2011, the WHO adopted the Pandemic Influenza Preparedness (PIP) Framework,[56] which calls on the international community to share access to vaccines and other benefits.[57] Finally, the outbreak of the Ebola virus disease across West

48 WHO Regional Office for Europe, 'Health Emergencies', <https://www.euro.who.int/__data/assets/pdf_file/0009/393705/Action-Plan_EN_WHO_web_2.pdf>.

49 Eg the Strategic Plan for the Eastern Mediterranean 21.

50 Severe acute respiratory syndrome (SARS).

51 Eg WHO guidelines for the global surveillance of severe acute respiratory syndrome (SARS). Updated recommendations, October 2004, WHO/CDS/CSR/ARO/2004.1.

52 F Mahoney, J W Le Duc, 'Multinational Outbreak Investigations' in The CDC Epidemiology Manual, Centers for Disease Control (CDC), <https://www.cdc.gov/eis/field-epi-manual/chapters/Multinational-Outbreak.html>.

53 Eg UNGA, UN Doc A/RES/60/262 (17 August 2006); UN Doc A/RES/65/277 (8 July 2011); UN Doc A/70/266 (8 June 2016). See also ch 17 by De Guttry in this volume.

54 Eg World Health Assembly (WHA) Resolution WHA64.14 (2011) on a global health sector strategy on HIV/AIDS, 2011–2015; WHA Resolution (2016), Global health sector strategies on HIV, viral hepatitis and sexually transmitted infections for the period 2016–2021.

55 Eg OHCHR and Joint United Nations Programme on HIV/AIDS, International Guidelines on HIV/AIDS and Human Rights (2006).

56 WHO, Pandemic Influenza Preparedness Framework for the Sharing of Influenza Viruses and Access to Vaccines and other Benefits (2011). See also ch 17 by De Guttry in this volume. <https://apps.who.int/iris/bitstream/handle/10664/44976/9789241503082_eng.pdf?sequence=1> (hereafter: 'PIP Framework').

57 Ibid 3.

Africa from 2014 to 2016 highlighted important shortcomings in the global response, due to a lack of preparedness at the national level and shortcomings in the WHO's response.[58] The UN Security Council, in its Resolution 2177/2014, determined, for the first time, that a major infectious disease could constitute a threat to international peace and security, by classifying the Ebola outbreak as such.[59] This resolution sets out recommendations for both affected and assisting States, concerning the delivery of appropriate, coordinated health care. Efforts were made to ensure a more effective response to the Ebola outbreak in the DRC in 2018–2019.[60] Also, regional response strategies for these epidemics were implemented.[61]

A concrete example of recovery measures adopted in Liberia after the Ebola outbreak, was the creation of Social Reconnection Groups (SRGs), which focus on supporting individual psychosocial well-being and strengthening community relationships and community capacity to handle problems.[62] In the Liberian village of Mawah, the International Medical Corps (IMC) sought to provide a safe platform that community members could use to 'reflect their experiences, build trust, address resulting problems and move towards re-establishing mechanisms of social support which existed before the outbreak'.[63] This sort of intervention adopts a community-based approach,[64] which could be used in similar settings.

2.2.3 Response and Recovery Rules Related to COVID-19

Although the general instruments addressing epidemic outbreaks (see Section 2.2.1.) also apply to COVID-19, its rapid spread and the high death-toll from this novel virus have spurred additional responses. At the international level, the UNGA first adopted, on 3 April 2020, Resolution 74/270,[65] recognising that 'the COVID-19 pandemic requires a global response based on unity, solidarity and renewed multilateral cooperation'.[66] This same formulation was later

58 See Mahoney, Le Duc (n 52).

59 UNSC, S/RES/2177 (2014).

60 Eg WHO Strategic Response Plan for Ebola Virus Disease Outbreak (2018) – DRC; UNSC Resolution 2439 (2018); see also ch 17 by de Guttry in this volume.

61 Eg SADC, Regional Strategy for HIV Prevention, Treatment and Care (2018), ASEAN Regional SARS Plan (2003).

62 WHO, 'Culture and Mental Health in Liberia: A Primer' (2017) WHO/MSD/MER/17.3.

63 M Morelli, 'Recovering from the Ebola crisis: "Social Reconnection Groups" in a rural Liberian community' (2019) Global Mental Health <https://doi.org/10.1017/gmh.2019.13>.

64 Ibid 7.

65 UNGA Res 74/270 (3 April 2020) UN Doc A/RES/74/270.

66 Ibid, Preamble, last para.

repeated by the Security Council in its Resolution 2532.[67] In a second resolution, the UNGA called for international cooperation to ensure global access to medicines, vaccines and medical equipment to face COVID-19.[68] Six months later, the Assembly adopted more detailed guidance,[69] urging States to adopt 'responses that are people-centred, gender-responsive, with full respect for human rights',[70] and encouraging them to partner with stakeholders to strengthen scientific cooperation. The resolution also urges States 'to adopt a climate- and environment-sensitive approach to COVID-19 recovery efforts'.[71] Furthermore, the Security Council adopted a Resolution[72] demanding 'a general and immediate cessation of hostilities in all situations on its agenda'[73] and calling upon all parties to armed conflicts 'to engage immediately in a durable humanitarian pause for at least 90 consecutive days, in order to enable the safe, unhindered and sustained delivery of humanitarian assistance'[74] for COVID-19-related relief.

The WHO also formulated guidance for States' response actions,[75] including sharing information with the WHO and other States on 'COVID-19 related knowledge, lessons learned, experiences, best practices, data, materials and commodities needed in the response',[76] and providing timely and adequate public health information to the population[77] and to the WHO.[78] It also recommends ensuring adequate working conditions for health workers, access to protective equipment,[79] and implementing 'whole of society' responses through a cross-sectoral national plan addressing both short-term and long-term actions.[80] However, references to 'recovery' are limited to the preparation for the recovery phase, and to the need to mainstream a gender perspective in response and recovery actions.[81]

67 UNSC (n 3).
68 UNGA Res 74/274 (20 April 2020) UN Doc A/RES/74/274.
69 UNGA Res A/74/L.92* (11 September 2020) UN Doc A/RES/74/L92.
70 Ibid para 2.
71 Ibid para 47.
72 UNSC (n 3).
73 Ibid para 1.
74 Ibid para 2.
75 WHO, World Health Assembly, A73/CONF./1 Rev.1 (18 May 2020), 'COVID-19 Response'.
76 Ibid para 7.11.
77 Ibid para 7.6.
78 Ibid para 7.10.
79 Ibid para 7.8.
80 Ibid para 7.1.
81 Ibid para 7.14.

As part of the global response measures, COVAX should also be mentioned. It is a global collaboration of governments, global health organisations, manufacturers, scientists, private sector actors and civil society, set up by the WHO, the European Commission and France to accelerate the development, production, and equitable worldwide access to COVID-19 tests, treatments, and vaccines.[82] At the regional level, strategic plans for COVID-19 response have been adopted with the support of WHO Regional Offices.[83] In addition, the Organisation for Economic Co-operation and Development (OECD) has published a series of 'Key Policy Responses', providing guidance for both short-term measures and longer-term impacts, paving the way to recovery with coordinated policy responses across countries.[84] Furthermore, NATO has established a Pandemic Response Trust Fund, enabling it to quickly acquire and donate medical supplies and services to allies and partners.[85] Despite these numerous instruments, the response to the ongoing pandemic has been extremely uneven across the world.

3 Some Initial Results and Remaining Challenges with Respect to COVID-19-Related Response and Recovery

The implementation by States and IOs of their COVID-19 related international response obligations has been reviewed by several expert committees.[86] The 'Review Committee on the Functioning of the International Health Regulations (2005) during the COVID-19 Response' published a report on the implementation of the IHR by States and by the WHO.[87] It highlighted that lack of compliance with States' obligations under the IHR – including early

82 COVAX is co-led by Gavi, the Coalition for Epidemic Preparedness Innovations (CEPI) and WHO, <https://www.who.int/initiatives/act-accelerator/covax>.

83 Eg COVID-19 Strategic Response Plan in the WHO African Region (4 May 2020); COVID-19: operationalization of the global response strategy in the WHO European Region (September 2020); Strategic Preparedness and Response Plan for the South- East Asian Region (2019); PAHO/WHO Regional Office for the Americas, Response to COVID-19 Outbreak in the Region of the Americas (28 august 2020).

84 OECD, Tackling Coronavirus (COVID-19), Contributing to a Global Effort <https://www.oecd.org/coronavirus/en/policy-responses>.

85 See <https://www.nato.int/nato_static_fl2014/assets/pdf/2020/10/pdf/2010-factsheet-COVID-19_en.pdf>.

86 Sere also 'Lex-Atlas: Covid-19' <https://lexatlas-c19.org>.

87 WHO, 'WHO's work in health emergencies: Strengthening preparedness for health emergencies: implementation of the International Health Regulations (2005)', A74/9 Add.1 (5 May 2021).

notification to the WHO, ensuring adequate health capabilities, and creating effective National Focal Points – contributed to the pandemic becoming a global health emergency, and confirmed the need for a robust accountability mechanism. Moreover, the Committee emphasised that '(e)arly response requires better collaboration, coordination and trust'.[88] The Committee concluded that 'the inherent tension between the IHR's aim to protect health and the need to protect economies by avoiding travel and trade restrictions has been noted [...] as the most important factor limiting compliance with the Regulations'[89] and made detailed recommendations for improvements. Moreover, an analysis (covering 114 countries globally) of States' compliance with IHR obligations to ensure health-related capacities, concluded that a higher 'IHR capacity score' was significantly associated with more optimal control of transmission of COVID-19.[90]

Turning to some examples of individual States' compliance with their international response and recovery obligations, and of possible legal avenues for holding States to account for the lack of such compliance, China has received severe criticism for its failure to promptly and adequately inform the WHO in the initial stages of the COVID-19 outbreak.[91] The question whether a case could be brought against China before the International Court of Justice based on a violation of, *inter alia*, its notification obligations under the WHOC and IHR is the subject of discussion among legal commentators, raising both jurisdictional and substantive questions.[92] In this regard, it should be noted that both the WHOC and the IHR require regular annual reporting by States to the World Health Assembly (WHA) and the IHR offers additional voluntary external evaluations and 'After Action Reviews (AAR)' through its Monitoring and

88 Ibid 10.

89 Ibid 60.

90 MCS Wong et al., 'The potential effectiveness of the WHO International Health Regulations capacity requirements on control of the COVID-19 pandemic: A cross-sectional study of 114 countries', *Journal of the Royal Society of Medicine* (2021) Vol. 114(3) 121–131, 128. See also L Hirschhorn, 'Integrating implementation science into COVID-19 response and recovery' (2020) TheBmj <https://doi.org/10.1136/bmj.m1888; T Oyeniran, 'Novel coronavirus disease 2019 (COVID-19) outbreak in Nigeria: How effective are government interventions?' (2020) (14) Ethics, Medicine and Public Health <http://doi.org/10.1016/j.jemep.2020.100515>.

91 Reuters, 5 January 2021 <https://www.reuters.com/article/health-coronavirus-china-who-int-idUSKBN29A0LX>.

92 M Videler, 'ICJ Jurisdiction over Obligations to Share Information with the WHO', *Ejiltalk!*, 21 January 2021; V Mazzuoli, 'State Responsibility and COVID-19: Bringing China to the International Court of Justice?' International Law Blog, 15 May 2020. See also P Tzeng, 'Taking China to the International Court of Justice over COVID-19', *Ejiltalk!*, 2 April 2020.

Evaluation Framework.[93] However, there is no formal enforcement or compliance mechanism which could lead to any form of sanctions for a State that does not properly implement its legally binding obligations under the IHR, except for the dispute settlement clause of Article 56 IHR.[94] Thus, whereas the WHO is the leading coordinating agency for international COVID-19 response, it does not have sufficiently effective powers to ensure compliance with the IHR, nor with the specific guidelines that it has adopted.[95]

In the United States, at least 14 civil lawsuits were brought against China based on its perceived culpability in causing the pandemic.[96] These lawsuits currently face the challenge that sovereign States generally enjoy immunity under the Foreign Sovereign Immunities Act of 1976 (FSIA). However, in July 2020, the US Senate Judiciary Committee approved the Civil Justice for Victims of China-Originated Viral Infections Diseases (COVID) Act, which would amend the FSIA to permit lawsuits against a foreign government for claims related to the coronavirus. Even though it is uncertain whether this law will ultimately be adopted, it could potentially open the way for numerous additional claims against China, regarding its actions related to the COVID-19 outbreak.[97]

Another legal issue concerns the discriminatory distribution of vaccines in breach of the IHR and human rights law. For instance, in Israel, Palestinians were virtually excluded from the vaccine rollout, as all the available jabs were reserved for the Israeli settlers in the West Bank and Gaza.[98]

Regarding the implementation of international guidance on recovery, several States, IOs and NGOs have recognised the need for a Build Back Better approach to the recovery from COVID-19, integrating it with other objectives,

---

93 See <https://www.euro.who.int/en/health-topics/health-emergencies/international-health-regulations/monitoring-and-evaluation>.

94 States Parties can resort to mediation, conciliation, or good offices, and, thereafter, ask the Director-General for a brokered resolution; States Parties also have an option to accept arbitration for their disputes.

95 See J Lee, 'IHR 2005 in the Coronavirus Pandemic: A Need for a New Instrument to Overcome Fragmentation?', in 24 ASIL16 (2020) <https://www.asil.org/insights/volume/24/issue/16/ihr-2005-coronavirus-pandemic-need-new-instrument-overcome-fragmentation>.

96 S Mirski, S Anderson, 'What's in the Many Coronavirus-Related Lawsuits Against China?', *Lawfare Blog* (24 June 2020) <https://www.lawfareblog.com/whats-many-coronavirus-related-lawsuits-against-china>.

97 See <https://www.law360.com/articles/1294068/sens-advance-bill-allowing-suits-against-china-over-covid>, and <https://www.congress.gov/bill/116th-congress/senate-bill/4212>.

98 BBC News 'COVID-19: Palestinians lag behind in vaccine efforts as infections rise' <bbc.com/news/55800921>.

in particular the SDGs and climate change mitigation and adaptation. Examples include the policies adopted in France and Germany, linking public funding for economic recovery to increased investments in the renewable energy sector.[99] Also in the context of development cooperation programmes, some States are increasingly providing COVID-related recovery support and seeking to integrate it with SDGs and climate action, such as Australia,[100] Japan,[101] Canada[102] and the USA.[103]

4 Concluding Remarks

This chapter has provided an overview of the specific obligations of States and international organisations, included in international and regional normative instruments, with respect to the response and recovery phases of naturally occurring CBRN events, with a focus on epidemics, including COVID-19. The analysis shows that the normative framework for the response to epidemic outbreaks is quite specific, with the WHO's International Health Regulations providing clear, legally binding obligations for, *inter alia*, two essential aspects: information-sharing and international cooperation. With the occurrence of epidemics, such as SARS, Ebola and HIV/AIDS, more specific rules have been adopted to further improve and operationalise such information-sharing and international cooperation. With the ongoing COVID-19 pandemic, even more detailed and elaborated guidelines have been developed. However, as recognised by the WHA, enforcement and accountability mechanisms for ensuring better compliance with these international instruments need to be

99 German Federal Ministry of Finance, 'German Recovery and Resilience Plan' <https://www.bundesfinanzministerium.de/Content/EN/Downloads/2021-01-13-german-recovery-and-resilience-plan.pdf?__blob=publicationFile&v=4> (13 January 2021); French Ministry of Economy and Finance, 'France: Recovery Plan' (3 September 2020) <https://www.gouvernement.fr/sites/default/files/locale/piece-jointe/2020/09/french-recovery-plan-press-kit.pdf>.

100 Government of Australia, Department of Foreign Affairs and Trade, 'Partnerships for Recovery: Australia's COVID-19 Response' <https://www.dfat.gov.au/publications/aid/partnerships-recovery-australias-COVID-19-development-response>.

101 H Kondoh, T Yamagata 'Japan's Oda to Fight against COVID-19: Its Implications for Developing Countries', UN ESCA (24 December 2020) <https://www.unescap.org/sites/default/d8files/eventdocuments/Policy%20Brief_JASID%20Yamagata%20and%20Kondoh.pdf>.

102 'Canada's global response to COVID-19: Investing in aid' (21 September 2020) <https://cooperation.ca/canadas-global-response-to-COVID-19-investing-in-aid/>.

103 'USAID's COVID-19 Response' <https://www.usaid.gov/coronavirus>.

strengthened, and the implementation of the adopted rules can only succeed through increased cooperation and solidarity.[104]

As put forward by UN Secretary-General Antonio Guterres in his 'Remarks to Member States on Priorities for 2021': 'Science is succeeding – but solidarity is failing. To defeat COVID-19 is possible. We must make it happen. Together'.[105]

Bibliography

Hirschhorn L, 'Integrating implementation science into COVID-19 response and recovery' (2020) TheBmj <https://doi.org/10.1136/bmj.m1888>.

Lee J, 'IHR 2005 in the Coronavirus Pandemic: A Need for a New Instrument to Overcome Fragmentation?' 24 ASIL16 (2020).

Morelli M, 'Recovering from the Ebola crisis: "Social Reconnection Groups" in a rural Liberian community' (2019) Global Mental Health <https://doi.org/10.1017/gmh.2019.13>.

Winser B, '"Build Back Better?' The challenge of Goma and beyond' (2019) International Journal of Disaster Risk Reduction.

Wong MCS, 'The potential effectiveness of the WHO International Health Regulations capacity requirements on control of the COVID-19 pandemic: A cross-sectional study of 114 countries' (2021) 114 (3) Journal of the Royal Society of Medicine.

104 WHA, 'Strengthening WHO preparedness for and response to health emergencies', WHA 74.7 (21 May 2021).

105 UN Secretary General, António Guterres, Remarks to Member States on Priorities for 2021 (28 January 2021) <https://www.un.org/sg/en/content/sg/speeches/2021-01-28/remarks-member-states-priorities-for-2021>.

CHAPTER 19

Regional Perspective: Obligations under EU Law as Applicable to Naturally Occurring CBRN Events

Federico Ferri

1 Introduction: The Applicable Legal Framework

Until now, the European Union has not developed a clear and consistent set of obligations dedicated to naturally occurring CBRN events. Behind this lacuna are some 'constitutional' constraints that hinder the possibility for the EU to take comprehensive initiatives in this sector.[1] Accordingly, to complete the present analysis, it is necessary to dig into some EU secondary law acts. Three target areas are addressed in this chapter.

First, the main rules are contained in the legal framework governing the Union Civil Protection Mechanism (UCPM), currently regulated by Decision 2013/1313/EU,[2] as amended by Decision (EU) 2019/420[3] (implemented – in particular – through Commission implementing Decision 2014/762/EU)[4] and Regulation (EU) 2021/836.[5]

1 See ch 6 by Casolari.

2 Decision No 1313/2013/EU of the European Parliament and of the Council of 17 December 2013 on a Union Civil Protection Mechanism [2013] OJ L347/924. For a thorough analysis of the mechanism, see, *inter alia*, M Gestri, 'EU Disaster Response Law: Principles and Instruments' in A de Guttry, M Gestri and G Venturini (eds), *International Disaster Response Law*, (Springer 2012) 105–128.

3 Decision (EU) 2019/420 of the European Parliament and of the Council of 13 March 2019 amending Decision No 1313/2013/EU on a Union Civil Protection Mechanism [2019] OJ L 77l/1.

4 Commission Implementing Decision 2014/762/EU of 16 October 2014 laying down rules for the implementation of Decision No 1313/2013/EU of the European Parliament and of the Council on a Union Civil Protection Mechanism and repealing Commission Decisions 2004/277/EC, Euratom and 2007/606/EC, Euratom [2019] OJ L 320/1.

5 Regulation (EU) 2021/836 of the European Parliament and of the Council of 20 May 2021 amending Decision No 1313/2013/EU on a Union Civil Protection Mechanism [2021] OJ L 185/1.

There is no doubt that this set of rules applies also to naturally occurring CBRN events,[6] even if it is no mystery that the 2017 Action Plan on CBRN risk preparedness[7] places a major emphasis on man-made disasters and terrorist attacks.[8] Article 4(1) of Decision 2013/1313 determines that the UCPM covers, among other things, 'disasters', that is to say, 'any situation which has or may have a severe impact on people, the environment, or property, including cultural heritage'.

As a matter of interest, while chemical and biological events do not raise particular issues (*ie* the UCPM is entirely applicable to them), with respect to nuclear and radiological events, the UCPM is 'without prejudice to the adoption of legally binding acts under the Treaty Establishing the European Atomic Energy Community, setting out specific emergency measures in case of nuclear or radiological disasters'.[9] Furthermore, for consequences of radiological disasters, the UCPM may cover only preparedness and response actions.[10]

Now, despite the growing importance of the UCPM, some gaps were detected even after the 2013 reform, as the mechanism was not considered to be a sufficient tool to face transboundary threats and crises.[11] And, as regards practice, it can be said that, although the UCPM was activated multiple times, until 2019, assistance between Member States was generally provided bilaterally.[12] Only in 2020, the number of activations has increased considerably; more precisely,

---

6 See, in particular, R Roffey, 'The EU as an Actor?', in D O'Mathuna and I de Miguel Beriain (eds), *Ethics and Law for Chemical, Biological, Radiological, Nuclear & Explosive Crises* (Springer 2019) 26.

7 Communication from the Commission to the European Parliament, the Council, the European Economic and Social Committee and the Committee of the Regions, Action Plan to enhance preparedness against chemical, biological, radiological and nuclear security risks, COM/2017/0610 final.

8 Issues concerning CBRN terrorism at the EU level will not be discussed here. See ch 10 by Villani.

9 Decision 2013/1313 (n 2), recital 28. For more information on nuclear safety and security in Europe, see ch 15 by Balboni.

10 Ibid recital 3.

11 European Commission, Interim evaluation of the Union Civil Protection Mechanism, 2014–2016: Final Report, August 2017. Indeed, the overall cooperation framework has long been fragmented, primarily due to differences in the organisation of national civil protection systems. C Parker, T Persson and S Widmalm, 'The Effectiveness of National and EU-level Civil Protection Systems: Evidence from 17 Member States' (2017) 26(9) Journal of European Public Policy 1312.

12 C Beaucillon, 'International and European Emergency Assistance to EU Member States in the COVID-19 Crisis: Why European Solidarity Is Not Dead and What We Need to Make It both Happen and Last' (2020) 5(1) European Papers 387, 391.

in the period 2007–2019, there were 284 cases of activations, while in 2020 the UCPM was triggered 102 times by Member States and third countries (with 85 activations due to the COVID-19 pandemic).[13]

The second target area is represented by the so called 'EU solidarity clause' enshrined in Article 222 TFEU. Council Decision 2014/415 concerning the implementation of the EU solidarity clause[14] is thus of much importance with respect to this chapter, even if, so far, this clause has never been activated.[15]

Decision 2014/415 has effect on the territory of Member States to which the Treaties apply[16] and it seems that it primarily applies to CBRN-related issues connected to terrorist attacks.[17] However, the rules established by the Decision also apply to natural disasters, pursuant to the definition provided by Decision 2013/1313.[18] Furthermore and not by chance, the UCPM might well overlap with secondary law acts adopted to enhance the effectiveness of the solidarity clause.[19] This remains true despite the fact that, as pointed out in recital 1, this act concerns only the implementation 'by the Union' of the solidarity clause.[20]

In addition, the Decision implementing the EU solidarity clause tackles 'crises', which means disasters (or terrorist attacks) of such a wide-ranging impact or political significance that they require 'timely policy coordination and response at Union political level'.[21] Therefore – if conditions permit – Council Decision 2014/415 could be applied to naturally occurring CBRN events.

Finally, the framework analysed in the present chapter is enriched by Decision 2013/1082 on serious cross-border threats to health,[22] by means

---

13 See <https://www.consilium.europa.eu/en/infographics/civil-protection/>.

14 Council Decision 2014/415/EU of 24 June 2014 on the arrangements for the implementation by the Union of the solidarity clause [2013] OJ L192/53. See also recital 5, highlighting the links between this act and the UCPM.

15 See ch 6 by Casolari.

16 Council Decision 2014/415 (n 14), art 2, which adds that the Decision applies also when the terrorist attack or the disaster affects infrastructures situated in the territorial sea, the exclusive economic zone or the continental shelf of a Member State.

17 Ibid recital 7.

18 Ibid art 3(a).

19 Although some argued (at least for some time) that Article 222 TFEU provided the potential for a rather more robust system of solidarity compared to the UCPM. N Von Ondarza and R Parkes, 'The EU in the Face of Disaster, Implementing the Lisbon Treaty's Solidarity Clause' (SWP comments, 9 April 2010) 2.

20 On the contrary, the implementation of the solidarity clause by Member States pursuant to Article 222(2) TFEU does not fall within the scope of this Decision.

21 Council Decision 2014/415 (n 14), art 3(c).

22 Decision No 1082/2013/EU of the European Parliament and of the Council of 22 October 2013 on serious cross-border threats to health and repealing Decision No 2119/98/EC [2013] OJ L193/1.

of which the list of dangerous sources was expanded to include, alongside communicable diseases, also biological and chemical events (together with environmental events, or events of unknown origin) that may pose a risk to EU citizens across the entire Union.[23] Consequently, this Decision is meant to cover, at least in part, naturally occurring CBRN events.

Overall, before the COVID-19 pandemic, the mechanisms and structures established under this act proved to operate effectively and up to the quality level required to deal with a serious cross-border threat to health, in particular, during the during the Ebola outbreak, the Middle East Respiratory Syndrome caused by coronavirus (MERS CoV) and the poliomyelitis threat.[24]

Furthermore, Decision 2013/1082 and Decision 2013/1313 are intertwined[25] and have enabled the evolution of a coherent and unitary approach[26] which also acknowledges the need to take into account the relevant international law legal framework.

In light of the above, the analysis will be carried out by delving into all these Decisions, in an attempt to find out if and to what extent the EU institutions/bodies and the Member States are subject to *ex ante* and *ex post* obligations in relation to naturally occurring CBRN events.

2 Obligations of Prevention

The point of departure is to identify and assess prevention obligations stemming from the UCPM.

To start with, it must be pointed out that *ex ante* obligations (including also those referring to preparedness) are quite underdeveloped in this framework. Although the legal basis under which the UCPM was adopted – Article 196 TFEU – also refers to the need to prevent disasters, the UCPM was designed, in principle, to operate in post-incident scenarios.[27] Nevertheless, the UCPM has gradually been underpinned by a general policy framework for supranational

23 Ibid recital 3 and art 2(1).

24 Report from the Commission to the European Parliament and the Council, Report on the implementation of Decision No 1082/2013/EU of the European Parliament and of the Council of 22 October 2013 on serious cross-border threats to health and repealing Decision No 2119/98/EC, COM(2015) 617 final.

25 There are also connections between Decision 2013/1082 (n 22) and Decision 2014/415 (n 14); see for instance recital 5 of the latter).

26 F Casolari, 'Prime considerazioni sull'azione dell'Unione ai tempi del Coronavirus' (2020) 7(1) Eurojus 95, 101.

27 European Parliament – Policy Department for Citizen's Rights and Constitutional Affairs (2018), EU Civil Protection Responding to EU CBRN Incidents and Attacks. In-depth Analysis, 28.

actions on disaster risk prevention, also with a view to fostering a culture of prevention.[28] In addition, the reforms brought about through the adoption of Decision (EU) 2019/420 and Regulation (EU) 2021/836 seem to be justified also by the need to strengthen the efficiency of *ex ante* activities belonging to the overall disaster management cycle.[29]

The pillars of prevention consist of the sharing of information on risks and risk management capabilities. The main prevention obligations in this domain can be found in Articles 5 and 6 of Decision 2013/1313.[30]

Article 5 provides for a list of rather generic duties/powers belonging to the European Commission exclusively. The aim of this article is to foster the production of, access to and sharing of knowledge, in particular, as regards the identification, assessment, mapping and management of risks. In the EU legislator's mind, the Commission should not act only as a mere facilitator; it is required to take some decisive initiatives, such as establishing and regularly updating a cross-sectoral overview and map of disaster risks the Union may face; compiling and disseminating the information made available by Member States; and promoting the use of various EU funds to support sustainable disaster prevention.

Article 6 provides for activities that became mandatory with the 2013 Decision. This provision was significantly changed in particular by Decision (EU) 2019/420; however, and even after the adoption of Regulation (EU) 2021/836, the major amendments do not concern general obligations, thereby falling outside the scope of this contribution. It should not be overlooked that Article 6(1) refers to obligations of a hybrid nature, in the sense that they entail both prevention and preparedness initiatives to be performed, in the first place, by Member States.

Nevertheless, the current version of Article 6 is also characterised by the lack of clear requirements and indicators. This means that Member States keep enjoying a broad margin of manoeuvre. As evidence of that, Member States are asked to 'further' develop, either at national or appropriate sub-national level, core activities, such as risk assessments, the assessment of risk management capability and disaster risk management planning. However, it is not specified with accuracy what Member States are actually expected to deliver and to what extent the European Commission can exercise control powers. The only

28 Decision 2013/1313 (n 2), recital 8. See also Communication from the Commission to the European Parliament and the Council, A Community approach on the prevention of natural and man-made disasters, COM(2009) 82 final.

29 See, in particular, Decision 2019/420 (n 3), recitals 5 and 6, and Regulation 2021/836 (n 5), recitals 5 and 7.

30 These provisions were amended by ibid arts 1(3) and 1(4).

thing that appears to be beyond any doubt is that now Member States' disaster prevention activities must go beyond the standards reached before 2019.

Therefore, the clearest obligation on preventing (natural) disasters – which is actually halfway between prevention and preparedness – is laid down in the new Article 6(1)(d), which requires Member States to produce a summary of the relevant elements of their assessments concerning risks and risk management capabilities.[31] This document must be consistent with new guidelines drafted by the Commission in cooperation with Member States[32] and it was due by 31 December 2020.[33]

3 Obligations of Preparedness

Starting with civil protection issues, preparedness rests on the joint work of the Commission and Member States to improve cross-sectoral disaster risk management planning, as provided by Article 10 of Decision 2013/1313.[34] In general terms, the prerogatives enshrined in the most relevant provisions may be seen as powers and obligations at the same time; therefore, the EU legislator decided to call them 'actions'.

Article 8 of said Decision refers to the Commission's general actions. In particular, the Commission is tasked with multiple functions, such as: ensuring coordination between national contact points, which are to be established to comply with the legal framework on civil protection, and the two pillars of the Union Mechanism, namely the Emergency Response Coordination Centre (ERCC)[35] and the Common Emergency Communication and Information

31 Decision 2013/1313 (n 2), art 6(1)(d) – as amended by Decision 2019/420 (n 3), art 1(4) – now adds that, for key risks having cross-border impacts (and, where appropriate, for low probability risks with a high impact), Member States shall describe priority prevention and preparedness measures.

32 Reporting Guidelines on Disaster Risk Management, art 6(1)d of Decision 1313/2013/EU [2019] C428/9.

33 Then, it shall be submitted every three years thereafter (and whenever there are important changes).

34 According to Article 10(1), as amended by Regulation 2021/836 (n 5), art 1(8), the Commission and the Member States shall work together and that planning shall include scenario-building at Union level for disaster prevention, preparedness and response, taking into account the work carried out in relation to the Union disaster resilience goals.

35 The ERCC's main function is to coordinate the delivery of assistance in case of disasters by operating 24/7. See Decision 2013/1313 (n 2), art 7. After the amendments to the UCPM legal framework, the ERCC has become crucial to guarantee operational and logistical support. Furthermore, the strengthening of the ERCC witnesses the Commission's intention to ensure close coordination between civil protection and humanitarian aid. See

System (CECIS);[36] establishing and managing the capability to mobilise and dispatch expert teams to provide assistance either to the Member States or to the ERCC; working with Member States to improve transnational detection and early warning systems, maintain and further develop situational awareness and analysis capability, and provide advice on scientific knowledge about disasters and climate change impacts on the basis of joint monitoring activities; facilitating host nation support, which also includes the development and update of guidelines based on operational experience; developing and maintaining a network of trained experts from the Member States, who can assist the ERCC with monitoring information and facilitating coordination.

Article 9 sets out some general preparedness actions to be taken by Member States. So that they are properly prepared to respond to possible disasters, Member States shall – in advance and on a voluntary basis – develop modules and identify experts within their competent services, in particular, within their civil protection or other emergency services.[37] Article 9(1) states that other response capacities shall also be identified; however, according to Article 9(4) Member States shall simply 'consider providing' those additional capacities, and only where necessary. To increase the degree of coordination between national and supranational levels, Member States are required to submit to the Commission information on the modules, experts and other response capacities made available in the framework of the Union Mechanism. Apart from that, Member States shall designate contact points tasked with communication and sharing of information with the ERCC. More generally, Member States are asked to take the appropriate preparedness actions to facilitate host nation support.

It is clear that the Chapter on preparedness of the UCPM was particularly targeted for amendment by Decision (EU) 2019/420. However, those amendments are largely linked to the response phase. The two primary innovations are the 'European Civil Protection Pool' (ECPP) and 'rescEU'.

S Villani *The Concept of Solidarity Within EU Disaster Response Law: A Legal Assessment* (forthcoming), 177–178.

36 CECIS is a web-based application for alert and notification enabling real time exchange of information.

37 Commission implementing Decision 2014/762 (n 4) establishes specific requirements for the capacity, functioning and self-sufficiency of the modules. In this framework, the Member States and the Commission must cooperate to develop quality criteria and a certification process for the different teams, with a view to achieving high quality and interoperable standards.

The ECPP was introduced by Article 1(6) of the 2019 Decision, thereby amending Article 11 of Decision 2013/1313. It is 'a pool of voluntarily pre-committed response capacities of the Member States and include modules, other response capacities and categories of experts'. In a nutshell, the European Civil Protection Pool is the new version of the former European Emergency Response Capacity (EERC).

rescEU is a last-resort set of capacities aimed at assisting any State participating in the Union Mechanism that faces an overwhelming situation where overall existing capacities at national level and those under the ECPP are not sufficient to ensure an effective response. Chemical, biological, radiological and nuclear incidents are expressly referred to in Article 1(10) of Regulation (EU) 2021/836.

Initially, the composition of rescEU consisted of aerial forest firefighting capacities,[38] medical aerial evacuation capacities and emergency medical team capacities.[39] After the outbreak of COVID-19, rescEU reserves were expanded to also include medical team and medical stockpiling capacities[40] and capacities established to respond to low probability risks with a high impact,[41] with the idea being to turn rescEU into a more appropriate tool for tackling large-scale disasters (including naturally occurring CBRN events), as well as more localised events.

As a rule, rescEU capacities shall be acquired, rented or leased by Member States, but according to Article 1(10) of Regulation (EU) 2021/836 the same may be done by Commission to the extent necessary to address the gaps in the area of transport and logistics or, more in general, in duly justified cases of urgency.

The voluntary dimension of the ECPP and rescEU should be neither forgotten nor underestimated. Member States are free to decide how to contribute to both reserves. However, while ECPP capacities remain available for national purposes at all times and it is up to the Member States concerned to take the

38 Commission Implementing Decision (EU) 2019/570 of 8 April 2019 laying down rules for the implementation of Decision No 1313/2013/EU of the European Parliament and of the Council as regards rescEU capacities and amending Commission Implementing Decision 2014/762/EU [2019] OJ L99/41.

39 Commission Implementing Decision (EU) 2019/1930 of 18 November 2019 amending Implementing Decision (EU) 2019/570 as regards rescEU capacities [2019] OJ L299/55.

40 Commission Implementing Decision (EU) 2020/414 of 19 March 2020 amending Implementing Decision (EU) 2019/570 as regards medical stockpiling rescEU capacities [2020] OJ L82I/1.

41 Commission Implementing Decision (EU) 2020/452 of 26 March 2020 amending Implementing Decision (EU) 2019/570 as regards capacities established to respond to low probability risks with a high impact [2020] OJ L94I/1.

ultimate decision on their deployment,[42] rescEU capacities may only be used for national purposes 'if not being used or needed for response operations under the Union Mechanism'[43] and can be deployed and demobilised pursuant to a Commission's decision.[44]

In any case, clear preparedness obligations behind the ECPP and rescEU are not easy to detect, especially where Member States are considered. The most relevant provisions from the preparedness standpoint are those addressing the Commission and they only imply prerogative powers that are of limited scope, at least compared to the original intention of the Commission.[45] At most, the Commission defines the 'capacity goals'[46] (and with regard to this aspect Decision (EU) 2019/420 indicates that CBRN events constitute a priority area) and response capacities and it establishes the key requirements these resources must have under the ECPP and rescEU.[47] The Commission recently established the rules governing both reserves by means of an implementing act.[48]

Member States are responsible for ensuring the quality of their response capacities where they decide to contribute to the ECPP. Moreover, Member States that have acquired, rented or leased rescEU capacities must ensure

---

42 Decision 2013/1313 (n 2), arts 11(5) and 11(7).

43 Ibid new art 12(5), as amended by Decision 2019/420 (n 3), art 1(7).

44 This decision is taken in close coordination with the requesting Member State and the Member State owning, renting or leasing the capacity, according to ibid new art 12(6), as amended by Decision 2019/420 (n 3), art 1(7).

45 For example, the proposal leading to Decision 2019/420 (n 3) was highly criticised by certain Member States, since it assigned the Commission a meaningful role for the management of rescEU capacities, in particular, with reference to their acquisition and in terms of command and control over the Member States: see European Commission, Proposal for a Decision of the European Parliament and of the Council amending Decision No 1313/2013/EU on a Union Civil Protection Mechanism, COM(2017) 772. See on this point F Casolari, 'Europe (2018)' (2018) 1 Yearbook of International Disaster Law 346, 347–349.

46 This expression refers to the types and the number of key response capacities required for the European Civil Protection Pool: Regulation 2021/836 (n 5), art 1(9).

47 Decision 2013/1313 (n 2), art 11(3–4) and (new) art 12(4). The Commission has to rely on international standards that may apply to establish qualitative requirements and, in case of rescEU capacities, those requirements are set forth in consultation with the Member States. Only in respect to the ECPP, the Commission shall establish and manage a process for certification and registration of the response capacities made available by the Member States. As for the Member States, they are responsible for ensuring the quality of their response capacities where they decide to contribute to the ECPP. Moreover, Member States that have acquired, rented or leased rescEU capacities must host them accordingly.

48 Commission implementing decision (EU) 2019/1310 of 31 July 2019 laying down rules on the operation of the European Civil Protection Pool and rescEU [2019] OJ L204/94.

they are properly maintained[49] and ensure their availability for deployment in UCPM operations. In sum, Member States are subject to a sort of custody duty over rescEU capacities in order to properly comply with preparedness obligations.

Finally, activities in the field of training, exercises, lessons learnt and knowledge dissemination must be carried out by the new UCPM Network.[50]

It is worth noting that a preparedness obligation may also be spotted in Decision implementing the EU solidarity clause. By virtue of Article 8 of Decision 2014/415, the European Council may request reports on specified threats from, depending on the case, the Commission, the High Representative of the Union for Foreign Affairs and Security Policy, and/or Union agencies. However, unless the European Council decides otherwise, this does not imply that the relevant institutions have to search for additional information beyond that which is compiled as standard; according to Article 8(2), 'any such reports shall be based solely on available assessments of threats compiled by relevant Union institutions, bodies and agencies under existing arrangements, and on information provided voluntarily by the Member States'.[51]

A few preparedness obligations are established also by Decision 1082/2013 on serious cross-border threats to health. In fact, even though the aim was to cover both the *ex ante* phases (plus, of course, the response phase) this Decision appears to focus more on preparedness than prevention.[52] In this framework, Member States first have to designate national authorities and representatives responsible for certain key activities to be carried out to comply with preparedness and response obligations under the Decision.[53] Apart from that, preparedness obligations in the context of Decision 1082/2013 mainly relate to information exchanges and communications.[54]

49 They also have to register those capacities in the CECIS.

50 Decision 2013/1313 (n 2), art 13, as amended by Decision 2019/420 (n 3) and Regulation 2021/836 (n 5).

51 In any case, 'in accordance with point (a) of Article 346(1) TFEU, no Member State shall be obliged to supply information the disclosure of which it considers contrary to the essential interests of its security'.

52 European Commission (Health and Food Safety Directorate-General), Annex – Policy expectations for a Joint Action to Strengthen Health Preparedness and Response to Biological and Chemical Terror Attacks, Ref. Ares(2019)3071424; COM(2015) 617 (n 24).

53 Decision 1082/2013 (n 22), art 15.

54 It should also be mentioned that, in light of ibid art 5, the institutions of the Union and various Member States agreed to engage in a joint procurement procedure for the purchase of medical countermeasures for serious cross-border threats to health. The agreement at stake could be concluded on a voluntary basis but once in force it became the source of multiple obligations (more details can be found here <https://ec.europa

In this respect, Article 4 of the Decision prescribes that consultations must be regularly held among the Commission and Member States within the Health Security Committee (HSC) – established by Article 17 of the Decision[55] – to coordinate their efforts aimed at developing, strengthening and maintaining their capacities for the monitoring, early warning, assessment of, and response to, serious cross-border threats to health. In particular, Member States have to provide the Commission with all relevant information indicated in Article 4(2). This information contributes to illustrating the evolution of the situation with regard to preparedness and response planning at national level; in general, reporting obligations become more urgent when a Member State substantially revises national preparedness planning, as specified by Article 4(3).[56]

According to a report issued by the Commission,[57] by late October 2015, 26 Member States and one EEA Country had provided the requested information via a dedicated website (while Member States that failed to supply this information were just 'reminded' to proceed). It was also noted that, in general, the overall communication in the HSC was 'reasonably effective' and that there were important lessons learned from the process, especially during the peak of the Ebola outbreak.

4 Obligations of Response

Obligations concerning the management cycle of naturally occurring disasters mainly refer to the response phase. At the same time, recovery obligations almost do not exist.

In the framework of the UCPM, the first response obligation is provided in Article 14(1) of Decision 2013/1313 and must be fulfilled by the Member State in case of an actual or imminent disaster 'which causes or is capable of causing

.eu/health/preparedness_response/joint_procurement/jpa_signature_en>). Increasing preparedness of Member States for cross-border threats to health via joint procurement of medical countermeasures was also encouraged by the Commission in the 2017 Action Plan on CBRN (p. 9).

55 According to this provision, the Health Security Committee is composed of representatives of the Member States and chaired by a representative of the Commission. It serves to facilitate the coordination of the response in the event of serious cross-border health threats. Decision 1082/2013 (n 22), art 17 seeks to respond to the need for formalisation of this group and clarification of its role (see recital 4).

56 The information referred to by Article 4 (paras 2 and 3) is particularly sensitive, to the extent that Member States are requested to apply national security regulations to anyone handling it.

57 COM(2015) 617 final (n 24) 5.

trans-boundary effects or affects or is capable of affecting other Member States'. In these situations, the Member State concerned shall, without delay, notify the potentially affected Member States, while the Commission shall be notified only if the effects are potentially significant.[58] Thus, in the event of calamities, including naturally occurring CBRN disasters, response obligations are primarily aimed at avoiding negative effects outside the Member State (initially) affected.

Where the (actual or potential) disaster lacks the abovementioned trans-boundary nature, the Member State wishing to be assisted under the UCPM has the burden of submitting a specific request, especially to the ERCC. However, asking for assistance when a disaster occurs – regardless of its effects – does not seem to constitute an obligation and nothing in the 2013 Decision appears to suggest that the EU legislator adopted a different approach.[59]

The Commission is also subject to some obligations. Article 15(3) of Decision 2013/1313 provides that as soon as a request for assistance has been received by a Member State, the Commission shall, 'as appropriate and without delay', forward the request to the contact points of other Member States and facilitate the coordination of the response, in particular, by ensuring an efficient circulation of relevant information. The Commission cannot exercise decisional powers *vis à vis* the other Member States but is required to make recommendations (in consultation with the requesting Member State) for the provision of assistance through the UCPM.

If UCPM assistance is required for disasters taking place or likely to occur outside the Union, the Union coordination 'shall be fully integrated with the overall coordination provided by the United Nations Office for the Coordination of Humanitarian Affairs (OCHA), and shall respect its leading role'.[60] Hence, the Commission becomes subject to additional obligations, especially

58 Furthermore, according to art 14(2), '(i)n the event of a disaster within the Union, or of an imminent disaster, which is likely to result in a call for assistance from one or more Member States, the Member State in which the disaster occurs or is likely to occur shall, without delay, notify the Commission that a possible request for assistance through the ERCC can be expected, in order to enable the Commission, as appropriate, to inform the other Member States and to activate its competent services'.

59 However, it was also suggested that interpreting Decision 2013/1313 (n 2), art 15, in light of EU general principles and fundamental rights aimed at protecting some rights that could be put at serious risk in such situations (especially the right to life) might well lead to a different conclusion. M Gatti, 'L'obbligo di proteggere le persone dalle calamità nell'Unione europea' in A Spagnolo and S Saluzzo (eds), *La responsabilità degli Stati e delle organizzazioni internazionali: nuove fattispecie e problemi di attribuzione e di accertamento* (Ledizioni, 2017) 127, 134–135.

60 Decision 2019/420 (n 3), art 1(10), amending Decision 2013/1313 (n 2), art 16(2).

in order to guarantee consistency in the delivery of the assistance and to respect the 'imperative for an immediate operational response' through the UCPM.[61] The European External Action Service shall also be informed and the competent Union delegation may be required to provide logistical support.[62] It has to be pointed out that maybe the only exception to the lack of recovery obligations is represented by Article 16(3)(e), according to which the Commission shall ensure a certain degree of consistency also in the closing phase of the assistance intervention under the Union Mechanism, to facilitate a 'smooth handover'.[63]

Besides that, the Commission provides financial assistance, which usually covers more than half of the costs and, under certain circumstances, may cover all the costs deriving from the activation of the UCPM, especially where rescEU capacities are used.[64]

There is also an obligation incumbent on the Member States that are in the position to provide assistance when the UCPM is activated. This obligation is quite controversial, at least as far as its scope of application is concerned and – as will be explained later in this section – due to possible links between the UCPM and the solidarity clause.

In principle, it seems safe to state that the only actual obligation for the Member State(s) eventually required to intervene is to decide what to do in a timely fashion and to make the Member State affected by the disaster aware of that decision through the CECIS.[65] That practically serves to secure proper organisation and management of response activities. Furthermore, the Member State rendering assistance must observe the general guidelines laid

61 Decision 2013/1313 (n 2), art 16(3). However, pursuant to art 16(10), '(t)he role of the Commission referred to in this Article shall not affect the Member States' competences and responsibility for their teams, modules and other support, including military capacities. In particular, the support offered by the Commission shall not entail command and control over Member States' teams, modules and other support, which shall be deployed on a voluntary basis in accordance with the coordination at headquarters level and on site'.

62 Ibid arts 16(4) and 16(5).

63 European Court of Auditors, Union Civil Protection Mechanism: the coordination of responses to disasters outside the EU has been broadly effective (Special report 2016) 24.

64 Decision 2013/1313 (n 2) arts 19–21; Decision 2019/420 (n 3) arts 1(12)–1(14); Regulation 2021/836 (n 5), art 1(19).

65 Decision 2013/1313 (n 2) art 15(4). As established by Commission implementing Decision 2014/762/EU (n 4), art 35(9), the deadline 'shall be based on the nature of the disaster and shall in any case not be less than two hours'.

down by the requesting Member State,[66] which is also responsible for the coordination on site.

It can be argued that when a Member State chooses to make response capacities available, as a general rule, it cannot then prevent those resources from being used when a disaster occurs and the assistance of this voluntary pool is required.[67] Such interpretation of Article 11(7) of Decision 2013/1313 appears to be the most logical outcome of the application of the loyal cooperation and *effet utile* principles, although it is hard to argue that if the Member State fails to comply with this requirement, the Commission would be enabled to trigger an infringement procedure.

Similar considerations apply if rescEU is activated, except that, while the ultimate decision to deploy ECPP response capacities is taken by the Member States which registered them, rescEU capacities are deployed and demobilised on the basis of a Commission decision (to be taken in close coordination with the Member States concerned).[68]

However, there are also important differences concerning the legal regimes applicable to the deployment of ECPP and rescEU response capacities. Pursuant to Article 11(8), a Member State does not have to make ECPP capacities available for a specific disaster in the event that it is itself affected by domestic emergencies, force majeure or, in 'exceptional cases', cannot do so for 'other serious reasons'; however, the same does not go for the provision of capacities under rescEU. At the same time, the ECPP response capacities (once deployed) remain under the command and control of the Member State that made them available; on the contrary, rescEU response capacities are subject to more intensive powers of the Commission.[69]

Finally, assistance under the UCPM can be requested by virtue of Article 11(4) of Decision 1082/2013 on serious cross-border threats to health, but only when such a threat overwhelms the response capacities of the requesting Member State. So, the UCPM and the mechanism applicable to serious cross-border threats to health are connected, but the latter is, in principle, characterised by autonomous rules concerning the response phase, including response obligations.

Also, in the framework of Decision 1082/2013, the first obligation incumbent on the Member State concerned is notifying an alert of the emergence

66 Ibid art 15(5). However, this provision adds that it is up to the person in charge, appointed by the Member State rendering assistance, to decide the details of the execution of those tasks.

67 Villani (n 35) 191.

68 Decision 2019/420, (n 3) art 1(7).

69 Ibid.

or development of a serious cross-border threat to health fulfilling the criteria listed in Article 9(1) of the Decision.[70] The Commission also has the same obligation to notify an alert where it becomes aware of such a threat. The alert notification must comprise all relevant and available information that may be useful for coordinating the response[71] and it has to be submitted in the Early Warning and Response System (EWRS). This mechanism, established by Article 8, was designed to enable the Commission and the national competent authorities to be in permanent communication for managing the events tackled by Decision 1082/2013.

With respect to the majority of threats covered by Decision 1082/2013, following an alert, all Member States must fulfil ad hoc monitoring obligations. Article 7 clarifies that these activities mainly involve the transmission of relevant information, such as any change in geographical distribution, spread and severity of the threat concerned, as well as information on the means of detection being used, if available.

To complete the regime guiding the response after the notification of an alert, Article 10 of Decision 1082/2013 provides for a possible additional obligation for the Commission: to make available through the EWRS a risk assessment of the potential severity of the threat to public health, including possible public health measures. Two aspects deserve to be further explained. First, this risk assessment does not have to be automatically produced when the early warning is raised; basically, it is up to the HSC to decide on the matter 'where necessary for the coordination of the response at Union level'.[72] Second, according to Article 10, the Commission is a sort of 'driver', while the risk assessment is formally carried out by relevant Union agencies in lieu of the Commission.

Following the transmission of the information indicated in Articles 7 and 9 and, potentially, the risk assessment mentioned in Article 10, Member States are free to decide upon the national measures to take. That said, under Article 11, the Member States still have to comply with an obligation of consultation. To

70 The alert must be notified when the following criteria exist which characterise a threat to health: 'a) it is unusual or unexpected for the given place and time, or it causes or may cause significant morbidity or mortality in humans, or it grows rapidly or may grow rapidly in scale, or it exceeds or may exceed national response capacity; and (b) it affects or may affect more than one Member State; and (c) it requires or may require a coordinated response at Union level'.

71 See Decision 1082/2013 (n 22), art 9(3).

72 The Commission can provide the risk assessment on its own initiative but, should that be the case, this would no longer be an obligation.

put it briefly, Member States must consult each other within the HSC and in liaison with the Commission, with a view to coordinating national responses to the serious cross-border threat to health, as well as providing risk and crisis communications. In particular, consultations should refer to the nature, purpose and scope of response measures; if the need to protect public health is so urgent that the immediate adoption of the measures is necessary, the Member State concerned shall inform the other Member States and the Commission on these aspects.

A last-resort response instrument that may be triggered in the event of a disaster, including a naturally occurring disaster, is the solidarity clause. For the purposes of this analysis, reference must be made to Council Decision 2014/415, in order to highlight the obligations to be fulfilled either by the Member States or EU institutions and bodies when a disaster (or a crisis) occurs.

The rationale behind the implementation of the solidarity clause by the Union is that response initiatives taken under it should rely on existing instruments; therefore, the idea is not to use additional resources.[73] But the fact remains that recital 5 of Council Decision 2014/415 also refers to the UCPM (and Decision 1082/2013), while recital 4 of Decision 2013/1313 anticipates that the UCPM should also contribute to the implementation of Article 222 TFEU, 'by making available its resources and capabilities as necessary'.[74] Therefore, the activation of the solidarity clause could undermine the Member States' discretion to deny assistance through the UCPM, thereby giving rise to a correspondent obligation when intensive interventions are necessary to face a crisis.

This interpretation may be counterbalanced by the text of Declaration 37 on Article 222 of the TFEU, according to which none of the provisions of this Article is intended to affect the right of a Member State to choose the most appropriate means to comply with its own solidarity obligation towards the Member State affected by the disaster. Probably, the solution to such conundrum is that – once again in harmony with the principles of loyal cooperation and *effet utile* – 'each Member State, in the presence of a formal request from another one, is invested with a legal obligation to provide assistance, but keeps the right to choose those measures deemed appropriate', even though '(i)n exercising this choice, the State in question is, however, obliged to act in

73 It was thus observed that, contrary to the rather open-textured formulation of Article 222 TFEU, Council Decision 2014/415 (n 14) 'takes a clear – and pronouncedly restrictive – stance'. P Hilpold, 'Filling a Buzzword with Life: The Implementation of the Solidarity Clause in Article 222 TFEU' (2020) 42(3) LIEI 209, 224.

74 For useful considerations on the interplays between the solidarity clause and the instruments of disaster response (in particular, the UCPM), see Villani (n 35) 221–224.

good faith and in a spirit of sincere cooperation as prescribed in Article 4(3) TEU'.[75]

At the heart of Council Decision 2014/415 are Articles 4 and 5, regulating, respectively, the invocation and the implementation *stricto sensu* of the solidarity clause. Both provisions show that, contrary to the response mechanisms construed through the UCPM and the Decision on serious cross-border threats to health, the role played by the Council is of major importance, while the Commission's powers are a little weaker.[76] That is testament to the more intergovernmental nature characterising the solidarity clause.

Article 4 points out that the Member State affected by a disaster 'may' (hence, is not obliged to) invoke the solidarity clause. However, this option can be chosen only if all the possibilities offered by existing means and tools at the national and Union levels have been exploited. Furthermore, the solidarity clause can be invoked if the Member State concerned considers that the crisis clearly overwhelms the response capabilities available to it. The invocation of the solidarity clause must be addressed to the Presidency of the Council and to the President of the European Commission through the ERCC. Thus, the ERCC performs important functions also outside the UCPM framework.[77]

Article 5 sets out the main initiatives constituting the response phase, but, within this provision, the Council strived to safeguard the prerogatives of the other institutions and bodies involved. In sum, the Council 'shall ensure the political and strategic direction of the Union response [...] taking full account of the Commission's and the HR's competences'. At the same time, the Commission and the HR are mainly tasked with the identification of the resources (already available) to use and are requested to advise the Council on whether existing resources provide sufficient means to assist the affected Member State. As for the types of resources to be identified, there are no particular limitations.

On the basis of Articles 1(2) and 5 (paras 1 and 4), the overall response at Union political level shall be guided by EU Integrated Political Crisis Response (IPCR) Arrangements. This single set of arrangements was approved by the Council on 25 June 2013 to coordinate responses at the highest political level

75 S Villani, 'The EU Civil Protection Mechanism: Instrument of Response in the Event of a Disaster' (2017) 26 Revista Universitaria Europea 121, 140.

76 Conversely, the approach followed in the proposal leading to Council Decision 2014/415 (n 14) seemed to be the opposite. See Joint Proposal for a Council Decision on the arrangements for the implementation by the Union of the Solidarity clause, JOIN(2012)39 final.

77 In particular, according to art 5(6), the ERCC shall act as the central 24/7 contact point at Union level with Member States' competent authorities and other stakeholders.

during major cross-sectoral crises,[78] even the solidarity clause is not invoked.[79] This flexible and tailor-made instrument was designed to ensure uniform, efficient and timely responses to any kind of crisis and in multiple ways: for example, through information exchange, political coordination or the adoption of decisions.

The basic rules applicable to the IPCR Arrangements are now included in Council implementing Decision (EU) 2018/1993.[80] In particular, the activation of the IPCR shall be decided by the Presidency of the Council, while the Committee of Permanent Representatives is the default level at which oversight of the implementation of the IPCR arrangements is carried out.[81] However, where the solidarity clause has been invoked, the Presidency of the Council is not free to choose whether or not to activate the IPCR; this becomes an obligation and, what is more, it has to be performed 'immediately'.[82]

5 Conclusions and Perspectives

The obligations applicable within the management cycle of naturally occurring CBRN events are indirect, short-term and rather weak in terms of enforceability. Binding provisions expressly concerning this type of event have still not been adopted, so it is necessary to refer to a set of secondary EU law norms which have evolved considerably since the entry into force of the Lisbon Treaty. In addition, the vast majority of the obligations identified do not concern prevention initiatives. Finally, failure to respect them will generally not be likely to produce any particular legal consequence.

---

78 More information can be found here <https://www.consilium.europa.eu/media/29699/web_ipcr.pdf>. See also A Nimark, 'Post-Lisbon Developments in EU Crisis Management: The Integrated Political Crisis Response (IPCR) Arrangements', in O'Mathuna and de Miguel Beriain (n 6) 75.

79 The ongoing COVID-19 pandemic constitutes a case in point, since, in March 2020, the then-Presidency of the Council activated the IPCR mechanism in 'full mode', although outside the solidarity clause legal framework (<https://www.consilium.europa.eu/en/press/press-releases/2020/03/02/covid-19-outbreak-the-presidency-steps-up-eu-response-by-triggering-full-activation-mode-of-ipcr/>). This modality was maintained by the following Presidency of the Council (<https://www.consilium.europa.eu/en/policies/ipcr-response-to-crises/>).

80 Council implementing Decision (EU) 2018/1993 of 11 December 2018 on the EU Integrated Political Crisis Response Arrangements [2018] OJ L320/28.

81 Ibid arts 4(1) and 6(1) of.

82 Council Decision 2014/415 (n 14), art 5(1) and ibid art 4(2).

These findings may lead one to consider the opinions of some renowned scholars who argue that the EU should be given a more robust role to properly deal with large-scale crises in general. Resorting to the flexibility clause (as for the Directive on critical infrastructures) or to an enhanced cooperation could be suitable ways to increase the Union's powers in the field of 'emergencies'. For example, the viewpoint of these authors is that a sort of 'general regulation' on disasters could be a valuable option. At the same time, the EU should be put in the position to exercise more effective urgency powers where certain serious situations occur.[83]

Theoretically, a trend is visible which shows how the European Union is gradually trying to develop a more unitary framework characterised by a stronger supranational governance. Indeed, there is currently a very real risk that the system of mutual European solidarity may be insufficient in situations where multiple Member States are impacted by the same emergency simultaneously, thereby being unable assist each other. That, of course, applies also to naturally occurring CBRN-events.

However, on the practical level things are quite different. A case in point is the main initiative completed so far within the areas addressed above, namely, the last reform of the UCPM. Regulation (EU) 2021/836 has not produced major changes in terms of obligations, as it simply amends the existing legal framework (without substituting it) and increases the powers of the Commission only to a limited extent.

Time will tell how quick progress will be and how the reforms (already adopted or still under discussion)[84] will be implemented and/or shaped, bearing in mind the limits arising from the legal bases generally applicable in the fields considered in this chapter.

83 G Tesauro, 'Senza Europa nessun Paese andrà lontano' (2020) Aisdue (Dibattito 'Coronavirus e diritto dell'Unione') 10, 16.

84 For example with regard to cross-border threats to health: see Communication from the Commission to the European Parliament, the Council, the European Economic and Social Committee and the Committee of the Regions, Building a European Health Union, COM(2020)724 final; Reinforcing the EU's resilience for cross-border health threats; Proposal for a Regulation of the European Parliament and of the Council on a reinforced role for the European Medicines Agency in crisis preparedness and management for medicinal products and medical devices, COM(2020)726 final; Proposal for a Regulation of the European Parliament and of the Council amending Regulation (EC) No 851/2004 establishing a European Centre for disease prevention and control, COM(2020)726 final; Proposal for a Regulation of the European Parliament and of the Council on serious cross-border threats to health and repealing Decision No 1082/2013, COM(2020) 727 final.

Bibliography

Åhman T, 'The Treaty of Lisbon and Civil Protection in the European Union' (FOI-R-2806-SE, November 2009) 1.

Beaucillon C, 'International and European Emergency Assistance to EU Member States in the COVID-19 Crisis: Why European Solidarity Is Not Dead and What We Need to Make It both Happen and Last' (2020) 5(1) European Papers 387.

Casolari F, 'Europe (2018)' (2018) 1 Yearbook of International Disaster Law 346.

Casolari F, 'Prime considerazioni sull'azione dell'Unione ai tempi del Coronavirus' (2020) 7(1) Eurojus (2020) 95.

Gatti M, 'L'obbligo di proteggere le persone dalle calamità nell'Unione europea' in A Spagnolo and S Saluzzo (eds), *La responsabilità degli Stati e delle organizzazioni internazionali: nuove fattispecie e problemi di attribuzione e di accertamento* (Ledizioni, 2017) 127.

Gestri M, 'EU Disaster Response Law: Principles and Instruments' in A de Guttry, M Gestri and G Venturini (eds), *International Disaster Response Law* (Springer 2012).

Hilpold P, 'Filling a Buzzword with Life: The Implementation of the Solidarity Clause in Article 222 TFEU' (2020) 42(3) LIEI 209.

Nimark A, 'Post-Lisbon Developments in EU Crisis Management: The Integrated Political Crisis Response (IPCR) Arrangements', in D O'Mathuna and I de Miguel Beriain (eds), *Ethics and Law for Chemical, Biological, Radiological, Nuclear & Explosive Crises* (Springer 2019) 75.

Parker C, Persson T and Widmalm S, 'The Effectiveness of National and EU-level Civil Protection Systems: Evidence from 17 Member States' (2017) 26(9) Journal of European Public Policy 1312.

Roffey R, 'The EU as an Actor? in D O'Mathuna and I de Miguel Beriain (eds), *Ethics and Law for Chemical, Biological, Radiological, Nuclear & Explosive Crises* (Springer 2019) 15.

Tesauro G, 'Senza Europa nessun Paese andrà lontano' (2020) Aisdue (Dibattito 'Coronavirus e diritto dell'Unione') 10.

Villani S, 'The Concept of Solidarity Within EU Disaster Response Law: A Legal Assessment' (forthcoming).

Villani S, 'The EU Civil Protection Mechanism: Instrument of Response in the Event of a Disaster' (2017) 26 Revista Universitaria Europea 121.

Von Ondarza N and Parkes R, 'The EU in the Face of Disaster, Implementing the Lisbon Treaty's Solidarity Clause' (SWP comments, 9 April 2010) 1.

PART 3

International Obligations Applicable to CBRN Weapons

CHAPTER 20

The Challenge to *Jus ad Bellum* Posed by the Development or Use of CBRN Weapons

Laura Magi

1 Introduction

The development of CBRN weapons is a significant challenge to international stability. They have overwhelming effects causing terrible suffering to those who are exposed to them. Moreover, they have protracted negative consequences on human health and the environment. New delivery systems have made their use still more harmful. For these reasons, sometimes States have invoked their right to act in order to prevent an enemy State from developing and using CBRN weapons against them. In other cases, the employment of CBRN weapons in an internal conflict against insurgents and civilians brought third States to react militarily against the responsible State.

A widespread debate has arisen on the lawfulness of military interventions to counter the proliferation of CBRN weapons and prevent their use against combatants and civilians. Some authors have judged such a debate useless.[1] They believe that *jus ad bellum* has become 'paper rules', *ie* 'rules that lay out aspirational goals for the management of state-sponsored force rather than binding precepts of international law.'[2]

Moving from the opposite opinion, this chapter assumes that the rules prohibiting the use of force are still alive and have not lost their compulsory nature.[3]

Against this background, the present chapter will examine whether State practice concerning the development and use of CBRN weapons has brought (or is in the process of bringing) the emergence of new rules allowing States to

1 M Walzer, *Just and Unjust Wars: A Moral Argument with Historical Illustrations* (5th edn, Basic Books 2015); MJ Glennon, 'The UN Security Council in a Unipolar World' (2003–2004) 44 VandJTransnatlL 91 98–100.

2 MJ Glennon, 'Pre-empting Proliferation: International Law, Morality and Nuclear Weapons' (2013) 24 EJIL 109, 111.

3 For an interesting reply to Glennon, see PCR Terry and KS Openshaw, 'Nuclear Non-Proliferation and Preventive Self-Defence: Why Attacking Iran Would Be Illegal' (2013) 51 ACDI 165, especially 181 ff.

DOI:10.1163/9789004507999_021

use military force with the limited aim of preventing the occurrence of imminent or possible CBRN attacks against them or thwarting their use against civilians and combatants.

In what follows, the expression 'anticipatory self-defence' will be used to refer to the use of force in order to repel an attack that is imminent.[4] The concept of imminence adopted is time-related. An imminent attack will be considered as one that is going to occur and that can be stopped only by neutralising it by means of a military counter-action. In contrast, the expression 'preventive self-defence' will be employed to describe the use of force to counter the risk of an attack that might materialise in the future.

Proponents of preventive self-defence try to blur the dividing line between it and anticipatory self-defence by broadening the concept of 'imminence'. According to them, the requirement of imminence should consider the nature of the threat or the gravity of the threatened attack, precisely in order to take into account current threats like the use of weapons of mass destruction[5] (WMD). On the contrary, this chapter will refer only to a time-related notion of imminence.

The term 'pre-emptive self-defence' will not be used. While it has frequently been interpreted as meaning the same as preventive self-defence, according to a rigorous approach, the term would be synonymous with anticipatory self-defence in the *Caroline* case sense.[6] Thus, to avoid confusion, this chapter will not refer to it.

2 Preventive Military Actions against States That Develop and May Use CBRN Weapons

States have voiced their right to act in self-defence against the threat posed by the (alleged) development of CBRN weapons by other States. In 1981, Israel

4 As famously stated by US Secretary of State Webster in 1841, in relation to the *Caroline* incident, a State is permitted to use force in order to counter an attack that has not yet commenced provided there exists 'a necessity of self-defence, instant, overwhelming, leaving no choice of means, and no moment for deliberation' : Letter from Daniel Webster to Lord Ashburton (27 July 1842): Yale Law School, The Avalon Project <https://avalon.law.yale.edu/19th_century/br-1842d.asp> (all links were last accessed 20 January 2021).

5 White House Archives, 'National Security Strategy of the United States' (September 2002), <https://georgewbush-whitehouse.archives.gov/nsc/nss/2002/nss5.html>; Chatham House, 'Principles of International Law on the Use of Force by States in Self-Defence', 2005, Principle No. 4 and the Commentary to it, <https://www.chathamhouse.org/2005/10/principles-international-law-use-force-states-self-defence>; D Bethlehem, 'Self-Defence Against an Imminent or Actual Armed Attack by Non-state Actors' (2012) 106 AJIL 774.

6 M Sapiro, 'Iraq: The Shifting Sands of Preemptive Self-Defense' (2003) 97 AJIL 599 at 599.

justified the bombing of the Osirak reactor as preventive self-defence against the purported development of nuclear weapons by Iraq. In 2003, a coalition of States led by the US and the UK attacked Iraq claiming it possessed WMD. Among the intervening States, the US and Australia invoked the right to act in preventive self-defence. In 2007, Israel allegedly bombed the Al-Kibar nuclear reactor in Syria but did not formulate any legal justification.

2.1 *Osirak (1981)*

Israel bombed an Iraqi nuclear reactor which – Iraq maintained – was for peaceful use only. Israel justified its action by invoking the so called 'Begin doctrine', named after the Israeli Prime Minister Begin who drafted it in the '80s.[7] Before the United Nations Security Council (UNSC), the Israeli representative acknowledged that the attack was preventive, and justified it as a lawful act of self-defence. Furthermore, it claimed a right to act similarly in the future.[8]

In the debate that followed in the UNSC, many States explicitly and strongly condemned the Israeli strike as an act of aggression contrary to the UN Charter.[9] They included Middle Eastern States[10] and the nuclear weapons States (France,[11] China,[12] the United Kingdom,[13] the USSR[14] and the US). The US delegate remembered the words of the US President ('Israel might have sincerely believed it was a defensive move'); meanwhile, he declared that the US was shocked by the Israeli attack and condemned it.[15] SC Resolution 487 (19 June 1981), adopted unanimously, vigorously criticised the Israeli attack as an act in 'clear violation of the UN Charter' and called upon Israel to refrain from similar actions and to grant an appropriate redress to Iraq. A few months later, on the 13th of November 1981, the United Nations General Assembly (UNGA) adopted Resolution 36/27 that condemned Israel for its 'premeditated and unprecedented act of aggression' against Iraq. The latter was adopted with a large majority, even though 34 States abstained; significantly, the US – that had previously condemned the attack – voted against it.

---

7 A Yadlin, 'The Begin Doctrine: The Lessons of Osirak and Deir ez-Zor', INSS Insight (21 March 2018) <https://www.inss.org.il/publication/the-begin-doctrine-the-lessons-of-osirak-and-deir-ez-zor/>.

8 UNSC 'Complaint by Iraq' (1981) UN Doc S/PV.2280, para 58.

9 See from UN Doc S/PV.2280 to UN Doc S/PV.2288 (12–19 June 1981).

10 See the opinion of the delegates of Tunisia, Jordan, Algeria (UN Doc S/PV.2280), Kuwait (UN Doc S/PV.2281), Syria (UN Doc S/PV.2284), Turkey (UN Doc S/PV.2286), Libya and Kuwait (UN Doc S/PV.2288).

11 UN Doc S/PV.2288, 15 June 1981, para 39 ff.

12 Ibid, para 89.

13 Ibid, para 104 ff., especially para 106.

14 UN Doc S/PV.2283, 15 June 1981, para 63.

15 UN Doc S/PV.2288, 19 June 1981, para 27.

2.2 *Iraq (2003)*

A coalition of States led by the US and the UK (and originally joined by Australia, Spain and Poland) attacked Iraq in March 2003.[16] The military action was connected with Iraqi non-compliance with SC Resolution 687 (1991).[17] The latter laid down the obligation for Iraq to destroy nuclear, biological and chemical weapons it allegedly possessed and to accept a long-term monitoring system to ensure its compliance with the previously mentioned obligations. In addition, Resolution 687 (1991) established the ceasefire between Iraq, Kuwait and the States authorised by SC Resolution 678 (1990) to use force to repel the Iraqi invasion of Kuwait.

The aggressors formally justified their military actions by invoking the theory of the 'material breach' of the terms of SC Resolution 687 (1991).[18] They claimed that Iraq had not fulfilled the obligation to destroy WMD it possessed as laid down in Resolution 687 (1991) and had repeatedly failed to co-operate with the UN inspectors and the International Atomic Energy Agency (IAEA). In their view, the failure of Iraq to fulfil its obligations re-vitalised the original SC authorisation to use force against Iraq contained in Resolution 678 (1990).[19] The States which supported the military aggression against Iraq, grounded it on the 'material breach' argument.[20]

The US had also paved the way for a military action by adopting declarations asserting its right of defence in light of the risk to its security represented by the possession of WMD by Iraq.[21] In the same vein, the Australian 2003 National Security Strategy had provided that the Australian Government was ready to consider requests to support coalition military operations to prevent the proliferation of WMD by rouge States or terrorists.[22]

---

16 For a list, see E MacAskill, 'US Claims 45 Nations in "Coalition of Willing"', *The Guardian* (19 March 2003) <https://www.theguardian.com/world/2003/mar/19/iraq.usa>.

17 UNSC Res 687 (3 April 1991) UN Doc S/RES/1687.

18 M Weller, 'The Iraq War – 2003' in T Ruys, O Corten and A Hofer (eds), *The Use of Force in International Law. A Case-Based Approach* (OUP 2018) 641 ff.

19 UN Doc S/1998/1181 and S/1998/1182, 16 December 1998. See also the statements of the delegates of Australia, Spain and Poland before the SC in UN Doc S/PV.4726, 26 March 2003 and S/PV.4726 (resumption 1), 27 March 2003.

20 See the statements of the delegates of Singapore, South Korea, Japan, Macedonia, Iceland, Mongolia, Marshal Islands, El Salvador, Uganda and Bulgaria in UN Doc S/PV.4726, 26 March 2003 and S/PV.4726 (resumption 1), 27 March 2003.

21 See, *ie*, the statement of the US Permanent Representative to the UN after the adoption of the SC Resolution 1441 (2002), UN Doc S/PV.4644, 8 November 2002, 3. See also the statements of US President quoted by J A Ramírez, 'Iraq War: Anticipatory Self-Defense or Unlawful Unilateralism?' (2003) 34 CalWIntlLJ 17 and footnote 81.

22 Ministry of Defence, 'National Security: A Defence Update 2003' 16, quote in WM Reisman and A Armstrong, 'The Past and Future of the Claim of Preemptive Self-Defense' (2006) Faculty Scholarship Series, Paper 957, 539.

The majority of States condemned the coalition's military action as a unilateral use of force in violation of international law and the UN Charter.[23] Among those that complained against the Western-led military attack, were a number of Middle Eastern States, namely, Yemen, Libya, Iran, Lebanon and Syria, some of which, arguably, might have been the most threatened by Iraq's possession of WMD. The majority of States rejected the 'material breach' argument and some of them (Iran and Lebanon) expressly excluded the legality of the preventive self-defence justification as well.

2.3 *Al-Kibar* (2007)

Some years later, in September 2007, Israel bombed the Al-Kibar nuclear reactor in Syria. Syria formally complained about the 'flagrant violation by Israel of its airspace' sending letters to the UNSC and the UNGA.[24] Nonetheless, it denied the Israeli attack had caused material damage.[25] Later, the Syrian President admitted that Israel had hit a military building.[26] Syria is a non-nuclear weapon State Party to the Treaty on the Non-Proliferation of Nuclear Weapons (NPT), which prohibits States from developing nuclear weapons. Syria's non-compliant conduct explains why it carefully protested against the Israeli attack and did not reveal the real target of it. Syria denied the existence of a nuclear facility until the circulation, in 2008, of a video of a US intelligence briefing, which revealed that the 2007 military attack by Israel destroyed a covert nuclear reactor;[27] shortly followed by the IAEA's inspection discovering uranium particles at the Al-Kibar site.[28]

Differently from what happened after the attack on the Osirak reactor, only one month later, in October 2007, Israel admitted that there had been an attack

23 See the debate before the SC after the beginning of the attack as recorded in UN Doc S/PV.4726, 26 March 2003 and S/PV.4726 (resumption 1), 27 March 2003, especially the statements of the Permanent Representative of Malaysia, also speaking on behalf of the Non-Aligned Movement, and those of the delegates of Algeria, Yemen, Libya, Indonesia, Cuba, Switzerland, Sudan, Viet Nam, Jamaica, Iran, Lebanon, Belarus, Laos, Tanzania, Costa Rica, Sri Lanka, Russian Federation, France, China and Syria. On the 24th of March 2003 the Council of the League of Arab States adopted a decision condemning the aggression against Iraq: UN Doc S/2003/365, annex, paras 1 and 2.

24 UN Doc S/2007/537 and A/61/1041.

25 Ibid.

26 'Assad Sets Conference Conditions' *BBC News* (1 October 2007) <http://news.bbc.co.uk/2/hi/middle_east/7021986.stm>.

27 Office of the Director of National Intelligence, 'Background Briefing with Senior U.S. Officials on Syria's Covert Nuclear Reactor and North Korea's Involvement' (24 April 2008) <https://www.dni.gov/files/documents/Newsroom/Speeches%20and%20Interviews/20080424_interview.pdf>.

28 IAEA, 'Implementation of the NPT Safeguards Agreement in the Syrian Arab Republic' GOV/2008/60, GOV/2009/36, GOV/2009/56, GOV/2010/11.

on an unspecified military installation;[29] nevertheless, it continued to deny that the attack was against a nuclear facility until 2018, when the Israeli Prime Minster acknowledged Israel's responsibility.[30] Nonetheless, Israel has never justified the attack by invoking preventive self-defence. Because of the reticent conduct of both States involved, the Israeli strike has never been brought up for debate before the SC. Nor has the First Committee of the UNGA, which deals with disarmament and international security, ever addressed it. The outcome was that, in the aftermath of the attack, third States did not take any position on whether or not the Israeli action was lawful,[31] except for North Korea which condemned it.[32] Nonetheless, two years later, in 2009, the 118 Member States of the Non-Aligned Movement (NAM) protested against Israel's conduct. The declaration adopted at the end of the NAM's Heads of State Summit qualified the Israeli action as a flagrant violation of the UN Charter.[33]

3 Preventive Military Actions against States 'Unwilling or Unable' to Prevent Non-State Actors from Developing and Using CBRN Weapons

In 1998, the US invoked its right to act in self-defence in accordance with Article 51 of the UN Charter, as a justification for its military airstrike against a facility being used by Al-Qaeda, with the tolerance of the Sudanese Government, to produce chemical weapons in Sudan. In 2014 and 2015, the US, Australia, Canada, Turkey and Germany launched military attacks against the Islamic State of Iraq and the Levant's (ISIL) enclaves on Syrian territory, claiming Syria was 'unwilling or unable' to prevent ISIL from organising military actions against them.

29 'Israel Admits Air Strikes on Syria', *BBC News* (2 October 2007) <http://news.bbc.co.uk./1/hi/7024287.stm>.

30 'Israel Admits Striking Suspected Syrian Nuclear Reactor in 2007' *BBC News* (21 March 2018), <https://www.bbc.com/news/world-middle-east-43481803>.

31 Surprisingly, when the Syrian Government accused Israel of aggression during the October 2007 session of the UNGA, no other States replied: see UN Doc A/62/PV.12, 1 October 2007.

32 R Weitz, 'Israeli Airstrike in Syria: International Reactions', James Martin Center for Nonproliferation Studies, 1 November 2007, 7 <https://www.inss.org.il/he/wp-content/uploads/sites/2/systemfiles/Israeli%20Airstrike%20in%20Syria%20%20International%20Reactions%20-%201.11.pdf>.

33 15th Summit of the Heads of States and Governments of the Non-Aligned Movement, Sharm el Sheik, 11–16 July 2009, NAM2009/FD/Doc.1, <http://cns.miis.edu/nam/documents/Official_Document/15Summit-Final-_Compiled.pdf>.

3.1 *Al-Shifa (1998)*

In August 1998, in the context of a missile attack against military bases and facilities connected to Al Qaeda in Afghanistan and Sudan, the US targeted a pharmaceutical plant in Al-Shifa, allegedly used to secretly produce chemical weapons. In the letter, dated 20 August 1998, from the US Permanent Representative to the SC President, the US justified its military actions as an exercise of its right of self-defence in accordance with Article 51 of the UN Charter. It invoked its right to respond to a series of armed attacks against United States embassies and nationals by the terrorist organisation of Bin Laden and to prevent and deter their continuation. The letter provided that the 'attacks were carried out only after repeated efforts to convince the Government of the Sudan and the Taliban regime in Afghanistan to shut these terrorist activities down and to cease their cooperation with the Bin Ladin organization.'[34]

Later, the US President justified the attack officially, stating that Al Qaeda was seeking to acquire chemical weapons and other dangerous weapons;[35] the US Department of State also released an official statement saying that, as far as the Al-Shifa factory was concerned, 'the U.S. has reliable intelligence that the Bin Laden network has been actively seeking to acquire weapons of mass destruction – including chemical weapons – for use against United States interests'.[36]

Sudan qualified the US action as an aggression and asked for the convening of an urgent meeting of the UNSC to discuss the matter.[37] It also called upon the UNSC to send a fact-finding mission to the Sudan.[38]

The States belonging to the Islamic Group and the African Group supported the Sudanese request.[39]

The SC met at the end of August 1998 to discuss the situation in Afghanistan, but no Member States referred to the bombing in Sudan.[40] Only one month after the attack, the delegate of Burkina Faso made a general reference to the

34 UN Doc S/1998/780, 20 August 1998.

35 'Statement of President Clinton Concerning U.S. Military Action in Afghanistan and Sudan', as recorded by the Federal Document Clearing House, <https://apnews.com/article/6dcb03c4a2713bed29f3a32f552f11cb>.

36 Coordinator for Counterterrorism, U.S. Department of State, 'Fact Sheet: U.S. Strike on Facilities in Afghanistan and Sudan' United States Information Agency, 21 August 1998, <https://1997-2001.state.gov/regions/africa/fs_binladin_facilities.html>.

37 E Cannizzaro and A Rasi, 'The US Strike in Sudan and Afghanistan – 1998' in T Ruys, O Corten and A Hofer (n 18) 542.

38 UN Doc S/1998/786, 21 August 1998.

39 UN Doc S/1998/790, 21 August 1998 and UN Doc S/1998/802, 25 August 1998.

40 UN Doc S/PV.3921 and S/PV.3921 (Resumption), 28 August 1998.

US strike before the SC and qualified it as an 'unacceptable reprisal carried out indiscriminately.'[41]

The Arab States condemned the US military action. In a statement dated 21 August 1998, the Secretariat of the League of Arab States qualified it as 'a blatant violation of the sovereignty of a State member of the League of Arab States, and of its territorial integrity, as well as against all international laws and tradition, above all the Charter of the United Nations.'[42] A few days later, the Council of the League of Arab States adopted Resolution 5781, which reiterated the condemnation expressed by the Secretariat and qualified the US action as an act of aggression against Sudan.[43]

Nuclear States reacted in different ways. The UK and Israel approved the US conduct; France did not express either open favour or a clear condemnation; the Russian Federation, China and Pakistan harshly criticised the US attack.[44]

3.2 *Syria (2014–2015)*

In 2014, 15 States used military force against the territory of Syria where ISIL was preparing and launching military attacks against Iraq and – according to the intervening States – where the same entity was preparing terrorist attacks against them. Some of the States which acted in a preventive way, namely, the US,[45] Australia,[46] Canada,[47] Turkey[48] and Germany[49] grounded their conduct on their right under Article 51 of the UN Charter to act in individual self-defence. In their view, they were entitled to use force to prevent the occurrence of military attacks coming from the territory of a State that was 'unwilling or unable' to prevent non-State actors from threatening their security.[50] The same States declared their intent to destroy any facility terrorists were suspected of using in order to develop and store CBRN weapons.[51] Syria protested against

41 UN Doc S/PV.3931, 24 September 1998.
42 UN Doc S/1998/789, Annex, 21 August 1998.
43 UN Doc S/1998/800, Annex, 24 August 1998. The condemnation was reiterated in the Resolution 5794 of the 17th of September 1998: see UN Doc S/1998/894, 28 September 1998.
44 J Lobel, 'The Use of Force to Respond to Terrorist Attacks: The Bombing of Sudan and Afghanistan' (1999) 24 YaleJIntlL 582 at 583.
45 UN Doc S/2014/695, 23 September 2014.
46 UN Doc S/2015/693, 9 September 2015.
47 UN Doc S/2015/221, 3 March 2015.
48 UN Doc S/2015/563, 24 July 2015.
49 UN Doc S/2015/946, 10 December 2015.
50 O Corten, 'The "Unwilling or Unable" Test: Has it Been, and Could it be, Accepted?' (2016) 29 LJIL 777.
51 White House, 'US National Strategy to Combat Weapons of Mass Destruction' (December 2002), <https://fas.org/irp/offdocs/nspd/nspd-17.html>; see also 'US National Strategy for Countering Weapons of Mass Destruction Terrorism' (2018) 2, 7 f. <https://www.hsdl.org/?abstract&did=819382>.

the US-led strikes in its territory, but not until one year after they began:[52] in December 2015, it also rejected any justification based on the self-defence doctrine.[53] Before the SC, third States did not dwell on the foundation of a right to act in self-defence against an 'unwilling or unable' State. Nonetheless, some States[54] and the League of Arab States[55] considered the attack as unlawful. The majority of States did not express either a legal or a political position on the issue.

4 Military Actions against States That Use CBRN Weapons against Their People

4.1 *Syria (2017–2018)*

The Syrian armed forces have used chemical weapons against their own people several times since December 2012.[56] As a reaction, in April 2017, the US army launched an attack against the Al-Shayrat military airbase in Syria. The US stated that this was in response to the Syrian Government's use of chemical weapons from this airbase against the city of Khan Shaykhun.[57] One year later, in April 2018, a coalition of States, composed of the US, France and the UK, carried out military airstrikes against sites alleged to be connected with the development, production and stockpiling of WMD in Syria.[58] The 2018 attacks

52 UN Doc A/70/385-S/2015/727, 22 September 2015.

53 UN Doc A/70/673 and UN Doc S/2015/1048, 4 January 2016; see also UN Doc S/2016/31, 12 January 2016.

54 UN Doc S/PV.7527, 30 September 2015, at 4, 6, 18 and 50; UN Doc S/PV.7504, 17 August 2015, at 4; UN Doc S/PV.7501, 7 August 2015, at 6; UN Doc S/PV.7419, 27 March 2015, at 24.

55 Resolution No. 7987 adopted at the Ministerial Meeting of the Council of the League of Arab States, 'Unified Arab Position on the Violation by Turkish Forces of the Sovereignty of Iraq', 24 December 2015, annexed to UN Doc S/206/16, 11 January 2016.

56 'Timeline of Syrian Chemical Weapons Activity' (2012–2020) <https://www.armscontrol.org/factsheets/Timeline-of-Syrian-Chemical-Weapons-Activity>; see also the reports of the Fact-Finding Mission established in 2014 by the Organisation for the Prohibition of Chemical Weapons (OPCW), <https://www.opcw.org/fact-finding-mission>.

57 UN Doc S/PV.7919, 7 April 2017. See also 'Letter of President Trump to Congressional Leaders on United States Military Operations in Syria', 8 April 2017 <https://www.gpo.gov/fdsys/pkg/DCPD-201700244/pdf/DCPD-201700244.pdf>.

58 Statement of the 14th of April 2018 the UK Ministry of Defence <https://www.gov.uk/government/news/raf-jets-strike-chemical-weapon-facility-in-syria>. See also the statement of Lt. Gen. McKenzie <https://www.defense.gov/News/Transcripts/Transcript-View/Article/1493749/department-of-defensepress-briefing-by-pentagon-chief-spokesperson-dana-w-whit/>.

were justified as reactions to the chemical attack against Douma, which had occurred few days before, in early April 2018.[59]

The acting States invoked a mix of legal arguments to justify their conduct. They expressed their intent to bring the Syrian regime to justice because of the commission of serious crimes against its population. The chemical attacks in Khan Shaykhun and Douma were pictured as 'the tip of the iceberg', the 'red line' that had been crossed by the Syrian Government and that did not permit any State – even taking the blockage of the SC by Russia into account – to wait for other horrific crimes to be committed. The military reaction was intended as a means of last resort to degrade the Syrian military's ability to conduct further chemical attacks and to dissuade the Syrian Government from using chemical weapons again.[60] The language used, especially during the 2017 US military action, brings to an international lawyer's mind the punitive use of armed reprisals.[61] Instead, following the 2018 attacks, the US expressly excluded a punitive intent as a rationale behind the attacks.[62] Only the UK expressly invoked the humanitarian intervention justification. Its limited aim was to prevent other 'chemical attacks' against the Syrian people.[63] The other

59 'U.S. Says Air Strikes Cripple Syria Chemical Weapons Program', *Reuters* (12 April 2018) <https://www.reuters.com/article/us-mideast-crisis-syria/trump-says-ordered-precision-strikes-against-syria-chemical-weapons-capabilities-idUSKBN1HJ0ZS>; Prime Minister's Office, 'Syria action: UK Government Legal Position', 14 April 2018, <https://www.gov.uk/government/publications/syria-action-uk-government-legal-position/syria-action-uk-government-legal-position>. For an overview of States' opinions regarding the authorship of the chemical attacks in Douma, see A de Guttry, 'The Western-led Military Operations in Syria in Response to the Use of Chemical Weapons: A Critical Assessment of the Claim for New Exceptions to the Prohibition on the Use of Force' (2018) 56 Archiv des Völkerrechts, especially 477–481; see also OPCW, 'Interim Report on the Progress of the Fact-Finding Mission Regarding an Incident of Alleged Use of Toxic Chemicals as a Weapon in Douma, Syrian Arab Republic, on 7 April 2018', OPCW Doc S/1645/2018, 6 July 2018 <https://www.opcw.org/sites/default/files/documents/S_series/2018/en/s-1645-2018_e_.pdf>.

60 As for the 2017 military reaction, see the statement released the 5th of April 2017 by the US representative before the UNSC, UN Doc S/PV.7917, 5 April 2017. In the same vein, the US statement of the 7th of April 2017 that followed the US military reaction, UN Doc S/PV.7919. A similar language was used by the representatives of the UK, France, Italy, Japan and Ukraine during the abovementioned SC meeting (UN Doc S/PV.7919, 7 April 2017).

61 For example, see UN Doc S/PV.7919, 7 April 2017.

62 UN Doc S/PV.8233, 14 April 2018.

63 As regards the 2018 attack, see the UK official statement justifying the military action: Prime Minister's Office, 'Syria action: UK Government Legal Position', 14 April 2018 <https://www.gov.uk/government/publications/syria-action-uk-government-legal-position/syria-action-uk-government-legal-position>.

intervening States partly alluded to the humanitarian intervention, though they did not refer to it *expressis verbis*.[64] Some of the States which supported the airstrikes did the same.[65]

Both military interventions gathered expressions of approval and of clear condemnation.[66]

A survey carried out by international law scholars on the reactions of 133 Sates to the 2018 attacks, reveals a number of elements that are very useful for assessing the consequence of this event on the possible development of a customary rule permitting the use of force against a State that has employed chemical weapons against its people. It discloses that the number of States that definitely considered the attacks as lawful was limited, but the number of States that definitely regarded them as unlawful was also limited. A significant number of States explicitly supported the airstrikes, although they did not explicitly refer to any legal ground in order to justify them. At the same time, a comparable number of States provided expressions of commitment to the UN Charter or other norms involving principles of non-intervention or sovereignty, but did not explicitly condemn the military intervention.[67]

64 As for the US position, see footnote n 60 and White House, 'Statement by President Trump on Syria', April 13, 2018 <https://www.whitehouse.gov/briefings-statements/statement-president-trump-syria/>. As for France's legal justification, see 'Communiqué de presse du Président de la République sur l'intervention des forces armées françaises en réponse à l'emploi d'armes chimiques en Syrie', 14 Avril 2018 <https://www.elysee.fr/emmanuel-macron/2018/04/14/communique-de-presse-du-president-de-la-republique-sur-l-intervention-des-forces-armees-francaises-en-reponse-a-l-emploi-d-armes-chimiques-en-syrie>. See also the joint declaration of the French Minister for European and Foreign Affairs and of the Minister for Defence, issued on 14 April 2018 <https://www.diplomatie.gouv.fr/fr/dossiers-pays/syrie/article/declaration-de-m-jean-yves-le-drian-ministre-de-l-europe-et-des-affaires>.

65 See footnote n 60.

66 In support of the 2017 military attack, the UK, France, Italy, Japan, Ukraine (see UN Doc S/PV.7919, 7 April 2017); against the Russian Federation, Bolivia (see UN Doc S/PV.7919, 7 April 2017), Iran and North Korea. In favour of the 2018 attacks, Côte d'Ivoire, Kuwait, Netherlands, Poland, Sweden, which voted against a draft resolution proposed by the Russian Federation to condemn the aggression by the United States and its allies over suspected chemical weapons use in Syria. The draft proposal was instead approved by Bolivia and China: UN Doc SC/13296, 14 April 2018. Iran condemned the attack, 'Iran's Supreme Leader Says Western Attack on Syria a Crime' *Reuters* (14 April 2018) <https://www.reuters.com/article/us-mideast-crisis-syria-iran-guards/irans-supreme-leader-says-western-attack-on-syria-a-crime-idUSKBN1HL0DO>.

67 A Gurmendi Dunkelberg, R Ingber, P Pillai and E Pothelet, 'Mapping States' Reactions to the U.S. Strikes Against Syria of April 2018: A Comprehensive Guide' (7 May 2018) <https://www.justsecurity.org/55835/mapping-states-reactions-syria-strikes-april-2018-a-comprehensive-guide/>.

5 States' Inaction

5.1 *Iraq (1987), Iran (2002–), Sudan (2016) and North Korea (2016–)*

In cases other than those just recalled, States have declared themselves to be under a serious threat because of the development of CBRN weapons by other States. This is the case of Israel which, in the last 15 years, has frequently declared that it regards a nuclear-armed Iran as an existential threat[68] and that it is in the process of evaluating whether to act in preventive self-defence.[69] In July 2016, North Korea tested intercontinental ballistic missiles, posing a serious nuclear threat to the United States and Japan. The US Secretary of State declared that the US was keeping all options, including a military strike, on the table.[70]

Fortunately, neither Israel nor the US and Japan have reacted to the threats militarily.

In other cases, States made use of CBRN weapons against their people. Iraq employed chemical weapons (during the Iran-Iraq war) to repress the Kurdish insurgency in 1988.[71] Suspected chemical attacks have been carried out by the Sudanese army as part of a major military offensive launched in January 2016 in Jebel Marra against the Sudan Liberation Army.[72] Third States did not react either to the Iraqi attack against the Kurdish people or to the Sudanese alleged use of chemical weapons in Darfur.

68 L Schloss, 'The Limits of the Caroline Doctrine in the Nuclear Context: Anticipatory Self-Defense and Nuclear Counter-Proliferation' (2012) 43 Georgetown Journal of International Law 555, 568.

69 See, for instance, the interview released by Ehud Barak (at that time in charge as Israeli Minister of defence) to *The New York Times* in 2012: 'Will Israel Attack Iran?' New York Times Magazine (25 January 2021) <https://www.nytimes.com/2012/01/29/magazine/will-israel-attack-iran.html>.

70 R Tillerson, 'Military Action against North Korea Is 'on the Table'' *NBC News* <https://www.nbcnews.com/news/north-korea/rex-tillerson-military-action-against-north-korea-table-n734771>.

71 J Hiltermann, 'The 1988 Anfal Campaign in Iraqi Kurdistan' <https://www.sciencespo.fr/mass-violence-war-massacre-resistance/fr/document/1988-anfal-campaign-iraqi-kurdistan.html>; see also 'Report of the Mission Dispatched by the Secretary-General to Investigate Allegations of the Use of Chemical Weapons in the Conflict between the Islamic Republic of Ira and Iraq' UN Doc S/19823, 25 April 1988.

72 According to an Amnesty International investigation, the Sudanese forces committed at least 30 attacks employing chemical weapons: Amnesty International, *Scorched Earth, Poisoned Air: Sudanese Government Forces Ravage Jebel Marra, Darfur*, 2016, <https://www.amnesty.org/download/Documents/AFR5448772016ENGLISH.PDF>.

6 Cyber-Attacks and Targeted Killings as New Means to Prevent States from Developing and Using CBRN Weapons or Allowing Non-State Actors to Do So

6.1 *Iran* (2010–)

According to media reports, the United States and Israel are widely believed to have developed the Stuxnet computer virus which cyber-attacked an Iranian nuclear facility, the Natanz uranium-enrichment site in 2010.[73] Other cyber-attacks have been launched since then against Iranian nuclear plants.[74] Most recently, in July 2020, Israel was suspected of being behind the cyber-attack that triggered a fire at the same facility.[75] Except for Iran's warning that it is ready to 'retaliate' against its cyber-enemies, other States did not protest against the alleged US-Israeli cyber-attacks. The latter have never taken responsibility for the attacks; therefore, no legal justification was submitted for them.

Since 2010, Israel's intelligence service is widely believed to have carried out a series of targeted killings against Iranian scientists, purported to be agents of the Iranian State who have been developing Iranian atomic weapons.[76] No official protest has ever been advanced against Israel, except by Iran.

7 Assessment of State Practice

7.1 *Three Preliminary Methodological Issues*

Three preliminary issues have to be considered before evaluating the State practice mentioned above. The first concerns State conduct which hasn't been accompanied by legal justifications. Can such conduct be taken into account in order to support the creation of a new customary rule? The second question concerns what weight to give to the practice and the *opinio juris* of States which have a 'legal interest' in the respect of a rule, although they are not specifically

73 'Stuxnet Was Work of U.S. and Israeli Experts, Officials Say' *The Washington Post* (2 June 2012) 'The Secret History of the Push to Strike Iran' *New York Times Magazine* (4 September 2019) <https://www.nytimes.com/2019/09/04/magazine/iran-strike-israel-america.html>.

74 'Obama Order Speed Up Wave of Cyberattacks Against Iran' *The New York Times* (1 June 2012) <https://www.nytimes.com/2012/06/01/world/middleeast/obama-ordered-wave-of-cyberattacks-against-iran.html>.

75 <https://akegroup.com/2020/07/08/iran nantaz-nuclear-nightmare/>.

76 F Fassihi, D E Sanger, E Schmitt and R Bergman, 'Iran's Top Nuclear Scientist Killed in Ambush, State Media Say', *The New York Times* (27 November 2020) <https://www.nytimes.com/2020/11/27/world/middleeast/iran-nuclear-scientist-assassinated-mohsen-fakhrizadeh.html#link-235350d7>. See also UN Doc A/66/656–S/2012/27, 12 January 2012.

affected by a specific conduct. To what extent is their conduct relevant in the development of a new customary rule?

The third question concerns the value an interpreter should give to States' inaction in the development of customary international law. When a State infringes an existing customary rule or initiates a new practice and the main reaction by third States is silence (or inaction), how should this silence be interpreted? Should it mean tacit acceptance, implied condemnation, lack of interest or absence of a legal opinion?

7.1.1 Express Legal Justifications

According to a formalistic approach, as followed by the ICJ in the *Nicaragua* case, an interpreter does not have the authority to 'ascribe to States legal views which they do not themselves advance.'[77] It has also been observed that it is only on the basis of a State's legal view justifying its own conduct, that the other States may express their own legal opinions in favour or against it. In the absence of the acting State's legal justification, approval or lack of condemnation by third States could not have any 'bearing on the formation of customary international law.'[78] This should be the dividing line between law and politics.[79]

This methodological question is relevant for the present analysis. It has been contended that the acting States have not defended the Al-Kibar attack or the military actions against Syria in 2017 and 2018 on legal grounds (more exactly, only some have not in the Syrian case).[80] The outcome of this reasoning would be that the Israeli attack on the Al-Kibar facility, as well as third States' reactions to it, could not be taken into account as elements of State practice supporting or denying the emergence of a customary norm authorising

77 ICJ, *Case Concerning military and Paramilitary Activities in and against Nicaragua* (*Nicaragua v US*) (Merits) 27 June 1986, para 207, <https://www.icj-cij.org/en/case/70/judgments>. In this vein K J Heller, 'Why al-Kibar Does Not Contribute to Pre-Emptive Self-Defence', *Opiniojuris*, <www.opiniojuris.org>; M Milanovic, 'The Syria Strikes: Still Clearly Illegal', *EJILTalk!*, 15 April 2018 <https://www.ejiltalk.org/the-syria-strikes-still-clearly-illegal/>.

78 Ibid. See also A Garwood-Gowers, 'Israel's Airstrike on Syria's Al-Kibar Facility: A Test Case for the Doctrine of Pre-emptive Self-Defence?', (2011) 16 JC&SL 263, at 284 who believes that because of the absence of a legal justification by Israel for the Al-Kibar attack, the international community's lack of protest cannot be considered acceptance of the Israeli action.

79 Ibid.

80 J Bellinger, 'The Trump Administration Should Do More to Explain the Legal Basis for the Syrian Airstrikes' *Lawfare* (14 April 2018) <https://www.lawfareblog.com/trump-administration-should-do-more-explain-legal-basis-syrian-airstrikes>.

States to act in preventive self-defence.[81] In the same vein, in the case of the military attacks against Syria, the fact that both the intervening States and their supporters (except for the UK) avoided the language of humanitarian intervention, would mean that their conduct could not be considered as relevant for the creation of a humanitarian exception to the prohibition on the use of force.

The above-mentioned argument is convincing, so long as it is applied in a non-formalistic way. While it is not for international lawyers to invent justifications for States' conduct,[82] it is for them to take into account the substantial meaning of statements States make, without limiting their analysis to look only at the employment of standardised formula (*ie* humanitarian intervention theory).

Furthermore, it is appropriate for international lawyers to consider opinions expressed by States in various ways, *ie* not just when they resort to formal statements.

Israel has never withdrawn from the Begin doctrine and has repeatedly asserted its right to act in preventive self-defence against any threat to its existence. Therefore, the absence of an official justification for the Al-Kibar attack can hardly be intended as a change of mind. In such a case, the State's real conduct reasonably includes its *opinio juris* on the matter.

As regards the US and France's statements on the legal justification of their military actions against Syria, while it is definitely true that they were quite general and did not expressly make use of the 'humanitarian intervention' formula, they nonetheless repeatedly referred – among the possible justifications – to their intent to bring an end to the humanitarian crisis affecting the Syrian people. Thus, the humanitarian intervention purpose was sufficiently clear.

7.1.2 Can Conduct of Some States Count More Than That of Others?

In the introduction of its survey on *Customary International Humanitarian Law*, the International Committee of the Red Cross (ICRC) acknowledged that one of the requirements for a customary rule to come into existence 'is that the state practice concerned must be both *extensive and representative*.'[83] In the ICRC's view, 'representative' means, in the words of the International

81 E Chachko, 'The Al-Kibar Strike: What a Difference 26 Years Make', *Lawfare* (2 April 2018) <https://www.lawfareblog.com/>. This is also the opinion of Andrew Garwood-Gowers, footnote 79.

82 Ibid.

83 J-M Henckaerts and L Doswald-Beck (eds.), *Customary International Humanitarian Law, Volume I, Rules* (CUP 2009) xliv.

Court of Justice in the *North Sea Continental Shelf* cases, that the practice must 'include that of States whose interests are *specially affected*.'[84] According to the ICRC's survey, which States are specifically affected will vary depending on the circumstances:[85] when rules concern conduct that all States can be held to have a 'legal interest' in, like in the case of humanitarian law rules, 'all States must be considered, whether or not they are "specially affected" in the strict sense of that term.'[86]

This position reflects what Judge Shahabuddeen wrote in his Dissenting Opinion attached to the ICJ's Advisory Opinion on the *Legality of the Threat or Use of Nuclear Weapons*, where he suggested that '[w]here what is in issue is the lawfulness of the use of a weapon which could annihilate mankind and so destroy all States, the test of which States are specially affected turns not on the ownership of the weapon, but on the consequences of its use. From this point of view, all States are equally affected, for, like the people who inhabit them, they all have an equal right to exist.'[87]

The interests in countering the proliferation of CBRN weapons and avoiding a serious prejudice to peace and security – which may be the result of a military intervention aimed at countering the proliferation of CBRN weapons – are undoubtedly States' shared interests. It is for this reason that the practice of all States, not only of those specifically affected in the strict meaning of this term, is relevant for a new customary rule authorising the use of force to come into existence.[88]

---

84 Ibid, xlv. See also ICJ, *North Sea Continental Shelf Cases* (Germany v Denmark; Germany v Netherlands) (Merits), 20 February 1969, 43, para 74 <https://www.icj-cij.org/public/files/case-related/52/052-19690220-JUD-01-00-EN.pdf>.

85 Ibid, xliv.

86 Ibid, xlv.

87 ICJ, *Legality of the Threat or Use of Nuclear Weapons* (Advisory Opinion) [1996] ICJ Rep 1996 at 414.

88 The Commentary to the ILC Draft Conclusion 8 on the identification of customary international law adopted in 2018 clarifies that 'in assessing generality, an indispensable factor to be taken into account is the extent to which those States that are particularly involved in the relevant activity or are most likely to be concerned with the alleged rule ("specially affected States") have participated in the practice'. Nevertheless, no reference is made to cases where all States ought to be considered 'specially affected' because they have a 'legal interest' in a rule being respected: ILC, Draft Conclusions on Identification of Customary International Law with Commentaries, UN Doc. A/73/10, Yearbook of the International Law Commission, 2018, vol. II, Part Two.

7.1.3 Value of Third States' Silence

As just concluded, when conduct that is contrary to a rule providing for an *erga omnes* obligation is at stake, the practice of every State counts in order to develop an exception to this rule. But what form may State conduct and *opinio juris* assume? Do silence or inaction count?

A recent survey by Harvard Law School on the 'Quantum of Silence: Inaction and *Jus ad Bellum*', has persuasively observed that 'the general complexities of imbuing silence with legal significance [...] are amplified in the field of *jus ad bellum*.'[89] It is not a surprise that, in this field, international law scholars have given opposite meanings to third States' silence.

In its work on the 'Identification of Customary International Law', the International Law Commission (ILC) has laid down that State practice may, in certain circumstances, include inaction (Draft conclusion 6, para 1).[90] In the ILC's Commentary, the Commission has clarified that the State that does not react has to be conscious of refraining from acting in a certain situation because the inaction may count as an element of State practice. Examples include States that abstain from using force.[91]

Failure to act may also count as evidence of State *opinio juris* 'provided that States were in a position to react and the circumstances called for reaction' (Draft conclusion 10, para 3). The ILC refers to cases where States which do not react have a direct interest in the issue, so that their inaction is considered as acquiescence. This position has also been held by the ICJ in the *Temple of Preah Vihear* case and, recently, in the *Pedra Branca* case.[92]

No specific Draft conclusion deals with the value of States' silence or inaction before conduct which is in contrast with an *erga omnes* obligation actually takes place.

Among governments that commented on the Draft conclusions, as adopted by the ILC in 2016, some expressed perplexities that, under certain circumstances, silence could be regarded as acquiescence. In particular, the Governments of the Czech Republic and New Zealand replied that States may not react to conduct of other States due to political and diplomatic considerations or simply because they have not been directly affected (in the strict

89 D A Lewis, N K Modirzadeh and G Blum, 'Quantum of Silence: Inaction and *Jus ad Bellum*', Harvard Law School Program on International Law and Armed Conflict, 2019, 33.

90 ILC Draft Conclusions (n 88).

91 Ibid.

92 ICJ, *Temple of Preah Vihear* (*Cambodia v Thailand*) (Merits) [1962] ICJ Rep.; ICJ, *Sovereignty over Pedra Branca/Pulau Batu Puteh,Middle Rocks and South Ledge* (*Malaysia v Singapore*), (Merits) [2008] ICJ Rep., para 121.

meaning of this term) by the action taken by other States, namely, if they lack a direct interest in the issue.[93]

These observations suggest that a cautious approach is warranted before giving silence a specific meaning when rules providing for *erga omnes* obligations – like the prohibition against military attacks – are at stake. In fact, where *erga omnes* obligations are concerned, the silence of third States is questionable evidence to establish their approval of the acting State's conduct.[94] Specifically affected States are expected to react to certain conduct; their inaction – if they have the capacity to react – may rightly be considered as an expression of acquiescence. However, States that have a legal interest in the respect of rules protecting shared values may be prevented by international or domestic political calculations from expressing their opinions about the legality of another State's conduct, even though the conduct is in contrast with the importance they attach to the rules.[95] For all these reasons, silence by States which have a legal interest in the respect of *erga omnes* obligations is much more enigmatic than in other cases,[96] and extreme caution should be used to assign it a legal meaning. Thus, in such cases, it is preferable not to invoke silence in support of or against the development of a new rule.

7.2 *Assessment of Preventive Self-Defence Claims*

7.2.1 Claims against Proliferating States

As the previous paragraphs have shown, the Israeli preventive attack on the Iraqi nuclear facility in 1981 encountered widespread condemnations by third States.

Israel did not claim any legal ground after the 2007 attack to the Al-Kibar nuclear plant, although – for the reasons just said – it is reasonable to believe that it was another application of the Begin doctrine. Third States did not react

---

93 UN Doc A/CN.4/716, 14 February 2018, 39 and 41.

94 ILC, Draft Conclusions (n 88) 133.

95 N S Marques Antunes, 'Acquiescence', *Max Planck Encyclopedia of Public International Law* (Rüdiger Wolfrum ed, 2006) para 16, who refers to *jus cogens* rules, believes that silence should not be 'legally tolerable' where 'overarching issues in which the interests of the international order as a whole' are concerned. Buzzini ('Les comportement passifs des Etats et leur incidence sur la reglementation de l'emploi de la force en droit international general', E Cannizzaro and P Palchetti, *Customary International Law on the Use of Force. A Methodological Approach* (Martinus Nijhoff, 2005), 93–96), observes that while States are expected to react in case of serious violations of *erga omnes* obligations, general international law only recognises a right to react (not an obligation), leaving States some leeway to take into account other interests.

96 A Bianchi, 'The International Regulation of the Use of Force: The Interpretive Method' (2009) 22 LJIL 651, at 663.

immediately after the 2007 Israeli attack. This has led some to consider third States' silence as a telling element of States' support for the development of a right to act in preventive self-defence against nuclear threats.[97] This conclusion is not convincing because – as said above – when the violation of a rule providing for an *erga omnes* obligation occurs, silence of third States is enigmatic. Third States' absence of complaint might be explained by practical and political considerations. No information on the strike was provided by the governments involved. For Arab States, the close ties developed between Syria and Iran might have been perceived as having a 'disruptive influence in the region', 'making [Syria] a less sympathetic victim of Israeli pre-emption than Iraq in 1981.'[98]

Be that as it may, it must not be forgotten that an important number of States condemned the Israeli attack (the 118 States Parties of the NAM), although this was two years later and so might be considered too late to have any value in the creation of a customary rule.

As for the 2003 attack against Iraq, only two intervening States invoked the plea of preventive self-defence, while the others turned to other legal excuses (namely, the 'material breach' theory). More generally, the attack was widely reputed as unlawful.

The only reasonable conclusion to draw is, therefore, that current international law does not permit States to forcefully and preventively counter the proliferation of CBRN weapons in self-defence. This conclusion is supported by the development, in recent years, of nuclear programmes by Iran and North Korea. States like the US and Israel – which had attacked Iraq and Syria and which might be among those more directly at risk from a nuclear Iran or North Korea – have refrained – at least up to now – from forcefully intervening. This tells us that the practice of the intervening States is not coherent, another element which supports excluding the development of a new exception to the prohibition of the use of force.

Furthermore, this conclusion is also in line with the emergence of new strategies some States have developed to limit the proliferation of their enemies, like the spreading of malware to affect the functioning of nuclear facilities and the targeted killing of individuals, such as eminent scientists believed to have a fundamental role in the development of States' CBRN weapons capabilities. States seem to prefer alternative strategies to that of targeted military attacks against alleged CBRN facilities. Although the lawfulness of the latter

97 E Chachko (n 81).

98 L S Spector and A Cohen, 'Israel's Airstrike on Syria's Reactor: Implications for the Nonproliferation Regime' <https://www.armscontrol.org/>.

measures remains doubtful as well, they nevertheless mark a new approach, which might diminish the risk of further armed actions against alleged CBRN weapons plants.

7.2.2 Claims against 'Unwilling or Unable' States

The 'unwilling or unable' test has been discussed in scholarly writings for the last couple of decades.[99] However, a wider debate has since been started by the former Legal Adviser to the United Kingdom Foreign and Commonwealth Office, Daniel Bethlehem, who has advocated in favour of self-defence not only against non-State actors who perpetrate armed attacks, but also against States materially supporting them (at least hosting them).[100] The proposal has several followers.[101]

The State practice referred to above is not sufficient to support the idea that a customary rule has developed, permitting States to act in self-defence against States 'unwilling or unable' to prevent non-State actors from possessing or developing CBRN weapons. On the other hand, less criticism was expressed against the intervening States acting against non-State actors and facilities allegedly used by them. States that condemned these attacks were numerically speaking less than in the other cases and a larger number of them decided not to take any legal position. Silence is far from meaning support of State conduct. Therefore, the legality of the self-defence plea has to be excluded. However, this silence definitely expresses a higher degree of uncertainty about the current stance of international law and may leave the door more open for further developments of the law.[102]

---

99 A Deeks, 'Unwilling or Unable: Toward a Normative Framework for Extraterritorial Self Defense', (2002) 52 VaJIntlL 483.

100 D Bethlehem (n 5) 770.

101 The Chatham House Principles (n 5), point 6; N Schrijver and L van den Herik, 'Leiden Policy Recommendations on Counter-terrorism and International Law', (2010) 57 NYIL 531; L Moir, 'Action Against Host States of Terrorist Groups', in M Weller (ed), *The Oxford Handbook of the Use of Force in International Law* (OUP 2015), 720; E Chachko and A Deeks, 'Which States Support the 'Unwilling and Unable' Test?' *Lawfare*, 10 October 2016 <https://www.lawfareblog.com/which-states-support-unwilling-and-unable-test>.

102 According to P Starski, 'Silence within the Process of Normative Change and Evolution of the Prohibition on the Use of Force: Normative Volatility And Legislative Responsibility' (2016) MPIL Research Paper Series 2016–20, 42 f., the ambiguity inherent in the claims made by the intervening States and their supporters do not permit 'treating mere silence of in-active States as acquiescence': <https://papers.ssrn.com/sol3/papers.cfm?abstract_id=2851809>. *Contra* T Ruys and L Ferro, 'Divergent Views on the Content and Relevance of the Jus Ad Bellum in Europe and the United States? The Case of the U.S.-Led Military Coalition Against "Islamic State"' (10 February 2016) at 23, <https://ssrn.com/abstract=2731597>.

7.3 *Is a Rule Authorising States to Act in Anticipatory Self-Defence in Cases of Imminent CBRN Attacks Desirable?*

Counter-proliferating military attacks are always justified by concerns over potential threats to the national security of the intervening States. However, in no case has clear and irrefutable evidence of an imminent attack been found. Nevertheless, is it reasonable to expect a State, faced with proof of the imminence of an armed attack (by a State or a non-State actor), not to intervene? A wait-and-see attitude is far from reasonable, at least when States have interceptive military capacities.

Especially because of the nefarious effects of CBRN weapons, scholars have upheld the lawfulness of an action in anticipatory self-defence. The idea has taken hold not only among those who believe that Article 2(4) of the UN Charter has not precluded the applicability of the pre-Charter era customary rule allowing for anticipatory self-defence,[103] or among those who argue such a right is in accordance with Article 51.[104] It has also been supported by those who believe that, for the UN Member States, the Charter has swept away the pre-existing customary rule permitting States to act in anticipatory self-defence.[105] However, among the holders of such a view, some have pointed out some conditions the acting States must respect, in addition to those of necessity and proportionality, in order to assess the imminence of the threat. The most interesting of these conditions is that the anticipatory use of force ought to require 'clear and convincing' evidence of an imminent military attack.[106]

This opinion is based on a realist evaluation of States' conduct, and convincingly tries to shape legal prohibitions to take into account the need for military defence and, at the same time, to prevent abuses. The real weakness of it is, nonetheless, twofold.

---

103 This seems to be the opinion of the High-level Panel on Threats, Challenges and Change the UN Secretary-General established in 2004: High-level Panel Report, *A More Secure World: Our Shared Responsibility*, UN Doc A/59/565, 2 December 2004, para 188.

104 Among the supporter of this opinion see, *ie*, D W Bowett, *Self-defence in International Law* (Univ. Press, 1958); S M Schwebel, 'Aggression, Intervention and Self Defence in Modern International Law' 136 RdC (1972-III), 463.

105 A Cassese, 'Una modesta proposta sulla legittima difesa preventiva', M Spinedi, A Gianelli and M L Alaimo (eds), *La codificazione della responsabilità internazionale degli Stati alla prova dei fatti* (Giuffré, 2006), 189 ff.

106 Ibid; D A Sadoff, 'Striking a Sensible Balance on the Legality of Defensive First Strikes' (2009) 42 VandJTransnatlL 441, 442 (2009); M E O'Connell, 'Lawful Self-Defense to Terrorism' (2002) 63 UPittLRev 889, 889–90, 893.

It does not seem to be applicable to biological and chemical weapons, whose production is easy to hide.[107] Moreover, biological weapons cause more contamination if the pathogens are dispersed by means of air spraying methods other than explosions, the former being more difficult to monitor and prevent. Since biological weapons can be used without warning, it may not be possible to distinguish the temporal proximity of a threat.[108]

Furthermore, a military action aimed at destroying a facility from which a radio-nuclear or chemical attack is going to be launched, might cause as much health and environmental damage as the anticipatory attack is intended to prevent. But how to make an *a priori* assessment of the human and material costs of an anticipatory self-defence intervention? How to assess whether the remedy would be worse than the disease?

7.4 *Assessment of Humanitarian Intervention Claims*

As the previous paragraphs have pointed out, in recent years, CBRN weapons have been used by Iraq, Syria and Sudan against their own people; third States have replied by using military force only against Syria.[109] Political and strategic interests might dictate third States' inaction. It makes this practice useless for those who want to ascertain whether a customary rule permitting humanitarian intervention is in the process of developing.

In contrast, the April 2018 airstrikes against Syria have been considered a 'transformative event that may have changed international law concerning humanitarian intervention.'[110] Some would argue that the airstrikes have crystallised a new exception in which force is allowed, 'namely to respond to and prevent future use of chemical weapons against civilians when the UNSC is blocked from authorizing humanitarian intervention by a Permanent Member's veto'.[111] This conclusion is based on a reading of the State practice that gives an important role to the silence of many States before the 2018 attacks. M.P. Scharf, one of the main holders of this view, writes that 'international law considers States that elect not to weigh in on an issue of general concern as providing silent support or acquiescence.'[112]

107 M C Waxman, 'The Use of Force Against States That Might Have Weapons of Mass Destruction' (2009) 31 MichJIntlL, 11–14 and 19.

108 Ibid, 13.

109 For a general summary of State practice, see N S Rodley, 'Humanitarian Intervention' in M Weller (n 101) 775.

110 M P Scharf, 'Striking a Grotian Movement: How the Syrian Airstrikes Changed International Law Relating to Humanitarian Intervention' (2019) 19 ChiJIntlL 586.

111 Ibid, 593.

112 Ibid, 609.

Scharf undoubtedly focuses on one of the thorny issues every international lawyer has to tackle once he/she confronts the emergence of a new customary rule, even more so in respect to *jus ad bellum* rules. In this field of law, silence is of particular concern.

As already said, while many States considered the attacks against chemical facilities in Syria as legitimate, they were silent on the legal justification for it. Their silence cannot be considered as an element in favour of a right to humanitarian intervention for the reasons already given above.

Furthermore, many States did not invoke the unlawfulness of the attacks, but reiterated the UN Member States' obligations to respect the Charter and the principle of non-intervention. These references suggest the authors of the statements believed the strikes violated at least Article 2(4).

In light of these elements, it is hard to conclude that a right to humanitarian intervention has arisen from the ashes of the 2018 airstrikes against Syria. This should not lead one to underestimate the important precedential value that States' material and verbal reactions to the use of chemical weapons against the Syrian people may have in the future, for the development of a further exception to the prohibition on the use of force.

7.5 *Does the 'Illegal but Legitimate' Argument Work?*

The imminence of an attack with CBRN weapons has paved the way for a debate on the advantages of a customary rule allowing for anticipatory self-defence when specific conditions have been met (see *supra*). The use of the same weapons against civilians and combatants has led to a different debate on the 'unlawful but legitimate' use of force to prevent further uses of them.[113]

The argument is based on the premises that humanitarian intervention is prohibited, but it can be morally justified in exceptional circumstances, since the law may not reflect elementary considerations of justice and humanity.[114]

Proponents of the 'unlawful but legitimate' argument move from a different perspective than those who are in favour of the development of a right to act in

---

113 Another interesting debate, that cannot be dealt with within the limited confines of this study, concerns the occurrence of a 'paradigm shift' in the international legal order, from a law for States to a 'law of humanity' (RG Teitel, *Humanity's Law* (OUP 2011) that would justify humanitarian intervention. For an interesting reply to this opinion, see C O'Meara, 'Should International Law Recognize a Right of Humanitarian Intervention' (2017) 66 ICLQ 441.

114 The 'unlawful but legitimate' claim was advanced in 2000 by the Report of the Independent International Commission on Kosovo, co-chaired by Richard Goldstone and Carl Tham, <https://www.law.umich.edu/facultyhome/drwcasebook/Documents/Documents/The%20Kosovo%20Report%20and%20Update.pdf>.

anticipatory self-defence. The former admit to breaking the law without trying to justify the military action on legal grounds, as they advocate for the raising of a new rule permitting the use of force as a moral imperative. The development of a legal exception to the prohibition on the use of force is instead at the core of the latter approach. Nonetheless the 'unlawful but legitimate' argument shares with the anticipatory self-defence claim the same weakness. Proponents of the 'unlawful but legitimate' formula include among the criteria of legitimacy a cost-benefit analysis intended to assess whether the consequences of an intervention are not worse than the consequences of inaction.[115] But how to make an *a priori* assessment of the human and material costs of a humanitarian intervention to prevent further use of CBRN weapons? How to assess if it will produce less damage and suffering than the employment of CBRN weapons will cause (or has already caused)?

When CBRN weapons are at stake, the negative and long-term effects on human health and the environment that their use or their destruction may produce make it more difficult to apply the cost-benefit analysis as a criterion for deciding whether or not to intervene. Moreover, *ex post facto* assessments of the costs and benefits of an intervention always relate to a specific case; their use to foresee the 'costs' of military intervention in different scenarios would be wrong.[116]

8 Concluding Remarks

The present survey has disclosed that the development of CBRN weapons and the risk of their employment has represented a momentous temptation for States to use force, both to protect their security interests and to defend civilian populations under attack. This chapter has shown that current customary international law does not provide for specific exceptions to the ban on the use of force to respond to the proliferation of CBRN weapons or their use against human beings. It has also brought to the fore that where States have reacted against States that were 'unwilling or unable' to limit the acquisition of CBRN weapons by non-State actors on their own territory or against States that used chemical weapons against their own people, third States have

115 G Evans, 'When Is It Right to Fight? Legality, Legitimacy and the Use of Military Force', 2004 Cyril Foster Lecture, Oxford University, 10 May 2004, <http://www.gevans.org/speeches/speech105.html>.

116 M Milanovic, 'Illegal but Legitimate' (*EJILTalk!* 10 April 2017) <https://www.ejiltalk.org/illegal-but-legitimate/>.

supported them more than in cases of military actions justified by preventive self-defence. Yet, even in the latter scenario, third States' inaction and silence prevailed; however, this does not justify concluding that the development of new rules permitting the use of force are in the process of emerging. Moreover, accepting that compelling reasons and needs – like the dire humanitarian situation in Syria – might pave the way for the development of new rules, based on limited and contested State practice and *opinio juris*,[117] would lead to the abusive application of coercive military force.

Bibliography

Bethlehem D, 'Self-Defence Against an Imminent or Actual Armed Attack by Non-state Actors' (2012) 106 AJIL 774.

Bianchi A, 'The International Regulation of the Use of Force: The Interpretive Method' (2009) 22 LJIL 651, at 663.

Bowett D W, *Self-defence in International Law* (Univ. Press, 1958).

Buzzini, 'Les comportement passifs des Etats et leur incidence sur la reglementation de l'emploi de la force en droit international general', E Cannizzaro and P Palchetti, *Customary International Law on the Use of Force. A Methodological Approach* (Martinus Nijhoff, 2005), 93–96.

Cannizzaro E and Rasi A, 'The US Strike in Sudan and Afghanistan – 1998' in T Ruys, O Corten and A Hofer (eds), *The Use of Force in International Law. A Case-Based Approach* (OUP 2018) 542.

Cassese A, 'Una modesta proposta sulla legittima difesa preventiva', M Spinedi, A Gianelli and M L Alaimo (eds), *La codificazione della responsabilità internazionale degli Stati alla prova dei fatti* (Giuffré, 2006), 189 ff.

Corten O, 'The "Unwilling or Unable" Test: Has it Been, and Could it be, Accepted?' (2016) 29 LJIL 777.

de Guttry A, 'The Western-led Military Operations in Syria in Response to the Use of Chemical Weapons: A Critical Assessment of the Claim for New Exceptions to the Prohibition on the Use of Force' (2018) 56 Archiv des Völkerrechts, especially 477–481.

Deeks A, 'Unwilling or Unable: Toward a Normative Framework for Extraterritorial Self Defense', (2002) 52 VaJIntlL 483.

117 This is instead the opinion expressed by Daniel Bethlehem, 'Stepping Back a Moment: The Legal Basis in Favour of a Principle of Humanitarian Intervention' *EJILTalk!* 12 September 2013, <https://www.ejiltalk.org/stepping-back-a-moment-the-legal-basis-in-favour-of-a-principle-of-humanitarian-intervention/>.

Garwood-Gowers A, 'Israel's Airstrike on Syria's Al-Kibar Facility: A Test Case for the Doctrine of Pre-emptive Self-Defence?', (2011) 16 JC&SL 263, at 284.

Glennon M J, 'Pre-empting Proliferation: International Law, Morality and Nuclear Weapons' (2013) 24 EJIL 109, at 111.

Glennon M J, 'The UN Security Council in a Unipolar World' (2003–2004) 44 VandJTransnatlL 91 at 98–100.

Henckaerts J-M and Doswald-Beck L (eds.), *Customary International Humanitarian Law, Volume I, Rules* (CUP 2009).

Lobel J, 'The Use of Force to Respond to Terrorist Attacks: The Bombing of Sudan and Afghanistan' (1999) 24 YaleJIntlL 582 at 583.

Marques Antunes N S, 'Acquiescence', *Max Planck Encyclopedia of Public International Law* (Rüdiger Wolfrum ed, 2006) para 16.

Moir L, 'Action Against Host States of Terrorist Groups', in M Weller (ed), *The Oxford Handbook of the Use of Force in International Law* (OUP 2015), 720.

O'Connell M E, 'Lawful Self-Defense to Terrorism' (2002) 63 UPittLRev 889, 889–90, 893.

O'Meara C, 'Should International Law Recognize a Right of Humanitarian Intervention' (2017) 66 ICLQ 441.

Ramírez J A, 'Iraq War: Anticipatory Self-Defense or Unlawful Unilateralism?' (2003) 34 CalWIntlLJ 17 and footnote 81.

Reisman W M and Armstrong A, 'The Past and Future of the Claim of Preemptive Self-Defense' (2006) Faculty Scholarship Series, Paper 957, 539.

Rodley N S, 'Humanitarian Intervention' in M Weller (ed), *The Oxford Handbook of the Use of Force in International Law* (OUP 2015), 775.

Ruys T and Ferro L, 'Divergent Views on the Content and Relevance of the Jus Ad Bellum in Europe and the United States? The Case of the U.S.-Led Military Coalition Against "Islamic State"' (10 February 2016) at 23, <https://ssrn.com/abstract=2731597>.

Sadoff D A, 'Striking a Sensible Balance on the Legality of Defensive First Strikes' (2009) 42 VandJTransnatlL 441, 442 (2009).

Sapiro M, 'Iraq: The Shifting Sands of Preemptive Self-Defense' (2003) 97 AJIL 599 at 599.

Scharf M P, 'Striking a Grotian Movement: How the Syrian Airstrikes Changed International Law Relating to Humanitarian Intervention' (2019) 19 ChiJIntlL 586.

Schloss L, 'The Limits of the Caroline Doctrine in the Nuclear Context: Anticipatory Self-Defense and Nuclear Counter-Proliferation' (2012) 43 Georgetown Journal of International Law 555, 568.

Schrijver S and van den Herik L, 'Leiden Policy Recommendations on Counter-terrorism and International Law', (2010) 57 NYIL 531.

Schwebel S M, 'Aggression, Intervention and Self-Defence in Modern International Law' 136 RdCours (1972-III), 463.

Starski P, 'Silence within the Process of Normative Change and Evolution of the Prohibition on the Use of Force: Normative Volatility And Legislative Responsibility' (2016) MPIL Research Paper Series 2016–20, 42 f.

Teitel R G, *Humanity's Law* (OUP 2011).

Terry P C R and Openshaw K S, 'Nuclear Non-Proliferation and Preventive Self-Defence: Why Attacking Iran Would Be Illegal' (2013) 51 ACDI 165, especially 181 ff.

Walzer M, *Just and Unjust Wars: A Moral Argument with Historical Illustrations* (5th edn, Basic Books, 2015).

Waxman M C, 'The Use of Force Against States That Might Have Weapons of Mass Destruction' (2009) 31 MichJIntlL, 11–14 and 19.

Weller M, 'The Iraq War – 2003' in T Ruys, O Corten and A Hofer (eds), *The Use of Force in International Law. A Case-Based Approach* (OUP 2018) 641 ff.

CHAPTER 21

The Use of CBRN Weapons in Armed Conflict

Diego Mauri

1 Introduction

One of the bedrock rules of international humanitarian law (IHL) is that the right of parties to an armed conflict 'to choose methods and means of warfare is not unlimited':[1] limitations exist. While, intuitively, the goal of warfare is to overcome the enemy, IHL imposes certain constraints on parties to a conflict: their ultimate rationale is to curb State and non-State actors' tendency to resort to whatever tactic or weapon to succeed in their effort. The whole history of IHL – also known as *jus in bello* or, as it is still referred to, Law of Armed Conflict (LOAC) – is thus a history of *limitation*.[2]

This is made clear by the evolution of this branch of international law through the last century and a half, a period in which the limitation of tactics and weapons has literally blossomed: a quick tour of the International Committee of the Red Cross (ICRC)'s online databases suffices to make one aware of the large number of treaties and customs regulating hostilities.[3] What is more, the rules on methods and means are held to be drafted 'in a peremptory manner' (thus qualifying as *jus cogens*) and to apply to situations of both international armed conflict (IAC) and non-international armed conflict

1 Convention (IV) respecting the Laws and Customs of War on Land and its annex: Regulations concerning the Laws and Customs of War on Land (adopted 18 October 1907, entered into force 26 January 1910) 187 CTS 227 art 22; Protocol Additional to the Geneva Conventions of 12 August 1949, and Relating to the Protection of Victims of International Armed Conflicts (adopted 8 June 1977, entered into force 7 December 1978) 1125 UNTS 3 (hereinafter: AP I) art 35(1).

2 H McCoubrey, *International Humanitarian Law. Modern Development in the Limitation of Warfare* (2nd ed, Routledge 2019); A Alexander, 'A Short History of International Humanitarian Law' (2015) 26 EJIL 109; ME O'Connell, 'Historical Development and Legal Basis', in D Fleck (ed), *The Handbook of International Humanitarian Law* (2nd ed, OUP 2013).

3 See <https://www.icrc.org/en/icrc-databases-international-humanitarian-law> (all links accessed on 20 May 2021). As for customary law, see JM Henckaerts and L Doswald-Beck (eds), *Customary International Humanitarian Law* (CUP 2005), and also <https://ihl-databases.icrc.org/customary-ihl/eng/docs/home> (hereinafter CIHL).

(NIAC).[4] The advent of new technologies, while a constant challenge throughout the history of IHL, is more worrisome today than ever before due to the rapid development of weapons and the unprecedented capabilities they give their users.[5]

The purpose of the present chapter is to provide a fresh appraisal of how Chemical, Biological, Radiological and Nuclear (CBRN) weapons are regulated by existing IHL. To begin with, the extent to which CBRN 'agents' can be considered as 'weapons' or 'means of warfare' pursuant to IHL will be tackled, and relevant definitions will be provided that build upon the premises laid down at the beginning of the present book.[6] The analysis will then turn to IHL rules and principles of IHL dealing with *specific* weapons and prohibiting (or restraining) *specific* means of warfare, without losing sight of general rules and core principles Finally, the chapter will deal with current challenges posed by new technologies in the specific field of CBRN weapons, including considerations of up and coming advancements in military applications of CBRN agents, and will identify and discuss a normative tool for addressing them (4), before turning to conclusions (5).

Before raising anchor, some coordinates are due. First, this chapter is interested solely in armed conflict: uses of CBRN weapons in different scenarios, such as the no less turbulent waters of law-enforcement operations, are left for other contributions.[7] Second, accepting the traditional difference between *jus ad bellum* and *jus in bello*, little reference will be made to norms regulating whether and to what extent force can be used in international relations, as this will be addressed in chapters dealing with norms on disarmament and arms control.[8] The main (but not exclusive) normative framework this chapter is concerned with is IHL; however, the reader must be alerted to possible docking at other ports of international law. Third, the topic of CBRN weapons in armed conflict may intersect with the issue of the protection of the natural environment, which again, is the subject of a specific contribution in this volume and will not be tackled here.[9]

---

4 Y Sandoz, C Swinarski, and B Zimmermann (eds), *Commentary on the Additional Protocols of 8 June 1977 to the Geneva Conventions of 12 August 1949* (Martinus Nijhoff 1987) (AP I Commentary) para 1405.

5 W Wallach, *A Dangerous Master. How to Keep Technology from Slipping Beyond Our Control* (Basic Books 2015).

6 See ch 1 by Frulli.

7 See Part 4 on horizontal issues.

8 See ch 20 by Magi and ch 23 by Poli.

9 See ch 22 by Saluzzo.

2 Setting the Stage: CBRN 'Agents' as 'Weapons'

It may come as a surprise that, despite the fact that wars are naturally fought through them and they are integral to the use of force (and thus a mainstream term in literature on that topic), the term 'weapon' has never been made the object of a universally-accepted definition in IHL.[10] While intuitively understood as an instrument designed or used for inflicting harm or damage, either offensively or defensively, no specific definition is provided either by customary or treaty IHL, to the point that the ICRC has claimed that any guidance is to be sought not 'across the international community' but, rather, within domestic legal orders.[11]

A distinction that is accepted in IHL is between 'weapons' and 'means' of warfare, and 'methods' of warfare.[12] The first two categories may be treated as synonyms, as they both refer to the *instruments* through which force is used in hostilities.[13] However, the term 'methods' refers to the *tactics* that are employed in those contexts.[14] To put it differently, the rules dealing with the former relate to the 'is the tool *itself* lawful?' question, while rules dealing with the latter relate to the (subsequent) 'is *the way* in which that tool is employed lawful?' question.[15] According to a definition proposed by the United States Department of Defence (US DoD), the term 'weapon' would include 'all arms, munitions, materiel, instruments, mechanisms or devices that have an intended effect of injuring, damaging, destroying or disabling personnel or property'.[16] The very fact that so many terms are employed demonstrates that, rather than the object in itself, what matters is the *purpose* for which the

10 S Casey-Maslen, 'Weapons', in B Saul and D Akande, *The Oxford Guide to International Humanitarian Law* (OUP 2020). See also W Boothby, *Weapons and the Law of Armed Conflict* (OUP 2009).

11 ICRC, 'A Guide to the Legal Review of New Weapons, Means and Methods of Warfare: Measures to Implement Article 36 of Additional Protocol I of 1977' (Geneva, 2006) (hereinafter: ICRC Guide) 47.

12 AP I, art 36.

13 S Haines, 'The Developing Law of Weapons. Humanity, Distinction and Precautions in Attack', in A Clapham and P Gaeta (eds), *The Oxford Handbook of International Law in Armed Conflict* (OUP 2014).

14 MN Schmitt, 'International Humanitarian Law and the Conduct of Hostilities', in Saul and Akande (n 10).

15 Haines (n 13) 277 (using the example of white phosphorous).

16 Cited in ICRC Guide, 8. The term 'weapon' is not included in the recent US DoD, 'DoD Dictionary of Military and Associated Terms' (June 2020) <https://www.jcs.mil/Doctrine/DOD-Terminology-Program/>. This definition is only partially satisfying as it leaves outside weapons causing damage to the environment as such, which is a topical issue today: see ch 22 by Saluzzo.

object is used, namely to project force against human or non-human targets. Consequently, it has been argued that any working definition of 'weapon' must be sufficiently open-textured, so as to include, for instance, devices that cause harm by means of kinetic energy (eg bullets) and those that do so by other means (eg heat, sound, electricity or electromagnetism, bacteria).[17] Long story short, for an 'object' to qualify as a weapon, the essential feature is its capability of directly causing harm.

Turning now to CBRN agents, the ICRC has proposed a definition that – while acknowledging the differences in nature, origins and properties of various agents, as well as in the type of injury or illness the exposure to them can produce – identifies four common properties, namely: (i) toxicity, (ii) latency, (iii) persistency, and (iv) transmissibility.[18] Although conceived for training purposes only, this definition has the merit of highlighting 'toxicity' as the first common property of all CBRN agents, *ie* the 'ability [...] to cause harmful effects or death'.[19] The above definition of 'weapons' immediately rings in the ears: CBRN agents are *inherently* capable of causing harm, and thereby make a formidable weapon to be used against an enemy. As a confirmation of this, the very notion of 'Weapons of Mass Destruction' (WMD) – though not a term of art in IHL – is commonly employed to identify CBRN weapons capable of causing high orders of destruction and mass casualties.[20] In other words, no one would question that CBRN agents are extremely suitable for 'weaponisation'.

Therefore, IHL regulates the use of CBRN agents as 'weapons' and, from a theoretical standpoint, it makes sense to investigate CBRN weapons through the lens of IHL. To date, however, there is no treaty or customary rule addressing the use of CBRN weapons in armed conflict *as a whole*; rather, their regulation is scattered in various legal instruments that consider the use of those 'agents' separately.

3 IHL Norms Regulating CBRN Weapons

In the landmark Advisory Opinion rendered in the *Nuclear Weapons* case, the International Court of Justice (ICJ) fixed the two 'cardinal principles [...] constituting the fabric of [IHL]'.[21] The first one is the principle of discrimination,

17 Casey-Maslen (n 10) 261.

18 ICRC, 'Chemical, Biological, Radiological and Nuclear Response. An Introductory Guidance' <https://www.icrc.org/en/publication/4175-chemical-biological-radiological-and-nuclear-response-introductory-guidance>.

19 Ibid 8.

20 US DoD (n 16); see also ch 1 by Frulli.

21 *Legality of the Threat of Use of Nuclear Weapons* (1996) ICJ Reports 66, para 78.

including both the prohibition against directly targeting civilians and civilian objects,[22] and the prohibition on using indiscriminate weapons, namely those 'that are incapable of distinguishing between civilian and military targets'.[23] The second principle also prohibits using weapons that cause legitimate targets superfluous injury or unnecessary suffering (aka the 'SIrUS rule' in the ICRC's jargon),[24] or, in other words, cause 'a harm greater than that unavoidable to achieve legitimate military objectives'.[25] As is evident, these rules enshrine the idea of limitation as illustrated above, and have to be read in conjunction with other key principles of IHL applicable to targeting, namely proportionality and precautions in attack.[26]

These rules establish *general* prohibitions on the use of certain weapons: provided that it is demonstrated that a weapon is inherently indiscriminate (eg poison),[27] or that its use causes superfluous injury or unnecessary suffering (such as explosive projectiles weighing less than 400 grammes),[28] that weapon cannot be used in conformity with IHL, even absent a specific prohibition. There is also a general prohibition on the use of weapons that are intended, or may be expected, to cause widespread, long-term and severe damage to the natural environment.[29] Last but not least, the overarching principle of humanity as encapsulated by the so-called Martens Clause deserves mention. By placing combatants and civilians 'under the protection and authority of the principles of international law derived from established customs, from the principles of humanity and from the dictates of public conscience',[30] the Martens Clause proscribes weapons recognised as abhorrent, even absent specific treaty rules.[31]

In addition to these general rules, IHL also prohibits and restricts *specific* weapons or means of warfare, both in separate treaties and in customary

22 AP I, art 48; CIHL rule 1.

23 AP I, art 35(2); CIHL, rule 71.

24 Convention (IV) (n 1) art 23(2); AP I, art 35(2). As for the ICRC, see R Coupland and P Herby, 'Review of the Legality of Weapons: A New Approach. The SIrUS Project' (1999) 81 IRRC 583.

25 *Legality of the Threat of Use of Nuclear Weapons* (n 21) para 78.

26 AP I, arts 51(5)(b) and 57(2); CIHL, rules 14 and 15.

27 AP I Commentary, para 1402.

28 Declaration Renouncing the Use, in Time of War, of Explosive Projectiles under 400 Grammes Weight (adopted 11 December 1868, entered into force 11 December 1868) 138 CTS 297.

29 AP I, arts 35(3) and 55; CIHL, rule 45. See more extensively ch 22 by Saluzzo.

30 AP I, art 1(2).

31 Literature on the Martens Clause and its legal implications is immense: see A Cassese, 'The Martens Clause: Half a Loaf or Simply Pie in the Sky?' (2000) 11 EJIL 187.

norms. An interesting example is provided by the 1980 Convention on Certain Conventional Weapons (CCW), an 'umbrella' treaty composed of only a few procedural obligations and completed by its Protocols.[32] This variable-geometry instrument is supposed to encourage the participation of as many States as possible, leaving them free to choose which Protocols to ratify; in addition, it really renders the CCW a living instrument, capable of adapting to new technologies.[33] Weapons specifically prohibited in their own Protocols include those leaving non-detectable fragments, booby-traps, landmines, incendiary weapons, blinding lasers, explosive remnants of war, and cluster munitions.[34] Most of these instruments have been adopted on the basis that the weapon under scrutiny was found to be in contrast with the general rules above, to the point that a clear and explicit prohibition by way of treaty was considered as the optimal normative choice: overlaps between general and specific rules are thus unavoidable and even auspicious, as they reinforce the prohibition on certain weapons.

With this distinction between general and specific prohibitions in mind, let us now tackle each weapon in turn.

3.1 *Chemical Weapons*

The prohibition on the use of chemical agents as weapons is probably among the most ancient ones in IHL. In addition to being indiscriminate in nature, chemical weapons produce lifelong damage whose effects on the human person and the environment remain after the end of the conflict. The fact that, if air is contaminated with chemical agents, people can simply not breathe was a sufficient ground for invoking a ban on those weapons.

'Asphyxiating gases', such as chlorine and sulphur mustard (having a blistering effect on skin or the moisture in lungs), were first prohibited by the 1899 Hague Declaration (IV, 2), yet with two major limitations.[35] First, the prohibition concerned the use of projectiles the 'sole' object of which was the diffusion of such gases, while it was questionable whether projectiles causing their release as a side-effect were lawful. Second, the prohibition ceased to have effect if one party to the conflict was joined by a State that had

32 Convention on Prohibitions or Restrictions on the Use of Certain Conventional Weapons Which May Be Deemed to Be Excessively Injurious or to Have Indiscriminate Effects (adopted 10 October 1980, entered into force 2 December 1983) 1342 UNTS 137.

33 Haines (n 13) 281.

34 For more details, see N Melzer, *International Humanitarian Law. A Comprehensive Introduction* (coordinated by E Kuster) (ICRC 2016) 111ff.

35 Declaration (IV,2) concerning Asphyxiating Gases (adopted 29 July 1899, entered into force 4 September 1900) 18 CTS 453.

not been a Contracting Party to the Declaration: this is a typical example of a *si omnes* clause ('either every one or no one'), an expression of the logic of *reciprocity* that used to animate IHL back then,[36] and was subsequently abandoned during the nineteenth century.[37]

Due to these limitations, and in spite of a strong international movement against them, chemical agents were employed as weapons in WWI. Under the auspices of the League of Nations, a new binding instrument dealing specifically with these weapons was negotiated at an international conference in Geneva, namely the 1925 Geneva Protocol.[38] The Protocol extended the scope of the prohibition by including 'asphyxiating, poisonous or other gases, and all analogous liquid materials or devices', as well as 'bacteriological methods of warfare'. However, more than 20 States made reservations to the Protocol, declaring that they maintained the right to use these weapons in retaliation.[39] Again, a logic of reciprocity – *de facto* reducing the prohibition to a ban on first use – re-surfaced. After WWII, most of these reservations were withdrawn, and the UN General Assembly repeatedly invited all States to accede to the Protocol. Several (bilateral, multilateral, regional and universal) instruments have been proposed and adopted to ban not only the *use* of chemical weapons but also their development *lato sensu*.[40]

A key turning point was represented by the adoption of the Chemical Weapons Convention (CWC) in 1993.[41] This instrument establishes the first and most comprehensive regulatory regime for chemical weapons, which is relevant not only from the standpoint of IHL (in that it prohibits the *use* of chemical agents as weapons) but also from the standpoint of disarmament law (in that the prohibition covers also the development, production, stockpiling, and transfer).[42] To begin with, the CWC defines 'chemical weapons' as 'toxic chemicals and their precursors, except where intended for purposes not

36 T Meron, *The Humanization of International Law* (Martinus Nijhoff 2006) 9ff.

37 See, for instance, AP I, art 96(2); AP I Commentary, para 3753.

38 Protocol for the Prohibition of the Use of Asphyxiating, Poisonous or Other Gases, and of Bacteriological Methods of Warfare (adopted 17 June 1925, entered into force 8 February 1928) 94 LNTS 65. The prohibition on these weapons had already been re-stated by Article 171 of the Treaty of Versailles *vis-à-vis* Germany, and in other peace treaties in the aftermath of WWI: see <https://ihl-databases.icrc.org/applic/ihl/ihl.nsf/INTRO/280>.

39 Casey-Maslen (n 10) 272.

40 CIHL, rule 74.

41 Convention on the prohibition of the development, production, stockpiling and use of chemical weapons and on their destruction (adopted 13 January 1993, entered into force 29 April 1997) 1974 UNTS 317.

42 CWC, art 1. See Casey-Maslen (n 10) 272; Melzer (n 34) 120.

prohibited', munitions and devices designed to cause death and injury through the toxic properties of the substances above, and other connected equipment.[43] Mortal agents such as nerve agents (sarin, or VX) and blood agents like cyanide – both causing death from suffocation – are included in the definition.[44] Herbicides as a method of warfare are included as well, at least when they amount to chemical weapons.[45]

Among the CWC's strengths, it is important to mention that Article I establishes that the prohibitions apply 'under any circumstances', that is, not only with regard to IAC but also NIAC (where many contemporary abuses, such as Saddam Hussein's use of chemical weapons against the Kurds in 1998 and more recently their use in Syria, have infamously occurred).[46] This is in line with a recent trend towards the gradual overcoming of the differences between rules and principles applicable to IAC and NIAC.[47] Another important innovation is the institution of a body tasked with overseeing the implementation of the CWC, namely the Organisation for the Prohibition of Chemical Weapons (OPCW).[48] The OPCW has been endowed with verification and inspection powers, and it represents – at least in principle – a key tool for ensuring respect for the obligations set forth by the CWC.[49]

As for its weakness, while the use of riot control agents (such as tear gas) is specifically prohibited as a 'method of warfare',[50] an exception is made for law-enforcement purposes, 'including domestic riot control'.[51] In other words, what is prohibited during the conduct of hostilities may be allowed in law-enforcement scenarios. Due to the 'grey areas' between armed conflict and law enforcement – more frequent than ever, in an era characterised by asymmetrical conflicts – the regime established by the CWC may provide unclear

43 CWC, art II.

44 ICRC, 'An effective killer: Five things you need to know about chemical weapons' (9 April 2018) <https://www.icrc.org/en/document/effective-killer-five-things-you-need-know-about-chemical-weapons>.

45 CWC, Preamble; CIHL, rule 76.

46 CWC, art I(1). For more on the situation in Syria, see UNSC Res 2118 (27 September 2013) UN Doc S/RES/2118 (2013); M Sossai, 'Come assicurare la punibilità dell'uso di armi chimiche in Siria?' (2017) 11 Diritti umani e diritto internazionale 419.

47 *Prosecutor v Tadić* (Decision on Defence Motion for Interlocutory Appeal on Jurisdiction) IT-94-1-AR72 (2 October 1995) paras 65–142. See also K Watkin, 'Chemical Agents and "Expanding" Bullets: Limited Law Enforcement Exceptions or Unwarranted Handcuffs?' (2006) 82 Int'l L Studies 196.

48 CWC, art VIII.

49 Melzer (n 34) 120. For a critical assessment of the OPCW's action in Syria, see Casey-Maslen (n 10) 273, and more extensively Sossai (n 47).

50 CWC, art I(5).

51 CWC, art II(9). See also CIHL, rule 75.

guidance, in particular, in cases of internal disturbances of a level of violence that approaches (but does not reach) the threshold of NIAC.[52]

Lastly, it is important to recall that the use of chemical weapons is also a war crime pursuant to the Statute of the International Criminal Court (ICC).[53] In light of all of the above, today, the prohibition on chemical weapons – including, with some disagreement, herbicides – is considered part of customary IHL.[54]

3.2 *Biological Weapons*

As the (sadly still ongoing at the time of writing) SARS-CoV2 pandemic teaches, it is hard to prevent viruses and bacteria from spreading. This demonstrates the inherently indiscriminate nature of biological weapons, whose effects 'cannot be limited' to the legitimate target of an attack.[55] Moreover, biological (or bacteriological) agents contain living organisms that reproduce and release toxins that are dangerous not only to humans but also to animals, plants, and the environment at large.[56]

The first IHL instrument on biological weapons dates back to the 1925 Geneva Protocol.[57] In addition to the previous prohibitions on poison and asphyxiating gases, the Geneva Protocol banned 'bacteriological methods of warfare'; however, the instrument had a limited impact on the reality of warfare, as illustrated above.[58] Immediately after WWII, numerous resolutions and declarations, mostly adopted within the UN framework, restated the prohibition on biological weapons.[59] The subject was also dealt with in the context of proposals for general disarmament but, through the 1950s and 1960s, this remained inconclusive.[60]

52 Watkin (n 48). More extensively, compare N Ronzitti, 'La Convention sur l'interdiction de la mise au point, de la fabrication, du stockage et de l'emploi des armes chimiques et sur leur destruction' (1995) 99 RGDIP 881, and M Pedrazzi, 'The Chemical Weapons Convention and International Humanitarian Law: A Brief Overview of Some Critical Issues', in International Institute of Humanitarian Law, *The Chemical Weapons Convention: Between Disarmament and International Humanitarian Law* (2008).

53 Rome Statute of the International Criminal Court (adopted 17 July 1998, entered into force 1 July 2002) 2187 UNTS 3, arts 8(2)(b)(xviii) and 8(2)(e)(xiv). See ch 32 by Vierucci.

54 CIHL, rules 74–6.

55 AP I, art 51(5)(c).

56 See ch 22 by Saluzzo.

57 See Casey-Maslen (n 10) 272.

58 See *supra* 3.1.

59 CIHL, rule 73.

60 J Goldblat, 'The Biological Weapons Convention – An overview' (1997) 318 IRRC 251.

A major development occurred when, in late 1969, the US unilaterally renounced biological weapons and decided to destroy its entire stockpile. Subsequent negotiations at the Conference of the Committee on Disarmament (CCD) led to the adoption, some 30 years before the CWC, of the Convention on Biological Weapons (BWC).[61] The BWC prohibits the development, production, stockpiling, acquisition and retention of 'microbial or other biological agents, or toxins' in such qualities and quantities that they have no justification for 'peaceful purposes', as well as 'weapons, equipment or means of delivery' designed to spread those agents.[62] Like the CWC, the BWC also prohibits such conduct 'under any circumstances', in a general and *absolute* fashion.[63] Contrary to the CWC, the BWC failed to establish any independent monitoring and verification authority;[64] however, the continuing need to ensure its effectiveness led the parties to adopt subsequent agreements that established, *inter alia*, consultative processes; annual exchanges of information to enhance transparency and build confidence among States; and, eventually, an Implementation Support Unit (ISU).[65]

Admirable though the above prohibitions are, one may question whether they make the BWC effective as an IHL instrument, as at no point is the 'use' of such agents proscribed. As a matter of fact, any reference to the 'use' of biological weapons is confined to the Preamble, where – as befits preambular clauses – it is solemnly proclaimed that the use of such weapons 'would be repugnant to the conscience of mankind'.[66] Preambles are a formidable hermeneutical tool, but they could hardly be used to argue for the existence of obligations that are absent from the text. This major shortcoming has, however, been fixed by the Final Documents of the fourth, sixth and seventh Review Conferences, which affirmed that 'the use by States Parties, in any way and under any circumstances, of [biological agents]' that cannot be justified as above 'is effectively a violation of Article I'.[67] Furthermore, in all cases, it is acknowledged that the use of biological weapons is prohibited by customary

61 Convention on the Prohibition of the Development, Production and Stockpiling of Bacteriological (Biological) and Toxin Weapons and on their Destruction (adopted 16 December 1971, entered into force 26 March 1975).

62 BWC, art I.

63 Ibid.

64 Casey-Maslen (n 10) 273. See also L Vierucci, 'Offensive Military Applications of Biotechnologies: Loopholes in the Law?', in F Francioni (ed), *Biotechnologies and International Human Rights* (Hart Publishing 2007), at 377.

65 BWC Implementation Support Unit, 'Additional agreements reached by previous Review Conferences relating to each article of the Convention' (28 September 2011).

66 BWC, Preamble.

67 'Additional agreements' (n 65) para 8.

IHL.[68] By the same token, as a matter of customary law, the violation of that prohibition amounts to a war crime, even though it was not specifically included in the Statute of the ICC.[69]

Lastly, while it sounds entirely reasonable that the prohibition on biological agents employed as weapons should have no prejudicial effect on the 'peaceful' uses of such agents (eg to produce vaccines, to fight against diseases, to enhance health security), the reality is that it is not that easy to keep permissible ('peaceful') and impermissible ('military') uses of biological agents clearly distinct. One of the major challenges that the BWC is facing right now is how to ban the 'weaponisation' of biological agents without hampering biological research in other fields.[70] All things considered, it appears that an effective regulation of biological hazards can be ensured only through a comprehensive and multi-disciplinary legal approach, going beyond IHL: the point will be further explored below.

3.3 *Nuclear Weapons*

Radiological and nuclear agents are radioactive materials that are ultra hazardous both for humans and for other living organisms. While the former are generated typically as by-products and waste from the mineral processing industries or occur naturally in the environment, the latter are generated from nuclear fission or fusion.[71] This sub-paragraph will tackle nuclear weapons and will leave radiological weapons for later.

When weaponised, nuclear agents bestow an unprecedented power upon their users – a power so destructive that the nuclear bomb conjures up the image of 'the absolute weapon', developed by 'wizards' eager to drag the entire planet to an 'Armageddon' scenario and consign mankind to 'oblivion'.[72] And it was precisely because of the impact that nuclear weapons had on targeted populations and, broadly, on public opinion that the doctrine of nuclear deterrence was born.[73] After the terrifying experiences of Hiroshima and Nagasaki, States, international organisations (first and foremost, the UN) and other

68 CIHL, rule 73.

69 CIHL, rule 156.

70 P Millett, 'The Biological Weapons Convention: Securing Biology in the Twenty-first Century' (2010) 15 Journal of Conflict & Security L 25.

71 ICRC (n 18) 7.

72 B Brodie, *The Absolute Weapon: Atomic Power and World Order* (Harcour, Brance and Company 1972); F Kaplan, *The Wizards of Armageddon* (Stanford University Press 1991); HF York, *Race to Oblivion: A Participant's View of the Arms Race* (Simon and Schuster 1970).

73 D Jordan and ors, *Understanding Modern Warfare* (2nd edition, CUP 2016), 405 ff (explaining historical bases and dynamics of deterrence, with a focus on platforms designed to carry nuclear weapons but intended to avoid their use, instead of incentivising it).

actors (such as the ICRC) strove to prohibit all recourse to such weaponry,[74] beginning by halting nuclear proliferation through an ad hoc binding instrument, the Nuclear Non-Proliferation Treaty (NPT).[75] More recently, the Treaty on the Prohibition on Nuclear Weapons (TPNW) has been adopted with the aim of providing, for the first time in history, a comprehensive ban on nuclear weapons on a global scale.[76]

It is hard to think of a weapon whose use in armed conflict is more likely to fail to discriminate between permissible and impermissible targets, to provoke superfluous injury and unnecessary suffering, and to cause widespread, long-term and severe damage to the natural environment, than nuclear weapons. In sum, nuclear weapons stand in the most stark opposition to IHL rules and principles. One might thus expect a written prohibition on such weapons, clearly spelled out in a binding instrument; yet, and maybe surprisingly, this is not the case.

When the drafting process of Additional Protocol I (AP I) was about to start, the ICRC clearly stated, in its first submission, that 'problems relating to atomic, bacteriological and chemical warfare [would remain the] subject of international agreements or negotiations by governments', thus it was considered more appropriate not to tackle them.[77] Some States – such as the US, the UK, and other NATO Members – understood the rules contained in the Protocols as 'not intended to have effect' on nuclear weapons, as their application was limited to 'conventional' weapons.[78] To an extent, this view was confirmed by scholars who, after surveying customary IHL in depth, were able to conclude, as late as the mid-1980s, that 'the wartime use of nuclear weapons [was] not categorically prohibited under the existing rules of positive international law'.[79]

An important contribution was given by the ICJ in the famous *Nuclear Weapons* case.[80] The ICJ had received two requests to render an Advisory Opinion, from the World Health Organization (WHO) and from the UN General Assembly. The Court declined the former and delivered its opinion only with

74 Boothby (n 10) 215–6.

75 Treaty on the Non-Proliferation of Nuclear Weapons (adopted 1 July 1968, entered into force 5 March 1970) 729 UNTS 169.

76 Treaty on the Prohibition of Nuclear Weapons (adopted 7 July 2017, entered into force 22 January 2021) CN.478.2020.TREATIES-XXVI-9. See M Pedrazzi, 'The Treaty on the Prohibition of Nuclear Weapons: a Promise, a Threat or a Flop?' (2018) 27 Ital YIL 215.

77 Boothby (n 10) 216.

78 Ibid, at 217. More extensively, see J Gaudreau, 'The Reservations to the Protocols Additional to the Geneva Conventions for the Protection of War Victims' (2003) 849 IRRC 143.

79 F Kalshoven, 'Arms, armaments and international law' (1985-II) 191 Recueil des Cours 271.

80 *Legality of the Threat of Use of Nuclear Weapons* (n 21).

regard to the latter.[81] The Opinion is a complex piece of international law, touching upon various issues – *jus ad bellum*, the relationship between IHL and human rights law, even the qualification of the use of nuclear weapons as a crime of genocide – that cannot be discussed here due to space constraints.[82] For our purposes, two key findings – both adopted with the President's casting vote – tackled the use of nuclear weapons in armed conflict. First, the Court found that 'the threat or use of nuclear weapons would *generally* be contrary to the rules of international law applicable in armed conflict, and in particular the principles and rules of humanitarian law'.[83] Second, the Court found that '[h]owever, in view of the current state of international law [...] the Court cannot conclude definitively whether the threat or use of nuclear weapons would be lawful or unlawful in an *extreme* circumstance of self-defence, in which the very survival of a state would be at risk'.[84] Most commentators – both in favour of and against the existence of a customary norm prohibiting nuclear weapons in IHL – have expressed their discomfort *vis-à-vis* this actual *non liquet*.[85]

The Advisory Opinion depicts the proverbial image of an elephant in the room: everyone sees how the use of nuclear weapons contravenes the core rules and principles of IHL, yet States are reluctant to recognise the prohibition in customary law, let alone in treaty instruments. However, a recent and important step forward deserves to be mentioned. As already discussed, the TPNW, which entered into force in January 2021, contains a legal obligation to refrain from using or threatening to use nuclear weapons, which applies also during hostilities.[86] In this sense, the TPNW can be considered not only as a key disarmament treaty but also as an IHL instrument. This contention is also confirmed by the Preamble, where rules and principles applicable to armed conflict are expressly cited. In particular, it is remarkable that reference is made to a bedrock rule of IHL, namely that the right of parties to a conflict to

81 Boothby (n 10) 220.

82 E Louka, *Nuclear Weapons, Justice and The Law* (Edward Elgar Publishing 2011) 308ff. See also D Akande, 'Nuclear Weapons, Unclear Law? Deciphering the Nuclear Weapons Advisory Opinion of the International Court' (1997) 68 BYbIL 165.

83 *Legality of the Threat of Use of Nuclear Weapons* (n 21) para 105(2)(E), italics added.

84 Ibid, italics added.

85 C Greenwood, 'The Advisory Opinion on Nuclear Weapons and the Contribution of the International Court to International Humanitarian Law' (1997) 316 IRRC 65 (arguing that to say that nuclear weapons cannot be used lawfully under any circumstances would be an unwarranted contention); S Casey-Maslen, 'The use of nuclear weapons under rules governing the conduct of hostilities', in G Nystuen, S Casey-Maslen, and A Golden Bersagel (eds), *Nuclear Weapons under International Law* (CUP 2014).

86 TPNW, art 1(1)(d).

choose means and methods of warfare is not unlimited.[87] However, the TPNW, despite having been adopted by a vote of 122 States in favour in 2017 (84 of which are signatories) and ratified by 50 States, is far from enjoying universal support, especially from nuclear weapons States.[88] On the contrary, and quite tellingly, the US has recently engaged in a man-marking tactic to push States that have already ratified the TPNW to withdraw their ratifications.[89] Thus, there is a very real risk of the Treaty being sabotaged and it is highly doubtful that the prohibition on the use of nuclear weapons will make its way into customary IHL any time soon; indeed, even the ICRC was unable to elaborate a customary rule on nuclear weapons.[90]

At the root of such stubborn resistance is that nuclear weapons States want to retain the capabilities to react in self-defence in case of nuclear attack and to employ tactical nuclear weapons. With particular regard to the latter, one may think of equipping missiles with nuclear explosives in order to target submarines or other naval targets located far from civilians and civilian objects, or enemy military installations situated in a desert. While in such scenarios – curiously, taken into account by Judge Schwebel in his separate opinion in the *Nuclear Weapons* case, as an argument for the non-existence of a general prohibition on nuclear weapons under IHL[91] – there would be little risk of using such weaponry in an indiscriminate manner,[92] it must be recalled that nuclear blasts cause long-lasting effects on human health and on the environment. These begin soon after the fireball and the initial release of neutron radiation, and continue with a significant increase of cancer mortality throughout the life of survivors and those who happened to be in the blast radius.[93]

---

87 See n 1.

88 At the regional level, there are treaties containing the prohibition on the use of nuclear weapons in any circumstances. See Treaty for the Prohibition of Nuclear Weapons in Latin America and the Caribbean (Tlatelolco Treaty) (adopted 14 February 1967, entered into force 25 April 1969), reproduced in UN Doc A/6333 (23 February 1967), art 1(1)(a); Treaty on the Southeast Asia Nuclear-Weapon-Free Zone (Bangkok Treaty) (adopted 15 December 1995, entered into force 28 March 1997) 1981 UNTS 129, art 3(1)(c).

89 G Lythgoe, 'Nuclear Weapons and International Law: The Impact of the Treaty on the Prohibition on Nuclear Weapons' (2 December 2020) EJIL: Talk! <https://www.ejiltalk.org/nuclear-weapons-and-international-law-the-impact-of-the-treaty-on-the-prohibition-of-nuclear-weapons/>.

90 ICRC, 'Nuclear Weapons', <https://ihl-databases.icrc.org/customary-ihl/eng/docs/v1_rul_nuwe>.

91 *Legality of the Threat of Use of Nuclear Weapons* (n 21), Separate Opinion of Judge Schwebel at 98.

92 *Legality of the Threat of Use of Nuclear Weapons* (n 21), Written Statement of the United States (20 June 1995) at 23.

93 International Law and Policy Institute and Geneva Academy of International Humanitarian Law and Human Rights, 'Nuclear Weapons Under International Law: An Overview' (October 2014) 5–6.

In sum, while it may be argued that resistance *vis-à-vis* the prohibition of nuclear weapons in *jus ad bellum* may end up reflecting on *jus in bello*, the case can be convincingly made that, from the IHL viewpoint, nuclear weapons – even the most tactical ones – could hardly be used in a lawful way.

3.4 *Radiological Weapons*

In contrast to the attention that scholarship has dedicated to nuclear weapons, far fewer pages have been written on radiological weapons. Explanations for this include, on the one hand, the fact that no treaty has ever been adopted on the topic and, on the other hand, that the weaponisation of radiological agents is not at the top of the list of priorities of States' departments of defence.

As a matter of fact, discussions on radiological weapons were started by the then Committee (today Commission) on Disarmament back in 1979, with the inclusion of 'radioactive material weapons' in the definition of WMD.[94] At that time, the US and the USSR were negotiating a treaty prohibiting the development, production, stockpiling and use (merging, as usual, disarmament and IHL perspectives) of radiological weapons, understood as any device other than nuclear explosives that is capable of disseminating radioactive material.[95] Due to disagreements relating to the object and scope of the treaty, as well as to the definition of radiological weapons, the proposal was eventually dropped. After the 9/11 attack, a last attempt was made at reviving the issue in the Commission on Disarmament, but with limited success.[96]

A combination of radiological and chemical agents is present in depleted uranium (DU), which is the by-product of the manufacture of enriched uranium from uranium ore. According to some States, DU weapons can be regarded as strategic weapons with limited impact on health and environment due to their limited radiation hazard. For instance, the US Air Force considers that its proportional use does not violate relevant IHL.[97] On the opposite side, it has been argued that DU weapons' effects have to be evaluated against the precautionary principle, to the point that, even if their negative impact on human life and environment is scientifically uncertain, their use may be limited nonetheless.[98]

94 Report of the Committee on Disarmament (9 October 1979) A/RES/34/27 at 17.

95 J Herbach, 'The Evolution of Legal Approaches to Controlling Nuclear and Radiological Weapons and Combating the Threat of Nuclear Terrorism' (2014) 17 Yb IHL 45, 61.

96 Ibid 61–2.

97 Boothby (n 10) 243.

98 L Wexler, 'Limiting the Precautionary Principle: Weapons Regulation in the Face of Scientific Uncertainty' (2006) 39 UC Davis LR 459.

DU weapons aside, no State has been known to develop radiological weapons for use in armed conflict. Rather, as technically speaking radiological agents can be efficiently employed to build a so-called 'dirty bomb' (where conventional explosives are used to detonate the bomb and provoke the release of radiation), such technology is believed to be more attractive to terrorist groups.[99] While this could suggest that this topic would be better dealt with in other fields of international law (such as the use of force against non-State actors), it is important to recall that non-State groups engaged in NIAC – commonly referred to as 'organised armed groups' – are under the obligation to respect relevant IHL norms. Even though Article 3 common to the Geneva Conventions and the Second Additional Protocol to them do not contain any provisions on the use of specific weapons in NIAC, the 'cardinal principles' discussed above (distinction and the SIrUS rule above all), which are of a customary nature, continue to govern the law applicable on weapons even absent a specific treaty.[100] This is confirmed also by the International Criminal Tribunal for the former Yugoslavia in a key passage in the *Tadić* case: '[w]hat is inhumane, and consequently proscribed, in international wars cannot but be inhumane and inadmissible in civil strife'.[101]

Against this background, any use of radiological weapons – in the most known forms of DU weapons or 'dirty bombs' – is actually regulated by existing IHL, namely by rules and principles that apply generally to all kinds of armed conflict. The absence of specific treaty provisions on them, commensurate with the scarce State practice of employing such weapons, does not affect that general regulation. It may be true that radiological weapons are likely to raise less alarming issues than nuclear weapons, but parties in a conflict that decide to resort to them remain bound by IHL.

4 How to Address Future Technologies in the Field of CBRN Weapons?

Our journey across the 'four quadrants' of CBRN weapons may appear fragmented: each agent, when turned into a weapon, is subject to a specific set of rules. However, the analysis above has shown that this might be true only *prima facie*. On closer inspection, those weapons are regulated by rules and principles constituting the 'bedrock' norms of IHL, such as the principle of

99 Ibid.

100 Melzer (n 34) 128.

101 *Prosecutor v Tadić* (n 48) para 119.

distinction and the prohibition on the use of indiscriminate weapons and those causing superfluous injury or unnecessary suffering. Those norms came to the fore not only with regard to weapons that are not *per se* prohibited or limited by dedicated legal instruments (eg nuclear and radiological weapons), but also with regard to weapons that treaty and customary IHL have prohibited, or significantly limited, for decades now (eg chemical and biological weapons). In sum, there are norms providing interpreters with basic coordinates to navigate safely through all four quadrants.

These same coordinates are all the more needed when sailing the waters of emerging military technologies. Current scientific research is making tremendous progress in CBRN-related technologies. Just to give a few examples, one may think of nanotechnology and, more generally, synthetic biology, which study how to 'assemble' natural and synthetic materials to engineer functional organisms.[102] Advances in the field of biochemistry make it possible to develop non- or less-lethal agents to be employed as weapons. Along the same lines, another emerging (and promising) field of research relates to microfluidics and nanofluidics, which allow for enhanced control over potentially ultra-hazardous reactions (that occur on a microscopic scale).[103] Little to no attention has been dedicated to such advances, from either a disarmament or IHL perspective.

In light of this, and bringing the discussion to a more general level, the question remains on how IHL regulates new technologies, that is, weapons that do not (apparently) fit in existing legal categories. A mainstream approach to new technologies is to present – and thus study – them as if they were something of a totally unprecedented nature: the newness of a weapon, or a weapon system, is believed to be enough to justify dedicating many time and energy-consuming pages. However, to the siren song of those who predict legal 'singularities' (that is, the impossibility of adopting legal categories as we know them) with respect to new military technology (for instance, technology associated with the exponential development of autonomous weaponry),[104] this writer prefers remaining lashed to the mast of the ship, that is, to stick with the existing norms of IHL – even when ploughing the waters of CBRN-related technologies.

102 H Nasu, 'Nanotechnology and the Future of the Law of Weaponry' (2015) 91 Int'l L Stud 486.

103 C Jabbari and PC Bleek, 'Honey, I Shrunk the Lab: Emerging Microfluidics Technology and its Implications for Chemical, Biological, and Nuclear Weapons' (May 2019) Emergence & Convergence Research Paper No 5 1.

104 B Kastan, 'Autonomous Weapons Systems: A Coming Legal "Singularity"' (2013) Journal of Law, Technology and Policy 45.

As a matter of fact, applying existing rules to the development of new technology is a core provision of IHL, namely Article 36 AP I, which establishes the obligation to conduct a legal review of new weapons:

> In the study, development, acquisition or adoption of a new weapon, means or method of warfare, a High Contracting Party is under an obligation to determine whether its employment would, in some or all circumstances, be prohibited by this Protocol or by any other rule of international law applicable to the High Contracting Party.[105]

While the issue of whether Article 36 corresponds to customary IHL still remains open,[106] the fact that, today, AP I counts on 174 signatory parties renders the obligation to conduct a legal review of new weapons almost universal in scope. This obligation presents several strengths. Firstly, it covers different phases of weapons manufacture and procurement (ranging from the 'study' to the 'adoption' thereof), which may be relevant, for instance, if a particular weapon is developed by private actors (typically companies operating as defence contractors): in this case, the State is under an obligation to ensure that those actors act in compliance with applicable norms. Secondly, the rules against which new weapons are to be assessed encompass those contained in AP I and IHL in general, including the core rules on distinction, proportionality, precautions in attack, but also the principle of humanity.[107] Article 36's scope is even broader than this, as it also covers other international norms applicable to the State under scrutiny. This is of particular importance *vis-à-vis* CBRN weapons, as CBRN agents and events are regulated by disparate branches of international law (from disarmament and arms control to human rights and environmental law). States are, therefore, under a duty to take into account all these other norms when developing CBRN weapons.

If 'taken seriously', Article 36 AP I provides States with a unique device for testing the compatibility of new CBRN capabilities with international law at large. Engaging with comprehensive, multi-disciplinary and integrated legal

105 AP I, art 36.

106 N Jevglevskaja, 'Weapons Review Obligation under Customary International Law' (2018) 94 Int'l L Stud 186 (concluding negatively).

107 I Daoust, R Coupland and R Ishoey, 'New wars, new weapons? The obligation of States to assess the legality of means and methods of warfare' (2002) 84 IRRC 345. As for the principle of humanity, see *Legality of the Threat of Use of Nuclear Weapons* (n 21), particularly paras 86–7 (affirming that the Martens Clause 'has proved to be an effective means of addressing the rapid evolution of military technology' and refuting the argument whereby 'new' technologies would escape the application of IHL).

reviews of CBRN weapons may thus incentivise respect for other international norms and, indirectly, also favour prevention, preparedness, response and recovery *vis-à-vis* CBRN events in general, not only in the battlefield. For all these reasons, the fact that, as has been lamented for years now, only few States carry out legal reviews pursuant to Article 36 is disheartening.[108] However, it is worth noting that the duty to conduct legal reviews of weapons has been gaining momentum recently, especially in the debates around autonomous weapons systems (AWS).[109] Within the framework of the CCW, several meetings of experts have been convened in recent years to discuss the implications related to the development and deployment of AWS. One of the cornerstones that virtually all States and other involved actors agree upon is that such next-generation weaponry has to be reviewed to ensure compliance with international law, and IHL in particular.[110] Article 36 obligations are held to be key to ensuring that technological advances in various fields comply with IHL.[111]

Extending these remarks to our field, revitalising the duty to conduct legal reviews of new weapons may prove beneficial for CBRN security. An important step forward could be for States to implement domestic measures to undertake legal reviews of new weapons and to disseminate results, with a view not only to sharing information on procedures and mechanisms but also – and more importantly – facilitating cooperation among States in the CBRN field.

5 Concluding Remarks

Through the above analysis, the present chapter has managed to demonstrate three main arguments, in ascending order of relevance. First, it makes sense to speak in terms of 'CBRN weapons': while the notion does not exist in IHL, the agents' properties are such that a unitary label is conceptually founded. Second, when turned into weapons, CBRN agents are governed by a wide spectrum of IHL norms, both treaty and customary. The historical trend of

108 ICRC (n 11).

109 For more information, see <https://www.un.org/disarmament/the-convention-on-certain-conventional-weapons/background-on-laws-in-the-ccw/>.

110 Group of Governmental Experts of the High Contracting Parties to the Convention on Prohibitions or Restrictions on the Use of Certain Conventional Weapons Which May Be Deemed to Be Excessively Injurious or to Have Indiscriminate Effects, 'Report of the 2019 session of the Group of Governmental Experts on Emerging Technologies in the Area of Lethal Autonomous Weapons Systems', 25 September 2019, CCW/GGE.1/2019/3 Annex IV lit e).

111 W Boothby, 'Dehumanization: Is There a Legal Problem Under Article 36?', in W Heintschel von Heinegg, R Frau and T Singer (eds), *Dehumanization of Warfare. Legal Implications of New Weapon Technologies* (Springer 2018).

limiting – in some cases, prohibiting – the weapons that may be used in armed conflict, which characterises IHL, is confirmed by existing rules and principles applicable to CBRN weapons. Third, IHL is part of a larger set of norms dealing with CBRN-related risks. Certainly, IHL provides an effective legal framework for addressing CBRN events occurring in (at least) one specific domain, that is, the battlefield. While one may argue that the scope of this branch of international law is inherently limited – after all, it deals solely with armed conflicts – it has been noted, with respect to all four agents, that touchpoints between IHL and other branches are recurring. The need for a multi-faceted approach is confirmed also by those obligations expressly requiring States to take into consideration other rules and principles of international law, for instance, when manufacturing or procuring new weapons, means or methods of warfare, pursuant to Article 36 AP I. All in all, this chapter's main findings confirm the key intuition lying at the very basis of the entire book: against any logic of strict compartmentalisation, only a comprehensive and integrated legal approach to CBRN events is adequate for coping with the complexities – and the dangers – associated with such matters.

Bibliography

Akande D, 'Nuclear Weapons, Unclear Law? Deciphering the Nuclear Weapons Advisory Opinion of the International Court' (1997) 68 BYbIL 165.

Alexander A, 'A Short History of International Humanitarian Law' (2015) 26 EJIL 109.

Boothby W, 'Dehumanization: Is There a Legal Problem Under Article 36?', in W Heintschel von Heinegg, R Frau and T Singer (eds), *Dehumanization of Warfare. Legal Implications of New Weapon Technologies* (Springer 2018).

Boothby W, *Weapons and the Law of Armed Conflict* (OUP 2009).

Casey-Maslen S, 'Weapons', in B Saul and D Akande, *The Oxford Guide to International Humanitarian Law* (OUP 2020).

Casey-Maslen S, 'The use of nuclear weapons under rules governing the conduct of hostilities', in G Nystuen, S Casey-Maslen, and A Golden Bersagel (eds), *Nuclear Weapons under International Law* (CUP 2014).

Cassese A, 'The Martens Clause: Half a Loaf or Simply Pie in the Sky?' (2000) 11 EJIL 187.

Coupland R and Herby P, 'Review of the Legality of Weapons: A New Approach. The SIrUS Project' (1999) 81 IRRC 583.

Daoust I, Coupland R and Ishoey R, 'New wars, new weapons? The obligation of States to assess the legality of means and methods of warfare' (2002) 84 IRRC 345.

Gaudreau J, 'The Reservations to the Protocols Additional to the Geneva Conventions for the Protection of War Victims' (2003) 849 IRRC 143.

Goldblat J, 'The Biological Weapons Convention – An overview' (1997) 318 IRRC 251.

Greenwood C, 'The Advisory Opinion on Nuclear Weapons and the Contribution of the International Court to International Humanitarian Law' (1997) 316 IRRC 65.

Haines S, 'The Developing Law of Weapons. Humanity, Distinction and Precautions in Attack', in A Clapham and P Gaeta (eds), *The Oxford Handbook of International Law in Armed Conflict* (OUP 2014).

Henckaerts JM and Doswald-Beck L (eds), *Customary International Humanitarian Law* (CUP 2005).

Herbach J, 'The Evolution of Legal Approaches to Controlling Nuclear and Radiological Weapons and Combating the Threat of Nuclear Terrorism' (2014) 17 Yb IHL 45.

ICRC, 'A Guide to the Legal Review of New Weapons, Means and Methods of Warfare: Measures to Implement Article 36 of Additional Protocol I of 1977' (Geneva, 2006).

Jabbari C and Bleek PC, 'Honey, I Shrunk the Lab: Emerging Microfluidics Technology and its Implications for Chemical, Biological, and Nuclear Weapons' (May 2019) Emergence & Convergence Research Paper No 5 1.

Jevglevskaja N, 'Weapons Review Obligation under Customary International Law' (2018) 94 Int'l L Stud 186.

Jordan D and ors, *Understanding Modern Warfare* (2nd edition, CUP 2016).

Kalshoven F, 'Arms, armaments and international law' (1985-II) 191 Recueil des Cours 271.

Kastan B, 'Autonomous Weapons Systems: A Coming Legal "Singularity"' (2013) Journal of Law, Technology and Policy 45.

Louka E, *Nuclear Weapons, Justice and The Law* (Edward Elgar Publishing 2011).

McCoubrey H, *International Humanitarian Law. Modern Development in the Limitation of Warfare* (2nd ed, Routledge 2019).

Melzer N, *International Humanitarian Law. A Comprehensive Introduction* (coordinated by E Kuster) (ICRC 2016).

Meron T, *The Humanization of International Law* (Martinus Nijhoff 2006).

Millett P, 'The Biological Weapons Convention: Securing Biology in the Twenty-first Century' (2010) 15 Journal of Conflict & Security L 25.

Nasu H, 'Nanotechnology and the Future of the Law of Weaponry' (2015) 91 Int'l L Stud 486.

O'Connell ME, 'Historical Development and Legal Basis', in D Fleck (ed), *The Handbook of International Humanitarian Law* (2nd ed, OUP 2013).

Pedrazzi M, 'The Chemical Weapons Convention and International Humanitarian Law: A Brief Overview of Some Critical Issues', in International Institute of Humanitarian Law, *The Chemical Weapons Convention: Between Disarmament and International Humanitarian Law* (2008).

Pedrazzi M, 'The Treaty on the Prohibition of Nuclear Weapons: a Promise, a Threat or a Flop?' (2018) 27 Ital YIL 215.

Ronzitti N, 'La Convention sur l'interdiction de la mise au point, de la fabrication, du stockage et de l'emploi des armes chimiques et sur leur destruction' (1995) 99 RGDIP 881.

Sandoz Y, Swinarski C, and Zimmermann B (eds), *Commentary on the Additional Protocols of 8 June 1977 to the Geneva Conventions of 12 August 1949*.

Schmitt, 'International Humanitarian Law and the Conduct of Hostilities', in B Saul and D Akande, *The Oxford Guide to International Humanitarian Law* (OUP 2020).

Sossai M, 'Come assicurare la punibilità dell'uso di armi chimiche in Siria?' (2017) 11 Diritti umani e diritto internazionale 419.

Vierucci L, 'Offensive Military Applications of Biotechnologies: Loopholes in the Law?', in F Francioni (ed), *Biotechnologies and International Human Rights* (Hart Publishing 2007).

Wallach W, *A Dangerous Master. How to Keep Technology from Slipping Beyond Our Control* (Basic Books 2015).

Watkin K, 'Chemical Agents and "Expanding" Bullets: Limited Law Enforcement Exceptions or Unwarranted Handcuffs?' (2006) 82 Int'l L Studies 196.

Wexler L, 'Limiting the Precautionary Principle: Weapons Regulation in the Face of Scientific Uncertainty' (2006) 39 UC Davis LR 459.

CHAPTER 22

CBRN Weapons and the Protection of the Environment during Armed Conflicts

Stefano Saluzzo

1 Introduction

During the Vietnam War, more than 20 million gallons of herbicides were sprayed over the Vietnamese rain forests, wetlands and croplands. The campaign, aimed at destroying food resources and depriving the enemy of concealment, was initially started at the request of the South Vietnamese Government and then turned into a US White House programme under the name of Operation Ranch Hand. Within the latter, the US developed the well-known Agent Orange, a dioxin-contaminated herbicide capable of defoliating thick jungle vegetation.[1] A recent study has investigated the long-lasting effects of the dioxin used during the Vietnam War and how it is still affecting soils, water, sediment, fish, aquatic species, the food supply, and Vietnamese health.[2] The environmental legacy of Agent Orange could potentially last for decades or even centuries.

The connection between the use of CBRN weapons and the role of international humanitarian law (IHL) in protecting the environment is not expressed in clear terms in the rules applicable to armed conflicts. Nonetheless, the use of Agent Orange in Vietnam represents one of the key moments in history that led to the drafting of these rules,[3] together with the threat posed by nuclear

1 See P Sills, *Toxic War – The Story of Agent Orange* (Vanderbilt University Press 2014); AL Young, *The History, Use, Disposition and Environmental Fate of Agent Orange* (Springer 2009) 57.

2 KR Olson and LW Morton, 'Long-Term Fate of Agent Orange and Dioxin TCDD Contaminated Soils and Sediments in Vietnam Hotspots' (2019) 9(1) *Open Journal of Soil Science* 1. Other studies recently demonstrated the long-term environmental effects of mustard gas and other chemical agents employed during WWII. See P Vanninen *et al* 'Exposure status of sea-dumped chemical warfare agents in the Baltic Sea' (2020) 161 *Marine Environmental Research* 105112.

3 In 1969, the UN General Assembly adopted a resolution widening the scope of the 1925 Geneva Gas Protocol and recognising it as part of international customary law. UNGA Res 2603 A (1969) GAOR 24th session Supp 30, 16. Nevertheless, all actions brought before US courts to claim damages deriving from the use of Agent Orange have been dismissed, on the

weapons during the Cold War. In 1976, the Conference on Disarmament adopted the Convention on the Prohibition of Military or Any Hostile Use of Environmental Modification Techniques (ENMOD), while the Diplomatic Conference on the Reaffirmation and Development of International Humanitarian Law (1974–1977) was able to reach an agreement on the introduction of certain rules on environmental protection within the newly adopted text of Additional Protocol I (AP I) to the Geneva Conventions.

It is worth recalling that, throughout history, environmental damage has been an inherent element of any armed conflict, not necessarily linked to the use of specific weapons.[4] The present chapter will deal exclusively with environmental damage arising out of the use of CBRN weapons and it does not aim at addressing all the problems related to environmental protection in armed conflicts.

The aim of the present chapter is to understand the extent to which the rules on environmental protection in armed conflicts could provide a further layer of restrictions on the use of CBRN weapons. Moreover, the chapter addresses the relevance of international environmental law (IEL) principles that could provide a more detailed regulation of the different phases of a CBRN event occurring during an armed conflict.

2 The Provisions on Environmental Protection during Armed Conflicts

For quite a long time, the law of armed conflict (LOAC) paid little if no attention to environmental issues arising from war. Whether damage to the environment was directly intentional (with the aim of gaining a specific military advantage) or caused indirectly by the hostilities (as a type of collateral damage), it was never addressed by any rules on armed conflict until the seventies. Even instruments dealing with chemical weapons, such as the Geneva Gas Protocol of 1925, were not based on environmental concerns.[5]

---

ground that at the time no prohibition on the use of herbicides existed in the law of armed conflict. See eg United States Court of Appeals for the Second District, *Vietnam Association for Victims of Agent Orange*, 05-1953-cv, judgment of 22 February 2008.

4 See J Wyatt, 'Law-Making at the Intersection of International Environmental, Humanitarian and Criminal Law: the Issue of Damage to the Environment in International Armed Conflicts' (2010) 92 *IRRC* 596–598.

5 Even more recent international instruments, such as the 1972 Biological Weapons Convention or the 1993 Chemical Weapons Convention do not mention the protection of the environment as one of their main objectives.

The first set of rules expressly dealing with the protection of the environment was introduced in the 1977 AP I to the Geneva Conventions, regulating international armed conflicts, together with the adoption of the ENMOD Convention in 1976. These two frameworks follow a common pattern, although with major differences as to the scope of protection provided therein.

2.1 *Additional Protocol I and the ENMOD Convention*

Under Article 35 AP I, devoted to the basic rules on choice of means and methods of warfare,[6] paragraph 3 forbids the parties 'to employ methods or means of warfare which are intended, or may be expected, to cause widespread, long-term and severe damage to the natural environment'. The provision is to be read in conjunction with Article 55(1) AP I, expressly dealing with the protection of the environment:

> Care shall be taken in warfare to protect the natural environment against widespread, long-term and severe damage. This protection includes a prohibition of the use of methods or means of warfare which are intended or may be expected to cause such damage to the natural environment and thereby to prejudice the health or survival of the population.

Moreover, under Article 55(2) AP I, attacks against the environment by means of reprisals are equally prohibited. During the Diplomatic Conference that led to the adoption of AP I, concerns were raised against having two provisions of almost identical content; however, an attempt to incorporate Article 35(3) into Article 55 failed: while Article 55 was dealing with the protection of the natural environment, Article 35 was dealing with the prohibition of unnecessary suffering.[7]

Whereas the provisions enshrined in AP I only apply to international armed conflict, the prohibitions deriving from the ENMOD Convention apply in both times of peace and times of war. The Convention requires States Parties 'not to engage in military or any other hostile use of environmental modification techniques having widespread, long-lasting or severe effects as the means of destruction, damage or injury to any other State Party' (Article I) and forbids 'any technique for changing – through the deliberate manipulation of natural

6 On choice of means and methods of warfare in relation to CBRN weapons, see ch 21 by Mauri.

7 See Official Records of the Diplomatic Conference on the Reaffirmation and Development of International Humanitarian Law Applicable in Armed Conflicts, CDDH/III/GT/35, 3 para. 11. See also J de Preux, 'Protocol I – Article 35' in Y Sandoz, C Swinarski and B Zimmermann (eds.), *Commentary on the Additional Protocols of 8 June 1977 to the Geneva Conventions of 12 August 1949* (ICRC/Martinus Nijhoff Publishers 1987) 414 (para 1449).

processes – the dynamics, composition or structure of the Earth, including its biota, lithosphere, hydrosphere and atmosphere, or of outer space' (Article II).

Notwithstanding the similar phrasing on environmental protection and the threshold of damage, the protection offered by the two instruments is quite different. In fact, ENMOD requires 'widespread, long-lasting *or* severe' damage and it is thus sufficient for a State's behaviour to meet alternatively one of the three criteria to be considered illegal. On the contrary, the three criteria in AP I are jointly considered as cumulative.[8] This difference determines different scopes of application of the two sets of rules. While, on the one hand, the rules in AP I have a wider scope in terms of the types of conduct covered, as they do not refer specifically to certain techniques, the threshold of damage triggering their application is certainly higher than the one set forth by the ENMOD Convention.[9] As we will see, the need to assess the entirety of the damage caused by CBRN events and weapons is essential to the application of the AP I rules to them.[10]

Finally, an additional protection from CBRN events during armed conflict might be found in Article 56 AP I, prohibiting attacks against works and installations that may release dangerous forces, such as nuclear power stations or chemical factories. Although the provision refers expressly to the consequences such a release may have for the civilian population, the prohibition can also be construed in terms of an indirect environmental protection.[11] Furthermore, such protection would not be subject to the strict requirements set forth by the above-mentioned rules of AP I.

2.2 *Customary Law*

In the *Nuclear Weapons* Advisory Opinion, the International Court of Justice (ICJ) referred to IHL rules on environmental protection as 'powerful constraints for all the States having subscribed to these provisions'.[12] The statement casts some doubt as to whether the prohibition of environmental damage during armed conflict could have reached the status of customary law.[13] However,

8 M Bothe, C Bruch, J Diamond and D Jensen, 'International law protecting the environment during armed conflict: gaps and opportunities' (2010) 92 *IRRC* 572.

9 See E David, *Principes de droit des conflits armés* (Bruylant 2012) 351.

10 See Section 4 below.

11 S Oeter, 'Methods and Means of Combat' in D Fleck (ed), *The Handbook of International Humanitarian Law* (Oxford University Press 2013) 216.

12 ICJ, *Legality of the Threat or Use of Nuclear Weapons* (Advisory Opinion) [1996], para 31. The ICJ instead recognised the customary nature of certain principles of international environmental law, in particular referring to the *Trail Smelter* principle (para 29).

13 See J Gaudreau, 'The reservations to the Protocols additional to the Geneva Conventions for the protection of war victims' (2003) 849 *IRRC* 143.

several efforts have been made with the aim of recognising the customary nature of IHL rules on the environment.

First of all, the International Committee of the Red Cross (ICRC) has confirmed that the relevant principles on the conduct of hostilities apply also to the environment, even extending the scope of the original rules enshrined in AP I. Aware of the fact that during an armed conflict the environment could easily be affected by the hostilities, Rule 43 of the *Study on Customary Law* establishes that no part of the natural environment can be attacked, unless it is a military objective, thus confirming the civilian nature of the environment.[14] The protection is further strengthened by reference to the principles of military necessity and proportionality, that must be applied in assessing the legitimacy of armed force used against the environment.[15] Rule 45 confirms the customary nature of the provision enshrined in Article 35 of AP I, also specifying that the destruction of the environment may not be used as a weapon. The ICRC's study has layered a double level of protection for the natural environment in Rule 45, joining the specific provisions of Article 35 and of the ENMOD Convention with the general principles on the conduct of hostilities.[16] Finally, an innovative perspective has been taken in drafting Rule 44, which draws upon the precautionary principle of Article 57 AP I and entails certain features inspired by IEL.

Quite a different approach is to be found in the work of the International Law Commission (ILC) on the protection of the environment in relation to armed conflict, which resulted in the drafting of 28 principles adopted at first reading in 2019.[17] The work is based on a careful assessment of the interplay of IHL with other fields of international law, especially human rights and IEL,[18] thus offering a complementary legal framework to the work of the ICRC.[19]

The identification of customary rules plays an essential role also in relation to non-international armed conflict, especially because Additional Protocol II does not contain any reference to environmental protection.[20]

14 See Rule 43(A). See also Bothe/Brunch/Diamond/Jensen (n 8) 576–577.

15 Rule 43(B) and 43(C).

16 See, however, Wyatt (n 4) 613 (fn 95).

17 See ILC 'Report of the International Law Commission, Seventy-first Session' UN Doc A/74/10 (2019) (ILC 71st Session Report) 208–296.

18 See M Lehto, 'Armed conflicts and the environment: The International Law Commission's new draft principles' (2020) 29 *Review of European, Comparative and International Environmental Law* 69.

19 ILC, 'Text of the draft principles on Protection of the environment in relation to armed conflicts and commentaries thereto', in ILC 71st Session Report 215, Introduction, para 3.

20 An indirect protection for the environment could be derived by rules on the conduct of hostilities mirroring those provided for in AP I. See J Pretorius, 'Enhancing Environmental Protection in Non-International Armed Conflict: The Way Forward' (2018) 78 ZaöRV 903.

The ICRC Commentary to the *Study on Customary Law* affirms that the principle of due regard for the environment 'applies in non-international armed conflicts if there are effects in another State'.[21] As to the rules on choice of means and methods that may affect the environment, their application in non-international armed conflicts is still subject to debate.[22]

3 Interactions between International Environmental Law and the LOAC

The development of IEL in the seventies was certainly a major factor in introducing environmental considerations into the LOAC. As early as 1969, the UN General Assembly made an effort to extend the scope of the 1925 Gas Protocol to 'chemical or biological agents of warfare intended to cause disease in or have effect on man, animals or plants'.[23] The awareness of the natural environment's fragility in armed conflict was also recognised at the Stockholm conference of 1972, with Principle 22 calling for international cooperation to further develop the law on liability for environmental damage and, more importantly, Principle 26 recognising that '[m]an and his environment must be spared the effects of nuclear weapons and all other means of mass destruction'.[24]

In addition, a major issue is to what extent IEL rules and principles can be applied during an armed conflict.[25] The general trend of extending the applicability of peacetime international law instruments to armed conflict has involved IEL as well.[26] However, defining the scope of application of such rules and principles may prove particularly complex. Firstly, it will depend on the provisions of the treaty itself and on their interpretation; secondly, it might be subject to the general rules on the law of treaties, especially on suspension (or termination) of international agreements; finally, once established that a

21 The argument would be supported by the applicability in armed conflicts of general principles of IEL. See J-M Henckaerts and L Doswald-Beck, *Customary International Humanitarian Law – Volume I: Rules* (Cambridge University Press 2009) 148–149.

22 Ibid 156–157.

23 General Assembly Resolution 2603 (XXIV) of 16 December 1969, 24th Session, 1836th plenary meeting.

24 Declaration of the United Nations Conference on the Human Environment, 16 June 1972, 1972 UNYB 319, ('Stockholm Declaration').

25 The content of rules and principles of IEL is beyond the scope of this chapter. For a detailed overview, see ch 34 by Capone in this volume.

26 See in this regard also the Rio Declaration on Environment and Development, 13 June 1992, UN Doc. A/CONF.151/26, Vol. I, Principle 24.

certain rule of IEL applies to the armed conflict, the relationship of that rule with other IHL rules must be established.[27]

A general principle in this regard was adopted by the ILC in 2008 in its work on the effects of armed conflicts on treaties.[28] Under Draft Article 3, the existence of an armed conflict 'does not *ipso iure* terminate or suspend the operation of treaties as between States parties to the conflict and as between a State party to the conflict and a State that is not'.[29] Based on this premise, the continuity of IEL agreements during armed conflicts will have to be determined on a case-by-case analysis, in light of both objective and subjective elements.

The object and purpose of a specific treaty on environmental protection may provide guidance as to its applicability during armed conflict, whenever the intention of the parties does not expressly exclude it.[30] However, although certain international environmental agreements contain provisions confirming their continuing application directly or indirectly,[31] most of them remain silent on the issue.[32]

As far as the subjective application is concerned, international environmental rules may continue to regulate the relationships between belligerent and non-belligerent States. Since the law of neutrality plays a key role in granting to non-belligerent States the right not to be adversely affected by the conflict, the legal relationships between a belligerent State and a neutral State are governed by the law of peace.[33] In relation to the use of nuclear weapons

27 Bothe/Brunch/Diamond/Jensen (n 8) 579–580.

28 ILC, Effects of Armed Conflicts on Treaties, UN Doc. A/CN.4/L.727/Rev.1, 6 June 2008.

29 The ILC hereby confirmed the approach already adopted by the *Institut de droit international* in 1985 during the Helsinki session. See *Institut de droit international*, Yearbook, vol. 61, Part II (1985), 278.

30 See art 9 Convention on Third Party Liability in the Field of Nuclear Energy (1960, amended 1964).

31 See, for instance, art 236 of the UN Convention on the Law of the Sea. See also International Institute of Humanitarian Law, *San Remo Manual on International Law Applicable to Armed Conflict at Sea* (Cambridge University Press 1995), paras 34–35. In the context of the conflict between Iraq and Iran, the Security Council required all belligerents to 'refrain from any action that may endanger peace and security as well as marine life in the region of the Gulf'. See UNSC Res 540 (31 October 1983), para 5.

32 Examples include the Convention on Biological Diversity (1992), the UN Convention to Combat Desertification (1994) and the Convention on the Conservation of Migratory Species of Wild Animals (1979). For a detailed analysis of IEL agreements that may be considered applicable in armed conflicts, see S Vöneky, 'A New Shield for the Environment: Peacetime Treaties as Legal Restraints of Wartime Damage' (2000) 9 *RECIEL* 20.

33 M Bothe, 'The Law of Neutrality' in D Fleck (ed), *The Handbook of International Humanitarian Law* (Oxford University Press 2013) 549.

during an armed conflict, the ICJ highlighted the relevance of the law of neutrality while recalling that 'the principle of neutrality applies with equal force to transborder incursions of armed forces and to the transborder damage caused to a neutral State by the use of a weapon in a belligerent State'.[34] Accordingly, a non-belligerent State could expect a State participating in a conflict to comply with its environmental obligations and invoke the consequences attached to an internationally wrongful act in the event of a breach.[35]

Different considerations concern customary principles of environmental law. Certain principles might be deemed applicable even during an armed conflict, due to their formulation or related State practice. An example is offered by the so-called *Trail Smelter* principle, requiring States not to allow the use of their territory to harm the territory of other States.[36] The preventive obligations encapsulated in the principle may afford protection to neutral States in case of environmental damage deriving from the hostilities conducted on the territory of the parties to the conflict,[37] as foreseen by the ICJ in the *Nuclear Weapons* advisory opinion.[38] In such context, the applicability of customary principles on environmental protection would also be confirmed by reference to the Martens Clause, which has formed part of the LOAC since the 1899 II Hague Convention.[39]

This leads to a final question, regarding the precise scope of interaction between the rules of IHL and those of IEL. It has been claimed that, even once the applicability of IEL obligations during an armed conflict has been accepted in principle, it could be difficult to resort to the *lex specialis* criterion to determine the exact relationship between the two sets of rules. The LOAC is generally considered special as regards other rules of international law. Some commentators have questioned this construction in relation to IEL rules, the

34 ICJ, *Nuclear Weapons*, para 88, quoting the written statement of the Government of Nauru (p. 35) in the advisory proceeding on *Legality of the Use by a State of Nuclear Weapons in Armed Conflict*.

35 With the only exceptions being suspension or termination of a treaty by means of the *rebus sic stantibus* clause or by conduct justified under a state of necessity.

36 *United States v. Canada*, 3 RIAA 1907 (1941).

37 Bothe/Brunch/diamond/Jensen (n 8) 585. See the example of the law of occupation in Draft Principle 22 ('Due Diligence') of the ILC's work on Protection of the environment in relation to armed conflicts.

38 ICJ, *Nuclear Weapons*, para 29.

39 The Martens Clause is often recalled as a legal basis for the application of fundamental rights in armed conflict. See David (n 9) 94–95; A Cassese, 'The Martens Clause: Half a Loaf or Simply Pie in the Sky' (2000) 11 *EJIL* 212.

latter being special as well, in relation to environmental concerns not specifically addressed by IHL.[40]

However, the *lex specialis* criterion is relevant only to address concrete and specific normative conflicts, that is, when a material case is regulated by two conflicting rules. In the scenario where IHL rules do not provide an answer to certain aspects of environmental damage occurring in armed conflict, one could resort to rules and principles of IEL as a complementary tool. If, for instance, consequences of an environmental damage are not regulated by IHL, elements such as remedial duties and liability might be regulated by IEL. This is particularly evident when considering that IHL rules on the conduct of hostilities are mostly preventive in nature and do not address the material and legal consequences of environmental damage. As regards CBRN events occurring in armed conflicts, while obligations of prevention will mainly flow from the rules of IHL on the conduct of hostilities, other phases of the disaster management cycle will fall under the authority of the applicable rules of international law.[41]

4 The Damage Threshold

Most of the criticisms regarding IHL rules on environmental protection are related to the high threshold that the environmental damage must meet in order to trigger their application.[42] As already mentioned, the cumulative conditions set forth by Article 35(3) AP I show a particularly restrictive approach, that might jeopardise the concrete effectiveness of the prohibition. Different

40 See Bothe/Brunch/diamond/Jensen (n 8) 581 (fn 41) and SN Simonds, 'Conventional Warfare and Environmental Protection: A Proposal for International Legal Reform' (1992) 29 *StanJIntlL*188.

41 In the case of an oil slick that affected Lebanon's coastline, caused by the 2006 Israeli operation in Lebanon against Hezbollah, the UN General Assembly recognised the duty upon Israel 'to assume responsibility for prompt and adequate compensation to the Government of Lebanon and other countries directly affected by the oil slick for the costs of repairing the environmental damage caused by the destruction, including the restoration of the marine environment'. See UNGA Res 62/88 (19 December 2007), UN Doc. A/RES/62/88, para 4. See also UNSC Res 687 (1991), UN Doc. S/RES/687 (1991), where the UN Security Council held Iraq accountable 'under international law for any direct loss, damage, including environmental damage and the depletion of natural resources'.

42 See R Falk, 'The Inadequacy of the Existing Legal Approach to Environmental Protection in Wartime' in JE Austin and CE Brunch (eds), *The Environmental Consequences of War – Legal, Economic and Scientific Perspectives* (Cambridge University Press 2000) 137.

interpretations have also been advanced as far as the ENMOD Convention and AP I are concerned.[43]

As to the temporal element, the long-term duration of the damage is measured in months under the ENMOD Convention and in decades under AP I.[44] However, while the 'wide-spread' element encompasses 'an area on the scale of several hundred square kilometers' for the purpose of the ENMOD Convention,[45] AP I would require a lower scale. Finally, the gravity of the environmental damage envisaged is rather ambiguous: according to the ENMOD Convention, it should involve 'serious or significant disruption or harm to human life, natural and economic resources or other assets',[46] while, under Article 55(1) AP I, the damage should 'prejudice the health or survival of the population'.

The terminological uncertainty of such provisions, together with the need to conduct an assessment of these elements *ex ante*,[47] have contributed to their lack of practical relevance, with authors highlighting the impossibility of calculating the consequences of environmental damage under IHL even in the case of nuclear weapons.[48] Moreover, given the civilian character of the natural environment, the ambiguity also affects the application of the general principles on the conduct of hostilities.

As far as the principle of proportionality is concerned, an attack would only be lawful when the damage to the environment is not excessive in relation to the concrete and direct military advantage. While assessing the scope of incidental environmental consequences might prove difficult, authors have also raised doubts as to whether the proportionality assessment should encompass all the requirements defining environmental damage under AP I.[49] Some

43 A Bouvier, 'Protection of the Natural Environment in Time of Armed Conflict' (1991) 31 *IRRC* 575–6.

44 David (n 9) 351; WH Boothby, *Weapons and the Law of Armed Conflict* (Oxford University Press 2016) 80, 83.

45 See the Understandings attached to the Convention.

46 Ibid.

47 Damage to the environment which is not intended nor expected would fall outside the prohibition of the Protocol. See Y Dinstein, *The Conduct of Hostilities under the Law of International Armed Conflicts* (Cambridge University Press 2004) 183.

48 Oeter (n 11) 216. The environmental damage caused during the First Gulf War, related to the bombing of hundreds of oil wells, is generally considered to fall outside the scope of arts 35 and 55 AP I. See E Crawford, A Pert, *International Humanitarian Law* (Cambridge University Press 2020) 208.

49 Bothe (n 33) 578.

States seem to consider the criteria set forth by Articles 35 and 55 AP I as an integral part of the proportionality test.[50]

The multiple complexities surrounding the application of IHL rules on environmental protection lead inevitably to the need to reconsider the role of IEL principles in guiding the belligerents' behaviour, also in a preventive perspective. This can only be achieved by a reassessment of the implications deriving from the precautionary principle.

5 The Precautionary Principle and Environmental Care

It is easily arguable that the principle of precaution under Article 57 of AP I is also applicable to attacks against the natural environment.[51] The principle of precaution entails specific duties on the belligerent, namely to take all feasible measures to distinguish between civilian and military objectives and to avoid attacks expected to cause excessive collateral damage. The principle places upon belligerents a duty of due diligence in all phases of the attack, from the planning to the concrete execution. In the context of attacks that may provoke damage to the environment, the question becomes whether the precautionary duties can be construed and applied in line with the approach usually adopted in IEL. Such an attempt has been made by the ICRC *Study on Customary Law*, with customary Rule 44 enshrining the principle of 'due regard' in relation to potential environmental damage:

> Methods and means of warfare must be employed with due regard to the protection and preservation of the natural environment. In the conduct of military operations, all feasible precautions must be taken to avoid, and in any event to minimize, incidental damage to the environment. Lack of scientific certainty as to the effects on the environment of certain military operations does not absolve a party to the conflict from taking such precautions.

---

50 See US Army, Civilian Casualties Mitigation, July 2012 (available at <www.armypubs.us.army.mil/doctrine/index.html>). In relation to the war crime of environmental damage, the Rome Statute also codified an additional requirement regarding proportionality, according to which the damage must be 'clearly excessive in relation to the concrete and direct overall military advantage anticipated' (art 8(2)(b)(iv)). See Wyatt (n 4) 633.

51 As confirmed by the 1996 ICRC *Guidelines for Military Manuals and Instructions on the Protection of the Environment in Times of Armed Conflict* (<www.icrc.org/en/doc/resources/documents/article/other/57jn38.htm>).

This formulation represents an effort to apply the precautionary obligations of IEL to the IHL duty to take precautions in armed conflicts,[52] as also confirmed by the Commentary to the Study.[53] A precautionary approach could already be derived from the reference in Article 55 AP I to the duty of 'care'.[54] The value of Rule 44, however, lies in the clarification of specific elements of such a precautionary approach.

Firstly, the provision bridges the gap between the notion of due regard and the obligations of conduct placed upon the belligerents by virtue of the principle of precaution. Moreover, both the notion of 'care' and of 'due regard' are flexible enough to allow environmental considerations to change and develop over time,[55] in accordance with scientific knowledge and common sensitivity. Indeed, this is confirmed by the final clause of Rule 44, containing a reference to the precautionary approach derived from IEL: belligerents may not invoke the lack of scientific certainty to disregard the duties stemming from the principle of precaution. The choice of words mirrors the text of the 1992 Rio Declaration, whose Principle 15 codifies the precautionary approach.[56] Although the latter is generally invoked as a parameter for regulatory choices, the reference in Rule 44 adapts the approach to more dynamic decisions, such as those related to the planning and the execution of an attack.[57] In this sense, the reference to the precautionary approach also entails an extension of the scope of application of the duties of precaution set forth in IHL. At the same time, it constitutes a complementary element of environmental protection in

52 Bothe/Brunch/diamond/Jensen (n 8) 575. The wording of Rule 44 has also been adopted in other codification: see L. Doswald-Beck (ed), *San Remo Manual on International Law Applicable to Armed Conflict at Sea* (Cambridge University Press 1995), Rule 44; Harvard University, Program on Humanitarian Policy and Conflict Research (HPCR), *Manual on International Law Applicable to Air and Missile Warfare*, Bern, 2009, Rule 88.

53 The Commentary highlights that the entire framing of Rule 44 stems from the development of international environmental law and from the need to protect the environment not just as a civilian object, but mostly as a common good in itself. See Henckaerts/Doswald-Beck (n 21) 147.

54 K Hulme, 'Taking Care to Protect the Environment against Damage: a Meaningless Obligation?' (2010) 92 *IRRC* 679.

55 R Desgagné, 'The Prevention of Environmental Damage in Time of Armed Conflicts: Proportionality and Precautionary Measures' (2000) 3 *YIntlHL* 116.

56 See P Sands, *Principles of International Environmental Law* (Cambridge University Press 2003) 266.

57 Moreover, the precautionary approach would also entail a shift in the burden of proof. See Sands (n 56) 273.

armed conflicts with respect to unforeseeable results, together with preventive duties that are instead related to expected outcomes.[58]

A second issue raised by Rule 44 is the absence of any reference to the threshold of damage that characterises Articles 35(3) and 55(1) AP I (and the corresponding customary rules). Consequently, States would be required to abide by precautionary obligations even when the expected damage is below the wide-spread, long-term and severe threshold.[59] If construed this way, Rule 44 would certainly constitute a major innovation to be welcomed. However, one could still consider that the threshold would remain implicitly required. Especially because Rule 44 relies on a general principle of IHL, it would be questionable for such a rule to bypass requirements set forth by special rules of AP I addressing a specific case, such as those on environmental protection. On the other hand, it is also true that the two readings are not inconsistent with each other: while Articles 35(3) and 55(1) incorporate a prohibition on causing damage of a certain expected gravity, the principle of precaution (as phrased in Rule 44) would require belligerents to undertake a careful assessment of the situation during the targeting process. In other words, while the threshold of damage is part of an obligation of result, the precautionary principle entails obligations of means (or best effort obligations), which are necessarily wider in scope even when applied to environmental protection. More importantly, it is precisely the performance of precautionary duties that would allow the parties to conduct the prognostic evaluation of the attack required by the other provisions.

6 Concluding Remarks

The vagueness and restrictiveness of environmental protection standards in IHL have attracted much criticism and debate over the decades. It is hard to deny the flaws of the current legal framework, which has been eroded by many years of controversies and non-compliance. However, the rules provided in IHL could receive new life and attention if cautiously bridged with duties flowing from general obligations of IEL, with the aim of better regulating all the phases of a CBRN threat that could materialise during an armed conflict.

---

58 On the relationship between the prevention and the precautionary principles, see JE Viñuales, 'Legal Techniques for Dealing with Scientific Uncertainty in Environmental Law' (2010) 43 *VandJTransnatlL* 437; L-A Duvic-Paoli, *The Prevention Principle in International Environmental Law* (Cambridge University Press 2018) 263.

59 Hulme (n 54) 686.

First, the approaches and the mechanisms regulating the functioning of IEL are frequently used as a tool to implement IHL obligations related to the environment. As to CBRN weapons, this tool may prove particularly valuable, by shaping the duties of belligerents in all phases of the attack and by requiring a careful assessment of the consequences deriving from it. The construction of the principle of precaution under Article 57(1) AP I seems to move precisely in this direction.

Furthermore, there are still many aspects related to the use of CBRN weapons that IHL does not have the capacity to regulate. Instead of waiting for a reform of the existing legal framework, a much better solution lies in exploring the interactions between the LOAC and IEL. Rules and procedures established by the latter in relation to response and liability issues could be relied upon to mitigate the environmental impact of CBRN events that occur during a conflict.

This approach has already been adopted by the ICRC in its Study on Customary Law and in the 1996 Guidelines and it is still at the core of the ILC's work on the protection of the environment in armed conflict. It appears to be the only viable approach to address the full range of environmental risks deriving from war, especially in cases that would fall outside the restrictive scope of IHL rules.

Bibliography

Boothby WH, *Weapons and the Law of Armed Conflict* (Oxford University Press 2016).

Bothe M, 'The Law of Neutrality' in D Fleck (ed), *The Handbook of International Humanitarian Law* (Oxford University Press 2013) 549.

Bothe M, Bruch C, Diamond J and Jensen D, 'International law protecting the environment during armed conflict: gaps and opportunities' (2010) 92 *IRRC* 572.

Bouvier A, 'Protection of the Natural Environment in Time of Armed Conflict' (1991) 31 *IRRC* 567.

Cassese A, 'The Martens Clause: Half a Loaf or Simply Pie in the Sky' (2000) 11 *EJIL* 187.

Crawford E, Pert A, *International Humanitarian Law* (Cambridge University Press 2020).

David E, *Principes de droit des conflits armés* (Bruylant 2012).

de Preux J, 'Protocol I – Article 35' in Y Sandoz, C Swinarski and B Zimmermann (eds), *Commentary on the Additional Protocols of 8 June 1977 to the Geneva Conventions of 12 August 1949* (ICRC/Martinus Nijhoff Publishers 1987) 389.

Desgagné R, 'The Prevention of Environmental Damage in Time of Armed Conflicts: Proportionality and Precautionary Measures' (2000) 3 *YIntlHL* 109.

Dinstein Y, *The Conduct of Hostilities under the Law of International Armed Conflicts* (Cambridge University Press 2004).

Doswald-Beck L (ed), *San Remo Manual on International Law Applicable to Armed Conflict at Sea* (Cambridge University Press 1995).

Duvic-Paoli LA, *The Prevention Principle in International Environmental Law* (Cambridge University Press 2018).

Falk R, 'The Inadequacy of the Existing Legal Approach to Environmental Protection in Wartime' in JE Austin and CE Brunch (eds), *The Environmental Consequences of War – Legal, Economic and Scientific Perspectives* (Cambridge University Press 2000) 137.

Gaudreau J, 'The reservations to the Protocols additional to the Geneva Conventions for the protection of war victims' (2003) 849 *IRRC* 143.

Harvard University, Program on Humanitarian Policy and Conflict Research (HPCR), *Manual on International Law Applicable to Air and Missile Warfare*, Bern, 2009.

Henckaerts J-M and Doswald-Beck L, *Customary International Humanitarian Law – Volume I: Rules* (Cambridge University Press 2009).

Hulme K, 'Taking Care to Protect the Environment against Damage: a Meaningless Obligation?' (2010) 92 *IRRC* 675.

International Institute of Humanitarian Law, *San Remo Manual on International Law Applicable to Armed Conflict at Sea* (Cambridge University Press 1995).

Lehto M, 'Armed conflicts and the environment: The International Law Commission's new draft principles' (2020) 29 *RECIEL* 67.

Oeter S, 'Methods and Means of Combat' in D Fleck (ed), *The Handbook of International Humanitarian Law* (Oxford University Press 2013) 115.

Olson KR and Morton LW, 'Long-Term Fate of Agent Orange and Dioxin TCDD Contaminated Soils and Sediments in Vietnam Hotspots' (2019) 9(1) *Open Journal of Soil Science* 1.

Pretorius J, 'Enhancing Environmental Protection in Non-International Armed Conflict: The Way Forward' (2018) 78 *ZaöRV* 903.

Sands P, *Principles of International Environmental Law* (Cambridge University Press 2003).

Sills P, *Toxic War – The Story of Agent Orange* (Vanderbilt University Press 2014).

Simonds SN, 'Conventional Warfare and Environmental Protection: A Proposal for International Legal Reform' (1992) 29 *StanJIntlL* 165.

Vanninen P *et al* 'Exposure status of sea-dumped chemical warfare agents in the Baltic Sea' (2020) 161 *Marine Environmental Research* 105112.

Viñuales JE, 'Legal Techniques for Dealing with Scientific Uncertainty in Environmental Law' (2010) 43 *VandJTransnatlL* 437.

Vöneky S, 'A New Shield for the Environment: Peacetime Treaties as Legal Restraints of Wartime Damage' (2000) 9 *Review of European, Comparative and International Environmental Law* 20.

Wyatt J, 'Law-Making at the Intersection of International Environmental, Humanitarian and Criminal Law: the Issue of Damage to the Environment in International Armed Conflicts' (2010) 92 *IRRC* 593.

Young AL, *The History, Use, Disposition and Environmental Fate of Agent Orange* (Springer 2009).

CHAPTER 23

Chemical and Biological Weapons' Disarmament

Ludovica Poli

1 Introduction

The use of pathogenic microbes, toxins and chemical agents in warfare has ancient roots in human history[1] and still represents a serious concern for international security today, as chemical and biological weapons 'might prove attractive in [...] new conflict situations, particularly because they lend themselves to tactics such as terror, population displacement, and wider forms of social/economic destabilization'.[2]

From a legal point of view, a synergy does exist between international humanitarian law (IHL) and arms control and disarmament law (ACDL): both fields of law ban the use of biological and chemical weapons, although with a different approach. While, under IHL, the use of these weapons is considered contrary to fundamental principles, such as the prohibition of superfluous injury or unnecessary suffering,[3] under ACDL, the ban is rather linked to the general aim of lowering the risk of war by reducing the overall number of weapons.[4]

The definition of States' disarmament obligations in this field gained momentum with the adoption of the 1972 Convention on the Prohibition of the Development, Production, Stockpiling and the Use of Bacteriological (Biological) and Toxin Weapons and on their Destruction (BWC),[5] while it took more time to reach an international consensus on chemical weapons. The Convention on the Prohibition of the Development, Production, Stockpiling and the Use of Chemical Weapons and on their Destruction (CWC) was open

1 SM Block, 'The Growing Threat of Biological Weapons' (2001) 89 American Scientist 28; V Pitschmann 'Overall View of Chemical and Biochemical Weapons' (2014) 6 Toxins 1761.

2 C McLeish and R Trapp, 'The life sciences revolution and the BWC' (2011) 18 The Nonproliferation Review 534.

3 See ch 21 by Mauri.

4 E Myjer and J Herbach, 'Arms Control Law as the Common Legal Framework for CBRN Security' in A Malizia, M D'Arienzo (eds), *Enhancing CBRNE Safety & Security: Proceedings of the SICC 2017 Conference* (Springer 2018).

5 Convention on the prohibition of the development, production, stockpiling and the use of bacteriological (biological) and toxin weapons and on their destruction (1972) (Biological Weapons Convention, BWC). The BWC currently has 183 States Parties.

© LUDOVICA POLI, 2022 | DOI:10.1163/9789004507999_024

for signature only in 1993.[6] Unlike the BWC, the CWC imposes a stringent verification mechanism on States as a necessary condition of their renunciation of chemical weapons, because such weapons are perceived to be a more concrete military option than biological armaments.[7] As a matter of fact, despite pathogenic microbes having a significant comparative advantage over chemicals (since they do not need to be produced in large quantities to be weaponised because they replicate within the host and they are more powerful per unit weight[8]) they still appear to not really be practicable for military purposes, as their effect might easily spread beyond any control.[9] Historical records seem to confirm this point: 'the few known cases since World War II of countries using biological weapons mostly have involved small-scale operations in support of internal regime security, whether through assassinations of dissidents, regime rivals, or in counterinsurgency operations'.[10] However, risks connected to the potential use of biological weapons remain topical, in particular, with reference to non-State actors.

The present chapter aims at exploring the role of ACDL in combating the use of chemical and biological weapons and in ensuring their destruction. It analyses the two Conventions, assessing their different compliance monitoring systems, identifying challenges to their implementation and contextualising them in a broader non-proliferation regime, where other multilateral and institutional initiatives take place.

---

6 Convention on the prohibition of the development, production, stockpiling and the use of chemical weapons and on their destruction (1993) (Chemical Weapons Convention, CWC). With its 193 States Parties, it is the arms-control and disarmament agreement with the largest participation today. For an overview: P Gargiulo, 'Le armi chimiche. Aspetti di diritto internazionale e disarmo. Pt. I' (1987) 42 *La comunità internazionale*, 9; P Gargiulo, 'Le armi chimiche. Aspetti di diritto internazionale e disarmo. Pt. II' (1987) 42 *La comunità internazionale*, 167.

7 NA Sims, 'A simple treaty, a complex fulfillment: A short history of the Biological Weapons Convention Review Conferences' (2011) 67 Bulletin of the Atomic Scientists 10.

8 JB Tucker 'Strengthening the BWC: Moving Toward a Compliance Protocol' (1998) Arms Control Today <https://www.armscontrol.org/act/1998-01/arms-control-today/strengthening-bwc-moving-toward compliance-protocol> (all links were last accessed on 4 May 2021).

9 Pitschmann (n 1) 1766.

10 G Cross and L Klotz, 'Twenty-first century perspectives on the Biological Weapon Convention: Continued relevance or toothless paper tiger' (2020) 76 Bulletin of the Atomic Scientists 187; AR Fooks and LK Holmstrom, 'United Nations Secretary-General's Mechanism' (2017) 36 Revue scientifique et technique de l'Office international des épizooties 630.

2 Treaty Obligations and Verification Regimes: A Comparison

The use of chemical and biological weapons in armed conflicts was banned, for the first time, with the adoption of the 1925 Geneva Protocol, at the Conference for the Supervision of the International Trade in Arms and Ammunition, held under the auspices of the League of Nations.[11] The agreement, however, prohibited only the use and not the development of these weapons. Additionally, some States made reservations to the Protocol, with the intention to limit the non-use obligation only with respect to other States Parties and/or to preserve the possibility of using such means of war in response to an attack involving them.[12]

In 1968, the issue of chemical and biological weapons was included on the agenda of the then Eighteen-Nation Committee on Disarmament in Geneva. It then took four years to adopt the BWC, prohibiting the development, production, acquisition, transfer, retention and stockpiling of biological and toxin weapons and implicitly banning their use in warfare. According to Article IX of the BWC, States undertook to renew negotiations on an agreement to destroy chemical weapons and prohibit their development and stockpiling. In the following years, efforts continued within the UN Conference on Disarmament to prepare a draft convention on chemical weapons. Many events, in the late 1980s, contributed to reinforce this intention, including the use of chemical weapons during the Iran-Iraq War. An agreement was finally adopted in 1993, explicitly banning the use of chemical weapons, along with their development, production, acquisition, retention, transfer or stockpiling.

If three main elements are usually at stake in arms control treaty negotiations – namely, political concerns over security and sovereignty; economic issues, connected to potential financial and commercial gain or loss as the outcome of adherence to the treaty; and effectiveness of the arms control regime, to be assessed via verification mechanisms[13] – the two Conventions couldn't be more different. While the BWC can be described as an arrangement driven mainly by political considerations, the CWC, on the contrary, 'represents a

11 Protocol for the Prohibition of the Use in War of Asphyxiating, Poisonous or Other Gases, and of Bacteriological Methods of Warfare ('1925 Geneva Protocol') (1925).

12 TM Rajah, G Dawson and L Aylett, 'The Chemical Weapons Convention and the Contribution of the Organisation for the Prohibition of Chemical Weapons to Sustainable Development' (2019) 24 Journal of Conflict & Security Law 619.

13 T Taylor, 'The Chemical Weapons Convention and prospects for implementation' (1993) 42 Int'l & Comp LQ 918.

treaty where there is more balance between the three elements[14] [...] which was possible only in the political climate of the 1990s'.[15]

A major difference between the two agreements concerns the verification regime.

2.1 *The Biological Weapons Convention and the Meaning of Transparency in* ACDL

The adoption of the BWC was aimed at achieving 'effective progress towards general and complete disarmament, including the prohibition and elimination of all types of weapons of mass destruction'.[16] It was also based on the idea that an agreement on the prohibition of bacteriological (biological) and toxin weapons would represent 'a first possible step towards the achievement of agreement on effective measures also for the prohibition of the development, production and stockpiling of chemical weapons'.[17]

Under Article I, the BWC bans the development, production, stockpiling, acquisition or retention of 'microbial or other biological agents, or toxins whatever their origin or method of production, of types and in quantities that have no justification for prophylactic, protective or other peaceful purposes'. Weapons, equipment or means of delivery designed to use these agents or toxins for hostile purposes or in armed conflict are also outlawed under Article I. While the BWC does not openly ban the use of biological and toxin weapons, it prohibits that implicitly, recalling the 1925 Geneva Protocol in the Preamble and reaffirming the obligations assumed under it by States Parties (art VIII). Furthermore, as stressed by Sims, 'the treaty does not limit its scope to existing biological agents and toxins, but instead anticipates future developments. It bans any weaponization of disease, as well as preparatory steps toward weaponization'.[18]

Insisting on the intended purpose of bioagents and equipment, the Convention cannot be read as banning biodefence programmes, designed to develop defensive measures against bio-threats.[19] In fact, the Convention recognises the right of States Parties to participate 'in the fullest possible exchange of equipment, materials and scientific and technological information for the

14 In particular, only the CWC includes provisions on economic and technological development: see art XI.

15 Taylor (n 13) 918.

16 BWC, Preamble.

17 Ibid.

18 Sims (n 7) 9.

19 D Kimball, 'The Biological Weapons Convention (BWC) At A Glance' (2020) Arms Control Today <https://www.armscontrol.org/factsheets/bwc>.

use of bacteriological (biological) agents and toxins for peaceful purposes' and promotes international cooperation in the scientific development 'in the field of bacteriology (biology) for the prevention of disease, or for other peaceful purposes' (art X).

According to the BWC, each State Party should also take any necessary measures to prohibit and prevent the development, production, stockpiling, acquisition or retention of the prohibited substances and equipment 'within the territory of such State, under its jurisdiction or under its control anywhere' (art IV). States' obligations, therefore, extend to the potential activity of non-State actors within their territory. Additionally, per Article III, States Parties undertake 'not to transfer to any recipient whatsoever, directly or indirectly, and not in any way to assist, encourage, or induce any State, group of States or international organizations to manufacture or otherwise acquire' any of the banned substances or equipment.

Finally, the Convention requires States Parties to destroy or, at least, divert to peaceful purposes the prohibited agents, toxins, weapons, equipment, and means of delivery, within nine months after the Convention's entry into force (art II).

Rather than establishing a specific verification mechanism, the Convention mandates States Parties to consult with one another and cooperate, bilaterally or multilaterally, to solve compliance concerns (art V). They are also called upon to provide or support assistance to a victim of bioweapons attack, whenever the Security Council has established that a State Party has been exposed to danger as a result of violation of the Convention (art VII). Lastly, the Convention allows States Parties to lodge a complaint with the UN Security Council, providing the relevant evidence, whenever they believe that another Member is violating the Convention's obligations. The Security Council can investigate such complaints and States Parties have to cooperate with it. Nevertheless, this power has never been invoked and, indeed, its limits are self-evident: 'if one of the five permanent members of the Security Council were to be the subject of an accusation, its veto power in the Council could block any possible resolution of the issue'.[20]

In the years since the adoption of the BWC, States Parties have maintained their efforts in promoting cooperation in the field and exploring the possibility of establishing a proper verification mechanism, in particular during the review conferences held every five years.[21]

---

20 MI Chevrier & I Hunger, 'Confidence-building measures for the BTWC: performance and potential' (2000) 7 The Nonproliferation Review 29.

21 Rather than being convened to amend the BWC, the review conferences contributed to insisting on the treaty's binding power and to tracing its implications: Sims (n 7) 10–11.

During the Second Review Conference, while some countries supported the idea of creating a specific procedure for verification, others considered this approach not feasible and many delegations stressed the urgency of concluding the negotiations on the CWC, which could then offer a model for a possible future BWC verification protocol.[22] As a result, a set of Confidence-Building Measures (CBMs)[23] have been introduced by way of *an interim* solution to encourage transparency about relevant national biological activities and facilities.[24] Confidence-building measures mainly consist in the exchange of information and data on relevant facilities, programmes, legislation, as well as on outbreaks of infectious diseases.[25] These measures were considered important in order to reduce secrecy and, therefore, increase confidence among States, with the final aim to reinforce reliance on the treaty and improve international cooperation in the field of peaceful biological activities. The CBMs system has been modified during the subsequent review conferences, with slight changes in the formulation of the measures and, more importantly, with the establishment, during the Sixth Review Conference in 2006, of a BWC Implementation Support Unit (ISU), within the Geneva branch of the UN Office for Disarmament Affairs, tasked to receive and distribute confidence-building measures from and to States Parties.[26]

Since the introduction of the CBMs, States Parties' negotiations on a more structured verification mechanism have continued.[27] Between 1995 and 2001, an ad hoc Group engaged in negotiations on a Compliance Protocol to the BWC, with the aim of establishing an international body to receive declarations of treaty-relevant facilities and activities; to conduct routine on-site visits; to conduct challenge inspections in case of doubtful activities; and to investigate suspicious outbreaks of diseases.[28] However, the draft issued by the

22 F Lentzos, 'Hard to prove' (2011) 18 The Nonproliferation Review 573.

23 Confidence-Building Measures can be described as 'arrangements designed to enhance [...] assurance of mind and belief in the trustworthiness of states and the facts they create': JJ Holst, 'Confidence-Building Measures: A Conceptual Framework' (1983) 25 Survival 2.

24 Lentzos (n 22) 573.

25 For a comment on the use of the Convention as a platform for addressing infectious disease threats arising naturally, and malicious dissemination of pathogenic microorganisms: C Enemark, 'The role of the Biological Weapons Convention in disease surveillance and response' (2010) 25 Health Policy and Planning 486.

26 Sims (n 7) 13.

27 JP Zanders & AE Smithson, 'Ensuring the future of the Biological Weapons Convention' (2011) 18 The Nonproliferation Review 480.

28 Tucker (n 8).

ad hoc Group in 2001 was rejected by the US[29] and the negotiations to adopt a BWC Protocol have definitely failed. Interestingly enough, while early drafts of the Protocol used the word 'verification', it soon became clear that this term would not only raise the opposition of some States Parties,[30] but that it also did not necessarily recall the proper concept for assessing compliance with a treaty in the field of biological weapons. In fact, if the heart of verification is seen as 'the ability to detect a militarily significant violation of a treaty's limits',[31] this standard usually works well 'for arms reduction treaties involving weapons that take a long lead-time to develop, produce, and deploy'.[32] In the case of biological weapons, because pathogenic microbes replicate within the host, the scope of the conduct that will constitute a suspected violation might be extremely different and 'even small illegal stockpiles may have significant military consequences'.[33] Indeed, promoting transparency, rather than implementing verification, appeared as a more concrete aim for the measures envisaged in the Protocol.[34]

Thus, the current system is not conceived as a verification apparatus but rather as a compliance regime,[35] aimed at strengthening transparency. As explained by Hunger and Dingli, the system includes, on the one hand, a monitoring tool (the CBMs) through which States can demonstrate compliance on a regular basis and, on the other, alternative 'transparency-enhancing mechanisms'[36] – the consultative process under Article V and the UN-led investigations under Article VI – can be activated in case of suspicions, ambiguities, or compliance concerns. Confidence-building measures are commonly defined as *politically* binding, meaning that, while they are not mandatory under international law, States have formally agreed to abide by them. Indeed, this 'formal agreement adds political muscle and a certain degree of moral suasion to push countries to fulfill their commitments'.[37] More generally, transparency might help to reinforce adherence to the treaty and, despite the low

29 KD Mahley, 'Statement of the United States to the Ad Hoc Group of Biological Weapons Convention States Parties' Geneva, July 25, 2001, <https://2001-2009.state.gov/t/ac/rls/rm/2001/5497.htm>.

30 Lentzos (n 22) 577.

31 Zanders & Smithson (n 27) 480.

32 Ibid 481.

33 Ibid 481.

34 The final protocol draft does not mention the word verification even once but uses the word transparency dozens of times: Cross & Lynn Klotz (n 10) 186.

35 F Lentzos 'Strengthening the Biological Weapons Convention confidence-building measures: Toward a cycle of engagement' (2011) 67 Bulletin of the Atomic Scientists 27.

36 I Hunger & S Dingli, 'Improving Transparency' (2011) 18 The Nonproliferation Review 515.

37 Chevrier & Hunger (n 20) 26.

use of biological weapons in past decades, this is of major importance in view of potential evolution of science and technology, as will be stressed below.

2.2 *The Chemical Weapons Convention and Institutionalised Verification*

The structure and style of the CWC are very different from the BWC. While the BWC is a lean text, the CWC appears to be a very comprehensive agreement, completed by three annexes (namely the Annex on Chemicals, the Annex on Implementation and Verification and the Annex on the Protection of Confidential Information) in which, along with States obligations, practical steps for disarmament are envisaged in detail.

Article I CWC states the general obligations of States Parties: it is a broad provision containing a variety of duties. First, it bans development, production, acquisition, stockpiling, retention and transfer of chemical weapons (art I.1 a). Second, it prohibits the use of such weapons, as well as any military preparations to utilise them (art I.1 b and c). It also makes clear that using riot control agents as a method of warfare is prohibited (art I.5). As one scholar has underlined, a certain flexibility was necessary in dealing with the issue of riot control agents, defined as 'chemicals not listed in a Schedule which can produce rapidly in humans sensory irritation or disabling physical effects which disappear within a short time following termination of exposure' (art II, para 7). During negotiations, while most States wanted to maintain the right to use riot control agents, some delegations believed that they should be used only by the police, while others reaffirmed the need for armed forces to have access to them, especially whenever the military is deployed to support civil power.[38] In any case, it was clear that allowing riot control agents for general use in warfare might result 'in an unscrupulous State Party concealing a chemical warfare capability in the form of an incapacitant'[39] and, therefore, the solution was to ban riot control agents in war, while law enforcement, including domestic riot control, was defined as a permitted purpose (art II, para 9). This produced a bizarre effect, as the Convention prohibits a means of warfare against combatants, which conversely can be applied against non-combatants.[40]

In addition to the abovementioned prohibitions, Article I also requires States Parties to destroy chemical weapons and chemical weapons production facilities they own or possess, or that are located under their jurisdiction or control (art I.2 and para 4), as well as all chemical weapons they have abandoned on

38 Taylor (n 13) 913.
39 Ibid 914.
40 Ibid 914.

the territory of another State Party. Finally, it prohibits parties to assist, encourage or induce, in any way, anyone to engage in any activity prohibited under the Convention (art I.1 d).

Article VII of the CWC extends the States' obligations with reference to the activity of non-State actors. While the spirit of the norm is the same as Article IV of the BWC, this provision – resulting from an intense negotiation[41] – goes further, in detailing that each State Party shall enact criminal legislation to forbid natural and legal persons, under its jurisdiction, from undertaking any prohibited activity (art VII.1.a) and shall also extend such legislation to any activity 'undertaken anywhere by natural persons, possessing its nationality' (art VII.1.c).[42] In addition, States Parties shall not to permit such activities in any place under their control, such as foreign bases and occupied territories (art VII.1.b).

The CWC defines the prohibited chemical weapons by reference to their purpose: all toxic chemicals and their precursors are banned, with the exception of those 'intended for purposes not prohibited under [the] Convention' (art II.1.a). Munitions, devices and other equipment designed to cause death or other harm through the banned toxic chemicals are included in the definition (art I b and c).

Articles III, IV, and V itemise the disarmament undertakings in different operative phases (starting from the declarations on existing chemical weapons and chemical weapons production facilities) and require the elimination of chemical weapons and facilities within a defined timeframe.

Article VI regulates legitimate activities in the field of chemical industry: while enunciating the right of each State Party 'to develop, produce, otherwise acquire, retain, transfer and use toxic chemicals and their precursors for purposes not prohibited under [the] Convention', it also subjects chemicals and chemical production facilities to verification measures provided in the Verification Annex.

The verification regime is at the heart of the agreement. As highlighted by Krutzsch, Myjer and Trapp, 'there is no other subject of the Convention that has been developed in more detail in the treaty text'.[43] Most of the relevant rules are contained in the Verification Annex, but also some CWC provisions (arts VIII, IX, XII) contribute to defining a normative framework, aimed at

41 Ibid 917.

42 According to Taylor, some delegations wanted the extension of criminal legislation also to legal persons, focusing on the activities of multinational companies: Taylor (n 13) 917.

43 W Krutzsch, E Myjer, R Trapp, 'The Chemical Weapons Convention – Objectives, Principles, and Implementation Practice' in W Krutzsch, E Myjer, R Trapp (eds), *The Chemical Weapons Convention: A Commentary* (OUP 2014) 8.

managing compliance concerns. In addition, the Chemicals Annex lists toxic chemicals and their precursors, for the application of verification measures, and the Confidentiality Annex deals with the need to protect – in the verification process – security interests of the States Parties, as well as the business priorities of their industries.[44]

Contrary to the compliance regime developed with reference to the BWC, verification under the CWC has an institutionalised nature, with an independent international supervisory organisation – the Organisation for the Prohibition of Chemical Weapons (OPCW) – tasked with ensuring the implementation of the Convention. The OPCW is responsible for the international verification of compliance with the CWC, and it also provides a forum for consultation and cooperation among States Parties. Article VIII of the CWC contains the statutory provisions of the OPCW, establishing its three main organs, namely, the Conference of the States Parties, the Executive Council and the Technical Secretariat.

Notwithstanding the institutionalised nature of the verification procedure under the CWC, dialogue among States Parties is encouraged. Under Article IX, the States Parties undertake to consult and cooperate to resolve any doubts about compliance with the treaty. Different mechanisms are considered in the provision, ranging from bilateral consultations to multilateral procedures.

Article IX also regulates the so-called 'challenges inspections', which are fact-finding missions in relation to concerns raised by a State Party that another State Party may be violating the Convention. These inspections must be 'carried out for the sole purpose of determining facts relating to the possible non-compliance' (art IX, para 9). Each State Party can request 'an on-site challenge inspection of any facility or location in the territory or in any other place under the jurisdiction or control of any other State Party for the sole purpose of clarifying and resolving any questions concerning possible non-compliance with the provisions of this Convention' (art IX, para 9). The inspected State, on its part, has the 'the right and the obligation to make every reasonable effort to demonstrate its compliance' and, to this end, to allow the inspection team to accomplish the mandate, providing access to the requested site, while adopting measures 'to protect sensitive installations, and to prevent disclosure of confidential information and data' (art IX, para 11). This system is unique for two main reasons. First, there is no pre-condition (such as a suffered injury or a concrete threat to national security) that must be satisfied before a State Party can request a challenge inspection. Although the requesting State must refrain from unfounded inspection requests (art IX, para 9) and the OPCW Executive

44 Krutzsch, Myjer, Trapp (n 43) 8.

Council is called upon to prevent misuse of these instruments (including by requiring the requesting State to bear part of the 'financial implications' of a challenge inspection that is found to have been abusive (art IX, para 17)), it is undeniable that 'all that is needed for a request is the political will of a state to make one'.[45] Secondly, the challenge inspections are to be carried out on the territory of a State Party anytime, anywhere and without possible refusal, as the requested Party is obligated to accept the inspection. These instruments represent a powerful intrusion into State sovereignty, justified as 'a means to uncover clandestine activities and provide a safety net in the event that routine verification fails, as well as to reach facilities beyond the scope of routine inspections'.[46]

In case of non-compliance with the treaty obligations, the Conference of the OPCW may adopt measures envisaged under Article XII, restricting or suspending the non-compliant State Party's rights and privileges under the Convention, recommending collective measures to States Parties in conformity with international law or, in cases of particular gravity, bringing the case to the attention of the United Nations General Assembly and the United Nations Security Council.

A particular feature of the CWC is the protection of confidentiality, assured through the provisions contained in the Confidentiality Annex, which details the duties of the OPCW in collecting data and information; the measures to be adopted by the inspected States and the inspection teams to protect sensitive installations and to prevent disclosure of confidential data in the course of on-site verification activities; and the procedures to be followed in case of breaches, or alleged breaches, of confidentiality.

3 Challenges to Verification: Dual-Use and Developments in Science and Technology

Although the ACDL normative corpus appears to be solid and consistent, challenges to its proper application come from inherent limits to its enforcement, recognisable both in the 'soft' treaty compliance monitoring system established for the BWC, and in the more structured verification mechanism of the CWC.

---

45 T Abe, 'Challenge inspections under the Chemical Weapons Convention: between ideal and reality' (2017) 24 The Nonproliferation Review 170.

46 Ibid 168.

Scrutinising the implementation of disarmament obligations in relation to biological and chemical weapons is primarily made difficult by the dual use of most bioagents and chemicals. As already discussed, under both the regimes, the intended purpose is what makes the distinction between biological or chemical agents that can be legitimately produced, stockpiled or used and materials that are banned as outlawed weapons of mass destruction. Indeed, monitoring adherence to ACDL obligations in this field requires assessing whether the agent is produced for peaceful purposes or not, that is, whether the State has an offensive or defensive intent.

From this perspective, measures aimed at improving transparency around activities relevant to the core prohibition of the treaties are of a key importance. Due to the dual-use nature of most agents in biotechnology and chemistry, the 'state's transparency about these activities and its willingness to explain them are of utmost importance to increasing confidence in [their] peaceful nature of such activities'.[47] This notwithstanding, the compliance monitoring method established for the BWC presents some inherent limitations. To begin with, the confidence-building measures system still faces low and quite inconsistent participation,[48] although there have been slight improvements in submissions.[49] It is true that there is a growing international expectation of transparency which is 'transforming the past common practice of state secrecy about certain activities into an indicator of malevolent intent',[50] but it is also undeniable that the extent to which the release of data by a State will effectively increase confidence among other parties depends upon the reputation of that country for compliance, as well as the quality of the information provided.[51] Indeed, not all delivered information necessarily contributes to broadening transparency. In addition, it should be considered whether current CBMs are capable of addressing present security concerns, in which bio-weapons threats could come more easily from non-State actors than from central governments.[52]

Under the CWC, on the other hand, the institutionalised monitoring regime has increased cooperation among States and the very existence of the challenge

47 Hunger & Dingli (n 36) 514.

48 Lentzos (n 35) 29.

49 According to the Annual report of the Implementation Support Unit 2019 (BWC/MSP/2019/4), delivered on 8 October 2019, while the number of States Parties submitting CBMs forms in a timely manner is increasing, a total of 57 States Parties have never submitted them (para 23).

50 Zanders & Smithson (n 27) 481.

51 Chevrier & Hunger (n 20) 27.

52 Lentzos (n 35) 28; Lentzos (n 22) 578–579.

inspections might be considered a deterrence for non-compliant States,[53] despite the fact that it has never been put into practice. A major reason for this lack of practice is that bilateral consultations – not involving the OPCW institutional framework – are often preferred as an option, also considering that requesting a challenge inspection may complicate relations between the States involved.[54] Another issue are the different interpretations adopted, on the one hand, by the European Union, the United Kingdom, and the United States, which consider that consultative measures do not necessarily have to be exhausted before requesting a challenge inspection, and the opposite position held by Russia, China, and Iran (accepted also by the Non-Aligned Movement CWC States Parties and the China Group), which stress the need to take consultative measures before asking for a challenge inspection.[55] Although Article IX makes clear that challenge inspections are independent from other measures, the interpretative dichotomy might contribute to a certain resistance in requesting them.[56] In any case, even admitting that 'the more time that elapses without a request being made, the more difficult making such a request will become',[57] the challenge-inspection system still plays an important role in preventing noncompliance, rather than detecting it.[58]

Other and more pressing challenges to ACDL in the fields of biological and chemical weapons come from the continuous development of science and technology. For example, while biological weapons have, in the past, exploited infectious organisms from nature (like smallpox, plague and anthrax), genetic engineering might now open new possibilities for 'black biology', namely the application of new techniques of molecular biology to improve weapons. Similarly, in the chemical industry, advances in technology and the discovery of new compounds might be relevant to the object and purpose of the CWC.[59] According to one scholar, for example, 'it is thus possible to assume that in the future, new forms of the accumulation of stocks of chemical [...] weapons will occur, which will be produced by the virtual synthesis of new toxic substances from unmonitored chemical agents'.[60] Therefore, scientific and technological progress needs to be governed to prevent and avoid new threats, but it is also important to sustain peaceful research. Most chemicals and biological agents are commonly applied in commercial manufacturing and might

53 Abe (n 46) 168.
54 Ibid 174–175.
55 Ibid 173.
56 Ibid 174.
57 Ibid 184.
58 Ibid.
59 Krutzsch, Myjer, Trapp (n 43) 13.
60 Pitschmann (n 1) 1781.

be crucial to pursue public interests (such as the protection of public health, through the production of vaccines, antibiotics, biological pesticides, feed supplements, etc.), including the development of tools for countering the effects of biological and chemical weapons.[61] Considering gene editing, for example, the Meeting of Experts on review of developments in the field of science and technology related to the BWC has stressed that while this technique 'could make the acquisition, development, and production of biological weapons easier; it could also help to counter such risks, for example through the design of more effective medical countermeasures, or through improved means of detection'.[62]

A topic of special concern is the convergence of biology and chemistry,[63] as a source of new potential challenges in terms of development of biochemical weapons, namely, 'biologically active chemical compounds or compounds produced by a specific chemical mechanism in a living organism'.[64] In fact, there is already a clear convergence between chemistry and biology in the life sciences, which demonstrates the relationship between infectious disease, toxins, bioregulators and chemical agents, and determines, in practical terms, a growing overlapping of their corresponding industries.

From our perspective, this means not only that progress in fields such as synthetic biology, nanomaterials and additive manufacturing can make monitoring and inspections much more complex, but also that this progress may pose legal issues for verification and treaty implementation, as it inevitably questions the 'traditional understanding of the boundaries between the regimes that govern, respectively, the prohibition of chemical and biological weapons'.[65] Indeed, while the BWC and the CWC share the same origin (the Geneva Protocol) and are normatively linked (as proved by the reciprocal

61 A Üzümcü, 'The Chemical Weapons Convention-disarmament, science and technology' (2014) 406 Analytical and Bioanalytical Chemistry 5072.

62 Meeting of the States Parties to the Convention on the Prohibition of the Development, Production and Stockpiling of Bacteriological (Biological) and Toxin Weapons and on Their Destruction, Report of the 2018 Meeting of Experts on review of developments in the field of science and technology related to the Convention BWC/MSP/2018/MX.2/3, 12 November 2018, para 16.

63 Evans points out the distinction between convergence and dual-use technologies as independent concepts: '[…] a general rule is that "dual use" concerns a multiplicity of uses from a single piece of [science and technology], while "convergence" denotes a particular use arising from a multiplicity of [science and technology] developments': NG Evans, 'Models of scientific and technological review for the Biological and Toxin Weapons Convention' (2019) 26 The Nonproliferation Review 355.

64 Pitschmann (n 1) 1776.

65 Krutzsch, Myjer, Trapp (n 43) 13.

textual references),[66] a possible 'convergence' of the two different arms-control regimes has yet to be explored. For the time being, these developments 'may require combined action of both implementation systems, and [pose] conceptual questions about legal consequences for both treaties'.[67]

4 Other Elements of the Biological and Chemical Weapons Non-Proliferation Regime

Rules and procedures established through the adoption of the BWC and CWC have to be contextualised in what can be considered as a broader non-proliferation regime against the development and use of biological and chemical weapons.

First, different multilateral initiatives aim at reinforcing the rules established by the two Conventions. In particular, the G-8 Global Partnership against the Spread of Weapons and Materials of Mass Destruction promotes the adoption and full implementation of a range of multilateral treaties and other international instruments, seeking also to strengthen the institutions designed to implement them.[68] Similarly, the Australia Group represents a forum for coordination among its members on export controls on chemical precursors and dual-use chemical equipment, as well as on biological weapons agents and toxins, and related dual-use equipment.[69]

States' efforts have also been supplemented by initiatives undertaken by international organisations (other than the UN) which might significantly contribute to the fight against biological and chemical weapons due to their expertise and field of action. For example, the World Health Organization has developed global alert and response activities that are central to the detection, verification and containment of epidemics, elements which are vital to effective international containment efforts, also in the event of the intentional release of a biological agent. While the main focus of the WHO is on the public health aspects of preparedness and response,[70] its expertise might provide general

66 CWC, Preamble para 5 and Article XIII; BWC, Articles VIII and IX.

67 Krutzsch, Myjer, Trapp (n 43) 11.

68 CL Thornton, 'The G8 global partnership against the spread of weapons and materials of mass destruction' (2002) 9 The Nonproliferation Review 135.

69 DH Joyner, *International Law and the Proliferation of Weapons of Mass Destruction* (OUP 2009) 116–117; see also ch 25 by Viterbo.

70 See for example: World Health Organization, *Preparedness for the deliberate use of biological agents A rational approach to the unthinkable* (WHO 2002); *Public health response to biological and chemical weapons: WHO guidance* (WHO 2004).

support to States and the international community in implementing ACDL. Similarly, an important role is played by the World Organisation for Animal Health (OIE), as the continuous sharing of data on occurrence, prevention and control of zoonosis is extremely important. In addition, considering that biological agents could be weaponised with the intention of triggering agricultural sabotage and/or endangering food security,[71] the contribution of the Food and Agriculture Organization (FAO) is also crucial.

The role of international organisations was particularly stressed during the BWC Eighth Review Conference in 2016.[72] Moreover, since 2003, delegates from the abovementioned and other organisations (such as the World Trade Organization and the International Plant Protection Convention), along with representatives from the biopharmaceutical industry, research institutes and scientific organisations, have participated in the annual meetings of experts and BWC members. These meetings have been held since the collapse of the Compliance Protocol negotiations and are known as 'intersessional processes'. This broad participation confirms the 'diversity of actors that can make positive contributions to the policing of the BWC's prohibitions'[73] and that 'the prevention of biological weapons is becoming a more broadly shared responsibility'.[74]

Finally, two mechanisms within the UN system complete this scenario: the Committee established pursuant to Resolution 1540 (2004) and the Secretary-General's Mechanism for Investigation of Alleged Use of Chemical and Biological Weapons.

Resolution 1540 (2004) affirmed that the spread of nuclear, chemical and biological weapons and their means of delivery constitutes a threat to international peace and security and, thus, required States to adopt legislation to prevent their proliferation, calling also for a full implementation of multilateral treaties aimed at eliminating or avoiding their production.[75] The Resolution also represents 'the first legally binding international tool that targeted specifically the proliferation of all types of WMD to non-state actors'.[76] Although focusing on preventing non-State actors' access to prohibited

71 Fooks & Holmstrom (n 10) 630–631.

72 D Feakes, 'The Biological Weapons Convention' (2017) 36 Revue scientifique et technique de l'Office international des épizooties, 623.

73 Zanders & Smithson (n 27) 481 see also NA Sims & J Littlewood, 'Ambitious incrementalism', (2011) 18 The Nonproliferation Review 503.

74 Zanders & Smithson (n 27) 481.

75 UNSC Res 1540 (28 April 2004) UN Doc S/RES/1540.

76 B Kienzle, 'Effective Orchestration? The 1540 Committee and the WMD Terrorism Regime Complex' (2019) 10 Global Policy 487. On the criticism surrounding the role of the Security Council as an international legislator, with specific reference to Resolution 1540, see M Asada, 'Security Council Resolution 1540 to Combat WMD Terrorism: Effectiveness

weapons, Resolution 1540 (2004) generally contributes to the disarmament process by requiring States to establish national controls to prevent proliferation of WMD and their means of delivery.[77] The 1540 Committee monitors compliance with the Resolution and relies mainly on national reports when updating the Security Council on its implementation. According to one scholar, 'working from the reports, national legislation can be identified, patterns discerned, gaps revealed, and even the shortest and most poorly written reports can be indicative of a level of compliance and be a useful source of information'.[78] This mechanism contributes, therefore, to mapping implementation trends that might be relevant for assessing compliance with the CWC and BWC obligations as well.

Finally, the ACDL normative corpus is further complemented by the United Nations Secretary-General's Mechanism (UNSGM), developed in the late 1980s to undertake timely and evidence-based investigations on the use of chemical, bacteriological (biological) or toxin-based weapons.[79] The Mechanism consists in the dispatch by the Secretary-General of missions of experts – selected from a roster of specialists nominated by UN Member States – with the task of ascertaining facts related to an allegation (presented by any UN Member) of the use of such weapons.

The Secretary-General's Mechanism was activated in 2013 in the Syrian Arab Republic, upon request of the Syrian Government, to investigate the 19 March 2013 Khan al-Assal chemical attack, with the assistance of experts from the OPCW and WHO. The Report, delivered in September 2013, also considered the attack that occurred in Ghouta, immediately after the deployment of the mission, and confirmed that chemical weapons had been used on a relatively large scale, including against the civilian population. In the same month, the Syrian Arab Republic signed up to the CWC, while the USA and the Russian Federation reached an agreement to define a framework for destroying all chemical weapons held in that country, exceptionally allowing for the removal

and Legitimacy in International Legislation' (2009) 13 Journal of Conflict & Security Law 322. See ch 7 by Poltronieri Rossetti and ch 25 by Viterbo.

77 D Vitkauskaitė-Meurice, 'The UN-NATO cooperation in implementing the United Nations Security Council Resolution' (2014) 21 Jurisprudencija-Jurisprudence 336, 342.

78 A Viski, 'UNSCR 1540: Implementation Trends', in D Salisbury, I J Stewart, A Viski (eds), *Preventing the Proliferation of WMDs Measuring the Success of UN Security Council Resolution 1540* (London 2019) 40.

79 See, in particular: UNGA Res 42/37 (30 November 1987) UN Doc A/RES/42/37C; Report of the Secretary-General on chemical and biological weapons (4 October 1989) UN Doc A/44/561 Annex I; as well as UNSC Res. 620 (26 August 1988) UN Doc. S/Res/620.

of chemical weapons and their destruction outside of Syria.[80] Certainly, in this case, the Secretary-General's Mechanism contributed to launching the disarmament process in Syria. However, despite the success of such a 'complex, multinational disposal operation',[81] which certainly helped to eliminate 'the threat of further large-scale chemical weapons attacks by the Assad regime against the Syrian people and neighboring states',[82] smaller but still lethal chemical attacks have continued in Syria. Moreover, attribution and accountability remain hot topics.[83]

5 Concluding Remarks

The Syrian case demonstrates the pitfalls of a disarmament system with limited enforcement mechanisms, combined with the inability of UN sanctions to cope with the use of chemical and biological weapons, in particular, in case of both incidents of low intensity and incidents occurring in areas of very intense conflicts, which present serious difficulties in attribution of responsibility.[84]

This notwithstanding, a wider acceptance of the ACDL normative *corpus* can probably make a significant difference, also in view of the broader non-proliferation regime that has been described. As has rightly been stressed by

80 K Makdisi & C Pison Hindawi, 'The Syrian chemical weapons disarmament process in context: narratives of coercion, consent, and everything in between' (2017) 38 Third World Quarterly 1697.

81 A Sanders-Zakre, D Kimball, 'Responses to Violations of the Norm Against Chemical Weapons' (2019) Arms Control today <https://www.armscontrol.org/issue-briefs/2019-04/responses-violations-norm-against-chemical-weapons>. For details on the operation see: R Trapp, 'The Use of Chemical Weapons in Syria: Implications and Consequences', in B Friedrich, D Hoffmann, J Renn, F Schmaltz, M Wolf (eds), *One Hundred Years of Chemical Warfare: Research, Deployment, Consequences* (Springer 2017) 363.

82 Sanders-Zakre, Kimball (n 81).

83 A number of international bodies have been engaged in investigating alleged chemical weapons use in Syria. The Independent International Commission of Inquiry on the Syrian Arab Republic, established in 2011 by the Human Rights Council, released its Report in September 2018, documenting many chemical attacks, mostly perpetrated by the Syrian government. The OPCW Fact-Finding Mission was established in 2014 to determine if chemical weapons were used in reported attacks, while the OPCW-UN Joint Investigative Mechanism (JIM) was established by UN Security Council Resolution 2235 in 2015 to determine which party was responsible for chemical attacks. In its two years of operation, the JIM issued seven reports and found the Syrian government responsible for four chemical weapons attacks and the Islamic State guilty of two. Finally, in June 2018, a special session of CWC States Parties voted to establish the Investigation and Identification Team (IIT).

84 See ch 26 by Buscemi.

Sims and Littlewood, '[t]hese external mechanisms [...] do assist states to achieve the broader objectives of the regime'[85] established in the BWC and the CWC. The prospective success of the arms control and non-proliferation regime is conditioned by the synergy between the normative *corpus* and 'the wider world in which it operates'.[86]

In supporting the international efforts against the production and use of biological and chemical weapons, a major consideration of the 'normative role' of science and technology within the context of the Conventions is needed.[87] Considering the developments in life sciences and chemistry, timely adaptation of the Conventions provisions is of a keen importance and requires 'a new quality in the interaction between the OPCW and civil society, including chemical industry'.[88] In fact, with respect to these future prospects, the focus of disarmament needs to move from weapons elimination to weapons prevention and this probably requires a renewed engagement with different stakeholders[89] (science, industry, government, but also civil society), in order to reinforce the basis for 'compliance with the safe and responsible conduct and utilization of science'.[90]

Bibliography

Abe T, 'Challenge inspections under the Chemical Weapons Convention: between ideal and reality' (2017) 24 The Nonproliferation Review 167.

Asada M, 'Security Council Resolution 1540 to Combat WMD Terrorism: Effectiveness and Legitimacy in International Legislation' (2009) 13 Journal of Conflict & Security Law 303.

Block SM, 'The Growing Threat of Biological Weapons' (2001) 89 American Scientist 28.

Chevrier MI & Hunger I, 'Confidence-building measures for the BTWC: performance and potential' (2000) 7 The Nonproliferation Review 24.

Cross G & Klotz L, 'Twenty-first century perspectives on the Biological Weapon Convention: Continued relevance or toothless paper tiger' (2020) 76 Bulletin of the Atomic Scientists 185.

85 Sims & Littlewood (n 73) 501.

86 Ibid.

87 Evans (n 63).

88 Krutzsch, Myjer, Trapp (n 43) 13.

89 Ibid 14. Insisting on the need to support research on biodefence: C M Fraser & M R Dando, 'Genomics and future biological weapons: the need for preventive action by the biomedical community', (2001) 29 Nature Genetics 253.

90 McLeish & Trapp (n 2) 540.

Enemark C, 'The role of the Biological Weapons Convention in disease surveillance and response' (2010) 25 Health Policy and Planning 486.

Evans NG, 'Models of scientific and technological review for the Biological and Toxin Weapons Convention' (2019) 26 The Nonproliferation Review 351.

Feakes D, 'The Biological Weapons Convention' (2017) 36 Revue scientifique et technique de l'Office international des épizooties 621.

Fooks AR & Holmstrom LK, 'United Nations Secretary-General's Mechanism' (2017) 36 Revue scientifique et technique de l'Office international des épizooties 629.

Fraser CM & Dando MR, 'Genomics and future biological weapons: the need for preventive action by the biomedical community', (2001) 29 Nature Genetics 253.

Gargiulo P, 'Le armi chimiche. Aspetti di diritto internazionale e disarmo. Pt. I' (1987) 42 *La comunità internazionale*, 9.

Gargiulo P, 'Le armi chimiche. Aspetti di diritto internazionale e disarmo. Pt. II' (1987) 42 *La comunità internazionale*, 167.

Holst JJ, 'Confidence-Building Measures: A Conceptual Framework' (1983) 25 Survival 2.

Hunger I & Dingli S, 'Improving Transparency' (2011) 18 The Nonproliferation Review 513.

Joyner DH, *International Law and the Proliferation of Weapons of Mass Destruction* (OUP 2009).

Kienzle B, 'Effective Orchestration? The 1540 Committee and the WMD Terrorism Regime Complex' (2019) 10 Global Policy 486.

Krutzsch W, Myjer E, Trapp R, 'The Chemical Weapons Convention – Objectives, Principles, and Implementation Practice' in W Krutzsch, E Myjer, R Trapp (eds), *The Chemical Weapons Convention: A Commentary* (OUP 2014) 8.

Lentzos F, 'Strengthening the Biological Weapons Convention confidence-building measures: Toward a cycle of engagement' (2011) 67 Bulletin of the Atomic Scientists 26.

Lentzos F, 'Hard to prove' (2011) 18 The Nonproliferation Review 571.

Makdisi K & Pison Hindawi C, 'The Syrian chemical weapons disarmament process in context: narratives of coercion, consent, and everything in between' (2017) 38 Third World Quarterly 1691.

McLeish C & Trapp R, 'The life sciences revolution and the BWC' (2011) 18 The Nonproliferation Review 527.

Myjer E and Herbach J, 'Arms Control Law as the Common Legal Framework for CBRN Security' in A Malizia, M D'Arienzo (eds), *Enhancing CBRNE Safety & Security: Proceedings of the SICC 2017 Conference* (Springer 2018) 207.

Pitschmann V, 'Overall View of Chemical and Biochemical Weapons' (2014) 6 Toxins 1761.

Rajah TM, Dawson G and Aylett L, 'The Chemical Weapons Convention and the Contribution of the Organisation for the Prohibition of Chemical Weapons to Sustainable Development' (2019) 24 Journal of Conflict & Security Law 617.

Sims NA & Littlewood J, 'Ambitious incrementalism', (2011) 18 The Nonproliferation Review 499.

Sims NA, 'A simple treaty, a complex fulfillment: A short history of the Biological Weapons Convention Review Conferences' (2011) 67 Bulletin of the Atomic Scientists 8.

Taylor T, 'The Chemical Weapons Convention and prospects for implementation' (1993) 42 Int'l & Comp LQ 912.

Thornton CL, 'The G8 global partnership against the spread of weapons and materials of mass destruction' (2002) 9 The Nonproliferation Review 135.

Trapp R, 'The Use of Chemical Weapons in Syria: Implications and Consequences', in B Friedrich, D Hoffmann, J Renn, F Schmaltz, M Wolf (eds), *One Hundred Years of Chemical Warfare: Research, Deployment, Consequences* (Springer 2017) 363.

Üzümcü A, 'The Chemical Weapons Convention-disarmament, science and technology' (2014) 406 Analytical Bioanalytical Chemistry 5071.

Viski A, 'UNSCR 1540: Implementation Trends', in D Salisbury, IJ Stewart, A Viski (eds), *Preventing the Proliferation of WMDs Measuring the Success of UN Security Council Resolution 1540* (London 2019) 40.

Vitkauskaitė-Meurice D, 'The UN-NATO cooperation in implementing the United Nations Security Council Resolution' (2014) 21 Jurisprudencija-Jurisprudence 335.

Zanders JP & Smithson AE, 'Ensuring the future of the Biological Weapons Convention' (2011) 18 The Nonproliferation Review 479.

CHAPTER 24

International Legal Obligations Related to Nuclear Disarmament and Nuclear Testing

Andrea Spagnolo

1 Introduction

The present Chapter discusses and analyses the effectiveness of existing legal obligations related to nuclear disarmament and testing, starting with an overview of treaty obligations and then moving to and concluding with some reflections on the possibility that customary rules have evolved in *subiecta materia*. It will first present the current state of play on these issues in order to narrow down the main research questions; it then analyses the main legal issues arising from the two general international treaties on disarmament: the Non-Proliferation Treaty (NPT)[1] and the recent Treaty on the Prohibition of Nuclear Weapons (TPNW).[2] The analysis of treaty obligations then concludes with an overview of particular and bilateral treaty regimes, such as those establishing Nuclear Weapons Free Zones (NWFZ). In the concluding paragraph of the chapter, the possible evolution of a customary regime on disarmament will be addressed, with a view to offering some remarks *de lege ferenda*.

2 Nuclear Disarmament and Testing: Framing the Research Question(s)

There is no technical or normative definition of 'disarmament'. As we will see in this chapter, none of the relevant international treaties help in this regard. It is possibly in the light of this that scholars have elaborated their definition of disarmament, which can be found in the Encyclopaedia of Public International Law:

1 Treaty on the Non-Proliferation of Nuclear Weapons (1968).
2 Treaty on the Prohibition of Nuclear Weapons (2017).

> [t]he term disarmament embraces a variety of measures designed to limit or reduce, both quantitatively and qualitatively, eliminate, and cease the production of means of warfare.[3]

From the same encyclopaedia, it is possible to infer a more precise definition of 'disarmament' by reference to the definition of 'arms control'. The difference between the two terms is spelled out as follows:

> whereas disarmament seeks to reduce military capacity of all States – eventually to zero – arms control is primarily concerned with curbing the build-up of arms by introducing quantitative or qualitative ceilings for weapon systems, arms, and manpower.[4]

When it comes to nuclear disarmament, the absence of a normative definition is more sensitive. Despite some differences, scholars maintain that nuclear disarmament means that all nuclear arsenals must be dismantled.[5] Admittedly, such a view inspired the drafting of the NPT, which mentions in the Preamble, among its purposes, 'the cessation of the manufacture of nuclear weapons, the liquidation of all their existing stockpiles, and the elimination from national arsenals of nuclear weapons and the means of their delivery.'[6]

So, if 'disarmament' means nothing but … disarmament, what is the state of play on the dismantling of nuclear arsenals?

According to the most recent report published by the Stockholm International Peace Research Institute (SIPRI), at the beginning of 2020, the nine nuclear-weapons possessing States (NWS) – the United States, Russia, the United Kingdom, France, China, India, Pakistan, Israel and the Democratic People's Republic of Korea (North Korea) – could count on an arsenal of 13,400 nuclear weapons. Around 3,720 of those nuclear weapons are currently deployed with operational forces and nearly 1,800 of these are kept in a state of high operational alert.[7]

---

3 B Tuzmukhamedov, 'Disarmament', *EPIL* (May 2011), para 1.

4 A Loets, 'Arms Control', *EPIL* (July 2013), para 2.

5 See, for example, DH Joyner, *International Law and the Proliferation of Weapons of Mass Destruction* (Oxford University Press 2009) 64; see also and accordingly M Roscini, 'On certain legal issues arising from Article VI of the Treaty on the Non-Proliferation of Nuclear Weapons' in I Caracciolo, M Pedrazzi, T Vassalli di Dachenhausen (eds), *Nuclear Weapons: Strengthening the International Legal Regime* (eleven publishing 2016) 17.

6 Treaty on the Non-Proliferation of Nuclear Weapons (n 1), Preamble.

7 SIPRI, *Armaments, Disarmament and International Security*, Yearbook 2020, Summary (OUP 2020) see <https://www.sipri.org/yearbook/2020 14-15> (all links were last accessed on 31 May 2021).

The above numbers confirm a decreasing trend in the overall number of nuclear weapons, which can be explained by the reductions implemented by the USA and Russia, who still possess 90 per cent of nuclear weapons in the world, in execution of the 2010 Treaty on Measures for the Further Reduction and Limitation of Strategic Offensive Arms (New START). The recent administration change in the USA, and the consequent renewal of New START, which is now extended until 2026,[8] is surely a promising sign that channels of communication between the two Countries that possess the vast majority of nuclear weapons will be re-opened after a deadlock in the negotiations, reflecting the relationship between Russia and the previous USA administration.

However, that is the only good news about nuclear disarmament. The decision of the previous USA Administration to withdraw from the Joint Comprehensive Plan of Action (JCPOA)[9] that has curtailed Iran's ambition to become a NWS for years, weakens the ambition of the international community to avoid this scenario, which – according to some commentators – could push Saudi Arabia and Turkey to develop nuclear technologies for defending their national security interests in a geographical area (Middle East) that is not covered by any Nuclear Weapons Free Zone (NWFZ) treaty.[10]

Another reason for concern is the modernisation of NWS' arsenals. It is reported that China is in the middle of a significant transformation of its nuclear arsenal. Furthermore, India and Pakistan are slowly increasing the size and diversity of their nuclear forces, while North Korea continues to prioritise its military nuclear programme as a central element of its national security strategy and, in 2020, it conducted multiple flight tests of shorter-range ballistic missiles, including several new types of system, although it has since self-imposed a moratorium on testing.[11]

In the light of the above overview of the state of play, it appears immediately that, despite the slow decrease in the number of overall nuclear weapons, there are at least two reasons for concern: first, NWS are not abandoning the 'nuclear option' as they are modernising their arsenals and, at the same time, they are not speeding up the disarmament process; second, some non-nuclear weapons possessing States (NNWS) are developing plans to have their own nuclear weapons.

8 See New Start Treaty, <https://www.state.gov/new-start/>.

9 Remarks by President Trump on the Joint Comprehensive Plan of Action (8 May 2018), see <https://www.whitehouse.gov/briefings-statements/remarks-president-trump-joint-comprehensive-plan-action/>.

10 See *infra*, para 6.

11 SIPRI (n 7) 15.

From the viewpoint of international law, the above scenario demonstrates that the existing legal framework concerning disarmament can be questioned and its effectiveness can be the object of a critical scrutiny. In the most recent report of the Committee on Nuclear Weapons, Non-Proliferation and Contemporary International Law, the International Law Association (ILA) bluntly affirmed that '[e]fforts towards global and regional Nuclear Disarmament are still characterized by a lack of progress.'[12]

Evidence of a stalemate regarding the disarmament process can be found in the troublesome path leading up to the next NPT review conference, which is now postponed until 2022:[13] it is well known that NPT States Parties did not agree on the substance of a final document of the last review conference that took place in 2015.[14] Furthermore, the recent TPNW, despite its humanitarian aim, attracted much criticism from NWS and their allies.[15]

The stalemate is probably explained by the reliance of NWS on the doctrine of nuclear deterrence.[16] Just to give a few examples, in the 2018 Nuclear Posture Review of the USA, it is affirmed that '[t]he highest U.S. nuclear policy and strategy priority is to deter potential adversaries from nuclear attack of any scale.'[17] At NATO level, the 2010 Strategic Concept still considers deterrence as a 'core element'[18] of its overall strategy; more generally, NATO still regards itself as a nuclear alliance.[19]

---

12 Committee on Nuclear Weapons, Non-Proliferation and Contemporary International Law, 'Legal Challenges for Nuclear Deterrence and Security – Fifth Report' in International Law Association Report of the Seventy-Ninth Conference (Kyoto 2020) (International Law Association, Kyoto 2020) 4.

13 See Letter from the President-designate to all States Parties regarding the postponement of the NPT Review Conference (21 July 2021) <https://www.un.org/sites/un2.un.org/files/letter_from_president-designate_21072021.pdf>.

14 Ibid 8, para 8.

15 See *infra*, para 4.

16 On which, see ND White, 'Understanding Nuclear Deterrence Within the International Constitutional Architecture', in JL Black-Branch, D Fleck (eds), *Nuclear Non-Proliferation in International Law: Vol. V Legal Challenges for Nuclear Deterrence and Security* (Springer/Asser Press 2020) 254–258.

17 US Department of Defence, *Nuclear Posture Review 2018* (February 2018) <https://media.defense.gov/2018/Feb/02/2001872886/-1/-1/1/2018-NUCLEAR-POSTURE-REVIEW-FINAL-REPORT.PDF> 19.

18 NATO, *Active Engagement, Modern Force. Strategic Concept for the Defence and Security of the Members of the North Atlantic Treaty Organization* (2010) <https://www.nato.int/nato_static_fl2014/assets/pdf/pdf_publications/20120214_strategic-concept-2010-eng.pdf 14>, para 17.

19 Ibid.

In the light of this, it is plausible to identify some research questions that might help with building a research agenda: what are the main obstacles to a full implementation of the duties enshrined in the NPT? Is the TPNW going to change the current legal framework on disarmament? Does the whole set of international treaty and non-treaty rules suggest that, at least, there is room to argue for the evolution of a customary regime on disarmament?

3 The Legal Regime Envisaged by the 1968 Non-Proliferation Treaty

The governance of nuclear weapons has been the object of an intensive normative regulation through international treaties. Consequently, the analysis of existing treaty regulations is essential, beginning with the foundational text of the NPT. In the context of that treaty, it will be interesting to offer an analysis of the duty enshrined in Article VI to negotiate the cessation of the nuclear arms race.

Indeed, the NPT is still nowadays considered the cornerstone of the whole international legal nuclear non-proliferation regime.[20] The legal architecture envisaged by the NPT rests on three pillars and on a classification of States Parties into two categories: NWS and NNWS.[21]

The three pillars of the NPT are: civilian use of nuclear energy, non-proliferation of nuclear weapons, and disarmament of nuclear weapons.[22] As noted, there is no hierarchy between them and all of them, together, contribute to clarifying the object and purpose of the treaty.[23]

The structure of the NPT is reflected in the existence of two different prongs of obligations: on one side NWS are bound not to transfer to NNWS – or otherwise contribute or assist them to gain possess of – nuclear weapons (see Article I); on the other side, NNWS have the duty to refuse any such transfer or any other actions that might enable them to manufacture any nuclear weapons (Article III).

20 See *ex multis* I Caracciolo, 'The Limitations of the 1968 Treaty on the Non-Proliferation of Nuclear Weapons: International Law in Support of Nuclear Disarmament', in I Caracciolo, M Pedrazzi, T Vassalli di Dachenhausen (eds) (n 5) 6.

21 It must be noted, however, that not all the NWS States are Parties to the NPT. India and Israel never ratified the treaty and North Korea withdrew from it in 1993.

22 DH Joyner, *Interpreting the Nuclear Non-Proliferation Treaty* (Oxford University Press 2011) 75–76.

23 Ibid. See also ND White, 'Interpretation of Non-Proliferation Treaties', in DH Joyner, M Roscini (eds), *Non-Proliferation Law as a Special Regime* (Cambridge University Press 2012) 113.

Notwithstanding the above binary legal commitments, the NPT also contains provisions that bind at the same time both NWS and NNWS, namely Articles IV and V and Article VI. The first two articles set forth the inalienable right of all States to benefit from the development of nuclear energy when it is aimed at peaceful purposes. The most critical provision is surely Article VI, which states that:

> Each of the Parties to the Treaty undertakes to pursue negotiations in good faith on effective measures relating to cessation of the nuclear arms race at an early date and to nuclear disarmament, and on a treaty on general and complete disarmament under strict and effective international control.

Article VI is crucial as it binds NPT Parties to achieve three results: the cessation of the nuclear arms race; nuclear disarmament; and the conclusion of a treaty on general and complete disarmament. Article VI obliges the Parties to pursue negotiations in good faith on effective measures to achieve these aims. Despite some critical voices, there is agreement in legal scholarship that the text of Article VI suggests neither any prioritisation of the three results, nor any particular relationship between them.[24]

The interpretation of this provision is subject to a fierce debate among scholars and, primarily, between NWS and NNWS; therefore, its application is not univocal. The main contentions concern whether Article VI envisages a *pactum de negotiando* or a *pactum de contrahendo*;[25] what does the expression 'effective measures' mean; and, last but not least, whether the adoption of the TPNW might constitute a fulfilment of the obligation to conclude a general treaty on disarmament.

In this context, NWS have always maintained the position that the term 'pursue negotiations' means nothing but a good faith effort towards negotiations, hence an obligation 'of means.'[26] As a consequence, a failure to achieve a concrete result must not be attributed to any State in terms of international responsibility.

---

24 See again M Roscini (n 5) 16; DH Joyner (n 22) 101–102. For a contrary voice, see CA Ford, 'Debating Disarmament: Interpreting Article VI of the Treaty on the Non-Proliferation of Nuclear Weapons,' 14(3) Non-proliferation Review (November 2007) 404.

25 See specifically on the difference between *pactum de negotiando* and *pactum de contrahendo*, L Magi, 'L'obbligo di disarmo nucleare quale obbligo a realizzazione progressiva' (2018) 101 RivDirInt 58 ff.

26 See, for example, CA Ford (n 24) 403.

The ICJ had the occasion to pronounce itself on that provision in an *obiter dictum* in the Advisory Opinion on the *Legality of the Threat of Nuclear Weapons*.[27] The Court affirmed that:

> The legal import of that obligation goes beyond that of a mere obligation of conduct; the obligation involved here is an obligation to achieve a precise result – nuclear disarmament in all its aspects – by adopting a particular course of conduct, namely, the pursuit of negotiations on the matter in good faith.[28]

The ICJ consequently stated that Article VI contains a 'twofold obligation to pursue and to conclude negotiations.'[29] Although it appears that the ICJ interpreted Article VI as entailing an obligation *of result*, doubts have been raised as to the weight that can be accorded to the Court's pronouncement. As Ford notes,[30] the ICJ might have acted *ultra vires* in offering its interpretation of Article VI of the NPT, because it was not asked by the General Assembly to deliver an opinion on the NPT. Such a view can be justified also by the fact that the Court placed the above statements at the end of the Advisory Opinion, in a sort of *obiter dictum*[31] and by the debate among judges.[32]

Despite the disagreement on the interpretation of Article VI offered by the ICJ, it is important to look briefly at States' practice and, in particular, at the outcomes of the NPT Review Conferences to offer a realistic perspective on the interpretation of Article VI and to open legal questions on that basis.

In this regard, it must be recalled that at the 2000 NPT Review Conference, States Parties agreed on a final document that sets out the so-called 13 Practical Steps for the Implementation of Article VI, which range from the entry into force of the Comprehensive Nuclear-Test-Ban Treaty (CTBT) and the moratorium on nuclear tests pending the entry into force of the CTBT, to the negotiation of a treaty banning the production of fissile material for nuclear

27 *Legality of the Threat or Use of Nuclear Weapons* (Advisory Opinion) (1996) ICJ Report 226.

28 Ibid, para 99.

29 Ibid, para 100.

30 CA Ford (n 24) 402.

31 Ibid. See also DH Joyner (n 22) 97.

32 As noted by L Magi (n 25) 64, Judge Guillaume appended an individual opinion affirming precisely that the ICJ acted *ultra petita* (*Legality of the Threat or Use of Nuclear Weapons* (n 27) 287); to the contrary, Judge President Bedjaoui linked the need to interpret Article VI to the whole discourse on the legality of the use of nuclear weapons (ibid 267).

weapons, and finally to some steps that urge NWS to engage in measures aimed at the reduction and eventual total dismantling of their nuclear arsenals.[33]

The 13 Practical Steps were upheld in the course of the 2010 NPT Review Conference, where States agreed on an Action Plan to implement the 13 Practical Steps that were reduced to seven 'concrete steps.'[34] Significantly, those steps include 'the unequivocal undertaking of the nuclear-weapon States to accomplish the total elimination of their nuclear arsenals leading to nuclear disarmament, to which all States Parties are committed under article VI' and the 'continued validity of the practical steps agreed to in the Final Document of the 2000 Review Conference.' Also, for the first time in an NPT Review Conference, States Parties expressed deep concern at the catastrophic humanitarian consequences of any use of nuclear weapons, even though this is referenced in the Preamble of the NPT.[35]

As the 2015 NPT Review Conference did not produce any final document, the 2010 Action Plan still serves as the latest valid guidance agreed by States Parties.

In light of this situation, the main legal question that is still open is whether the outcomes of NPT Review Conferences can be used to interpret the obligations set forth in Article VI of the NPT and thus to clarify the fog that surrounds that provision. In particular, it is reasonable to ask whether the 13 Practical Steps and 2010 Action Plan could be the 'effective measures' that are to be negotiated by NPT States Parties, as advocated by some scholars.[36]

In this respect, one possibility is to consider the outcomes of the NPT Review Conferences as subsequent agreements or practice in the terms of Articles 31 or 32 of the Vienna Convention on the Law of Treaties (VCLT). According to the ILC's Draft Conclusion no. 11 on subsequent agreements and subsequent practice in the interpretation of treaties, it is possible that final documents of conferences of States Parties to a treaty constitute subsequent agreements or practice, depending on the circumstances of their adoption.[37] Furthermore, in the commentary to Draft Conclusion no. 11, the ILC explicitly mentioned

---

33 2000 Review Conference of the Parties to the Treaty on the Non-Proliferation of Nuclear Weapons, Final Document (New York 2000) NPT/CONF.2000/28 (Parts I and II) 14–15.

34 2010 Review Conference of the Parties to the Treaty on the Non-Proliferation of Nuclear Weapons, Final document (New York 2010) NPT/CONF.2010/50 (Vol. I) 19–20.

35 Ibid.

36 See M Roscini (n 5), L Magi (n 25) and DH Joyner (n 22) 102.

37 ILC, 'Draft conclusions on subsequent agreements and subsequent practice in relation to the interpretation of treaties' in 'Report of the International Law Commission on the Work of its the 70th Session' (30 April–1 June and 2 July–10 August 2018) UN Doc. A/73/10, 15.

the NPT Review Conferences to identify the category of conferences of States Parties whose outcome falls under the scope of application of the conclusion.[38]

Determining the interpretive value of the final documents is not merely a theoretical exercise: should States Parties agree on the above approach, failure to fulfil the 13 Practical Steps and/or the 2010 Action Plan could give rise to a violation of the obligations contained in Article VI of the NPT; moreover, there would be much more clarity on the content of a much-debated provision. In particular, this approach would definitely counter the NWS' argument that the obligation to disarm is dependent on the conclusion of a general treaty with this object and purpose.[39]

4 The Treaty on the Prohibition of Nuclear Weapons

However, a new general treaty on disarmament actually exists. The TPNW entered into force on the 21 January 2021. Its adoption represented the culmination of a path begun in 2010, known as 'The Humanitarian Initiative', fostered by 16 States Parties to the NPT, which tried to propose, with no success, a 'humanitarian' approach to nuclear weapons, in the course of the 2015 NPT Review Conference.[40] The contents of the initiative, which aimed at preventing 'catastrophic, persistent effects of nuclear weapons on our health, societies and the environment' through a complete ban on nuclear weapons originated in the already mentioned clause inserted in the 2010 NPT Review Conference that highlighted the 'catastrophic humanitarian consequences that would result from the use of nuclear weapons.'[41]

The content of the initiative was taken up at the UN level, thanks to the endorsement by the Council of Delegates of the ICRC,[42] and some UN agencies

38 Ibid 83.

39 The NWS' interpretation builds on the Preamble of the NPT, in which it is stated that States Parties desire to disarm 'pursuant to a Treaty on general and complete disarmament under strict and effective international control'. See again CA Ford (n 24) 403.

40 A Kmentt, 'The Development of the International Initiative on the Humanitarian Impact of Nuclear Weapons and its Effects on the Nuclear Weapons Debate' (2015) 97 IRRC 681. On the negotiating and drafting history of the TPNW, see S Casley Maslen, *The Treaty on the Prohibition of Nuclear Weapons: A Commentary* (OUP 2019) 47 ff.

41 2010 Review Conference of the Parties to the Treaty on the Non-Proliferation of Nuclear Weapons, Final document (New York 2010) NPT/CONF.2010/50 (Vol. I) 19.

42 See ICRC, *Working towards the elimination of nuclear weapons* (26 November 2011) <https://www.icrc.org/eng/resources/documents/resolution/council-delegates-resolution-1-2011.htm>. The resolution contains an appeal to all States 'to pursue in good faith and conclude with urgency and determination negotiations to prohibit the use

and NGOs, such as the International Campaign to Abolish Nuclear Weapons (ICAN), which was awarded the Nobel Peace Prize for its efforts.

The TPNW was, therefore, negotiated within the framework of a mandate given by the UNGA in Resolution 71/258, titled 'Taking forward multilateral nuclear disarmament negotiation', adopted with 113 votes to 35 and 13 abstentions.[43]

Significantly, none of the nine NWS joined the negotiation of the Treaty, though China abstained in the voting in the UNGA. The negotiations suffered from a boycott by States that have agreements with the USA on the stationing of nuclear weapons on their soil, except for the Netherlands, which participated in all the drafting conference under pressure from its Parliament but, at the end, voted against the adoption of the treaty.

As to the content of the treaty, it is important to devote some words to the approach that inspired its negotiation. Ambassador Whyte Gomez from Costa Rica, President of the negotiating conference, issued a non-paper to present the first draft of the treaty, stating that it would be built on four principles: complementarity with the existing disarmament regime, in particular the NPT; reinforcement of existing obligations; non-discrimination between NWS and NNWS; and a flexible design to endure for the long term.[44]

Building on these founding principles, the TPNW includes a comprehensive set of prohibitions on participating in any nuclear weapon activities, which can easily be associated with a complete ban on nuclear weapons. The restrictions – which are, for the most part, listed in Article 1 of the Treaty – include not to develop, test, produce, acquire, possess, stockpile, use or threaten to use nuclear weapons. Significantly – and critically, as we will see later – the Treaty prohibits the deployment of nuclear weapons on the national territory of States Parties and makes illegal the provision of assistance to any State in the conduct of prohibited activities.

It is immediately clear that the TPNW is built on a different rationale to that of the NPT: whereas the latter still considers the use of nuclear weapons as a viable option for defending national security, the former does not admit any reservation to Article 1 (see Article 16), hence it puts all the States – whether NWS or NNWS – on the same plane. The rationale of the TPNW is not the only feature of the treaty that deserves comment. Indeed, in the set of prohibitions,

---

of and completely eliminate nuclear weapons through a legally binding international agreement.'

43 UNGA Res 71/258 (11 January 2017) UN Doc A/RES/71/258.

44 Letter from Ambassador Elayne Whyte Gomez (Costa Rica) (Geneva 22 May 2017) <https://s3.amazonaws.com/unoda-web/wp-content/uploads/2017/05/Letter-from-the-Chair May-24-2017.pdf> 2.

the negotiating States agreed to include a ban on the use of nuclear weapons 'under any circumstances', an expression that with no interpretive doubts refers also to armed conflicts.[45] Such an inclusion, which is in line with the position of the ICRC, represents the first explicit prohibition of the use of nuclear weapons in armed conflict. Indeed, it is useful to recall that in the 1996 Advisory Opinion, the ICJ was not able to reach a similar conclusion, though it admitted that the use of nuclear weapons might violate the principle of proportionality.[46]

Last but not least, the TPNW, building on one of its founding principles, does not foresee any termination date: Article 17 sets an unlimited duration for the treaty. It is certainly possible for States Parties to withdraw, but to do so they have to justify the existence of 'extraordinary events' and to notify the other States Parties 12 months before the expected date of withdrawal. Moreover, the same article contains a safe clause that maintains the prohibition on using nuclear weapons in armed conflict if the withdrawing State is engaged in an armed conflict, until the expiration of the 12-month notification period.

According to its founding principles, the TPNW is meant to complement the already existing international legal obligations on disarmament, especially the NPT. This is confirmed by the Preamble of the treaty, in which the necessity to fully implement the NPT is reaffirmed and regarded as the cornerstone of international law on disarmament. To this end, the TPNW contains a saving clause, Article 19, according to which 'The implementation of this Treaty shall not prejudice obligations undertaken by States Parties with regard to existing international agreements, to which they are party, where those obligations are consistent with the Treaty.'

The content of the above-mentioned clause, though it was probably designed to link the NPT and the TPNW, reinforced the criticisms of NWS and their allies. Indeed, the wording of Article 19 clearly sets out that the TPNW shall not prejudice 'obligations' undertaken by States Parties, but it does not say that the TPNW shall not prejudice 'rights' conferred to States Parties under existing international agreements, implying that all the rights accorded to NWS are inconsistent with the TPNW.[47] This view is also confirmed by Article 4,

45 See, accordingly, M Pedrazzi, 'The Treaty on the Prohibition of Nuclear Weapons: A Promise, a Threat or a Flop?' (2017) ItYBIL 220. This interpretation is supported by the Preamble of the TPNW: 'Considering that any use of nuclear weapons would be contrary to the rules of international law applicable in armed conflict, in particular the principles and rules of international humanitarian law'.

46 See, again, M Pedrazzi (n 45) 221.

47 For an analysis from this angle, see S Casley Maslen, 'The Relationship of the 2017 Treaty on the Prohibition of Nuclear Weapons with other Agreements: Ambiguity,

which dictates that each State Party of the treaty must dismantle its nuclear arsenal 'in accordance with a legally binding, time-bound plan for the verified and irreversible elimination of that State Party's nuclear-weapon programme, including the elimination or irreversible conversion of all nuclear-weapons-related facilities.' Accordingly, NWS can theoretically adhere to the TPNW before the dismantling of their nuclear arsenals, but if they do so, they assume an obligation to eliminate their nuclear weapons' programmes.[48]

In light of the above, which is nothing but a confirmation that the TPNW builds on a non-discriminatory approach, it appears clear that the treaty admits no dedicated paths for NWS. Their reaction, therefore and predictably, has been a firm opposition to the TPNW. In a joint declaration, the USA, France and UK affirmed that:

> We do not intend to sign, ratify or ever become party to it. Therefore, there will be no change in the legal obligations on our countries with respect to nuclear weapons.[49]

Critically, the three States observed that:

> This initiative clearly disregards the realities of the international security environment. Accession to the ban treaty is incompatible with the policy of nuclear deterrence, which has been essential to keeping the peace in Europe and North Asia for over 70 years. A purported ban on nuclear weapons that does not address the security concerns that continue to make nuclear deterrence necessary cannot result in the elimination of a single nuclear weapon and will not enhance any country's security, nor international peace and security. It will do the exact opposite by creating even more divisions at a time when the world needs to remain united in the face of growing threats, including those from the DPRK's ongoing proliferation efforts. This treaty offers no solution to the grave threat posed

---

Complementarity, or Conflict?' (1st August 2017) *EJIL: Talk!*, <https://www.ejiltalk.org/the-relationship-of-the-2017-treaty-on-the-prohibition-of-nuclear-weapons-with-other-agreements-ambiguity-complementarity-or-conflict/>. More in general, see also M Sossai, 'Il rapporto tra il trattato sul divieto di armi nucleari e gli altri accordi in materia di non proliferazione e disarmo' (2018) 1 RivDirInt 185.

48 See M Sossai (n 47).

49 Joint Press Statement from the Permanent Representatives to the United Nations of the United States, United Kingdom, and France Following the Adoption (7 July 2017) <https://usun.usmission.gov/joint-press-statement-from-the-permanent-representatives-to-the-united-nations-of-the-united-states-united-kingdom-and-france-following-the-adoption/>.

> by North Korea's nuclear program, nor does it address other security challenges that make nuclear deterrence necessary. A ban treaty also risks undermining the existing international security architecture which contributes to the maintenance of international peace and security.

Russia took a similar stance: 'At that time, we saw the domination of a dangerous and delusive trend towards forcing the nuclear powers to abandon their nuclear stockpiles without any regard for their security interests and strategic realities.'[50] Similarly, China, who, it must be recalled, did not oppose the UNGA resolution that launched the negotiations of the TPNW, affirmed that a full nuclear disarmament must be achieved in the light of the 'principle of safeguarding global strategic stability and compromising the security of no country', which are best assured in the existing non-proliferation regimes.[51]

Significantly, India, which is regarded as a NWS, but is not a Party to the NPT 'supported the commencement of negotiations on a comprehensive Nuclear Weapons Convention in the Conference on Disarmament, which is the world's single multilateral disarmament negotiation forum working on the basis of consensus.'[52]

Criticisms towards the TPNW were also raised by NNWS, which nonetheless are allied to NWS. This is a critical factor that impacts, in particular, on NNWS having military agreements with NWS on the installation of nuclear facilities or devices on their territories, within the context of NATO. According to the 2010 Strategic Concept, whereas only three NATO Members are NWS, the whole alliance 'ensure the broadest possible participation of Allies in collective defence planning on nuclear roles, in peacetime basing of nuclear forces, and in command, control and consultation arrangements.'[53] In such a context, five NATO States – Belgium, Germany, Italy, the Netherlands and Turkey – still host on their territories nuclear weapons deployed by the USA in the context of the so-called NATO Nuclear Sharing policy.[54] Such a circumstance virtually makes

50 Foreign Minister Sergey Lavrov's remarks at a UN Security Council meeting on the Non-Proliferation of Weapons of Mass Destruction: Confidence Building Measures (18 January 2018) <https://russiaun.ru/en/news/sclav_1801>.

51 Foreign Ministry Spokesperson Hua Chunying's Regular Press Conference on March 20 (20 March 2017) <https://www.fmprc.gov.cn/ce/cenp/eng/fyrth/t1447146.htm>.

52 Response by the Official Spokesperson to a media query regarding India's view on the Treaty to ban nuclear weapons (18 July 2017) <https://www.mea.gov.in/media-briefings.htm?dtl/28628>.

53 NATO (n 18) 19.

54 See, for more details, Berlin Information-Center for Transnational Security (BITS), *NATO Nuclear Sharing and the NPT – Questions to be Answered* (June 1997) <http://www.bits.de/public/researchnote/rn97-3.htm>.

it impossible for those States to adhere to the TPNW. However, the domestic political dynamics of Germany,[55] Italy[56] and the Netherlands[57] deserve attention: in all three countries, national Parliaments are pushing their respective Governments to find ways to join the TPNW. In Belgium, the Government adopted a report in which it committed to explore the possibility of joining the TPNW.[58]

5 Regional and Bilateral Treaties on Disarmament and Testing

International treaty obligations on nuclear disarmament and testing can be found in a variety of international treaties. As of today, one can count a series of treaties establishing the so-called nuclear weapons free zones (NWFZ) agreements; treaties applicable only to pre-determined geographic areas; and two treaties specifically dedicated to nuclear testing.

According to UNGA Resolution 3472B of 1975,[59] a NWFZ is characterised by the total absence of nuclear weapons and by the existence of an international system of verification and control.[60] As it is the same UNGA Resolution to state that NWFZ must be the result of a 'free exercise of sovereignty',[61] their establishment must be achieved through the conclusion of international treaties. As of now, five such treaties are in force: the 1967 Treaty of Tlatelolco,[62] which creates a NWFZ in Latin America and the Caribbean; the 1985 Treaty of Rarotonga,[63] applicable in the South Pacific; the 1995 Treaty of Pelindaba,[64] applicable in Africa; the 1996 Treaty of Bangkok,[65] establishing the Southeast Asia Nuclear Weapons Free Zone; and finally the 2006 Treaty of Semipalatinsk,[66] which institutes a NWFZ in Central Asia. All five treaties share the same features: they are signed at a regional level, with the initial involvement of a small number of States but foreseeing the participation of NWS that can accept some

55 ICAN, Germany <https://www.icanw.org/germany>.
56 ICAN, Italy <https://www.icanw.org/italy>.
57 ICAN, Netherlands <https://www.icanw.org/netherlands>.
58 ICAN, Belgium <https://www.icanw.org/belgium_tpnw_shift>.
59 UNGA Res 3472B (XXX) (11 December 1975).
60 Ibid, para 1.
61 Ibid.
62 Treaty for the Prohibition of Nuclear Weapons in Latin America (1967).
63 South Pacific Nuclear Free Zone Treaty (1985).
64 The African Nuclear-Weapon-Free Zone Treaty (1996).
65 Treaty on the Southeast Asia Nuclear Weapon-Free Zone (1995).
66 Treaty on a Nuclear-Weapon-Free Zone in Central Asia (2006).

obligations related to the respect of denuclearised zones, through the ratification of apposite optional protocols. Regarding the content, NWFZ Treaties prohibit the possession and even the stationing on national territories of nuclear weapons; significantly, with exception of the Treaty of Tlatelololco, all the other NWFZ treaties oblige NWS Parties not to test any nuclear weapons in the zone delimited by the treaty itself.

The international legal regime concerning nuclear disarmament is also composed of three sectoral treaties: the 1959 Antarctic Treaty,[67] which was the first ever agreement on nuclear weapons; the 1966 Outer Space Treaty;[68] and the 1971 Seabed Arms Treaty.[69] The first is broad in scope as it provides that Antarctica 'shall be used for peaceful purposes only', with the consequence that 'any measures of military nature' are prohibited, including the use of nuclear weapons. Article IV of the Outer Space Treaty explicitly prohibits parties to place in orbit nuclear weapons or weapons of mass destruction, though it does not ban the use of nuclear weapons in outer space or prevent the launching of nuclear weapons from Earth into space. Similar provisions feature in the Seabed Arms Treaty, which prohibits any activities aimed at implanting on the seabed nuclear weapons or any other weapons of mass-destruction.

Nuclear testing is also specifically governed by the 1963 Partial Test Ban Treaty[70] and the 1996 Comprehensive Test Ban Treaty (CTBT)[71] that is not yet in force. The Test Ban Treaty of 1963 prohibits nuclear weapons tests 'or any other nuclear explosion' in the atmosphere, in outer space, and under water. Whereas it does not ban underground tests, the Treaty contains a general prohibition of nuclear explosions if they cause 'radioactive debris to be present outside the territorial limits of the State under whose jurisdiction or control' the explosions were conducted. In accepting limitations on testing, the nuclear powers accepted as a common goal 'an end to the contamination of man's environment by radioactive substances.' This treaty is in force and applies also to NWS, which are Parties to it; however, it does not foresee an international verification mechanism, leaving such an activity to States Parties. This circumstance prompted calls for the conclusion of the CTBT that entails an overall

67 The Antarctic Treaty (1959).

68 Treaty on principles governing the activities of States in the exploration and use of outer space, including the moon and other celestial bodies (1967).

69 Treaty on the prohibition of the emplacement of nuclear weapons and other weapons of mass destruction on the sea-bed and the ocean floor and in the subsoil thereof (1971).

70 Treaty banning nuclear weapon tests in the atmosphere, in outer space and under water (1963).

71 Comprehensive Nuclear-Test-Ban Treaty (1996).

prohibition on conducting nuclear tests and – most importantly – establishes the Comprehensive Nuclear Test Ban Treaty Organization (CNTBTO), an international monitoring system that may conduct on-site inspections. The CTBT requires ratification by all NWS to enter into force, which so far has not happened, hence a stalemate exists on this front. For the same reason, the CNTBTO is not yet operative, though a preparatory commission was envisaged and currently operates in Vienna.

Some last words can be spent on particular treaty-based regimes. As mentioned in the second paragraph of this chapter, the USA and Russia – which possess the majority of nuclear weapons or devices in the world – established a regime under the START treaty-regime by which they limit their respective nuclear warheads. The bilateral regime between the two nuclear powers is now regulated by the New START, which was negotiated in 2010 and renewed at the beginning of 2021. It must not be forgotten that the USA and Russia are still also part of the Intermediate-Range Nuclear Force Treaty (INF), signed in 1987 and entered into force in 1988, which still binds the two States to eliminate all nuclear and conventional ground-launched ballistic and cruise missiles with ranges of between 500 and 5,500 kilometres.

Another particular regime is represented by the already mentioned JCPOA, an agreement signed by Iran with the five permanent Members of the UN Security Council on 14 July 2015. The JPCOA was endorsed by UN Security Council Resolution 2231 and adopted on 20 July 2015. According to the plan, Iran is bound to reduce the enrichment of uranium. Iran's compliance with the nuclear-related provisions of the JCPOA will be verified by the International Atomic Energy Agency (IAEA) according to certain requirements set forth in the agreement.

6 Customary International Rules on Disarmament and Testing

As demonstrated by the analysis performed in previous paragraphs, it must be acknowledged that the existing international treaty regimes might not be sufficient to place effective limitations on the nuclear arms race or on testing, given that all NWS are still not bound by any treaty-based prohibition. This substantiates the necessity to investigate the existence of international legal obligations of a customary nature.

It is important to recall that the existence of a customary duty to disarm nuclear arsenals was at the core of the application of the Marshall Islands against India before the ICJ that never reached the merits stage due to the

Court's ruling on the absence of a dispute between the parties.[72] This issue, therefore, is still of practical relevance, especially in light of the entry into force of the TPNW which, according to a recent comment, could pave the way for the affirmation of a customary prohibition on using or threatening to use nuclear weapons.[73]

In this regard, one must not forget that the ICJ already had the chance to scrutinise whether a prohibition against using or threatening to use nuclear weapons had acquired customary status. In the 1996 Advisory Opinion, the Court ruled out the existence of a customary rule that prohibits using or threatening to use nuclear weapons, on the ground that a firm and consolidated *opinio juris* did not exist at that time. In particular, the ICJ found that all the UNGA Resolutions condemning the use of nuclear weapons, though potentially able to have a normative impact on the evolution of international law, were adopted with abstentions and contrary votes.[74] Moreover, the Court also noted that the same Resolutions did not contain any reference to such a customary rule.[75] This reasoning brought the ICJ to conclude that:

> [t]he emergence, as *lex lata*, of a customary rule specifically prohibiting the use of nuclear weapons as such is hampered by the continuing tensions between the nascent *opinio juris* on the one hand, and the still strong adherence to the practice of deterrence on the other.[76]

As more than 20 years have passed since the adoption of the Advisory Opinion, it is reasonable to verify if that finding is still valid. In this regard, some elements that emerge from the analysis performed in the previous paragraphs can be helpful. Indeed, the stalemate of the NPT Review Conferences, the consequent slowness in the disarmament process, and the emergence of new nuclear threats corroborate the Court's findings. Furthermore, the adoption and the entry into force of the TPNW, as seen above, were welcomed with

72 *Obligations concerning Negotiations relating to Cessation of the Nuclear Arms Race and to Nuclear Disarmament* (*Marshall Islands v. India*) (Jurisdiction of the Court and admissibility of the application) (2016) ICJ Report 255.

73 G Lythgoe, 'Nuclear Weapons and International Law: The Impact of the Treaty on the Prohibition of Nuclear Weapons' (2 December 2020) *EJIL: Talk!* <https://www.ejiltalk.org/nuclear-weapons-and-international-law-the-impact-of-the-treaty-on-the-prohibition-of-nuclear-weapons/>.

74 *Legality of the Threat or Use of Nuclear Weapons* (Advisory Opinion) (n 27) para 72.

75 Ibid.

76 Ibid, para 73.

strong critiques from the NWS and some declarations aimed precisely at denying a customary status to the rules contained in the new treaty. In the already mentioned joint statement, France, USA and UK clearly affirmed that:

> we would not accept any claim that this treaty reflects or in any way contributes to the development of customary international law. Importantly, other states possessing nuclear weapons and almost all other states relying on nuclear deterrence have also not taken part in the negotiations.[77]

The argument raised by France, USA and UK mirrors the usual approach of NWS regarding the evolution of customary rules in the field of nuclear disarmament. Indeed, despite an isolated statement from China,[78] NWS have always adhered to the doctrine of nuclear deterrence, in their exercise of their rights to self-defence, as seen in the second paragraph of this chapter. This, as seen above, was considered by the ICJ as a strong obstacle to the formation of a customary rule on the prohibition of nuclear weapons.

At this stage of the analysis, one must admit that the debate on the possible evolution of a customary prohibition of nuclear weapons suffers from the strong opposition of NWS to the TPNW.

However, one must not underestimate the fact that the new treaty may still produce normative effects. In the future, more States could potentially join the TPNW and its implementation practice might contribute to attracting consensus over the obligations listed therein. Consequently, a legal argument can be made in favour of the possibility that *per se* the TPNW could contribute to the formation of a customary rule prohibiting nuclear weapons. According to the *North Sea Continental Shelf* case, 'widespread and representative' participation in a treaty can be considered evidence of the formation of a customary rule, provided that 'States whose interests were specially affected' participate in the treaty.[79] The ICJ confirmed this approach to the relationship between

77 See *supra* footnote 48.

78 'Before the goal of complete prohibition and thorough destruction of nuclear weapons is achieved, nuclear-weapon states should commit themselves to no first use of nuclear weapons and undertake unconditionally not to use or threaten to use nuclear weapons against non-nuclear-weapon states or nuclear-weapon-free zones. Nuclear-weapon states should abandon the policies of nuclear deterrence based on the first use of nuclear weapons and reduce the role of nuclear weapons in their national security.' Statement of the Chinese Delegation on Draft Resolutions Related to Nuclear Disarmament before the Vote (New York, 24 October 2005) <https://www.fmprc.gov.cn/mfa_eng/wjb_663304/zzjg_663340/jks_665232/jkxw_665234/t219978.shtml>.

79 *North Sea Continental Shelf* (*Federal Republic of Germany/Netherlands*) (Merit) (1969) ICJ Report 3, para 73.

treaties and custom in a later judgment: 'multilateral conventions may have an important role to play in recording and defining rules deriving from custom, or indeed in developing them.'[80]

The doctrine of 'specially affected States' is therefore crucial.[81] It was invoked by the USA and the UK before the ICJ during the proceedings related to the *Nuclear Weapons* Advisory Opinion. In particular, the USA held that 'customary law could not be created over the objection of the nuclear weapon States, which are the states whose interests are most specially affected.'[82] The ICJ did not make recourse to that legal argument. Interestingly, in the recent 2016 judgment on the Preliminary Objections in the *Marshall Islands* case, the ICJ regarded the applicant in the proceedings (the Marshall Islands) as 'specially affected with regard to whether customary international law requires states to affirmatively pursue nuclear disarmament'.[83] The statement was made explicit by the Court when it held that the Marshall Islands 'has special reasons for concern about nuclear disarmament.'[84]

The ILC did not explicitly include the notion of 'specially affected States' in the *Draft Conclusions on the Identification of Customary International Law*, but it mentioned it in the Commentary to Draft Conclusion no. 8 on the requirement of generality of the practice:

> While in many cases all or virtually all States will be equally affected, it would clearly be impractical to determine, for example, the existence and content of a rule of customary international law relating to navigation in maritime zones without taking into account the practice of relevant coastal States and flag States, or the existence and content of a rule on foreign investment without evaluating the practice of the capital-exporting States as well as that of the States in which investment is made.[85]

80 *Continental Shelf* (*Libyan Arab Jamahiriya/Malta*) (Merit) (1985) ICJ Report 13, para 27.

81 See, extensively, KJ Heller, 'Specially-Affected States and the Formation of Custom' (2018) 11 AJIL 191 ff.

82 *See Legality of the Threat or Use of Nuclear Weapons* (n 27) Letter Dated 20 June 1995 from the Acting Legal Adviser to the Department of State, Together with Written Statement of the Government of the United States of America, 8–9.

83 *Obligations concerning Negotiations relating to Cessation of the Nuclear Arms Race and to Nuclear Disarmament* (*Marshall Islands v. India*) (n 72) para 44.

84 Ibid.

85 ILC, 'Draft Conclusions on the Identification of Customary International Law' in 'Report of the International Law Commission on the Work of its the 70th Session' (30 April–1 June and 2 July–10 August 2018) (n 37) 136–137. See, accordingly, T Treves, 'Customary Law', *EPIL* (2012), para 36.

The Commentary seems to confirm that in the formation of customs there is no univocal interpretation of the notion of 'specially affected States', which surely means that it is not necessarily only the practice of NWS that counts in the context of nuclear disarmament.[86] Accordingly, the TPNW could potentially be a vehicle for the evolution of a customary regime on nuclear weapons.[87]

This might be a long path as regards the full prohibition of nuclear weapons and the duty to disarm; however, that does not mean that the TPNW is not able already to confirm the existence of some customary rules related to nuclear disarmament.

Indeed, as noted, there has been no formal contestation, even by NWS, of the prohibition to transfer nuclear devices to NNWS or to Non-State Actors. The fact that such a prohibition is included in the NPT and the TPNW and in all the treaties establishing NWFZ, which for the most part are signed and ratified also by NWS, is evidence of the formation of custom. In addition, NWS' practice seems to be coherent with this prohibition: in a 2008 white paper, France, describing the *Proliferation Security Initiative* affirmed that:

> It now includes almost 90 signatories. It aims at improving operational cooperation among governmental actors in order to identify and prohibit the transfer of materials or equipment that may contribute to programmes on nuclear weapons and their means of delivery.

A similar reasoning can apply also to the prohibition on conducting nuclear tests, although the CTBT is not entered into force. States' practice seems to go in this direction: NNWS – and, in particular, States negatively affected by nuclear tests – have always maintained that NWS must not perform nuclear tests; the latter's resistance to this duty is fragile, as witnessed by France and the USA's declaration on testing. Whereas the first State already ratified the CTBT and calls for universal ratification,[88] the latter has not yet adhered to the treaty but has confirmed its commitment to a long-term prohibition of nuclear testing.[89]

86 See KJ Heller (n 81) 220–221; S Casley Maslen (n 40) 58.

87 See, accordingly, Gail Lythgoe (n 73).

88 Ministry of Defence, France, White Paper on 'Defence and National Security' (2008) <https://ihl-databases.icrc.org/customary-ihl/eng/docs/v2_rul_nuwea>.

89 United States, Report by the President, '201 National Security Strategy', (2010) 23 <https://ihl-databases.icrc.org/customary-ihl/eng/docs/v2_rul_nuwea>.

The ICJ, in the *Nuclear Tests* case, adopted interim measures that, at least, confirmed that nuclear testing violates sovereignty rights of the affected States:

> the French Government should avoid nuclear tests causing the deposit of radio-active fallout on the territory of New Zealand, the Cook Islands, Niue, or the Tokelau Islands.[90]

In this respect, one should also consider that nuclear testing threatens the respect of international environmental norms, which have already acquired the status of custom, such as Principle 21 of the Stockholm Declaration, under which States have the responsibility to 'ensure that activities within their jurisdiction or control do not cause damage to the environment[s] of other States or of areas beyond the limits of national jurisdiction.'[91]

7 Concluding Remarks

The main research questions raised in this Chapter concern the effectiveness of international legal obligations on disarmament. The answers are not univocal.

On one side, the effectiveness of international law on nuclear disarmament still rests on the implementation of the NPT, and in particular of Article VI. In this regard, the next NPT review conference will be called on to clarify crucial doubts, such as the legal value of the Action Plan agreed by States Parties in order to implement that provision.

On the other side, the stalemate characterising this phase of the disarmament process is affected by the entry into force of the TPNW. Whereas, at present, the treaty in itself has attracted severe critiques from NWS, in the future, it could catalyse States' practice and *opinio juris*, hence contributing to consolidate a customary regime that might potentially fill the gaps of a treaty regime that is not always capable of coping with the nuclear threat.

---

90 *Nuclear Tests (Australia v. France)* (Provisional Measures) (1974) ICJ Report 253, 106.

91 Report of the UN Conference on the human environment, UN Doc A/CONF.48/4 (1972) 2 ff. The customary nature of Principle 21 was confirmed by the ICJ in the Advisory Opinion on the *Legality of the Threat or Use of Nuclear Weapons* (para 30). See, accordingly, P Sands, J Peel, *Principles of International Environmental Law* (Cambridge University Press 2018) 196.

Bibliography

Caracciolo I, 'The Limitations of the 1968 Treaty on the Non-Proliferation of Nuclear Weapons: International Law in Support of Nuclear Disarmament', in I Caracciolo, M Pedrazzi, T Vassalli di Dachenhausen (eds), *Nuclear Weapons: Strengthening the International Legal Regime* (eleven publishing 2016) 1.

Casley Maslen S, *The Treaty on the Prohibition of Nuclear Weapons: A Commentary* (OUP 2019).

Ford CA, 'Debating Disarmament: Interpreting Article VI of the Treaty on the Non-Proliferation of Nuclear Weapons,' 14(3) Non-proliferation Review (November 2007) 401.

Heller KJ, 'Specially-Affected States and the Formation of Custom' (2018) 11 AJIL 191.

Joyner DH, *International Law and the Proliferation of Weapons of Mass Destruction* (Oxford University Press 2009).

Joyner DH, *Interpreting the Nuclear Non-Proliferation Treaty* (Oxford University Press 2011).

Kmentt A, 'The Development of the International Initiative on the Humanitarian Impact of Nuclear Weapons and its Effects on the Nuclear Weapons Debate' (2015) 97 IRRC 681.

Loets A, 'Arms Control', *EPIL* (July 2013).

Magi L, 'L'obbligo di disarmo nucleare quale obbligo a realizzazione progressiva' (2018) 101 RivDirInt 58.

Pedrazzi M, 'The Treaty on the Prohibition Of Nuclear Weapons: A Promise, a Threat or a Flop?' (2017) ItYBIL 215.

Roscini M, 'On certain legal issues arising from Article VI of the Treaty on the Non-Proliferation of Nuclear Weapons' in I Caracciolo, M Pedrazzi, T Vassalli di Dachenhausen (eds), *Nuclear Weapons: Strengthening the International Legal Regime* (eleven publishing 2016) 15.

Sands P, Peel J, *Principles of International Environmental Law* (Cambridge University Press 2018).

Sossai M, 'Il rapporto tra il trattato sul divieto di armi nucleari e gli altri accordi in materia di non proliferazione e disarmo' (2018) 1 RivDirInt 185.

Treves T, 'Customary Law', *EPIL* (2012).

Tuzmukhamedov B, 'Disarmament', *EPIL* (May 2011).

White ND, 'Interpretation of Non-Proliferation Treaties', in DH Joyner, M Roscini (eds), *Non-Proliferation Law as a Special Regime* (Cambridge University Press 2012) 267.

White ND, 'Understanding Nuclear Deterrence Within the International Constitutional Architecture', in JL Black-Branch, D Fleck (eds), *Nuclear Non-Proliferation in International Law: Vol. V Legal Challenges for Nuclear Deterrence and Security* (Springer/Asser Press 2020) 237.

CHAPTER 25

Obligations Related to Transfers of CBRN Weapons and Dual-Use Items

Annamaria Viterbo

1 Introduction

The purpose of this Chapter is to review the international legal framework on CBRN non-proliferation by focusing on export controls.[1]

Export controls are preventive measures used by governments to limit international trade in a number of controlled goods, the most important of which are CBRN weapons and dual-use items (*ie* goods, materials and technology that may be used for both civilian and military purposes). For the most part, export controls are deployed to protect international and national security, but they can also be used for purely economic strategic goals.

The description of the variety of forms that export controls can take (*ie* export bans, taxes, quotas, licensing requirements) will not be the object of this research. Nor is this chapter going to analyse and compare national legislation regulating the export of CBRN items.

Instead, we will describe the complex network of treaty-law and soft-law instruments that govern this field.

Indeed, lists and guidelines adopted by the so-called 'informal export control regimes' play a very important role. With this definition we describe the fora (the Zangger Committee, Nuclear Suppliers Group and Australia Group[2]) in which groups of industrialised countries convene to coordinate their trade

1 See in particular DH Joyner, *International Law and the Proliferation of Weapons of Mass Destruction*, (OUP 2009) 8. DH Joyner (ed), *Nonproliferation Export Controls: Origins, Challenges and Proposals for Strengthening* (Ashgate 2006).

2 The Missile Technology Control Regime (MTCR) and the Wassenaar Arrangement (WA) will not be analysed in this contribution. The MTCR was established in 1987 to slow the proliferation of ballistic and cruise missiles, rockets, unmanned aerial vehicles (UAV) and related technologies capable of delivering nuclear weapons, but in 2002 its focus was broadened to also cover the delivery of chemical and biological weapons. The WA was created in 1985 to promote the voluntary exchange of information on transfers of conventional arms and dual-use goods and technologies; it is intended to complement and reinforce, without duplication, the other existing informal regimes.

controls over the export of CBRN materials, items and technology (with the transfer of CBRN weapons being *per se* strictly prohibited).

Notably, these regimes are not treaty-based, they do not have international legal personality, their deliberations are not legally-binding and they do not establish any formal verification mechanism.

Informal regimes have often been established to 'complement' a treaty regime. However, the relationship of the informal export control regimes with multilateral non-proliferation treaties raises many problematic issues. Can their acts be considered supplementary – and therefore useful – means of treaty interpretation? Or are they facilitating the adoption of overly restrictive export control measures which are at odds with treaty provisions like the ones that encourage international cooperation for peaceful purposes?

2 Export Controls on Nuclear Weapons, Materials, Equipment and Dual-Use Items

The Treaty on the Non-Proliferation of Nuclear Weapons (NPT) entered into force in 1970 and currently binds 191 States Parties, with the notable absence of India, Israel and Pakistan (North Korea withdrew in 2003). The NPT's 'grand bargain' establishes two distinct sets of obligations: one for the five nuclear weapons States (NWS) that had exploded or were already in possession of nuclear weapons before 1 January 1967 and one for the non-nuclear weapons States (NNWS).[3]

According to the NPT's two-tiered structure, NWS are prohibited from transferring nuclear weapons and other nuclear explosive devices 'to any recipient whatsoever', as well as from sharing technologies, components and designs which could lead NNWS to develop nuclear weapons (art I).[4] Despite this broad prohibition, it has to be borne in mind that the treaty was negotiated to prevent proliferation among States and none of its provisions explicitly aims at preventing non-State actors from acquiring nuclear material or technology. This gap was closed by UN Security Council Resolution 1540 (2004), which, being adopted under Chapter VII, imposes on all UN members – even those that have not ratified the non-proliferation treaties – the obligation to refrain from providing any form of support to non-State actors that attempt

3 The five States that had manufactured or detonated a nuclear explosive device before 1 January 1967 are: China, France, Russia, the United Kingdom and the United States.

4 Notably, art I does not cover the sharing between NWS of components, means of transport or propulsion, technology and know-how.

to develop, acquire, manufacture, possess, transport, transfer or use CBRN weapons and their means of delivery, for terrorist purposes.[5]

In parallel, NNWS 'undertake not to receive' nuclear weapons or other nuclear explosive devices from any transferor, 'not to manufacture or otherwise acquire' such weapons or devices, as well as 'not to seek or receive any assistance' in their manufacturing (art II).

In exchange for these commitments, NWS are to cooperate with the other parties in the development of programmes for the peaceful use of nuclear energy (art IV). In addition, all parties to the NPT pledge to conduct negotiations on disarmament and ultimately stop the nuclear arms race (art VI).

According to Article III.2, each State Party commits not to supply a) 'source or special fissionable material' or b) 'equipment or material especially designed or prepared for the processing, use or production of special fissionable material' for peaceful purposes to any NNWS, unless the export is subject to International Atomic Energy Agency (IAEA) safeguards.

Furthermore, each NNWS has to accept IAEA safeguards on all nuclear materials in its territory or under its jurisdiction or control. To this end, it has to conclude with the IAEA a Comprehensive Safeguards Agreement under which the Agency's inspectors can access civilian nuclear power generation facilities for the exclusive purpose of verifying that nuclear material is not diverted to military uses.[6]

Since the NPT does not provide clear definitions, already in March 1971, a group of 15 supplier States (from both sides of the Cold War divide) gathered under the chairmanship of Professor Zangger to reach a common understanding on what constitutes 'equipment or material *especially designed or prepared* for the processing, use or production of special fissionable material' (EDPS). Soon, the Committee became a permanent forum for the interpretation of Article III.2 NPT and the harmonisation of national export control policies.

5 See D Salisbury and others (eds), *Preventing the Proliferation of WMDs: Measuring the Success of UN Security Council Resolution 1540* (Palgrave 2018). See ch 7 Poltronieri Rossetti and ch 23 Poli.

6 See IAEA INFCIRC/153, 'The Structure and Content of Agreements Between the Agency and States Required in Connection with the Treaty on the Non-Proliferation of Nuclear Weapons' and INFCIRC/540, 'Model Protocol Additional to the Agreement(s) between State(s) and the IAEA for the Application of Safeguards'. Agreements under the Model Additional Protocol grant the IAEA increased inspection authority on both declared and undeclared material and activities. However, their conclusion does not fall within the obligations arising from art III.4 NPT. See ch 24 Spagnolo and ch 26 Buscemi.

Currently, the Zangger Committee (ZC)[7] counts 39 Participating States that are also parties to the NPT, plus the European Union as an observer. The Committee's most important contribution to non-proliferation is the publication of the so-called 'Trigger List' of nuclear materials and equipment, the export of which 'triggers' IAEA safeguards pursuant to Article III.2 NPT.

The Trigger List comprises two Memoranda and one Annex.[8] Memorandum A and B respectively recommend a set of procedures to be followed with regards to the exports of source and special fissionable material and EDPs to NNWS not party to the NPT, while the Annex clarifies what equipment and material fall within the EDP category.

The export of nuclear items for peaceful purposes is subject to three requirements ('conditions of supply'): the assurance by the recipient State that the exported items will not be converted into nuclear weapons or other nuclear explosive devices, that they will be subject to IAEA safeguards, and that they will not be re-exported without applying the same conditions of supply.

The ZC soft-law instruments form the core of the legal framework on export controls for nuclear weapons and related equipment and materials. However, participating countries have always reserved the right to restrict the export of items other than those specified in the List.[9] Even more significantly, the instruments are not intended to create additional obligations beyond the NPT.

It has to be noted that, since 1975, the ZC Trigger List has been complemented by the soft-law guidelines adopted by the Nuclear Suppliers Group (NSG).[10] The main reason behind the formation of this additional informal regime was the failure of the ZC to prevent nuclear items from being transferred to countries acting in bad faith. In 1974, in fact, India had successfully

7 F Schmidt, 'NPT Export Controls and the Zangger Committee' (2000) 7(3) The Nonproliferation Review 136–145; F Schmidt, 'The Zangger Committee: Its History and Future Role' (1994) 2(1) The Nonproliferation Review 38–44.

8 The List is periodically updated to take into account technological development, proliferation sensitivity and changes in procurement practices. The last review was completed in 2020. Notably, the Trigger List is published by the IAEA among its information circulars in the INFCIRC/209 series. Information circulars are published by the IAEA to bring matters of general interest – in this case, the commitment of the Committee's members under art III.2 NPT – to the attention of its Member States. See IAEA, INFCIRC/209/Rev. 5, 5 March 2020.

9 This reservation allows States that are also members of the NSG to implement the stricter controls which are associated with that regime.

10 A Sultan, *Universalizing Nuclear Nonproliferation Norms* (Palgrave 2019) 64; DH Joyner, 'The Nuclear Suppliers Group: History and Functioning' (2005) IntTLR 33–42; DH Joyner, 'The Nuclear Suppliers Group: Present Challenges and Future Prospects' (2005) IntTLR 84–96.

diverted material and equipment designated for a nuclear power plant to the development of a nuclear weapon.

The NSG was therefore called upon to adopt more stringent instruments than those adopted by the ZC in order to meet the obligations set forth by Article III.2 NPT. Moreover, while the ZC comprised only States Parties to the NPT, the NSG aimed to also include third countries like France (which at that point had not yet joined the NPT).

Nowadays, the NSG consists of 48 nuclear supplier countries, with the European Commission and the ZC Chair participating as observers. Strict criteria must be met to become a member.[11]

The NSG adopts two sets of guidelines to ensure that trade of nuclear-related items and cooperation in the peaceful uses of nuclear energy will be carried out in a manner consistent with international non-proliferation rules.[12]

Part 1 Guidelines were first adopted in 1978 and concern nuclear transfers. Although largely mirroring the ZC Trigger List,[13] they are wider in scope (especially for what concerns EDPs) and cover transfers to any NNWS, not only those that have ratified the NPT.

Part 2 Guidelines concern transfers of dual-use equipment, materials, software and related technology, which could provide a major contribution to a nuclear explosive activity, an unsafeguarded nuclear fuel-cycle activity or acts of nuclear terrorism. These Guidelines were first adopted in 1992, after it had become clear that dual-use items were the most important to control. In fact, in the 1970s–1980s, Iraq – a party to the NPT – was able to pursue a clandestine nuclear weapons programme by purchasing dual-use items not covered by export controls. Up to that point, neither the ZC nor the NSG had addressed the issue because dual-use items could not be considered EDPs for the purposes of Article III.2 NPT. To close this gap, the NSG adopted a supplementary set of guidelines to establish harmonised export controls on nuclear-related dual-use items identified in a dedicated Annex. The decision prompted a heated reaction from developing countries which opposed further export restrictions on items falling outside the scope of Article III.2 NPT which were considered critical to developing their energy production capacities.

While all items are subject to a licensing requirement, the conditions of supply set by the NSG Guidelines differ for trigger list items and dual-use items.

---

11 In 2019, China formally affirmed that, in order to be admitted to the NSG, India should have first ratified the NPT.

12 The NSG Guidelines are published in the INFCIRC/254 series. See IAEA, INFCIRC/254/Rev.14/Part 1 and INFCIRC/254/Rev.11/Part 2, as lastly amended.

13 There is close cooperation between the NSG and the Zangger Committee on the review and amendment of their lists.

For trigger list items, the following apply. First, to become eligible for nuclear trade with NSG members, a recipient State needs to have in place a Comprehensive Safeguards Agreement.[14] This requirement is similar to the one established by Article III.1 NPT, but it is addressed to any recipient State (irrespective of it being an NPT member or not) and amounts to a significant tightening of the export control regime.[15] Moreover, this raises a particular issue for Israel and Pakistan, which have only entered into facility-specific arrangements with the IAEA. On the contrary, India – the very country which prompted the creation of the NSG – was unanimously granted a waiver from this requirement in 2008. The decision to exempt India greatly undermined the credibility of the NSG and violated the political commitment given by NSG members to the 1995 NPT Review Conference not to provide nuclear technology to States without full-scope safeguards.

The second requirement is that recipient governments have to provide adequate assurances on the peaceful use of trigger list items. Among these, two assurances are particularly important: that the items will not be used in any nuclear explosive device and that the recipient of potential retransfers will have to provide the same assurances as those required by the supplier for the original transfer. Complementary to these conditions, suppliers should require from the recipient country assurances that nuclear material and facilities will be placed under effective physical protection in order to prevent unauthorised use and handling. The transfers of enrichment and reprocessing facilities, equipment and technology are subject to stricter conditions than those applicable to trigger list items.

In addition, the Part 1 Guidelines also contain the so-called 'non-proliferation principle', according to which a supplier State can authorise a transfer only when satisfied that it would not contribute to the proliferation of nuclear weapons or be diverted to acts of nuclear terrorism.

For dual-use items, the conditions of supply established by the Part 2 Guidelines essentially consist of three types of government-to-government assurances: a statement from the end-user specifying the uses and the end-use locations of the items; an assurance explicitly stating that the proposed transfer will not be used for any nuclear explosive activity or unsafeguarded nuclear fuel-cycle activity; an assurance that the prior consent of the supplier

14 Even if under the NSG regime the adoption of safeguards based on the IAEA Additional Protocol does not constitute a condition of supply for trigger list items, such commitment is required by all EU Members States, in particular for the export of enrichment and reprocessing facilities, equipment and technology.

15 See IAEA, INFCIRC/405.

will be required before transferring any dual-use item to a State not adhering to the Guidelines.

In any case, according to the so-called 'basic principle' of the Part 2 Guidelines, suppliers are required not to authorise transfers of listed dual-use items when: a) there is an unacceptable risk of diversion to a nuclear explosive activity or unsafeguarded nuclear fuel-cycle activity; b) the transfers are contrary to the objective of averting the proliferation of nuclear weapons; or c) there is an unacceptable risk of diversion to acts of nuclear terrorism. To exercise the prudence required by the basic principle, several factors need to be considered, among which is whether the recipient State has failed to comply with UNSC Resolution 1540 (2004).

The Part 2 Guidelines also contain a 'catch-all clause', which requires an authorisation even for the transfer of items not listed in the Annex when such items 'are or may be intended, in their entirety or in part, for use in connection with a nuclear explosive activity'.[16]

NSG participants undertake to ensure the effective implementation of the Guidelines in their national legislation by adopting export licensing regulations, enforcement measures and penalties for violations. However, they also reserve their discretionary power to apply the Guidelines to items of concern other than those listed in the Annex, as well as to apply additional transfer conditions. All non-participating States are invited to adhere to the Guidelines.

The NSG Guidelines have been strongly criticised for being an attempt by nuclear technology holders to preserve their economic advantages and for being at odds with the reciprocal nature of the obligations arising from the NPT.

Before concluding this analysis, it has to be underlined that the NPT does not include a clear prohibition on the transfer of nuclear weapons or other nuclear explosive devices from one NNWS to another NNWS.

This lacuna was addressed by the Treaty on the Prohibition of Nuclear Weapons (TPNW), which entered into force in January 2021 and currently binds 52 States Parties,[17] with the notable absence of all NWS. The TPNW prohibits all States Parties – without distinction – from developing, testing, producing, manufacturing, acquiring, possessing, or stockpiling, using or threatening to use nuclear weapons or other nuclear explosive devices.

16 See IAEA, INFCIRC/254/Rev.11/Part 2, par. 5.

17 All the States Parties to the TPNW are also States Parties to the NPT, except for the Cook Islands. On the TPNW see M Pedrazzi, 'The Treaty on the Prohibition of Nuclear Weapons: A Promise, a Threat or a Flop?' (2018) 27 ItYBIL 215.

In particular, pursuant to Article 1.1(b) TPNW, States Parties are barred from directly or indirectly transferring 'to any recipient whatsoever' (*ie* a State, a natural or a legal person) nuclear weapons and other nuclear explosive devices, or control over them. In parallel, Article 1.1(c) TPNW prohibits all States Parties from receiving, directly or indirectly, the transfer or control over any such weapons or devices.

These two prohibitions are broader than the ones set forth by the NPT, as they cover non-State actors and do not require full ownership, or the execution of a payment or another form of consideration. Moreover, they also extend to transfers made through intermediaries or third parties where there is knowledge that they will be used to produce a nuclear weapon or other nuclear explosive device.

3 Export Controls on Biological and Chemical Weapons, Materials, Equipment and Dual-Use Items

Export controls on biological and chemical weapons, materials and equipment are regulated respectively by the Convention on the Prohibition of the Development, Production and Stockpiling of Bacteriological (Biological) and Toxin Weapons and on Their Destruction (BWC) and the Convention on the Prohibition of the Development, Production, Stockpiling and Use of Chemical Weapons and on Their Destruction (CWC).[18] The two abovementioned treaties are complemented by the informal regime of the Australia Group (AG).

The BWC entered into force in 1975, categorically banning for the very first time an entire category of weapons of mass destruction.[19] However, the BWC did not establish an implementation body or a verification regime.[20]

The Convention, which currently binds 183 States Parties, prohibits the development, production, stockpiling or acquisition[21] of biological weapons,

18 Both the BWC and CWC rest on and supplement the 1925 Geneva Protocol for the Prohibition of the Use in War of Asphyxiating, Poisonous or Other Gases, and of Bacteriological Methods of Warfare.

19 See ch 23 Poli; J Littlewood, 'The Biological and Toxin Weapons Convention' in M Crowley and others (eds), *Preventing Chemical Weapons: Arms Control and Disarmament as the Sciences Converge* (Royal Society of Chemistry 2018) 69–100; A Kelle, *Prohibiting Chemical and Biological Weapons: Multilateral Regimes and Their Evolution* (Lynne Rienner Publishers 2014).

20 A proposal to put in place a verification mechanism – the draft Protocol negotiated within the Ad Hoc Group – was ultimately shelved in 2001 due to US opposition.

21 Although the BWC does not contain an explicit prohibition, the 1996 Fourth Review Conference affirmed that the use of biological weapons will certainly be considered a breach of the Convention.

equipment or means of delivery, as well as of microbial or other biological agents or toxins 'whatever their origin or method of production, of types and in quantities that have no justification for prophylactic, protective or other peaceful purposes' (art I).

This general-purpose definition of prohibited items was reaffirmed by the Eighth Review Conference, which declared that all naturally or artificially created or altered microbial and other biological agents and toxins, as well as their components, regardless of whether they affect humans, animals or plants, which are not used for peaceful purposes, are unequivocally covered by Article I.[22]

Article III obliges States not to transfer to any recipient whatsoever, directly or indirectly, such bioagents, toxins, weapons, equipment or means of delivery. States are also prohibited from assisting, encouraging, or inducing any other State or group of States to manufacture or otherwise acquire such equipment and materials.

At the same time, Article X requires States: a) to facilitate the fullest possible exchange of equipment, materials and scientific and technological information for the peaceful use of biological agents and to cooperate on the prevention of diseases; and b) to implement the Convention 'in a manner designed to avoid hampering the economic or technological development of State parties.'

Unfortunately, even though BWC Review Conferences can reach additional understandings and agreements to interpret, define, or elaborate the meaning or scope of a provision of the Convention or to provide instructions, guidelines, or recommendations on how a provision should be implemented, they have never adopted lists of bioagents to facilitate the implementation of the obligations arising from Articles I and III BWC.[23] While the general-purpose criterion adopted by Article I allows the BWC to catch scientific and technological advances, the absence of legal clarity remains a major challenge both for non-proliferation and scientific research. As we will see, this gap is addressed – not without controversy – by the Australia Group.

The CWC, which currently applies to 193 States Parties, entered into force in 1997 after years of lengthy negotiations which accelerated only with the easing

22 The treaty provides for regular Review Conferences to assess national implementation measures and to establish confidence-building measures. On the outcome of the last Review Conference, see GS Pearson, 'Time for Structural Changes to Make the Biological and Toxin Weapons Convention More Effective' (2016) 1(1) Global Security: Health, Science and Policy 23–38.

23 The BWC Implementation Support Unit (ISU) regularly updates a document that provides information on the understandings and additional agreements reached by Review Conferences.

of tensions between superpowers and as a reaction to the threat of chemical warfare during the first Gulf War.

In marked contrast to the BWC, not only was the Organisation for the Prohibition of Chemical Weapons (OPCW) formally established but also a very stringent inspection regime.[24]

Pursuant to Article I.1, States Parties undertake 'never under any circumstances' to use, develop, produce, otherwise acquire, stockpile or retain chemical weapons, or to transfer, directly or indirectly, chemical weapons to anyone.

These prohibitions have to be balanced with the right to develop, produce, transfer and use toxic chemicals and their precursors for all the purposes not prohibited by the Convention (art VI CWC). In addition, the CWC reaffirms the freedom of scientific research on chemicals and encourages States Parties to cooperate and not to maintain trade restrictions that would hamper economic and technological development (art XI CWC).

With respect to transfers, reference must be made to: a) the broad definition of chemical weapons provided by Article II; b) the three Schedules contained in the Annex on Chemicals, where toxic chemicals and precursors are grouped by relevance to chemical weapons production and potential legitimate peaceful use; and c) the Annex on Implementation and Verification (in particular, Parts VI, VII and VIII).

Schedule 1 chemicals are those of the highest lethal or incapacitating toxicity and/or risk to the object and purpose of the Convention. They have a primary military use and very few commercial applications. They may only be transferred between States Parties for research, medical, pharmaceutical or protective purposes. Transfers have to be promptly notified to the Technical Secretariat. Retransfer is not allowed.

On 7 June 2020, the first 'change'[25] ever adopted to the CWC Annex on Chemicals entered into force, adding Novichok (the nerve agent used in the

24 See ch 23 Poli; W Krutzsch and others (eds), *The Chemical Weapons Convention: A Commentary*, (Oxford 2014); J Littlewood, *The Biological Weapons Convention: A Failed Revolution* (Ashgate 2004); R Trapp, 'The Chemical Weapons Convention – Past Success, Current Challenges', in M Crowley and others (eds), *Preventing Chemical Weapons: Arms Control and Disarmament as the Sciences Converge* (Royal Society of Chemistry 2018) 27–68.

25 These changes were adopted in accordance with the simplified amendment procedure established by art XV.4 and .5 CWC. See OPCW Technical Secretariat, 'Note by the Technical Secretariat: Consolidated Text of Adopted Changes to Schedule 1 of the Annex on Chemicals to the Chemical Weapons Convention', S/1820/2019, December 23, 2019.

2018 attempted assassination of a former Russian agent in Salisbury, UK) and carbamate agents to the Schedule 1 list of toxic chemicals.[26]

Schedule 2 chemicals are those of the next highest relative toxicity which pose a significant risk to the object and purpose of the Convention. They have some commercial uses and may only be transferred between States Parties. The exporting State is required to obtain from the recipient State an end-use and end-user certificate and the assurance that transferred chemicals will only be used for purposes not prohibited under the Convention. No retransfers are permitted.

Schedule 3 chemicals are those of lowest relative toxicity and/or risk to the object and purpose of the Convention. Since they have wide commercial uses, they may be transferred also to third States but under the conditions required for Schedule 2 chemicals.[27]

Even if they do not list all the chemicals and precursors prohibited by the Convention (which are defined in a very comprehensive way by Article II), the Schedules of the Annex on Chemicals play a very important role for the regime's effectiveness as they identify the agents subject to declaration requirements and verification measures. Keeping these Schedules up to date is, therefore, key for the CWC to stay abreast of new developments.

Notably, in 2013, after Bashar al-Assad's regime crossed the red line by carrying out a ruthless chemical attack in Ghouta against the civilian population, Syria was forced by international pressure to ratify the Convention. Subsequently, UN Security Council Resolution 2118 (2013) called on Syria to relinquish its arsenal of sarin, mustard gas and other nerve agents, and authorised Member States to acquire, control, transport, transfer and destroy all the Syrian chemical weapons, materials and equipment identified by the OPCW. The UN-OPCW Joint Mission made possible the transfer of chemical weapons and their components out of an unstable country ravaged by a civil war, for their safe neutralisation and destruction at sea or in specialised facilities. The OPCW clarified that the decision to allow such transfers was due to the

26 See S Costanzi and Gregory D Koblentz, 'Controlling Novichoks After Salisbury: Revising the Chemical Weapons Convention Schedules' (2019) 26(5–6) The Nonproliferation Review 599–612.

27 Ammonium nitrate and other explosive precursors are not included in the CWC lists. Ammonium nitrate was used in the deadly Oklahoma City bombing of April 1995 and was the cause of the devastating explosion in the port of Beirut in 2020. It is the main component of ammonium nitrate fuel oil (ANFO) and can easily be turned into an improvised explosive device (IED).

extraordinary character of the situation and did not create any precedent for the future.[28]

The BWC and CWC provisions on non-proliferation of biological and chemical weapons are complemented by the soft-law instruments adopted by the Australia Group (AG).[29]

The creation of this new informal regime was prompted by the discovery that Iraq had used tabun, sarin and mustard gas against Iran, in stark violation of the 1925 Geneva Protocol. In the 1980s, Iraq was in fact able to legitimately buy industrial chemicals on the international market for its WMD programme. In response, 15 countries introduced export controls on certain chemicals, but these measures lacked an overall strategy. Therefore, in 1985, while the negotiations on the CWC were still ongoing, those 15 countries and the European Commission decided to meet under the AG umbrella to further minimise the risk of proliferation of chemical weapons, coordinate their national export control laws and enhance their cooperation (for example, by sharing intelligence about the risk of CBW proliferation and terrorism).

By 1990, the scope of the AG activities was broadened to cover, together with chemicals, also bioagents and dual-use chemical and biological technologies and equipment. After 9/11, the AG started to focus also on items that could potentially be used by terrorists.

Today the AG counts 42 members, which are all parties to the BWC and CWC, plus the European Union.

Members commit to use licensing measures to ensure that the exports of certain bioagents, chemicals and dual-use manufacturing facilities, equipment, technology and software do not contribute to the development or use of CBW. To these ends, the AG issues common control lists on chemical weapons precursors (Novichok was added to this list in 2020); dual-use chemical manufacturing facilities and equipment and related technology and software; human and animal pathogens and toxins (which include the MERS- and SARS-related coronaviruses);[30] plant pathogens; and dual-use biological equipment and related technology and software.

28 OPCW Executive Council Decision, 'Destruction of Syrian Chemical Weapons', EC-M-33/DEC.1, 27 September 2013.

29 RJ Mathews, 'Chemical and Biological Weapons Export Controls and the "Web of Prevention": A Practitioner's Perspective' in B Rappert and C McLeish (eds), *A Web of Prevention: Biological Weapons, Life Sciences and the Governance of Research* (Routledge 2007) 163–171; J Seevaratnam, 'The Australia Group' (2006) 13(2) The Nonproliferation Review 401–415; A Kelle, 'CBW Export Controls: Towards Regime Integration?' in Joyner (2006) (n 1) 101–118.

30 To date, the AG has not clarified whether export controls should apply to samples of the SARS-CoV-2 virus or related genetic sequences. This lack of clarity is particularly

In addition, the AG Guidelines for Transfers of Sensitive Chemical or Biological Items outline some of the factors that members have to take into account when evaluating export requests. Members are expected to deny export licences when there is persuasive information that an item is intended to be used in a CBW programme or for CBW terrorism, or that a significant risk of diversion exists.

Participants have no legal obligation to apply AG lists and guidelines and they have often used their discretion when implementing national export controls, also adopting more restrictive measures than those agreed to within the Group.

Overall, the AG's activities have attracted strong criticism, especially from countries in the Non-Aligned Movement (NAM), which consider it to be essentially a cartel restricting trade and hampering international cooperation in an illegitimate way. In particular, NAM countries contend that export control measures adopted by AG members are inconsistent with the obligations they had assumed under the BWC and CWC and result in a breach of the right of the other treaty parties to benefit from the fullest possible exchange of equipment, materials and scientific and technological information for peaceful purposes (as provided by Article X.1 BWC and, even more clearly, by Articles XI.1 and XI.2(c) CWC[31]). Furthermore, they deem the application of more stringent restrictions than those envisaged by treaty law capable of altering the already precarious balance between the two parallel goals of non-proliferation and international scientific cooperation.[32] The inclusion in the AG control lists of almost 50 precursors that do not appear in the CWC Schedules is seen as particularly problematic.[33]

On the contrary, AG members consider the establishment of national export licensing mechanisms integral to the proper implementation of the obligations arising from Article I.1(a) and (d) CWC and Articles I and III BWC. In particular, they argue that their export controls effectively ensure that the legitimate

---

worrisome at a time when access to samples or fragments is critical to develop vaccines, drug treatments and diagnostic tools.

31 Art XI.2(c) CWC establishes that CWC parties shall not maintain among themselves any restrictions incompatible with the obligations arising from the Convention which would restrict or impede trade and the development and promotion of scientific and technological knowledge in the field of chemistry for peaceful purposes.

32 J Husbands, 'Cooperation on Biosecurity as Part of a Strategy to Prevent Misuse of the Life Sciences' in O Meier (ed), *Technology Transfers and Non-Proliferation: Between Control and Cooperation* (Routledge 2014) 155–175; JP Zanders, 'Chemical Weapons Convention (CWC) Article XI and the Future of the CWC', in O Meier (ed), *Technology Transfers and Non-Proliferation: Between Control and Cooperation* (Routledge 2014) 176–203.

33 Joyner (2009) (n 1) 120.

trade of materials, equipment and technology used for peaceful purposes can proceed unhindered.

The fact that the BWC still lacks a multilateral monitoring and verification mechanism may support this argument, but the same does not stand for chemical weapons, given that the OPCW is the sole body responsible for verifying States Parties' compliance with the CWC.

4 Concluding Remarks

From all of the above, it appears clear that the interaction between CBRN treaties and informal export control regimes raises several important issues, especially when the latter have been established to 'complement' a treaty regime.

When a treaty and an informal regime are intertwined, two views are possible:

On the one hand, the adoption of lists, guidelines and understandings by a subset of States Parties to the relevant treaty can be deemed inconsistent with the obligations arising from multilateral non-proliferation treaties. This is the standpoint adopted, for instance, by some NNWS, which contend that the NSG has exceeded the terms of NPT Article III.2 when setting additional conditions for exports of nuclear dual-use items; and by NAM countries, which argue against the restrictions adopted by members of the Australia Group on bioagents and chemical precursors that do not appear in the CWC Schedules.

In particular, export controls implemented by NSG and AG members are considered to result in a breach of the right of the other treaty parties to benefit from the fullest possible exchange of equipment, materials and scientific and technological information for peaceful purposes.

Similarly troublesome is the 2008 NSG decision to allow India to resume nuclear trade despite the fact that this country did not have IAEA full-scope safeguards in place. This exception, which amounts to a divorce of the NSG from the NPT, increased tensions among NPT parties and likely postponed India's accession to the Treaty as a NNWS.

On the other hand, the soft-law instruments adopted by informal regimes can be considered a useful tool to clarify the provisions set forth by the non-proliferation treaty to which they are connected.

In particular, lists of controlled items can help the interpreter to shed light on the meaning of certain treaty terms. In fact, such lists constitute subsequent practice adopted by a group of States Parties in the application of the treaty after its conclusion and, therefore, they can certainly be considered a supplementary means of treaty interpretation under Article 32 of the Vienna Convention on the Law of Treaties (VCLT), at least with respect to the application of the treaty provisions to members of the informal regime.[34] However, it remains doubtful whether these lists can be employed as a supplementary means of treaty interpretation to solve a potential dispute between a member of the informal regime and a treaty party that does not participate in the regime.

In our view, the said lists cannot be considered instruments adopted by one or more treaty parties 'in a close temporal and contextual relation with the conclusion of the treaty' which are accepted by the other parties as an instrument related to the treaty. Therefore, they cannot be used to provide a contextual interpretation of the treaty to which they are connected, according to Article 31.2(b) VCLT.[35]

Nor can such lists be treated as subsequent practice under Article 31.3(b) VCLT, since this would require a common understanding regarding the interpretation of the treaty accepted by *all the parties* to the treaty.[36] This reading of Article 31.3(b) VCLT, which requires the support of all States Parties, was confirmed by the ICJ in the *Whaling in the Antarctic case*.[37]

Bibliography

Bown CP, 'Export Controls: America's Other National Security Threat', PIIE Working Paper 20-8, May 2020, 2.

34 Pursuant to art 32 of the VCLT, one may resort to supplementary means of interpretation to confirm or corroborate the meaning resulting from the application of art 31 VCLT, or to determine the meaning when the interpretation according to art 31 VCLT a) 'leaves the meaning ambiguous or obscure', or b) 'leads to a result which is manifestly absurd or unreasonable'.

35 See ILC, 'Draft conclusions on subsequent agreements and subsequent practice in relation to the interpretation of treaties, with commentaries' (2018) 13.

36 For a different opinion, according to which the lists and guidelines adopted by informal regimes fall within art 31.3(b) VCLT, see T Marauhn, 'Global Governance of Dual-Use Trade: The Contribution of International Law' in O Meier (ed), *Technology Transfers and Non-Proliferation: Between Control and Cooperation* (Routledge 2014) 58 and Joyner (2009) (n 1) 34–6.

37 International Court of Justice (ICJ), *Whaling in the Antarctic case* (2014) para 83. The conclusion reached by the Court on the resolutions adopted by the International Whaling Commission does not exclude, however, that they can be used as supplementary means of treaty interpretation pursuant to art 32 VCLT.

Costanzi S and Koblentz GD, 'Controlling Novichoks After Salisbury: Revising the Chemical Weapons Convention Schedules' (2019) 26(5–6) The Nonproliferation Review 599.

Crowley M and others (eds), *Preventing Chemical Weapons: Arms Control and Disarmament as the Sciences Converge* (Royal Society of Chemistry 2018).

d'Argent P, 'Les enseignements du Cocom' (1993) 26(1) RBDI 147.

Førland TE, *Cold Economic Warfare: CoCom and the Forging of Strategic Export Controls 1948–1954* (Republic of Letters Publishing 2009).

Husbands JL, 'Cooperation on Biosecurity as Part of a Strategy to Prevent Misuse of the Life Sciences' in O Meier (ed), *Technology Transfers and Non-Proliferation: Between Control and Cooperation* (Routledge 2014) 155.

Jones S, 'Emptying the Haunted Air: The Current and Future Missile Control Regime' in DH Joyner (ed), *Nonproliferation Export Controls: Origins, Challenges and Proposals for Strengthening* (Ashgate 2006) 75.

Joyner DH (ed), *Nonproliferation Export Controls: Origins, Challenges and Proposals for Strengthening* (Ashgate 2006).

Joyner DH, 'The Nuclear Suppliers Group: History and Functioning' (2005) IntTLR 33.

Joyner DH, 'The Nuclear Suppliers Group: Present Challenges and Future Prospects' (2005) IntTLR 84.

Joyner DH, *International Law and the Proliferation of Weapons of Mass Destruction* (OUP 2009).

Kelle A, 'CBW Export Controls: Towards Regime Integration?' in DH Joyner (ed), *Nonproliferation Export Controls: Origins, Challenges and Proposals for Strengthening* (Ashgate 2006) 101.

Kelle A, *Prohibiting Chemical and Biological Weapons: Multilateral Regimes and Their Evolution* (Lynne Rienner Publishers 2014).

Krutzsch W and others (eds), *The Chemical Weapons Convention: A Commentary* (Oxford 2014).

Lipson M, 'The Wassenaar Arrangement: Transparency and Restraint through Trans-Governmental Cooperation?' in DH Joyner (ed), *Nonproliferation Export Controls: Origins, Challenges and Proposals for Strengthening* (Ashgate 2006) 49.

Littlewood J, 'The Biological and Toxin Weapons Convention' in M Crowley and others (eds), *Preventing Chemical Weapons: Arms Control and Disarmament as the Sciences Converge* (Royal Society of Chemistry 2018) 69.

Littlewood J, *The Biological Weapons Convention: A Failed Revolution* (Ashgate 2004).

Marauhn T, 'Global Governance of Dual-Use Trade: The Contribution of International Law' in O Meier (ed), *Technology Transfers and Non-Proliferation: Between Control and Cooperation* (Routledge 2014) 45.

Mathews RJ, 'Chemical and Biological Weapons Export Controls and the 'Web of Prevention': A Practitioner's Perspective' in B Rappert and C McLeish (eds), *A Web of Prevention: Biological Weapons, Life Sciences and the Governance of Research* (Routledge 2007) 163.

McLeish C and Trapp R, 'The life sciences revolution and the BWC' (2011) 18 The Nonproliferation Review 527.

Meier O, 'India, the Nuclear Suppliers Group and the Legitimacy of the nuclear non-proliferation regime' in O Meier (ed), *Technology Transfers and Non-Proliferation: Between Control and Cooperation* (Routledge 2014) 116.

Meier O, *Technology Transfers and Non-Proliferation: Between Control and Cooperation* (Routledge 2014).

Pearson GS, 'Time for structural changes to make the biological and toxin weapons convention more effective' (2016) 1(1) Global Security: Health, Science and Policy 23.

Quentin M and others, *Controlling the Trade of Dual-Use Goods: A Handbook* (Peter Lang 2013).

Rappert B and McLeish C (eds), *A Web of Prevention: Biological Weapons, Life Sciences and the Governance of Research* (Routledge 2007).

Salisbury D and others (eds), *Preventing the Proliferation of WMDs: Measuring the Success of UN Security Council Resolution 1540* (Palgrave 2018).

Schmidt F, 'NPT Export Controls and the Zangger Committee' (2000) 7(3) The Nonproliferation Review 136.

Schmidt F, 'The Zangger Committee: Its History and Future Role' (1994) 2(1) The Nonproliferation Review 38.

Seevaratnam J, 'The Australia Group' (2006) 13(2) The Nonproliferation Review 401.

Sultan A, *Universalizing Nuclear Nonproliferation Norms* (Palgrave 2019).

Trapp R, 'The Chemical Weapons Convention – Past Success, Current Challenges', in M Crowley and others (eds), *Preventing Chemical Weapons: Arms Control and Disarmament as the Sciences Converge* (Royal Society of Chemistry 2018) 27.

Wrubel WA, 'The Toshiba-Kongsberg Incident: Shortcomings of Cocom, and Recommendations for Increased Effectiveness of Export Controls to the East Bloc' (1989) 4(1) AmUJIntlL&Pol 241.

Zanders JP, 'Chemical Weapons Convention (CWC) Article XI and the Future of the CWC', in O Meier (ed), *Technology Transfers and Non-Proliferation: Between Control and Cooperation* (Routledge 2014) 176.

CHAPTER 26

Ensuring Compliance with International Obligations Applicable to CBRN Weapons: Supervisory Mechanisms, Sanctions, and Inter-State Litigation

Martina Buscemi

1 Introduction

The effectiveness of international rules aimed at eliminating or curbing the build-up of CBRN weapons is ultimately dependent on the extent to which States are compelled to comply with the binding international obligations. Whilst arms control and disarmament law (ACDL) forms an assorted net of highly technical and detailed obligations,[1] its enforcement remains today a sticking point. On the one hand, supervisory mechanisms, entrusted to verify that States Parties to relevant agreements abide by their terms, rely on a cooperative strategy and consensual solutions to achieve compliance, rather than on unilateral or multilateral enforcement.[2] On the other hand, the use of coercive powers by the Security Council, as an enforcement mechanism of last resort, may face being vetoed, or simply may not succeed in bringing violators back in line.[3]

It is, therefore, the purpose of this chapter to piece together the patchy framework of different mechanisms aimed at inducing compliance with international obligations applicable to CBRN weapons, mapping them according to the four phases of the emergency management cycle and highlighting deficiencies, strengths, and connections. The chapter examines, firstly, the verification system devised for the most relevant multilateral ACDL treaties (Section 2.1), as well as the investigative bodies established by the United Nations (UN) to determine the circumstances surrounding the development or use of CBRN

1 For a detailed analysis of the relevant obligations, see Part 3 of this volume on CBRN weapons.

2 T Marauhn, 'Dispute resolution, compliance control and enforcement of international arms control law' in G Ulfstein, T Marauhn, A Zimmermann (eds), *Making Treaties Work. Human Rights, Environment and Arms Control* (CUP 2007) 243, 271.

3 See Sections 3.2 and 4 in this contribution.

weapons (Section 2.2). It will then look at the adoption of sanctions, as 'socially organised acts of constraint',[4] to counter CBRN weapons, namely, the collective measures laid down in relevant treaty regimes (Section 3.1) and the coercive measures imposed by the Security Council (Section 3.2), often adopted as a consequence that is triggered by the violation of an international obligation, with a view to ensuring, and/or restoring, full compliance with the law. The soundness of the foregoing instruments will be tested against a case study dealing with one of the most recent dire uses of chemical weapons, which prompted numerous investigations from different international institutions, thus bringing forth the issue of coordination and cooperation among the tasks entrusted to them (Section 4). Lastly, some final remarks will be devoted to inter-State dispute settlement mechanisms concerning the application or interpretation of obligations applicable to CBRN weapons, in light of some recent (and prospective) litigation brought before the International Court of Justice (Section 5).

2 A Bird's-Eye View of Supervisory Mechanisms

2.1 *Verification under Arms Control and Disarmament Regimes*

Genuine compliance with ACDL is usually tested through institutionalised supervision, made up of inspections or other fact-finding activities. Supervisory mechanisms have been envisioned in a wide array of international agreements. Focusing on multilateral treaties with a universal reach,[5] monitoring systems have been included in 'conventional weapons' agreements,[6] treaties banning

---

4 While the notion of 'sanction' in international law is still fraught with ambiguity, it is here intended to encompass 'coercive measures taken in execution of a decision of a competent social organ, ie an organ legally empowered to act in the name of the society or community that is governed by the legal system', as defined by Abi-Saab (A Pellet, A Miron, 'Sanctions', *Max Planck Encyclopedia of Public International Law* (August 2013) para 8). Therefore, 'unilateral sanctions', as well as measures undertaken by States within the scheme of international responsibility, more properly labelled as 'countermeasures', are not examined in the present analysis.

5 The analysis of bilateral and regional agreements goes far beyond the scope of this chapter. For a comprehensive list of relevant treaties and related compliance mechanisms, see <https://www.nti.org/learn/treaties-and-regimes/treaties/> (all links were last accessed on 31 May 2021).

6 See eg the Arms Trade Treaty (2013) which envisages a verification system based on reporting obligations (art 13).

nuclear tests,[7] or prohibiting certain emplacement of nuclear weapons,[8] as well as disarmament conventions, such as the 2017 Treaty on the Prohibition of Nuclear Weapons (TPNW), which has just entered into force.[9] In particular, there are two instruments – the 1968 Treaty on the Non-Proliferation of Nuclear Weapons (NPT) and the 1993 Convention on the Prohibition of the Development, Production, Stockpiling and Use of Chemical Weapons and on their Destruction (CWC) – that deserve closer attention, as they incorporate the most sophisticated verification system based on the mantra 'trust but verify', which encompasses obligations of notification, reporting duties, routine inspections and more intrusive ad hoc procedures. Conversely, the treaty regime covering biological weapons – the 1972 Convention on the Prohibition of the Development, Production and Stockpiling of Bacteriological (Biological) and Toxin Weapons and on their Destruction (BWC) – lacks an international monitoring system and the attempt to integrate one failed definitively in 2001.[10]

As far as the CWC is concerned, the Organisation for the Prohibition of Chemical Weapons (OPCW) supervises an international monitoring verification apparatus, which is arguably the most intrusive control regime established thus far in the field of ACDL.[11] In order to validate the information given by States in their initial and annual declarations,[12] the OPCW Technical Secretariat, acting as an independent and impartial fact-finder, conducts routine verification actions, which range from on-site inspections to regular

7 For instance, the Comprehensive Nuclear-Test-Ban Treaty (1996), albeit not yet in force, provides for several measures of verification, including the International Monitoring System (art IV). By contrast, the Treaty Banning Nuclear Tests in the Atmosphere, in Outer Space and Under Water (1963) does not foresee any international verification system.

8 See eg Treaty on the Prohibition of the Emplacement of Nuclear Weapons and Other Weapons of Mass Destruction on the Seabed and Ocean Floor and in the Subsoil Thereof (1971), which envisages verification through observation and inspections.

9 The TPNW does not establish new verification mechanisms but relies on the existing safeguards agreements established with the International Atomic Energy Agency. On the TPNW, in general, see M Pedrazzi, 'The Treaty on the Prohibition of Nuclear Weapons: A Promise, a Threat or a Flop?' (2018) 27 ItYBIL 215.

10 On the BWC regime, see more in-depth ch 23 by Poli. It should be noted that, in order to support implementation of the BWC, review conferences (which take place once every five years), an Implementation Support Unit and confidence-building measures play a crucial role (G Venturini, 'Control and Verification of Multilateral Treaties on Disarmament and Non-Proliferation of Weapons of Mass Destruction' (2011) 17 UC Davis JIntL & Policy 345, 371–372).

11 L Tabassi, 'The Convention on the Prohibition of the Development, Production, Stockpiling and Use of Chemical Weapons and on their Destruction' in G Ulfstein, T Marauhn, A Zimmermann (n 2) 273.

12 Art III, VI CWC.

visits by teams selected by trained inspectors, whose final reports are usually confidential to the State under inspection.[13] The CWC also provides a procedure whereby any State Party can request the OPCW Executive Council to help clarify situations of possible non-compliance of another State Party with the CWC, through consultation and mediation.[14] Remarkably, a further special safety net offered by the CWC's monitoring system are the so called 'challenge inspections'. As a matter of fact, at the request of a State Party, the OPCW Secretariat may conduct inspections of any facility or location, without the right of refusal, to clarify any questions of possible non-compliance,[15] except if the request is considered frivolous, abusive or beyond the scope of the CWC by a three-quarters majority vote by the Executive Council.[16] Although a powerful tool capable of introducing an element of enforcement, challenge inspections have never been requested in practice – probably due to their perception as hostile acts[17] – not even with regard to the critical situation concerning the Syrian Arab Republic, where, instead, several ad hoc investigative actions have been put in place.[18]

In case of doubts or concerns regarding non-compliance with the CWC arising from the verification activities, the OPCW can take 'corrective' actions made up of several incremental steps. Firstly, the Technical Secretariat can try to solve a non-compliance issue through dialogue and consultation with the State concerned before informing the Executive Council.[19] Subsequently, if the issue is not solved, the Executive Council can consult with the State involved, and may request the latter to take measures to remedy the critical situation within a specified time.[20] Moreover, it can inform all States Parties, bring the issue to the attention of the Conference, make recommendations regarding 'measures to redress a situation and to ensure compliance, including sanctions', as stipulated in Article XII,[21] and, eventually, in cases of particular gravity, it shall bring the situation directly to the attention of the UN General

13 According to D Feakes, 'Evaluating the CWC Verification System' (2002) Disarmament Forum 11, 17 'much of the regime of international monitoring is conducted bilaterally between the Secretariat and individual states parties without the involvement of other states parties'.

14 Art IX, paras 3–7 CWC.

15 Art IX, paras 8–25 CWC.

16 Art IX, para 17 CWC.

17 Tabassi (n 11) 286.

18 On the use of chemicals as weapons in Syria, see more in-depth Section 4 in this contribution.

19 Art VIII, para 40 CWC.

20 Art VIII, para 36 CWC.

21 On these measures, see Section 3.1 in this contribution.

Assembly and the Security Council. The possibility to address the Security Council is foreseen also in Article VI BWC, whereby a State Party, which finds that any other State Party is acting in breach of the obligations established therein, is empowered to lodge a complaint directly with the Security Council for further investigation.[22]

By a similar token, the NPT compliance control system, although limited to non-proliferation obligations, provides for verification to be carried out by a competent international institution, the International Atomic Energy Agency (IAEA), and possibly for the enforcement phase to be carried out under the authority of the Security Council.[23] As already discussed in this volume,[24] bilateral Comprehensive Safeguards Agreements, or other types of agreements on safeguards, are concluded with the IAEA, whereby non-nuclear weapons States declare the existence of materials which are then subject to safeguards, including reporting duties, routine inspections, as well as unannounced inspections, aimed at verifying the fulfilment of the obligations assumed under the NPT, with a view to preventing the diversion of nuclear material for peaceful uses to nuclear weapons or other nuclear explosive devices.[25] Pursuant to the IAEA Statute, the IAEA Board has the competence to assess whether a State is not complying with the safeguards agreement and, if so, to request that the State remedy the situation.[26] In case of failure, the Board of Governors has no purely coercive means to restore compliance – except by issuing 'penalties', which will be analysed later[27] – although it can notify the UN Security Council or the General Assembly of non-compliance with safeguards undertakings. Notwithstanding its control system, the IAEA didn't prevent two particularly troublesome situations occurring in relation to Iraq in 1991 and the Democratic People's Republic of Korea (DPRK) in 1993, the latter ultimately withdrawing from the NPT in 2003.[28] Only on certain occasions, has the supervisory activity conducted by the IAEA led the Security Council to adopt a sanctions regime

22 Art VI BWC requires States Parties to cooperate in carrying out any investigation initiated by the Security Council.

23 On the IAEA verification procedure, see, generally, J L Black-Branch, D Fleck (eds), *Nuclear Non-Proliferation in International Law. Volume II: Verification and Compliance* (Asser Press 2016); L Rockwood, 'The Treaty on the Non-Proliferation of Nuclear Weapons (NPT) and IAEA Safeguards Agreements' in G Ulfstein, T Marauhn, A Zimmermann (n 2) 301.

24 See ch 24 by Spagnolo.

25 Art III IAEA Statute.

26 Art XII.C IAEA Statute.

27 See Section 3.1 in this contribution.

28 For an overview of these cases, see L Rockwood (n 23) 315–319; M Bothe, 'Weapons of Mass Destruction, Counter-Proliferation', *Max Planck Encyclopedia of Public International Law* (August 2016) para 15.

under Chapter VII of the UN Charter, sometimes within the NPT regime and sometimes outside.[29]

There is no doubt that the verification systems under consideration represent a crucial 'negative' incentive to induce compliance with the agreements, to enhance transparency and to build confidence between States Parties. Yet, a key role in ensuring fulfilment of the terms set out in the agreements is also played by the so-called 'positive' incentives, which consist of a number of benefits, including technical and economic assistance, granted to diligent States that meet their obligations. To give a few examples, the CWC provides emergency assistance and protection should a chemical weapons attack, or a threatened attack, occur;[30] moreover, it promotes economic and technological development of States Parties, by establishing an obligation to facilitate, and the right to participate in, 'the fullest possible exchange of chemicals, equipment and scientific and technical information relating to the development and application of chemistry for purposes not prohibited under [the CWC]'.[31] Likewise, States Parties to the NPT undertake to facilitate, and have the right to participate in, the fullest possible exchange of equipment, materials and scientific and technological information for the peaceful uses of nuclear energy, and also cooperate, if possible, in contributing to further development of nuclear energy for peaceful purposes, with due consideration for the needs of the developing countries.[32] Furthermore, the NPT ensures that non-nuclear-weapon States have access to research and development on the benefits of nuclear explosions conducted for peaceful purposes.[33]

By verifying, and inducing, State compliance with the CWC and NPT provisions, supervisory mechanisms are primarily concerned with the 'prevention' phase of the CBRN emergency management cycle. However, if a CBRN event is likely to have occurred, eg chemical weapons are believed to have been used, there are a number of mechanisms that can be activated, namely, the investigation of alleged use and emergency assistance, which relate more to the 'recovery' and 'response' phases of the cycle, respectively. At any rate, the most critical issue of the international verification system relates to the scope of its application which, evidently, excludes States not party to relevant agreements, in relation to which investigations and coercive measures can be undertaken autonomously under the UN aegis.

29 See Section 3.2 in this contribution.

30 Art X CWC.

31 Art XI CWC, para 2(b).

32 Art IV, para 2 NPT.

33 Art V NPT.

2.2 *The UN Investigative Mechanisms*

In response to the risk posed by CBRN weapons, the UN has developed a wide spectrum of investigative bodies, managed by the UN itself or jointly with other organisations, to shed light on the development or use of CBRN weapons and to ensure accountability for serious violations of human rights and international humanitarian law.[34] To that end, the Security Council; the General Assembly; the Human Rights Council; the Secretary-General; and the High Commissioner for Human Rights, can establish commissions of inquiry, fact-finding missions, inspection regimes, and similar bodies.

A key instrument that stands out in the UN practice is the Secretary-General's Mechanism for Investigation of Alleged Use of Chemical and Biological Weapons (SGM), established in the late 1980s with the mandate to launch a prompt investigation into allegations concerning the possible use of chemical, bacteriological (biological) and toxin weapons, upon request from any UN Member State, and to report the results of any investigation to all Member States.[35] In great detail, the SGM grants the Secretary-General the authority to deploy a fact-finding team to the site of the alleged incident, with approval and coordination from the territorial State, in order to ascertain in an objective and scientific manner, the facts of alleged violations of the 1925 Geneva Protocol, which bans the use of chemical and biological weapons, or other violations of relevant rules of customary international law.[36] Once the SGM is triggered, a mission team, selected from a roster of experts and laboratories provided by Member States, is composed, according to the Guidelines and Procedures adopted by the General Assembly in 1989.[37] From the very first

34 On this trend, in general, see Z D Kaufman, 'The Prospects, Problems and Proliferation of Recent UN Investigations of International Law Violations' (2018) 16 JICJ 93, and, more recently, G Le Moli, 'From "Is" to "Ought": The Development of Normative Powers of UN Investigative Mechanisms' (2021) 19 Chinese JIntL 625.

35 The authority granted to the Secretary-General, which can be traced to art 99 UN Charter, was first provided by the General Assembly in 1987 (UNGA Res 42/37 (30 November 1987) UN Doc A/RES/42/37C), and one year later, by the Security Council (UNSC Res 620 (26 August 1988) UN Doc S/RES/620(1988)).

36 <https://www.un.org/disarmament/wmd/secretary-general-mechanism/>.

37 UN Doc A/44/561. The Guidelines have recently undergone a process of review, conducted by the Office for Disarmament Affairs in 2007, together with other organisations, resulting in a revision only of the Appendices to take into account the developments in the biological area. A proposal to revise the mechanism, tabled by the Russian Federation in October 2020, which aimed at awarding the Security Council a much more prominent role (UN Doc A/C.1/75/L.65/Rev.1), has recently been rejected (<https://www.un.org/press/en/2020/gadis3657.doc.htm>). The motion faced strong opposition from several Member States, including European countries that noted that 'the SGM is an independent

time the Secretary-General carried out investigations into the use of chemical and biological weapons in the Iran-Iraq war, the SGM has been activated on a (limited) number of occasions: in Mozambique and Azerbaijan in 1992,[38] and more recently in Syria.[39]

For its part, the Security Council, whose investigative and fact-finding powers are expressively stipulated in Article 34 of the UN Charter, has established a variety of commissions to handle critical situations related to the maintenance of international peace and security, including those arising from the (threat of) use of 'weapons of mass destruction' (WMD). By way of example, the Security Council set up monitoring systems to verify that Iraq was complying with disarmament obligations in the aftermath of the Gulf war,[40] and an investigative body to identify the perpetrators of chemical attacks that occurred during the Syrian conflict.[41] In relation to the chemical attacks in Syria, even the General Assembly took investigative action, taking a historic step by setting up a special mechanism entrusted to collect and analyse evidence of international crimes committed therein that could be preserved for future criminal investigations.[42] Lastly, bodies capable of investigating human rights and humanitarian law violations resulting from the use of CBRN weapons can be commanded to investigate a situation by the UN Human Rights Council (HRC), in the form of an ad hoc commission of inquiry.[43]

All in all, the blossoming of the UN investigative mechanisms has become critical to the promotion of accountability for CBRN incidents involving weapons, especially the most serious ones. By determining the occurrence of CBRN incidents and the facts surrounding any allegations of the use of CBRN weapons, and, at times, even carrying out legal assessments, UN investigative powers can be instrumental to ensuring, or to laying the groundwork for ensuring, the prosecution of those responsible. Though pertaining more to the 'recovery' phase of the CBRN emergency cycle, the UN investigative powers end up exercising also a crucial deterrent function to 'prevent' future similar CBRN events.

---

instrument separate from the [BWC], with a different mandate and different membership' (<https://eeas.europa.eu/delegations/un-new-york/88134/node/88134_bs>).

38 UN Doc S/24065, S/24344 respectively detail the results of those two investigations.

39 See Section 4 in this contribution.

40 See the UNMOVIC, which replaced the UNSCOM (Section 3.2 in this contribution).

41 See Section 4 in this contribution.

42 Ibid.

43 Ibid.

3 An Overview of Collective Measures of Constraint

3.1 *Institutional Penalties under Arms Control and Disarmament Regimes*

Once non-compliance with ACDL agreements is suspected or found, graduated measures can be taken by competent institutional organs as an incentive to remedy incorrect behaviour, starting from the removal of treaty benefits to the adoption of penalties as the last stage of the compliance-control system. Accordingly, their goal is to 'reinforce' the prevention phase of the CBRN emergency management cycle. By contrast, when a CBRN event actually occurs, the exercise of sanctioning powers by the supervisory bodies may step more into the 'recovery' phase of the cycle.

For the purpose of this chapter, the constraint measures adopted by the OPCW, and those endorsed by the IAEA, are worth examining. With regard to the in-built sanctions handled by the OPCW, the approach followed appears, as already anticipated, to be more managerial than truly coercive. Specific tools aimed at leading the violator back to compliance are clearly provided in Article XII CWC, titled 'measures to redress a situation and to ensure compliance, including sanctions', which set forth a three-step procedure. Firstly, in cases where a State has been requested by the Executive Council to take measures to redress a situation raising problems with regard to its compliance,[44] and where the State concerned fails to fulfil the request within the specified time, the OPCW Conference may, upon the recommendation of the Executive Council, restrict or suspend the State Party's rights and privileges under the CWC until it undertakes the necessary action to conform with its obligations under the Convention.[45] The measures can impinge on a wide set of membership benefits with the only limitation being the deprival of State membership. In doing this, the Conference doesn't necessarily need to ascertain a violation of the Convention and may depart from recommendations received by the Executive Council, although an attempt to solve the issue through consultation between the latter and the State concerned is required in order to take action under Article XII. A further initiative that the Conference may embark upon, in cases where serious damage to the object and purpose of the Convention results from activities prohibited therein, is to recommend 'collective measures' to States Parties, such as the withholding of any exports of chemicals from the concerned State.[46] Although the recommendations are *per*

44 See art VIII, para 36 CWC, and Section 2.1 in this contribution.

45 Art XII, para 2 CWC.

46 Art XII, para 3 CWC.

se not legally binding, a State Party that doesn't comply with them, by assisting and cooperating with the State concerned, can be found to be in breach of Article I, para 1(d) CWC. In cases of particular gravity, the Conference, as a last resort, shall bring the issue, including relevant information and conclusions, to the attention of the UN General Assembly and the Security Council.[47] Despite the detailed and sophisticated procedure offered by the CWC in the event of non-compliance, Article XII had never been implemented, until very recently. Indeed, on 20 April 2021, the OPCW Conference adopted a groundbreaking decision, whereby it suspended certain rights and privileges of the Syrian Arab Republic under the CWC, thus marking the first application of Article XII, para 2.[48] At times, allegations of the breach of the CWC have been discussed during Review Conferences, though without Article XII being formally triggered.[49]

A different kind of centralised penalty applies with regard to the NPT regime, with the IAEA playing the role of 'nuclear watchdog' of an 'early warning system' which does not, strictly speaking, involve an enforcement procedure.[50] Under the verification system established in Article XII.C of the IAEA Statute, in cases where non-compliance issues are reported by the inspectors, and in the event of failure of the concerned State to take fully corrective action within a reasonable time, the IAEA Board may directly curtail or suspend assistance being provided by the Agency or by a member and call for the return of materials and equipment made available to the recipient State. Moreover, in accordance with Article XIX, a member which has persistently violated the provisions of this Statute, or of any agreement entered into by it pursuant to the IAEA Statute, may be suspended from the exercise of the privileges and rights of membership by the General Conference, acting by a two-thirds majority of the members present and voting upon a recommendation by the Board of Governors.[51]

In light of the above overview, it emerges that the relationship between the supervisory organisations and the UN, especially the Security Council, is highly 'institutionalised', so that the former's sanctioning powers can never encroach upon the prerogatives of the latter. This is clear from Article XII, para 3

47 Art XII, para 4 CWC.

48 <https://www.opcw.org/media-centre/news/2021/04/conference-states-parties-adopts-decision-suspend-certain-rights-and>. As for the backdrop against which the OPCW adopted the decision, see Section 4 in this contribution.

49 On such allegations, see G den Dekker, 'Art. XII' in W Krutzsch, E Myjer, R Trapp (eds), *The Chemical Weapons Convention: A Commentary* (OUP 2014) 365, 376.

50 L Rockwood (n 23) 319.

51 Art XIX.B IAEA Statute.

CWC, affirming that measures taken by the OPCW should be 'in conformity with international law', which implies, on the one hand, that the Conference can only recommend peaceful measures and, on the other hand, that measures under the CWC should complement, not undermine, the prerogatives of the Security Council. Needless to say, the Security Council can take actions not only on the basis of 'referral' from the IAEA or the OPCW, but also autonomously under Chapter VII, as long as the risk posed by CBRN weapons constitutes a threat or breach of international peace and security, or an act of aggression, thus overcoming the lack of universality of treaty obligations.

3.2 *Sanctions Imposed by the Security Council*

As is known, the reawakening of the Security Council in the 90s resulted in a more frequent triggering of Chapter VII and in a progressive enlargement of what constitutes a threat to, or breach of, peace pursuant to Article 39 of the UN Charter. The notion came into play in a variety of different situations, including the proliferation of nuclear, chemical, and biological weapons,[52] and, most recently, the spread of biological pathogens causing communicable diseases.[53] With particular regard to WMD, the milestone is the widely discussed Resolution 1540 (2004), whereby the Security Council enacted counter-proliferation measures of a general and abstract character.[54]

On quite a few occasions, the Security Council was able to adopt sanctions pursuant to Article 41 of the UN Charter, mostly of an economic nature, targeting specific CBRN threats, thus preserving and re-establishing international peace and security.[55] The Security Council has, thus, become a major actor in counter-proliferation by intervening in several problematic situations, to begin with, the well-known comprehensive economic embargo imposed against Iraq for the possession of nuclear, chemical and biological weapons, following the invasion of Kuwait in 1990–1991.[56] In the aftermath of the

52 On proliferation of nuclear, chemical and biological weapons, see UNSC Res 825 (1993), 1540 (2004), 1695 (2006), 1718 (2006), 1887 (2009), 2087 (2013), 2094 (2013).

53 The Security Council dealt with the HIV emergency in UNSC Res 1308 (2000), with the Ebola outbreak in UNSCR Res 2177 (2014) and, recently, with the Covid-19 virus in UNSC Res 2535 (2020). The Security Council, while openly employing the language of Chapter VII amid the Ebola crisis, used a more nuanced approach with regard to the Covid-19 outbreak (on this issue, see M Arcari, 'Some thoughts after SC resolution 2532 (2020) on Covid-19' (2020) 70 QIL 59, 62–63).

54 See ch 7 by Poltronieri Rossetti.

55 From the perspective of the CBRN emergency management cycle, these sanctions can be considered as part of the prevention phase, if the CBRN event has not yet occurred, and in between the response and the recovery phase, if the event has occurred, depending on the sanctions' specific purpose.

56 See UNSC Res 661 and 670 (1990), Res 1284 (1999).

controversial use of global sanctions against Iraq, which raised several concerns due to the humanitarian consequences suffered by its population, the Security Council converted the economic embargo into a 'smart' sanctions regime targeting senior officials of the former Iraqi regime and their immediate family members, including entities owned or controlled by them or by persons acting on their behalf.[57] Selective embargoes and scaling-down of diplomatic relations have also been imposed on Libya for developing WMD during the 90s,[58] and on two other problematic situations related to the development of nuclear programmes by Iran and the DPRK. With respect to the Iranian nuclear programme, the Security Council adopted sanctions in 2006, partially pursuant to the NPT regime and partially outside that system,[59] and it established the 1737 Committee to monitor the implementation of the measures, which worked in cooperation with the IAEA. The Iranian sanctions regime was eventually lifted in 2016, when the Security Council approved the Joint Comprehensive Plan of Action (JPCOA) in 2015,[60] and when the IAEA reported that Iran had taken the necessary steps to allow verification and monitoring as a result of the implementation of the JPCOA. However, the effectiveness of the JPCOA was steadily undermined in 2018, when the US withdrew from it,[61] claiming that Iran infringed the deal, and reimposed unilateral sanctions against Tehran, and when the latter, in response, exceeded agreed-upon limits and moved away from its nuclear pledges, especially during a period of particular unrest between the two States exacerbated by the killing of Iranian Major General Qasem Soleimani. As for the situation in the DPRK, which withdrew from the NPT in 2003, albeit through dubious procedures,[62] its nuclear programme has been the object of a specific sanctions regime established by the

57 States are required to implement asset freezes and transfer measures in connection with individuals and entities included in the List established pursuant to UNSC Res 1483 (2003), managed by the 1518 Committee.

58 See UNSC Res 748 (1992) and 883 (1993). The sanctions regime was suspended in 1999 and formally lifted in 2003.

59 See UNSC Res 1696 (2006), 1737 (2006), 1747 (2007), 1803 (2008), 1835 (2008), 1929 (2010).

60 UNSC Res 2231 (2015) provided a 'snap-back' mechanism which leads to the re-imposition of sanctions in case of a violation of the JPCOA, according to a peculiar procedure defined as an 'inversed veto' (H Blix, 'UN Security Council vs. Weapons of Mass destruction' (2016) 85 ActScandJurisGent 147, 160). In April 2020, the US announced its intention to trigger that mechanism, but it encountered objections from other permanent members of the Security Council.

61 See M Arcari, E Milano, 'The Joint Comprehensive Plan of Action five years on: Legal questions and future prospects' (2020) 66 QIL Zoom-in 1, introducing the contributions written by M Sossai and T Cullis and S Noorbaloochi.

62 See, among many, T Coppen, 'Good faith and withdrawal from the Non-Proliferation Treaty' (2014) 2 QIL Zoom-in 21.

Security Council in 2006,[63] overseen by the 1718 Committee, which remains in force today. Recently, Resolutions 2270 (2016) and 232 (2016), following several nuclear tests by the DPRK, set up one of the most comprehensive sanctions regimes ever imposed by the UN, composed of both a selective embargo and targeted measures.[64] On the contrary, in the aftermath of the chemical attacks in Syria, the Security Council, whilst condemning such incidents, failed to adopt a resolution that would have imposed sanctions against parties using chemical weapons, due to the veto powers exercised by permanent members (namely Russia and China).[65]

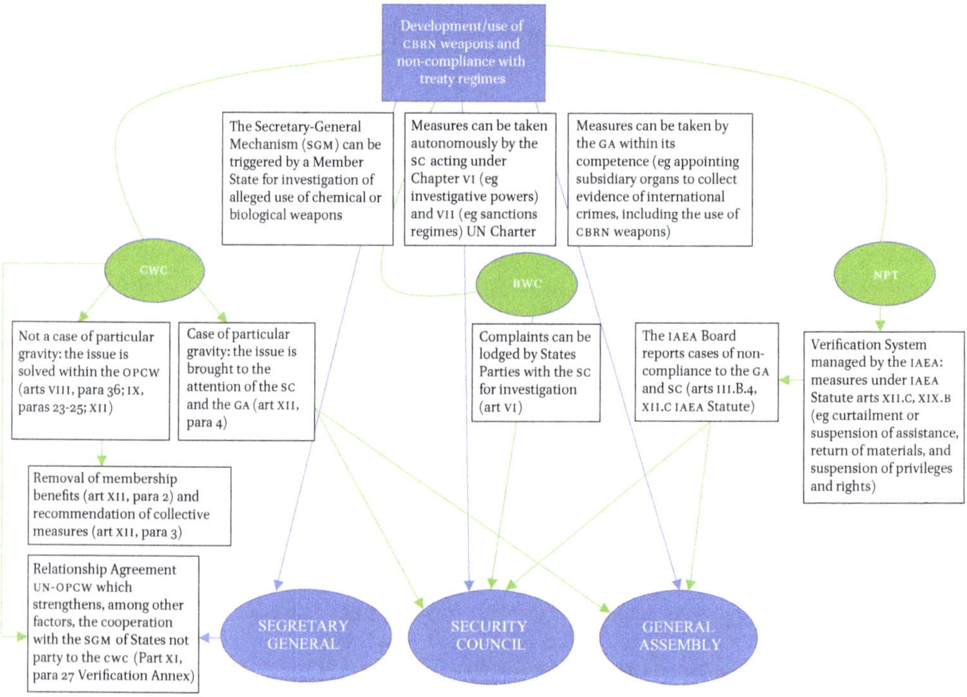

DIAGRAM 1 Non-compliance with international obligations applicable to CBRN weapons. An overview of the 'institutionalised' cooperation between the UN and treaty regimes

63 UNSC Res 1605 (2006), 1718 (2006), 1874 (2009).

64 L Borlini, 'The North Korean Gauntlet, International Law and the New Sanctions Imposed by the Security Council' (2016) ItYBIL 319. Apart from expanding the obligations resulting from the NPT, the resolutions promoted the BWC, to which the DPRK is a party, and the CWC, to which it is not.

65 <https://news.un.org/en/story/2017/02/552362-russia-china-block-security-council-action-use-chemical-weapons-syria>.

4 The Use of Chemical Weapons in Syria as a Catalyst for Multiple Investigations

As shown in the foregoing graphic, the 'institutionalised' relationship between the UN and the CWC regime is articulated on a number of different levels. The 2000 Relationship Agreement signed between the OPCW and the UN aims at further coordinating their respective tasks, through mutual information and reporting obligation schemes, making clear that there is no exclusivity in terms of the sphere of action between one organisation or the other, but that the range of powers entrusted to the OPCW can complement the mandate of the UN. The inter-governmental response to the use of chemical weapons in Syria during the deadly civil war illustrates how the cooperation between the UN and the OPCW has worked in practice, setting up a unique disarmament process, implemented under exceptional circumstances, notwithstanding that the stalemate of the Security Council led to the failure to adopt coercive measures.[66]

In March 2013, the Government of Syria officially made allegations of the use of chemical weapons in the Aleppo area and requested the Secretary-General to investigate under the SGM scheme.[67] With the assistance of the OPCW and the WHO, the Secretary-General dispatched a team mission to Syria in August 2013, which also investigated, as a priority, the second alleged use of chemical weapons, occurring later the same month, in the Ghouta area of Damascus. The mission presented a report on 13 September 2013, which confirmed that chemical weapons (namely sarin) had been used in a large-scale attack against the civilian population, including numerous children.[68] Shortly after, on 14 September 2013, Syria, under great international pressure, signed the CWC and provided notification of its intention to apply the Convention provisionally,[69] while the Russian Federation and the United States reached a historic agreement-framework for the elimination of chemical weapons in Syria. Immediately, the OPCW Executive Council adopted a

66 The assessment of the military reactions to the use of chemical weapons in Syria, and their possible legal justifications, clearly exceeds the scope of this contribution (on this topic see, among many, A de Guttry, 'The Western-led Military Operations in Syria in Response to the Use of Chemical Weapons: A Critical Assessment of the Claim for New Exceptions to the Prohibition on the Use of Force' (2018) Archiv des Voelkerrechts 472).

67 On the SGM, see Section 2.2.

68 UN Doc A/67/997 – S/2013/553.

69 On the question of the provisional application of the CWC, and the alleged 'instant accession' by Syria, see W Krutzsch, E Myjer, R Trapp, 'Annex to The Commentary, Issues Raised by the Accession of Syria to the Chemical Weapons Convention' in W Krutzsch, E Myjer, R Trapp (n 49) 689, 693–694.

decision,[70] fully endorsed and 'hardened' by Security Council Resolution 2118 (2013), which established special procedures for the expeditious destruction of Syria's chemical weapons programme and stringent verification thereof, with reference to the agreement-framework.[71] To oversee the timely elimination of the chemical weapons programme in the safest and most secure manner possible, a special mission, the OPCW-UN Joint Mission on the elimination of Syrian chemical weapons (JMIS), was established[72] and completed its task on 30 September 2014.[73]

Despite the dismantling activities, persistent allegations of chemical weapon attacks in Syria continued and, therefore, the OPCW set up a further investigative body in 2014, namely, the Fact-Finding Mission (FFM), mandated 'to establish facts surrounding allegations of the use of toxic chemicals, reportedly chlorine, for hostile purposes in the Syrian Arab Republic'.[74] Over the last six years, the FFM has looked into several incidents of use of chemical weapons in Syria, and it has confirmed with a 'high degree of confidence' that chlorine and mustard gas have been deployed as weapons.[75] The FFM's findings, in turn, constituted the basis for the work of the OPCW-UN Joint Investigative Mechanism (JIM), an independent body created by Security Council Resolution 2235 (2015), with a groundbreaking mandate to identify the perpetrators of chemical weapon attacks where the FFM determines or has determined that a specific incident in Syria involved or likely involved the use of chemicals as weapons.[76] In its reports presented to the Security Council, the JIM was able to attribute responsibility of four chemical incidents to the Syrian Government.[77] What stands out is that, unlike the FFM which is meant to establish only facts surrounding chemical incidents, the JIM's mandate, for the first time ever, was to determine the attribution of specific chemical incidents,

70 OPCW EC EC-M-33/Dec.1.

71 For the timelines for the elimination of the chemical weapons programme, see <https://opcw.unmissions.org/mandate-and-timelines>.

72 The mandate of the JMIS was based on recommendations developed in close consultations between the UN Secretary-General and the OPCW Director-General and pursuant to the 2000 UN-OPCW Relationship Agreement (see EC-M-33/DEC.1 and UNSC Res 2118 (2013)). On the legal basis from which the JMIS came to light, see R Trapp, 'Elimination of the Chemical weapons Stockpile of Syria' (2014) 19 JC&SL 7, 13–14.

73 A subsequent agreement was signed between the UN and the OPCW to foster closer cooperation between the two organisations (OPCW EC EC-M-34/DG.1 para 17).

74 <https://www.opcw.org/fact-finding-mission>.

75 Ibid.

76 UNSC Res 2235 (2015).

77 On the main findings of the JIM, see Y Naqvi, 'Crossing the red line: The use of chemical weapons in Syria and what should happen now' (2017) 99 IRRC 959, 971–974.

albeit without making any formal or binding judicial determination of criminal liability.[78] Therefore, it comes as no surprise that JIM's special mandate has been harshly criticised, leading to its expiration in November 2017, after the Russian Federation vetoed its renewal.

In the wake of the JIM's non-renewal, an alternative solution was found, in 2018, for identifying the perpetrators of the use of chemical weapons, the so-called Investigation and Identification Team (IIT). This time, the mechanism was created within the OPCW Technical Secretariat, under the authority of the Director-General.[79] After having begun its work in June 2019, the ITT submitted its first 82-page report, confirming that three chemical attacks which occurred in 2017 were launched 'pursuant to orders from the highest levels of the Syrian Arab Armed Forces'.[80] The second report, issued on 12 April 2021, with regard to the incident in Saraqib in 2018, drew a similar conclusion.[81] Given its unique task of identifying perpetrators, the IIT's mandate was also criticised, leading to complaints that the OPCW had exceed its powers. While it's undeniable that the OPCW, in the Syrian crisis context, moved away from purely technical verification and took on the functions of gathering and preserving evidence of chemical attacks, as well as attributing the attacks, in support of possible future judicial determination, the creation of the IIT could not be considered as an *ultra vires* act, since, as convincingly argued by scholars,[82] it pertains to the (implied) powers of the OPCW, set out in Articles VIII, IX, and XII CWC.

The UN efforts to conduct an inquiry into the brutal chemical incidents taking place in Syria have tremendously multiplied over the last decade. In fact, the UN HRC had already activated its own investigative powers with regard to the critical situation in Syria, back in August 2011, by establishing

78 For a thorough discussion on the JIM and its breakthrough mandate, see M Sossai, 'Identifying the Perpetrators of Chemical Attacks in Syria: The Organisation for the Prohibition of Chemical Weapons as Part of the Fight Against Impunity?' (2019) 17 JICJ 211, 214–215.

79 The IIT, established pursuant to OPCW Conference C-SS-4/DEC.3, has been entrusted with the mandate to 'identif[y] and repor[t] on all information potentially relevant to the origin of those chemical weapons in those instances in which the FFM determines or has determined that use or likely use occurred, and cases for which the OPCW-UN JIM has not identified the perpetrators of chemical weapons use in Syria' (<https://www.opcw.org/iit>).

80 OPCW TS S/1867/2020.

81 OPCW TS S/1943/2021.

82 Sossai (n 78) 220–221. For a critical reading of the OPCW Decision (n 79), and the powers delegated to the IIT concerning the determination of responsibility and attribution, see A Orakhelashvili, 'The Attribution Decision Adopted by the OPCW's Conference of States Parties and Its Legality' (2020) 17 IntlOrgLRev 664.

the Independent International Commission of Inquiry on the Syrian Arab Republic (HRC-COI).[83] Interestingly enough, the UN General Assembly, for its part, condemned the use of chemical weapons in Syria on several occasions and, in December 2016, took the groundbreaking decision to institute the 'International, Impartial and Independent Mechanism to ensure due Punishment to the Persons Responsible for the Most Serious Crimes under International Law Committed in the Syrian Arab Republic since March 2011' (known in shorthand as IIIM).[84] The mechanism arguably falls within the boundaries of the General Assembly's competence, despite the fact that Russia and Syria have persisted in objecting to the step made as being *ultra vires*.[85] The IIIM is neither a prosecutor's office nor a court, but it collects, and analyses, information and evidence of international crimes committed in Syria, including those deriving from the use of chemical weapons, with the ultimate goal of assisting national, regional or international courts that have or will have jurisdiction over these crimes. The HRC-COI and the IIIM are complementary despite having distinct mandates: the former collects information, reports on broad patterns of violations and makes recommendations, notably to Member States; in contrast, the IIIM assists courts, based on the information collected by others – notably the HRC-COI – and it is not expected to publicly report on its substantive work.[86] Additionally, the OPCW made arrangements to connect the work of the IIT to the IIIM mandate, as the former is requested to preserve and provide information to the latter or to any relevant investigatory entities established under the auspices of the UN.[87]

This brief overview clearly indicates how multi-layered the cooperation among the UN and international institutions dealing specifically with CBRN agents can be. It also shows how pragmatic and innovative solutions can be found together, within and beyond the UN institutions, to circumvent, on the one hand, the inability or unwillingness of domestic authorities to prevent and investigate CBRN weapon incidents and, on the other hand, the Security Council's inertia, which may block the establishment of an ad hoc tribunal,

---

83 UN Doc A/HRC/RES/S-17/1 (reports are available at <https://www.ohchr.org/EN/HRBodies/HRC/IICISyria/Pages/Documentation.aspx>).

84 UNGA Res 71/248 (21 December 2016) UN Doc A/RES/71/248.

85 Whilst is true that the General Assembly cannot itself create a body that prosecutes crimes, it is entitled, under arts 10 and 22 of the UN Charter, to establish subsidiary organs to collect and assess the available evidence of international crimes in order to inform its own discussion and recommendations on these matters. On the legitimacy of the General Assembly's action, see A Whiting, 'An Investigation Mechanism for Syria. The General Assembly Steps into the Breach' (2017) JICJ 231.

86 <https://www.ohchr.org/en/NewsEvents/Pages/DisplayNews.aspx?NewsID=21241>.

87 See C-SS-4/DEC.3 (n 79) para 12.

the referral to the International Criminal Court, and the adoption of sanctions under Chapter VII. The establishment of investigative mechanisms, such as the IIIM for Syria, can be seen, ultimately, as 'a marker that reminds future political actors and diplomats that the crimes in Syria will not easily be forgotten or brushed aside',[88] hence creating an important bridge and setting the stage for a future criminal prosecution.[89] By establishing investigative mechanisms empowered to determine attribution of chemical weapons use, the OPCW has shown an inclination to deal not only with 'disarmament' issues but also with 'accountability'.

From this perspective, the international law framework applicable to CBRN weapons seems to have antibodies, if not to prevent, at least to pave the way to recover from CBRN events, through investigation and fact-finding activities, especially with regard to the most serious incidents that may constitute crimes under international law and gross human rights violations. Therefore, it remains to be seen whether and to what extent the valuable amount of data collected by the international investigative bodies will be used, as evidence, to hold perpetrators accountable before national and international courts. In this regard, the latest claims brought before national prosecutors (namely German) by Syrian victims of sarin gas attacks will certainly deserve attention in the future.[90] Alongside the remedies available for the victims,[91] some final thoughts should be devoted to inter-State litigation concerning CBRN events before international courts, namely, the International Court of Justice (ICJ).

5 New Routes to Enforce CBRN Obligations? Concluding Remarks on Inter-State Litigation

The analysis conducted above shows that most of the ACDL treaties endorse a 'carrot and stick' approach by envisaging, on the one hand, a number of benefits deriving from full compliance with the provisions established therein ('positive' incentives), and, on the other hand, a centralised system of supervision in order to ensure compliance with the provisions laid down in the agreements ('negative' incentives). If positive and negative incentives do

88 Whiting (n 85) 235.

89 On the relationship between fact-finding activities and criminal prosecution, see, among many, M Frulli, 'Fact-Finding or Paving the Road to Criminal Justice. Some reflections on United Nations Commissions of Inquiry' (2012) 10 JICJ 1323.

90 <https://www.justiceinitiative.org/litigation/german-criminal-investigation-into-chemical-weapons-attacks-in-syria>.

91 On this issue, see ch 34 by Capone.

not achieve their purpose, and non-compliance is suspected or found, treaty regimes provide also for progressive constraint measures that seek to restore full compliance and bring the violator back in line. Yet, these latter procedures fit into a rather 'soft-enforcing' dynamic. In fact, under the CWC and NPT regimes analysed above, the OPCW and the IAEA, lacking purely coercive powers, and envisaging only 'institutional penalties', offer a forum for debates among States Parties to help with clarifying doubts or solving disputes, through mediation and dialogue, in order to implement the agreements in a cooperative manner. From this perspective, supervisory organisations play much more of a 'managerial' role than a truly 'confrontational' one in their efforts to ensure compliance.[92]

In the event that an actual dispute arises between the parties, it is worth examining, finally, whether and to what extent dispute settlement clauses come into play. Many multilateral treaties dealing with CBRN events contain compromissory clauses that defer the settlement of disputes between the parties to the ICJ. This holds true especially with regard to CBRN industrial accidents,[93] as well as naturally occurring events, including communicable diseases.[94] Conversely, their insertion in disarmament and arms control agreements is less frequent and they have 'never played a major role in the context of implementation and compliance'.[95] Generally speaking, ACDL is more focused on the prevention of situations likely to give rise to disputes, through multiple levels of continuous dialogue, rather than on the resolution of disputes. Compliance control and dispute settlement mechanisms work in parallel, yet the *raison d'être* of the former is to avoid resorting to the latter in the first place.[96]

---

92 G den Dekker, 'The Effectiveness of International Supervision in Arms Control Law' (2004) 9 JC&SL 315, 322.

93 Eg Convention on the Transboundary Effects of Industrial Accidents (1992) art 21; Basel Convention on the Control of Transboundary Movements of Hazardous Wastes and their Disposal (1989) art 20.

94 For instance, with respect to potential litigation concerning health events, State compliance with WHO law (in particular with the 2005 International Health Regulations) could be challenged before the ICJ, relying on the compromissory clause contained in Article 75 of the WHO Constitution. With regard to the COVID-19 outbreak, see recently P Tzeng, 'Taking China to the International Court of Justice over COVID-19' (*EJIL:Talk!*, 2 April 2020) <https://www.ejiltalk.org/taking-china-to-the-international-court-of-justice-over-covid-19/>.

95 T Marauhn (n 2) 251.

96 As argued by scholars, '[t]he effectiveness of the whole [CWC] will to some extent depend on the ability of the system to avoid disputes' (T Kurzidem, 'Conflict management and the Chemical Weapons Convention' in M Bothe, A Rosas, N Ronzitti (eds), *The New Chemical*

As for treaty regimes explored in this chapter, neither the NPT,[97] nor the CWC or the BWC,[98] enshrine compromissory clauses that refer disputes to the ICJ, but, rather, they provide for diplomatic means to resolve differences. At most, institutional organs are often empowered, subject to authorisation from the General Assembly, to trigger the ICJ advisory function on any legal question arising within the scope of the activities of the respective institutions.[99] Yet, in recent years, nuclear weapons issues, in particular, have been brought to the attention of the ICJ on a number of occasions, both in litigation cases, based on different grounds of jurisdiction,[100] and in advisory opinions.[101] On the whole, the Court has taken a cautious attitude in dealing with such matters. However, some recent disputes may bring forward new questions relating – albeit only indirectly – to prohibited nuclear and chemical activities. With respect to nuclear activities, Iran recently sued the United States for violation of the 1955 Treaty of Amity,[102] as a result of the decision undertaken by the Trump administration to terminate its participation in JPCOA and to reimpose on Tehran sanctions lifted in connection with the JPCOA. The case is still pending and it remains to be seen whether the dispute falls within the material scope of the Treaty of Amity and its compromissory clause.[103] With respect to chemical activities, the Netherlands announced in September 2020 that it was seeking to hold Syria responsible for gross human rights violations, namely, for committing torture and using chemical weapons, by resorting to the compromissory clause contained in Article 30 of the Convention against Torture

Weapons Convention: Implementation and Prospects (Kluwer Law International 1998) 287).

97 Yet, art XVII.A IAEA Statute refers to the ICJ disputes not settled through negotiation. The Comprehensive Safeguards Agreements provide also for arbitration as a means to solve disputes between the parties, subject to a prior negotiation.

98 Art XIV CWC, art V BWC.

99 Art XIV CWC para 5 and art XVII.B Statute IAEA.

100 *Nuclear Tests* (*Australia v France*) (1974) ICJ Rep 253; *Obligations concerning Negotiations relating to Cessation of the Nuclear Arms Race and to Nuclear Disarmament* (*Marshall Islands v India*) (2016) ICJ Rep 255. The ICJ in both cases did not address the merits of the claims.

101 *Legality of the Threat or Use of Nuclear Weapons* (1996) ICJ Rep 226.

102 *Alleged Violations of the 1955 Treaty of Amity, Economic Relations, and Consular Rights* (*Islamic Republic of Iran v United States of America*).

103 So far, the ICJ has affirmed that it has *prima facie* jurisdiction to grant provisional measures. Recently, it rejected the preliminary objections to jurisdiction and admissibility raised by the United States of America and found, consequently, that it has jurisdiction to entertain the application filed by the Islamic Republic of Iran. See ibid (Preliminary Objections).

and Other Cruel, Inhuman or Degrading Treatment or Punishment (CAT).[104] Interestingly, in March 2021, Canada declared its intention to take the same steps.[105] Although the scope of the dispute will be confined to a violation of the CAT, the ICJ, if it finds itself to have jurisdiction, would be indirectly asked to pronounce on the chemical attacks that occurred in Syria and it could make good use of the significant amount of factual evidence collected thus far by the several investigative bodies mentioned above.

Although litigation in this field is still rather scant, it is worth noting that applicant States, even if not 'specifically affected' by a given CBRN event, may, nevertheless, be willing to protect collective interests enshrined in treaties whose interpretation and application is at the centre of the dispute. Litigating 'communitarian' obligations on behalf of the international community in matters that deal, even indirectly, with CBRN weapons seems to have motivated both the applications filed by the Marshall Islands, with respect to the cessation of the nuclear arms race, and the forthcoming application announced by the Netherlands (and Canada) for the chemical attacks in Syria. If successful, this kind of litigation can, incidentally, contribute to implementing the recovery phase of the CBRN emergency management cycle, by requiring the non-compliant State to respect relevant obligations and to provide for reparation. Moreover, litigating CBRN events before international courts can induce the implementation of the obligation to give assurances and guarantees of non-repetition, with a view to preventing any similar events in the future, an obligation that, in the CBRN law field, is of paramount importance.

Bibliography

Arcari M, 'Some thoughts after SC resolution 2532 (2020) on COVID-19' (2020) 70 QIL Zoom-in 59.

Arcari M, Milano E, 'The Joint Comprehensive Plan of Action five years on: Legal questions and future prospects' (2020) 66 QIL Zoom-in 1.

Black-Branch J L, Fleck D (eds), *Nuclear Non-Proliferation in International Law. Volume II: Verification and Compliance* (Asser Press 2016).

104 <https://www.government.nl/latest/news/2020/09/18/the-netherlands-holds-syria-responsible-for-gross-human-rights-violations>.

105 <https://www.canada.ca/en/global-affairs/news/2021/03/backgrounderjoint-statement-of-canada-and-the-kingdom-of-the-netherlands-regarding-their-cooperation-in-holding-syria-to-account.html>.

Blix H, 'UN Security Council vs. Weapons of Mass destruction' (2016) 85 ActScand-JurisGent 147.

Borlini L, 'The North Korean Gauntlet, International Law and the New Sanctions Imposed by the Security Council' (2016) ItYBIL 319.

Bothe M, 'Weapons of Mass Destruction, Counter-Proliferation', *Max Planck Encyclopedia of Public International Law* 2016.

Coppen T, 'Good faith and withdrawal from the Non-Proliferation Treaty' (2014) 2 QIL Zoom-in 21.

de Guttry A, 'The Western-led Military Operations in Syria in Response to the Use of Chemical Weapons: A Critical Assessment of the Claim for New Exceptions to the Prohibition on the Use of Force' (2018) Archiv des Voelkerrechts 472.

den Dekker G, 'Art. XII' in W Krutzsch, E Myjer, R Trapp (eds), *The Chemical Weapons Convention: A Commentary* (OUP 2014) 365.

den Dekker G, 'The Effectiveness of International Supervision in Arms Control Law' (2004) 9 JC&SL 315.

Feakes D, 'Evaluating the CWC Verification System' (2002) Disarmament Forum 11.

Frulli M, 'Fact-Finding or Paving the Road to Criminal Justice. Some reflections on United Nations Commissions of Inquiry' (2012) 10 JICJ 1323.

Kaufman Z D, 'The Prospects, Problems and Proliferation of Recent UN Investigations of International Law Violations' (2018) 16 JICJ 93.

Krutzsch W, Myjer E, Trapp R, 'Annex to The Commentary, Issues Raised by the Accession of Syria to the Chemical Weapons Convention' in W Krutzsch, E Myjer, R Trapp (eds), *The Chemical Weapons Convention: A Commentary* (OUP 2014) 689.

Kurzidem T, 'Conflict management and the Chemical Weapons Convention' in M Bothe, A Rosas, N Ronzitti (eds), *The New Chemical Weapons Convention: Implementation and Prospects* (Kluwer Law International 1998) 287.

Le Moli G, 'From "Is" to "Ought": The Development of Normative Powers of UN Investigative Mechanisms' (2020) 19 Chinese JIntL 625.

Marauhn T, 'Dispute resolution, compliance control and enforcement of international arms control law' in G Ulfstein, T Marauhn, A Zimmermann (eds), *Making Treaties Work. Human Rights, Environment and Arms Control* (CUP 2007) 243.

Naqvi Y, 'Crossing the red line: The use of chemical weapons in Syria and what should happen now' (2017) 99 IRRC 959.

Orakhelashvili A, 'The Attribution Decision Adopted by the OPCW's Conference of States Parties and Its Legality' (2020) 17 IntlOrgLRev 664.

Pedrazzi M, 'The Treaty on the Prohibition of Nuclear Weapons: A Promise, a Threat or a Flop?' (2018) 27 ItYBIL 215.

Pellet A, Miron A, 'Sanctions', *Max Planck Encyclopedia of Public International Law* 2013.

Rockwood L, 'The Treaty on the Non-Proliferation of Nuclear Weapons (NPT) and IAEA Safeguards Agreements' in G Ulfstein, T Marauhn, A Zimmermann (eds), *Making Treaties Work. Human Rights, Environment and Arms Control* (CUP 2007) 301.

Sossai M, 'Identifying the Perpetrators of Chemical Attacks in Syria: The Organisation for the Prohibition of Chemical Weapons as Part of the Fight Against Impunity?' (2019) 17 JICJ 211.

Tabassi L, 'The Convention on the Prohibition of the Development, Production, Stockpiling and Use of Chemical Weapons and on their Destruction' in G Ulfstein, T Marauhn, A Zimmermann (eds), *Making Treaties Work. Human Rights, Environment and Arms Control* (CUP 2007) 273.

Trapp R, 'Elimination of the Chemical weapons Stockpile of Syria' (2014) 19 JC&SL 7.

Tzeng P, 'Taking China to the International Court of Justice over COVID-19' (*EJIL:Talk!*, 2 April 2020).

Venturini G, 'Control and Verification of Multilateral Treaties on Disarmament and Non-Proliferation of Weapons of Mass Destruction' (2011) 17 UC Davis JIntL & Policy 345.

Whiting A, 'An Investigation Mechanism for Syria. The General Assembly Steps into the Breach' (2017) JICJ 231.

PART 4

Horizontal Issues

CHAPTER 27

Positive Obligations under Human Rights Law to Protect against CBRN Risks

Silvia Venier

1 Introduction

In a recent essay on the human rights framework for emergency situations (HRFE), Nickel suggests that there are many grounds for dissatisfaction, including that the rights are undifferentiated (*ie* not targeted to different hazards), mostly negative (*ie* focusing on negative obligations) and rather simplistic (*ie* suggesting that the main danger is overreaction while unpreparedness and inadequate response are never addressed).[1] The traditional way of looking at the interplay between human rights law (HRL) and emergency situations is, indeed, to assess limitations and derogations, *ie* to focus on negative obligations (NO) as duties to refrain from acting in a way that impacts on human rights in a disproportionate or unnecessary manner.[2] However, the State has the responsibility not only to refrain from violating rights when implementing emergency management measures but, more generally, to provide what is needed to protect or secure rights. In other words, under HRL, NO are complemented by positive obligations (PO), as duties to take active steps to protect against violations committed by third parties or deriving from a dangerous situation. As recognised in previous chapters in this volume, HRL is, indeed, one of the most important sources of the obligations to prevent, prepare for, respond to and recover from emergency situations. By clarifying States' duties with respect to the persons under their jurisdiction, PO under HRL complement horizontal obligations enshrined in other relevant areas of international law. The added value of looking at PO is that HRL is endowed with stronger enforcement mechanisms, and this is particularly the case for regional HR courts.

It is now acknowledged that any type of right demands a mix of negative and positive duties for its complete realisation, but the positive dimension took some time to develop. It was first proposed by Shue in 1980, expanded by

1 JW Nickel, 'Two models of normative frameworks for Human Rights during Emergencies', in EJ Criddle (ed.) *Human Rights in Emergencies* (CUP 2016).
2 See ch 28 by Sommario.

 | DOI:10.1163/9789004507999_028

Eide in the late 1980s, and then extensively relied upon by the Committee on Economic, Social and Cultural Rights (CESCR), which developed a tripartite typology of obligations (*ie* to respect, protect and fulfil) under the International Covenant on Economic, Social and Cultural Rights (ICESCR).[3] While the positive dimension is explicitly recognised under ICESCR Article 2(1),[4] PO related to civil and political rights are usually seen as implicit in the wording of those provisions requiring States Parties to 'ensure' or to 'secure' human rights.[5] Key challenges in the development of PO include the arbitrariness of the negative/positive distinction or of framing a violation as resulting from an act or an omission; the potentially open-ended scope of PO; the difficulties in adjudicating over resource-demanding obligations; and the potential impact on the separation of powers.[6] As noted by Fredman, 'there is still much to be done to develop a full understanding of the implications of positive duties triggered by human rights, both from a theoretical and practical legal perspective'.[7] An important contribution to this debate was offered by Pisillo Mazzeschi with the categorisation of three types of PO under HRL (obligations of immediate result, of conduct or due diligence, and of progressive realisation, ranging from the most definite and justiciable to the more vague that imply less strict responsibilities) that allow States to understand what is required and according to which timescale.[8] The categorisation is subject to changes over time, as our understanding of the role of the State in relation to HR protection evolves.

3 H Shue, *Basic Rights* (Princeton University Press 1980); UN Special Rapporteur for the Right to Food, 'The right to adequate food as a human right: final report submitted by Asbjørn Eide' (1987) UN Doc E/CN.4/Sub.2/1987/23; International Covenant on Economic, Social and Cultural Rights (1966).

4 Pursuant to ICESCR art 2(1), 'Each State Party to the present Covenant undertakes to take steps, individually and through international assistance and co-operation, especially economic and technical, to the maximum of its available resources, with a view to achieving progressively the full realization of the rights recognized in the present Covenant by all appropriate means, including particularly the adoption of legislative measures'.

5 See ICCPR art 2(1); European Convention on Human Rights (1951) art 1; American Convention on Human Rights (1969) art 1(1).

6 On the challenges to develop PO, see S Besson, 'Les obligations positives de protection des droits fondamentaux – Un essai en dogmatique comparative' (2003) 1(49) *Revue de droit Suisse* (on the legal basis for PO); D Xenos, *The Positive Obligations of the State under the European Convention of Human Rights* (Routledge 2012) (on PO open-ended scope); L Lavrysen, *Human Rights in a Positive State. Rethinking the Relationship between Positive and Negative Obligations under the European Convention on Human Rights* (Intersentia 2018) (on the negative/positive distinction).

7 S Fredman, *Human Rights Transformed* (OUP 2008) 3.

8 R Pisillo Mazzeschi, 'Responsabilité de l'état pour violation des obligations positives relatives aux droits de l'homme' (2008) 333 *Collected Courses of the Hague Academy of International Law*.

PO applicable to emergency management are currently being identified by human rights' supervising authorities at the universal and regional levels but have not attracted much attention from the academic community. Their exact scope and content and their applicability to specific types of emergency situations are not yet completely clear. More attention to PO is thus required in order to realise the full potential of HRL in relation to emergency situations, also in consideration of the fact that treaties and international instruments directly applicable to CBRN risks are now making explicit reference to HR protection, but this is usually understood only in terms of NO. References to HRL are enshrined in the Sendai Framework on Disaster Risk Reduction (DRR)[9] and in the Draft Articles on the Protection of Persons in the Event of Disasters adopted by the International Law Commission (ILC) in 2016;[10] in the Paris Agreement on Climate Change (and this is also relevant as climate change adaptation implies adapting to disasters resulting from extreme weather events);[11] in the Treaty on the Prohibition of Nuclear Weapons (TPNW);[12] and in the revised International Health Regulations (IHR).[13]

This contribution investigates the role of PO under HRL to enhance protection in relation to emergency situations, including those of CBRN origin. It first looks at the provisions under HRL that enshrine relevant PO and at the practice of UN human rights treaty monitoring bodies and Charter-based mechanisms (2) and at the identification of relevant PO within regional human rights regimes (3). It then classifies PO according to the phase of the emergency management cycle (prevention, preparedness, response and recovery) and the type of obligation (of immediate result, due diligence and progressive realisation), and it finally offers some conclusive remarks on the role of PO under HRL in CBRN protection.

9 Differently from the previously adopted DRR frameworks, an explicit reference to the requirement for DRR activities to be carried out 'while promoting and protecting all human rights' is included among the Sendai Framework's guiding principles. Sendai Framework for Disaster Risk Reduction 2015–2030 (2015) UN Doc A/CONF.224/L.2, para 19(c).

10 ILC Draft Articles 5 and 6.

11 On the linkages between climate change adaptation and disaster risk reduction, see G Forino, J von Meding, G Brewer, 'A Conceptual Governance Framework for Climate Change Adaptation and Disaster Risk Reduction Integration' (2015) 6 Intl J Disaster Risk Science 372. See also D Cubie, 'Promoting Dignity for all: Human Rights Approaches in the Post-2015 Climate Change, Disaster Risk Reduction and Sustainable Development Frameworks' (2014) 8(36) Human Rights and International Legal Discourse.

12 Treaty on the Prohibition of Nuclear Weapons (2017).

13 B Toebes, 'Human rights and public health: towards a balanced relationship' (2015) 19(4) The International Journal of Human Rights 488.

2 PO Relevant to Emergency Situations Identified within the UN System

Back in 1982, the Human Rights Committee (HRCtee) asserted that a State has to take positive action to protect the right to life, including measures 'to reduce malnutrition and epidemics'.[14] Similarly, the CESCR recently indicated that 'core obligations' under the right to health include 'the creation of a system of urgent medical care in cases of accidents, epidemics and similar health hazards, and the provision of disaster relief and humanitarian assistance in emergency situations'.[15] The General Comment (GC) on the right to life adopted in 2019 by the HRCtee confirmed that PO under that right include to 'develop, when necessary, contingency plans and disaster management plans designed to increase preparedness and address natural and manmade disasters that may adversely affect enjoyment of the right to life, such as hurricanes, tsunamis, earthquakes, radioactive accidents and massive cyberattacks resulting in disruption of essential services.'[16] Among the most serious threats to the right to life, the GC identifies risks of CBRN origin, including CBRN weapons and environmental degradation.[17]

UN human rights Treaty Monitoring bodies are paying increasing attention to the links between HRL and emergency situations and are proposing recommendations to States. Recurring DRR themes in their Concluding Observations refer to taking into account the views and needs of the most vulnerable groups (*ie* persons with disabilities, ethnic minorities, women and children, the elderly, who are likely to be disproportionately affected by disasters); collecting data on disaster losses that are disaggregated by factors of vulnerability; and training emergency service personnel to meet the needs of these groups.[18] The analysis of this practice reveals that a set of HRL recommendations are

---

14 HRCtee, 'General Comment No. 6, The right to life (Article 6)' (1982) para 6.

15 CESCR, 'General Comment 14, The Right to the Highest Attainable Standard of Health' (2000) UN Doc E/C.12/2000/4, para 12.

16 Ibid para 26.

17 Substantial and procedural obligations related to the right to a healthy environment have been recognised by the Independent Expert on the enjoyment of a safe, clean, healthy and sustainable environment and by the Special Rapporteur on toxic waste. See HRC, 'Report of the Independent Expert on the issue of human rights obligations relating to the enjoyment of a safe, clean, healthy and sustainable environment' (2013) A/HRC/25/53; HRC, 'Report of the Special Rapporteur on the implications for human rights of the environmentally sound management and disposal of hazardous substances and wastes' (2017) UN Doc A/HRC/3641.

18 E Sommario and S Venier, 'Human Rights Law and Disaster Risk Reduction' (2018) 49 QIL Zoom-in.

being identified that correspond to some of the priorities put forward by the Sendai Framework.[19]

The most detailed document on DRR measures required under HRL is the General Recommendation no. 37, adopted in 2018 by the Committee on the Elimination of Discrimination against Women (CEDAW),[20] which identifies three different but mutually reinforcing areas for action: (i) the general principles of the Convention applicable to disaster risk and climate change; (ii) specific measures to address disaster risk reduction and climate change; and (iii) specific areas of concern. Key principles applicable to any DRR initiative (i) refer to equality and non-discrimination, participation and empowerment, accountability and access to justice. As far as (ii) is concerned, the document provides recommendations on data collection and information sharing, policy coherence, extraterritorial obligations and international cooperation, resource allocation, capacity development and access to technology. Finally, the last section (iii) discusses the implementation of specific rights, such as to live free from gender-based violence against women and girls, to education and information, to work and social protection, to health, to an adequate standard of living and freedom of movement.

Recent developments within the Convention on the Rights of Persons with Disabilities have to be mentioned, since Article 11 under this treaty explicitly (and uniquely) establishes the obligation to 'take [...] all necessary measures to ensure the protection and safety of persons with disabilities in situations of risk, including situations of armed conflict, humanitarian emergencies and the occurrence of natural disasters'. In addition to the recommendations regularly offered to States by the Committee on the Rights of Persons with Disabilities

19 The need for the continuing implementation of the Sendai Framework and its references to HR was affirmed by the resolution on human rights and climate change adopted by the UN Human Rights Council (HRC) in 2017, which encouraged the UN HR monitoring bodies 'to provide technical assistance to States, upon their request, to help to better promote and protect human rights when taking action to address the adverse impact of climate change'. The resolution called upon States to enhance international cooperation and assistance for adaptation measures to help both developing countries and persons in vulnerable situations 'including migrants and persons displaced across international borders in the context of the adverse impact of climate change'. See UN HRC, Res 35/20 'Human Rights and Climate Change' (2017) UN Doc A/HRC/35/L.32 paras 5 and 6.

20 UN CEDAW, 'General Recommendation No. 37 on Gender-Related Dimensions of Disaster Risk Reduction in the context of climate change' (2018) CEDAW/C/GC/37. It is interesting to note that the Recommendation adopts a very broad definition of disaster situations and explicitly mentions 'environmental, technological and biological hazards and risks [...] as well as any other chemical, nuclear and biological hazards and risks [...] testing and use of all types of weapons by State and non-State actors' (para 13).

(CRPD),[21] a recent report by the Special Rapporteur on the rights of persons with disabilities recalled the importance of international cooperation to support the implementation of rights and provided guidance to States on how to ensure that international cooperation is inclusive of and accessible to persons with disabilities.[22] The year 2019 was also important as the Security Council adopted a landmark resolution on the situation of persons with disabilities in armed conflicts and humanitarian crises, which emphasised the need to ensure both access to emergency assistance and participation in recovery and reconciliation efforts.[23]

With regards to response and recovery, the obligation to ensure that emergency response efforts are carried out in a non-discriminatory manner was pointed out by the HRCtee while commenting on the United States' response to Hurricane Katrina[24] and on the denial of assistance to undocumented migrants in Thailand during the 2004 Indian Ocean Tsunami.[25] UN human rights monitoring bodies have stressed the need to ensure genuine consultation and participation of victims of disasters in the design and implementation of all decisions affecting them and to guarantee that the rights of the most marginalised groups are fully taken into account in reconstruction plans, with particular attention to access to housing, education and healthcare.[26] Of note is also the research-based report presented in 2015 by the HRCtee on best practices and main challenges in the promotion and protection of HR in post-disaster and post-conflict situations.[27]

21 For an overview, see Sommario and Venier (n 16).

22 Special Rapporteur on the rights of persons with disabilities, 'Right of persons with disability' (2020) UN Doc A/75/186. The report notes that international cooperation 'includes a wide range of activities between States, such as development assistance, humanitarian aid, economic and trade cooperation, military aid, counter-terrorism, peacebuilding assistance and cultural exchanges' (para 18).

23 SC Resolution 2475 (2019). The same year, the Inter-Agency Standing Committee adopted its first set of guidelines on the inclusion of persons with disabilities in humanitarian action, see Inter-Agency Standing Committee, *Guidelines: Inclusion of Persons with Disabilities in Humanitarian Action.*

24 HRCtee 'Concluding Observations of the Human Rights Committee on the United States of America' (2006) UN Doc CCPR/C/USA/CO/3/Rev.1, para 26.

25 HRCtee, 'Concluding Observations Thailand' (2005) UN Doc CCPR/CO/84/THA, para 23.

26 See eg HRCtee, UN Doc. CCPR/C/USA/CO/3/ Rev.1 (n 861) para 26; CERD, 'Concluding observations of the Committee on the Elimination of Racial Discrimination on the United States of America' (2008) UN Doc CERD/C/USA/CO/6 para 28; CESCR, 'Concluding Observations Japan' (2001) UN Doc E/C.12/1/Add.67, para 27.

27 HRCtee, 'Final research-based report of the Human Rights Council Advisory Committee on best practices and main challenges in the promotion and protection of human rights in post-disaster and post-conflict situations' (2015) UN Doc A/HRC/28/76.

Human rights monitoring bodies and Special Rapporteurs have looked at CBRN emergencies more specifically. Looking at the obligations to mitigate the risks posed by CBRN weapons, only very recently the HRCtee clarified the incompatibility of 'the threat or use of weapons of mass destruction, in particular nuclear weapons' with the right to life and related obligations.[28] As far as nuclear weapons (NW) are concerned, it has been noted that '[t]he existence of international human rights mechanisms means that the adverse effects of these weapons are directly justiciable'.[29] This would also be relevant in respect to PO to protect the right to life against the likely negative impacts of nuclear testing and the risks inherent in the mere possession of NW. The practice of the HRCtee on NW, however, has been rather controversial especially when the Committee was confronted with individual complaints.[30] Recent developments in terms of chemical weapons (CW) include instead the establishment of the Independent International Commission of Inquiry on the Syrian Arab Republic by the HRC, which has being reporting on CW use against civilians since the first attack occurred in the Ghouta district in 2013 and has been complementing the work carried out by the UN-OPCW Joint Investigative Mechanism (JIM) since 2015.[31] The Commission was tasked with investigating and recording all violations of HRL and allegations of crimes against humanity and war crimes and with identifying, where possible, those responsible for these violations, but it has never addressed PO enshrined under HRL to protect against the development and use of CW.

Turning our attention to industrial accidents, while commenting on the response to the Fukushima disaster, the CESCR raised the concern that 'the specific needs of disadvantaged and vulnerable groups, such as older persons, persons with disabilities, and women and children, were not sufficiently met during the evacuation and in the rehabilitation and reconstruction efforts' and requested Japan to provide comprehensive data disaggregated by factors of vulnerability, as well as information on how victims' right to justice has

28 HRCTee, 'General comment no. 36, Article 6 (Right to Life)' (3 September 2019) CCPR/C/GC/35 para 66. This obligation also covers the prohibition of the use of chemical agents in individual poisoning cases, as occurred in the Skrypal and Navalny cases.

29 L Doswald-Beck, 'Human Rights Law and Nuclear Weapons' in Nystuen G, Casey-Maslen S and Golden Bersagel A (eds), *Nuclear Weapons under International Law* (CUP 2014).

30 T Wright, 'Do Nuclear Weapons Violate the Right to Life under International Law?' (2008) 3 *Australian Journal of Peace Studies*.

31 Independent International Commission of Inquiry on the Syrian Arab Republic, 'Human rights abuses and international humanitarian law violations in the Syrian Arab Republic' (2017) UN Doc A/HRC/34/CRP.3. See ch 23 by Poli.

been guaranteed.[32] The Special Rapporteur on the right to health identified several aspects in which the action of the Japanese government could have been (or could be) improved, which may be understood in terms of PO as they point out some recommendations on steps that have to be taken to ensure respect of the right to health. The recommendations referred to the nuclear emergency response system; the scope and extent of the basic and detailed health management surveys; the dose limits of radiation and relevant decisions on evacuations and decontamination; access to accurate information on radiation and its health effects; transparency and accountability of the nuclear industry and regulatory authority; and participation of affected communities and vulnerable groups in decision-making processes (including those related to recovery).[33] More recently, UN human rights experts have called on the Japanese government 'to delay any decision on the ocean-dumping of nuclear waste water from the reactors at Fukushima Daiichi until after the COVID-19 crisis has passed and proper international consultations can be held'.[34]

Finally, the Office of the High Commissioner for Human Rights (OHCHR), while commenting on the responses to the Ebola outbreak in 2014, called for the adoption of a human rights-based approach (HRBA) 'to analyse and revise the actions taken by State authorities to contain and combat the Ebola outbreak, thus considering the individual as a rights holder and correlate her/his rights with the State's obligation to respect, fulfil and protect life, as embodied in international human rights conventions'.[35] PO are identified as referring to the duties to provide adequate healthcare, food and education; to ensure adequate working conditions for health workers; and to ensure that information is provided in an accurate and timely manner, targeted to the needs of the local audience, accessible from a wide variety of sources, and disseminated with the support of the local population and the press.

The COVID-19 pandemic is offering the opportunity to clarify requirements under HRL related to a public health emergency. UN human rights actors have provided guidance notes, detailed advice and statements on how to ensure a

---

32 CESCR, 'Concluding Observations on the third periodic report of Japan' (2013) UN Doc E/C.12/JPN/CO/3 para 24.

33 HRC, Report of the Special Rapporteur on the right of everyone to the enjoyment of the highest attainable standard of physical and mental health. Mission to Japan' (2013) UN Doc A/HRC/23/41/Add.

34 OHCHR, 'Fukushima: Japan must not ignore human rights obligations on nuclear waste disposal' (2021) <https://www.ohchr.org/EN/NewsEvents/Pages/DisplayNews.aspx?NewsID=25940&LangID=E>.

35 OHCHR West Africa Regional Office, 'A human rights perspective into the Ebola outbreak' (OHCHR 2014) 3.

HRBA to the global health crisis, and respect of PO in preparedness, response and recovery. The OHCHR has made available a compilation of these guidance documents[36] and has issued a Guidance on COVID-19 that puts emphasis on the need to adopt specific measures to protect the most vulnerable, to share relevant information on the emergency response and to ensure participation of all persons in the decision-making that affects their lives.[37] The OHCHR also prepared a 'toolkit on treaty law perspectives and jurisprudence in the context of COVID-19' that offers an operational contribution to strengthen the HRBA to both UN and States' responses to the COVID-19 pandemic.[38]

To sum up, UN human rights supervising authorities are dealing with PO under HRL applicable to emergency management and are starting to take into consideration the human rights implications of specific emergency situations. Recommendations are being proposed to States on how to implement PO in these contexts in Concluding Observations, General Comments, and Reports. The recommendations identified by UN human rights monitoring mechanisms have, however, some limitations. First, they specifically cover DRR activities, while other phases of the emergency management cycle do not receive the same attention. To date, they have not heard any individual complaints on disaster-related matters, which would help to further crystallise and apply these requirements to real-life situations. Such complaints would also help to focus more attention on analysing to what extent States are actually implementing, for instance through legal and policy instruments, international recommendations offered. Finally, as noted by Cubie and Hesselman, this effort remains ad hoc and there might be the 'need for a coordinated international approach to recognise and enumerate the rights-holders and duty-bearers in disaster settings, and to provide practical support and guidance to States and humanitarian actors on how best to ensure all human rights are respected in the complex context of disaster preparation and response'.[39]

36 OHCHR, 'Compilation of statements by human rights treaty bodies in the context of COVID-19' (September 2020).

37 See <https://www.ohchr.org/EN/NewsEvents/Pages/COVID19Guidance.aspx> (last accessed January 2020).

38 OHCHR, 'Internal HRTB toolkit of treaty law perspectives and jurisprudence in the context of COVID-19' (May 2020).

39 D Cubie and M Hesselman, 'Accountability for the Human Rights Implications of Natural Disasters: A Proposal for Systemic International Oversight' (2015) 33(1) Netherlands Quarterly of Human Rights.

3 PO Identified within Regional Human Rights Regimes

Regional human rights instruments include provisions on the wide variety of rights that have to be protected against emergency situations and some PO to act in a certain way have been identified within these regional regimes.[40] In Africa, the Kampala Convention on the Protection and Assistance of Internally Displaced Persons includes provisions on early warning systems, the establishment and implementation of DRR strategies and disaster preparedness. The African Charter on Human and Peoples' Rights has been made relevant to disasters in the context of its Reporting Guidelines[41] and under Article 24 which establishes that '[a]ll peoples shall have the right to a general satisfactory environment favourable to their development'. The African Commission on Human and Peoples' Rights (ACHPR) underscored the different obligations stemming from this provision, including the obligation to take reasonable measures to prevent pollution and ecological degradation and to monitor projects that could affect the environment,[42] and to provide access to information on activities that are hazardous to health and the environment, in the understanding that this gives communities exposed to a specific risk the opportunity to take part in the decision-making that affects them.[43]

A number of disaster settings have been immediate cause for discussion within the Inter-American human rights system, such as in the US, Venezuela and Haiti.[44] Within the Inter-American Court of Human Rights (IACtHR) system, recent decades have seen the emergence of a growing body of substantive rules related to environmental protection, including rules on preventing and investigating environmental harm. In 2017, the landmark Advisory Opinion OC-23/17 and the *Lhaka Honhat* case represented turning points in the Court's jurisprudence as they establish the autonomous right to a healthy environment.

---

40 For an overview, see M Hesselman, 'Regional human rights regimes and humanitarian obligations of states in the event of disaster', in Zwitter et al (eds) *Humanitarian Action: Global, Regional and Local Legal Responses* (CUP 2014).

41 See ibid 213. African Union Convention for the Protection and Assistance of Internally Displaced Persons (2009); African Charter on the Rights and Welfare of the Child (1986); African Charter on Human and Peoples' Rights (1981).

42 ACHPR, Case of the Social and Economic Rights Center (SERAC) and Center for Economic and Social Rights (CESR) v. Nigeria, Communication 155/96 (2001), paras 52 and 53.

43 ACHPR, Social and Economic Rights Center (SERAC) and Center for Economic and Social Rights (CESR) v. Nigeria. Communication 155/96. Decision of October 27, 2001, para 53.

44 OAS, Inter-American Commission on Human Rights, Hearing on 'Protection of Human Rights in Natural Disasters' (3 March 2006); OAS, Inter-American Commission on Human Rights, 'Human Rights Situation during the Natural Disaster in Venezuela' (2000); OAS, 'Economic and Social Rights in Haiti following the Earthquake', 138th Period of Sessions (2010).

In the Advisory Opinion, the Court not only affirmed the existence of the right to a healthy environment but also provided a systematic account of States' obligations in environmental protection, by incorporating environmental law principles and rules within HRL.[45] States have not only a primary obligation of prevention (to adopt adequate legislative and administrative frameworks and monitor their implementation; to require and approve environmental impact assessments; to prepare a contingency plan; and to mitigate impacts if environmental damage occurs), but also duties to adhere to the precautionary principle and to cooperate in environmental protection. Procedural obligations include the duty to provide access to information, public participation in decision making, and access to justice.

Turning our attention to the European system, the European Court of Human Rights (ECtHR) is the authority that has contributed the most to clarifying the scope and content of obligations to take active steps to protect in emergency situations. Since the notion of PO under the European Convention on Human Rights (ECHR) appeared for the first time in the *Belgian linguistic case* in 1968, the ECtHR has broadened this category of obligations and expanded its rulings against States, to the point where it is recognised that 'all the standard setting provisions of the Convention have now a dual aspect in terms of their requirements, one negative and one positive'.[46] The imposition of PO is inextricably linked with the effective application of the Convention, which 'is intended to guarantee not rights that are theoretical or illusory but rights that are practical and effective',[47] and a constant recalibration of the scope and content of PO may be required in light of the Court's interpretation of the Convention as a 'living instrument'.[48] Interestingly, the ECtHR has explicitly refused to propose a clear theoretical basis for the development of PO under the ECHR,[49] while always emphasising the need not to impose an impossible or disproportionate burden upon public authorities.

The ECtHR jurisprudence relevant to the present discussion includes cases related to individual exposure to dangerous activities conducted by the State;[50] public concern over exposure to an actual risk; loss of life due to disasters

45 IACtHR, 'The Environment and Human Rights Advisory Opinion' (15 November 2017).

46 JF Akandji-Kombe, 'Positive obligations under the European Convention on Human Rights. A guide to the implementation of the European Convention on Human Rights' (Council of Europe 2007).

47 ECtHR, *Airey v Ireland* (1979–80) 2 EHRR 305 para 24.

48 *Tyrer v. United Kingdom* (1979–80) 2 EHRR 1.

49 *Plattform Ärzte für das Leben v. Austria* (1991) 13 EHRR 204.

50 *L.C.B. v. The United Kingdom* (1999) 27 EHRR 212 and *McGinley and Egan v the United Kingdom* (1999) 27 EHRR concerned the atmospheric tests of NW carried out in the Christmas Islands by the United Kingdom (1952–1967).

caused by natural or man-made hazards; and counter-terrorism operations. Within the ECtHR jurisprudence, PO emerge from the rights to life (Article 2), to private and family life (Article 8) and to the right of access to justice (Article 6). As far as prevention is concerned, the criteria for State responsibility include the existence of a life-threatening risk (*ie* real and immediate and concerning an identifiable individual or group) and the knowledge element (the authorities knew or ought to have known about the risk and 'failed to take measures within the scope of their powers which, judged reasonably, might have been expected to avoid that risk').[51]

Along with previous cases on CBRN weapons testing, in the *Roche* case (concerning CW tests carried out on service personnel in the early 1960s as part of the UK's chemical and biological warfare research programme) the Court found that the UK had not fulfilled its PO under Article 8 to ensure that the applicant had access to relevant and appropriate information on the risks.[52] A similar case, *Burdov* (the applicant was called on to take part in emergency operations at the site of the Chernobyl nuclear disaster in 1986, was entitled due to health problems to social benefits, but the authorities failed to pay those fully or on time), may be read as highlighting 'the importance of having proper mechanisms in place for the compensation of victims of catastrophes, including the use of the insurance schemes'.[53]

In the sub-set of cases concerning public concerns over present risks, the ECtHR has shown increasing interest in taking into consideration the environmental dimension under the ECHR, especially in terms of procedural obligations under Article 8. In the well-known cases of *Lopez Ostra* and *Guerra*, the Court, for the first time, pointed out that severe environmental pollution may affect individuals' well-being and private and family life[54] and found a

---

51 *Osman v. the United Kingdom* (2000) 29 EHRR 245 para 116. The application of the Osman test to scenarios for which it was not originally conceived has given rise to conceptual confusion, and a more coherent doctrine of risk prevention is needed also in consideration that the importance of PO is likely to increase. FC Ebert and RI Sijniensky, 'Preventing Violations of the Right to Life in the European and Inter-American Systems: From the Osman test to a coherent doctrine of risk prevention?' (2015) 15 HRLRev. For a discussion of the knowledge element, see V Stoyanova, 'Fault, knowledge and risk within the framework of positive obligations under the European Convention on Human Rights' (2020) 33 LJIL.

52 *Roche v The United Kingdom* (2006) 42 EHRR 30 para 157.

53 E Sommario, 'Conclusions. One law to bind them all: International Law and Disaster Resilience', in Herwig and Simoncini (eds), *Law and the management of disasters. The challenge of Resilience* (Routledge 2016), 348.

54 *Lopez Ostra v. Spain* (1995) 20 EHRR 277 para 49; *Guerra and others v. Italy* (1998) 26 EHRR 357 para 60.

violation of Article 8, considering the lack of information provided that would have enabled citizens to assess the relevant risks. The duties to assess environmental and health implications of hazardous activities and to share relevant information with the public were confirmed in recent case law.[55] In *Cordella* (concerning the lack of measures to protect the environment around the Ilva factory in Taranto), the Court expanded the scope of these obligations by integrating the broad concept of 'community welfare'.[56] However, in the sub-set of cases involving nuclear risks (*ie* rail transport of nuclear waste in *L.M.R* and the extension of the licence of an ageing nuclear power plant in *Balmer-Schafroth* and *Athanassoglou*), the Court took a more cautious approach, finding no violations of Article 6 on access to justice, which was invoked by the applicants with the aim of finding avenues to revise the government's decisions.[57]

Looking at the cases related to loss of life due to technological and natural risks, in *Öneryildiz* (involving the death of 39 people caused by a methane explosion at a municipal rubbish tip close to a slum area of Istanbul), the Court stated that the primary duty is 'to put in place a legislative and administrative framework designed to provide effective deterrence against threats to the right to life'.[58] More precisely, in this field, domestic regulations must govern 'the licensing, setting up, operation, security and supervision of the activity and must make it compulsory for all those concerned to take practical measures', while 'particular emphasis should be placed on the public's right to information' and on 'appropriate procedures for identifying shortcomings in the processes concerned and any errors committed by those responsible at different levels'.[59]

In *Budayeva* (involving deaths caused by a mudslide), the authorities failed to comply with PO under Article 2, since they omitted to implement land planning and emergency relief policies, despite the fact that that area was particularly vulnerable to mudslides.[60] Similarly to *Öneryildiz*, PO were identified in all phases of the emergency management cycle. In the *ex-ante* phase, PO include not only to put in place an adequate legislative framework but also more concrete ad-hoc risk mitigation measures (eg engineering works to

55 *Fedayeva v Russia*, App. n. 55723/00 (ECtHR 30 November 2005); *Dubetska and others v Ukraine* (2015) 61 EHHR 11; *Tatar c. Roumanie*, App n. 67021/ 01 (ECtHR 27 January 2009) para 88.

56 *Affaire Cordella Et Autres C. Italie*, Requêtes nos 54414/13 et 54264/15 (ECtHR, 24 January 2019) para 174.

57 *Balmer-Schafroth v. Switzerland* (1998) 25 EHRR 598; *Athanassoglou v Switzerland* (2001) 31 EHRR 13.

58 *Öneryildiz v. Turkey* (2005) 41 EHHR 20, para 89.

59 Ibid para 90.

60 *Budayeva and others v Russia* (2014) 59 EHRR 2 paras 135–136.

maintain protection structures). Furthermore, the Court found that States have 'a positive obligation to adequately inform the public about any life-threatening emergency' and that there was a 'causal link between the serious administrative flaws, including the lack of early warning, and the death of and injuries to the applicants'.[61] After the calamitous event, PO include the primary duty to carry out an independent and effective investigation. All these requirements were confirmed and further clarified in more recent case law.[62] Considering the Court's finding in *Budayeva* that natural hazards are 'beyond human control', it has recently been proposed that the Court should more explicitly adopt an 'all-hazards approach' towards protecting human life in the face of all hazards, since the difference between man-made and natural hazards is less clear-cut than one might assume. When determining the required level of protection, the Court should instead rely 'on three basic criteria: the foreseeability, gravity and mitigability of the threat/hazards in question',[63] which are already traceable in the Court's case law but have not been systematically set out yet.

Looking at counter-terrorism operations, *Finogenov* concerned the use of an anaesthetic gas by Russian authorities in October 2002, when storming a theatre in Moscow where hundreds of civilians had been taken hostage by Chechen terrorists.[64] Russian authorities killed all the terrorists and rescued hundreds of hostages but approximately 130 hostages died due to adverse reactions to the incapacitating chemical agent used. The Strasbourg Court clarified that 'it was not in a position to indicate to member States the best policy in dealing with a crisis of this kind' and found that the use of the chemical agent was not in breach of Article 2 ECHR.[65] However, interestingly, it affirmed that this conclusion 'does not preclude the Court from examining whether the ensuing rescue operation was planned and implemented in compliance with the authorities' positive obligations under Article 2 of the Convention, namely whether the authorities took all necessary precautions to minimise the effects

---

61 Ibid para 182.

62 *Kolyadenko and others v Russia* (2013) 56 EHRR 2; *Ozel and others v Turkey*, App. n 14350/05 and 2 others (2 May 2016).

63 K Cedervall Lauta and J Elo Rytter, 'A Landslide on a Mudslide? Natural Hazards and the Right to Life under the European Convention on Human Rights' (2016) 7(1) Journal of Human Rights and the Environment.

64 *Finogenov v. Russia* (2015) 61 EHRR 4.

65 Ibid para 223. Rietiker however suggests that the Court should have been keen to discuss the use of incapacitating agents under HRL in law enforcement operations, see D Rietiker, 'Strange Bedfellows? The Cross-Fertilization of Human Rights and Arms Control. The European Court of Human Rights on Cases Involving Chemical Weapons and Anti Personnel Mines' (2014) 3 Cyprus Human Rights Law Review.

of the gas on the hostages, to evacuate them quickly and to provide them with necessary medical assistance'.[66] Indeed, the Court found a violation of PO under Article 2 because of the inadequate planning and conduct of the rescue operation, including in consideration of the limited on-site coordination between various services ('the absence of any centralised coordination on the spot');[67] the inadequate information exchange on the type of gas that was used ('the original evacuation plan did not appear to contain any instructions as to how information on the victims and their condition was to be exchanged between members of various rescue services'); and the lack of appropriate medical treatment ('it is unclear what order of priorities was set for the medics', no medical assistance was provided on the bus from the theatre to the hospitals, and 'everything suggests that there was no clear plan for the distribution of victims amongst various hospitals').[68]

Finally, in *Tagayeva* (concerning a dramatic hostage taking that occurred in 2004 in a school in the town of Beslan, North Ossetia, which lasted three days and involved at least 1,100 persons, including more than 700 children, and ended with the death of more than 300 persons), the Court found unanimously that there had been a violation of Article 2 of the Convention because of the authorities' failure to try to prevent an event which had been planned days before and about which they had knowledge and because of the inadequacy of the response operation.[69] More precisely, the Court found that '[n]o single sufficiently high-level structure was responsible for the handling of the situation, evaluating and allocating resources, creating a defence for the vulnerable target group and ensuring effective containment of the threat and communication with the field teams'.[70]

To sum up, this section has discussed the practice of regional human rights courts relevant to PO applicable to emergency situations. The European context is the most developed, with the Strasbourg Court being very active in the identification of PO in all phases of the emergency management cycle. A number of disaster settings have been discussed within the Inter-American human rights system, which develops PO particularly in relation to protection of the environment. Along similar lines, the African system also imposes on States obligations to act in the face of environmental risks, such as the duties to take reasonable measures to prevent pollution and ecological degradation, to

66 Ibid para 237.

67 Ibid para 247.

68 Ibid paras 250–251.

69 *Tagayeva and others v. Russia* App. n 26562/07 and 6 other applications (ECtHR 18 September 2017).

70 Ibid para 491.

monitor projects that could affect the environment and to provide the potentially affected population with relevant information.

4 Classification of PO under HRL Relevant to CBRN Protection

The analysis in the previous sections suggests that PO relevant to all phases of the emergency management cycle (prevention, preparedness, response and recovery) and of all types (of immediate result, of conduct and of progressive realisation) are currently being identified by HR supervising authorities, both at the universal and regional levels. The following paragraphs present an overview of such PO.

Generally speaking, the adoption of a HRBA to emergency management means to mainstream in all relevant activities key principles deriving from HRL, such as equality and non-discrimination (with particular regard to the needs and views of the most vulnerable groups); participation and empowerment (through the adoption of effective processes and the allocation of necessary resources); and accountability and access to justice (requiring the provision of appropriate and accurate information and mechanisms to ensure that victims have access to adequate remedies).[71] Furthermore, the duty to cooperate at the international level has been discussed by UN human rights monitoring bodies, and has been included in ILC Draft Articles 7 (Duty to cooperate) and 8 (Forms of cooperation in the response to disasters) and in the Sendai Framework's guiding principles.[72] States have to devote efforts to cooperating with other States (especially in view of common threats) and with international organisations (IOs), not only in the acute response phase but in DRR initiatives and in recovery efforts. For instance, in relation to the current pandemic outbreak, the CESCR has affirmed that 'international cooperation is critical in preventing, addressing and following up to the effects of the pandemic, in medical, economic, social and other areas'.[73] The ILC classifies the duty to cooperate as an obligation of conduct.[74]

71 On integrating a HRBA into disaster management, see A Creta, 'Integrating human rights into disaster management: normative, operational and methodological aspects', in F Z Giustiniani et al (eds), *Routledge Handbook of Human Rights and Disasters* (Routledge 2018).

72 Sendai Framework para 19(l) and Section VI.

73 OHCHR (n 37) 7.

74 ILC, 'Fifth report on the protection of persons in the event of disasters, by Mr. Eduardo Valencia-Ospina, Special Rapporteur' (2012) UN Doc A/CN.4/652, ch III(B).

Looking at PO applicable to the pre-disaster phase, States are under the primary obligation to prevent disasters by adopting, amending and implementing adequate laws and policies, and by ensuring their independent supervision, which can be understood as primarily obligations of immediate result with some components of due diligence.[75] Prevention obligations of due diligence include performing accurate and timely risk assessments, which should take into consideration the worst-case scenarios and all potential implications on the wide variety of human rights that may be impacted by emergency situations. As suggested by UN human rights monitoring bodies, risk assessment should be based on the collection of data on disaster losses that should be disaggregated according to different factors of vulnerability. Once the results of the risk assessment are available, ad hoc risk mitigation measures should be adopted, targeted to the threat under consideration. As indicated by both UN actors and regional human rights courts, the outcomes of risk assessments must be widely disseminated: particular attention has to be paid to keeping the population regularly informed of any life or health-threatening risks. The ECtHR has clarified that the scope of relevant PO depends on the origin of the risk (is this beyond human control?), the extent to which it is foreseeable (can the threat be anticipated? is this a regularly recurring calamity or is its occurrence unpredictable?) and whether it is susceptible to mitigation (would risk mitigation measures have served the aim of avoiding harm?).

Preparedness obligations under HRL include having in place a contingency plan (which shall take into account the views and needs of vulnerable populations) and conducting training and education programmes. The IACtHR has indicated that emergency plans must be elaborated in cooperation with other potentially affected States and with responsible IOs. The ECtHR case law also emphasised the importance of having in place early warning systems, which according to the Sendai Framework should be multi-hazard and people-centred. In general, preparedness duties also appear to be a mix of obligations of immediate result and due diligence.

In the acute emergency response phase, human rights actors have pointed out that having in place a system of urgent medical care is a 'core obligation' to protect the rights to life and to health.[76] The contingency plan must be implemented with due diligence, with particular attention paid to those

75 See ch 3.

76 Although there is no authoritative distinction of core/peripherical duties under HRL, core obligations generally refer to duties that are more immediate and more compelling than other obligations that are of a more flexible or programmatic nature. See M Scheinin, 'Core Rights and Obligations', in D Shelton, *The Oxford Handbook of International Human Rights Law* (OUP 2011).

marginalised groups that are likely to be the most affected during emergency situations. The ECtHR has indicated that lack of coordination among different authorities during the response operation may also amount to a violation of the right to life. Furthermore, particularly serious emergencies, such as nuclear accidents or public health crises, may imply more specific obligations, such as obligations to protect health care workers or to ensure adequate working conditions. In any case, throughout the crisis, PO under HRL require that information is provided in an accurate and timely manner, targeted to the needs of the local audience, accessible from a wide variety of sources, and disseminated with the support of the local population and the press. PO applicable to the response phase are generally to be understood as obligations of conduct.

Finally, in the post-disaster phase, UN human rights monitoring bodies have stressed the need to ensure genuine consultation and participation of victims of disasters in the design and implementation of all decisions affecting them and to guarantee that the rights of the most marginalised groups are fully taken into account in reconstruction plans, with particular attention to access to housing, education and healthcare. Regional human rights courts have put emphasis on the procedural obligation to conduct effective investigations in cases of alleged violations of rights during emergency situations.[77] While these duties can be considered as PO of immediate result, it may be expected that PO of progressive realisation will also be involved in recovery efforts, especially for those duties related to the fulfilment of economic, social and cultural rights that might have been impacted by disaster situations and might need long-term projects for their complete realisation.

5 Concluding Remarks

This chapter has reviewed the practice of international and regional human rights supervising authorities, which offers abundant references to the rights of persons and to the corresponding States' obligations in all phases of the emergency management cycle. These references are dispersed among a wide range of general comments (providing guidance on obligations as resulting from treaty provisions); recommendations, concluding observations and special reports (providing guidance on specific themes or country situations); as well as in advisory opinions and the jurisprudence of regional courts (identifying human rights standards under regional instruments). It may reasonably be expected that some matters will be subject to further crystallisation and

77 On prosecutions and remedies in the context of CBRN events, see Part 5.

clarification in the near future, as our understanding of human rights implications raised by risk and emergency management evolves and the opportunities for hearing individual complaints on these matters emerge.

It has been argued that PO under HRL deserve deeper attention in order to realise the full potential of HR in relation to emergency situations. Detailed analysis of the scope and content of PO under specific circumstances; of their role in protecting against serious risks; and of their interplay with NO can make a valuable contribution by offering greater conceptual and operational clarity on what is needed to implement a HRBA to emergency management. PO as identified in this chapter include a mix of obligations of immediate result, due diligence and progressive realisation that are applicable to the different phases of the emergency management cycle. The analysis has shown that specific types of PO may be applicable to specific types of emergency situations. Through the overview of PO relevant to disaster situations, as developed within the global and regional systems, it is hoped that this chapter has contributed to the discussion on how to elaborate a more positive, differentiated and complex HRFE.

Bibliography

Akandji-Kombe JF, 'Positive obligations under the European Convention on Human Rights. A guide to the implementation of the European Convention on Human Rights' (Council of Europe 2007).

Besson S, 'Les obligations positives de protection des droits fondamentaux – Un essai en dogmatique comparative' (2003) 1(49) Revue de droit Suisse 49.

Cedervall Lauta K and Elo Rytter J, 'A Landslide on a Mudslide? Natural Hazards and the Right to Life under the European Convention on Human Rights' (2016) 7(1) Journal of Human Rights and the Environment 111.

Creta A, 'Integrating human rights into disaster management: normative, operational and methodological aspects', in Giustiniani FZ et al(eds), *Routledge Handbook of Human Rights and Disasters* (Routledge 2018).

Cubie D and Hesselman M, 'Accountability for the Human Rights Implications of Natural Disasters: A Proposal for Systemic International Oversight' (2015) 33(1) Netherlands Quarterly of Human Rights 9.

Cubie D, 'Promoting Dignity for all: Human Rights Approaches in the Post-2015 Climate Change, Disaster Risk Reduction and Sustainable Development Frameworks' (2014) 8(36) Human Rights and International Legal Discourse 36.

Doswald-Beck L, 'Human Rights Law and Nuclear Weapons' in Nystuen G, Casey-Maslen S and Golden Bersagel A (eds), *Nuclear Weapons under International Law* (CUP 2014).

Ebert FC and Sijniensky RI, 'Preventing Violations of the Right to Life in the European and Inter-American Systems: From the Osman test to a coherent doctrine of risk prevention?' (2015) 15 HRLRev 343.

Forino G, von Meding J, Brewer G, 'A Conceptual Governance Framework for Climate Change Adaptation and Disaster Risk Reduction Integration' (2015) 6 Intl J Disaster Risk Science 372.

Fredman S, *Human Rights Transformed* (OUP 2008).

Hesselman M, 'Regional human rights regimes and humanitarian obligations of states in the event of disaster', in Zwitter et al (eds) *Humanitarian Action: Global, Regional and Local Legal Responses* (CUP 2014).

Lavrysen L, *Human Rights in a Positive State. Rethinking the Relationship between Positive and Negative Obligations under the European Convention on Human Rights* (Intersentia 2018).

Nickel JW, 'Two models of normative frameworks for Human Rights during Emergencies', in EJ Criddle (ed.) *Human Rights in Emergencies* (CUP 2016).

Pisillo Mazzeschi R, 'Responsabilité de l'état pour violation des obligations positives relatives aux droits de l'homme' (2008) 333 Collected Courses of the Hague Academy of International Law.

Rietiker D, 'Strange Bedfellows? The Cross-Fertilization of Human Rights and Arms Control. The European Court of Human Rights on Cases Involving Chemical Weapons and Anti Personnel Mines' (2014) 3 Cyprus Human Rights Law Review 130.

Scheinin M, 'Core Rights and Obligations', in D Shelton, *The Oxford Handbook of International Human Rights Law* (OUP 2011).

Shue H, *Basic Rights* (Princeton University Press 1980).

Sommario E and Venier S, 'Human Rights Law and Disaster Risk Reduction' (2018) 49 QIL Zoom-in 29.

Sommario E, 'Conclusions. One law to bind them all: International Law and Disaster Resilience', in Herwig and Simoncini (eds), *Law and the management of disasters. The challenge of Resilience* (Routledge 2016).

Stoyanova V, 'Fault, knowledge and risk within the framework of positive obligations under the European Convention on Human Rights' (2020) 33 LJIL 601.

Toebes B, 'Human rights and public health: towards a balanced relationship' (2015) 19(4) The International Journal of Human Rights 488.

Xenos D, *The Positive Obligations of the State under the European Convention of Human Rights* (Routledge 2012).

CHAPTER 28

Ordinary and Extraordinary Limitations on Human Rights Introduced to Tackle CBRN Threats

Emanuele Sommario

1 Introduction

The present contribution intends to illustrate the extent to which human rights can be restricted to respond to CBRN threats and events, looking at both the preventive and reactive measures that States can introduce. The chapter will start by briefly illustrating the legal framework concerning ordinary limitations on the enjoyment of human rights, and then will use concrete examples taken from the practice of human rights courts and monitoring bodies to elucidate how these standards have been applied to CBRN threats and events (Section 2). The same methodology will be followed with respect to cases in which States have made use of derogation clauses to react to major CBRN events, hence introducing exceptional limitations that would otherwise be incompatible with conventional standards (Section 3). In sketching the applicable legal framework, particular reference will be made to the Human Rights Committee's (HRComm) General Comment No. 29 on 'States of Emergency'[1] and to the *Siracusa Principles on the Limitation and Derogation Provisions in the International Covenant on Civil and Political Rights* (*Siracusa Principles*), a soft-law tool that elaborates on the standards developed by treaty monitoring bodies.[2] The chapter will end with a few general comments on the practice reviewed (Section 4).

The analysis will adopt the open-ended definition of CBRN threats and events identified for the purpose of the present study.[3] However, CBRN events occurring in situations of armed conflict will not be considered, both because the applicable legal framework is compounded by the concurrent application of international humanitarian law, and because other contributions in this

1 HRComm, General Comment No. 29. States of Emergency (Article 4), UN Doc. CCPR/C/21/Rev.1/Add.11 (2001).

2 The *Siracusa Principles* were adopted by a group of 31 eminent legal experts in 1984 and are reproduced in *Human Rights Quarterly*, Vol. 7, 1985, pp 5–17.

3 See ch 1 by Frulli.

volume have looked at the legal implications of the use of CBRN weapons in armed conflicts.[4] Finally, while CBRN events may also severely affect the enjoyment of economic, social and cultural rights,[5] for reasons of expediency, we will limit our discussion to civil and political rights.

2 Ordinary Limitations on Human Rights and CBRN Events

Ordinary limitations are usually made possible by including within a human rights treaty the possibility to interfere with individual rights if certain qualifying conditions are met. Thus, formal and substantial requirements must be respected or else a given limitation will amount to a treaty violation. These include the requirements that the limitation (a) is provided by law; (b) pursues a legitimate aim (*ie* that it serves one of the purposes for interference listed in the specific provision at hand); and (c) is necessary to achieve said aim, which requires a proportionality test, *ie* a balancing between the extent to which a right is restricted and the interest that the limitation seeks to protect.

A second way to impose ordinary limitations is to determine that certain conduct falls outside the protection of the treaty. For instance, Article 5(1) of the European Convention on Human Rights (ECHR, 1950) protects the right to personal liberty, but also features a list of circumstances which would not constitute violations of the right. These include the 'lawful detention of persons for the prevention of the spreading of infectious diseases' (Article 5(1)(e)). The example is pertinent for our purposes, as 'the spreading of infectious diseases' might well be considered a CBRN event.

As we shall see, in essence, the legal tests carried out by monitoring bodies to assess the legality of a given restriction under a specific human rights treaty do not distinguish between the first and the second category of limitations. In the following two subsections, we will first review the contents of the three-pronged test illustrated above and then analyse how it has been applied in cases concerning CBRN threats or events.

2.1 *Formal and Substantial Requirements for Legitimate Human Rights Limitations*

Any restriction of human rights requires a *formal legal basis*, *ie* the limitation must be 'provided by law'. The 'law' must be 'formulated with sufficient

4 See ch 21 by Mauri and ch 22 by Saluzzo.

5 See A Müller, 'Limitations to and Derogations from Economic, Social and Cultural Rights', in Human Rights Law Review, Vol. 9, 2009, pp. 557–601.

precision to enable citizens to regulate their conduct'.[6] Moreover, it must be framed with sufficient clarity and specify the manner in which it will be applied.[7]

The second leg of the test requires States to clearly identify the purpose of the limitation it wishes to introduce. Each provision protecting limitable rights presents an exhaustive list of aims on which restrictions can be based. These include public order (*ordre public*), public health, public morals, national security, public safety and the rights and freedoms of others. Limitations are obviously only permitted on the basis of grounds that are expressly listed in the specific provision.[8]

It should be noted that the scope of most of the grounds for interference is rather wide, and States can usually make a plausible case that they have a legitimate reason for limiting a specific right. In cases of interference imposed to counter CBRN events, one of the most frequently invoked reasons is the preservation of public health.[9] For instance, the HRComm recently stated that '[t]he protection of "public health" may exceptionally permit restrictions [on the right to peaceful assembly] to be imposed, for example where there is an outbreak of an infectious disease and gatherings are dangerous.'[10]

In addition to being lawful and serving a legitimate purpose, any restriction must be 'necessary' to achieve said purpose. When restrictions are introduced, States 'must demonstrate their necessity and only take such measures as are proportionate to the pursuance of legitimate aims'.[11] To meet this test, a limitation must respond to a 'pressing social need' and the interference with the right protected must be no greater than is necessary to address such need.[12] The latter element is usually referred to as the test of *proportionality*, which

6 European Court of Human Rights (ECtHR), *Sunday Times v. UK*, Judgment of 26 April 1979, para 49. The same principles have been endorsed by the HRComm as valid for limitations imposed under the International Covenant on Civil and Political Rights (ICCPR, 1966), see HRComm, General Comment No. 34, Article 19: Freedoms of opinion and expression, UN Doc. CCPR/C/GC/34 (2011) para 25.

7 See, for instance, ECtHR, *Big Brother Watch and Others v. UK*, Judgment of 3 September 2018, para 306.

8 This is confirmed by art 18 ECHR, according to which 'restrictions permitted under this Convention to the said rights and freedoms shall not be applied for any purpose other than those for which they have been prescribed'.

9 See ECtHR, *Solomakhin v. Ukraine*, Judgment of 15 March 2012.

10 HRComm, General Comment No. 37 on the right of peaceful assembly, UN Doc. CCPR/C/GC/37 (2020) para 45.

11 HRComm, General Comment No. 31: The Nature of the General Legal Obligation Imposed on States Parties to the Covenant, UN Doc. CCPR/C/21/Rev.1/Add.13 (2004) para 6.

12 See ECtHR, *Sunday Times v. UK* (supra n 6) para 59.

treaty monitoring bodies apply to balance the severity of the interference against the importance of the public interest at stake.[13]

Under the ECtHR case law, States have been granted a 'margin of appreciation' in deciding on the nature and scope of the limitations required to protect certain general interests. The Strasbourg Court has stressed that State authorities:

> [b]y reason of their direct and continuous contact with the vital forces of their countries [...] are in principle in a better position than the international judge to give an opinion on the exact content of these requirements as well as on the 'necessity' of a 'restriction' or 'penalty' intended to meet them.[14]

The margin of appreciation doctrine is applied both with respect to limitations and derogations from the ECHR, but its exact meaning and scope is sometimes obscure.[15] The discretion left to States may, in fact, vary depending on the nature of the rights at issue and on the balancing of competing rights.[16] Indeed, the Court has clarified that the margin of appreciation is not unlimited, and that it will be narrower 'where the right at stake is crucial to the individual's effective enjoyment of intimate or key rights'.[17]

2.2 *The Practice of Human Rights Mechanisms Concerning Limitations Imposed to Tackle CBRN Events*

There is, so far, relatively little practice concerning ordinary limitations imposed to tackle CBRN events strictly speaking. Our analysis will be divided into two parts, looking first at measures directed at preventing a CBRN emergency and then at those employed to respond to a crisis once it has erupted.

---

13 On the proportionality test, as applied by the ECtHR, see JH Gerards, 'How to Improve the Necessity Test of the European Court of Human Right', in *International Journal of Constitutional Law*, Vol. 11, 2013, pp. 466–90.

14 ECtHR, *Handyside v. UK*, Judgment of 7 December 1976, para 48.

15 See A Legg, *The Margin of Appreciation in International Human Rights Law* (Oxford University Press, 2012). According to this author, even the IACtHR (at p. 32) and the HRComm (at p. 81), while not explicitly endorsing this doctrine, have granted States a certain margin of appreciation when deciding cases before them. However, in one of its more recent General Comments, the HRComm has explicitly dismissed the doctrine. See HRComm, General Comment No. 34, Article 19: Freedoms of opinion and expression, UN Doc. CCPR/C/GC/34 (2011) para 36.

16 See B Rainey, E Wicks and C Ovey, *Jacobs, White and Ovey: The European Convention on Human Rights* (6th edn, Oxford University Press, 2014), pp. 325–333.

17 ECtHR, *Connors v. UK*, Judgment of 27 May 2004, para 82.

Starting with preventive measures, one interesting case concerns a compulsory vaccination campaign aimed at eradicating the risk of diphtheria, a highly infectious and virulent disease. In *Solomakhin v. Ukraine*, the applicant complained, *inter alia*, that there had been no reason for vaccinating him, as there had not been an outbreak of diphtheria in his hometown at the relevant time and the vaccine had been strongly contraindicated for him.[18] In the months following the vaccination, he suffered a bad state of health and maintained that it was linked to the vaccine he had received. The ECtHR decided to address the case under Article 8 of the Convention, which protects respect for private life.[19]

The Government agreed that the compulsory vaccination had constituted an interference with the applicant's private life but contended that this was made necessary by the complicated epidemiological situation in the region.[20] The Court agreed with the respondent State. Elaborating on the issue of proportionality, it recalled that the medical staff had checked the applicant's suitability for vaccination prior to carrying it out, which suggests that necessary precautions had been taken to ensure that the medical treatment would not be to his detriment to an extent that could upset the balance of interests between the applicant's personal integrity and the public interest of protecting the health of the population.[21] Another decisive element in the Court's reasoning was the fact that the applicant's allegations had been thoroughly examined by the domestic courts. Their findings were based on a large amount of medical data that had not been properly challenged by the applicant.[22]

A similar case was recently the object of a pivotal judgment rendered by the Grand Chamber of the Strasbourg Court. In the case of *Vavřička and Others v. the Czech Republic*,[23] the Court held that there had been no violation of Article 8 with respect to the compulsory vaccination regime for children against nine common and potentially very serious diseases. The high-profile ruling confirmed the compatibility with conventional standards of national rules imposing vaccination and setting negative consequences in the case of non-compliance. The applicants were several children and one father. In none of the cases were the vaccines given, due to the applicants' objections which were based on concerns over possible serious damage arising from their side-effects. The applicant children were forbidden from attending nursery school, while the father was fined for non-compliance with the vaccination duty. The

18 ECtHR, *Solomakhin v. Ukraine* (supra n 9), para 30.

19 Ibid, para 28.

20 Ibid, para 32.

21 Ibid, para 36.

22 Ibid, para 38.

23 ECtHR [GC], *Vavřička and Others v. the Czech Republic*, Judgment of 8 April 2021.

applicants argued that Czech rules on compulsory vaccination lacked a sufficient legal basis and sufficiently robust scientific justification.

The ECtHR found that the restriction pursued a legitimate aim, as the impugned legislation had the objective to protect against diseases posing a serious risk to health. In particular, the campaigns aimed at protecting both the health of those receiving the vaccination, as well as of those who cannot be vaccinated due to medical reasons and who need to rely on 'herd immunity' to be protected.[24] With respect to the requirement that the interference is 'necessary in a democratic society', the ECtHR noted that 'there is no doubt about the importance of the interest at stake' because 'there is a general consensus among the Contracting Parties, strongly supported by the specialised international bodies, that vaccination is one of the most successful and cost-effective health interventions and that each State should aim to achieve the highest possible level of vaccination among its population'.[25]

Other important elements highlighted in the Court's assessment of whether the restriction imposed was reasonable concerned the fact that vaccinations could not be forcibly administered, as exemptions were foreseen, accompanied by procedural safeguards. Children with a permanent contraindication to vaccination were not asked to undergo the procedure[26] and parents who refused to vaccinate their children had at their disposal both administrative appeals, as well as judicial remedies before the administrative courts and ultimately the Constitutional Court.[27] Moreover, precautions were taken throughout the process, including the monitoring of the safety of the vaccines in use and the checking for possible contraindications in each individual case.[28] Finally, in cases of refusal to allow the required vaccination, the repercussions were not deemed to be excessive. The parents could only receive a fine which, in the case of Mr. *Vavřička*, the Court did not consider 'unduly harsh or onerous',[29] and the effects on the child applicants were of limited duration, as admission to primary school was not affected by vaccine status.[30]

Also relevant in the Court's findings was the fact that no consensus exists among States on whether vaccination should be voluntary or compulsory, which implied that, on this sensitive topic, the national authorities should enjoy a wide margin of appreciation.[31] It is expected that the decision will have

24 Ibid, para 272.
25 Ibid, para 277.
26 Ibid, para 291.
27 Ibid, para 295.
28 Ibid, para 301.
29 Ibid, para 293.
30 Ibid, para 302.
31 Ibid, para 280.

an impact on the approach of European States to compulsory vaccinations, at a time when the debate on the COVID vaccination campaign is particularly heated.[32]

Another pertinent example of a limitation that States might impose to pursue preventive aims can be found in the practice of the UN Special Rapporteur on human rights and hazardous substances. One of his most recent reports concerns the scope and content of the right to information throughout the life cycle of hazardous substances and wastes.[33] The document underlines that information about hazardous substances 'is essential to prevent risks, mitigate harms, conduct focused research on safer alternatives, provide treatment and remedy, and ensure transparency, participation and consent in decision- and policymaking'.[34] The corresponding right to seek information – protected under Article 19 ICCPR – should not be unduly restricted. An example of illegitimate limitation would be the refusal to disclose information because it would adversely affect the value of intellectual property or the confidentiality of commercial businesses or industrial information, in a situation where such refusal may hamper public health or the overall public interest. After recapitulating the relevant rules in matters of limitations to human rights,[35] the report concludes that '[i]t is not legitimate to protect a competitive advantage of businesses that create risks to public health and other public interests'.[36]

Turning to the second type of limitations, *ie* those introduced to tackle a threat that has already materialised, an illustrative example comes from a case concerning the deprivation of liberty of an HIV-positive homosexual man.[37] In *Enhorn v. Sweden*,[38] the applicant had unknowingly infected another man, which led medical authorities to issue him with a number of instructions in order to minimise the risk that he might transmit the virus to others. Among

---

32 Deutsche Welle, *ECHR rules obligatory vaccination may be necessary*, available at <https://www.dw.com/en/echr-rules-obligatory-vaccination-may-be-necessary/a-57128443>. See also S Katsoni, 'Do compulsory vaccinations against COVID-19 violate human rights?: An assessment of the measure's compatibility with the European Convention on Human Rights', *Völkerrechtsblog*, 2 December 2020, available at <https://voelkerrechtsblog.org/do-compulsory-vaccinations-against-covid-19-violate-human-rights/>.

33 Report of the Special Rapporteur on the implications for human rights of the environmentally sound management and disposal of hazardous substances and wastes, Başkut Tuncak, UN Doc. A/HRC/30/40, 8 July 2015.

34 Ibid, para 7.

35 Ibid, para 38–39.

36 Ibid, para 45.

37 Admittedly, the measures adopted in the case under scrutiny could also be considered as preventive ones, as they aimed at reducing the risk of a further spreading of the disease.

38 ECtHR, *Enhorn v. Sweden*, Judgment of 25 January 2005. For an accurate discussion, see R Martin, 'The Exercise of Public Health Powers in Cases of Infectious Disease: Human Rights Implications' 14 Medical Law Review (2006) 132–143.

them, was the requirement to attend periodical medical appointments. When the applicant failed to attend some of the meetings, the Swedish authorities issued an order imposing on him compulsory hospital isolation for three months. He was then arrested and interned, and the detention order was renewed several times. However, he frequently absconded thereafter, with the result that he was, in fact, deprived of his liberty for a total of about 18 months over a seven-year period.

Having accepted that Enhorn's detention potentially fell under the exception provided by Article 5(1)(e) ECHR, the ECtHR had to determine whether it was also 'prescribed by law'. The Court acknowledged that, if deprivation of liberty is involved, it is particularly important that the principle of legal certainty be satisfied. It was, therefore, essential that the conditions for detention be clearly defined and that the law be foreseeable in its application. At the same time, however, the Court accepted that it is for national courts to interpret and apply domestic law. In the case at hand, the Swedish courts had carefully examined the instructions given to the applicant and had concluded that the requirements of the relevant domestic legislation were fulfilled.

The Court then turned to the substantive requirements of Article 5 and determined that the essential elements when assessing the 'lawfulness' of the detention of a person for sanitary purposes are (a) whether the disease 'is dangerous to public health or safety' and (b) whether detention of the person infected is 'the last resort in order to prevent the spreading of the disease, because less severe measures have been considered and found to be insufficient to safeguard the public interest'.[39] Regarding the first leg of the test, the Strasbourg judges had no problems in recognising that HIV constituted a serious threat to public health. Yet, with respect to the necessity of the measure, the judgment found that 'the compulsory isolation of the applicant was not a last resort in order to prevent him from spreading the HIV virus because less severe measures had not been considered and found to be insufficient to safeguard the public interest'.[40] As mentioned above, while the proportionality test is not expressly foreseen by Article 5 ECHR, the judgment attempted to strike a balance between the interference with the right to personal liberty and the need to preserve the general interest of society, thereby mirroring the process adopted for other limitation clauses.

Another right that could suffer undue limitations in the aftermath of a massive CBRN event is freedom of expression. Discussing the issue in the framework of the COVID-19 pandemic, the UN Special Rapporteur on the promotion and

39 ECtHR, *Enhorn v. Sweden* (supra n 38), para 44.

40 Ibid, para 55.

protection of the right to freedom of opinion and expression stressed that access to information, independent media and other free expression rights are critical to meeting the challenges posed by the disease.[41] The report underscores that individuals 'cannot protect themselves against disease when information is denied to them, when they have diminished trust in sources of information, and when propaganda and disinformation dominate the statements of public authorities'.[42] After recapitulating the scope and form that legitimate limitations on the right to seek information must take, the document sets out State obligations with respect to government-held information. If it intends to restrict access to information on an ongoing crisis, a Government must justify such deprivation 'only on the narrowest grounds and with the greatest degree of necessity to protect a legitimate interest'.[43] However, even where authorities are legitimately concerned about releasing information that could cause individuals to panic, it is likely that failure to disclose is not the only option. To the contrary, sharing information that is properly contextualised may advance both public policy and freedom of expression guarantees.[44] It is suggested that a similar approach should inform the conduct of public authorities in many other CBRN-related emergencies.

This brief overview has strived to demonstrate the complex and delicate nature of the reasoning underpinning the assessment of the legality of restrictive measures adopted to tackle biological threats. While different hazards might present certain peculiarities (especially if CBRN material is used with criminal or malicious intent), it is submitted that certain features in the proportionality assessment will be present in most (if not all) of the relevant legal analyses. On one hand, States are required to properly assess the nature and danger of the threat, taking into account expert advice based on scientifically sound information. Human behaviour will obviously be an integral part of said calculation, as hostile, illegal or even simply negligent attitudes on the part of the end-user will inevitably increase the danger associated with CBRN material. Also relevant is the likelihood of an event actually materialising, and the perceived seriousness of the hazard will clearly be more intense for events that are already ongoing. On the other hand, appropriate weight should be given to a) the specific right subject to restriction (with more 'essential' rights – such as personal liberty – calling for increased levels of protection); b) the scope

41 Report of the Special Rapporteur on the promotion and protection of the right to freedom of opinion and expression, UN Doc. A/HRC/44/49, 23 April 2020.

42 Ibid, para 5.

43 Ibid, para 20.

44 Ibid.

and length of the limitations imposed; c) the way in which the limitation is applied (*eg* by offering differential treatment based on reasonable and objective grounds) and enforced (*eg* in terms of the consequences attached to a lack of compliance);[45] d) the attempt to identify the least intrusive measure to cope with the threat; e) the availability of procedural safeguards that allow individuals to challenge any restrictive measure. In addition, national authorities might rely on a margin of appreciation in deciding which measures to adopt and how to implement them, especially if there is no consensus between States Parties to a treaty regarding the relative importance of the interest at stake or as to the best means of protecting it.

3 Extraordinary Limitations on Human Rights and CBRN Events

Some CBRN events may have exceptionally severe consequences that call for the adoption of extraordinary measures. These may entail restrictions of individual rights and freedoms to an extent which goes beyond what is allowed by limitation clauses and which is not compatible with the affected State's international obligations under human rights law treaties. The drafters of human rights conventions acknowledged that the texts needed to provide States facing this sort of predicament with a mechanism that would enable them 'to loosen the stranglehold of their obligations without running the risk of their membership of the community of States parties being called into question'.[46] This is why the principal human rights instruments include a derogation clause.[47]

The derogation clause sets out the requirements States need to respect if they intend to avail themselves of it, as well as a list of those rights that cannot be derogated from under any circumstances. The use of the clause exonerates the State invoking it from international responsibility for failing to fully respect its treaty obligations, provided that certain substantial and procedural

45 For instance, UN Human Rights Special Rapporteurs have recently criticised Cambodia's anti-COVID legislation, which allows 20-year prison terms and fines of up to USD 5,000 for those convicted of violations of said law. In their joint press release, they stressed that '[a]ll measures taken to fight the pandemic, including possible punishments, should be necessary and proportionate and not be used excessively', see OHCHR Press release, UN experts urge Cambodia to review approach to COVID-19, 12 April 2021, available at <https://www.ohchr.org/EN/NewsEvents/Pages/DisplayNews.aspx?NewsID=26985&LangID=E>.

46 N Questiaux, Study of the Implications for Human Rights of Recent Developments Concerning Situations Known as States of Siege or Emergency, UN Doc. E/CN.4/Sub.2/1982/15 (1982) 11, para 37.

47 See, for instance, art 15 of the ECHR, art 4 of the ICCPR, or art 27 of the American Convention on Human Rights (ACHR, 1969).

rules are complied with.[48] Before looking at the actual practice concerning the application of the clause, it must be underlined that natural or human-made CBRN events might be qualified as 'public emergencies' in the sense of IHRL. While the clause was predominantly used in the context of armed conflicts or other situations of violence,[49] it is clear that major CBRN events having the potential to seriously undermine the functioning of the State could also create an appropriate context for the application of the derogation clause. This view is supported by the preparatory works of the ACHR[50] and is also reflected in legal literature.[51] However – most importantly – it has gained traction in view of the widespread resort to the derogation clause in response to the COVID-19 pandemic.[52]

3.1 *The Normative Framework: Substantial and Procedural Requirements*

When can a CBRN event prompt resort to the derogation clause? As the HRComm points out, 'not every disturbance or catastrophe qualifies as a public emergency which threatens the life of the nation'.[53] When it was called on to work out this notion in relation to Article 15 ECHR, the European Commission on Human Rights (ECommHR) established that a 'public emergency' must possess the following features:

48 For a general introduction to the derogation clauses and their operation, see AL Svensson-McCarthy, *The International Law of Human Rights and States of Exception* (Martinus Nijhoff Publishers, 1998); G Cataldi, 'Art. 15 – Deroga in caso di urgenza' in S Bartole, P De Sena and V Zagrebelsky (eds), *Commentario breve alla Convenzione europea dei diritti dell'uomo* (CEDAM, 2012), pp. 555–564; E Sommario, *Stati d'emergenza e trattati a tutela dei diritti umani* (Giappichelli, 2018).

49 For a list of situations in which States have resorted to derogation clauses, see A Siehr, 'Derogation Measures under Article 4 ICCPR, with Special Consideration of the "War against International Terrorism"', in *German YB of International Law*, Vol. 47, 2004, p. 550.

50 See Conferencia Especializada Interamericana Sobre Derechos Humanos, San Josè, Costa Rica, 7–22 de noviembre de 1969, Actas y Documentos , Doc OEA/Ser.K/XVI/1.2, 264–265 (1969).

51 Commenting on Article 15 ECHR, Boisson de Chazournes expresses the view that '[e]nvironmental disasters can give rise to the right of derogation if the conditions of Article 15 are met', L Boisson De Chazournes, 'Non-Derogable Rights and the Need to Protect the Environment', in D Premont (ed), *Droits Intangibles et Etats d' Exception: Non-Derogable Rights and States of Emergency* (Editions Bruylant, 1996), p. 465. The same view is held by, among others, SR Chowdhury, *Rule of Law in a State of Emergency: The Paris Minimum Standards of Human Rights Norms in a State of Emergency* (St. Martin's Press, 1989), pp. 16–17.

52 See infra, Section 3.2.

53 HRComm, General Comment No. 29, (supra n 1) para 3.

1. It must be actual or imminent.
2. Its effect must involve the whole nation.
3. The continuance of the organised life of the community must be threatened.
4. The crisis or danger must be exceptional, in that the normal measures or restrictions, permitted by the Convention for the maintenance of public safety, health and order, are plainly inadequate.[54]

A quick review of these four elements is called for in order to clarify their actual import. The 'actual' or 'imminent' nature of the emergency implies that derogation is not allowed when the threat is merely 'latent' or 'perceived'.[55] The requirement that the emergency must involve 'the whole nation' has been somewhat loosened, as it is accepted that the crisis situation may have a geographically limited scope while still affecting the entire population of the interested area.[56] According to the *Siracusa Principles*, the third criterion demands that the situation is so serious as to imperil 'the physical integrity of the population, the political independence or the territorial integrity of the State or the existence or basic functioning of institutions indispensable to ensure and protect the rights recognised in the Covenant'.[57] The last condition requires that a crisis be truly 'exceptional', a feature that is assessed on the basis of the quality and scope of the measures required to avert the emergency. Measures that are incompatible with conventional standards must be the last resort and can only be enacted when all ordinary measures are exhausted and have not been adequate to deal with the threat. As we shall see, this element might be decisive with respect to the assessment of the restrictive regimes introduced to tackle the COVID pandemic. Indeed, while considering the prospect of derogation from the ICCPR during a natural catastrophe or a major industrial accident, the HRComm expressed the opinion that:

> the possibility of restricting certain Covenant rights under the terms of, for instance, freedom of movement [...] or freedom of assembly [...] is generally sufficient during such situations and no derogation from the provisions in question would be justified by the exigencies of the situation.[58]

54 ECommHR, *Denmark, Norway, Sweden and the Netherlands v. Greece*, Report of 5 November 1969, para 113.

55 See J Hartman, 'Derogation from Human Rights Treaties in Public Emergencies', in *Harvard International Law Journal*, Vol. 22, 1981, p. 16; and *Siracusa Principles* (supra n 2) N 39.

56 ECtHR, *Ireland v. UK*, Judgment of 18 January 1978, para 205.

57 *Siracusa Principles* (supra n 2) N 39.

58 HRComm, General Comment No. 29 (supra n 1) para 5.

Therefore, when (even major) CBRN events can be dealt with by resorting to ordinary restrictions, the crisis cannot be deemed to be 'exceptional', and derogation from HR treaties should not be allowed.

Once it is established that a given event constitutes a 'public emergency', it must be asked whether the measures adopted to confront it are 'strictly required by the exigencies of the situation'. As with ordinary limitations, the severity of the measures resorted to must strictly depend on – and correspond to – the gravity of the threat. The HRComm has deemed the principle of strict necessity to be 'a fundamental requirement for any measures derogating from the Covenant' and one which relates 'to the duration, geographical coverage and material scope of the state of emergency and any measures of derogation resorted to because of the emergency'.[59] Looking first at the temporal dimension, the requirement stipulates that derogation measures can only be kept in place as long as the emergency persists.[60] As to the 'geographic' element, the principle of strict necessity demands that the applicability of any derogation measure be limited to the areas where the emergency actually unfolds. Moving to the scope of the derogation measures enacted, States are again required to strike a balance between individual rights and the public interest endangered by the emergency. In reviewing State compliance with the principle, treaty bodies have developed a number of criteria.

First, each measure of derogation must bear some relation to the threat and be apt to contribute to the solution of a specific problem that forms part of the emergency. In the words of the ECommHR, '[t]here must be a link between the facts of the emergency on the one hand and the measures chosen to deal with it on the other'.[61] Second, when more than one measure appears acceptable, the least interfering measure must be chosen.[62] While assessing the requirement of strict necessity, much emphasis has been put on the availability of sufficient safeguards against the abuse of derogation measures. The need for a proper assessment of emergency legislation and for a periodic review of emergency powers by the legislature or by the judiciary have been identified as essential factors in this respect.[63] Closely linked to this requirement is that effective remedies remain available to persons affected by emergency legislation.[64]

59 Ibid, para 4.

60 ECommHR, *De Becker v. Belgium*, Report of 8 January 1960.

61 ECommHR, *Ireland v. UK*, Report of 25 January 1976, p. 97.

62 ECommHR, *Lawless v. Ireland*, Report of 19 December 1959, p. 123 (Opinion of Mr Waldock).

63 ECtHR, *Ireland v. UK* (supra n 56) para 220.

64 *Siracusa Principles* (supra n 2) NN 55–56.

Another requirement foreseen for derogation measures is that they must be in line with the derogating State's other obligations under international law. These will obviously vary from State to State, depending on their level of participation in multilateral and bilateral treaties. The requirement of consistency has generated very little case law by treaty bodies. Yet, treaties pertaining to the field of international disaster law would appear to be particularly relevant in the context of CBRN events.[65]

One of the cornerstones of the derogation regime is the principle of non-derogability of certain key rights. The different derogation clauses each contain a list of these rights, which display certain differences.[66] Those which are common to all human rights treaties are: the right to life; the prohibition of torture and cruel, inhuman and degrading treatment and punishment; the prohibition of slavery; and the prohibition of retroactive application of criminal law, most of which are considered to reflect norms of *jus cogens*.[67]

Looking at the procedural steps that are required from States intending to derogate from certain rights, Article 15 ECHR requires such a State to keep the Secretary-General of the Council of Europe 'fully informed' of the measures it has taken and of the reasons for doing so. This is usually done by filing a so-called 'derogation notice', which the Secretary-General then circulates to other Member States.

3.2 *State Practice Regarding Derogations Prompted by CBRN Events*

As mentioned above, State practice under human rights treaties suggests the permissibility of derogations in cases of major CBRN events. Article 4 ICCPR was invoked as early as 2006 to deal with a dangerous epidemic. On that occasion, Georgia derogated from the Covenant when authorities felt they had to suspend – in one of the country's districts – constitutional guarantees related to freedom of movement and to the right to property, in order to prevent further spread of the Avian Flu virus.[68] Three years later, it was Guatemala's turn

65 See E Sommario, 'Limitation and Derogation Provisions in International Human Rights Law Treaties and their Use in Disaster Settings', in F Zorzi Giustiniani et al. (eds), *Routledge Handbook of Human Rights and Disasters* (Routledge, 2018), p. 110.

66 The longer lists in the ICCPR, the ACHR and the Arab Charter are also explained by the different rationale behind the inclusion of certain rights, which were added not because they were perceived as being absolutely central to the protection of individuals in emergency situations, but rather because their suspension could never be justified in such contexts; see HRComm, General Comment No. 29 (supra n 1) para 11.

67 See Questiaux (supra n 46) p. 19.

68 See ICCPR, Notification under Article 4(3) of the Covenant: Georgia (7 March 2006) 2363 UNTS 465. Note that, in relation to the same events, Georgia also invoked art 15 ECHR; see Georgia: ECHR, Derogation to the Convention on the Protection of Human Rights and Fundamental Freedoms, Notification – JJ6239C Tr./005-166 (13 March 2006). The

to declare a 'public health emergency' for a period of 30 days, with a view to 'preventing and mitigating the effects of the influenza A (H1N1) epidemic'. The Guatemalan government suspended Article 12 (right to liberty of movement), Article 19 (right to freedom of expression) and Article 21 (right of peaceful assembly).[69] Yet, the most significant use of derogations linked to a CBRN event occurred in 2020, when more than 25 States[70] made resort to the various derogation clauses to justify the introduction of anti-COVID measures.

The rights derogated from include freedom of assembly, the right to education, freedom of movement, the right to property, the right to private and family life, the right to personal liberty and the right to fair trial. Interestingly, while all States have introduced measures of confinement, just a few have chosen to expressly suspend the right to personal liberty, perhaps reflecting the idea that quarantines and similar measures rather correspond to restrictions on freedom of movement. The frequent amendments to the derogation regimes seem to reflect the requirement for a constant reconsideration of the measures needed to confront the emergency, in line with the principle of proportionality. Also, the withdrawal of derogation notices by many States testifies to a strict adherence to the principle of necessity.

4 Conclusions

The substantive compliance of the various suspension regimes introduced to confront the COVID virus with the rules regulating derogations has not yet been tested by any human rights body. Moreover, the decision by the majority

derogation was withdrawn about three weeks later; see ECHR, Georgia: Withdrawal of Derogation to the Convention on the Protection of Human Rights and Fundamental Freedoms, Notification – JJ6268C Tr./005–168 (7 April 2006). Both notifications are available at <https://wcd.coe.int>. Neither the affected individuals nor other States Parties to the Convention have voiced opposition to Georgia's conduct.

69 ICCPR, 'Notification under Article 4(3) of the Covenant: Guatemala, UN Doc. C.N.347. 2009. TREATIES-8 (Depositary Notification)' (20 May 2009), available at <https://treaties.un.org/doc/Publication/CN/2009/CN.347.2009-Eng.pdf>.

70 For instance, Latvia, Romania, Armenia, Estonia, Moldova, Georgia, Albania, North Macedonia, Serbia, and San Marino notified derogations from the ECHR. The texts of the notifications are all available at the following link: <https://www.coe.int/en/web/conventions/full-list/-/conventions/webContent/62111354>. Ecuador, Bolivia, Guatemala, Peru, Columbia, Panama, Chile, the Dominican Republic, Honduras, Argentina and El Salvador invoked Article 27 of the ACHR. The derogation notices are available at the following link: <http://www.oas.org/en/sla/dil/inter_american_treaties_suspension_guarantees.asp>. At least 25 States have derogated from the ICCPR. The notifications are available here: <https://treaties.un.org/Pages/CNs.aspx?cnTab=tab1&clang=_en>.

of States not to use the derogation clause has prompted a lively debate among human rights scholars. Can the pandemic be addressed by using 'only' ordinary limitations to human rights? Some scholars seem to support this view, arguing that '[o]ne can insist on the principle of normalcy and on full respect for human rights. What can be done under the framework of permissible restrictions, should be preferred'.[71] On the other hand, other commentators disagree, rejecting the argument that 'everything can and should be accommodated through the proportionality test' as it would render derogations 'a dead-letter' and, in so doing, 'increase the possibility of exceptional powers becoming normalised'.[72]

It is submitted that the answer to this question should be based on a careful analysis of the measures adopted and of their compatibility with ordinary conventional standards. As mentioned above, it is only when the normal measures or restrictions on rights, which are permitted by human right treaties, are 'plainly inadequate' to tackle the emergency that derogation measures are justified. The decision to derogate must, therefore, depend on the specific set of measures introduced.[73] Yet, it should be borne in mind that, where measures which restrict rights are adopted to respond to exceptional situations of crisis, the ECtHR has generally allowed States to interpret the scope of the permitted restrictions under the relevant articles broadly.[74] A derogation may, therefore, be unnecessary given that extensive interferences with rights may be justifiable in pursuit of the legitimate aim of protecting public health. On the other hand, the distinction between limitations and derogations is difficult to draw because principles such as proportionality and non-discrimination are

71 See M Scheinin, COVID-19 Symposium: To Derogate or Not to Derogate?, Opinio Juris, <https://opiniojuris.org/2020/04/06/covid-19-symposium-to-derogate-or-not-to-derogate/>; see also K Dzehtsiarou COVID-19 and the European Convention on Human Rights, Strasbourg Observers, 27 March 2020, <https://strasbourgobservers.com/2020/03/27/covid-19-and-the-european-convention-on-human-rights/>.

72 A Greene, 'States should declare a State of Emergency using Article 15 ECHR to confront the Coronavirus Pandemic', Strasbourg Observers, 1 April 2020, <https://strasbourgobservers.com/2020/04/01/states-should-declare-a-state-of-emergency-using-article-15-echr-to-confront-the-coronavirus-pandemic/>.

73 See for example GM Farnelli, 'Proporzionalità ed emergenza sanitaria da COVID-19 nei parametri CEDU', in *La Comunità Internazionale*, Vol. 75, 2020, p. 110, arguing that quarantine measures as applied by many States are not in line with the ECHR and must thus be legitimised through a derogation.

74 For instance, the Court was ready to accept an extensive interference with the right to property where a State adopted measures in response to 'the existence of an exceptional crisis without precedent', ECtHR, *Koufaki and Adedy v. Greece*, Judgment of 7 May 2013, para 37.

applicable to both. The lack of a clear standard may lead to Member States issuing a notice of derogation in a situation where it might not be required, in essence using the derogation as a safety net.[75]

Whatever the answer to this question, States must always give priority to human rights protection as they attempt to prevent and to react to CBRN events. Respect for the international legal system as a whole and of individual rights in particular should inform any plan or policy directed at curbing CBRN risks. The main human rights treaties provide that, in times of public emergency, States may restrict rights protected by the treaty in order to respond more effectively to a possible crisis. However, resort to derogation clauses should be a measure of last resort and is unlikely to be required when reacting to minor CBRN events or when introducing preventive measures against CBRN threats. These types of situations are probably better addressed by making use of the ordinary limitations foreseen by the provisions of all major treaties protecting civil and political rights.

Irrespective of the kind of restriction used, public authorities should strive to be transparent in justifying their line of conduct. In this context, human rights monitoring mechanisms play an important role and should guide States in deciding which sort of restrictive regime is better attuned to achieve the desired aim of effectively tackling CBRN threats. Hopefully, the COVID-19 crisis will provide opportunities to shed further light on what appears to be a largely uncharted legal territory.

Acknowledgement

Associate Professor of International Law at the Scuola Superiore Sant'Anna in Pisa. The author wishes to thank the editors for their useful comments on earlier drafts of this chapter. All errors remain the author's sole responsibility. All links included in the footnotes were last checked on 15 June 2021.

75 See Sommario (supra n 65) p. 110, noting that certain derogation notices are not entirely clear as to the intention of the State authorities to expressly suspend the enjoyment of certain rights. The same stance is taken by E Richardson and C Devine, 'Emergencies End Eventually: How to Better Analyze Human Rights Restrictions Sparked by the COVID-19 Pandemic Under the International Covenant on Civil and Political Rights', in Michigan Journal of International Law, Vol. 42, 2020, pp. 128–130; and by A Spadaro, COVID-19: testing the limits of human rights, in *European Journal of Risk Regulation*, Vol. 11, 2020, p. 322.

Bibliography

Boisson De Chazournes L, 'Non-Derogable Rights and the Need to Protect the Environment' in D Premont (ed) *Droits Intangibles et Etats d' Exception: Non-Derogable Rights and States of Emergency* (Editions Bruylant, 1996) 463.

Cataldi G, 'Art. 15 – Deroga in caso di urgenza' in S Bartole, P De Sena and V Zagrebelsky (eds) *Commentario breve alla Convenzione europea dei diritti dell'uomo* (CEDAM, 2012) 555.

Chowdhury SR, *Rule of Law in a State of Emergency: The Paris Minimum Standards of Human Rights Norms in a State of Emergency* (St. Martin's Press, 1989).

Farnelli GM, 'Proporzionalità ed emergenza sanitaria da COVID-19 nei parametri CEDU' (2020) 75 La Comunità Internazionale 97.

Gerards JH, 'How to Improve the Necessity Test of the European Court of Human Right' (2013) 11 International Journal of Constitutional Law 466.

Hartman J, 'Derogation from Human Rights Treaties in Public Emergencies' (1981) 22 Harvard International Law Journal 1.

Legg A, *The Margin of Appreciation in International Human Rights Law* (OUP 2012).

Martin R, 'The Exercise of Public Health Powers in Cases of Infectious Disease: Human Rights Implications' (2006) 14 Medical Law Review 132.

Müller A, 'Limitations to and Derogations from Economic, Social and Cultural Rights' (2009) 9 Human Rights Law Review 557.

Rainey B, Wicks E and Ovey C, *Jacobs, White and Ovey: The European Convention on Human Rights* (6th edn) (OUP 2014).

Richardson E and Devine C, 'Emergencies End Eventually: How to Better Analyze Human Rights Restrictions Sparked by the COVID-19 Pandemic Under the International Covenant on Civil and Political Rights' (2020) 42 Michigan Journal of International Law 105.

Siehr A, 'Derogation Measures under Article 4 ICCPR, with Special Consideration of the "War against International Terrorism"' (2004) 47 German YB of International Law 545.

Sommario E, *Stati d'emergenza e trattati a tutela dei diritti umani* (Giappichelli 2018).

Sommario E, 'Limitation and Derogation Provisions in International Human Rights Law Treaties and their Use in Disaster Settings', in F Zorzi Giustiniani et al. (eds) *Routledge Handbook of Human Rights and Disasters* (Routledge, 2018) 98.

Spadaro A, 'COVID-19: testing the limits of human rights' (2020) 11 European Journal of Risk Regulation 317.

Svensson-McCarthy AL, *The International Law of Human Rights and States of Exception* (Martinus Nijhoff Publisher 1998).

CHAPTER 29

CBRN Events and International Environmental Law: From Fragmentation to Mutual Supportiveness and Coordination

Chiara Tea Antoniazzi

1 Introduction

The prevention of, preparedness for, response to and recovery from CBRN events intersect with the protection of the environment (consisting of all living and non-living natural components and factors surrounding humans) in many ways. At the same time, international environmental law (IEL) does not address the CBRN threat holistically, so that – similarly to what happens with several other environment-related issues – the regulation of CBRN activities and events is scattered throughout a multiplicity of universal, regional and sectoral treaties, while the legal status of unifying principles and norms of general application in IEL remains contested.[1]

Whether the piecemeal nature of IEL is detrimental to its effectiveness or, conversely, allows for flexibility in dealing with issues that are inherently technical and evolving is still very much debated.[2] The former argument might, nonetheless, have become prevailing, as the UN Secretary-General was recently entrusted – at the urging of a group of experts – with the preparation of a report on gaps in IEL and, on this basis, discussions are ongoing on the need for a comprehensive Global Pact for the Environment.[3]

1 U Beyerlin, 'Different Types of Norms in International Environmental Law Policies, Principles, and Rules' in D Bodansky, J Brunnée and E Hey (eds), *The Oxford Handbook of International Environmental Law* (OUP 2012); P Sands and J Peel, *Principles of International Environmental Law* (4th edn, CUP 2018) ch 6.

2 On the problems deriving from 'treaty congestion' in IEL, E Brown Weiss, 'International Environmental Law: Contemporary Issues and the Emergence of a New World Order' (1993) 81 GeoLJ 697ff.; conversely, on the advantages of IEL fragmentation, T Gehring, 'Treaty-Making and Treaty Evolution' in Bodansky, Brunnée and Hey (n 1) 474ff especially.

3 UNGA 'Gaps in international environmental law and environment-related instruments: towards a global pact for the environment. Report of the Secretary-General' (2018) UN Doc A/73/419; and UNGA Res 72/277 (10 May 2018) UN Doc A/RES/72/277. For information on the Global Pact's progress, see the dedicated websites: <https://globalpactenvironment.org/en/> and <https://globalpact.informea.org/> (all links were last accessed on 29 November 2021).

As things stand, however, the actors concerned are still confronted with a complex web of IEL-based obligations relating to CBRN activities and events – obligations which Section 2 of this chapter identifies and systematises, to the extent possible, by focusing on those that are aimed at protecting the environment as such, separately from any injury to persons or their property. The chapter then zooms in on two highly topical issues that exemplify the interconnections between IEL and CBRN events, but which have rarely been considered in this light: epidemic outbreaks of zoonotic origin (Section 3) and climate change (Section 4).

In drawing some conclusions, Section 5 underlines the importance of an interpretation and application of IEL norms that adequately consider the prevention of, preparedness for, response to and recovery from CBRN events, on the basis of mutual supportiveness among CBRN-related IEL norms, as well as between IEL and non-IEL norms that are relevant to CBRN hazards – as has been put forward by the UN Secretary-General with respect to international instruments that more or less directly address the protection of the environment.

2 CBRN Events and International Environmental Law: An Overview

If a comprehensive notion of CBRN risks and events is adopted,[4] it becomes apparent that IEL is of the utmost relevance for their management. In general terms, areas of IEL that pertain to CBRN activities and events include transboundary environmental harm; the generation, movement, and disposal of hazardous substances and waste; nuclear waste and accidents; the marine environment; fresh water; the atmosphere; climate change; biodiversity; and the production and use of specific substances, such as mercury and persistent organic pollutants. While much has been written on these areas individually, it appears appropriate here to look at this complex body of rules from a CBRN-oriented perspective and, specifically, in light of the four phases of the CBRN emergency management cycle, *ie* prevention, preparedness, response and recovery.[5]

Prevention plays a crucial role in IEL in general. As recovery following environmental damage is more often than not impossible or extraordinarily difficult, IEL aims to prevent such damage from occurring in the first place, to the extent that this is possible. Accordingly, the obligation not to cause (significant)

4 See ch 1 by Frulli in this volume.
5 Ibid.

transboundary environmental harm is one of the main tenets of IEL and its oldest customary rule.[6] Such a broad due diligence obligation is related to a number of more specific procedural obligations that, while autonomous, could also be interpreted as giving substance to the prevention of transboundary environmental harm.[7] These encompass the obligations to conduct an environmental impact assessment (EIA) prior to authorising a hazardous activity;[8] notify potentially affected States and/or international organisations prior to authorising a hazardous activity;[9] exchange information with other States regarding the conditions of and dangers to shared resources or other States' resources;[10] and consult and/or negotiate with them on planned hazardous activities with potential transboundary effects.[11] All of these obligations also clearly embody the principle of cooperation, which is one of the cornerstones of the prevention of emergency situations in international law in general.[12]

6 The prohibition of transboundary environmental harm was first recognised in *Trail smelter case (United States, Canada)* (1938, 1941) III RIAA 1905, and it has since been applied repeatedly as a customary rule by the ICJ, most recently, in *Certain Activities Carried Out by Nicaragua in the Border Area (Costa Rica v Nicaragua)* [2015] ICJ Rep 665, para 118. The no-harm rule is laid down in numerous IEL instruments: eg, UN Convention on the Law of the Sea (1982) (UNCLOS) art 194; Declaration of the UN Conference on the Human Environment (1992) (Stockholm Declaration) principle 21; Rio Declaration on Environment and Development (1992) (Rio Declaration) principle 2; Convention on Biological Diversity (1992) (CBD) art 3; Draft articles on Prevention of Transboundary Harm from Hazardous Activities (2001) (Draft Articles on Prevention) art 3.

7 I Plakokefalos, 'Prevention Obligations in International Environmental Law' (2012) 23(1) YIntlEnvL. On the principle of prevention in IEL and its articulations, see also *The Environment and Human Rights*, Advisory Opinion OC-23, IACtHR Series A No 23 (15 November 2017) paras 127ff.

8 UNCLOS, art 206; Convention on Environmental Impact Assessment in a Transboundary Context (1991) (Espoo Convention); CBD, art 14(1)(a) (referring to biodiversity as such, as opposed to the biodiversity of other States); Draft Articles on Prevention, art 7; Directive 2014/52/EU [2014] OJ L124/1 (EIA Directive).

9 Basel Convention on the Control of Transboundary Movements of Hazardous Wastes and their Disposal (1989) (Basel Convention) art 6; Espoo Convention, arts 2(4), 3; Convention on the Transboundary Effects of Industrial Accidents (1992) (UNECE Industrial Accidents Convention) art 4(1); CBD, art 14(1)(c); Convention on the Law of the Non-Navigational Uses of International Watercourses (1997) (Watercourses Convention) arts 12–16; Draft Articles on Prevention, art 8.

10 UNCLOS, art 200; CBD, art 14(1)(c); Watercourses Convention, arts 9, 11; Draft Articles on Prevention, art 12.

11 Convention on Long-range Transboundary Air Pollution (1979) (LRTAP Convention) art 5; Espoo Convention, art 5; UNECE Industrial Accidents Convention, art 4(2)–(3) and annexes II–III; CBD, art 14(1)(c); Watercourses Convention, arts 11, 17; Draft Articles on Prevention, arts 9, 10.

12 See ch 3 by Venier in this volume.

At the domestic level, the prohibition of transboundary harm translates into the obligation for States to adopt all appropriate measures, including laws and regulations, to prevent the occurrence of such harm,[13] thereby also regulating the conduct of private actors, who are to be required to take all necessary steps to avoid or minimise environmental damage.[14]

As a reinforcement of the principle of prevention, precaution still suffers from ambiguities regarding its scope and legal status but is increasingly found in legal instruments and judgments.[15] By requiring States to adopt, without delay, measures to prevent (serious or irreversible) environmental damage, even in the absence of full scientific certainty that the damage will, in fact, occur, the precautionary principle or approach may very well apply to CBRN substances – such as chemicals[16] and various products of synthetic biology[17] – whose adverse effects on the environment are not fully known yet.

---

13 UNCLOS, arts 207, 208, 210–212; Basel Convention, art 4; Espoo Convention, art 2(2); UNECE Industrial Accidents Convention, arts 3(4), 6(1), 7; UNECE Convention on the Protection and Use of Transboundary Watercourses and International Lakes (1992) (UNECE Water Convention) art 3; CBD, art 10(a)–(b); Draft Articles on Prevention, art 5.

14 Basel Convention, art 4(2)(c); UNECE Industrial Accidents Convention, arts 3(3), 6 and annexes IV–V; UNECE Water Convention, art 3; Directive 2012/18/EU [2012] OJ L197/1 (Seveso III Directive) art 5(1). On private actors and CBRN-related activities and risks, see ch 2 by Di Francesco Maesa and ch 30 by Corcione in this volume.

15 The precautionary principle or approach can be found in several IEL instruments, including the UN Framework Convention on Climate Change (1992) (UNFCCC) art 3(3); Rio Declaration, principle 15; UNECE Water Convention, art 2(5)(a); 1996 Protocol to the Convention on the Prevention of Marine Pollution by Dumping of Wastes and Other Matter (1972) (London Convention) art 3(1); Cartagena Protocol on Biosafety to the CBD (2000) (Cartagena Protocol) arts 10(6), 11(8); Stockholm Convention on Persistent Organic Pollutants (2001) (Stockholm Convention) arts 1, 8(7)(a). The precautionary principle has also been recognised and applied in the case law of international courts: *Southern Bluefin Tuna (New Zealand v Japan; Australia v Japan)* (Provisional Measures) [1999] ITLOS Rep 280, para 77; *Pulp Mills on the River Uruguay (Argentina v Uruguay)* [2010] ICJ Rep 14, para 164; and *Responsibilities and Obligations of States with respect to Activities in the Area* (Advisory Opinion) [2011] ITLOS Rep 10, para 135. In the literature, among many, D Freestone and E Hey (eds), *The Precautionary Principle and International Law: The Challenge of Implementation* (Kluwer Law International 1996).

16 Eg, the European Commission purports that the REACH Regulation (Regulation No 1907/2006 [2006] OJ L396/1) is based on the precautionary approach, even though this claim has been contested: S Foss Hansen, L Carlsen and JA Tickner, 'Chemicals regulation and precaution: does REACH really incorporate the precautionary principle' (2007) 10 Environmental Science and Policy.

17 CBD, arts 8(g), 19(3)–(4) in particular; and Cartagena Protocol. On synthetic biology in the CBD context, F Keiper and A Atanassova, 'Regulation of Synthetic Biology: Developments Under the Convention on Biological Diversity and Its Protocols' (2020) 8 Frontiers in Bioengineering and Biotechnology.

Additionally, both prevention and precaution rely on or benefit from public participation in environmental decision-making, which broadens the sources of input and lends greater legitimacy to the relevant measures. Public participation is, in turn, connected to the provision of access to environmental information, and to the availability of remedies against decisions contrary to environmental law and decisions restricting the rights to information/participation. While, until recently, the most comprehensive codification of the rights to information, participation and remedy in environmental matters could be found in the Aarhus Convention,[18] adopted in the UNECE context, similar provisions have now been incorporated in the Escazú Agreement, concluded under the auspices of UNECLAC in 2018.[19] If one considers that these rights have also been recognised in several IEL sectoral treaties and non-binding instruments,[20] it can be said that 'environmental democracy' is becoming an increasingly important pillar of IEL. Nevertheless, the exercise of 'environmental democracy' rights can be restricted on a number of grounds, including national security and industrial or commercial secrecy,[21] which are of special relevance to CBRN-related activities. Thus, particularly in relation to nuclear activities, access to information and public participation regarding the activities and their effects on the environment and human health might be severely restricted.

As for preparedness, response and recovery, these phases of the CBRN emergency management cycle are considered jointly in several environmental treaties – a fact which highlights the functional interconnectedness of the cycle's phases, but, on the other hand, might result in the relative neglect of some phases compared to others (particularly of preparedness compared to

---

18 Convention on Access to Information, Public Participation in Decision-Making and Access to Justice in Environmental Matters (1998).

19 Regional Agreement on Access to Information, Public Participation and Justice in Environmental Matters in Latin America and the Caribbean (2018). Besides, in the Inter-American context, the IACtHR had already derived 'environmental democracy' rights from the American Convention on Human Rights in its advisory opinion on *The Environment and Human Rights*, paras 211ff. While no comparable instrument exists in the African context, participatory rights have been recognised in the African Convention on the Conservation of Nature and Natural Resources (2003) art XVI.

20 Rio Declaration, principle 10; UNECE Water Convention, art 16; Rotterdam Convention on the Prior Informed Consent Procedure for Certain Hazardous Chemicals and Pesticides in International Trade (1998) (Rotterdam Convention) art 15(2); Stockholm Convention, art 10; Draft Articles on Prevention, art 13; Minamata Convention on Mercury (2013) (Minamata Convention) art 18(1); Paris Agreement (2015) art 12.

21 Aarhus Convention, art 4(4); Escazú Agreement, art 5(6). See also Espoo Convention, art 2(8); Draft Articles on Prevention, art 14; Seveso III Directive, art 22.

response). As far as the international plane is concerned, the relevant norms essentially provide for obligations of cooperation – first of all, through the notification of the CBRN incident by the State of origin to other affected States and/or to international organisations.[22] As a first step of the response, notification can also contribute to the prevention of (further) environmental harm. Following notification, assistance in the response to the emergency comes into play. While the request for and provision of assistance are both generally voluntary (although conventions and complementary regulations might prescribe the form and modalities of the request or offer), there exist instances where the provision of assistance is compulsory.[23]

With more specific regard to preparedness, some conventions ask States – 'where appropriate' – to adopt joint contingency plans.[24] In practice, several bilateral instruments have been concluded to prepare for pollution incidents at sea, together with some multilateral ones (such as the 2018 ASEAN Regional Oil Spill Contingency Plan), and a 'Checklist for contingency planning for accidents affecting transboundary waters' has been developed by UNECE.

IEL treaties dealing with preparedness for, response to and recovery from CBRN incidents also give rise to obligations for States at the domestic level, including the obligation to establish appropriate national systems to respond to incidents[25] and the obligation to require that the private actors in charge of hazardous activities report any incidents and have contingency plans in place to deal with such incidents.[26]

---

22 UNCLOS, art 198; Convention on Early Notification of a Nuclear Accident (1986) arts 2, 5; Basel Convention, art 13(1); International Convention on Oil Pollution Preparedness, Response and Co-operation (1990) (OPRC) art 5(1)(c)–5(4); CBD, art 14(1)(d); UNECE Industrial Accidents Convention, art 10 and annex IX; Watercourses Convention, art 28(2); Draft Articles on Prevention, art 17.

23 Eg, UNECE Water Convention, art 15(1). Albeit 'subject to their capabilities and the availability of relevant resources' and 'when the severity of such incident so justifies', Parties to the OPRC are also required to cooperate in the response to a pollution incident (art 7). In the UNECE Industrial Accidents Convention, the provision of assistance remains voluntary, but the requested Party 'shall promptly decide and inform the requesting Party whether it is in a position to render the assistance required' (art 12(1); similarly, Convention on Assistance in the Case of a Nuclear Accident or Radiological Emergency (1986) art 2).

24 UNCLOS, art 199; OPRC, art 10; CBD, art 14(1)(e); Watercourses Convention, art 28(4); Draft Articles on Prevention, art 16.

25 OPRC, art 6; CBD, art 14(1)(e); UNECE Industrial Accidents Convention, arts 8, 10, 17.

26 OPRC, arts 3–4; UNECE Industrial Accidents Convention, art 8 and annex VII; Nagoya-Kuala Lumpur Supplementary Protocol on Liability and Redress to the Cartagena Protocol (2010) (Nagoya-Kuala Lumpur Protocol) art 5(1); Seveso III Directive, arts 12, 16 and annex IV.

Further IEL-based obligations that intersect with more than one phase of the CBRN emergency management cycle, or are not specifically related to the cycle, include monitoring the conditions of shared resources and the (potential) effects of hazardous activities and pollution;[27] exchanging information and reporting;[28] cooperating in research and training, especially in favour of developing countries;[29] and assisting developing countries financially.[30]

Arguably, the least developed component of IEL consists of liability and compensation regimes for environmental damage – a state of affairs which is made evident by the number of IEL instruments where the parties commit to support (future) international efforts to establish such regimes[31] and by the circumstance that those agreements on liability and redress which have been concluded have mostly yet to enter into force.[32] This does not mean that, at present, responsibility for violations of IEL is not recognised. However, as shown by recent ICJ jurisprudence,[33] traditional State responsibility might not be the most effective means of enforcement and redress in environmental matters, as uncertainties still surround the scope and legal status of various IEL primary norms; the assessment of environmental damage and compensation

27 UNCLOS, art 204; Basel Convention, art 10(2)(b); CBD, art 7; UNECE Water Convention, arts 4, 11; Stockholm Convention, art 11.

28 Basel Convention, art 13; LRTAP Convention, art 8; UNECE Industrial Accidents Convention, art 15 and annex XI; UNECE Water Convention, arts 6, 13; CBD, art 17; Rotterdam Convention, art 14; Stockholm Convention, arts 9, 15; Minamata Convention, arts 17, 21.

29 LRTAP Convention, art 7; UNCLOS, arts 200, 202; OPRC, arts 8–9; Espoo Convention, art 9; UNECE Water Convention, arts 5, 12; CBD, arts 12, 18; Rotterdam Convention, art 16.

30 CBD, art 20; Stockholm Convention, art 13(2)–(8); Minamata Convention, art 13; Paris Agreement, art 9.

31 Stockholm Declaration, principle 22; London Convention, art X; 1996 Protocol to the London Convention, art 15; UNCLOS, art 235(3); Rio Declaration, principle 13; CBD, art 14(2); UNECE Industrial Accidents Convention, art 13; UNECE Water Convention, art 7.

32 UNECE Convention on Civil Liability for Damage Caused during Carriage of Dangerous Goods by Road, Rail and Inland Navigation Vessels (1989; one ratification); CoE Convention on Civil Liability for Damage Resulting from Activities Dangerous to the Environment (1993; no ratifications); Protocol on Liability and Compensation for Damage Resulting from Transboundary Movements of Hazardous Wastes and Their Disposal (1999; 12 parties, all developing countries); UNECE Protocol on Civil Liability for Damage and Compensation for Damage Caused by Transboundary Effects of Industrial Accidents on Transboundary Waters (2003; one ratification); International Convention on Liability and Compensation for Damage in Connection with the Carriage of Hazardous and Noxious Substances by Sea (1996, as amended by its 2010 Protocol; five parties).

33 *Costa Rica v Nicaragua* (Compensation) [2018] ICJ Rep 15; for a critical appraisal of the judgment, K Kindji and M Faure, 'Assessing reparation of environmental damage by the ICJ: A lost opportunity?' (2019) 57 QuestIntlL, Zoom-in.

is still far from satisfactory; and the actual breach of an international norm is often immaterial to the environmental harm and its severity.[34]

The broadening of strict liability for environmental damage might thus be needed in the face of legal but hazardous activities.[35] Further, a number of international instruments call for the strengthening of civil liability regimes which, by incorporating the 'polluter pays' principle,[36] make the private operators responsible for the environmental harm bear the costs of restoration and compensation (at least up to a certain ceiling), thus at the same time incentivising preventive action.[37] Ultimately, a reinforcement of liability and redress regimes, in terms of both general principles and sector-specific norms, is needed.[38] The gaps in this area of IEL constitute a serious problem for CBRN incidents, which can cause devastating harm to the environment.

Overall, it can be said that IEL is the source of multiple obligations for States and, indirectly, private actors dealing with CBRN substances, activities and emergencies. The incremental process by which IEL and CBRN-related IEL, in particular, have come into existence – following discrete, major incidents – has resulted in a patchwork of regimes that often lack coherence and give rise to both overlaps and gaps. While waiting for a possible future Global Pact for the

34 On these and other challenges facing State responsibility for environmental harm, M Fitzmaurice, 'International Responsibility and Liability' in Bodansky, Brunnée and Hey (n 1); T Scovazzi, 'State Responsibility for Environmental Harm' (2001) 12 YIntlEnvL.

35 This is the path taken by the ILC Draft principles on the allocation of loss in the case of transboundary harm arising out of hazardous activities (2006). See also the resolution by the Institute of International Law, 'Responsibility and Liability under International Law for Environmental Damage' (4 September 1997).

36 On the content and functions of the 'polluter pays' principle, N de Sadeleer, *Environmental Principles: From Political Slogans to Legal Rules* (OUP 2002) 33ff. The principle is mentioned, *inter alia*, in TFEU (1957, as amended) art 191(2); Alpine Convention (1991) art 2(1); Rio Declaration, principle 16; UNECE Water Convention, art 2(5)(b); Convention on Nuclear Safety (1994) art 9; 1996 Protocol to the London Convention, art 3(2); Nagoya-Kuala Lumpur Protocol, art 12.

37 Civil liability regimes currently in force mainly focus on nuclear activities and oil pollution at sea: Convention on Third Party Liability in the Field of Nuclear Energy (1960) and its Supplementary Convention (1963); Vienna Convention on Civil Liability for Nuclear Damage (1963, as amended by the 1997 Protocol); Convention Relating to Civil Liability in the Field of Maritime Carriage of Nuclear Material (1971); International Convention on Civil Liability for Oil Pollution Damage (1992) and International Convention on the Establishment of an International Fund for Compensation for Oil Pollution Damage (1992). See also Directive 2004/35/EC [2004] OJ L143/56.

38 *Contra*, for a pessimistic view on the role that liability regimes can play in protecting the environment and even in making compensation easier, J Brunnée, 'Of Sense and Sensibility: Reflections on International Liability Regimes as Tools for Environmental Protection' (2004) 53 ICLQ.

Environment, the UN Secretary-General has identified the way forward in the mutual supportiveness of obligations, both within IEL and between IEL and related branches of international law. The following sections of this chapter put forward two areas of test ground for this approach – areas that are related to CBRN hazards and require the coordination of different IEL and non-IEL regimes: the prevention of zoonotic epidemics and the mitigation of and adaptation to climate change.

3 Zoonotic Epidemics and International Environmental Law

The fact that a pathogen originating from animals would spill over to humans and give rise to a deadly pandemic had long been predicted by experts, but – clearly – that prediction was not followed by the appropriate prevention and preparedness measures.[39] The foreseeability of the COVID-19 pandemic is connected, essentially, to the growing rates of urbanisation and globalisation. The shrinking of natural habitats to make room for farmland, mining, and human settlement, together with poaching and wild meat consumption, have multiplied contacts between humans and wildlife, which, in turn, considerably increase the risk that animal-borne (zoonotic) diseases will make the jump to human hosts. International trade and travel then cause these diseases to spread globally.[40]

What is the role of IEL in such a scenario? The international community has at its disposal two main IEL instruments to prevent the recurrence of zoonotic epidemics by ensuring an appropriate balance between nature and humans: the Convention on Biological Diversity (CBD) and the Convention on International Trade in Endangered Species of Wild Fauna and Flora (CITES).[41]

39 See ch 16 by Venier and ch 17 by de Guttry in this volume.

40 On zoonoses and their links with the destruction of ecosystems and the increase in contacts between humans and wildlife, KE Jones and others, 'Global trends in emerging infectious diseases' (2008) 451 Nature; WB Karesh and others, 'Ecology of zoonoses: natural and unnatural histories' (2012) 380 Lancet; D Quammen, *Spillover: Animal Infections and the Next Human Pandemic* (WW Norton 2013); M Everard and others, 'The role of ecosystems in mitigation and management of Covid-19 and other zoonoses' (2020) 111 Environmental Science and Policy.

41 A role could also be played by the Convention on the conservation of migratory species of wild animals (1979), as spillovers might originate from migratory species and migrations can facilitate the spread of zoonoses; at the same time, migrations have also been shown to reduce the risk of disease transmission: KD Reed and others, 'Birds, Migration and Emerging Zoonoses: West Nile Virus, Lyme Disease, Influenza A and Enteropathogens'

In order to attain the primary aims of conserving and sustainably using biological diversity, several obligations are established in the CBD for States Parties – from the development of national conservation plans to the monitoring of biodiversity and the conduct of environmental impact assessments (EIAS) for hazardous activities – which, however, are hardly specific and are often qualified by expressions such as 'as far as possible and as appropriate'.

Therefore, work is ongoing within the CBD system on the development of a post-2020 global biodiversity framework, which should set out specific biodiversity goals and targets. Whereas the current draft of the framework does not emphasise the nexus between the conservation of biodiversity and human health,[42] most of the targets included would have an indirect positive impact on the prevention of zoonoses, eg those concerning the restoration of degraded ecosystems, the conservation and sustainable management of wildlife, and the eradication of invasive alien species.[43] Much will, nonetheless, depend on the final definition of the (quantifiable) targets and on the mobilisation of sufficient financial resources and capacity-building.

Furthermore, it should be considered that, within the latest three Conferences of the Parties to the CBD, decisions were adopted on 'Biodiversity and Human Health'[44] that acknowledge the link between the two and promote the inclusion of biodiversity in the so-called One Health approach, whereby cross-sectoral research and policies are undertaken with a view to ensuring higher health protection.[45] Accordingly, States are, *inter alia*, encouraged to adopt national biodiversity strategies and action plans conforming to the

(2003) 1(1) Clinical Medicine & Research; S Altizer, R Bartel and BA Han, 'Animal Migration and Infectious Disease Risk' (2011) 331 Science.

Other potentially relevant IEL instruments include the Convention on Wetlands of International Importance especially as Waterfowl Habitat (1971) (Ramsar Convention on Wetlands) and the UN Convention to Combat Desertification (1994): P Horwitz, CM Finlayson and P Weinstein, *Healthy wetlands, healthy people: A review of wetlands and human health interactions* (Secretariat of the Ramsar Convention on Wetlands and WHO 2012); J Patz and others, *Our Planet, Our Health, Our Future. Human health and the Rio Conventions: biological diversity, climate change and desertification* (WHO 2012) 34ff especially.

42 Although Targets 8 and 11 refer to human health and well-being: CBD 'Update of the Zero Draft of the Post-2020 Global Biodiversity Framework. Note by the Co-Chairs' (17 August 2020) CBD/POST2020/PREP/2/1, 5–6.

43 Ibid, ss D and E.

44 CBD COP: Decision XII/21 (17 October 2014) UNEP/CBD/COP/DEC/XII/21; Decision XIII/6 (14 December 2016) CBD/COP/DEC/XIII/6; Decision 14/4 (30 November 2018) CBD/COP/DEC/14/4.

45 On the One Health approach, see WHO 'One Health' <https://www.who.int/news-room/questions-and-answers/item/one-health>.

One Health approach; promote inter-ministerial and inter-agency dialogue; undertake capacity-building and raise awareness on the biodiversity-health nexus; and consider linkages between biodiversity and health within EIAs.[46] Therefore, even though the decisions in question use soft-law language, it appears that there is broad agreement among the CBD Parties on the relevance of the Convention's obligations to the protection of human health. Additionally, the decisions have promoted the increasing engagement of the CBD system in the matter, starting with the establishment in 2012 of a Joint Work Programme with the World Health Organization.[47] In light of such progress and of the current circumstances, it is somewhat surprising that the draft post-2020 global biodiversity framework does not underline more strongly the connection between healthy ecosystems and human health.

As to the Convention on International Trade in Endangered Species of Wild Fauna and Flora (CITES), since the initial spread of COVID-19 was traced back to a wet market, multiple calls have been made to ban – or radically change the conditions of – trade in wildlife,[48] which is considered to exacerbate the risk of spillovers by multiplying unnatural and unsanitary interactions between animals and humans and between different species of animals.[49] Those calls were also directed at CITES, whose Secretariat, however, rather hastily refused to comment on the possible connection between the ongoing pandemic and the handling or consumption of wild meat, by maintaining that zoonotic diseases are out of the purview of CITES, which is only concerned with regulating trade at the international level.[50]

---

46 CBD COP, Decision 14/4 (n 44) paras 3, 5, 6, 8, 9; and CBD SBSTTA, 'Guidance on Integrating Biodiversity Considerations into One Health Approaches' (13 December 2017) CBD/SBSTTA/21/9.

47 CBD COP, Decision XI/6 (5 December 2012) UNEP/CBD/COP/DEC/XI/6, para 29. For the work of CBD bodies on the biodiversity-health nexus, see CBD 'Health and Biodiversity' <www.cbd.int/health/>.

48 Most recently, the WHO, OIE and UNEP recommended the suspension of trade in live wild mammals for food: WHO 'Food safety: Sale of live wild mammals in traditional food markets' <https://www.who.int/news-room/questions-and-answers/item/sale-of-live-wild-mammals-in-traditional-food-markets> (12 April 2021). Caution is at any rate required, as bans risk fuelling illegal trade and endangering indigenous and local communities relying on wildlife trade and consumption for their livelihoods: D Challender and others, 'Coronavirus: why a blanket ban on wildlife trade would not be the right response' (*The Conversation*, 8 April 2020)<https://theconversation.com/coronavirus-why-a-blanket-ban-on-wildlife-trade-would-not-be-the-right-response-135746>.

49 S Broad, *Wildlife Trade, COVID-19, and Zoonotic Disease Risks* (TRAFFIC 2020) <https://www.traffic.org/site/assets/files/12764/covid-19-briefing-vfinal.pdf>.

50 CITES 'CITES Secretariat's statement in relation to COVID-19', 17 March 2020 <https://cites.org/eng/CITES_Secretariat_statement_in_relation_to_COVID19>.

While *prima facie* solid, the Secretariat's argument appears to emphasise what divides and downplay what unites zoonotic epidemics and CITES. Although uncertainty persists over the identity of the intermediate host(s) for COVID-19, various reservoirs and intermediate hosts for past zoonotic diseases are included among the 'species threatened with extinction' in CITES Appendix I and are thus generally banned from international trade. Whereas spillovers might take place in the context of domestic trade, the CITES Secretariat itself, in the above-mentioned statement, recognised that the regulation of wildlife trade at domestic level 'will also contribute to the effective implementation and enforcement of the Convention and the conservation of CITES-listed species'. At any rate, after its rather timid initial stance, the CITES Secretariat appears to have engaged more closely with the causes and effects of the pandemic, starting by contributing to a workshop report by the Intergovernmental Platform on Biodiversity and Ecosystem Services (IPBES) on biodiversity and pandemics.[51]

In light of the link between uncontrolled or unsustainable wildlife trade and the exacerbation of the risk of zoonotic epidemics, the reinforced monitoring and implementation of CITES obligations concerning the international trade of endangered species would contribute to the minimisation of zoonotic spillovers, together with a more coherent regulation of the breeding of at-risk animal species in captivity for commercial purposes.[52] The explicit expansion of the CITES mandate to regulate the trade of species that are not endangered but are at high risk of transmitting diseases to humans has also been proposed by some commentators; however, the issue is still debated among experts,[53] whereas the relevant intergovernmental debate does not appear to have even started. Undoubtedly, further steps are required for CITES to take the lead in the prevention of zoonotic epidemics. Meanwhile, the effective monitoring and implementation of existing CITES obligations – especially regarding

51 IPBES, *IPBES Workshop on Biodiversity and Pandemics – Workshop Report* (IPBES 2020).

52 As recognised by the CITES system and crudely shown by the culling of millions of farmed minks in Denmark and the Netherlands after a mutated form of COVID-19 was found in animals and farmers: C Lesté-Lasserre, 'Mutant coronaviruses found in mink spark massive culls and doom a Danish group's research' (*ScienceMag.org*, 11 November 2020) <https://www.sciencemag.org/news/2020/11/mutant-coronaviruses-found-mink-spark-massive-culls-and-doom-danish-group-s-research>.

53 See, among others, the following opinions published on the Scientific American website (<scientificamerican.com>): S Lieberman, 'CITES, the Treaty that Regulates Trade in International Wildlife, Is Not the Answer to Preventing Another Zoonotic Pandemic' (22 May 2020); D Ashe and JE Scanlon, 'A Crucial Step Toward Preventing Wildlife-Related Pandemics' (15 June 2020); BJ Weissgold and others, 'How We Can Use the CITES Wildlife Trade Agreement to Help Prevent Pandemics' (24 August 2020).

species known to host potentially zoonotic pathogens, or high-risk places such as wet markets or wildlife farms – would still greatly contribute to reducing the risk of spillovers.

In closing, mention should also be made of the fact that the conservation, sustainable management, and restoration of forests play a considerable role in ensuring healthy ecosystems, forests being some of the richest areas in terms of biodiversity. Accordingly, commitments undertaken by States in order to conserve these biomes also contribute to the prevention of epidemics[54] and should be considered in this light. Indeed, even though no dedicated treaty exists, forests fall within the purview of various conventions (such as the CBD)[55] and are the subject of an increasing number of soft-law instruments and programmes, such as REDD+, whereby developing countries receive funding for conserving and sustainably managing their forests.

The same applies to climate change instruments. As climate change increasingly contributes to the destruction of ecosystems, the realisation of climate change commitments by States is critical to the protection of biodiversity; at the same time, care should be taken to ensure that climate action does not conflict with, and adequately considers, biodiversity conservation. In this respect, whereas climate change adaptation planning in a growing number of countries is incorporating an ecosystem-based approach,[56] mitigation strategies still too often ignore biodiversity concerns (eg the production of biofuel has proved particularly problematic).[57] Further, climate change is going to have particularly direct effects on the survival and spread of climate-sensitive pathogens, vectors and hosts.[58]

---

54 On the links between deforestation (and mismanagement of forests) and zoonotic epidemics, S Morand and C Lajaunie, 'Outbreaks of Vector-Borne and Zoonotic Diseases Are Associated With Changes in Forest Cover and Oil Palm Expansion at Global Scale' (2021) 8 Frontiers in Veterinary Science.

55 For relevant COP decisions, workshops, reports, guidelines and partnerships, see CBD 'Forest Biodiversity' <https://www.cbd.int/forest/>. Regarding other international instruments on forests, see Sands and Peel (n 1) 428–431.

56 This is especially the case for developing countries, which, however, frequently lack the resources to fully implement such nature-based solutions; also, national adaptation plans submitted in the UNFCCC context often omit quantifiable targets: see CBD SBSTTA, 'Biodiversity and Climate Change. Note by the Executive Secretary' (19 August 2019) CBD/SBSTTA/23/3, para 52.

57 On the negative impact of biofuel production and use on biodiversity, CBD COP, Decision X/37 (29 October 2010) UNEP/CBD/COP/DEC/X/37; in the literature, LM Verdade, CI Piña and LM Rosalino, 'Biofuels and biodiversity: Challenges and opportunities' (2015) 15 Environmental Development.

58 UNEP and ILRI, *Preventing the Next Pandemic: Zoonotic Diseases and How to Break the Chain of Transmission* (UNEP 2020) 17, and the literature mentioned there.

One Health and EcoHealth[59] approaches would appear particularly suitable to incorporate all of these cross-sectoral interactions and – it is posited here – to offer a lens through which to consider the obligations incumbent on States in these interrelated areas with a view to effectively preventing and preparing for zoonotic epidemics. Much remains to be done in this respect, however, especially at the domestic level, where genuinely integrated national implementation plans are lagging behind.[60]

4 CBRN Events and Climate Change

Climate change is not only relevant to CBRN events inasmuch as, by threatening biodiversity or otherwise impacting on pathogens, it heightens the risk of zoonotic epidemics. The thawing of permafrost caused by climate change is believed to have contributed to the release of 20,000 tonnes of oil in the Siberian tundra in May 2020, after the collapse of a fuel tank whose maintenance likely did not sufficiently consider the increasingly yielding nature of the soil. On the other side of the Pacific Ocean, the US Department of Defense has increasingly engaged with the potential impacts of climate change on US military operations, equipment and facilities.[61] In the latter respect,

59 EcoHealth approaches investigate the interconnectedness of human health and ecosystems health by focusing on environmental and socioeconomic issues: J Lebel, *Health: An Ecosystem Approach* (International Development Research Centre 2003). On similarities and differences between One Health and EcoHealth (and Planetary Health), H Lerner and C Berg, 'A Comparison of Three Holistic Approaches to Health: One Health, EcoHealth, and Planetary Health' (2017) 4 Frontiers in Veterinary Science.

60 According to WHO and CBD Secretariat, 'Background paper for the Regional capacity-building workshop on Biodiversity and Health for the WHO European region' (2017), '[i]nternal analyses [...] have shown that the integration of biodiversity and health linkages is generally poorly reflected in national action plans' to implement the CBD domestically.

61 The interest demonstrated by the US Department of Defense can be traced back at least to 2010, when its 'Quadrennial Defense Review Report' identified climate change as a priority issue. In the following years, the Department has remained seized of the matter; among the most recent initiatives are a memorandum and a handbook to assist the US military in adapting their installations to the impacts of climate change: Secretary of the Army, 'Army Directive 2020–08 (U.S. Army Installation Policy to Address Threats Caused by Changing Climate and Extreme Weather)' (11 September 2020); and AO Pinson and others, *Army Climate Resilience Handbook* (US Army Corps of Engineers 2020). See also MT Klare, *All Hell Breaking Loose: The Pentagon's Perspective on Climate Change* (Metropolitan Books, 2019). In Europe, too, increasing attention is devoted to the impacts of climate change on defence and security: EEAS, 'Climate Change and Defence Roadmap' (9 November 2020) EEAS(2020)1251.

climate change is directly threatening several critical military installations on US soil: from the hurricane that ravaged Tyndall Air Force Base (Florida) in October 2018 to the wildfire that threatened the Vandenberg Air Force Base (California) a couple of years earlier, and the repeated flooding of the Norfolk Naval Station and various other facilities.[62] The risk of CBRN events occurring as a result of damage to military installations – which not infrequently store chemical and even nuclear substances – is tangible and bound to rise with the acceleration of climate change.

The heightened risk of CBRN incidents as a consequence of climate change is, in turn, fuelled by CBRN-related activities, which increase the concentration of greenhouse gases (GHGs) in the atmosphere and thus exacerbate climate change. This especially applies to the chemical sector, which is responsible for 7% of global GHG emissions and 20% of industrial GHG emissions;[63] whereas nuclear energy is considered relatively 'green', even though assessments vary as to its actual carbon footprint over the whole fuel cycle.[64]

This state of affairs, first of all, requires that States undertake appropriate mitigation action, *ie* that they pursue emission reductions to avoid excessive global warming, including by regulating CBRN activities. According to the most recent binding instrument on climate change, the Paris Agreement, parties must '[hold] the increase in the global average temperature to well below 2°C above pre-industrial levels and [pursue] efforts to limit the temperature increase to 1.5°C above pre-industrial levels' (Article 2(1)(a)). To attain this objective, parties are required to draft ambitious national plans to cut emissions (so-called nationally determined contributions; Article 4).

However, as climate change is already taking place and its effects will increasingly be felt, States are also required to *adapt* to climate change, namely, to address those impacts that are occurring and will occur notwithstanding mitigation efforts. In relation to States' adaptation actions, the prevention of and preparedness for CBRN incidents appear particularly relevant. In drawing up their national adaptation plans (Article 7), States should duly assess and prepare for CBRN risks that might materialise as a consequence of climate change, eg the release of CBRN substances following damage to facilities, changes in soil composition, or chemical and physical alterations of watercourses and water basins.

62 Union of Concerned Scientists, 'The US Military on the Front Lines of Rising Seas', 27 July 2016 <https://www.ucsusa.org/resources/us-military-front-lines-rising-seas>.

63 IEA, ICCA and DECHEMA, *Technology Roadmap: Energy and GHG Reductions in the Chemical Industry via Catalytic Processes* (IEA Publications 2013) 6.

64 BK Sovacool, 'Valuing the greenhouse gas emissions from nuclear power: A critical survey' (2008) 36 Energy Policy.

In relation to those impacts that will not be avoided through either mitigation or adaptation – so-called loss and damage (Article 8) – parties are asked to cooperate and facilitate understanding, action and support in areas such as early warning, emergency preparedness, risk assessment and management, and insurance solutions (Article 8(3)–(4)). It is submitted here that loss and damage should be interpreted as including climate-induced CBRN events, so that preparedness for and response to the latter can be usefully included in the cooperation and information-sharing activities that are to take place in the above-mentioned areas.

While private actors are not the direct addressees of obligations under the international climate change regime,[65] they are subject to the limitations adopted by States to curb their overall emissions; additionally, an increasing number of corporations are voluntarily adhering to stringent climate targets with a view to helping meet the temperature goal of the Paris Agreement. Private entities are further expected to play a significant role in climate finance, as well as technology development and transfer.

Symmetrically to the involvement in climate change mitigation efforts of public and private entities carrying out CBRN activities and to the mainstreaming in States' adaptation actions of the prevention of, preparedness for and response to CBRN events, international norms addressing CBRN hazards should be interpreted in light of the growing threat represented by climate change. Accordingly, environmental impact assessments (EIAS) could be usefully employed to evaluate the impact that CBRN-related projects might have on climate change, eg through direct GHG emissions, deforestation, alteration of surrounding soil or waters; as well as to consider the potential impact of climate change on projects, by assessing the vulnerability of projects to climate variables and thus allowing the adoption of the necessary measures to prevent, or at least minimise, CBRN events.[66] While the latter function might appear peculiar for EIAS, which are normally concerned with the impact of activities on the environment and not vice versa, the need for incorporating climate change in EIAS in both ways is increasingly recognised in national and

65 But, on 26 May 2021, the District Court of The Hague ordered Shell to cut its emissions by 45% by 2030, relative to 2019, by interpreting the corporation's duty of care in light of the temperature goals of the Paris Agreement: *Milieudefensie et al v Royal Dutch Shell Plc*, ECLI:NL:RBDHA:2021:5337.

66 CW Christopher, 'Success by a Thousand Cuts: The Use of Environmental Impact Assessment in Addressing Climate Change' (2008) 9 Vermont Journal of Environmental Law; S Agrawala and others, *Incorporating Climate Change Impacts and Adaptation in Environmental Impact Assessments: Opportunities and Challenges* (OECD Publishing 2010).

supranational guidelines.[67] The fact remains that these instruments mostly do not specifically deal with CBRN-related activities and risks.

Furthermore, in the context of the preparedness phase of CBRN management, contingency plans drawn up by States and private operators should adequately take into account climate-induced CBRN risks. Finally, climate change is bound to have an impact on the response to CBRN emergencies as well, insofar as it is likely to cause an increase in certain kinds of incidents (eg epidemic outbreaks), as well as affecting the environmental conditions in which the emergency teams operate (eg extreme heat can compromise equipment, droughts can endanger water supplies).

Whereas the nexus between climate change and CBRN activities and events is not often considered, as such, in international legal instruments, it remains the case that obligations in this domain can be derived from both the international climate change regime and IEL and non-IEL norms that specifically address CBRN threats, which should be read in a mutually supportive way and rely on the synergies of the relevant actors from both areas.

5 Conclusions

CBRN activities, substances and events sit at the crossroads of multiple IEL regimes, thus raising several issues in terms of gaps and overlaps. Setting aside any assessment of the feasibility and appropriateness of a Global Pact for the Environment, this chapter has shown that the prevention of, preparedness for, response to and recovery from CBRN events would benefit from greater coordination in the interpretation and application of the relevant norms, both within IEL and at the intersection of IEL and other branches of international law, as well as from enhanced synergies between the competent actors.

Two phenomena have been examined more in depth that provide the litmus test for such an appraisal: zoonotic epidemics and climate change. The COVID-19 pandemic has provided incontrovertible proof of the dangers for human health that lie in the increasing destruction of ecosystems and,

67 See the compilations made available by the Sabin Center for Climate Change Law, respectively at <https://climate.law.columbia.edu/content/eia-guidelines-assessing-impact-project-climate-change> and <https://climate.law.columbia.edu/content/eia-guidelines-assessing-impact-climate-change-project>. At the supranational level, the EIA Directive – which specifically refers to the incorporation of climate change considerations in EIAs – is particularly significant; see also European Commission, *Guidance on Integrating Climate Change and Biodiversity into Environmental Impact Assessment* (EU 2013).

correspondingly, of the importance of legal instruments that protect biodiversity and of the conceptual and practical need for holistic solutions. On this basis, new approaches have been developed – such as the One Health approach, which, however, has yet to be put to full use.

Climate change is another primary example of the close interrelations between CBRN activities and events and the protection of the environment: CBRN activities exacerbate climate change, while simultaneously being threatened by its manifestations. However, to date, the international climate change regime and the regulation of CBRN emergencies appear to have mainly travelled on separate tracks. Therefore, ongoing discussions within climate fora would benefit from attentive consideration of CBRN hazards, while well-established procedures to avoid, minimise or respond to CBRN events (such as EIAs, contingency plans, emergency assistance) risk becoming fundamentally inadequate if they do not factor in the impacts of climate change.

The CBRN emergency management cycle thus heavily relies for its effectiveness on the harmonious interaction between norms from different IEL regimes and between IEL and non-IEL norms, as well as on the coordinated work of several actors. CBRN, as an inherently cross-cutting area, would therefore undoubtedly benefit from a certain systemisation of the IEL patchwork and could, indeed, offer a valuable perspective – if not an ordering criterion – within such a process.

Bibliography

Agrawala S and others, *Incorporating Climate Change Impacts and Adaptation in Environmental Impact Assessments: Opportunities and Challenges* (OECD Publishing 2010).

Altizer S, Bartel R and Han BA, 'Animal Migration and Infectious Disease Risk' (2011) 331 Science 296.

Ashe D and Scanlon JE, 'A Crucial Step Toward Preventing Wildlife-Related Pandemics' (*Scientific American*, 15 June 2020).

Beyerlin U, 'Different Types of Norms in International Environmental Law Policies, Principles, and Rules' in Bodansky D, Brunnée J and Hey E (eds), *The Oxford Handbook of International Environmental Law* (OUP 2012) 426.

Broad S, *Wildlife Trade, COVID-19, and Zoonotic Disease Risks* (TRAFFIC 2020).

Brown Weiss E, 'International Environmental Law: Contemporary Issues and the Emergence of a New World Order' (1993) 81 GeoLJ 675.

Brunnée J, 'Of Sense and Sensibility: Reflections on International Liability Regimes as Tools for Environmental Protection' (2004) 53 ICLQ 351.

Challender D and others, 'Coronavirus: why a blanket ban on wildlife trade would not be the right response' (*The Conversation*, 8 April 2020).

Christopher CW, 'Success by a Thousand Cuts: The Use of Environmental Impact Assessment in Addressing Climate Change' (2008) 9 Vermont Journal of Environmental Law 549.

de Sadeleer N, *Environmental Principles: From Political Slogans to Legal Rules* (OUP 2002).

European Commission, *Guidance on Integrating Climate Change and Biodiversity into Environmental Impact Assessment* (EU 2013).

Everard M and others, 'The role of ecosystems in mitigation and management of Covid-19 and other zoonoses' (2020) 111 Environmental Science and Policy 7.

Fitzmaurice M, 'International Responsibility and Liability' in Bodansky D, Brunnée J and Hey E (eds), *The Oxford Handbook of International Environmental Law* (OUP 2012) 1011.

Foss Hansen S, Carlsen L and Tickner JA, 'Chemicals regulation and precaution: does REACH really incorporate the precautionary principle' (2007) 10 Environmental Science and Policy 395.

Freestone D and Hey E (eds), *The Precautionary Principle and International Law: The Challenge of Implementation* (Kluwer Law International 1996).

Gehring T, 'Treaty-Making and Treaty Evolution' in Bodansky D, Brunnée J and Hey E (eds), *The Oxford Handbook of International Environmental Law* (OUP 2012) 469.

Horwitz P, Finlayson CM and Weinstein P, *Healthy wetlands, healthy people: A review of wetlands and human health interactions* (Secretariat of the Ramsar Convention on Wetlands and WHO 2012).

IEA, ICCA and DECHEMA, *Technology Roadmap: Energy and GHG Reductions in the Chemical Industry via Catalytic Processes* (IEA Publications 2013).

IPBES, *IPBES Workshop on Biodiversity and Pandemics – Workshop Report* (IPBES 2020).

Jones KE and others, 'Global trends in emerging infectious diseases' (2008) 451 Nature 990.

Karesh WB and others, 'Ecology of zoonoses: natural and unnatural histories' (2012) 380 Lancet 1936.

Keiper F and Atanassova A, 'Regulation of Synthetic Biology: Developments Under the Convention on Biological Diversity and Its Protocols' (2020) 8 Frontiers in Bioengineering and Biotechnology 310.

Kindji K and Faure M, 'Assessing reparation of environmental damage by the ICJ: A lost opportunity?' (2019) 57 QuestIntlL, Zoom-in 5.

Klare MT, *All Hell Breaking Loose: The Pentagon's Perspective on Climate Change* (Metropolitan Books, 2019).

Lebel J, *Health: An Ecosystem Approach* (International Development Research Centre 2003).

Lerner H and Berg C, 'A Comparison of Three Holistic Approaches to Health: One Health, EcoHealth, and Planetary Health' (2017) 4 Frontiers in Veterinary Science 163.

Lieberman S, 'CITES, the Treaty that Regulates Trade in International Wildlife, Is Not the Answer to Preventing Another Zoonotic Pandemic' (*Scientific American*, 22 May 2020).

Morand S and Lajaunie C, 'Outbreaks of Vector-Borne and Zoonotic Diseases Are Associated With Changes in Forest Cover and Oil Palm Expansion at Global Scale' (2021) 8 Frontiers in Veterinary Science 230.

Patz J and others, *Our Planet, Our Health, Our Future. Human health and the Rio Conventions: biological diversity, climate change and desertification* (WHO 2012).

Pinson AO and others, *Army Climate Resilience Handbook* (US Army Corps of Engineers 2020).

Plakokefalos I, 'Prevention Obligations in International Environmental Law' (2012) 23(1) YIntlEnvL 3.

Quammen D, *Spillover: Animal Infections and the Next Human Pandemic* (WW Norton 2013).

Reed KD and others, 'Birds, Migration and Emerging Zoonoses: West Nile Virus, Lyme Disease, Influenza A and Enteropathogens' (2003) 1(1) Clinical Medicine & Research 5.

Sands P and Peel J, *Principles of International Environmental Law* (4th edn, CUP 2018).

Sovacool BK, 'Valuing the greenhouse gas emissions from nuclear power: A critical survey' (2008) 36 Energy Policy 2950.

UNEP and ILRI, *Preventing the Next Pandemic: Zoonotic Diseases and How to Break the Chain of Transmission* (UNEP 2020).

Union of Concerned Scientists, 'The US Military on the Front Lines of Rising Seas', 27 July 2016.

Verdade LM, Piña CI and Rosalino LM, 'Biofuels and biodiversity: Challenges and opportunities' (2015) 15 Environmental Development 64.

Weissgold BJ and others, 'How We Can Use the CITES Wildlife Trade Agreement to Help Prevent Pandemics' (*Scientific American*, 24 August 2020).

CHAPTER 30

Private Corporations and CBRN Risk Management: An Overview from the Perspective of the UN Guiding Principles on Business and Human Rights

Elena Corcione

1 Introduction

Among CBRN actors,[1] private corporations are playing an increasing role, both because of their potential to be sources of CBRN risks and because of their ability to intervene once a CBRN event has occurred, since they can be 'drivers of disaster risk reduction and resilience building';[2] in other words, they play a twofold part, as both 'risk carriers and risk managers'.[3] Given the potential impact of industrial activities on human rights, States have a duty under international law to regulate the conduct of private corporations.[4] More recently, a growing corpus of international soft-law instruments has called directly on corporations to respect human rights when carrying out their activities, by preventing harmful effects and providing remedies when they occur.[5] Although

1 Ch 2 by Di Francesco Maesa.

2 UNDRR, ARISE Annual Report 2020, 13 April 2021.

3 A Telesetsky, 'Beyond voluntary Corporate Social Responsibility: Corporate Human Rights Obligations to Prevent Disasters and to Provide Temporary Emergency Relief' (2015) VandJTransnatlL, 1010; see also M Hesselman, L Lane, 'Disasters and non-state actors – human rights-based approaches' (2017) Disaster Prevention and Management, 526–539; T Miyaguchi, R Shaw, 'Corporate community interface in disaster management – a preliminary study of Mumbai, India' (2007) Risk Management, 209–222; T Izumi, R Shaw, *Disaster Management and Private Sectors: Challenges and Potentials* (Springer, 2016).

4 UNGA, 'State responsibilities to regulate and adjudicate corporate activities under the United Nations core human rights treaties: an overview of treaty body commentaries' (13 February 2007) UN Doc. A/HRC/4/35/Add.1; *ex multis* R McCorquodale, P Simons, 'Responsibility Beyond Borders: State Responsibility for Extraterritorial Violations by Corporations of International Human Rights Law' (2007) ModLRev, 598–625; D Augenstein, L Dziedzic, 'State Obligations to Regulate and Adjudicate Corporate Activities under the European Convention on Human Rights' (2017), EUI Working Papers 2017/15.

5 *ex multis*, A Clapham, *Human Rights Obligations of Non-state actors* (OUP, 2006); D Kinley, J Tadaki, 'From Talk to Walk: The Emergence of Human Rights Responsibilities for Corporations at International Law' (2004) VandJTransnatlL 931–1023; S Droubi, 'Transnational Corporations and International Human Rights Law' (2016) Notre Dame Journal

such provisions largely remain voluntary standards, the shift towards the acknowledgement of corporations' human rights obligations is endorsed by recent developments in domestic case law and national legislation calling for mandatory human rights due diligence (HRDD).[6] The question is of particular importance, considering that the adverse human rights impacts of hazardous business activities involve both workers and the general population and may harm the right to life (including situations that threaten life without necessarily resulting in loss of life), the right to health (including the right to the prevention of diseases) and the right to enjoy a life with dignity.[7] In relation to the collective rights of communities, the rights to a healthy environment, access to safe water, clean air, and adequate food can also be recalled.[8]

This notwithstanding, several documents focusing on disaster management look at corporations through the lens of corporate resilience and the disaster risk management in business policies follows accordingly, instead of fostering a human rights-based approach to disaster management.[9]

Drawing from the UN Guiding Principles on Business and Human Rights (UNGPs) and the OECD Guidelines for Multi-National Enterprises (OECD Guidelines), the aim of this chapter is to understand how private businesses operating in CBRN-relevant sectors should be regulated by States and how corporations should be involved in CBRN emergency management cycle through a human rights-based approach.[10] In order to draw a comparison

---

of International and Comparative Law, 119–144; C Bright et al, 'Toward a corporate duty to respect human rights in their global value chains?' (2020) Business and Politics, 667–697.

6 See the first landmark case brought by Nigerian farmers against Shell on the responsibility of a parent company to respect human rights and the environment in relation to oil spills, delivered on 29 January 2021 by the Court of Appeal in The Hague, *Four Nigerian Farmers and Milieudefensie v. Shell*. For a resumé of the judgment, see L Roorda, 'Wading through the (polluted) mud: the Hague Court of Appeals rules on Shell in Nigeria' available at <www.rightasusual.com> (all web links were last accessed on February 2021); for an assessment of developments in domestic laws, see European Coalition for Corporate Justice, 'Evidence for mandatory Human Rights and Environmental Due Diligence legislation' (January 2021), available at <https://corporatejustice.org>.

7 UNGA, Report of the Special Rapporteur on the implications for human rights of the environmentally sound management and disposal of hazardous substances and wastes (7 October 2019) UN Doc. A/74/480, para 8; HRC, General Comment no. 36 (2018) on article 6 of the International Covenant on Civil and Political Rights, on the right to life, (30 October 2018) UN Doc CCPR/C/GC/36, para 3.

8 UNGA (n 7), para 2.

9 UNDRR, Reducing Risk and building resilience of SMEs (2020).

10 For an overview of obligations related to prevention and preparedness in relation to industrial accidents, see ch 11 by Creta and ch 12 by Domaine. The SFDRR calls for shared responsibility between governments and stakeholders, through an all-of-society partnership, articulating responsibilities across public and private actors including

between the obligations stemming from business and human rights instruments and those of the risk management cycle, Section 3 will recall the obligations of States to regulate the activity of businesses (3.1), especially in the CBRN sector (3.2), while Section 4 will be devoted to businesses' responsibility to respect human rights in the CBRN context, addressing prevention, preparedness (4.1), response and recovery (4.2) obligations in the light of business and human rights instruments.

The tentative outcome of this analysis is that the business and human rights approach (BHRA) may contribute to understanding, and to fill with specific meaning, the obligations pertaining to each phase of the disaster risk management cycle in relation to CBRN events linked to industrial activities, by engaging corporations in prevention, preparedness and response as a consequence of their duty to respect human rights.

Before getting into the specific obligations of States and businesses, it is, therefore, worthwhile to trace a perimeter of the main industry sectors involved and the main human rights potentially impacted by CBRN events.

2 Defining the Scope of the Analysis: Broadening the Labels of CBRN 'Actors' and 'Events'

CBRN agents are currently used in a number of business sectors and the private sector is involved in different phases of the CBRN risk management cycle; as a consequence, business enterprises are necessarily included in the definition of 'CBRN actors'. This is indirectly confirmed, *inter alia*, by explicit references to the private business sector made in the Sendai Framework for Disaster Risk Reduction (SFDRR). Even though the Sendai document does not explicitly make reference to CBRN events, it calls for businesses to integrate disaster risk into their management practices. Furthermore, in order to facilitate the implementation of the SFDRR at the national and local levels,

businesses. UN Third World Conference on Disaster Risk Reduction, 'Sendai Framework for Disaster Risk Reduction 2015–2030' UN Doc. A/CONF.224/L.2, General Principles, 19 (b), (d), (e). On the interplay between Human Rights Law and Disaster Risk Reduction, see A Telesetsky, (n 2); E Sommario, S Venier 'Human Rights Law and Disaster risk reduction' (2018) QIL, Zoom-in, 29–47; C Shucksmith, 'Methods to Incorporate Human Rights Law into Disaster Prevention and Reduction Strategies', *EJIL:Talk*! (28 February 2017); M Hesselman, L Lane (n 2), 528 ff; F Zorzi Giustiniani, E Sommario, F Casolari, G Bartolini (eds), *Routledge Handbook of Human Rights and Disasters* (Routledge, 2018).

the Private Sector Alliance for Disaster Resilient Societies was created under the auspices of the UNDRR in 2015.[11]

This notwithstanding, the question is not only to be seen through the prism of disasters due to sudden and exceptional events, involving mass death or devastation. In addition to these disasters – such as the explosion of a chemical plant in India and the subsequent exposure of the population to toxic substances; radiation exposure from nuclear power plants in Japan; and the collapse of a dam in Brazil releasing tons of toxic chemicals into the water supply – CBRN agents are silently used in everyday practice, causing large-scale impacts on human rights in the long-term. Indeed, according to the Special Rapporteur on the implications for human rights of the environmentally sound management and disposal of hazardous substances and wastes, 'one worker dies every minute from exposure to hazardous substances'.[12] In this sense, the potential human rights harm related to CBRN substances used by certain business has been defined as a 'silent pandemic', given its widespread harmful effects on the population.[13] In this context, 'hazardous substances' are understood to 'include, *inter alia*, toxic industrial chemicals and pesticides, pollutants, contaminants, explosive and radioactive substances, certain food additives and various forms of waste', as well as 'non-toxic but hazardous substances'.[14] Such a broad definition allows for the inclusion of all CBRN agents and enterprises using such agents.

Consistently, following an all-hazards approach, a 'CBRN event' can be described as the spread of CBRN substances intentionally, accidentally or due to natural phenomena, including the release of CBRN agents following industrial accidents, natural disasters and calamities, or the improper disposal of toxic waste.[15] However, when it comes to man-made hazards related to industrial activities, the spread of CBRN substances may not be limited to 'accidents' or 'disasters'. A broader definition of CBRN event is necessary to include cases of release of hazardous agents either voluntary or as an avoidable consequence of negligent conduct. This broader concept of CBRN event seems to be implicitly endorsed in the Sendai Framework, which applies to 'small-scale

11 SFDRR, para 7; ARISE <ariseglobalnetwork.org>. See also UNISDR, 'Creating Shared Value: the Business Case for Disaster Risk Reduction' (GAR 2013).

12 UNGA, Report of the Special Rapporteur on the implications for human rights of the environmentally sound management and disposal of hazardous substances and wastes (5 August 2020) UN Doc. A/75/290, para 59.

13 UNGA (n 7).

14 Ibid, para 6 note 1.

15 Ch 1 by Frulli.

and large-scale, frequent and infrequent, sudden and slow-onset' disasters, whether caused by natural or man-made events.[16]

So interpreted, the list of industry sectors potentially contributing to human rights violations through the use or release of CBRN agents is exceptionally wide. The following is a brief overview of the main sectors involved.

The chemical industry is obviously a crucial sector in the realm of CBRN-related business and possibly the one to which international instruments have mostly devoted their attention. The Special Rapporteur has called several times on the chemical industry to abide by its obligations to undertake proper human rights due diligence to prevent harmful consequences on human rights.[17] Similarly, much attention has been paid to the nuclear sector, since the intrinsic nature of activity in nuclear plants makes it automatically a high-risk industry sector, especially when it comes to radiation exposure and radioactive decontamination activity.[18]

The release of hazardous chemicals is also a major human rights issue in the garment and textile industry, as a by-product of the production process, due to the release into the environment of toxins as production waste.[19] Lastly, the agri-business sector is an overly underestimated field as a source of CBRN risks deriving from corporate conduct, but it deserves special attention for its growing consequences in terms of adverse human rights impacts. Indeed, besides agrochemicals production, the massive use of pesticides and fertilizers in agriculture entails both a biological and chemical risk, since pesticides have been defined as 'any substance or mixture of substances of chemical and biological ingredients intended to repel, destroy or control any pest or regulate plant growth'.[20] Cases of poisoning from exposure to pesticides and fertilizers have multiplied in recent years;[21] the issue is particularly important in light of the accountability of the whole supply chain for human rights violations, given the reported systematic export and use of banned pesticides

16 SFDRR, para 15.

17 UNGA (n 12), paras 63–64.

18 Ibid, para 79.

19 See references of sector risks in OECD, Due Diligence Guidance for Responsible Supply Chains in the Garment and Footwear sector (2017).

20 FAO-WHO, International Code of Conduct on Pesticide Management: Guidelines on Highly Hazardous Pesticides (2016), according to which 'Pesticide means any substance, or mixture of substances of chemical or biological ingredients intended for repelling, destroying or controlling any pest, or regulating plant growth'.

21 Including a communication 2751/2016 ended in the adoption of view from the Committee under Article 5(4) of the Optional Protocol versus Paraguay on exposure of campesinos to agrochemicals dispersed by extensive cultivation of genetically modified soybeans (20 September 2019) UN Doc. CCPR/C/126/D/2751/2016.

in developing countries.[22] Intensive agriculture entails the use of pesticides and chemical agents that are likely to cause adverse effects on human rights, including permanent damage to human health and the environment.[23] Both the enterprises producing pesticides and those using pesticides, may be responsible for adverse human rights effects connected to such agents, although the nature and extent of the responsibilities will be different at different phases: the responsibility of the chemical industry producing pesticides will mostly be connected to the safety of workers in handling toxic substances during the production process. In this sense, doubts have been raised as to the possibility of ever producing such toxic substances safely.[24] Furthermore, recent pandemic events shed a light on the biological risks related to intensive livestock farming and the trade in wildlife for consumption, where spill-over of biological agents, such as viruses and bacteria, can easily happen, increasing the risk of zoonotic diseases and anti-microbial resistance.[25]

The foregoing list shows how a wide range of businesses may be included in the definition of 'CBRN actor', whether the CBRN-related risks directly stem from the company's operations or are rather linked to its value chain.

3 States' Positive Obligations to Regulate Private Actors and Their Application to CBRN Business Activities

Negotiations to draft an international agreement imposing explicit obligations on States to prevent and control harmful effects of business activities on human rights are still underway. The Working Group on the issue of human rights and transnational corporations, established by the Human Rights Council in 2011, is currently working on a third draft of a Legally Binding Instrument to Regulate, in International Human Rights Law, the activities of Transnational Corporations and other Business Enterprises.[26] In the words of the current

22 UNGA (n 12), para 68.

23 It is estimated that pesticides cause 200,000 acute poisoning death each year, the vast majority of which in developing countries, not to include chronic diseases and long-term effects on human health not resulting into death, UNGA, Report of the Special Rapporteur on the Right to Food (24 January 2017) UN Doc. A/HRC/34/48.

24 C Terwindt et al, 'Health Rights Impacts by Agrochemical Business: Legally Challenging the "Myth of Safe Use"' (2018) Utrecht Journal of International and European Law, 130–145.

25 For a recent assessment of anthropogenic causes of zoonotic diseases, see UNEP, Preventing the next pandemic: zoonotic diseases and how to break the chain of transmission (2020), 15.

26 OEIGWG Chairmanship third revised draft, 17 August 2021.

draft of the treaty, its purpose is to 'clarify and facilitate effective implementation of the obligation of State to respect, protect and promote human rights in the context of business activities' (Article 2(1)a), thus confirming that such obligations already exist in the realm of international human rights law and the treaty merely reinforces and fosters existing obligations.

Indeed, even pending the ratification of a legally binding instrument, it is already accepted that States have the positive obligation to protect individuals and communities from human rights violations due to industrial activities.[27] Such obligations derive implicitly from the international human rights framework[28] and, *inter alia*, from the European Convention on Human Rights (ECHR), the International Covenant on Civil and Political Rights (ICCPR) and the International Covenant on Economic, Social and Cultural Rights (ICESCR), which have been interpreted as including positive obligations to regulate the conduct of private actors.[29] This is supported by the European Court of Human Rights (ECtHR) in its case law and the recommendations of the Committee of Ministers,[30] as well as by the General Comments of the treaty bodies, such as General Comment no. 24 on State obligations under the International Covenant on Economic, Social and Cultural Rights in the context of business activities.[31]

In the following two paragraphs, States' positive obligations to regulate business activities will be reviewed from the point of view of business and human rights instruments, primarily the UNGPS, devoting particular attention to the application of such standards in the context of CBRN-related business activities.

27 On States' positive obligations see ch 27 by Venier.

28 UNGA (n 7), para 6.

29 While the present analysis focuses on ECHR, ICCPR and ICESCR, as the main references where States' positive obligations in relation to business conduct have been defined, it is nonetheless worth recalling relevant case law from other regional systems of human rights protection, such as the Inter-American Court of Human Rights, *Advisory opinion on the environment and human rights*, OC-23/17, 15 November 2017 and the African Commission on Human and Peoples' Rights, Social and Economic Rights Center (*SERAC*) *et al v. Nigeria, Communication* 155/96, 27 October 2001.

30 Recommendation of the Council of Europe's Committee of Ministers to Member States on Human Rights and Business (2 March 2016), CM/Rec(2016)3.

31 UNCESCR, General Comment no. 24 (2017) on State obligations under the International Covenant on Economic, Social and Cultural Rights in the context of business activities, (10 August 2017), UN Doc. E/C.12/GC/24.

3.1 *States' Obligations* vis-à-vis *Private Corporations under Business and Human Rights Instruments*

Besides negative obligations,[32] international human rights law provides that States have positive obligations to regulate the activity of private enterprises under their jurisdiction.[33] The relevant concept through which the State addresses its positive obligations in international law to protect individuals from human right violations by other private actors is that of due diligence. This concept implies that States have substantial obligations to provide for a coherent legislative and administrative framework, adopting all appropriate measures to effectively protect human rights from hazardous business activities, together with the procedural obligations to provide effective remedies to victims when such violations occur.[34]

The duty of States to regulate the activity of businesses has been particularly recognised in the case law of the ECtHR, where several cases have dealt with hazardous industrial business activities, involving substances that falls into the definition of 'CBRN agents'.[35] Generally, the obligations of

32 Ch 28 by Sommario.

33 The existence of a positive obligation to regulate the conduct of business extraterritorially is currently still under discussion. The question has been addressed by UNCESCR (n 31); ICJ, Maastricht Principles on Extraterritorial Obligations of States in the Area of Economic, Social and Cultural Rights (2011); and O De Schutter et al, 'Commentary to the Maastricht Principles on Extraterritorial Obligations of States in the Area of Economic, Social and Cultural Rights' (2012) HumRtsQ 34, 1134 ff.

34 On the concept of due diligence, *ex multis*, J Kulesza, *Due Diligence in International Law* (Brill, 2016). While there is no need to turn to the 'due diligence' concept in case of negative obligations, where the violation of human rights is the result of an interference or excessive interference in the enjoyment of human rights, J Bonnitcha, R McCorquodale, 'The concept of "Due Diligence" in the UN Guiding Principles on Business and Human Rights' (2017) EJIL 905.

35 See, *ex multis*, *Fadeyeva v Russia*, app no 55723/00 (ECHR, 9 June 2005) where the Court found a violation by the State for not taking adequate steps to regulate the activity of a steel plant whose levels of pollution caused severe health issues to the applicants; *Tatar v Romania*, app no 67021/01 (ECHR, 27 January 2009) where the Court dealt with the spill of chemical agent from a goldmine operated by a corporation and the consequent pollution of rivers, finding a violation of Article 8 in that no sufficient risk assessment of the corporate activity was carried out and no appropriate measures were taken by public authorities in violation of the precautionary principle; *Öneryildiz v Turkey*, app no 48939/99 (ECHR, 30 November 2004) the Court clarified that corporate activities related to the use of hazardous substances entail an intrinsic risk that must be faced accordingly by putting in place all the relevant specific regulations to control the activity in question. In particular the release of licences, and the setting up, operation, security and supervision of the activity must be controlled by State authorities. Furthermore, providing the potentially affected community with appropriate information on the risks is of

the State towards such activities have been summarised as follows: (a) regulating and controlling corporate activity through the release and control of licences and permissions, supervision of dangerous activities, and provision of proper information to the general public; (b) ensuring informed decision-making processes and public investigations, and imposing environmental impact assessment obligations; (c) making available effective remedies, including ensuring access to justice for the victims.[36]

More specifically, the obligation to adequately regulate the activities of businesses to prevent human rights abuses consists not only in imposing criminal or administrative sanctions and providing other deterrent or incentive methods, but also in 'a positive duty to adopt a legal framework requiring business entities to exercise human rights due diligence in order to identify, prevent and mitigate the risk of violations of [UN] Covenants rights, to avoid such rights being abused and to account for the negative impacts caused or contributed to by their decisions and operations and those of entities they control on the enjoyment of Covenants rights'.[37]

The findings of the UN treaty bodies and the ECtHR reflect the provisions contained in soft-law instruments that directly call upon States to regulate the activities of businesses. The UNGPs are 'the first global standard for preventing and addressing the risk of adverse impacts on human rights linked to business activity'[38] and they still remain the key reference in the international framework as far as the duties of corporations are concerned. The first pillar entails the State duty to protect against human rights abuses and provides for both foundational principles (Part A, Principles 1–2) and operational principles (Part B, Principles 3–10). The standard of conduct requires States to take appropriate steps 'to prevent, investigate, punish and redress human rights abuses' perpetrated by business enterprises 'through effective policies, legislation, regulations and adjudication' (Principle 1). The range of preventative measures to be implemented is discretionary, but the UNGPs suggest adopting a 'smart mix of measures' to foster human rights compliance by business enterprises (Principle 3, commentary). Lastly, the third pillar of the UNGPs adds important obligations upon States as regards access to remedy, requiring States to ensure that effective remedies are accessible when corporate abuses occur within their territory or jurisdiction (Principle 25). In addition, the OECD Guidelines

importance. More recently, see also the case *Cordella and others v. Italy*, app no 54414/13 et al (ECHR 24 January 2019) related to ILVA steel plant.

36 D Augenstein, L Dziedzic (n 4), 13.

37 UNCESCR (n 31), para 16.

38 UNGPs interpretative guide, 2012, 2.

bind States to create a non-judicial, State-based complaints mechanism via National Contact Points, thus further implementing the UNGPs (Principle 27).

The abovementioned standards in terms of prevention, mitigation and access to remedy are further set forth in the current draft of the Legally Binding Instrument to Regulate, in International Human Rights Law, the activities of Transnational Corporations and other Business Enterprises.[39]

The foregoing framework takes on a particular meaning when applied to CBRN-related enterprises, as will be shown in the next subsection looking deeper into this context.

3.2 *Regulating Private Corporations in a CBRN-Risk Context*

First of all, it is worth noting that CBRN-related businesses are often operating in strategic sectors of national importance, such as extractive or energy sectors, and thus are often fully or partially owned or controlled by the State.[40] In these cases, questions can be raised whether the violation is directly attributable to the State, calling negative obligations into play and requiring additional steps by the State to protect human rights.[41]

Apart from the particular case of State-owned enterprises (where the State may be directly responsible), the Special Rapporteur on hazardous substances and wastes has provided recommendations on how to shape States' positive obligations in the CBRN context. As for the prevention phase, he reiterated that the human rights obligations of States are met only if they compel business and other private actors to 'transition to cleaner, safer, healthier and more sustainable chemical production, use and disposal'.[42] Furthermore, he added that

39 At the time of writing, the third draft of the text provides for prevention obligations under Article 6, requiring States to regulate effectively the activities of business enterprises domiciled within their territory or jurisdiction in order to ensure their respect of internationally recognised human rights (art 6.1). In this sense, States shall require business enterprises to undertake human rights due diligence and, to this end, proceed with regular environmental and human rights impact assessments (arts 6.2 and 6.3). In addition, the draft treaty requires States to enable victims of corporate abuses to have access to adequate, timely and effective remedy and, to this end, to update their domestic laws accordingly with legal liability provisions (art 7 and art 8).

40 UNGA, 'Report of the Working Group on the issue of human rights and transnational corporations and other business enterprises' (4 May 2016) UN Doc. A/HRC/32/45, 13; L C Backer, 'The human rights obligations of State-Owned Enterprises (SOEs): emerging conceptual structures and principles in national and international law and policy' (2017) VandJTransnatlL, 827–888; M Barnes, 'The United Nations Guiding Principles on Business and Human Rights, the State Duty to Protect Human Rights and the State-Business Nexus' (2018) Reveista de Direito Internacional, 42.

41 UNGPs, Guiding Principle 4.

42 UNGA (n 12), para 60.

this obligation on States to compel should be imposed on businesses 'whether in their territory or abroad', thus strengthening the extraterritorial reach.

At the practical level, where the protection of public health is at risk, specific measures such as market restrictions may be required.[43] For example, the recent pandemic sheds light on biological risks related to intensive livestock farming and trade and consumption of wildlife. States may therefore bear the obligation to positively act and regulate business activities involved in wildlife trade as a necessary measure to protect public health. Preparedness obligations also emerge from the case law of the ECtHR, in relation to the set up and maintenance of functioning early-warning systems, as part of substantial obligations under Article 2,[44] as well as the duty to inform the population on actions to be taken in case of accidents, as part of obligations under Article 8.[45]

As for specific groups of rights-holders, workers employed in companies operating in CBRN sectors are particularly vulnerable and therefore deserve special attention. In 2019, the Human Rights Council adopted the 'Principles on human rights and protection of workers from exposure to toxic substances'.[46] The principles build on workers' rights and, especially, the right to safe and healthy working conditions (art 7 ICESCR) which implies the respect of interrelated rights (para 21). The document reiterates that States have the obligation 'to adopt measures to prevent occupational exposure to toxic substances', while also addressing 'threats emanating from private persons and entities' and 'taking preventive measures in respect of occupational accidents and diseases and the prevention and reduction of the population's exposure to harmful substances such as radiation and harmful chemicals' (para 29). Interestingly, the document also calls upon States to prevent exposure to toxic substances occurring outside their territory, where they are able to exercise control and reasonably foresee the potential harm of a business activity, thus reinforcing the extraterritorial reach of obligations to regulate CBRN business activity (para 44). Besides prevention measures, the Principles also specify preparedness obligations, by recognising the right to information and training for workers on the use and disposal of toxic substances. To this end, States also bear an obligation to 'generate, collect, assess and update information on hazards and risks encountered by workers as well as epidemiological and other evidence of occupational diseases and disabilities' (paras 55–57).

---

43 UNCESCR (n 31), para 19.

44 *Budayeva and others v. Russia*, App no 15339/02 et al (ECHR, 20 March 2008), para 155.

45 *Tatar v Romania*, App no 67021/01 (ECHR, 27 January 2009), para 124.

46 UNGA, Principles on human rights and the protection of workers from exposure to toxic substances (17 July 2019), UN Doc. A/HRC/42/41.

Furthermore, within the International Labour Organization (ILO), several specific conventions aim at protecting the health and safety of workers in the context of hazardous industrial activities; in particular, ILO Chemicals Convention, ILO Convention on Prevention of Major Industrial Accidents (no. 174), ILO Safety and Health in Mines Convention (no. 176), and ILO Safety and Health in Agriculture Convention (no. 184). All those instruments include the necessity to further protect the right to information of workers, which extends to the right to be informed and trained about the risks in the workplace.[47]

As for the response and remediation phase,[48] in the context of CBRN-related business activities, some remedies may additionally prove to be particularly effective as sanctions to deter further violations of human rights due diligence requirements by companies. In particular, revoking licences or revising public procurement contracts[49] can be used by the State as both reaction tool to and deterrent against the infringement of human rights by companies. Indeed, licenses are also relevant in the prevention phase, since granting exploitation permits without previously requesting the company to assess the potential adverse human rights impacts of its activity, where the business activity has the 'foreseeable effect' of harming human rights, is a clear violation of the Covenants.[50]

A separate issue that may involve the regulation of private corporations in a CBRN-risk context is where States have a duty to engage corporations that provide equipment, goods and support that the State cannot otherwise provide.[51] By way of example, in the event of a pandemic, the protection of public health may require States to engage private businesses and impose rules upon them in order to ensure the supply of medical treatment and the accessibility of life-saving medicines[52] or personal protective equipment. In relation to the Covid-19 pandemic, in a recent note, the OHCHR called for States to prioritise public health over private profits. This entails interpreting accordingly relevant provisions of Trade-Related Aspects of Intellectual Property Rights and preventing high costs of life-saving medicines and vaccines by providing

47 Ibid, para 55.

48 See ch 13 by Bakker and ch 34 by Capone.

49 UNCESCR (n 31), para 15.

50 Ibid, para 18.

51 Triggering the symmetric 'indirect' duty upon companies, see M Hesselman, L Lane (n 2), 531.

52 UNCESCR (n 31), para 24; according to UNGA, 'Report of the Special Rapporteur on the right of everyone to the enjoyment of the highest attainable standard of physical and mental health, Anand Grover, on access to medicines' (1 May 2013) UN Doc. A/HRC/23/42, para 3, access to medicines is an integral component of the right to health, as enunciated under Article 12 ICESCR.

support to research and production.[53] The use of private healthcare centres may also go in this direction.

In this sense, the engagement of the private sector through public-private partnership is crucial, as recognised in the SFDRR.[54]

4 Corporate Duty to Respect and Remedy the Adverse Impacts on Human Rights Deriving from CBRN Events

Although the responsibility to protect human rights primarily lies on States, it is nowadays established that enterprises must prevent human rights abuses deriving from their activity as well, independently from the will or the ability of the host State to enforce human rights protection.[55] The most important developments in this regard have been accomplished within the United Nations with the adoption of the UNGPs and a number of General Comments of the Human Rights Committees recommending standards of human rights protection for both States and companies, and within the OECD, through the OECD Guidelines directly calling on enterprises to undertake steps to prevent harmful consequences of their activities and to remedy such harms when they occur.

According to the definition provided in the UNGPs, corporations have a responsibility to respect human rights. This is the so-called 'second pillar' of the 'Protect, Respect and Remedy' Framework of the United Nations. The same obligation has been acknowledged in the OECD Guidelines, which provide that enterprises should 'avoid infringing on the human rights of others and should address adverse human rights impacts with which they are involved'.

Preliminarily, it is worth recalling that, currently, there are no obligations under international human rights law that are directly imposed on businesses, even though businesses are nonetheless called upon to commit to respect human rights. However, a different trend is emerging. Recently, a number of States have adopted national laws that go beyond the mere transparency

53 OHCHR, Human Rights and Access to Covid-19 Vaccines, 17 December 2020, 4.

54 Principle 19(e), 30(o), 36(c). See also UNISDR, Private Sector Activities in Disaster Risk Reduction: Good Practices and Lessons Learned (2008); UNISDR, Disaster Risk Reduction Private Sector Partnership (2015); UNDRR ARISE, ARISE focus areas and key performance indicators (KPIS) 2020–2021. NE Busch, AD Givens, 'Achieving Resilience in Disaster Management: the Role of Public-Private Partnership' (2013) Journal of Strategic Security, 1–19; J Chen et al, 'Public-Private Partnerships for the development of Disaster Resilient Communities' (2013) Journal of Contingencies and Crisis Management, 130–143.

55 UNGA (n 7), para 7; OECD Guidelines, General Policies, para 11.

requirements and effectively require human rights due diligence. Similarly, the Parliament of the European Union called for a legislative proposal on mandatory due diligence, in preparation for which the European Commission commissioned a Study in 2020.[56] Up to now, mandatory due diligence regulations within the EU have only been adopted for businesses operating in timber and conflict minerals markets.

The fragmentation that results from such a wide range of private actors and sectors using CBRN agents prevents the elaboration of one comprehensive set of standards on CBRN risks to be observed by all corporations. However, there can be no doubt about the necessity of involving private businesses in disaster risk reduction, as well as in the subsequent phases of response and recovery. The aim of this section is therefore to analyse the UNGPs and the OECD Guidelines standards as potentially fitting the different phases of the CBRN management cycle.

4.1 *Prevention and Preparedness through HRDD*

Respecting human rights means that business enterprises should prevent adverse effects of their activities, by avoiding causing or contributing to such adverse effects, mitigating those effects where they are not avoidable, and remediating adverse impacts that have already occurred. To do so, business enterprises should undertake HRDD. The process, embodied in Principle 17 of the UNGPs, requires companies to take all necessary steps to identify, prevent, mitigate and account for adverse impacts on human rights which 'the enterprise may cause or contribute to through its own activities or which may be directly linked to its operations, products or services by its business relationships' by 'assessing actual and potential human rights impacts, integrating and acting upon the findings, tracking responses, and communicating how impacts are addressed'. In other words, due diligence is intended as a 'standard of conduct that business must meet to discharge their responsibility to respect human rights'.[57] The identification of risks through a human rights impact assessment is the first step to carry out HRDD that aims to be effective in the specific context and towards the specific people that may be adversely impacted by a given operation.[58]

The same requirement to carry out HRDD is provided in the OECD Guidelines, asking enterprises to address actual and potential adverse impacts on

56 European Parliament report on sustainable finance (2018) and L Smit et al, 'Study on due diligence requirements through the supply chain', Final Report (2020).

57 J Bonnitcha, R McCorquodale (n 34) 909.

58 UNGPs, Principle 18, Commentary.

human rights, by taking adequate measures to identify, prevent and, where possible, mitigate potential human rights impacts and remediate actual impacts.[59] HRDD should be risk-based, meaning that it should be adequate to the severity and the likelihood of the adverse impacts concerned and tailored to the specific risk, taking into account different groups affected.[60] The nature and extent of the HRDD is further influenced by the context of the enterprise's operations and the nature of its activities.[61]

The responsibility of businesses to respect human rights is not limited to harm directly caused by their activities, but extends to their 'sphere of influence'.[62] According to Principle 13 of the UNGPs, companies are also responsible for adverse impacts on human rights that they contributed to or to which their activities are linked, thus extending the need to control risks of human rights violations along their value chain and within the activities of their business partners.[63] In such cases, businesses are called on to use leverage when they have power to influence third parties' conduct in preventing and avoiding human rights violations. It has been argued that this obligation is weaker upon companies, which must only 'seek to prevent' violations committed by others they have a relationship with, compared to the obligation to 'avoid' adverse impacts directly caused by their own business activities.[64]

The issue of leverage is particularly important in relation to activities of private actors that entail CBRN risks, since it is common for multinational enterprises to outsource production phases to countries where lower standards of human rights protection apply, thus benefiting from the legislative gap.[65] This general trend has been addressed as a 'toxic divide', whereby the most vulnerable are 'legally poisoned'.[66] By way of example, it is estimated that the use of agrochemicals has much higher impacts on the Global South than elsewhere.[67] Therefore, exercising leverage is particularly crucial to prevent potential CBRN adverse impacts caused by the misconduct of business partners operating abroad with risky agents, especially where the State is unwilling or unable to adopt and enforce appropriate business regulations.

59 OECD Guidelines, Chapter IV, Commentary para 41.
60 OECD Due Diligence Guidance, 17.
61 Ibid, 18.
62 A Telesetsky (n 2) 1022.
63 S Wood, 'The case for leverage-based corporate human rights responsibility' (2012) Business Ethics Quarterly, 63–98.
64 J Bonnitcha, R McCorquodale (n 34) 912.
65 UNGA (n 46), para 42 ff.
66 UNGA (n 12), para 85.
67 C Terwindt (n 24).

The abovementioned framework not only fits the emergency management cycle, but also adds important elements to a proper BHRA to disaster management. The process of HRDD is, indeed, essential to both the prevention and preparedness phases of the emergency management cycle. First of all, the responsibility of companies is recalled in the disaster risk management framework – especially in the Hyogo Framework for Action and the SFDRR – which calls for businesses to engage with disaster risk reduction.[68] The Hyogo Framework includes risk assessment as a necessary pre-disaster activity (11, 19 (ii)L). The risk assessment in the context of disaster risk reduction (DRR) can be equated to the human rights impact assessment, which is a necessary precondition for carrying out appropriate human rights due diligence in order to prevent human rights impacts and mitigate them where risks cannot be eliminated. A BHRA to DRR also contributes to the engagement with potentially involved communities and individuals, as this is a necessary part of HRDD. With respect to CBRN, specific agents can have particular effects on the enjoyment of human rights by some categories of individuals, which should be taken into account when developing prevention plans. For example, farm workers and their families, and communities living near agricultural lands are particularly exposed to the adverse human rights impacts caused by the use of pesticides[69] (as well as consumers of products sprayed with pesticides[70]) and therefore deserve special protection. Also, indigenous people must be involved in negotiations and their free, prior and informed consent must be obtained when CBRN-related industries want to operate near to indigenous communities. As for workers, personal protective equipment must be provided, together with proper information and training – provided in accessible language – on the use and management of toxic substances, as well as emergency planning.

HRDD is also necessary to enhance preparedness. When a potential CBRN event falls outside the 'disaster' sphere and the relevant DRR preparedness obligations, it may still be caught by the UNGPs, which provide for measures and actions to be undertaken when an adverse human rights impact occurs as an integral part of HRDD. The UNGPs (Principle 19) provide that business enterprises should integrate the findings of their human rights impact assessments by assigning responsibility for addressing adverse impacts to the appropriate level and function within the business, and by providing the necessary processes and resources to enable effective responses to such

68 A Telesetsky (n 2) 1009 ff.
69 UNGA (n 23), para 15 ff.
70 Ibid, para 27 ff.

impacts. But more importantly, the UNGPs and the related provisions of the OECD Guidelines, identify further obligations pertaining to the prevention and preparedness phase. For example, proper HRDD requires an ongoing activity, prescribing the assessment of risks to be an ongoing process (Principle 18 commentary), with clearly identified responsibilities at appropriate levels and functions (Principle 19.a.i).

The necessity for the private sector to address potential adverse impacts on human rights related to CBRN events is specifically delineated in several documents.[71] Outside the UN framework, documents outlining applications of the OECD Guidelines in the context of particular business activities have been adopted, including CBRN-related business activities. The OECD Guiding Principles for Chemical Accident Prevention, Preparedness and Response (2003),[72] address the prevention of accidents involving chemical substances, as well as preparedness and mitigation measures for when such accidents occur, and response guidance for the stakeholders potentially involved. As for the preparedness and mitigation, the Guidelines ask businesses to have an 'adequate on-site emergency plan', covering all possible scenarios (5.b.1), to identify roles and responsibilities in the chain of command and coordination (5.b.2), and to ensure employees have necessary information about the plan (5.b.3).

The OECD/FAO Guidelines (2016), recognising the risk of adverse impacts on the human right to health from exposure to toxic substances in agriculture, calls for the implementation of specific measures for risk mitigation and prevention in the agricultural supply chain.[73] For example, measures to avoid or minimise exposure of workers, third parties and the community to hazardous

71 See UNGA (n 46), para 38 related to exposure of workers to toxic agents, the Human Rights Council called upon businesses to prevent occupational exposures as part of their due diligence process expected under the UNGPs. Where the elimination of exposure is not possible, hazards should be controlled and mitigated as far as possible, by providing personal protective equipment to workers and proactively investigate working conditions along their supply chain.

72 OECD Environment, Health and Safety Publications, Series on Chemical Accidents, no. 10 (2003).

73 Other mitigation measures relevant to the CBRN sector may be: '[…] avoid or minimise the potential for community exposure to water-borne, water-based, water-related, vector-borne and communicable diseases that could result from operations, taking into consideration differentiated exposure to and higher sensitivity of vulnerable groups; […] consider observing global food safety standards, such as the Codex Alimentarius, and global animal health standards, such as OIE standards; promote traceability to ensure food safety but also to facilitate social and environmental management and increase trust', OECD-FAO, Guidance for Responsible Agricultural Supply Chain (2016), 59.

materials and substances that may be released by business operations, including modifying, substituting, or eliminating the condition or material causing the potential hazards; exercising reasonable efforts to control the safety of delivery, transportation and disposal of hazardous materials and waste; and assisting and collaborating with affected communities, local government agencies, and other relevant parties, in their preparations to respond effectively to emergency situations, especially when their participation and collaboration are necessary to respond to such emergency situations. Similarly, the OECD Due Diligence Guidance for Responsible Supply Chains in the Garment and Footwear Sector (2018) identifies the handling and disposal of hazardous chemicals as one of the main risks in this sector and calls for corrective action plans – developed with the assistance of experts and tailored to specific processes – for the disposal of hazardous chemicals.

In relation to the recent pandemic, most of the attention has been on the role of businesses in adopting mitigation measures, after the spread of the virus, and on human rights violations related to safety in the workplace or redundancies. Little attention has been devoted to the role of companies in preventing such an event. The spread of the pandemic, as a biological threat, should also be analysed in the light of prevention measures. In this sense, intensive livestock farming and international trade of wildlife for human consumption are business activities that imply the biological hazard of potential spread of biological agents from animals to humans, as well as indirect consequences related to antimicrobial resistance.

All these hazards, which may be considered CBRN hazards, can and should be prevented with responsible business conduct by integrating a BHRA to disaster risk management.

4.2 *Response and Recovery: Mitigating the Impact and Ensuring Access to Remedies*

The response and recovery phase is possibly the one where the business and human rights framework and the disaster management prism best cooperate and complete each other. On the one hand, calling on businesses to assist when a disaster occurs is a principle that can be drawn from disaster management obligations in the response phase,[74] while it would be harder to set proper obligations in this sense based on international human rights law in a case where the private actor did not itself cause the human rights harm.

74 Ch 13 by Bakker and ch 34 by Capone. S Silingardi, 'Responses by private corporations', in SC Breau et al (eds), *Research Handbook on Disasters and International Law* (Elgar, 2016), 225–248.

On the other hand, providing access to remedies, even within the company itself through non-State-based grievance mechanisms and operational level grievance mechanisms (Principles 28–29 UNGPs) does not sit easily within the response and recovery phases of disaster management as traditionally intended, while this is an essential part of the remedial aspects of the BHR framework. The following examples will clarify these assumptions.

In terms of response, enterprises are primarily required to mitigate adverse effects of their activities that cannot be avoided or eliminated and to put in place remedies to address adverse human rights impacts when they occur.[75] However, even when a corporation has not caused any adverse effects itself through its own activities, it may still be required to assist in the response phase, especially when the State concerned does not possess the necessary resources and competences to properly respond to an emergency.[76] If this is the case, private corporations may be called on to assist as part of their human rights obligations, since the concept of business 'activities' that may cause or contribute to adverse human rights impacts includes both actions and omissions.[77] Therefore, following a CBRN event, a corporation may be required to intervene by providing necessary means for the community to recover, since failing to do so may be considered as an omission with adverse impacts on human rights.[78] Furthermore, as already recalled, the SFDRR includes public-private partnerships as a necessary tool in disaster management, thus creating expectations not only upon States, but also indirect obligations upon companies to act accordingly.[79]

The recent COVID-19 pandemic provides a good example again. While agriculture and livestock farming bear the main responsibility in the prevention phase, since the specific risks related to their activities call for due diligence in avoiding biological and chemical hazards to health, it may also be the case that pharmaceutical industries and enterprises operating in the manufacturing of personal protective equipment (PPE) have the responsibility to contribute to re-establishing human rights in the post-disaster phase by providing adequate and sufficient life-saving medicines, vaccines and PPE. Although they did not 'cause' the adverse human rights impact, their activities (including their omissions/failure to act) may contribute to a different human rights violation, linked to the right of access to medicines and cures. In this sense,

75 OECD Guidelines, Chapter IV, Commentary para 46.
76 M Hesselman, L Lane (n 2), 531.
77 OECD Guidelines, Chapter IV, Commentary para 42.
78 Ibid.
79 See ch 2 by Di Francesco Maesa.

pharmaceutical enterprises have the responsibility to exercise due diligence in relation to the impacts of their activities in the response phase, for example, by assessing the potential adverse effects of pricing and distribution of vaccines and life-saving medicines, which must take into account the need to respect the right to health and act accordingly to mitigate an adverse impact and use leverage on other actors when necessary.[80]

Finally, a BHRA to CBRN events also impacts the obligations in that providing remedies is an integral part of the response to human rights violations,[81] as also provided in the Third Pillar of the UNGPs. Therefore, responding and recovering from adverse impacts on human rights cannot leave out the availability of remedies, whether judicial or non-judicial, State or corporate-based. In particular, UNGPs Principle 22 requires companies to provide for or cooperate in remediation, including through operational-level grievance mechanisms that possess the characteristics enshrined in Principle 31.

5 Concluding Remarks

The foregoing analysis highlights that the role of private corporations is crucial in the management of CBRN events. At the same time, international law still fails to regulate States' and companies' obligations accordingly through hard, binding instruments.

International human rights protection in the context of business activities has long been established in case law, which has defined States' positive obligations to regulate private businesses to prevent CBRN events, to adopt preparedness measures and to provide remedies when human rights are infringed as a consequence of such events. Similarly, international soft law instruments call on companies to undertake human rights due diligence, taking into account the specific risks of their activities. So far, no specific instrument to protect human rights in the context of CBRN activity has been adopted, thus leaving the matter in a fragmented scenario – where hard obligations and soft standards are blurred and uncertain.

However, existing instruments of human rights protection and disaster management could be read together to delineate the outline of an emerging field. Adopting a human rights-based approach to CBRN risk management in relation to business activity will help to improve protection of individuals

80 OHCHR, Human Rights and Access to COVID-19 Vaccines, 17 December 2020, 5.

81 D Shelton, *Remedies in international human rights law* (OUP, 2015).

in several aspects. First, such an approach covers events which do not fit the narrow limits of the disaster management framework, such as, for example, long-term or small-scale effects of industrial activities that nonetheless seriously impact human rights through the use of CBRN agents. Second, it requires the content of obligations to be adapted to better suit specific groups of rights-holders, such as workers or vulnerable people (migrants, women, children). Furthermore, it widens the business sectors involved as duty-bearers in CBRN management, depending on the different phases and fields of possible intervention. Lastly, State-based non-judicial remedies provided in the business and human rights framework, such as the OECD National Contact Points established pursuant to the OECD Guidelines, may also help victims to overcome the obstacles in obtaining proper redress after an industrial disaster.

The business and human rights framework is, therefore, essential in supporting the application of the principles governing disaster management and an intersection of the two sets of laws, regulations, international instruments and non-binding standards can pave the way for a full accountability and engagement of the private sector in CBRN event prevention, preparedness and response.

Bibliography

Backer LC, 'The human rights obligations of State-Owned Enterprises (SOEs): emerging conceptual structures and principles in national and international law and policy' (2017) VandJTransnatlL 827.

Barnes M, 'The United Nations Guiding Principles on Business and Human Rights, the State Duty to Protect Human Rights and the State-Business Nexus' (2018) Reveista de Direito Internacional 42.

Bonnitcha J, McCorquodale R, 'The concept of "Due Diligence" in the UN Guiding Principles on Business and Human Rights' (2017) EJIL 905.

Bright C et al, 'Toward a corporate duty to respect human rights' (2020) Business and Politics 667.

Busch NE, Givens AD, 'Achieving Resilience in Disaster Management: the Role of Public-Private Partnership' (2013) Journal of Strategic Security 1.

Chen J et al, 'Public-Private Partnerships for the development of Disaster Resilient Communities' (2013) Journal of Contingencies and Crisis Management 130.

Clapham A, *Human Rights Obligations of Non-state actors* (OUP, 2006).

De Schutter O et al, 'Commentary to the Maastricht Principles on Extraterritorial Obligations of States in the Area of Economic, Social and Cultural Rights' (2012) HumRtsQ 1134.

Droubi S, 'Transnational Corporations and International Human Rights Law' (2016) Notre Dame Journal of International and Comparative Law 119.

Hesselman M, Lane L, 'Disasters and non-state actors – human rights-based approaches' (2017) Disaster Prevention and Management 526.

Izumi T, Shaw R, *Disaster Management and Private Sectors: Challenges and Potentials* (Springer, 2016).

Kinley D, Tadaki J, 'From Talk to Walk: The Emergence of Human Rights Responsibilities for Corporations at International Law' (2004) VandJTransnatlL 931.

Kulesza J, *Due Diligence in International Law* (Brill, 2016).

McCorquodale R, Simons P, 'Responsibility Beyond Borders: State Responsibility for Extraterritorial Violations by Corporations of International Human Rights Law' (2007) ModLRev 598.

Miyaguchi T, Shaw R, 'Corporate community interface in disaster management – a preliminary study of Mumbai, India' (2007) Risk Management 209.

Shelton D, *Remedies in international human rights law* (OUP, 2015).

Silingardi S, 'Responses by private corporations', in SC Breau et al (eds), *Research Handbook on Disasters and International Law* (Elgar, 2016), 225.

Sommario E, Venier S, 'Human Rights Law and Disaster risk reduction' (2018) QIL Zoom-in 29.

Telesetsky A, 'Beyond voluntary Corporate Social Responsibility: Corporate Human Rights Obligations to Prevent Disasters and to Provide Temporary Emergency Relief' (2015) VandJTransnatlL 1003.

Terwindt C et al, 'Health Rights Impacts by Agrochemical Business: Legally Challenging the "Myth of Safe Use"' (2018) Utrecht Journal of International and European Law 130.

Wood S, 'The case for leverage-based corporate human rights responsibility' (2012) Business Ethics Quarterly 63.

Zorzi Giustiniani F, Sommario E, Casolari F, Bartolini G (eds), *Routledge Handbook of Human Rights and Disasters* (Routledge, 2018).

CHAPTER 31

New Technologies and CBRN Events: International Obligations in the Cybersecurity Domain

Gian Maria Farnelli

1 Introduction

Cyberspace has acquired increasing relevance since the introduction of the 'world wide web' in 1989. The ability of information and communication technology (ICT) to connect people and transmit data has become a key feature of current societies.

ICT has also become instrumental to managing industrial processes. Digitalisation in industrial activities started in the late 1950s with regard to CBRN facilities.[1] Automation and digital control systems are today essential in assuring that industrial CBRN materials are managed, exploited and stocked in a secure manner. Moreover, ICT is widely employed in disaster warning and response mechanisms,[2] thus being instrumental to States' compliance with obligations in the CBRN field.

The increasing role of ICT in every aspect of modern societies has attracted States' attention to its strategic and military applications. States have developed means to carry out malicious cyber activities short of traditional uses of force, while non-State actors have benefitted from the easy access to ICT to enhance their capacity to interfere with States' critical infrastructures. Cyberspace has thus become a new theatre for conflicts.[3]

Against this factual background, this chapter focuses on States' obligations and international recommendations regarding cybersecurity, qualified as the application of technologies aimed at preventing unauthorised access

1 TM Stout and TJ Williams, 'Pioneering Work in the Field of Computer Process Control' (1995) (17)1 *IEEE Annals of the History of Computing* 6.

2 G Gilibrays, G Mugeni and D Matovu, 'Role of ICT in Disaster Response and Management: A Review Study of ICT Challenges and Adoption Approaches by Developing Nations' (2016) 6(5) *International Journal of Advanced Research in Computer Science and Software Engineering* 196.

3 NATO, 'Warsaw Summit Communiqué Issued by the Heads of State and Government participating in the meeting of the North Atlantic Council in Warsaw 8–9 July 2016' (9 July 2016) paras 70–71.

and malicious uses of ICT.[4] Given the ongoing political debate on the issue at hand, the study will follow an 'evolutive interpretation'[5] approach to existing international law, so as to assess the existence of an international obligation to regulate and monitor the implementation of cybersecurity measures, in particular with regard to CBRN-related activities, with a view to preventing CBRN events.

Next to introductory and concluding sections, the chapter comes in three parts. First, an overview of recent cyber activities targeting CBRN facilities is presented, with a view to showing that their vulnerabilities have been the target of malicious cyber activities, and to substantiating the attention devoted by States and international bodies to cybersecurity issues. Second, the chapter addresses the ongoing debate on the application of rules of international law to cyberspace activities. On the basis of works within the UN and the most recent State practice, it is argued that international law is generally applicable to States' conduct in the cyber domain. Third, the study argues that States' obligation of prevention of CBRN events may be construed to encompass a due diligence obligation to take all appropriate measures concerning the cybersecurity of CBRN-related activities.

2 The Relevance of Cybersecurity for CBRN-Related Activities

One of the main consequences of the dependency of industrial control, monitoring, warning and response systems on ICT is that adequate cybersecurity protocols are an essential element of the security plan of any industrial activity. This is particularly true with regard to CBRN-related activities. Loopholes in the cybersecurity of a CBRN facility may easily allow an interference with its proper functioning, with potentially harmful consequences for human life and the environment.[6]

The relevance of cybersecurity in hazardous industrial processes was stressed in 1991 by Jim Bidzos' reference to the risk of a 'Digital Pearl Harbor'.[7]

---

4 R Siers, 'Cybersecurity' in PD Williams and M McDonald (eds), *Security Studies: An Introduction* (3rd edn; Routledge 2018) 556.

5 E Bjorge, *The Evolutionary Interpretation of Treaties* (OUP 2014).

6 On the risks for human life and the environment stemming from CBRN events, see International Committee of the Red Cross, *Chemical, Biological, Radiological and Nuclear Response. Introductory Guidance* (March 2014), available at <https://shop.icrc.org/icrc/pdf/view/id/1686>.

7 E Purchase and F Caldwell, 'Digital Pearl Harbor: A Case Study in Industry Vulnerability to Cyber Attack' in S Ghosh, M Malek and EA Stohr (eds), *Guarding Your Business. A Management Approach to Security* (Springer 2004) 47.

Such concerns were substantiated in 2002, when a malware successfully breached the cybersecurity of a US nuclear power plant and disabled safety monitoring systems for a few hours.[8] Years later, a water treatment plant was subjected to a similar attack aimed at increasing to poisonous levels the chlorine in water intended for domestic use.[9]

The number of malicious cyber operations targeting critical infrastructure and CBRN facilities has been increasing over the years. In 2010, the notorious Stuxnet attack caused physical disruption in control systems of the Iranian uranium enrichment plant in Natanz.[10] In 2011, the cybersecurity of several chemical companies worldwide was breached by a trojan-type malware to collect intellectual property data.[11] In 2012, a malware was employed to wipe essential data from 30.000 workstations of Aramco, highly reducing the capacity of the company to sell its 9.5 million barrels per day production for five months.[12] In 2015, one of the biggest reported 'Denial of Service'[13] attacks triggered a massive power outage in Ukraine which left all the residents of the Ukrainian city of Ivano-Frankivsk without power for six hours.[14] A similar attack hit and disrupted the British National Health Service for a few days in 2017, causing loses estimated at £92 million.[15]

---

8 K Poulsen, 'Slammer worm crashed Ohio nuke plant network' *Security Focus* (19 August 2003) available at <https://www.securityfocus.com/news/6767>.

9 R McMillan, 'Hackers break into water system network. Pennsylvania breach occurred via compromised laptop' *ComputerWorld* (31 October 2006) available at <https://www.computerworld.com/article/2547938/hackers-break-into-water-system-network.html>.

10 'Obama Order Sped Up Wave of Cyberattacks Against Iran' *The New York Times* (1 June 2012) available at <https://www.nytimes.com/2012/06/01/world/middleeast/obama-ordered-wave-of-cyberattacks-against-iran.html>.

11 G Keizer, '"Nitro" hackers use stock malware to steal chemical, defense secrets. Symantec traces one command-and-control server to China' *ComputerWorld* (31 October 2011) available at <https://www.computerworld.com/article/2499789/-nitro--hackers-use-stock-malware-to-steal-chemical--defense-secrets.html>.

12 J Pagliery, 'The inside story of the biggest hack in history' *CNN Business* (5 August 2015) available at <https://money.cnn.com/2015/08/05/technology/aramco-hack/>.

13 A 'Denial of Service' is an attack which 'aims to inundate the target with excessive calls, messages, enquiries, or requests in order to overload it and force its shut down' (M Roscini, *Cyber Operations and the Use of Force in International Law* (OUP 2014) 18).

14 N Tiptuk, S Hailes, 'The cyberattack on Ukraine's power grid is a warning of what's to come' *Phys.org* (13 January 2016) available at <https://phys.org/news/2016-01-cyberattack-ukraine-power-grid.html>.

15 'Global ransomware attack causes turmoil' *BBC News* (28 June 2017) available at <https://www.bbc.com/news/technology-40416611>; 'WannaCry, Petya, NotPetya: how ransomware hit the big time in 2017' *The Guardian* (30 December 2017) available at <https://www.theguardian.com/technology/2017/dec/30/wannacry-petya-notpetya-ransomware>; O Hughes, 'Government puts cost of WannaCry to NHS at £92m'

The above brief overview of malicious cyber activities and their economic consequences substantiates the attention that private experts have been devoting to the development of cybersecurity standards for private and public facilities.[16] The same awareness has been increasing amongst policymakers. Many States and international bodies have been working on 'cybersecurity strategies',[17] following the recommendations by the UN General Assembly concerning the '[c]reation of a global culture of cybersecurity'.[18]

For the purposes of this contribution, mention must be made of the United Nations Interregional Crime and Justice Research Institute studies on

---

digitalhealth (12 October 2018) available at <https://www.digitalhealth.net/2018/10/dhsc-puts-cost-wannacry-nhs-92m/>.

16 S Abaimov and M Martellini, 'Selected Issues of Cyber Security Practices in CBRNeCy Critical Infrastructure' in M Martellini and A Malizia (eds), *Cyber and Chemical, Biological, Radiological, Nuclear, Explosives Challenges. Threats and Counter Efforts* (Springer 2017) 11.

17 Eg Peoples' Republic of China, 'National Cyberspace security Strategy (2016)' available at <http://politics.people.com.cn/n1/2016/1227/c1001-28980829.html> (unofficial English translation available at <https://chinacopyrightandmedia.wordpress.com/2016/12/27/national-cyberspace-security-strategy/>); Russian Federation, 'Doctrine of Information Security of the Russian Federation' (5 December 2016) available at <https://www.mid.ru/en/foreign_policy/official_documents/-/asset_publisher/CptICkB6BZ29/content/id/2563163>; United States of America, 'National Cybersecurity Strategy of the United States' (September 2018) available at <https://trumpwhitehouse.archives.gov/wp-content/uploads/2018/09/National-Cyber-Strategy.pdf>; European Parliament and the Council, 'The EU's Cybersecurity Strategy for the Digital Decade' (15 December 2020) EU Doc. JOIN (2020) 18 final; Australia, 'Australia's Cybersecurity Strategy 2020' available at <https://www.homeaffairs.gov.au/cyber-security-subsite/files/cyber-security-strategy-2020.pdf>. By the same token, one may mention the Organization of American States' Cyber Security Initiative (<https://www.sites.oas.org/cyber/en/pages/default.aspx>), the Organization for Security and Co-operation in Europe Decision No. 5/17 on 'Enhancing OSCE Efforts to Reduce the Risk of Conflict Stemming from the Use of Information and Communication Technologies' (8 December 2017), and the ongoing dialogue on the matter in point between the EU and ASEAN ('ASEAN-EU Statement on Cybersecurity Cooperation' (1 August 2019) available at <https://asean.org/asean-eu-statement-cybersecurity-cooperation/>). For a comparative analysis of current trends in cybersecurity strategies, see OECD, *Cybersecurity policy making at a turning point. Analysing a new generation of national cybersecurity strategies for the Internet economy* (OECD 2012) available at <http://www.oecd.org/sti/ieconomy/cybersecurity%20policy%20making.pdf>; N Shafqat and A Massod, 'Comparative Analysis of Various National Cyber Security Strategies' (2016) 14(1) *International Journal of Computer Science and Information Security* 129.

18 UNGA 'Creation of a global culture of cybersecurity' (31 January 2003) UN Doc. A/RES/57/239; UNGA 'Creation of a global culture of cybersecurity and the protection of critical information infrastructures' (30 January 2004) UN Doc. A/RES/58/199; UNGA 'Creation of a global culture of cybersecurity and taking stock of national efforts to protect critical information infrastructures' (17 March 2010) UN Doc. A/RES/64/211.

'Information Security Best Practices for CBRN Facilities',[19] 'Information Security Management System Planning for CBRN Facilities'[20] and 'How to Implement Security Controls for an Information Security Program at CBRN Facilities'.[21] Such studies aim at providing guidance on developing and implementing best practices for protecting information security at CBRN facilities, for both private and public actors, including regulatory agencies. Though recommendatory in nature, such studies propose cyber security measures – such as the adoption of information security policies, standards and procedures,[22] and the integration of risk management plans[23] – which may also be considered as 'appropriate' for purposes of assessing the liability of the relevant actors. Without dwelling on the technical details of the recommended measures,[24] it is worth noting that the above studies refer to the need for balancing considerations of security with resource constraints, focusing on the greatest risk reduction possible with the resources available. These studies also highlight the importance of elaborating contingency and disaster recovery plans, as well as incident response processes, so as to return a given facility to its proper functionality in a timely manner and, thus, mitigate harmful consequences.[25]

3 The Debate over the Application of International Law in Cyberspace

The interest of States in cybersecurity issues has been coupled with a debate at the international level as to the applicability of international law to activities in cyberspace. Though this debate has not addressed CBRN-related cybersecurity issues specifically, the conclusions reached on the applicability of international law to cyberspace are relevant for assessing the existence and

19 UNICRI, *Information Security Best Practices for CBRN Facilities* (UNICRI 2015) available at <https://www.pnnl.gov/main/publications/external/technical_reports/PNNL-ACT-10019.pdf>.

20 UNICRI, *Information Security Management System Planning for CBRN Facilities* (UNICRI 2015) available at <https://www.pnnl.gov/main/publications/external/technical_reports/PNNL-24874.pdf>.

21 UNICRI, *How to Implement Security Controls for an Information Security Program at CBRN Facilities* (UNICRI 2015) available at <https://www.pnnl.gov/main/publications/external/technical_reports/PNNL-25112.pdf>.

22 UNICRI (n 19) 3.4.

23 UNICRI (n 20) 1 ff.

24 By way of example, the first UNICRI study stress the importance of 'identifying vectors of attack' using a threat modelling dubbed 'attack tree' (UNICRI (n 19) 3.5 ff.).

25 UNICRI (n 21) 44 ff.

contents of States' obligations concerning the prevention of harm stemming from malicious cyber activities.

The General Assembly has been warning against uses of ICT 'inconsistent with the objectives of maintaining international stability and security' since 1998,[26] calling upon States to 'develop [...] international principles' aimed at enhancing ICT security and reducing ICT-related criminality and terrorism.[27]

A few years later, General Assembly Resolution 58/32[28] instituted the Group of Governmental Experts (GGE),[29] tasked with addressing developments in ICT with regard to international peace and security, in consideration of States' increasing attention to the use of ICT for purposes of warfare and intelligence.[30]

Building on the ICJ reasoning in the *Nuclear Weapons* advisory opinion,[31] the work of the GGE has fostered the application of existing international law to cyberspace, rather than supporting the elaboration of a new legal framework. In its Second Report of 2013, the GGE maintained that general international law, and in particular the UN Charter, rules on State responsibility and sovereignty-related norms and principles apply in cyberspace.[32] The report further stressed the need for cooperation and information sharing aimed at timely response to and recovery from cyberattacks.[33]

The General Assembly endorsed such position in Resolutions 68/243[34] and 70/237.[35] The latter resolution also endorsed compliance with guidelines

26 UNGA 'Developments in the field of information and telecommunications in the context of international security' (4 December 1998) UN Doc. A/RES/53/70 PP 7.

27 Ibid para 2(c).

28 UNGA 'Developments in the field of information and telecommunications in the context of international security' (8 December 2003) UN Doc. A/RES/58/32.

29 The GGE was initially composed of experts from 15 States. The number was later increased to 20 in 2014 and 25 in 2016. For additional information, see the official page (<https://www.un.org/disarmament/ict-security/>).

30 UNGGE 'Report of the Group of Governmental Experts on Developments in the Field of Information and Telecommunications in the Context of International Security' (30 July 2010) UN Doc. A/65/201 para 7 ['2010 GGE Report'].

31 *Legality of the Threat or Use of Nuclear Weapons* (1996), ICJ Reports 226, para 86.

32 UNGGE 'Report of the Group of Governmental Experts on Developments in the Field of Information and Telecommunications in the Context of International Security' (24 June 2013) UN Doc. A/68/98 paras 19, 20 and 23 ['2013 GGE Report'].

33 Ibid para 26(c).

34 UNGA 'Developments in the field of information and telecommunications in the context of international security' (27 December 2013) UN Doc. A/RES/68/243 para 3.

35 UNGA 'Developments in the field of information and telecommunications in the context of international security' (23 December 2015) UN Doc. A/RES/70/237 para 4.

contained in the Third GGE Report,[36] which aimed at 'promoting an open, secure, stable, accessible and peaceful ICT environment'[37] and at fostering confidence building.[38] It also stressed that 'States have jurisdiction over the ICT infrastructure located within their territory'.[39]

The above debate within the UN was abruptly interrupted in 2017. Political tensions between the US and the Russian Federation as to the possibility of applying the law of armed conflict and the right to self-defence in cyberspace led to the adoption of two different GGE reports[40] and two resolutions.[41]

The divergence within the GGE and the call for a more inclusive and transparent debate, led to the institution of a second body, the 'Open-Ended Working Group' (OEWG), whose goal is to assess how international law applies to activities in cyberspace, and to elaborate capacity and confidence building measures. The first document produced by this body adopts the GGE approach according to which existing international law applies in cyberspace.[42] It also supports the development of '[v]oluntary, non-binding norms of responsible State behaviour' in cyberspace complementing existing international law.[43]

---

36 Ibid.

37 UNGGE 'Report of the Group of Governmental Experts on Developments in the Field of Information and Telecommunications in the Context of International Security' (22 July 2015) UN Doc. A/RES/70/174 para 13 ['2015 GGE Report'].

38 Ibid para 16 ff.

39 Ibid para 28(a).

40 The contrast may be inferred from statements by the US Coordinator for Cyber Issues, Mr Markoff, and the Russian Special Rapporteur for international cooperation in information security, Mr Kutskikh. See MG Markoff, 'Explanation of Position at the Conclusion of the 2016–2017 UN Group of Governmental Experts (GGE) on Developments in the Field of Information and Telecommunications in the Context of International Security' available at <https://usun.usmission.gov/explanation-of-position-at-the-conclusion-of-the-2016-2017-un-group-of-governmental-experts-gge-on-developments-in-the-field-of-information-and-tele/>; and A Kutskikh, 'Response of the Special Representative of the President of the Russian Federation for International Cooperation on Information Security Andrey Krutskikh to TASS' Question Concerning the State of International Dialogue in This Sphere' available at <https://coe.mid.ru/en_GB/sotrudnicestvo-v-sfere-pravoporadka/-/asset_publisher/jYpWpmrO5Zpk/content/otvet-specpredstavitela-prezidenta-rossijskoj-federacii-po-voprosam-mezdunarodnogo-sotrudnicestva-v-oblasti-informacionnoj-bezopasnosti-a-v-krutskih-n>.

41 UNGA 'Advancing responsible State behavior in cyberspace in the context of international security' (22 December 2018) UN Doc. A/73/266; UNGA 'Developments in the field of information and telecommunications in the context of international security' (5 December 2018) UN Doc. A/73/27.

42 UNOEWG 'Final Substantive Report' (10 March 2021) UN Doc A/AC.290/2021/CRP.2, para 34, available at <https://front.un-arm.org/wp-content/uploads/2021/03/Final-report-A-AC.290-2021-CRP.2.pdf>.

43 Ibid para 24.

The OEWG follows a 'multi-stakeholders approach'[44] geared towards ensuring the effectiveness of any regulatory decisions concerning States' activities in the cyber domain by inviting private stakeholders to participate in its work along with public ones.[45] This stems from the acknowledgement of the vital role of private enterprises in implementing cybersecurity measures. This is particularly the case in highly ICT-dependant CBRN activities.

4 States' Obligations on Cybersecurity in CBRN Facilities

Bearing the above considerations in mind, we can turn to whether international law imposes on States any obligations with regard to cybersecurity. Answering this question requires first to recall that the General Assembly has endorsed the conclusions reached by the GGE to the effect of applying existing international law in cyberspace. Such position, also supported by authoritative literature,[46] has been adopted within other *fora*.[47]

The relevant resolutions were adopted by consensus. Following the reasoning elaborated by the International Law Commission (ILC) in its works on 'Subsequent agreements and subsequent practice in relation to interpretation of treaties', and codified in Conclusion 12,[48] such resolutions may be taken as

44 Ibid paras 68 ff.

45 Several NGOs have already participated in the work of the OEWG and provided comments on its pre-draft report. See the OEWG official website (<https://www.un.org/disarmament/open-ended-working-group/>). It is to be noted that such approach follows the recommendations by the General Assembly in the field of cybersecurity (UNGA (n 18)). Some States have expressed perplexities on a regular institutional dialogue with private entities. See the Italian and Russian comments to the initial pre-draft report, available at <https://www.un.org/disarmament/open-ended-working-group/>.

46 MN Schmitt (ed), *Tallinn Manual 2.0 on the International Law Applicable to Cyber Operations* (2nd edn; CUP 2017).

47 Eg 'G7 Declaration on Responsible State Behavior in Cyberspace' (11 April 2017) available at <https://www.mofa.go.jp/files/000246367.pdf>; 'EU Statement – United Nations 1st Committee: Thematic Discussion on Other Disarmament Measures and International Security' (26 October 2018) available at <https://eeas.europa.eu/delegations/un-new-york/52894/eu-statement-%E2%80%93-united-nations-1st-committee-thematic-discussion-other-disarmament-measures-and_en>; ASEAN-EU Statement (n 17) paras 5–6. *Contra*, Organization of American States, 'Improving Transparency: International Law and State Cyber Operations – Fifth Report (Presented by Professor Duncan B. Hollis)' (7 August 2020) OAS Doc. OEA/Ser.Q/CJI/doc. 615/20 rev.1 para 3.

48 International Law Commission (ILC) 'Draft conclusions on subsequent agreements and subsequent practice in relation to the interpretation of treaties, with commentaries' (2018) II(2) UNYBILC, Draft Conclusion 12 and commentary thereto.

elements of subsequent practice to the effect of encompassing cyberspace within the 'spatial' scope of the UN Charter.[49] They might also be seen as evidence of *opinio juris*, to the effect of applying other general rules of international law, such as those on State responsibility, to cyberspace.

Some difficulties still arise, especially in the latter field. The reference made by the GGE to States' jurisdiction over ICT infrastructure on their territory[50] does not establish a presumption against the territorial State that it has responsibility for activities carried out through the said ICT.

With regard to CBRN events, a State would be responsible for cyber activities of its officials, or individuals under its direct control, that cause a CBRN event which constitutes a breach of a primary rule of international law.[51] The same apparently applies to cyber activities aimed at reducing early warning and response capacities prior to, or during, a CBRN event.[52] However, the nature of activities in cyberspace is such that attribution may be technically difficult, to the effect that cyber activities patently breaching international law may remain without an author.[53]

Such difficulties have led the literature to endorse the application of a 'due diligence standard of attribution', according to which unlawful conduct carried out from the territory of a State of which the territorial State is aware, or should have been aware, is attributable to it.[54] Though this construction represents a minority position, it has the merit of highlighting how the interest of avoiding ICT-related breaches of international law may be better served by applying due diligence obligations to cyber activities. Indeed, shifting the focus from negative State obligations to positive obligations of prevention would make

49 Roscini (n 13) 280; A Sardu 'L'*International Cybersecurity Law*: lo stato dell'arte' (2020) 75(1) *La Comunità Internazionale* 14.

50 Above (n 39).

51 Roscini (n 13) 33–40.

52 It is to be noted that such sabotage activity may reach the threshold for constituting an 'attack' under Article 2(4) UN Charter. See *inter alia* Roscini (n 13) 45–67.

53 Difficulties were acknowledged also by the GGE (2015 GEE Report (n 39) para 7). See *inter alia* Roscini (n 13) 33–40; C Antonopoulos, 'State responsibility in cyberspace' in N Tsagourias and R Buchan (eds), *Research Handbook on International Law and Cyberspace* (Edward Elgar 2015) 62–65; C Payne and L Finlay, 'Addressing Obstacles to Cyber-Attribution: A Model Based on State Response to Cyber-Attack' (2017) 49(3) Geo Wash Int'l L Rev 535; F Delerue, 'Attribution to State of Cyber Operations Conducted by Non-State Actors' in E Carpanelli and N Lazzerini (eds), *Use and Misuse of New Technologies* (Springer 2019) 233. Many States have called for the development of so-called 'common rules of technical attribution' (*eg* Argentina, Brazil, China, the Netherlands and Pakistan; see national comments to the initial OEWG Pre-Draft Report are available at <https://www.un.org/disarmament/open-ended-working-group/>).

54 L Chircop, 'A due diligence standard of attribution in cyberspace' (2018) 67(3) ICLQ 643.

it easier for the victim State to attribute responsibility, or liability,[55] and thus be compensated for damages suffered. It seems reasonable to argue that the results required by such obligations would be achieved through the implementation of adequate cybersecurity standards. The elaboration of due diligence obligations of prevention would thus indirectly impose on States obligations to develop cybersecurity regulations and strategies.[56]

It is well-known that due diligence requires States to take all reasonable measures aimed at preventing the occurrence of a given 'harm' stemming from private or public activities under its jurisdiction, and to mitigate the consequences thereof.[57] Furthermore, failure to comply with due diligence, including with regard to lawful activities, entails State liability. This is particularly relevant in the context of CBRN-related activities, which are mostly lawful in international law.

The application of due diligence obligations in cyberspace has been the object of many scholarly works,[58] as well as debate within the GGE.[59] The language of GGE reports[60] hints at difficulties in reaching an agreement as to the application of due diligence obligations to the territorial State with regard to malicious uses of ICT under its jurisdiction.[61]

During the work of the GGE, a consensus was reached with exclusive regard to obligations of prevention of activities threatening international peace and security.[62] It is therefore arguable that the international community has already accepted that States are bound to take all appropriate measures to

---

55 On the distinction between responsibility and liability, see A Tanzi, 'Liability for Lawful Acts', *Max Planck Encyclopedia of Public International Law* (February 2013), <https://opil.ouplaw.com/view/10.1093/law:epil/9780199231690/law-9780199231690-e1065>, para 2.

56 On obligations of prevention, see ch 3 by Venier.

57 R Pisillo Mazzeschi, *"Due diligence" e responsabilità internazionale degli Stati* (Giuffré 1989); R Barnidge, 'The due diligence principle in International Law' (2006) 8(1) ICLR 81; S Besson, 'La Due Diligence En Droit International' (2020) 409 Recueil des Cours de l'Académie de Droit International 159.

58 See, amongst the other, K Bannelier-Christakis, 'Cyber Diligence: A Low-Intensity Due Diligence Principle for Low-Intensity Cyber Operations?' (2014) 14(1) Baltic YBIL 28–39; Antonopoulos (n 53) 66–70; Chircop (n 54); Besson (n 57) 335 ff.

59 2013 GGE Report (n 32) para 20; 2015 GGE Report (n 37) para 27.

60 'States *should* take appropriate measures to protect their critical infrastructure from ICT threats' (2015 GGE Report (n 37) para 13(g); emphasis added); 'States *should* seek to ensure that their territories are not used by non-State actors for unlawful use of ICTs' (2013 GGE Report (n 32) para 23; 2015 GGE Report (n 37) para 28(e); emphasis added).

61 The issue of due diligence and cyberspace will be further developed below. For an overview of the issue, see Antonopoulos (n 53) 66–70; Schmitt (n 58) 68–81; Chircop (n 54) 643–668.

62 2015 GEE Report (n 39) para 13(a).

prevent ICT under their jurisdiction from being used to carry out activities threatening international peace and security, such as 'cyberattacks' in breach of Article 2(4) UN Charter.[63] Such obligations might include taking regulatory measures aimed at imposing upon private CBRN facilities the implementation of adequate cybersecurity, whenever malfunctions in those facilities may constitute a threat to international peace and security.[64]

Positions currently expressed within the OEWG show that a wider consensus is aggregating around the idea of applying due diligence rules of conduct to cyber activities for the protection of collective interests other than international peace and security. One may mention language to that effect in the national positions of Australia,[65] Finland,[66] France,[67] Germany[68] and The Netherlands,[69] as well as in the comments to the initial OEWG pre-draft report by the Republic of Korea.[70] The Chinese and United States Governments, too, support some forms of obligations of prevention concerning malicious cyber activities.[71] Other States, such as the United Kingdom, have not taken a clear stance on the issue in point.[72] Only a few States, such as New Zealand, have

---

63 This calls for the definition of activities short of a proper use of force. On the issue, see *inter alia*, Roscini (n 13) 44–69.

64 Such would be the case of malfunctions having harmful consequences akin to those of a kinetic armed attack. This hypothesis would also fall within the scope of potential obligations to prevent CBRN terrorism. See ch 7 by Poltronieri Rossetti.

65 Australia, 'Australia Paper – Open Ended Working Group on Developments in the Field of Information and Telecommunication in the Context of International Security' (2019) 9–11, available at <https://www.dfat.gov.au/sites/default/files/australian-oewg-national-paper-september-2019.pdf>.

66 Finland, 'International Law and Cyberspace. Finland's National Position' (2020) 4–5, available at <https://valtioneuvosto.fi/en/-/finland-published-its-positions-on-public-international-law-in-cyberspace>.

67 France (n 53) 6 and 10.

68 Germany, 'On the Application of International Law in Cyberspace' (2011) 3, available at <https://www.auswaertiges-amt.de/blob/2446304/2ae17233b62966a4b7f16d50ca3c6802/on-the-application-of-international-law-in-cyberspace-data.pdf>.

69 The Netherlands (n 53) 4–5.

70 Republic of Korea, 'Comments on the pre-draft of the OEWG Report' (2020) 5, available at <https://www.un.org/disarmament/open-ended-working-group/>.

71 BJ Egan, 'Remarks on International Law and Stability in Cyberspace' (2016) available at <https://2009-2017.state.gov/s/l/releases/remarks/264303.htm>; People's Republic of China, 'International Strategy of Cooperation on Cyberspace' (2017) available at <https://www.fmprc.gov.cn/mfa_eng/wjb_663304/zzjg_663340/jks_665232/kjlc_665236/qtwt_665250/t1442390.shtml>.

72 The British caution on the issue in point may be deduced from the language used by Attorney General Jeremy Wright's speech on international law and cyberspace, referring to State responsibility only with regard to: 'its internationally wrongful acts, and also for the acts of individuals acting under its instruction, direction or control' (J Wright,

expressed concerns as to the general applicability of due diligence to cyber activities.[73]

This is in line with the proposition that existing international law applies to activities carried out in cyberspace. As such, one may argue that States' obligations to prevent human rights or environmental law violations also apply if those breaches stem from a cyber activity. This means that States are under an obligation to take appropriate measures aimed at preventing cyber activities that may cause those harms.

Following this line of reasoning, the States' obligation to prevent malicious cyber activities targeting CBRN-related activities would stem from relevant obligations relating, *inter alia*, to the protection of the environment and human rights, as well as international disaster law. Amongst those rules, the 'no harm' rule,[74] as developed in the 2001 ILC Draft Articles on Prevention of Transboundary Harm from Hazardous Activities,[75] is of particular importance.[76] For the purpose of the argument put forward in this contribution, it is to be noted that the notion of 'appropriate measures' required by the 'no harm' rule encompasses legislative and administrative actions, including the establishment of 'suitable' monitoring mechanisms.[77] Accordingly, States are required to exercise control over private activities.[78] The degree of care required by States will depend on their material capacities and must be proportionate to the risk of transboundary harm.[79]

'Cyber and International Law in the 21st Century' (2018) available at <https://www.gov.uk/government/speeches/cyber-and-international-law-in-the-21st-century>).

73 New Zealand, 'The Application of International Law to State Activity in Cyberspace' (2020) para 17, available at <https://www.mfat.govt.nz/en/media-and-resources/ministry-statements-and-speeches/cyber-il>. The Author is not aware of any State explicitly excluding the application of existing due diligence obligations protecting collective interests other than international peace and security to activities in cyberspace.

74 The customary nature of 'no harm' has been acknowledged by the International Court of Justice in *Pulp Mills* (*Case concerning Pulp Mills on the River Uruguay* (*Argentina v Uruguay*) (*Pulp Mills*) (2010), ICJ Reports 14, para 101). On such rule, see A Tanzi and A Kolliopoulos, 'The No-Harm Rule' in A Tanzi *et al* (eds), *The UNECE Convention on the Protection and Use of Transboundary Watercourses and International Lakes* (Brill-Martinus Nijhoff 2015) 133.

75 ILC, 'Draft Articles on prevention of transboundary harm from hazardous activities' (2001) II(2) UNYBILC, Article 3, 154. On the application of such rule to CBRN events, see ch 3 by Venier.

76 On 'no harm', see ch 29 by Antoniazzi.

77 ILC (n 75) 156, Article 5.

78 Ibid para 3.

79 Ibid 155, paras 17–18. This is in line with ILC considerations, according to which the degree of diligence 'var[ies] from one context to another for reasons which essentially relate to the object and purpose of the treaty provision or other rule giving rise to the primary

Following the ILC reasoning, the high risk of transboundary harm stemming from CBRN-related activities calls for a high standard of care from the territorial State. In consideration of the dependence of CBRN facilities on ICT,[80] it is arguable that requirements concerning the level of cybersecurity to be implemented and related public monitoring activities would be essential to the aim of preventing CBRN events.

Such mechanisms would have to be balanced with other collective interests and the material implementation capacities of the territorial State and its national private actors.[81] Indeed, States are not required to achieve an absolute result concerning prevention, elimination or mitigation of harms caused by malicious uses of ICT targeting CBRN facilities. They are only required to act diligently in preventing the occurrence of such harm. As such, the standard of diligence required from States with limited capacities would be lower than the one required from technologically advanced States. Furthermore, this construction allows a balancing of interests between those protected by the primary rule of prevention and other interests, such as human rights. This appears of particular importance in the cyber domain, since any State activity of prevention would most probably constitute a restriction of, *inter alia*, the human right to privacy.

The issue remains as to assessment of the 'appropriateness' of given measures. In the absence of universal 'hard law' standards on the issue in point,[82]

---

obligation' (ILC, 'Draft Articles on Responsibility of States for Internationally Wrongful Acts, with Commentaries' (2001) 11(2) UNYBILC 34, para 3).

80 Above, Section 2.

81 On the need to balance considerations of security risk and resource constraints, see UNICRI (n 19).

82 'Hard law' standards have been adopted within the EU context with the so-called 'NIS Directive' (Directive (EU) 2016/1148 of the European Parliament and of the Council of 6 July 2016 concerning measures for a high common level of security of network and information systems across the Union). Member States are under obligations of notification and cooperation in the management and mitigation of incidents. Moreover, the Directive asks States to impose security requirements on operators of essential services and on digital services providers. On the basis of the NIS Directive, Italy has adopted Legislative Decree No 65 of 18 May 2018 (*Italian Official Gazzette General Series* No132 of 09 June 2018). The Commission has recently proposed a revision of the NIS Directive aimed at strengthening cooperation among Member States and enhancing supervision and enforcement of security requirements. See 'Proposal for a Directive of the European Parliament and of the Council on measures for a high common level of cybersecurity across the Union, repealing Directive (EU) 2016/1148' (EU Doc COM(2020) 823 final and EU Doc 2020/0359(COD)), as well as related factsheet, available at <https://ec.europa.eu/digital-single-market/en/news/revised-directive-security-network-and-information-systems-nis2>.

soft law instruments, such as studies by UNICRI[83] and NATO,[84] or regional diplomatic exercises aimed at confidence-building,[85] surely provide authoritative guidance, which may assist private and public actors in the CBRN sector to adopt appropriate security measures, thus avoiding liability.

5 Concluding Remarks

Building upon the consideration that '[t]he expanding use of ICTs in critical infrastructures and industrial control systems creates new possibilities for disruption',[86] the chapter at hand has presented the reasons why cybersecurity has been at the forefront of policymakers' minds since the early 21st Century. States and international bodies have increasingly addressed the issue at hand, with a view to preventing malicious uses of ICT inconsistent with the collective interest in the maintenance of international peace and security.

The present analysis has also addressed the ongoing debate over the application of international obligations to activities in cyberspace. It is commonly accepted that existing international law applies in cyberspace without the need to develop a new legal instrument. However, technical difficulties in attributing conduct in cyberspace make the application of secondary rules on State responsibility difficult, leaving space for 'malicious cyber operations without an author'.

Against this background, applying existing international due diligence obligations to ICT over which a State exercises jurisdiction appears reasonable. This would arguably mitigate the risk and the effect of malicious cyber activities targeting critical infrastructure, and provide the territorial State with legitimate reasons to exercise proportionate monitoring activities on data flows. Moreover, such approach would provide the victim State with a liable party from whom to seek compensation, absent a clear attribution of the cyber operation.

It has been argued that the application of existing obligations of due diligence, eg those stemming from the customary no harm rule, to highly

83 Above, notes 19–21.

84 The NATO Cooperative Cyber Defence Centre of Excellence (<https://ccdcoe.org/>) has devoted many studies to cybersecurity, with special regard to identification of threats. Reference is particularly to be made to the Tallin Manual (Schmitt (n 46)), which, *inter alia*, pinpoints as 'appropriate measures' the adoption of 'domestic legislation requiring companies to report cyber incidents' (ibid 46).

85 See initiatives referred to above (n 17).

86 2013 GGE Report (n 32) para 9.

ICT-dependent CBRN facilities requires the territorial State to exercise control over the appropriateness of the cybersecurity standards of any CBRN facility, irrespective of its private or public nature, with a view to fostering the prevention of CBRN events.

Following this line of reasoning, no new international legal instrument is necessary to require States to adopt cybersecurity regulations and strategies. Indeed, current international law concerning the prevention of harm and mitigation of consequences thereof may be easily construed as encompassing prevention of malicious cyber activities – *ie* cybersecurity. Moreover, the above line of reasoning would ground the assessment by existing compliance review mechanisms of the 'appropriateness' of States' cybersecurity strategies and plans, insofar as their inadequacy could generate a harmful event triggering States' liability under relevant international disaster, environmental or human rights law. However, the 'transboundary nature' of ICT implies that no State can tackle cyber-related issues alone. Initiatives aimed at fostering cooperation and harmonisation, in particular at a regional level,[87] are surely desirable and called for.

Bibliography

Abaimov S and Martellini M, 'Selected Issues of Cyber Security Practices in CBRNeCy Critical Infrastructure' in M Martellini and A Malizia (eds), *Cyber and Chemical, Biological, Radiological, Nuclear, Explosives Challenges. Threats and Counter Efforts* (Springer 2017) 11.

Antonopoulos C, 'State responsibility in cyberspace' in N Tsagourias and R Buchan (eds), *Research Handbook on International Law and Cyberspace* (Edward Elgar 2015) 62–65.

Bannelier-Christakis K, 'Cyber Diligence: A Low-Intensity Due Diligence Principle for Low-Intensity Cyber Operations?' (2014) 14(1) Baltic YBIL 28–39.

Barnidge R, 'The due diligence principle in International Law' (2006) 8(1) ICLR 81.

Besson S, 'La Due Diligence En Droit International' (2020) 409 Recueil des Cours de l'Académie de Droit International 159.

Bjorge E, *The Evolutionary Interpretation of Treaties* (OUP 2014).

Chircop L, 'A due diligence standard of attribution in cyberspace' (2018) 67(3) ICLQ 643.

87 See the OAS Cyber Security Initiative, OSCE Decision No. 5/17 and the recent EU Cybersecurity strategy and the ongoing ASEAN-EU dialogue on cybersecurity cooperation referred to above (n 17).

Delerue F, 'Attribution to State of Cyber Operations Conducted by Non-State Actors' in E Carpanelli and N Lazzerini (eds), *Use and Misuse of New Technologies* (Springer 2019) 233.

Gilibrays G, Mugeni G and Matovu D, 'Role of ICT in Disaster Response and Management: A Review Study of ICT Challenges and Adoption Approaches by Developing Nations' (2016) 6(5) *International Journal of Advanced Research in Computer Science and Software Engineering* 196.

Payne C and Finlay L, 'Addressing Obstacles to Cyber-Attribution: A Model Based on State Response to Cyber-Attack' (2017) 49(3) Geo Wash Int'l L Rev 535.

Pisillo Mazzeschi R, *"Due diligence" e responsabilità internazionale degli Stati* (Giuffré 1989).

Purchase E and Caldwell F, 'Digital Pearl Harbor: A Case Study in Industry Vulnerability to Cyber Attack' in S Ghosh, M Malek and EA Stohr (eds), *Guarding Your Business. A Management Approach to Security* (Springer 2004) 47.

Roscini M, *Cyber Operations and the Use of Force in International Law* (OUP 2014).

Sardu A, 'L'*International Cybersecurity Law*: lo stato dell'arte' (2020) 75(1) *La Comunità Internazionale* 14.

Schmitt MN (ed), *Tallinn Manual 2.0 on the International Law Applicable to Cyber Operations* (2nd edn; CUP 2017).

Siers R, 'Cybersecurity' in PD Williams and M McDonald (eds), *Security Studies: An Introduction* (3rd edn; Routledge 2018) 556.

Stout TM and Williams TJ, 'Pioneering Work in the Field of Computer Process Control' (1995) (17)1 *IEEE Annals of the History of Computing* 6.

Tanzi A, 'Liability for Lawful Acts', *Max Planck Encyclopedia of Public International Law* (February 2013).

Tanzi A and Kolliopoulos A, 'The No-Harm Rule' in A Tanzi *et al* (eds), *The UNECE Convention on the Protection and Use of Transboundary Watercourses and International Lakes* (Brill-Martinus Nijhoff 2015) 133.

PART 5

Responsibilities, Enforcement Mechanisms, Remedies

CHAPTER 32

Obligation to Prosecute CBRN-Related International Crimes

Luisa Vierucci

1 Introduction

International crimes are the most heinous offences undermining the values of the international community as a whole.[1] The core international crimes – that will be the focus of this contribution – are acts of genocide, crimes against humanity and war crimes. The gravity of these acts requires that the persons responsible be brought to justice. As stated in the Preamble to the International Criminal Court (ICC) Statute 'the most serious crimes of concern to the international community as a whole must not go unpunished and [...] their effective prosecution must be ensured by taking measures at the national level and by enhancing international cooperation.' More precisely, 'it is the duty of every State to exercise its criminal jurisdiction over those responsible for international crimes.' At the same time, the Statute creates an 'independent permanent International Criminal Court' to supplement, under certain conditions, States' jurisdiction to fight impunity for these abhorrent crimes.

As we shall see, some CBRN-related offences may amount to acts of genocide, crimes against humanity or war crimes.[2] After having identified the elements of the CBRN-related international crimes, the obligations incumbent upon States with respect to the prosecution of these crimes will be analysed by distinguishing the various stages of the criminal proceedings to which they are connected. The umbrella obligation to prosecute requires, in the first place, that the elements of the crime and the appropriate penalties be established in the national legal order; secondly, the submission of the case to the relevant authorities for the purposes of the investigation and, as the case may be, prosecution or extradition; thirdly, the cooperation and assistance with other States or the ICC.

1 A Cassese, *International Criminal Law* (OUP 2008) 11.

2 For the scope of the obligation to prosecute in case of CBRN-related offences not amounting to a war crimes, see ch 33 by Amoroso.

Finally, this contribution will address the legal consequences under international law of the violation of one of the above obligations.

2 Obligation to Criminalise

A number of treaties require States to establish the elements of certain international crimes and appropriate penalties into their national legal order. These treaties are analysed below under the headings of war crimes, genocide and crimes against humanity. Interestingly, the ICC Statute does not expressly demand that States Parties modify their national laws but should a State be 'unable' to prosecute one of the offences contained in Articles 6–8 of the Statute, the Court may admit the case on account of this very inability.[3] In practice, many States have incorporated the ICC Statute into their domestic law.[4] In most cases, the degree of national implementation of the Statute has been comprehensive, since not only have the elements of the crimes and penalties been incorporated but also the different modes of participation in the crimes, as well as cooperation and assistance with the Court.

When a State criminalises conduct on the basis of either an express treaty requirement or in order to be able to prosecute the ICC offences, it retains autonomy as to the concrete modalities of incorporation.[5] That said, the State's discretion cannot go so far as to limit the scope of application of the offence, as we shall see for each specific international crime.

2.1 *War Crimes*

The scope of the obligation to incorporate war crimes into national law differs depending on the typology of the crime. While the regime for grave breaches of the four 1949 Geneva Conventions is quite detailed, for non-grave breaches, the content of the obligation is more blurred.

Starting with the grave breaches, each of the four Geneva Conventions contains an identical provision whereby the High Contracting Parties 'undertake to enact any legislation necessary to provide effective penal sanctions for

3 The principle of complementarity between the ICC and the States Parties only implicitly requires States to criminalise the prohibited conduct. Failing to do so means that the Court might find the relevant State in a situation of inability to prosecute and hence may exercise jurisdiction in place of the State (see infra subpara 5).

4 See F Jessberger and G Werle, 'Principles of International Criminal Law' (OUP 2020, 4th ed) para 90 also for the extensive bibliography on this issue.

5 For details on the various modalities of implementation that States have adopted, see ibid paras 466–480.

persons committing, or ordering to be committed, any of the grave breaches of the present Convention defined in the following Article'.[6] A similar wording is included in the 1977 Additional Protocol I on the Protection of Victims of International Armed Conflicts, which extends and complements the four Conventions.[7]

The following acts are defined as 'grave breaches' in all four Conventions and may all be relevant for CBRN war crimes: 'wilful killing, torture or inhuman treatment, including biological experiments, wilfully causing great suffering or serious injury to body or health, and extensive destruction and appropriation of property, not justified by military necessity and carried out unlawfully and wantonly.'

A CBRN offence may constitute a grave breach of the 1949 Geneva Conventions, as included in Article 8(2)(a) of the ICC Statute. In particular, the use of a CBRN agent may amount to the grave breach of wilfully killing a protected person (art 8(2)(a)(i)); or of torture or inhuman treatment by way of biological experiments (art 8(2)(a)(ii)); or of wilfully causing great suffering, or serious injury to body or health (art 8(2)(a)(iii)).[8]

While the criminalisation regime for grave breaches of the Geneva Conventions is quite straight forward, the same cannot be said for war crimes other than grave breaches. This issue is delicate because the use of prohibited weapons relevant to CBRN offences, namely chemical and biological weapons, does not *per se* qualify as a grave breach of the Geneva Conventions. However, to some extent, the ICC Statute allows prosecution of these acts. Article 8(2)(b)(xvii) criminalises the use of 'poison or poisoned weapons' and subparagraph (xviii) the use of 'asphyxiating, poisonous or other gases, and all analogous liquids, materials or devices'. The wording of these two provisions, closely resembling those of earlier conventions, such as the 1925 Geneva Protocol for the Prohibition on the Use in War of Asphyxiating, Poisonous or Other Gases and of Bacteriological Methods of Warfare, purposefully excludes express reference to biological and chemical weapons. At the Rome diplomatic conference where the ICC Statute was adopted, the debate on this issue was very heated because closely linked to the criminalisation of such weapons is the employment of nuclear weapons. The decision to exclude express reference

6 Arts 49, 50, 129, and 146, respectively, of the First, Second, Third, and Fourth Geneva Conventions of 1949.

7 Art 85 (1), (3) and art 88 (2) of Additional Protocol I of 1977 to the four Geneva Conventions of 1949.

8 The prosecution of a CBRN-related war crime as a grave breach of the Geneva Conventions has the downside of not specifically stigmatising the abhorrent nature of the agent used because it focuses exclusively on the effects produced on the protected person.

to biological and chemical weapons, despite two widely ratified Conventions banning these weapons, respectively of 1972 and 1993,[9] as well as the customary nature of the prohibition, was mainly due to the attempt to avoid charges of 'hypocrisy' in light of the Statute's silence over nuclear weapons.

According to the majority view,[10] which is the most legally sound, Articles 8(2)(b)(xvii) and (xviii) do cover the use of biological and chemical weapons. This conclusion is warranted under an interpretation based on the literal reading of the two provisions, which should be preferred, on the basis of Article 31 of the Vienna Convention on the Law of Treaties, to an interpretation based on the legislative history of the treaty.[11] In addition, the ICC Elements of Crimes confirm that these articles cover any instance of 'death or serious damage to health'.[12]

In short, the use of biological and chemical weapons is criminalised by the ICC Statute, at least when such use entails consequences above a certain threshold, while herbicide and riot control agents would generally be excluded, at least when their use does not reach the relevant damage threshold.[13]

Different considerations apply with respect to nuclear weapons. Despite the fact that one cannot deny that the term 'poison' seems to attach also to the effects produced by this type of weapon, the pertinent practice shows that these weapons are not considered as included in the existing disarmament

---

9 See ch 21 by Mauri.

10 For the view that neither toxins nor chemicals or biological weapons fall under the category of 'poison' see P Webb and A Alamuddin, 'Expanding Jurisdiction over War Crimes under Article 8 of the ICC Statute' (2010) JICJ 1228 and K Allen, S Spence and R Escauriaza Leal, 'Chemical and biological weapons use in the Rome Statute: a case for change', Vertic Brief, 14 February 2011, 10, available at <http://www.vertic.org/media/assets/Publications/VB%2014.pdf>.

11 D Akande, 'Can the ICC Prosecute the Use of Chemical Weapons in Syria?', EJIL Blog, 23 August 2013, available at <https://www.ejiltalk.org/can-the-icc-prosecute-for-use-of-chemical-weapons-in-syria>. Cf also M Sossai, 'Identifying the Perpetrators of Chemical Attacks in Syria' (2019) JICJ 223; A Zimmermann and M Şener, 'Chemical Weapons and the International Criminal Court', (2014) AJIL 439. Along the same lines W Schabas and Y Askar, *Implementing International Humanitarian Law, From the Ad Hoc Tribunals to a Permanent International Criminal Court* (Routledge 2004) 189.

12 The relevant Element of Crimes provision reads as follows: 'The [gas, substance or device] was such that it causes death or serious damage to health in the ordinary course of events, through its [asphyxiating or toxic] properties' (available at <https://www.icc-cpi.int/nr/rdonlyres/336923d8-a6ad-40ec-ad7b-45bf9de73d56/0/elementsofcrimeseng.pdf>).

13 The use of herbicide and riot control agents are possibly excluded from the Court's jurisdiction, at least when they remain below the above threshold, see N Reid, F T Davis and V R Halek, 'Defining a War Crime Does the Department of Defense Law of War Manual Comply with the Rome Statute?' (2018) GWashIntlLRev 879.

treaties. Importantly, the *travaux préparatoires* of the ICC Statute indicate the drafters' intention not to criminalise their use.[14]

Nevertheless, the above considerations should not lead to the conclusion that no use of the nuclear weapon could ever come before the ICC. On the strength of Article 8(2)(b)(xx), the Court can scrutinise the legitimacy of the way in which the weapon is used.[15] This overarching provision contains two 'cardinal principles [...] constituting the fabric of humanitarian law',[16] namely the prohibition on causing superfluous injury or unnecessary suffering and the principle of distinction. The legislative history clarifies that this provision was not meant as a general clause to criminalise the use of any weapon that causes avoidable suffering to combatants, but rather to confine the criminalisation to two conditions: (i) the existence of a 'comprehensive prohibition' with respect to these weapons, and (ii) the inclusion of the specific weapon in an annex to the Statute.[17] Nuclear weapons would most probably meet the first condition and in this respect it is not without importance to refer to the International Court of Justice (ICJ), which, in 1996, had already determined the extreme difficulty of using nuclear weapons in conformity with the basic principles of International Humanitarian Law, including the ones under examination here.[18] By contrast, the annex specifying the type of weapons prohibited has not yet been approved by the ICC Assembly of the States Parties and for the time being this makes the prospects for the Court to adjudicate upon such crimes remote.

The principle of distinction appears in Article 8(2)(b)(xx), which prohibits weapons that are 'inherently indiscriminate in violation of the international law of armed conflict'. The indiscriminate nature of nuclear weapons can hardly be denied, yet this part of the provision is rendered moot by the fact that no annex listing the specific prohibited weapons has been adopted.

---

14 W Schabas, *The International Criminal Court: A Commentary on the Rome Statute* (OUP 2010) 244.

15 The Article defines as a war crime 'Employing weapons, projectiles and material and methods of warfare which are of a nature to cause superfluous injury or unnecessary suffering or which are inherently indiscriminate in violation of the international law of armed conflict, provided that such weapons, projectiles and material and methods of warfare are the subject of a comprehensive prohibition and are included in an annex to this Statute, by an amendment in accordance with the relevant provisions set forth in articles 121 and 123'.

16 *Legality of the Threat or Use of Nuclear Weapons*, Advisory Opinion of 8 July 1996, (1996) ICJ Reports, para 78.

17 R Clark, 'Building on Article 8(2)(b)(xx) of the Rome Statute of the International Criminal Court: Weapons and Methods of Warfare', (2009) New Criminal Law Review 376.

18 *Nuclear Weapons case* (n 16) para 95.

That said, the Court may qualify as a war crime a conduct consisting in the use of indiscriminate weapons by relying on Article 8(2)(b)(i)[19] that concerns an intentional attack directed against the civilian population as such.[20]

The above analysis has taken us from the crime of using a specific weapon to the rules concerning the way in which a weapon that does not fall into an express prohibition has to be used. This latter set of rules concerns not only nuclear but also all other types of weapons, including radiological ones. The modality of use of the weapons may be scrutinised by the ICC only if it amounts to a violation of the principle of proportionality (art 8(2)(b)(iv)) or, as just said, to a deliberate attack against a protected person or object.

In particular, the radioactivity released by radiological weapons risks polluting food to a degree that is conducive to the onset of cancer or to causing direct death.[21] Importantly, the detonation of an explosive enriched with a radioactive substance may contaminate a large area as a result of the propagation and deposition of aerosols produced by the explosion.[22]

The contamination may concern both the soil and buildings, as well as persons by way of inhalation of the radioactive molecules. This may amount to several distinct war crimes contemplated in Article 8 ICC St., in particular, the grave breach of wilfully causing great suffering or serious injury to body or health,[23] and/or the violation of the principle of proportionality with respect both to 'the incidental loss of life or injury to civilians or damage to civilian objects' and 'widespread, long-term and severe damage to the natural environment'.[24]

The articles of the ICC Statute concerning the means of warfare were amended in 2010 to apply also in non-international armed conflict.[25] This update still suffers from the lack of adoption of the annex listing the specific weapon that are prohibited and, in addition, comes into force only for those States that have ratified it. This means the ICC has jurisdiction over the crimes

19 Art 8(2)(e)(i) criminalises the same act when committed in non-international armed conflicts.

20 The wording used in the ICC Statute covers a broad range of conduct since it criminalises the mere launching of an indiscriminate attack regardless of the ensuing results, C Ponti, 'The Crime of Indiscriminate Attack and Unlawful Conventional Weapons: The Legacy of the ICTY Jurisprudence', (2015) Journal of International Humanitarian Legal Studies 126–127.

21 C Wirz and E Egger, 'Use of nuclear and radiological weapons by terrorists?' (2005) IRRC 504.

22 Ibid 505.

23 Art 8(2)(a)(iii).

24 Art 8(2)(b)(iv).

25 For a commentary, cf P Webb and A Alamuddin (n 10) 1219–1243.

contained in Article 8(2)(e)(xiii) and (xiv) only if the State of nationality of the accused or of the place of commission of the act has ratified the 2010 amendment or if the Security Council refers the situation to the Court.[26]

Also relevant to CBRN-related offences is the war crime of physical mutilation[27] or medical or scientific experiment[28] that is punishable under Article 8(2)(b)(x) ICC St.[29] This provision is limited to treatments carried out with respect to persons that are hospitalised or otherwise find themselves 'in the power or an adverse party.' Hence, regrettably, it seems not to cover attacks with CBRN agents whose purpose is to study the effects on the population in general. This crime, clearly relevant as far as the use of chemicals for medical experiments is concerned, is also significant with respect to biological agents, in particular in relation to biotechnology advances, inasmuch as it is possible to manipulate life processes, such as cognition, development, reproduction, and inheritance.[30]

Turning to the *mens rea*, according to Article 30 ICC St., unless otherwise specified, the required mental element is intent and knowledge, namely the intention to bring about a certain result or awareness that a certain event will occur in the ordinary course of events.[31] It is important to note, therefore, that with respect to the use of 'poison and poisonous weapons', as well as 'asphyxiating, poisonous or other gases, and all analogous liquids, materials or devices', awareness of the effects of such weapons is not required by the Elements of Crimes – contrary to the case, for example, with the use of other bullets.[32]

For medical experiments amounting to a grave breach, a specific *mens rea* must be proved (art 8(2)(a)(ii)), namely '[t]he intent of the experiment was non-therapeutic and it was neither justified by medical reasons nor carried out

26 Importantly, the Elements of Crimes for these added crimes in non-international armed conflicts are identical to those for international conflicts.

27 Mutilation is defined as an act which, in particular, causes permanent disfigurement or disability, or the removal of an organ or appendage (Elements of Crimes), circumstances that may be easily caused by the use of chemical and nuclear agents.

28 According to the Elements of Crimes, it suffices that the conduct 'seriously endangered the physical or mental health or integrity'.

29 S Mehring, 'Medical War Crimes', in A von Bogdandy and R Wolfrum (eds), (2011) MaxPlanckYrbkUNL 229–279.

30 L Vierucci, 'Offensive Military Applications of Biotechnologies: Loopholes in the Law?', in F Francioni (ed), *Biotechnologies and International Human Rights* (Hart 2007) 363–389.

31 In addition to the customary requirement of the nexus between the conduct and the armed conflict.

32 The Elements of Crimes concerning the employment of prohibited bullets require the perpetrator's awareness that 'the nature of the bullets was such that their employment would uselessly aggravate suffering or the wounding effect'.

in such person's or persons' interest' (Elements of Crimes), whereas no similar elements are envisaged for the 'medical or scientific experiment' consisting in a serious violation of the laws and customs of war (art 8(2)(b)(x)).

2.2 *Genocide*

The 1948 Convention on the Prevention and Repression of Genocide expressly requires States Parties 'to enact, in accordance with their respective Constitutions, the necessary legislation to give effect to the provisions of the present Convention and, in particular, to provide effective penalties' (art V).

The first question to be addressed is whether CBRN-related offences may qualify as acts of genocide. These are defined in Article II of the Convention as:

> any of the following acts committed with intent to destroy, in whole or in part, a national, ethnical, racial or religious group, as such:
> (a) Killing members of the group;
> (b) Causing serious bodily or mental harm to members of the group;
> (c) Deliberately inflicting on the group conditions of life calculated to bring about its physical destruction in whole or in part;
> (d) Imposing measures intended to prevent births within the group;
> (e) Forcibly transferring children of the group to another group.

All but the last count may be relevant to the use of CBRN agents and are therefore analysed separately in light of the ICC Statute that at Article 6 takes up *verbatim* the above clause of the Convention.

The first category of crime consists in 'killing members of the group'. The term 'killing' is a synonym for 'murder',[33] both intentional and voluntary, and is satisfied whether committed against one or more persons.[34] The extensive and usually lethal consequences of the use of CBRN agents obviously make this underlying offence central to our analysis, similarly to the second offence, which consists in 'causing serious bodily or mental harm to members of the group'.[35] With respect to this count, the fallout of the agents, be they radioactive or of another toxic nature, usually brings about harm that results in a 'grave and long-term disadvantage to a person's ability to lead a normal and

33 Art 6(a) ICC St.
34 See Elements of Crimes for art 6(a).
35 Art 6(b) ICC St.

constructive life',[36] therefore making it unproblematic to establish this material element of the crime.

Another relevant underlying offence is 'deliberately inflicting on the group conditions of life calculated to bring about its physical destruction in whole or in part'.[37] For our purposes, the ICC Elements of Crimes include an important specification to the effect that the infliction of 'conditions of life' includes, but is not limited to, 'intentional deprivation of resources indispensable for survival, such as deprivation of food or medical services'. The consequence of the employment of a CBRN agent may potentially be considered under this count. An illustrative example is the *Al-Bashir* case, where the ICC Trial-Chamber I has found that there are reasonable grounds to believe that the accused has committed this offence against several ethnic groups living in the Darfur region of Sudan by 'subjecting the group[s] to destruction of their means of survival in their homeland' through, among other acts, contamination of wells and water pumps.[38]

Under this count, the creation of circumstances that would lead to a 'slow death', such as poisoning with a low quantity of toxic material, would be prosecutable.[39] Moreover, this count may be invoked in relation to deliberate State policies that, in case of epidemics, deprive a certain group of access to medicine or protective equipment. Indeed, 'reduction of medical services below minimum requirement' has already been considered as a basis for conviction for genocide.[40]

Lastly, chemicals may be involved in the practice of forced sterilisation or measures of birth control, which are usually considered as amounting to the offence of 'imposing measures intended to prevent births within the group.'[41]

For each offence, the Elements of Crimes specify that the conduct does not have to take place as part of a pattern of similar conduct if it constitutes

---

36 This is the requirement threshold set out by the ICTY Trial Chamber, *Prosecutor v. Krstic* IT-97-24-T (Judgment), 31 July 2003, para 513. The ICC Elements of Crimes only specify that this offence is not limited to acts such as 'torture, rape, sexual violence or inhuman or degrading treatment'.

37 Art 6(c) ICC St.

38 ICC Pre-Trial Chamber I, *Prosecutor v. Al-Bashir* ICC-02/05-01/09, Second Decision on the Prosecution's Application for a Warrant of Arrest, 12 July 2010, paras 36–38.

39 In this sense, ICTY Trial Chamber, *Prosecutor v. Brdanin* IT-99-36-T (Judgment), 1 September 2004, para 691.

40 ICTR Trial Chamber, *Prosecutor v. Akayesu* ICTR-96-4 (Judgment), 2 September 1998, paras 505–6.

41 A Cassese (n 1) 134.

'conduct that could itself effect [...] destruction [of a group]'. This clarification possibly broadens the offence of genocide so as to cover a single use of a CBRN agent, provided that the other elements of the crime are satisfied.

The international crime of genocide requires a double intent: on the one hand, the intent of the underlying offence, on the other, the special intent (*dolus specialis*) of 'destroying, in whole or in part, a national, ethnical, racial or religious group, as such'. This means that, despite the enormously lethal potential of the agents under examination, a charge for genocide may fail if the agents are not employed against one or more persons because he or she is a member of a specific group. Membership in the protected group is thus an essential element of the crime, despite the despicable nature of the agent employed.

The question whether genocide requires a 'contextual element' of similar acts[42] or may be committed even by a lone individual is a long-debated issue that can be of relevance to some CBRN agents.[43] The scenario of a single individual detonating a radiological device, for example, is not implausible. In our opinion, the Elements of Crimes envisage the possibility of a single perpetrator committing an act of genocide when they spell out, for each material element of the crime, that 'a conduct that could itself effect [...] [destruction of a group]' is enough. The ICC Trial Chamber has corroborated this approach when it has found 'the lack of any irreconcilable contradiction between the definition of the crime of genocide of article 6 of the Statute and the contextual element provided for in the Elements of Crimes'.[44]

Having clarified which CBRN-related offences may amount to an act of genocide, let us turn to the scope of the duty to enact national legislation. Although States enjoy discretion as to the modalities of implementation of this crime into their national legal order, their autonomy is restricted by the need to preserve and respect the elements of the crime of genocide. This means that national re-formulation of the crime that, for example, requires a genocidal plan as a constitutive element or restricts the list of underlying offences constitutes a violation of the obligation to criminalise. Importantly, according to the

42 The contextual element refers to the broader environment in which the conduct has taken place, meaning that the single act forms part of other similar acts against the protected group.

43 For the position in favour of the 'lone génocidaire', see A Cassese (n 1) 140–141; for the opposite view, W Schabas, 'Darfur and the "Odious Scourge": The Commission of Inquiry's Findings on Genocide' (2005) LJIL 877.

44 ICC Pre-Trial Chamber II, *Prosecutor v. Al-Bashir* ICC-02/05-01/09-3, Decision on Arrest Warrant, 4 March 2009, para. 132. See C Kress, 'The Crime of Genocide and Contextual Elements: A Comment on the ICC Pre-Trial Chamber's Decision in the Al Bashir Case' (2009) JICJ 300–304.

1948 Genocide Convention, the obligation to criminalise does not only relate to the establishment of 'effective penalties' in domestic law but extends to the modalities of participation, namely: conspiracy to commit genocide, direct and public incitement to commit genocide, attempt to commit genocide and complicity in genocide.[45]

2.3 *Crimes against Humanity*

No general convention on crimes against humanity exists. In 2019, the Draft Articles on Prevention and Punishment of Crimes against Humanity were adopted by the UN International Law Commission (ILC)[46] and submitted to the UN General Assembly, which is currently analysing them. The Articles contain an articulate provision titled 'Criminalization under national law' that requires not only enactment at the domestic level of the specific underlying offences and modalities of participation but also exclusion of the relevance of the official capacity of the author, superior orders and statutes of limitation. Clearly it remains to be seen whether these Draft Articles will become the text of a Convention.[47]

In any case, there may be CBRN-related offences which amount to a crime against humanity, as can be illustrated by referring to Article 7 of the ICC Statute.

As to the *actus reus*, Article 7(1) ICC St. contains an exhaustive list of prohibited conduct amounting to crimes against humanity, none of which refers to the mere use of prohibited agents or weapons. Nonetheless, the effects that the use of a CBRN agent bring about may amount to several crimes against humanity, in particular murder[48] or extermination.[49] Also, the general residual

45 Art III of the Genocide Convention.

46 The text of the Draft Articles is available at <https://legal.un.org/ilc/texts/instruments/english/draft_articles/7_7_2019.pdf>.

47 See Article 6 of the Draft Articles. For a comment, cf. C Jalloh, 'The International Law Commission's First Draft Convention on Crimes Against Humanity: Codification, Progressive Development, or Both?' (2020) CaseWResJIntlL 331–405. To date, the only treaty that requires criminalisation of a crime against humanity is the 2006 International Convention for the Protection of All Persons from Enforced Disappearance, which is not relevant to CBRN offences.

48 The ICC jurisprudence has so far followed the well-established criterion whereby there must be a 'causal link between the act of murder and the victim's death' (ICC Pre-trial Chamber II, *Prosecutor v. Jean-Pierre Bemba Gombo* ICC-01/05-01/08, Decision Pursuant to Article 61(7)(a) and (b) of the Rome Statute, 15 June 2009, para 132). This link is probably easier to prove in the case of use of CBRN weapons than for conventional ones.

49 According to art 7(2)(b), extermination may be committed also by depriving access to food. A case in point may be contamination of food by adding chemical or radioactive substances, for example in production plants, during transport or even at shops. In such instances '[e]ven a selective and weak contamination of only a small number of items

provision criminalising 'other acts of a similar character intentionally causing great suffering, or serious injury to body or to mental or physical health'[50] is likely to cover the use of CBRN agents, given the large-scale effects especially of chemical, biological and nuclear agents.

Hence, although the use *per se* of CBRN agents is not an underlying offence of a crime against humanity, the consequences that this may have upon the civilian population may give rise to such an international crime.[51]

Article 7(1) ICC St. sets out an additional element for the crime, namely that the prohibited acts must be committed 'as part of a widespread or systematic attack against any civilian population'. The ICC Pre-Trial Chamber II has clarified that a widespread attack is 'large-scale', 'massive, frequent, carried out collectively with considerable seriousness and directed against a multiplicity of victims'.[52] By contrast, the term 'systematic' reflects 'the organised nature of the acts of violence and the improbability of their random occurrence'. It refers to the existence of 'patterns of crimes, evidenced by non-accidental repetition of similar criminal conduct on a regular basis'.[53]

The nature of CBRN agents makes the fulfilment of the 'widespread' requirement of the *chapeau* to Article 7(1) almost automatic. More troublesome may be the jurisprudential interpretation whereby the civilian population must be 'the primary object of the attack and not just an incidental victim',[54] because this would possibly exclude the use of CBRN agents against combatants as a crime against humanity.

For crimes against humanity, the ICC Statute adds a further requirement, namely that the attack be 'pursuant to or in furtherance of a State or organizational policy' (art 7(2)(a)). This component is explained in the Elements of Crimes as an 'active promotion or encouragement' of an attack against a civilian population on the part of a State or organisation. This is a narrow definition that may lead judges to exclude some scenarios, such as the employment of a CBRN agent through a practice that is simply tolerated or condoned

would have a considerable effect on the public', Wirz and Egger (n 21) 505. Most probably the use of chemical weapons during the armed conflict in Syria would constitute murder or extermination, cf Y Naqvi, 'Crossing the Red Line: The Use of Chemical Weapons in Syria and What Should Happen Now' (2017) IRRC 959.

50 Art 7(1)(k) ICC St.

51 C Harwood, 'The Use of Chemical Weapons is not a Crime against Humanity', 18 September 2013, available at <https://dovjacobs.com/2013/09/18/guest-post-the-use-of-chemical-weapons-is-not-a-crime-against-humanity>.

52 ICC Pre-trial Chamber II, *Prosecutor v. Jean-Pierre Bemba Gombo* (n 48) para 83.

53 ICC Trial Chamber IV, *Prosecutor v. Bosco Ntaganda* ICC-01/04-02/06 (Judgment) 8 July 2019 para 692.

54 ICC Pre-trial Chamber II, *Prosecutor v. Jean-Pierre Bemba Gombo* (n 48) para 76.

by the authorities,[55] or pursued in violation of superior orders, or that consists in a 'spontaneous or isolated act of violence.'[56] As a result, even if the use of CBRN weapons is interpreted widely to include the consequences they yield when used against a civilian population, it appears that only those consequences that are planned may qualify as a crime against humanity.[57]

Lastly, compliance with the ICC Statute also requires States Parties to incorporate into national law the criminalisation of modalities of participation in the crime other than its actual commission, as well as cooperation and assistance with the ICC with respect to the crime in question. The overwhelming practice of the States Parties to duly incorporate Article 7 ICC St. into national law is particularly important given the fact that most national legal orders do not allow the prosecution of an offence on the basis of an international customary law definition of a crime.

3 Obligation to Prosecute

The obligation to prosecute consists in the submission of the case to the relevant State's authorities for the purposes of prosecution. It comprises the obligation to investigate, apprehend, prosecute or extradite and, eventually, punish the perpetrators of the crime.[58]

The scope of the obligations differs depending on the qualification of the act as a war crime, or as genocide or a crime against humanity.

3.1 *War Crimes*

The first treaties concerning international crimes to establish the obligation to prosecute are the four Geneva Conventions of 1949, in the part instituting the grave breaches regime.[59] This obligation to prosecute arises as soon as

55 A Cassese (n 1) 135.

56 ICC Pre-trial Chamber II, *Prosecutor v. Jean-Pierre Bemba Gombo* (n 48) para 81.

57 Obviously, the *mens rea* requirements are the same whether the crime against humanity is committed through a CBRN agent or in another manner, namely, (i) the mental element proper to the underlying offence, and (ii) awareness of the existence of a widespread or systematic practice.

58 The possibility that the obligation to prosecute an international crime may be barred by immunities is not specific to CBRN-related international crimes. Generally on this obstacle to prosecution, see Jessberger and Werle (n 4) paras 820–849.

59 According to Articles 49, 50, 129, and 146 respectively of the First, Second, Third and Fourth Geneva Conventions of 1949, each Contracting Party 'is obligated to search for persons alleged to have committed, or to have ordered to be committed, grave breaches, and to bring such persons, regardless of their nationality, before its own courts'.

the alleged offender is present on the territory and the authorities have sufficient evidence to bring a criminal charge.[60] This means that no prosecutorial discretion may be exercised if the evidence requires opening a criminal case. Therefore, the obligation to search for and submit to prosecution an alleged offender is not conditional on any jurisdictional consideration, apart from the presence of the individual on the territory. However, upon receipt of a request for extradition, and provided the requesting State has established a *prima facie* case, the territorial State has discretion to choose between prosecution and extradition.[61]

3.2 *Genocide and Crimes against Humanity*

According to Article VI of the Genocide Convention, persons charged with committing genocide or another form of participation in the crime shall be tried by 'a competent tribunal of the State in the territory of which the act was committed'. Alternatively, the trial may take place before 'such international penal tribunal as may have jurisdiction with respect to those Contracting Parties which shall have accepted its jurisdiction.'

This 'rudimentary'[62] enforcement mechanism regime certainly imposes an obligation upon the States Parties to the Convention to bring to the attention of the relevant authorities an act of genocide on the basis of the territoriality principle of criminal jurisdiction. The question then arises whether such an obligation extends also to those States Parties whose territory was not involved in acts of genocide. On this point, practice is not uniform.[63] For example, while in the 1996 judgment in *Bosnia v Yugoslavia*, the ICJ stated that the obligation to punish the crime of genocide was 'not territorially limited by the Convention',[64] in the 2007 case of *Bosnia v Serbia* it opined that:

---

60 P Gaeta, 'Grave Breaches of the Geneva Conventions', in A Clapham, P Gaeta and M Sassoli (eds), *The 1949 Geneva Conventions – A commentary* (OUP 2015) 631.

61 As a matter of fact, the wording used in the Geneva Conventions is 'handing over' instead of extradition. However, the former is to be considered as a synonym for the latter with respect both to the actual transfer of the person under the control and authority of the requested State and to judicial involvement (the fact that 'a *prima facie* case' is established refers to such judicial involvement). This conclusion is corroborated by the fact that Additional Protocol I, that supplements and completes the Geneva Conventions, uses the term 'extradition' (art 88). For a different opinion, see M Henzelin, *Le principe de l'universalité en droi penal international* (Bruylant 2000) 353.

62 ILC, *The obligation to extradite or prosecute* (aut dedere aut judicare), 2014 Final Report, para 14.

63 For the debate, see Jessberger and Werle (n 4) paras 282–284.

64 ICJ, *Case concerning the Application of the Convention on the Prevention and Punishment of the Crime of Genocide* (*Bosnia and Herzegovina v. Yugoslavia*), Preliminary Objections (1996) ICJ Reports para 31.

> Article VI only obliges the Contracting Parties to institute and exercise territorial criminal jurisdiction; while it certainly does not prohibit States, with respect to genocide, from conferring jurisdiction on their criminal courts based on criteria other than where the crime was committed which are compatible with international law, in particular the nationality of the accused, it does not oblige them to do so.[65]

On account of the customary nature of the crime of genocide, the question is warranted whether a rule of custom has developed which obliges States to prosecute perpetrators of genocide. The same question extends to crimes against humanity, whose customary nature seems uncontroversial. There is no doubt that a similar custom exists, both for genocide and crimes against humanity,[66] as to the obligation of the territorial State to prosecute the alleged perpetrators of these crimes.[67]

Less clear is the existence of a similar obligation in the absence of any jurisdictional link with the State. The legal doctrine is divided on this issue,[68] whilst the works of the ILC on the *aut dedere aut iudicare* principle appear illustrative of an evolving trend. According to the Commission, on the one hand, the position of States seems quite clear-cut since only one State, Belgium, has 'claimed unambiguously that a customary obligation exists to prosecute or extradite for offences of genocide'; on the other, the Commission hints at the fact that its own position is in favour of the existence of a similar customary obligation.[69]

Turning specifically to the rules on extradition, the Genocide Convention spells out in Article VII that 'Genocide and the other acts enumerated in

65 ICJ, *Case concerning the Application of the Convention on the Prevention and Punishment of the Crime of Genocide (Bosnia and Herzegovina v. Serbia and Montenegro)*, Judgment (2007) ICJ Reports para 442.

66 Articles 10 and 13 of the Draft Articles on Prevention and Repression of Crimes against Humanity are very articulated with respect to the principle *aut dedere aut iudicare* and extradition.

67 Jessberger and Werle (n 4) para 277.

68 Favourable are C Bassiouni, 'Universal Jurisdiction for International Crimes', (2001) VaJIntlL 148ff. and O Ben-Naftali, 'The Obligation to Prevent and to Punish Genocide', in P Gaeta (ed), *The UN Genocide Convention* (OUP 2009), 47ff; against C Tomuschat, 'The Duty to Prosecute International Crimes Committed by Individuals', in H-J Cremer et al. (eds), *Tradition und Weltoffenheit des Rechts: Festschrift für Helmut Steinberger* (Springer 2002) 351 and J Dugard, 'Possible Conflicts of Jurisdiction with Truth Commissions', in A Cassese, P Gaeta and JR W D Jones (eds), *The Rome Statute of the International Criminal Court* (OUP 2002), vol. 1, 698.

69 2014 ILC Report (n 62) 17. It is noteworthy that Article 7 of the Draft Articles on Prevention and Repression of Crimes against Humanity requires States Parties to establish jurisdiction not only on the basis of the principle of territoriality but also active and passive nationality.

article III shall not be considered as political crimes for the purpose of extradition. The Contracting Parties pledge themselves in such cases to grant extradition in accordance with their laws and treaties in force.'

With respect to the ICC Statute, Article 89 clarifies that the request issued from the Court is 'surrender', not extradition, because it emanates from an international court instead of a national authority.

The possible co-existence of the obligations to surrender an individual to the ICC and to extradite that same person to a State may give rise to conflicting interests that are not easy to solve in legal terms. In order to address similar challenges, Article 89 of the ICC Statute indicates the priorities.

4 Obligation to Cooperate and Assist in Criminal Matters

The content of the obligation to cooperate and assist in criminal matters differs depending on the entity requiring cooperation and assistance: if the State has to entertain a request from the ICC, the cooperation develops along vertical lines, while it is of a horizontal nature when the requesting entity is another State.

Vertical cooperation requires compliance with Part 9 of the ICC Statute, which is a complex section detailing in 17 rich articles the obligations that ought to ensure a State Party's 'full cooperation' with the Court. These obligations follow all the phases of the Court's proceedings: from admissibility to the gathering of evidence stage, from the arrest and surrender of the suspect to the yielding of documents for trial purposes. Also, practical activities, such as logistical support, assistance with security of accused persons or witnesses and freezing of proceeds or instruments of crime are included.[70] Part 9 specifies also the modalities through which cooperation and assistance must be ensured, to the point that States Parties have often opted for the adoption of an internal law or modification of existing legislation in order to be able to discharge the multiform obligations stemming from this part of the Statute.

With respect to horizontal cooperation, the grave breaches regime established in Article 88 of Additional Protocol I of 1977 sets out the basic principle whereby States Parties 'shall afford one another the greatest measure of assistance in connection with criminal proceedings brought in respect of grave breaches of the Conventions or of this Protocol' and, more specifically, shall 'give due consideration to the request of the State in whose territory the alleged

---

70 The doctrine on the cooperation and assistance by States with the ICC is abundant, see for all G Sluiter, *International Criminal Adjudication and the Collection of Evidence: Obligations of States* (Intersentia 2002).

offence has occurred' and shall 'cooperate in the matter of extradition'. It also clarifies that the law of the requested State applies, subject to the priority to be given to relevant bilateral or multilateral treaties.

By contrast, the Genocide Convention is radically insufficient with respect to cooperation,[71] as it only sets out the option for a State Party to make recourse to the UN organs or the ICJ in case of a breach of the Convention, a problem with its interpretation or application or for preventive purposes.

In the absence of specific treaty obligations concerning horizontal cooperation with respect to the three core international crimes under examination, the rules relating to cooperation and assistance in criminal matters contained in bi- or multi-lateral treaties apply.[72]

5 Consequences in Case of Failure to Abide by the Obligations

With respect to the breach of a customary rule on genocide, crimes against humanity or war crimes, committed through recourse to a CBRN agent, the responsibility of the State arises *erga omnes* and the general rules of the 2001 Draft Articles on Responsibility of States for Internationally Wrongful Acts are applicable, including cessation and non-repetition of the act, reparation, as well as countermeasures.[73]

If the breached obligation is treaty-based, specific consequences may follow. For example, the Genocide Convention allows the parties to 'call upon the competent organs of the United Nations' to take such action under the Charter 'as they consider appropriate for the repression of genocide' (art VIII). In addition, in the terms of Article IX, the ICJ has jurisdiction over disputes between States concerning the interpretation or application of the Convention.

Most importantly, the ICC Statute creates a specific regime for situations when a State is 'unable' or 'unwilling' to genuinely investigate or prosecute a crime falling under the Court's jurisdiction, hence including CBRN-related international crimes. In this case, the principle of complementarity, based on respect for the primary jurisdiction of States, allows the Court to intervene in national proceedings in order to ensure that they are carried out in an effective and impartial manner. Article 17 clarifies the conditions of inability and unwillingness and implicitly requests States Parties to adequately incorporate

71 By contrast, the Draft Articles on the Prevention and Punishment of Crimes against Humanity contain detailed obligations of mutual assistance at Article 14.

72 A number of such multilateral treaties exist, *ie* the 1959 European Convention on Mutual Assistance in Criminal Matters.

73 A Cassese (n 1) 98.

into their national legislation the relevant provisions of the Statute: not only those relating to the elements of the crimes but also the ones concerning cooperation and assistance. Lack of incorporation of one of these aspects may give rise to the Court making a finding of 'inability' and thus trigger the Court's jurisdiction over a specific crime and person.

6 Conclusion

The enormously lethal potential of CBRN agents and the inherently indiscriminate nature of the weapons containing them make their use particularly likely to constitute the commission of a war crime, a crime against humanity or an act of genocide. Although the way in which the ICC Statute criminalises these conducts is not totally satisfactory, since it leaves a number of gaps with respect to the material element required, the obligations incumbent upon the States Parties to avoid letting these offences go unpunished are manifold.

These obligations consist primarily in the enactment of the legislative changes needed to incorporate the elements of the international crime of genocide as defined in the 1948 Convention, or the elements of war crimes amounting to grave breaches in the 1949 Geneva Conventions and the 1977 Additional Protocol I. For genocide, an additional obligation exists for States Parties to the Convention to determine also appropriate penalties for the modalities of participation in the crime other than commission.

Though no general obligations to criminalise conduct amounting to a crime against humanity or a war crime other than a 'grave breach' exist, States Parties to the ICC Statute ought to provide for national coverage of these conducts, lest they may be found 'unable' to prosecute a case, thus opening the way for the Court.

The obligation to prosecute, consisting in the need to investigate, submit the case to the authorities and, as the case may be, prosecute and punish or else extradite differs depending on the prosecuting State. There is no doubt that the territorial State has an obligation to prosecute. This duty is not only contained in all the relevant treaties dealing with genocide and war crimes, but it has also acquired a customary nature.

The existence of a similar obligation upon third States is more nuanced, at least when no traditional jurisdictional link exists. However, the fact that the prohibition of these crimes gives rise to *erga omnes* obligations bestows upon third States the right to open a criminal case on the basis of the principle of universality.

The other obligation incumbent upon States, both with respect to other States and the ICC, is to cooperate and assist the requesting entity at all levels of the criminal proceeding.

Failure to respect one of the above obligations gives rise to the responsibility of the State according to the general rules of international law. However, where the obligation stems from a treaty, such as the 1948 Genocide Convention or the ICC Statute, specific treaty-based consequences also attach to the violation.

Bibliography

Bassiouni C, 'Universal Jurisdiction for International Crimes', (2001) VaJIntlL 148.

Ben-Naftali O, 'The Obligation to Prevent and to Punish Genocide', in P Gaeta (ed), *The UN Genocide Convention* (OUP 2009) 47.

Cassese A, *International Criminal Law* (OUP 2008).

Clark R, 'Building on Article 8(2)(b)(xx) of the Rome Statute of the International Criminal Court: Weapons and Methods of Warfare', (2009) New Criminal Law Review 376.

Dugard J, 'Possible Conflicts of Jurisdiction with Truth Commissions', in A Cassese, P Gaeta and J R W D Jones (eds), *The Rome Statute of the International Criminal Court* (OUP 2002), vol. 1, 698.

Gaeta P, 'Grave Breaches of the Geneva Conventions', in A Clapham, P Gaeta and M Sassoli (eds), *The 1949 Geneva Conventions – A commentary* (OUP 2015) 614.

Henzelin M, *Le principe de l'universalité en droi penal international* (Bruylant 2000).

Jalloh C, 'The International Law Commission's First Draft Convention on Crimes Against Humanity: Codification, Progressive Development, or Both?' (2020) CaseWResJIntlL 331.

Jessberger F and Werle G, 'Principles of International Criminal Law' (OUP 2020, 4th ed).

Schabas W, *The International Criminal Court: A Commentary on the Rome Statute* (OUP 2010).

Schabas W and Askar Y, *Implementing International Humanitarian Law, From the Ad Hoc Tribunals to a Permanent International Criminal Court* (Routledge 2004).

Sluiter G, *International Criminal Adjudication and the Collection of Evidence: Obligations of States* (Intersentia 2002).

Sossai M, 'Identifying the Perpetrators of Chemical Attacks in Syria' (2019) JICJ 223.

Tomuschat C, 'The Duty to Prosecute International Crimes Committed by Individuals', in H-J Cremer et al. (eds), *Tradition und Weltoffenheit des Rechts: Festschrift für Helmut Steinberger* (Springer 2002) 315.

Vierucci L, 'Offensive Military Applications of Biotechnologies: Loopholes in the Law?', in F Francioni (ed), *Biotechnologies and International Human Rights* (Hart 2007) 363.

Webb P and Alamuddin A, 'Expanding Jurisdiction over War Crimes under Article 8 of the ICC Statute' (2010) JICJ 1228.

Wirz C and Egger E, 'Use of nuclear and radiological weapons by terrorists?' (2005) IRRC 504.

Zimmermann A and Şener M, 'Chemical Weapons and the International Criminal Court' (2014) AJIL 439.

CHAPTER 33

Criminal Repression of CBRN-Related Violations Which Do Not Amount to International Crimes

Alessandro Mario Amoroso

1 Introduction

This chapter focuses on international obligations concerning the criminal repression of individual conduct which violates applicable law on chemical, biological and radio-nuclear agents (CBRN-related violations) but does not amount to an international crime. A number of CBRN-related violations, indeed, fall within the scope of treaty and customary definitions of international crimes and must be prosecuted as such, either at the national or at the international level.[1] These, however, do not exhaust the full range of CBRN events which may entail criminal law liability pursuant to international law. Additional international norms, which have their source in either treaty or case law, require States to criminally repress in their domestic legal systems a broader array of conduct involving CBRN agents. Those norms and the obligations they provide form the object of the present contribution.

A survey of primary sources reveals the existence of two main international obligations concerning the domestic repression of CBRN-related violations not amounting to international crimes.[2] The first two sections of the chapter are devoted to them: the obligation to criminalise, *ie* to adopt domestic penal legislation making a given individual conduct a criminal offence (second section); and the obligation to prosecute, *ie* to activate the judicial system for the purpose of prosecution by, at least, submitting a case to the competent authorities (third section). Both of these obligations can be extraterritorial in

1 Obligations to prosecute CBRN-related international crimes are treated in ch 32 by Vierucci.

2 Several collections and databases of primary sources are available, although they greatly differ in scope. The following ones have been used for this chapter: EUROJUST, *CBRN-E Handbook* (version VI, EUROJUST 2017); International Disaster Law project, IDL Database <http://disasterlaw.sssup.it/disasters-database/>; UNODC, 'The International Legal Framework against Chemical, Biological, Radiological and Nuclear Terrorism' (United Nations 2016); ILO, International agreements in the field of chemical safety and the environment <https://www.ilo.org/safework/areasofwork/chemical-safety-and-the-environment/WCMS_118357/lang--en/index.htm> (all links were last accessed on 30 November 2021).

© ALESSANDRO MARIO AMOROSO, 2022 | DOI:10.1163/9789004507999_034 scope, as they may apply not only to conduct taking place in the territory of the State concerned, but also to that realised abroad. A further section considers the consequences of the failure to criminalise and/or to prosecute, which include State responsibility for breaches of treaty provisions and human rights responsibility for violating the right to life (fourth section). Some concluding remarks draw attention to the limits of a fragmented legal framework and to the increasing recourse to human rights case law as a source of general obligations (fifth section).

Obligations examined in this chapter can be found in several branches of international law which are relevant to CBRN events. They include arms control and disarmament law (ACDL), international counter-terrorism law (CTL), international environmental law (IEL), as well as other international conventions on hazardous activities. A considerable number of international treaties in these fields lay out obligations to criminalise and/or to prosecute, whose application is particular in scope as they concern either one kind of CBRN-related violation or one type of CBRN agent. Conversely, the case law of the European Court of Human Rights (ECtHR) developed an obligation to prosecute which is general in scope, in that it applies to all kinds of events, regardless of the CBRN agent released or the conduct realised.

A few remarks can be added to introduce the taxonomy of international obligations considered in this chapter. To begin with, it is argued that a relationship can be drawn between, on the one hand, obligations to criminalise and to prosecute and, on the other hand, the distinction between prescriptive and adjudicatory jurisdiction in international law.[3] The following sections endorse this distinction, insofar as it may be useful to illustrate how obligations to criminalise and obligations to prosecute affect the limits imposed by international law on domestic criminal jurisdiction.

Second, this chapter links obligations to criminalise and obligations to prosecute to the four phases of the CBRN emergency management cycle and argues that obligations to criminalise reinforce the prevention of and preparedness against CBRN events, while obligations to prosecute improve States' capacity to respond to and recover from CBRN events.[4]

---

3 The debate on the difference between prescriptive and adjudicatory jurisdiction and their further distinction from enforcement jurisdiction is broad and touches the meaning of jurisdiction itself, in national as well as in international law. Its consideration in this chapter is limited to the distinction as it applies in public international law concerning domestic criminal jurisdiction. For further elaboration see C Ryngaert, 'The Concept of Jurisdiction in International Law' in A Orakhelashvili (ed), *Research Handbook on Jurisdiction and Immunities in International Law* (Edward Elgar 2015) 54–60.

4 The CBRN emergency management cycle and its phases are introduced in Part I of this volume.

Finally, proper implementation also depends on a careful determination of the scope of each norm. To this end, the last section of the chapter adopts the distinction between obligations of conduct and obligations of result. It submits that obligations to criminalise shall be understood as obligations of result, while obligations to prosecute can be both obligations of result and obligations of conduct. Such a classification could provide guidance to national authorities in the implementation of relevant obligations and should help assess the level of State compliance.

2 Obligations to Criminalise

In international law, obligations to criminalise impose on States a duty to enact domestic legislation that makes certain individual conduct, as defined in the relevant international source, a criminal offence in the national legal system. Such obligations are not a novelty in the international sphere, as they arose from the need of States 'to better organize the joint repression of certain criminal offences, more specifically those that damaged their collective interests and had a strong transnational dimension'.[5] They have become progressively more detailed over time, placing stronger constraints on States' jurisdictional discretion.[6] In spite of this, international norms providing obligations to criminalise have multiplied and represent today a common feature of several discrete branches of public international law. This is particularly true when looking at those branches relevant to CBRN events, as CBRN-related violations are a typical example of transnational crime.

Obligations to criminalise CBRN-related violations are particular in scope, that is to say, they apply to CBRN-related violations in one particular branch of international law (eg CBRN terrorism) or to one type of CBRN agent only (*ie* chemical, biological, radiological or nuclear). Treaty-based obligations to criminalise appear in all major conventions on CBRN disarmament,[7] as well

5 P Gaeta, 'International Criminalization of Prohibited Conduct' in A Cassese (ed), *The Oxford Companion to International Criminal Justice* (OUP 2009) 63.

6 A Mills, 'Rethinking Jurisdiction in International Law' (2014) 84 BYIL 187, 210–13; and with reference to the European context D. Zerouki-Cottin, 'L'Obligation d'Incriminer Imposée par le Juge Européen, ou la Perte du Droit de ne pas Punir' (2011) 3 RSC.

7 Convention on the Prohibition of the Development, Production and Stockpiling of Bacteriological (Biological) and Toxin Weapons and on Their Destruction (1972) (BTWC) art IV; Convention on the Prohibition of the Development, Production, Stockpiling and Use of Chemical Weapons and on their Destruction (1993) (CWC) art VII(1)(a); Treaty on the Prohibition of Nuclear Weapons (2017) (TPNW) art 5(2).

as in most conventions dealing with CBRN terrorism[8] and in a few treaties on the protection of the environment from the release of CBRN agents, including as a result of hazardous activities.[9] Moreover, with Resolution 1540(2004), the UNSC, acting in a quasi-legislative capacity, further expanded the category of CBRN terrorist conduct that States are required to prohibit as criminal offences.[10] The EU also adopted a Directive on the protection of the environment through criminal law, which sought to harmonise national legislation by introducing, among other offences, specific crimes concerning the management of waste, nuclear materials and other radioactive substances.[11] All these provisions are worded differently and vary considerably in scope. Similarities between norms belonging to the same field do, however, allow some general considerations to be made.

Criminalisation clauses enclosed in CTL treaties show the highest level of accuracy. They provide details on the objective and subjective elements of the offence, modes of liability, nature of penalties and grounds of jurisdiction. Prohibited conduct includes not only the commission of terrorist acts by means of CBRN agents but extends to any activity in preparation for the terrorist act, for instance, the manufacturing, procurement, acquisition, receipt, possession, alteration, transfer, and delivery of CBRN materials for terrorist purposes, as well as the financing of nuclear terrorism. Most of these provisions

8 Convention on the Physical Protection of Nuclear Material (1979) (CPPNM) as amended art 7; International Convention for The Suppression of Terrorist Bombings (1997) (TBC) arts 2 and 4; International Convention for the Suppression of the Financing of Terrorism (1999) (TFC) arts 2 and 4; International Convention for the Suppression of Acts of Nuclear Terrorism (2005) (ICSANT) arts 2 and 5; Convention for The Suppression of Unlawful Acts of Violence Against the Safety of Maritime Navigation (1988) (SUA Convention) as amended arts 3, 3*bis*, 3*ter*, 3*quater* and 5; Protocol to the Protocol for the Suppression of Unlawful Acts against the Safety of Fixed Platforms Located on the Continental Shelf (2005) (SUA Protocol) arts 2–4; Convention on the Suppression of Unlawful Acts Relating to International Civil Aviation (2010) (Beijing Convention) arts 1 and 3.

9 International Convention for the Prevention of Pollution from Ships (1973) (MARPOL) as amended art 4; London Convention on the Prevention of Marine Pollution by Dumping of Wastes and Other Matter (1972) arts IV(1) and VII(2); London Protocol to the Convention on the Prevention of Marine Pollution by Dumping of Wastes and other Matter (1996) as amended arts 4(1) and 10(2); Basel Convention on the Control of Transboundary Movements of Hazardous Wastes and their Disposal (1989) (Basel Convention) arts 4(4) and 9(5); Stockholm Convention on Persistent Organic Pollutants (2001) (Stockholm Convention) art 3(1). See also the Council of Europe Convention on the Protection of the Environment through Criminal Law (1998) art 4, which however has not yet entered into force.

10 UNSC Res 1540 (28 April 2004) UN Doc S/RES/1540 paras 2 and 3(d).

11 Directive 2008/99/EC of the European Parliament and of the Council of 19 November 2008 on the protection of the environment through criminal law [2008] OJ L328/28 art 3.

require a general *mens rea*, namely the commission of the relevant conduct with intent, often assisted by a specific *mens rea* (for example, the intention to cause death, serious bodily injury or destruction).[12] Besides requiring criminalisation of preparatory conduct, CTL treaties, as is typical of counterterrorism legislation, also extend criminalisation beyond direct perpetration to include other modes of liability, from attempt to co-perpetration and various forms of complicity.[13] The same provisions go so far as to require the fixing of appropriate penalties that take into account the gravity of the conduct.[14] Finally, it must be noted that all criminalisation clauses provided in CTL treaties are followed by enabling provisions on grounds of jurisdiction, which allow States Parties to extend their penal legislation based on the passive personality principle and on universal jurisdiction.[15]

ACDL and IEL treaties do not have provisions comparable in scope to those of CTL conventions. Obligations to criminalise in disarmament treaties limit themselves to requiring the enactment of penal legislation that prohibits individuals from undertaking the same activities which are prohibited to States.[16] The *actus reus* in this case includes conduct such as the development, production, acquisition, stockpiling, transfer, and use of CBRN weapons; the provisions are silent on the *mens rea* of the offence. One treaty adopts an open formula on grounds of jurisdiction, which must be interpreted as simply leaving States Parties the choice of extending jurisdiction beyond their national territory.[17] IEL treaties are equally short on detail, only obliging States to introduce appropriate national legislation to punish conduct carried out in contravention of the convention. This includes the discharge, dumping, illegal traffic and any unauthorised transboundary movement of prohibited materials.[18] One treaty

12 The objective and subjective elements of the offences are described in the same provisions cited in n 8.

13 CPPNM as amended art 7(1)(h)–(k); TBC art 2(3); TFC art 2(4)–(5); ICSANT arts 2(3)–(4) and 7(1)(a); SUA Convention as amended art 3*quater*; SUA Protocol art 4(2); Beijing Convention art 1(4)–(5).

14 CPPNM as amended art 7(2); TBC art 4(b); TFC art 4(b); ICSANT art 5(b); SUA Convention as amended art 5; Beijing Convention art 3.

15 CPPNM as amended arts 8(2) and 8(4); TBC arts 6(2) and 6(4); TFC art 7; ICSANT arts 9(2) and 9(4); SUA Convention arts 6(2) and 6(4); SUA Protocol art 5; Beijing Convention art 8.

16 See for relevant provisions n 7. The obligation to criminalise is explicit in the CWC and the TPNW, whereas the BTWC in art IV only provides for a duty to 'take any necessary measures to prohibit' relevant conduct. This duty has been interpreted as an obligation to enact penal legislation, see T Dunworth, RJ Mathews and TLH McCormack, 'National Implementation of the Biological Weapons Convention' (2006) 11 JC&SL 100–05.

17 The TPNW art 5(2) allows States Parties to prohibit any activity undertaken 'by persons or on territory under its jurisdiction or control'.

18 See for relevant provisions n 10.

demands the adoption of penalties 'adequate in severity to discourage violations'.[19] It must be mentioned that these provisions stop short of explicitly requiring criminalisation, as they do not refer to 'criminal' sanctions but only to 'penalties' aimed at 'punishing' violations.[20] However, they have been consistently interpreted as introducing obligations to criminalise[21] and have been implemented in State practice through the adoption of penal legislation.[22] Finally, the abovementioned EU Directive on the protection of the environment through criminal law represents a notable exception in the field of IEL, as it lays down a detailed description of prohibited conduct, specifying the *mens rea*, modes of liability and type of penalties needed for each offence.[23]

A separate question is whether international law also provides for a general obligation to criminalise CBRN-related violations, *ie* an obligation applicable regardless of the CBRN agent released or the conduct realised. Customary international law does not provide the answer. While it is accepted nowadays that a customary rule exists requiring States to criminalise at least some international crimes,[24] the same cannot be said of CBRN-related violations which only amount to transnational crimes. Considering the large membership of CTL conventions and the consistency of criminalisation clauses provided therein, perhaps an argument can be made that a customary obligation is emerging to criminalise transnational terrorist conduct, including CBRN terrorism.[25] Alternatively, it has been submitted that an 'implicit' obligation to criminalise has developed in human rights law.[26] The argument relies

---

19 MARPOL art 4(4).

20 With the exception of the Basel Convention art 4(3).

21 B-S Cho, 'Emergence of an International Environmental Criminal Law?' (2000) UCLA Journal of Environmental Law and Policy 11, 15ff; F Mégret, 'The Problem of an International Criminal Law of the Environment' (2011) 36 Columbia Journal of Environmental Law 198.

22 MG Chalos and WA Parker, 'The Criminalization of Maritime Accidents and MARPOL + Violations in the United States' (2010) 23 USF Maritime Law Journal.

23 Directive 2008/99/EC (n 11) arts 3–5.

24 This is surely the case for war crimes, see *Furundžija case* (Judgement) ICTY-95-17/1 (10 November 1998) para 148.

25 The emergence of customary rules on the criminal repression of terrorist offences is arguably prevented by the absence of an agreed definition of terrorism in international law. In support of the opinion that CTL treaties, together with other sources, constitute practice of a customary rule on the international crime of terrorism in times of peace, see A Cassese and P Gaeta, *Cassese's International Criminal Law* (3rd edn, OUP 2013) 148.

26 See M Longobardo, 'The Italian Legislature and International and EU Obligations of Domestic Criminalisation' (2021) 21 IntlCLR, who builds the argument on ECtHR decisions and General Comment no. 36 of the Human Rights Committee. A similar analysis is proposed by D Zerouki-Cottin (n 6) 576–78, relying on case law from both the ECtHR and the Court of Justice of the European Union.

mainly on decisions of the ECtHR which found violations of the European Convention on Human Rights (ECHR) based on the lack of adequate criminalisation in the domestic legal system. To this end, the ECtHR interpreted some provisions of the Convention, including most notably Article 2, as imposing a duty to put in place 'effective criminal-law provisions to deter the commission of offences'.[27] Those judgments, however, are of little relevance to our analysis, as they do not concern CBRN events. Even if their findings were extended beyond the circumstances of the specific case to argue that human rights law requires the criminalisation of CBRN-related violations generally, this would not represent a substantive addition to the treaty-based obligations examined above. Nevertheless, the reasoning of the Court stresses the preventive role of positive obligations, which are deemed necessary to secure the right to life: this rationale surely applies *mutatis mutandis* to the prevention of CBRN-related violations.

Two final considerations can enrich the analysis of relevant obligations and facilitate their classification. First, obligations to criminalise can be conceived of as international norms on States' prescriptive jurisdiction, *ie* concerning the authority of States to define the scope of application of their laws to particular persons or conduct.[28] Contrary to the traditional view expressed in the *Lotus* judgment,[29] it is agreed today that States' authority to prescribe is limited by international norms, so that its extension beyond accepted grounds of jurisdiction (territoriality and active nationality) needs to rely on permissive rules.[30] This is particularly important when States seek to apply domestic criminal law extraterritorially, based on the passive personality principle and on universal jurisdiction.[31] From the point of view of prescriptive jurisdiction then, obligations to criminalise can be regarded as rules on permitted grounds

27 *Osman v. UK* ECHR 1998–VIII 3124 para 115, restated more recently in *Opuz v. Turkey* ECHR 2009-III 107 para 128; and in *Tunç and Tunç v. Turkey* App no 24014/05 (ECtHR, 14 April 2015) para 171.

28 The distinction between prescriptive, adjudicatory and enforcement jurisdiction has been used in international law primarily to clarify the different constraints placed on each of these three categories. In our analysis, it helps to better assess the impact of obligations to criminalise and obligations to prosecute on the reach of State criminal jurisdiction. See International Law Commission (ILC), 'Report of the International Law Commission on the Work of its 58th Session (1 May–9 June and 3 July–11 August 2006)', UN Doc A/61/10 517; C Ryngaert, *Jurisdiction in International Law* (2nd edn, OUP 2015) 14–21; WS Dodge, 'Jurisdiction in the Fourth Restatement of Foreign Relations Law' (2017) 18 Yearbook of Private International Law.

29 *The Case of the S.S. Lotus* (*France v. Turkey*) PCIJ Reports Series A No 10, 18–19.

30 P Gaeta (n 5) 70–71.

31 Ibid.

of jurisdiction. When a criminalisation clause allows States Parties to apply their legislation extraterritorially (as in CTL treaties), it provides a permissive rule on the exercise of passive personality and/or universal jurisdiction. Conversely, when the provision remains silent, the obligation to criminalise should be interpreted as limiting jurisdiction to the territoriality and active nationality principles.

Second, the latter remarks help disclose the functional relationship existing between the obligation to criminalise and the prevention and preparedness phases of the CBRN emergency management cycle. This connection stems from the purpose of the different provisions analysed in this section. On the one hand, criminalisation clauses enshrined in ACDL and IEL conventions seek to expand the scope of application of treaty-based prohibitions from States Parties to individuals subject to their jurisdiction. On the other hand, the aim of obligations to criminalise provided in CTL treaties is to create a web of prohibitions supported by competing claims of jurisdiction. What these norms have in common is the attempt to achieve maximum deterrence. It is precisely this objective that reinforces prevention because it supports States' efforts to avoid disaster risks and, at the same time, strengthens preparedness because it enhances their ability to effectively anticipate and respond to disasters. This conclusion is reflected in the ILC Draft Articles on the protection of persons in the event of disasters, which list the adoption of national legislation among the appropriate measures to prevent, mitigate, and prepare for disasters.[32]

3 Obligations to Prosecute

Obligations to criminalise provided in international law affect the traditional discretion enjoyed by States in choosing which individual conduct entails criminal law liability in their domestic legal systems. An even stronger restriction is imposed by those norms which, in addition to demanding criminalisation, require States to activate their judicial system for the purpose of prosecution. In the latter case, one can talk of obligations to prosecute and a number of them can be found in the international law applicable to CBRN events. They differ in scope and produce a varying degree of interference with Sates' prosecutorial discretion. A distinction should therefore be made between, on the one hand, norms that merely require a State to submit a case

32 ILC, 'Draft Articles on the Protection of Persons in Event of Disasters' (2016) II(2) UNYBILC, Draft Article 9.

to the competent authorities and, on the other hand, norms that provide a duty to bring the alleged offender to court. In the former case, the so-called 'Hague formula' is adopted:[33] it demands the intervention of law enforcement authorities (eg the launching of an investigation and/or the collection of evidence) but does not rule out prosecutorial discretion as to the initiation of criminal proceedings (so-called *opportunité de la poursuite*), provided such a discretionary power is recognised in the domestic legal system. Conversely, obligations to bring alleged culprits to court preclude prosecutorial discretion: they require that the suspect stands trial if sufficient evidence is gathered.[34] Both kinds of obligations to prosecute are reflected in international norms applicable to CBRN events. It is against this theoretical background that the considerations of this section should be read.

Obligations to prosecute CBRN-related violations are both particular and general in scope. The first appear mostly in treaties dealing with CBRN terrorism but can be found in IEL and ACDL conventions as well. As observed in the case of obligations to criminalise, provisions included in terrorism conventions tend to be much more detailed.

Starting our inquiry from CTL treaties, it is immediately clear that obligations to prosecute must be inferred from provisions offering an alternative between extradition or prosecution: prosecution is one out of two equivalent options to fulfil an obligation 'to extradite or prosecute' (*aut dedere aut iudicare*).[35] The provisions are phrased in almost identical terms in all CTL treaties[36] and the obligation to prosecute depends on three requirements: i) that an offence within the meaning of the convention has been committed, regardless of the territory where it took place; ii) that the alleged offender is found on the territory of the State Party; iii) that the offender is not extradited. If all three conditions are met, the State Party is under an obligation to submit the case to its competent authorities for the purpose of prosecution. These provisions thus leave it to the national authorities to decide whether or

33 From the Hague Convention for the Suppression of Unlawful Seizure of Aircraft (1970).

34 The distinction adopted in this section was first proposed by P Gaeta, 'Les Règles Internationales sur les Critères de Compétence des Juges Nationaux' in A Cassese and M Delmas-Marty (eds), *Crimes Internationaux et Juridictions Internationales* (PUF 2002).

35 CPPNM as amended art 10; TBC art 8(1); TFC art 10(1); ICSANT art 11; SUA Convention as amended art 10; Beijing Convention art 10.

36 See, for example, Beijing Convention art 10: 'The State Party in the territory of which the alleged offender is found shall, if it does not extradite that person, be obliged, without exception whatsoever and whether or not the offence was committed in its territory, to submit the case to its competent authorities for the purpose of prosecution'.

not to initiate criminal proceedings.[37] Still, most of these norms are combined with complementary obligations which, although not excluding prosecutorial discretion, commit the exercise of jurisdiction to the end of securing criminal liability. They concern in particular the obligation to ensure the presence of the alleged offender for the purpose of prosecution or extradition, including by taking the person into custody if necessary;[38] the obligation to make a preliminary inquiry;[39] the obligation to rule out the so-called political offence exception, *ie* to exclude that political and similar motivations may be used as a justification;[40] the obligation to afford the greatest measure of mutual legal assistance in order to make the repression of transnational conduct more effective.[41] States, moreover, bear a series of obligations aimed at the protection of victims of terrorism, including CBRN terrorism.[42]

Partly divergent considerations can be made as regards obligations to prosecute in the field of IEL. The Convention for the Prevention of Pollution from Ships requires States Parties under whose authority a ship operates to start proceedings upon being informed that a violation has occurred, provided they are satisfied that sufficient evidence is available.[43] If read carefully, this provision does not seem to leave room for the exercise of prosecutorial discretion. It should, therefore, be interpreted as precluding the *opportunité de la poursuite*. The obligation is, moreover, reinforced by a complementary duty to investigate.[44] Separate mention must be made of a convention on

---

37 The same is maintained by P Gaeta, 'National Prosecution of International Crimes: International Rules on Grounds of Jurisdiction' in *Studi di Diritto Internazionale in Onore di Gaetano Arangio-Ruiz* (Editoriale Scientifica 2004) 1939.

38 CPPNM as amended art 9; TBC arts 7(2) and 7(6); TFC arts 9(2) and 9(6); ICSANT arts 10(2) and 10(6); SUA Convention as amended art 7(1); Beijing Convention art 9(1).

39 TBC art 7(1); TFC art 9(1); ICSANT art 10(1); SUA Convention as amended art 7(2); Beijing Convention art 9(2).

40 TBC art 5; TFC art 6; ICSANT art 6.

41 CPPNM as amended art 13; TBC art 10; TFC art 12; ICSANT arts 7(1)(b) and 14; SUA Convention as amended art 8bis; Beijing Convention art 17. The need to enhance coordination against the illegal movement of nuclear, chemical, biological and other potentially deadly materials has been emphasised by the UN Security Council as a means to strengthen the global response against transnational crimes, see UNSC Res 1373 (28 September 2001) S/RES/1373 para 4.

42 For a restatement of existing international obligations and their sources, see Council of Europe, 'Revised Guidelines on the Protection of Victims of Terrorist Acts' (Council of Europe 2018).

43 MARPOL arts 4(1): 'If the Administration is informed of such a violation and is satisfied that sufficient evidence is available to enable proceedings to be brought in respect of the alleged violation, it shall cause such proceedings to be taken as soon as possible, in accordance with its law'.

44 MARPOL art 6(4).

cooperation between customs administrations concluded in the framework of the European Union (Naples II Convention). It compels States to permit cross-border cooperation for investigation and prosecution in cases of illicit traffic in prohibited goods; the latter include dangerous and toxic waste, nuclear material and materials or equipment intended for the manufacture of atomic, biological and/or chemical weapons.[45]

Finally, an obligation to prosecute has been read into the text of the Chemical Weapons Convention, where it requires each State Party to '[n]ot permit in any place under its control' activities prohibited by the Convention.[46] According to the Organisation for the Prohibition of Chemical Weapons, based on this provision Sates 'should enforce the measures taken to proscribe prohibited activity', including through criminal prosecution of alleged offenders.[47] This interpretation would exclude the *opportunité de la poursuite*.

Moving to the exploration of the possible sources of a general obligation to prosecute CBRN-related violations, it seems possible to conclude today that a customary rule concerning the repression of terrorist conduct has consolidated.[48] According to the Special Tribunal for Lebanon (STL), such a customary rule includes an obligation to prosecute, since it imposes on any State the duty 'to prosecute and try persons on its territory or in territory under its control who are allegedly involved in terrorism'.[49] The assessment of the STL is based on the analysis of multinational conventions on terrorism, including those examined in this section, as well as on resolutions of the UN Security Council and the UN General Assembly on the fight against terrorism.[50] If the existence of a customary obligation to prosecute is accepted, it would inevitably apply also to the CBRN-related violations covered by those conventions.[51]

---

45 Convention drawn up on the basis of Article K.3 of the Treaty on European Union, on mutual assistance and cooperation between customs administrations (1998) art 19(2)(a).

46 CWC art VII(1)(b).

47 OPCW, 'Note by the Director-General on Compliance with Article VII: Legislation, Cooperation and Legal Assistance', C III/ DG.1/Rev.1, 17 November 1998, 5–6.

48 MA Newton, 'Terrorist Crimes and The Aut Dedere Aut Judicare Obligation' in L van den Herik and N Schrijver (eds), *Counter-Terrorism Strategies in a Fragmented International Legal Order: Meeting the Challenges* (CUP 2013) 71.

49 Interlocutory Decision on the Applicable Law: Terrorism, Conspiracy, Homicide, Perpetration, Cumulative Charging, STL-11-01/I, 16 February 2011, para 102.

50 Ibid paras 88ff.

51 Note, however, that both the International Court of Justice and the International Law Commission refrained from taking a position on the existence of a customary obligation to extradite or prosecute, see *Questions relating to the Obligation to Prosecute or Extradite* (*Belgium v. Senegal*) (*Obligation to Prosecute or Extradite*) (2012) ICJ Reports 422, para 54; and ILC, 'Final Report of the International Law Commission on the Obligation to Extradite or Prosecute (*aut dedere aut judicare*)' (2014) II(2) UNYBILC.

The same conclusion cannot be reached in other fields of international law relevant to CBRN events, where there is a lack of sufficient practice to justify an argument to that end. It shall, therefore, be excluded that customary law provides a general obligation to prosecute CBRN-related offences independently from the nature of the event.

This makes it all the more important to call attention to a series of judgments of the ECtHR which have established a general obligation to prosecute in the context of dangerous activities. Out of five decisions in which the Court reiterated the same principles on the procedural aspect of the right to life (Article 2 ECHR), two judgments concern accidents involving the release of CBRN agents specifically;[52] three more deal with natural hazards.[53] The scholarship has duly emphasised the importance of this jurisprudence as a source of positive obligations to prevent infringements of the right to life resulting from dangerous activities.[54] Yet, one aspect deserves closer consideration. Besides imposing positive obligations to prevent disasters, the ECtHR extended its inquiry to the 'judicial response' required in the wake of a disaster. In a Grand Chamber decision, the Court found that, when violations of Article 2 result from the failure of public authorities to take measures that were necessary and sufficient to avert the risk inherent in a dangerous activity, '*the fact that those responsible for endangering life have not been charged with a criminal offence or prosecuted* may amount to a violation of Article 2'.[55] The paragraph clearly sets out an obligation to prosecute which precludes any exercise of prosecutorial discretion, since it requires pressing charges against State officials responsible for the failure to prevent. The judgments go so far as to require prosecution also in cases of negligence which 'goes beyond an error of judgment or carelessness', meaning that 'the authorities in question, fully realising the likely consequences and disregarding the powers vested in them' failed to adopt the necessary preventive measures.[56] Yet, in a recent decision concerning the transportation of dangerous goods, the Court nuanced its position, stating that 'where negligence has been shown, the obligation may also be satisfied if the legal system affords victims a remedy in the civil courts, either alone or

---

52 *Öneryıldız v. Turkey* [*GC*] ECHR 2004-XII 79 paras 93–94; *Mučibabić v. Serbia* App no 34661/07 (ECtHR, 12 July 2016) para 125.

53 *Budayeva and Others v. Russia* ECHR 2008-II 267 paras 140–142; *Kolyadenko and Others v. Russia* App nos 17423/05, 20534/05, 20678/05, 23263/05, 24283/05 and 35673/05 (ECtHR, 28 February 2012) paras 190–191; *Özel and Others v. Turkey* App nos 14350/05, 15245/05 and 16051/05 (ECtHR, 17 November 2015) paras 188–189.

54 See ch 27 by Venier. See also M Sossai, 'States' Failure to Take Preventive Action and to Reduce Exposure to Disasters as a Human Rights Issue' in F Zorzi Giustiniani and others (eds), *Routledge Handbook of Human Rights and Disasters* (Routledge 2018).

55 ECtHR, *Öneryıldız v. Turkey* [*GC*] (n 52) para 93 (emphasis added).

56 Ibid.

in conjunction with a remedy in the criminal courts'.[57] It is to be hoped that future case law will solve this ambiguity by clarifying whether the obligation to prosecute applies to negligent conduct.

It is important at this point to add some reflections that help to theoretically frame the survey of applicable international norms. First, it is submitted that obligations to prosecute can be regarded as rules on the exercise of adjudicatory jurisdiction, *ie* on the authority of States to apply their laws to specific cases through court adjudication, as opposed to obligations to criminalise which concern instead the exercise of prescriptive jurisdiction. As shown above, this classification is useful for assessing the different limits placed on different rules of jurisdiction. In this respect, it can be observed, first of all, that in criminal law, prescriptive and adjudicatory jurisdiction go hand in hand: because of the operation of the principle of legality, no adjudication is possible in the absence of previous criminalisation.[58] This has an often-overlooked implication: obligations to prosecute a given conduct are always necessarily also norms requiring the criminalisation of the same conduct, if it is not already treated as an offence in the applicable law.[59] Second, while this entails that all limits to prescriptive jurisdiction are also necessarily limits on adjudicatory jurisdiction, the opposite is not true: adjudicatory jurisdiction can be subjected to further limitations. This is, indeed, the case in the field of CBRN-related violations, where most treaty-based obligations to prosecute are made contingent upon the presence of the alleged offender on the territory of the State Party.

Second, in parallel to what has been argued for the obligation to criminalise, a connection can be identified also between obligations to prosecute and the phases of the CBRN emergency management cycle. Criminal justice intervenes after an offence has been committed as the preeminent reaction of a legal system to breaches of its rules. Such reaction is never purely retributive in scope, as it always plays also a limited restorative function, reaffirming the legitimacy of the legal system and rebuilding trust in the institutions. Obligations to prosecute seek to reinforce both these functions: they call on States to devise the domestic criminal system in a way that enables judicial authorities to take action immediately after disasters, thereby supporting response, and that ultimately helps restore the social fabric of disaster affected communities, accelerating recovery.

---

57 *Sinim v. Turkey* App no 9441/10 (ECtHR, 6 June 2017) paras 58–59. The circumstances of the case were, however, different from the abovementioned examples, because the activity in question was not carried out by or under the responsibility of public authorities.

58 International Covenant on Civil and Political Rights (1966) art 15.

59 This has been reaffirmed by the ILC with regard to obligations to extradite or prosecute, see ILC, 'Final Report on the Obligation to Extradite or Prosecute' (n 51) para 20.

4 National Implementation of Obligations to Criminalise and to Prosecute

This section seeks to complete the analysis of applicable law by offering a framework to measure the level of State compliance with the international norms at issue. For this purpose, it reviews the scope of the two obligations according to the distinction between obligations of conduct and obligations of result.[60] This distinction is based on an assessment of the different characters of the obligations and can be helpful in matters of international responsibility, as it sheds light on what constitutes a breach of international law (one of the two components of an internationally wrongful act) and on the precise moment when a breach takes place.[61] For the purpose of the present section, obligations of conduct (or means) are obligations requiring States to do their best (to show 'due diligence') to reach a certain result, without the guarantee that the goal will be ultimately attained. Conversely, obligations of result impose a duty to achieve a predetermined goal. Therefore, obligations of conduct are breached when, under given circumstances, the State did not exert the required diligence; obligations of result are breached when the result demanded by the norm is not achieved. It remains to be seen how this framework applies to obligations to criminalise and obligations to prosecute.

To begin with, both obligations to criminalise and obligations to prosecute are positive obligations: they require the performance of a particular (series of) act(s). Since not only actions but also omissions may constitute breaches of international obligations,[62] failure to implement obligations to criminalise and to prosecute, if attributable to a State, entails State responsibility. How and when a failure to criminalise or to prosecute engenders a breach is something which, as just said, depends on the character of the obligation.

60 On this, see, generally, R Kolb, *The International Law of State Responsibility* (Edward Elgar 2017) 41. For a discussion of the different meanings attributed to the terms, see P-M Dupuy, 'Reviewing the Difficulties of Codification: on Ago's Classification of Obligations of Means and Obligations of Result in Relation to State Responsibility' (1999) 10 EJIL.

61 Article 12 of the Articles on State Responsibility reads 'There is a breach of an international obligation by a State when an act of that State is not in conformity with what is required of it by that obligation, *regardless of its origin or character*' (emphasis added). The character of the obligation, indeed, does not determine whether a breach has taken place but gives indications as to how it comes into being.

62 ILC, 'Draft Articles on Responsibility of States for internationally wrongful acts, with commentaries' (2001) II(2) UNYBILC, Draft Article 2.

The outcome of our inquiry suggests that obligations to criminalise shall be understood as obligations of result. This view is supported in legal doctrine.[63] The same position has been implicitly taken by the International Court of Justice (ICJ) in *Belgium v. Senegal*, where the Court stressed that obligations to criminalise in international conventions have 'a preventive and deterrent character, since by equipping themselves with the necessary legal tools to prosecute this type of offence, the States parties *ensure that their legal systems will operate to that effect* and commit themselves to coordinating their efforts to eliminate any risk of impunity'.[64] The reading of treaty rules on criminalisation leaves no room for doubt: States are not simply required to show diligence in their attempt to pass national legislation; full implementation demands introducing the offence into the domestic legal system. Therefore, treaty-based obligations to criminalise, including those reflecting customary law as in the case of terrorism, are violated when States do not amend their laws (if necessary) upon the entry into force of the obligation. This was suggested also by the ICJ with regard to the obligation to criminalise torture, which 'has to be implemented by the State concerned as soon as it is bound by the Convention'.[65] Conversely, one commentator observed that the moment when a violation takes place may be different for 'implicit' obligations to criminalise. In this case, the breach would occur 'only when the prevention or protection fails because of the lack of a criminal law provision'.[66] This can be explained by the fact that implicit obligations to criminalise have been inferred in human rights case law from more generic duties to prevent, which only require State authorities to show diligent conduct.[67] The relevance of implicit obligations to our analysis is, however, limited, since no judicial decision establishing such obligations directly addressed CBRN-related violations.[68]

Nevertheless, the last remark points out a general issue. The second section argued that a functional link can be determined between obligations to criminalise (not only implicit ones) and the prevention phase of the CBRN emergency management cycle. The preventive function of such obligations

63 It has recently been adopted by M Longobardo (n 26). The same conclusion has been proposed and thoroughly discussed in the framework of human rights obligations by R Pisillo Mazzeschi, 'Responsabilité de l'État pour Violation des Obligations Positives Relatives aux Droits de l'Homme' (2008) 333 Recueil des Cours de l'Académie de Droit International, 311.

64 *Obligation to Prosecute or Extradite* (n 51), para 75 (emphasis added).

65 Ibid.

66 M Longobardo (n 26).

67 The same commentator pointed out a tendency to turn these obligations into implicit obligations of result which must be implemented immediately, ibid.

68 See above Section 2.

has been reaffirmed by the ICJ, as mentioned above. However, prevention rules typically set out due diligence obligations: they require State authorities to take all reasonable and necessary steps to prevent an event from occurring, not to guarantee that the event will eventually be averted.[69] Categorising obligations to criminalise as obligations of result may seem at odds with this conclusion. Yet, this contradiction, which is an ostensible one, can be easily explained by the purpose underlying obligations to criminalise. As a matter of fact, the criminalisation of transnational offences can only be effective when the greatest number of States has adopted the same conduct as an offence in their domestic legal systems; otherwise deterrence cannot be achieved.[70] Obligations of result, which leave States less flexibility in the implementation phase, serve precisely this purpose.

As far as obligations to prosecute are concerned, it is necessary to consider separately the two forms that they assume, as examined in the third section. On the one side, obligations to submit a case to the competent authorities better fit the category of obligations of conduct.[71] Here, what is required of States is not that criminal prosecution eventually takes place, but that the authorities are in a position to make a decision whether to initiate proceedings.[72] Therefore, the obligation is breached if States fail to take procedural steps for the purpose of prosecution, such as making a preliminary inquiry and apprehending the suspect when necessary.[73] Conversely, international norms requiring States to initiate proceedings against the alleged offender, which have been detected in both treaty[74] and case law,[75] are obligations of result. They impose a duty to bring charges against suspected persons, ruling out any exercise of prosecutorial discretion. This kind of obligation to prosecute, therefore, is breached when the authorities decide not to start court proceedings, even though sufficient evidence has been gathered to support a criminal trial.[76] This conclusion has seemingly been questioned in a later

---

69 See ch 3 by Venier.

70 See P Gaeta (n 5) 63–64.

71 For the opposite view, which, however, concerns the human rights obligation to set up a proper judicial system, rather than the specific duty to submit a case to the judicial authorities, see R Pisillo Mazzeschi (n 63) 352ff.

72 ILC, 'Final Report on the Obligation to Extradite or Prosecute' (n 51) para 21.

73 Ibid para 17.

74 See MARPOL art 4(1).

75 ECtHR, *Öneryıldız v. Turkey [GC]* (n 52) para 93.

76 A parallel can be drawn with the obligation to prosecute grave breaches of the Geneva Conventions. In that case, the same considerations offered lately by P Gaeta apply, see P Gaeta 'Grave Breaches of the Geneva Conventions' in A Clapham, P Gaeta and M Sassòli (eds), *The 1949 Geneva Conventions. A Commentary* (OUP 2016) 631.

decision of the ECtHR concerning violations of the right to life in the context of dangerous activities (although not activities related to CBRN events). In *Sinim v. Turkey*, the Court stressed that the judicial response to serious injury or death imposes obligations of means rather than result.[77] However, the reasoning of the Court is limited to the obligation 'to have in place an effective independent judicial system', a definition which does not reflect the meaning of obligations to prosecute adopted in this chapter.

It shall also be recalled that general obligations to prosecute drawn from the case law of the ECtHR additionally involve the human rights responsibility of the respondent State which failed to start proceedings. In the Grand Chamber judgment *Öneryıldız v. Turkey*, the Court found a violation of the procedural aspect of Article 2 ECHR because, although an effective investigation had been carried out, the necessary evidence had been collected and the person responsible had been identified, the national authorities only decided to commit the suspects to trial for 'negligence in the performance of their duties', bringing no charges related to the protection of the right to life.[78] In the execution of this, as well as of other judgments concerning the obligation to prosecute, the respondent States limited themselves to paying the amounts awarded in just satisfaction, but refrained from granting a retrial or from reopening the case or the investigation, due to domestic procedural limitations.[79] Yet, what is probably more relevant, the respondent State in the *Öneryıldız* case, in the wake of the ECtHR's decision, adopted 'general measures', including reforms of domestic criminal law which provided better prosecutorial options to try negligent conduct resulting in the loss of life.[80] General measures also resulted from the ECtHR's decision in *Özel v. Turkey*,[81] following which the respondent State extended prescription periods in respect of serious offences.[82]

Finally, most of the treaties examined above include provisions designed to promote national implementation of the obligations they introduce, including the obligations to criminalise and/or to prosecute. Such provisions generally pursue four objectives: to create monitoring organisations or other

77 ECtHR, *Sinim v. Turkey* (n 57) para 59.

78 ECtHR, *Öneryıldız v. Turkey* [*GC*] (n 52) para 116.

79 The status of execution of ECtHR judgments can be checked on the website of the Department for the Execution of Judgments of the ECtHR <https://hudoc.exec.coe.int/>.

80 Action report (15/05/2017) – Communication from Turkey concerning the case of Öneryıldız v. Turkey paras 38–44.

81 ECtHR, *Özel and Others v. Turkey* (n 53).

82 Action report (03/02/2017) – Communication from Turkey concerning the case of Özel and Others against Turkey paras 13–17.

mechanisms;[83] to facilitate State cooperation;[84] to set up implementation funds;[85] and to establish sanctions or activate sanction mechanisms in case of non-compliance.[86]

5 Concluding Remarks

This chapter has shown that States' efforts to repress CBRN-related violations not amounting to international crimes are guided by a rich set of international obligations, whose overarching purposes are to achieve deterrence through criminalisation and to attribute liability through prosecution. The outcome of our survey suggests two final considerations. First, although international law shows a strong tendency to govern the exercise of national criminal jurisdiction in response to CBRN events, the field is still marked by the extreme fragmentation of applicable rules, which is a consequence of the lack of a comprehensive instrument on the protection against CBRN disasters.[87] Second, the absence of general obligations, applicable regardless of the type of event or agent, encouraged the development of a case law which tried to fill the gap, aiming at a better protection of the right to life. This is a sign of the increasing recourse to human rights case law as a source of general obligations and may be yet more evidence of that shift from jurisdiction as a duty owed to other States to jurisdiction as a duty towards individuals, which is one achievement of international human rights law.[88] The status of execution of ECtHR judgments reviewed in this chapter indicates that States are open to reform their national criminal legislation to uphold a human rights-based obligation to prosecute. This consideration, however, rests on the limited number of cases decided so far on the matter and is only valid within a regional system, that of the Council

83 CWC art VIII; TPNW art 4; CPPNM as amended art 16; SUA Convention as amended art 15; Beijing Convention art 19; MARPOL art 11; London Convention arts VI(4) and XIV; London Protocol arts 9, 11 and 19; Basel Convention art 15(5); Stockholm Convention arts 15 and 16.

84 BTWC arts V and VII; CWC arts IX and X; TPNW art 7; CPPNM as amended art 5; TBC art 15; TFC art 18; ICSANT art 7; SUA Convention as amended art 13; SUA Protocol art 12; Beijing Convention art 18; MARPOL arts 6(1) and 17; London Convention art IX; London Protocol art 13; Basel Convention art 10; Stockholm Convention art 12.

85 CWC art X(7)(a); Basel Convention art 14; Stockholm Convention art 13.

86 BTWC art VI; CWC art XII; London Convention art X; London Protocol art 15; Basel Convention art 20; Stockholm Convention art 17.

87 E Sommario, 'One Law to Bind Them All: International Law and Disaster Resilience' in A Herwing and M Simoncini (eds), *Law and the Management of Disasters: The Challenge of Resilience* (Routledge 2016) 247.

88 A Mills, 'Rethinking Jurisdiction in International Law' (n 6) 209.

of Europe, with a powerful monitoring body and a vigilant mechanism for the execution of judgments. The existence and implementation of similar obligations outside the ECHR, within the framework of international human rights law generally, is an issue which deserves further exploration.

Bibliography

Cassese A and Gaeta P, *Cassese's International Criminal Law* (3rd edn, OUP 2013).

Chalos MG and Parker WA, 'The Criminalization of Maritime Accidents and MARPOL Violations in the United States' (2010) 23 USF Maritime Law Journal 206.

Cho B-S, 'Emergence of an International Environmental Criminal Law?' (2000) UCLA Journal of Environmental Law and Policy 11.

Dodge WS, 'Jurisdiction in the Fourth Restatement of Foreign Relations Law' (2017) 18 Yearbook of Private International Law 143.

Dunworth T, Mathews RJ and McCormack TLH, 'National Implementation of the Biological Weapons Convention' (2006) 11 JC&SL 93.

Dupuy P-M, 'Reviewing the Difficulties of Codification: on Ago's Classification of Obligations of Means and Obligations of Result in Relation to State Responsibility' (1999) 10 EJIL 371.

EUROJUST, *CBRN-E Handbook* (version VI, EUROJUST 2017).

Gaeta P, 'Les Règles Internationales sur les Critères de Compétence des Juges Nationaux' in Cassese A and Delmas-Marty M (eds), *Crimes Internationaux et Juridictions Internationales* (PUF 2002).

Gaeta P, 'National Prosecution of International Crimes: International Rules on Grounds of Jurisdiction' in *Studi di Diritto Internazionale in Onore di Gaetano Arangio-Ruiz* (Editoriale Scientifica 2004).

Gaeta P, 'International Criminalization of Prohibited Conduct' in A Cassese (ed), *The Oxford Companion to International Criminal Justice* (OUP 2009).

Gaeta P, 'Grave Breaches of the Geneva Conventions' in Clapham A, Gaeta P and Sassòli M (eds), *The 1949 Geneva Conventions. A Commentary* (OUP 2016).

International Law Commission, 'Draft Articles on Responsibility of States for internationally wrongful acts, with commentaries' (2001) II(2) UNYBILC.

International Law Commission, 'Report of the International Law Commission on the Work of its 58th Session (1 May–9 June and 3 July–11 August 2006)', UN Doc A/61/10.

International Law Commission, 'Final Report of the International Law Commission on the Obligation to Extradite or Prosecute (aut dedere aut judicare)' (2014) II(2) UNYBILC.

International Law Commission, 'Draft Articles on the Protection of Persons in Event of Disasters' (2016) II(2) UNYBILC.

Kolb R, *The International Law of State Responsibility* (Edward Elgar 2017).
Longobardo M, 'Italian Legislature and International and EU Obligations of Domestic Criminalisation' (2021) 21 IntlCLR 623.
Mégret F, 'The Problem of an International Criminal Law of the Environment' (2011) 36 Columbia Journal of Environmental Law 195.
Mills A, 'Rethinking Jurisdiction in International Law' (2014) 84 BYIL 187.
Newton MA, 'Terrorist Crimes and The Aut Dedere Aut Judicare Obligation' in van den Herik L and Schrijver N (eds), *Counter-Terrorism Strategies in a Fragmented International Legal Order: Meeting the Challenges* (CUP 2013).
Pisillo Mazzeschi R, 'Responsabilité de l'État pour Violation des Obligations Positives Relatives aux Droits de l'Homme' (2008) 333 Recueil des Cours de l'Académie de Droit International 175.
Ryngaert C, 'The Concept of Jurisdiction in International Law' in Orakhelashvili A (ed), *Research Handbook on Jurisdiction and Immunities in International Law* (Edward Elgar 2015).
Ryngaert C, *Jurisdiction in International Law* (2nd edn, OUP 2015).
Sommario E, 'One Law to Bind Them All: International Law and Disaster Resilience' in Herwing A and Simoncini M (eds), *Law and the Management of Disasters: The Challenge of Resilience* (Routledge 2016).
Sossai M, 'States' Failure to Take Preventive Action and to Reduce Exposure to Disasters as a Human Rights Issue' in Zorzi Giustiniani F and others (eds), *Routledge Handbook of Human Rights and Disasters* (Routledge 2018).
UNODC, 'The International Legal Framework against Chemical, Biological, Radiological and Nuclear Terrorism' (United Nations 2016).
Zerouki-Cottin D, 'L'Obligation d'Incriminer Imposée par le Juge Européen, ou la Perte du Droit de ne pas Punir' (2011) 3 RSC 575.

CHAPTER 34

Obligation to Provide Access to Adequate Remedies to Victims of CBRN Events under IHL and IHRL

Francesca Capone

1 Introduction

As spelled out in the United Nations Basic Principles and Guidelines on the Right to a Remedy and Reparation for Victims of Gross Violations of International Human Rights and Serious Violations of International Humanitarian Law (Basic Principles and Guidelines or UNBPG),[1] victims' remedies encompass: i) equal and effective access to justice; ii) adequate, effective and prompt reparation for harm suffered; iii) access to relevant information concerning violations and reparation mechanisms.[2] The UNBPG have the merit of illustrating, in clear terms, which are the remedies to which individual victims are entitled to, not only in the aftermath of gross or serious violations[3] but, more generally, as a consequence of breaches of international law that affect them directly.[4] Hence, victims of violations of international law[5] that stem from chemical, biological, radiological and nuclear (CBRN) events are entitled to remedies, which are foreseen under the current international

1 UNGA, 'Basic Principles and Guidelines on the Right to a Remedy and Reparation for Victims of Gross Violations of International Human Rights Law and Serious Violations of International Humanitarian Law' (2006), A/RES/60/147.

2 Ibid para 11.

3 L F Damrosch, 'Gross and Systematic Human Rights Violations', in R Wolfrum (ed), *Max Planck Encyclopedia of Public International Law* (OUP 2013); CF de Casadevante Romani 'International Law of Victims' (2010) 14 Max Planck UNYB 219. Notably, the terms are used, for example, in the jurisprudence of authoritative human rights bodies, but they are not defined in international binding instruments, although serious violations of international humanitarian law are classified as war crimes under the Rome Statute of the ICC. As specified in the Preamble to the UNBPG, gross violations of international human rights law and serious violations of international humanitarian law, by their very grave nature, constitute an affront to human dignity. UNBPG (n 1) Preamble. Thus, there is no closed list, but rather different factors that come into play to assess the gravity of a given violation, such as the character of the right, the magnitude of the violation, the type of victim (vulnerability) and the impact of the violation.

4 D Shelton, 'Human Rights, Remedies', in R Wolfrum (ed) (n 3).

5 Damrosch (n 3).

legal framework and represent the focus of this analysis.[6] Nonetheless, the venues and the mechanisms available are still scant and the focus so far has mainly been placed on inter-State disputes and secondary obligations deriving from breaches of norms at the inter-State level.[7]

The present contribution will not focus on the inter-State dimension nor on the municipal level,[8] but it rather aims at mapping and analysing the procedural and substantive aspects related to the international remedies that can be claimed directly by individual or groups of victims of CBRN-related violations as committed by States, private actors (eg terrorist organisations), business enterprises or individual perpetrators, in the various phases of a CBRN event.[9] In relation to those responsible for violations that directly cause (or contribute to) a CBRN event, it is worth underscoring that all the actors mentioned above bear an obligation to provide reparations, as spelled out by different sources of international law, eg the Articles on the Responsibility of States for Internationally Wrongful Acts (ARSIWA).[10]

Generally speaking, the identification of said obligation is rather straightforward when it comes to States.[11] In relation to individuals, the rise of international criminal law (ICL) has paved the way for the recognition of their international responsibility,[12] ultimately leading to the pioneering approach of the International Criminal Court (ICC) and its reparations regime. However, it should be borne in mind that ICL still regards the role of domestic courts

6 See generally, F Capone, 'Remedies', in R Wolfrum (ed) (n 3); D Shelton, *Remedies in International Human Rights Law* (OUP 2015 3rd edn).

7 G Bartolini, *Riparazione per violazione dei diritti umani e ordinamento internazionale* (Jovene 2009); M Iovane, *La riparazione nella teoria e nella prassi dell'illecito internazionale* (Giuffrè 1990).

8 C Evans, *The Right to Reparation in International Law for Victims of Armed Conflict* (CUP 2012) 39–43; J Sarkin, 'Reparation for Past Wrongs: Using Domestic Courts Around the World, Especially the United States, to Pursue African Human Rights Claims' (2004) 32 International Journal of Legal Information 426.

9 CBRN threats and events may include the use of chemical, biological, and nuclear weapons (weapons of mass destruction – WMD), both by State and non-State actors (including terrorist groups); the use of CBRN agents for smaller-scale crimes; industrial accidents involving release of CBRN agents into the environment; natural disasters or other calamities; and the disposal of toxic waste. See ch 1 by Frulli in this volume.

10 International Law Commission (ILC), 'Draft Articles on Responsibility of States for internationally wrongful acts, with commentaries' (2001) II(2) UNYBILC; D Shelton, 'Righting Wrongs: Reparations in the Articles on State Responsibility' (2002) 96 AJIL 833.

11 *Factory at Chorzów (Germany v Poland) (Judgment of 13 September 1928)* (Merits), PCIJ, Ser. A, No. 17, para 78.

12 See ch 32 by Vierucci in this volume.

as central and the engagement of the ICC as limited, in accordance with the principle of complementarity.[13]

Less straightforward is the obligation placed on non-State actors (NSAs), like terrorist groups and business enterprises, for which the current international legal framework clearly identifies, *de lege lata*, a subsidiary responsibility incumbent upon States, especially in those instances where the responsible actors are not able to, or are blatantly not interested in, providing reparations, like in the case of terrorist groups;[14] whereas, *de lege ferenda*, recent developments, eg in the field of business and human rights, point towards the recognition of NSAs' direct responsibility to provide redress.[15]

Ultimately, the present chapter will address the following key issues: an overview of victims' rights (or lack thereof) as enshrined in the current international and regional legal regimes applicable specifically to CBRN events; the role of international human rights law (IHRL) and international humanitarian law (IHL); and the potential contribution of ICL.[16]

2 Victims' Rights under the Current International Legal Regimes Applicable to CBRN Events

Some preliminary caveats must be made in relation to the scope of the current analysis. First, it is worth stressing that, since the present study pursues an

13 C McCarthy, *Reparations and Victim Support in the International Criminal Court* (CUP 2012); F Capone 'An Appraisal of the Al Mahdi Order on Reparations and Its Innovative Elements: Redress for Victims of Crimes against Cultural Heritage' (2018) 16 Journal of International Criminal Justice 645. On the principle of complementarity in general, see JK Kleffner, *Complementarity in the Rome Statute and National Criminal Jurisdictions* (OUP 2008).

14 UNBG (n 1) para 15; C Rose; 'An Emerging Norm: The Duty of States to Provide Reparations for Human Rights Violations by Non-State Actors' (2010) 33 Hastings Int'l & Comp. L. Rev. 307.

15 L Moffett 'Beyond Attribution: Responsibility of Armed Non-State Actors for Reparations in Northern Ireland, Colombia and Uganda' in N Gal-Or, C Ryngaert and M Noortmann (eds), *Responsibilities of the Non-State Actor in Armed Conflict and the Market Place: Theoretical Considerations and Empirical Findings* (Brill 2015) 323; Human Rights Council, 'Guiding Principles on Business and Human Rights, Implementing the United Nations Protect, Respect and Remedy Framework' (21 March 2011) UN Doc. A/HRC17/31; C Lopez, 'The Revised Draft of a Treaty on Business and Human Rights: A Big Leap Forward', OpinioJuris (15 August 2018), <http://opiniojuris.org/2019/08/15/the-revised-draft-of-a-treaty-on-business-and-human-rights-a-big-leap-forward/> (all links were last accessed on 8 January 2021).

16 McCarthy (n 13).

'all-hazards approach',[17] it does not only address CBRN events from a security or counter-terrorism perspective, but it deals with other emergencies, such as natural disasters, pandemic outbreaks, or hazardous activities carrying the risk of transboundary damage. Second, it is worth noting that the relevant actors can commit violations that pertain to the various phases of a CBRN event, *ie* prevention, preparedness, response and recovery; however, since the present contribution focuses only on remedies, *ie* secondary norms of international law, the description of the different primary norms and the corresponding obligations will not be carried out as it falls outside the purpose of the present analysis.[18]

Thus, the scope of the enquiry is rather broad, since it covers areas such as the arms control and disarmament regimes,[19] counter-terrorism law, international environmental law (IEL), and international disaster law (IDL).[20] Notably, none of these fields is particularly known for its contribution to the advancement of victims' rights; hence the need to further expand the analysis and discuss in the next section the venues for remedies under the current IHL and IHRL regimes.

2.1 *Defining the Victims of CBRN Events*

With regard to the definition of victims, the Basic Principles and Guidelines define them as:

> persons who individually or collectively suffered harm, including physical or mental injury, emotional suffering, economic loss or substantial impairment of their fundamental rights, through acts or omissions that constitute gross violations of international human rights law, or serious violations of international humanitarian law. Where appropriate, and in accordance with domestic law, the term "victim" also includes the immediate family or dependants of the direct victim and persons who have suffered harm in intervening to assist victims in distress or to prevent victimization.[21]

17 See ch 1 by Frulli in this volume.

18 See Part 1 on general obligations in the different phases of a CBRN event in this volume.

19 In particular, the Treaty on the Non-Proliferation of Nuclear Weapons (NPT) (1968), the Biological Weapons Convention (BWC) (1972), the Chemical Weapons Convention (CWC) (1993), and the Treaty on the Prohibition of Nuclear Weapons (TPNW) (2017) which will enter into force on 22 January 2021. Notably, the Comprehensive Nuclear-Test-Ban Treaty (CTBT) (1996) is not yet in force.

20 Other contributions in this book analyse responses connected to specific ambits, see ch 9 by Perrone, ch 5 by Bakker, ch 13 by Bakker, ch 30 by Corcione in this volume, and Part 3 on CBRN weapons.

21 UNBG (n 1) para 8.

The definition provided by the UNBPG is very wide and finds application in different settings, including IHRL and IHL violations that stem from CBRN events. Although no attempt has been made to draft a definition of victims of CBRN events, it is worth elaborating more on the different fields under investigation. The current arms control and disarmament regimes and the existing IEL framework fail to provide a definition of victim, and nor does IDL, in spite of the strong focus placed by the Draft Articles on the Protection of Persons in Event of Disasters on 'victims of disasters'.[22] Counter-terrorism law, a term traditionally used to refer to both the 'sectoral treaties'[23] and the relevant UN SC Resolutions,[24] is also silent on the definition of victims of terrorist offences. A notable exception at the regional level is represented by the European Union (EU) framework,[25] which provides a definition of victim of terrorism originally included in Directive 2012/29/EU[26] and later embedded in the 2017 Directive on combating terrorism.[27] According to this definition, the term victim refers to:

> a natural person who has suffered harm, including physical, mental or emotional harm or economic loss, insofar as that was directly caused by a terrorist offence, or a family member of a person whose death was directly caused by a terrorist offence and who has suffered harm as a result of that person's death.[28]

---

22 ILC, 'Draft Articles on the Protection of Persons in Event of Disasters' (2016) II(2) UNYBILC. On the Draft Articles see G Bartolini, 'A Universal Treaty for Disasters? Remarks on the International Law Commission's Draft Articles on the Protection of Persons in the Event of Disasters' (2017) 99(3) International Review of the Red Cross 1103; D Tladi, 'The International Law Commission's Draft Articles on the Protection of Persons in the Event of Disasters: Codification, Progressive Development or Creation of Law from Thin Air?' (2017) 16(3) Chinese Journal of International Law 425.

23 D O'Donnell, 'International Treaties against Terrorism and the Use of Terrorism during Armed Conflict and by Armed Forces' (2006) 88(864) International Review of the Red Cross 853, 854–859.

24 D Moeckli, 'The Emergence of Terrorism as a Distinct Category of International Law' (2008) 44 Texas International Law Journal 157; B Saul, *Defining Terrorism in International Law* (OUP, 2006).

25 See, in particular, ch 10 by Villani in this volume.

26 Directive 2012/29/EU of 25 October 2012 establishing minimum standards on the rights, support and protection of victims of crime.

27 Directive 2017/541/EU of 15 March 2017 on combating terrorism (2017 EU Directive on combating terrorism).

28 Ibid recital 27.

Lacking a more specific definition of victims of CBRN events, the current contribution favours the most comprehensive and general one, which is provided in the UNBPG.

2.2 *Victim Assistance in Lieu of Reparations within the Arms Control and Disarmament Regimes?*

Having dealt with those preliminary, although crucial, issues, the present analysis can now shift towards the venues and mechanisms in place for victims to claim remedies and reparations in the aftermath of a CBRN event. Prior to delving into the relevant instruments, it is worth stressing that, in some domains, when victims are mentioned the focus is always on victim assistance, and never on reparations. This represents a crucial point as it builds on the well-known difference between reparations, which are measures that are judicial in character and must address the harm caused by the violation committed by a specific actor, and provisions of assistance, which is a broader term that can refer to a number of measures provided in response to victims' needs.[29] As far as the arms control and disarmament regimes are concerned, it must be noted that victim assistance is nowadays regarded as a key provision of humanitarian disarmament treaties, placing a positive obligation on the States to ensure that victims' needs are met.[30] More specifically, the term 'victim assistance' first appeared in the text of the 1997 Mine Ban Treaty (MBT)[31] and, since then, it has been used in several humanitarian disarmament treaties.[32] As noted by some authors, the provision has gained momentum and evolved enormously, especially over the last two decades.[33]

In fact the 'core conventions', *ie* the NPT, the BWC and the CWC are all silent on the issue of victims' rights or needs, the only reference to victims appears in Article X of the CWC (assistance and protection against chemical weapons), according to which '[i]f the information available from the ongoing investigation or other reliable sources would give sufficient proof that there are

29 F Capone, *Reparations for Child Victims of Armed Conflict: State of the Field and Current Challenges* (Intersentia 2017) 125–130; PJ Dixon, 'Reparations, Assistance and the Experience of Justice: Lessons from Colombia and the Democratic Republic of the Congo' (2015) 10(1) the International Journal of Transitional Justice 88, 93–95.

30 Other positive obligations relevant for this book's analysis are, of course, obligations to prevent, see ch 3 by Venier in this volume.

31 Convention on the Prohibition of the Use, Stockpiling, Production and Transfer of Anti-Personnel Mines and on Their Destruction (1997) art 6.

32 Convention on Cluster Munitions (2008) art 5.

33 B Docherty, 'A Light for All Humanity: The Treaty on the Prohibition of Nuclear Weapons and the Progress of Humanitarian Disarmament' (2018) 30(2) Global Change, Peace & Security 163.

victims of use of chemical weapons and immediate action is indispensable', the Director-General shall notify all States Parties and shall take emergency measures of assistance. Notably, in 2011, the Organisation for the Prohibition of Chemical Weapons (OPCW) set up the International Support Network for Victims of Chemical Weapons and a voluntary trust fund to provide support to the victims of chemical weapons.[34] Whilst still framing the issue as 'assistance' and not reparations, the OPCW seems, at least, inclined to include victims on the non-proliferation and disarmament agenda. Quite surprisingly though, in the Ieper Declaration, issued by the OPCW in 2015 on the Occasion of the Centennial Commemoration of the First Large-Scale Use of Chemical Weapons, there is no reference to victims, but only the restatement of a 'strong conviction that those responsible for the use of chemical weapons should be held accountable'.[35]

With regard to the most recent treaties, whereas the CTBT includes no provision concerning victims,[36] the TPNW combines a comprehensive ban on nuclear weapons with obligations to assist victims and remediate the environment affected by use and testing. In so doing, the treaty aims both to prevent future harm and to address harm that has already occurred.[37] Drawing heavily from the Convention on Cluster Munitions (CCM),[38] the TPNW imposes comparable obligations on States Parties to provide assistance for nuclear weapons victims. The most relevant provisions are enshrined in Article 6 (victim assistance and environmental remediation)[39] and Article 7 (international cooperation and assistance). The latter has a much broader focus, which can be split into two different ambits. Article 7(4) of the TPNW places on each State

34 OPCW Conference of the States Parties, 'The Establishment of the International Support Network for Victims of Chemical Weapons and the Establishment of a Voluntary Trust Fund for this Purpose' (2011) UN Doc. C-16/DEC.13. No information is available on the activities carried out to support victims of chemical weapons and, currently, the Trust Fund for the International Support Network for Victims of Chemical Weapons stands at EUR 109,789. See OPCW Report by the Director-General 'Status of Implementation of the International Support Network for Victims of Chemical Weapons' (2019) UN Doc. EC-92/DG.17.

35 Declaration on the Occasion of the Centennial Commemoration of the First Large-Scale Use of Chemical Weapons at Ieper (Ieper Declaration) (2015) UN Doc. S/1262/2015.

36 T A Ruff, 'The Humanitarian Impact and Implications of Nuclear Test Explosions in the Pacific Region' (2015) 97(889) International Review of the Red Cross 775, 811–812.

37 N Singh, 'Victim Assistance under the Treaty on the Prohibition of Nuclear Weapons: An Analysis' (2020) 3(2) Journal for Peace and Nuclear Disarmament 265.

38 Convention on Cluster Munitions (2008) art 5, which places explicit obligations on States Parties affected by cluster munitions to provide assistance to victims in their territory and provides detailed guidance on how those obligations should be implemented.

39 TPNW (n 19) art 6(1) (emphasis added).

Party, in a position to do so, an obligation to provide assistance for the victims of the use or testing of nuclear weapons *or other nuclear explosive devices*. The scope of this provision is definitely wider than that of Article 6(1), which deals generally with 'victim assistance', as it encompasses both victims of nuclear weapons and victims of other nuclear explosive devices, *ie* any nuclear weapon or other explosive device capable of releasing nuclear energy, irrespective of the purpose for which it could be used.[40] Article 7(6) lays down the obligation on States, which have used or tested nuclear weapons or any other nuclear explosive devices, 'to provide adequate assistance to affected States for the purpose of victim assistance and environmental remediation'. This provision is a landmark in the field, as no other humanitarian disarmament treaty has put such an obligation on user States.[41] Nonetheless, it has been questioned whether the sentence 'shall have a responsibility to provide adequate assistance' actually undermines the effort by referring to a moral responsibility rather than a legal one.[42]

2.3 *Victims' Remedies under International Environmental Law and the Centrality of Civil Liability*

With respect to IEL, while the subject of reparation has been the focus of considerable attention in recent times, this has not yet resulted in the elaboration of detailed principles regarding the nature and quantification of reparations for environmental harm.[43] A preliminary consideration is that the main objective of international rules on the environment is to prevent damage rather than to provide the victim with an entitlement to receive redress.[44] Therefore, in addition to the principles of international law governing international responsibility, which apply also to obligations relating to environmental protection, the ILC's efforts have primarily been geared towards the issue of prevention of transboundary harm that results from activities not prohibited under international law.[45] Indeed, the ILC Articles on prevention fail to incorporate relevant

40 Singh (n 37) fn 13.

41 Ibid 271.

42 S Casey-Maslen, *The Treaty on the Prohibition of Nuclear Weapons: A Commentary* (OUP 2019) 224.

43 A Boyle, 'Reparation for Environmental Damage in International Law: Some Preliminary Problems' in M Bowman and A Boyle (eds), *Environmental Damage in International and Comparative Law: Problems of Definition and Valuation* (OUP 2002) 17.

44 T Scovazzi, 'State Responsibility for Environmental Harm' (2002) 12(1) Yearbook of International Environmental Law 43, 49. On CBRN risks and State obligations under IEL see ch 29 by Antoniazzi in this volume.

45 ILC, 'Draft Articles on prevention of transboundary harm from hazardous activities' (2001) II(2) UNYBILC (ILC Articles on prevention).

provisions on how to ensure reparations and compensation for harm arising out of activities *not prohibited by international law*.[46] However, the Commission did later take on the task of drafting a set of principles on the allocation of loss in the case of transboundary harm arising out of hazardous activities.[47] Both sets of provisions deal with activities not prohibited under international law, thus meaning that their scope of application is separated from that of the ARSIWA; nonetheless the non-fulfilment of the duty of prevention prescribed by the draft articles on prevention could engage State responsibility, meaning that the State ultimately will incur the well-known consequences of an internationally wrongful act.[48]

The ILC Principles allocate the liability for loss due to harm resulting from lawful economic or other activities, when the relevant State has complied with its due diligence obligations to prevent transboundary harm. More specifically, the principles provide a general framework for States to adopt domestic law or conclude international agreements to ensure prompt and adequate compensation for the victims of transboundary damage caused by lawful hazardous activities.[49] The principles support existing State practice, which largely channels liability to the owner or operator (or the State itself, if it is the operator)[50] and demands financial guarantees against future harm. Notably, the principles do not address the issue of how to guarantee victims' access to remedies, as they merely stress that to 'render access to justice more widespread, efficient and prompt suggestions have been made to establish special national or international environmental courts'.[51] Lacking an international environmental court, it is clear that said claims must be brought before domestic bodies, since, as part of arrangements for permitting hazardous activities within their jurisdiction and control, it is widely expected that States would make sure that adequate mechanisms are available to respond to claims for compensation in case of any damages.[52] This approach is in line with the one previously outlined by the Institute of International Law in its 1997 Resolution on Responsibility and

46 Ibid, Commentary to Draft Article 15, 167.

47 ILC Draft principles on the allocation of loss in the case of transboundary harm arising out of hazardous activities (2006) II(2)UNYBILC (ILC Principles on allocation of loss).

48 Ibid, Commentary to Principle 1, 62. Scovazzi (n 44) 50.

49 ILC Principles on allocation of loss (n 47) Commentary to Draft Principle 4, 76–81. D L Shelton and A Kiss, 'Strict Liability in International Environmental Law', in TM Ndiaye and R Wolfrum (eds) *Law of the Sea, Environmental Law and Settlement of Disputes: Liber Amicorum Judge Thomas A. Mensah* (Brill 2007) 1131, 1141–1145.

50 Ibid 1139.

51 ILC Principles on allocation of loss (n 47) 77–78.

52 Ibid 77.

Liability under International Law for Environmental Damage.[53] As stressed in the Resolution, 'civil liability of operators can be engaged under domestic law or the governing rules of international law regardless of the lawfulness of the activity concerned if it results in environmental damage'.[54] The Resolution further highlights that environmental regimes should include specific rules on responsibility and liability in order to ensure their effectiveness in terms of both encouraging prevention and providing for victims' restoration and compensation.[55] In other words, without precluding the application of rules of general international law, *ie* the principles governing international responsibility, environmental regimes should normally assign primary (civil) liability to operators.

In addition to the general framework delineated by the work of the ILC and the Institute of International Law, it is possible to find additional rules that follow this pattern in the relevant conventions. Across the many conventions that impose liability for damages to the environment, it is worth noting, for instance, that a number of multilateral treaties have been adopted in order to harmonise national laws in the area of civil liability for nuclear damage. Said treaties include the Paris Convention on Civil Liability of 1960 and the Vienna Convention of 1963, along with their amendments.[56] In 2015, the Convention on Supplementary Compensation for Nuclear Damage (CSC) entered into force,[57] marking a crucial milestone for the creation of a 'global nuclear liability regime'.[58] The CSC aims at establishing a minimum national compensation amount and at further increasing the amount of compensation through public funds to be made available by the Contracting Parties should

53 The Institute of International Law 'Resolution on the Responsibility and Liability under International Law for Environmental Damage' (1997) Session of Strasbourg.

54 Ibid, art 1.

55 Ibid, art 2.

56 The Convention on Third Party Liability in the Field of Nuclear Energy (Paris Convention) (1960), under the auspices of the Organisation for Economic Co-operation and Development (OECD); the Vienna Convention on Civil Liability for Nuclear Damage (Vienna Convention) (1963) under the auspices of the International Atomic Energy Agency (IAEA). In addition to the various protocols, and following the Chernobyl accident, a Joint Protocol Relating to the Application of the Vienna Convention and the Paris Convention (Joint Protocol) was adopted in 1988, under the joint auspices of the OECD and the IAEA, in order to create a 'treaty link' between the States Parties to the Paris and the Vienna Conventions.

57 Convention on Supplementary Compensation for Nuclear Damage (1997).

58 J Bellamy, 'Civil liability for nuclear damage in countries developing nuclear new build programmes' (2019) 12(1) The Journal of World Energy Law & Business 108.

the national amount be insufficient to compensate the damage caused by a nuclear incident.

According to the CSC, the so-called 'Installation State' is responsible for the redress of the following damages: loss of life or personal injury, and loss of or damage to property.[59] Moreover, compensation for nuclear damage shall be distributed by the Installation State equitably and without discrimination on the basis of nationality, domicile or residence.[60] Notably, the Convention is open not only to States Parties to the Paris and Vienna Conventions but also to other States, provided that their national legislation is consistent with uniform rules on civil liability laid down in the Annex to the Convention.[61] Under the international legal regime set up by the aforementioned treaties, some key principles have been established, including the strict and exclusive liability of the operator of a nuclear installation (meaning that the victims are not required to prove that the liable person was at fault); the existence of a minimum amount of liability; and the exclusive jurisdiction of one State, normally where the incident occurs, so that the victims, nationals as well as foreigners, do not need to bring their claims before multiple fora.[62]

Also relevant is the framework governing land-based activities, *ie* the Basel Convention on Hazardous Waste and its Liability Protocol.[63] The Protocol aims to provide a comprehensive regime for liability and for adequate and prompt compensation for damage resulting from transboundary waste movements, including illegal traffic. The Basel Protocol imposes strict liability on, first, the person who provides notification of a proposed transboundary movement according to Article 6 of the Basel Convention, and, thereafter, the disposer of the waste. The competent courts are those of the State where the damage was suffered, or the incident occurred, or the defendant has his habitual residence or has his principal place of business.[64]

Liability is also affirmed in relation to lawful activities taking place at sea that may involve CBRN elements. For example, the 1971 Convention relating to Civil Liability in the Field of Maritime Carriage of Nuclear Material provides

59 CSC (n 57) art 1(f).

60 Ibid art 3(2)(a).

61 Notably, an online calculator has been developed, which applies the formula in art IV of the CSC and assists users in running scenarios of actual and potential Contracting Parties to the CSC to determine the amounts to be contributed to the international fund in such cases, <https://www.iaea.org/publications/documents/treaties/convention-supplementary-compensation-nuclear-damage/online-calculator>.

62 Shelton and Kiss (n 49) 1141–1142.

63 Basel Convention on the Control of Transboundary Movements of Hazardous Wastes and their Disposal (1989) and the Basel Protocol on Liability and Compensation (1999).

64 Ibid art 17.

for shipowner liability if the shipowner committed or omitted an act with intent to cause damage.[65] Furthermore, the 1996 International Convention on Liability and Compensation for Damage in Connection with the Carriage of Hazardous and Noxious Substances by Sea (HNS Convention), and its amending Protocol of 2010, deal with claims for damage arising from the carriage, defined as that period during which the substances are on the ship or ship's equipment, of such substances at sea. Notably, the Convention's wide definition of hazardous and noxious substances makes it relevant for CBRN materials, with the exclusion of nuclear ones as they are covered by the 1971 treaty.[66] Under the 2010 HNS Convention, the shipowner is liable for the loss or damage up to a certain amount, which is covered by insurance (1st tier). A compensation fund (*ie* the HNS Fund) will provide additional compensation where the victims do not obtain full compensation from the shipowner or its insurer (2nd tier).[67]

Ultimately, what emerges from this overview of IEL's response to victims' rights, is that, in this field, there is a set of well-established principles and norms dealing with States and NSAs' civil liability and compensation obligations in cases of activities not prohibited under international law.[68]

2.4 *Victims' Rights under International Disaster Law*

With respect to disasters, man-made or natural,[69] the attention towards victims has grown significantly over recent decades, resulting in the effort to strengthen the connection between disasters and human rights.[70] However, as reflected by the contemporary view of the international community,[71] the focus rests mainly on the adequate and effective response to disasters and reduction of the risk, rather than on the rights of victims.[72]

65 International Convention relating to Civil Liability in the Field of Maritime Carriage of Nuclear Material (1971).

66 International Convention on Liability and Compensation for Damage in Connection with the Carriage of Hazardous and Noxious Substances by Sea (1996) as amended in 2010.

67 Ibid Preamble, para 8.

68 See ch 29 by Antoniazzi in this volume.

69 See ILC Draft Articles on the Protection of Persons in Event of Disasters (n 22) Article 3. G Bartolini, 'Il progetto di articoli della Commissione del diritto internazionale sulla "Protection of Persons in the Event of Disasters"' (2017) 100 Rivista di diritto internazionale 677.

70 See F Zorzi Giustiniani and others (eds), *Routledge Handbook of Human Rights and Disasters* (Routledge 2018).

71 Sendai Framework for Disaster Risk Reduction 2015–2030, (2015) UN Doc A/CONF. 224/L.2.

72 ILC Draft Articles on the Protection of Persons in Event of Disasters (n 22) art 2.

Thus, the work of the ILC on the protection of persons in the event of disasters, places the emphasis, first and foremost, on the measures that States must adopt to prevent, mitigate and prepare for such disasters. Furthermore, in the provisions dealing with human dignity (Article 4) and the protection which persons affected by disasters are entitled to under IHRL (Article 5), there is no explicit reference to victims' remedies and reparations. However, the importance of human rights protections in disaster situations is demonstrated by the increased attention paid to the issue by human rights bodies established under the auspices of the United Nations, as well as by regional courts. Hence, as will be discussed in Section 3, it is before those bodies that victims whose rights have been violated in a disaster context can claim redress.[73]

2.5 *Victims' Rights in the Counter-Terrorism Framework*

In the aftermath of the 9/11 attacks, the international community adopted the first-ever common strategic approach to combat terrorism, *ie* the UN Global Counterterrorism Strategy (UNGTS).[74] Beyond establishing mechanisms to fight the terrorist threat, the UNGTS recognised the importance of enhancing the rights of victims of terrorism, in order to counter the phenomenon in an effective way. Nevertheless, guarding the rights of victims of terrorism within a human rights framework has been largely neglected so far and few efforts have been made by States to answer the call of the UN strategy.

A bold and, unfortunately, isolated move in this sense is represented by the 2021 Report of the Special Rapporteur on the promotion and protection of human rights and fundamental freedoms while countering terrorism, Ben Emmerson, who attempted to lay down the 'framework principles for securing the human rights of victims of terrorism'.[75]

In a nutshell, according to Emmerson, there are 'sound reasons in favour of recognizing that States should accept a special obligation to victims of terrorism',[76] in light of the fact that 'there is almost always a direct or indirect motivational connection (however misguided) between acts of terrorism and

73 K Hausler, 'Indigenous Communities: from Victims to Actors of Disaster Management', in Zorzi Giustiniani and others (n 70) 291, 295–296.

74 UNGA 'The United Nations Global Counter-Terrorism Strategy' (20 September 2020) UN Doc. A/RES/60/288, para 8.

75 Human Rights Council, 'Report of the Special Rapporteur on the promotion and protection of human rights and fundamental freedoms while countering terrorism, Ben Emmerson' (4 June 2012) UN Doc. A/HRC/20/14.

76 Ibid para 53. See also E Lorenzana Del Villar and D Silfen Glasberg, 'Victims of Terrorism and the Right to Redress: Challenges and Contradictions in the 2012 Emmerson Report' (2015) 39(3) Humanity & Society 321.

policies of state'.[77] Thus, Emmerson urges States to voluntarily accept a binding international obligation to provide reparations to the victims of all acts of terrorism occurring on their territory in which a natural person has been killed or has suffered serious physical or psychological harm, irrespective of the nationality of the perpetrator or the victim, and thereby to fill an existing protection gap. Examples of such efforts are still scant in practice and only a few States, eg Spain,[78] have enacted a unified scheme setting out the assistance, support and protection to which victims of terrorism are entitled, recognising all victims of terrorism as being victims of human rights violations, irrespective of questions of State responsibility.[79]

Although it does not frame the issue in terms of breaches of IHRL, but rather in terms of provisions of assistance, the EU Directive on combating terrorism marks an important step in the direction of promoting and recognising victims' needs in the aftermath of a terrorist attack.[80] The aim of the Directive is, in fact, that of strengthening a uniform approach to the issue across the EU Member States, by requiring them to provide assistance and support to victims of terrorism in accordance with their specific needs.[81] In particular, the Directive asks States to amend their national frameworks and allow victims to obtain all the support they need.[82] Nonetheless, as revealed by the report on the implementation of the Directive, issued in 2020, whereas it is possible to ascertain a good level of enactment of most of the provisions enshrined in this instrument, 'there are deficiencies as regards the transposition of specific provisions for victims of terrorism, which could have the effect of victims of terrorism not receiving assistance or support tailored to their specific needs'.[83]

77 Human Rights Council (n 75) para 54.

78 Act No. 29/2011 of 22 September 2011 on the Recognition and Comprehensive Protection to Victims of Terrorism.

79 UNODC, 'Good Practices in Supporting Victims of Terrorism within the Criminal Justice Framework' (2015), 30 <https://www.unodc.org/documents/terrorism/Publications/Good%20practices%20on%20victims/good_practices_victims_E.pdf>.

80 2017 EU Directive on combating terrorism (n 27) arts 24–27.

81 CC Murphy, 'EU Counter-terrorism Law: What Kind of Exemplar of Transnational Law?' (2019) 21(1) Cambridge Yearbook of European Legal Studies 217, 222.

82 2017 EU Directive on combating terrorism (n 27) art 24.

83 Report from the Commission to the European Parliament and the Council based on Article 29(1) of Directive (EU) 2017/541 of the European Parliament and of the Council of 15 March 2017 on combating terrorism (30 September 2020) COM(2020) 619 final, 18–19.

3 Victims' Rights within the IHRL and IHL Frameworks: Residual Application or Way Forward?

Without providing an overview of the well-known and already widely discussed general aspects,[84] the present section will focus on the most recent developments in the fields of IHRL and IHL and their consequences on the access to remedies for victims of CBRN events. In relation to IHRL, notable progress includes the adoption on 3 September 2019 by the UN Human Rights Committee (HRC) of a new General Comment No. 36 on Article 6 (the right to life) of the International Covenant on Civil and Political Rights (ICCPR),[85] which concludes that the threat or use of nuclear weapons is incompatible with the right to life and may amount to a crime under international law. More specifically, paragraph 66 of the General Comment makes explicit reference to States Parties' obligation to take all necessary measures to stop the proliferation of weapons of mass destruction, including measures to prevent their acquisition by non-State actors. Furthermore, the HRC stresses the obligation incumbent on States to afford 'adequate reparation to victims whose right to life has been or is being adversely affected by the testing or use of weapons of mass destruction, in accordance with principles of international responsibility'.[86]

The HRC, consistently with its role and mandate, has placed the accent on States' responsibility, framing the discourse around violations of the ICCPR and the status of victims entitled to claim reparations and thus to exercise a legal right. Moreover, the HRC has in the past stressed States' responsibility to compensate victims of CBRN events. For example, in relation to the nuclear tests carried out by France, the HRC expressed its concern about the fact that the French Nuclear Test Victims Compensation Committee (CIVEN)[87] had dismissed a very high rate of cases (98.3 per cent) and stressed how France should take all necessary steps to ensure the effective recognition and compensation

84 With regard to IHRL, see for instance Shelton (n 6); in relation to IHL see Evans (n 8); EC Gillard 'Reparation for Violations of International Humanitarian Law' (2003) 85(851) International Review of the Red Cross 529; L Zegveld, 'Remedies for Victims of Violations of International Humanitarian Law' (2003) 85(851) International Review of the Red Cross 497.

85 HRC 'General comment No. 36 Article 6: right to life' (3 September 2019) UN Doc. CCPR/C/GC/36.

86 Ibid para 66.

87 Loi n° 2010–2 du 5 janvier 2010 relative à la reconnaissance et à l'indemnisation des victimes des essais nucléaires français.

of all the victims of French nuclear tests, especially the local population in Algeria and French Polynesia.[88]

In addition to the right to life, CBRN events can violate (or ultimately lead to the violation of) a plethora of other human rights, ranging from the right to freedom from torture or other forms of cruel, inhuman or degrading treatment, to the right to food, to an adequate standard of living, the right to freedom of movement or residence, the right to education and the right to family life.[89] In order for victims of human rights violations stemming from CBRN events to be able to access regional and international bodies, it is necessary to prove the connection between the CBRN event and the violation of IHRL.[90] This causal link appears to be particularly evident in some cases, for example, according to Doswald-Beck, 'any use of nuclear weapons will result in human rights violations';[91] whereas, it is more difficult to ascertain and to assess the responsibility of the actors involved in other situations, for instance, when the harm caused may originate from diverse sources, eg in the course of a global pandemic, and/or when the number of victims is potentially endless, eg in the aftermath of the accidental release of toxic agents from a chemical plant or a pipeline.[92]

Nonetheless, despite all the challenges to seeking remedies before regional and international human rights mechanisms, which apply also to victims of CBRN events,[93] it is often far easier to obtain individual redress for human

---

88 HRC, 'Concluding observations on the fifth periodic report of France' (17 August 2015) UN Doc. CCPR/C/FRA/CO/5 para 21. See also JM Collin and P Bouveret, 'The Waste From French Nuclear Tests in Algeria Radioactivity Under the Sand Analysis with regard to the Treaty on the Prohibition of Nuclear Weapons', Heinrich Böll Foundation, July 2020, 47.

89 L Doswald-Beck, 'Human Rights and Nuclear Weapons' in G Nystuen, S Casey-Maslen, A Golden Bersagel (eds) *Nuclear Weapons under International Law* (CUP 2014) 435, 453–456.

90 See ch 28 by Sommario in this volume.

91 Dowwald-Beck (n 89) 459.

92 The most serious chemical accident ever recorded is the 1984 Bhopal disaster, which occurred in 1984 in India, where more than 3,000 people died after a highly toxic gas (methyl isocyanate) was released from a Union Carbide Pesticides Factory. See M Frulli, 'The challenge of outlining the CBRN(E) definitional framework: agents, events and actors' (May 2020) <http://www.cbrn-italy.it/sites/default/files/The%20challenges%20of%20outlining%20CBRN%20definitional%20framework.pdf>.

93 I Bantekas and L Oette, 'Victims' Rights and Reparation' in I Bantekas and L Bette (eds), *International Human Rights Law and Practice* (CUP 2018) 598; Shelton (n 3); Capone (n 29); L Cornejo Chavez, 'New remedial responses in the practice of regional human rights courts: Purposes beyond compensation' (2017) 15(2) International Journal of Constitutional Law 372; C Sandoval, P Leach and R Murray, 'Monitoring, Cajoling and Promoting Dialogue: What Role for Supranational Human Rights Bodies in the Implementation of Individual Decisions?' (2020) 12(1) Journal of Human Rights Practice 71.

rights violations than for IHL violations. With regard to IHL, the dearth of mechanisms and the scant implementation of the right to reparation for victims of violations of the law of war have been discussed at length by several authors.[94] However, some additional thoughts can usefully be shared with regard to remedies for those affected by the use of CBRN materials in armed conflict.[95] In particular, it is worth highlighting two developments that might contribute to promoting victims' rights in the aftermath of violations of *jus in bello* and also *jus ad bellum*. The first development is the increased attention placed on environmental damages by Claims Commissions, *ie* ad hoc bodies established to deal with compensatory justice for violations of international law.[96] In particular, both the United Nations Claims Commission (UNCC) – set up to process claims and pay compensation for losses and damage suffered as a direct result of Iraq's unlawful invasion and occupation of Kuwait[97] – and the Eritrea–Ethiopia Claims Commission (EECC)[98] – established in 2000 by a treaty between the belligerents to settle claims for loss, damage, or injury of either government and its nationals – accepted environmental claims.[99] The successful, at least in part, experience of both Claims Commissions and the attention they shone on the often ignored devastation to the natural environment caused by armed conflict represent a model that can be pursued also when dealing with the widespread consequences of CBRN events.

The second development that is worth mentioning is the creation of new mechanisms to assist in the investigation and prosecution of the most serious crimes under international law, in particular, the crime of genocide, crimes against humanity and war crimes.[100] An example of said mechanisms is offered

94 See Hausler (n 73). See also S Casey-Maslen, 'The right to a remedy and reparation for the use of nuclear weapons' in G Nystuen, S Casey-Maslen, A Golden Bersagel (eds) (n 89) 461.

95 See ch 21 by Mauri in this volume.

96 L Brilmayer, C Giorgetti and L Charlton, *International Claims Commissions: Righting Wrongs after Conflict* (Edward Elgar 2017) 27; The International Bureau of the Permanent Court of Arbitration (ed) *Redressing Injustice through Mass Claims Processes. Innovative Responses to Unique Challenges* (OUP 2006); TJ Feighery and others (eds), *War Reparations and the UN Compensation Commission: Designing Compensation After Conflict* (OUP 2015).

97 CR Payne, 'Developments in the Law of Environmental Reparations. A Case Study of the UN Compensation Commission' in C Stahn, J Iverson and JS Easterday (eds), *Environmental Protecting and Transition from Conflict to Peace: Clarifying Norms, Principles and Practices* (OUP 2017) 329.

98 F Capone, 'The 17 August 2009 Final Awards of the Eritrea-Ethiopia Claims Commission' in A de Guttry, G Venturini and HG Post (eds), *The 1998–2000 War Between Eritrea and Ethiopia* (2nd edn Asser Press forthcoming).

99 See ch 22 by Saluzzo in this volume.

100 See ch 32 by Vierucci in this volume.

by the International, Impartial and Independent Mechanism (IIIM) set up by the UN General Assembly in 2016 and meant to bring to justice those responsible for international crimes perpetrated in the Syrian Arab Republic since March 2011.[101] In a nutshell, the Mechanism is mandated to collect evidence or relevant information pertaining to violations of international humanitarian law and human rights violations and abuse.

Until 2017, a Joint Investigative Mechanism (JIM) established by the OPCW and the UN was also deployed to determine responsibility for the use of chemical weapons in Syria.[102] The JIM,[103] however, unlike the IIIM, was not tasked with collecting and storing evidence to be used before judicial bodies and, therefore, its role, although equally relevant, was less prone to provide factual support to claims brought by victims before national or international fora.

4 International Criminal Law's (Potential) Contribution to Strengthening Victims' Rights

An aspect that is rarely considered in relation to CBRN events is the potential role that ICL might play with respect to enhancing victims' rights. The topic is probably deserving of a longer and more detailed analysis; however, it is worthwhile to include at least a reference to the increasingly important function that the ICC has been called upon to fulfil in the field of remedies.[104] The ICC is, in fact, the first international criminal body specifically tasked with providing reparations to victims of international crimes that fall under the Court's jurisdiction.[105] In light of this unique feature, the ICC has used its power to award reparations on a number of occasions, showing a significant inclination towards implementing a victim-friendly approach.[106]

101 UNGA 'International, Impartial and Independent Mechanism to Assist in the Investigation and Prosecution of Persons Responsible for the Most Serious Crimes under International Law Committed in the Syrian Arab Republic since March 2011' (21 December 2016) UN Doc. A/RES/71/248.

102 UNSC Res 2235/2015 (7 August 2015) UN Doc. S/RES/2235. See ch 26 by Buscemi in this volume.

103 Three consecutive vetoes by Russia led to its termination at the end of 2017.

104 Article 75 of the ICC Statute encapsulates the core provisions on reparation before the Court, stating, *inter alia*, that the Court may make an order directly against a convicted person specifying appropriate reparations to, or in respect of, victims, including restitution, compensation and rehabilitation.

105 McCarthy (n 13) see also Capone (n 13) 645. See ch 32 by Vierucci in this volume.

106 For an overview of the ICC's approach to reparations, see L Moffett and C Sandoval 'Tilting at Windmills: Reparations and the International Criminal Court' (2021) Leiden Journal of International Law 1.

When it comes to the ICC's role in relation to CBRN events, a preliminary and crucial clarification is needed about the Court's jurisdiction *ratione materiae* (or subject-matter jurisdiction). As is well known, the Rome Statute does not contain the words 'nuclear weapon', 'chemical weapon' or 'biological weapon.' During the drafting of what was to become Article 8 of the Rome Statute, the list of prohibited weapons proved to be among the most contentious questions. It was agreed to include express prohibitions of the use, in international armed conflicts, of 'poison or poisoned weapons' and 'asphyxiating, poisonous or other gases, and all analogous liquids, materials or devices'. Some States argued that listing chemical weapons, but not nuclear weapons, would be inherently 'unfair', given that chemical weapons were, in effect, considered the 'poor man's' weapon of mass destruction.[107] By contrast, nuclear weapons States, as well as those that were members of military alliances relying on nuclear weapons, rejected any inclusion of nuclear weapons in the list of prohibited weapons. In the final compromise, neither nuclear nor chemical weapons were expressly listed as weapons whose use was prohibited under the Rome Statute.[108]

Two provisions found in Article 8 of the Statute may refer to chemical and biological weapons (CBW) implicitly, but, according to some authors, it is unclear whether all chemical weapons are included, and whether biological weapons are included at all.[109] Other commentators found that, in practice, many and perhaps all uses of lethal chemical weapons in international armed conflicts will fall within the Article 8 prohibitions on the use of 'poison or poisoned weapons' and 'asphyxiating, poisonous or other gases, and all analogous liquids, materials or devices'.[110]

The Kampala Review Conference in 2010 led to the extension of the list of weapons whose use is prohibited in NIACs. The Kampala amendment to Article 8 inserts Article 8(2)(e)(xiii) and (xiv) into the Rome Statute, with the consequence that employing 'poison or poisoned weapons' and 'asphyxiating, poisonous or other gases, and all analogous liquids, materials and devices' constitutes a war crime in NIACs as well, at least for the States Parties that

107 A Zimmermann and M Şener 'Chemical Weapons and the International Criminal Court' (2014) 108 (3) The American Journal of International Law, 436, 439.

108 Ibid.

109 A Alamuddin and P Webb 'Expanding Jurisdiction over War Crimes under Article 8 of the ICC Statute' (2010) 8(5) Journal of International Criminal Justice 1219.

110 D Akande 'Can the ICC Prosecute for Use of Chemical Weapons in Syria?' (23 August 2013) <https://www.ejiltalk.org/can-the-icc-prosecute-for-use-of-chemical-weapons-in-syria/>. For more on the academic debate, see K J Heller 'The Rome Statute Does Not Criminalise Chemical and Biological Weapons' (5 November 2015) <http://opiniojuris.org/2015/11/05/why-the-rome-statute-does-not-criminalise-chemical-and-biological-weapons/>.

have ratified the Article 8 amendment. As a result, under the Rome Statute, as subsequently amended in Kampala, the ICC potentially has subject-matter jurisdiction over most uses of chemical weapons in both IACs and NIACs. In relation to the characterisation of conduct involving the use of certain WMD as a crime against humanity, if the requirement of a widespread or systematic attack against a civilian population is satisfied, then it will be possible to prosecute said conduct as a crime against humanity under Article 7(1)(a) or (k).

Notably, any punishment under these provisions, apart from being more difficult to prove, would not cover the specific wrongfulness inherent in the use of chemical or biological weapons. Assuming that the ICC has subject-matter jurisdiction over uses of CBW,[111] an issue that is still regarded as controversial by many, other relevant problems relate to, for instance, the possibility to convict the perpetrators and assess individual responsibility for the use of weapons, especially biological ones, that are more difficult to detect. In order for the ICC to realise its full potential, also in the field of victims' remedies, it would be helpful to recognise and act upon the need for a CBW-use amendment in the future.[112] Such an amendment would make the Court's jurisdiction over uses of chemical and biological weapons more effective and would provide the victims with an international forum for claiming reparations.

5 Concluding Remarks

Without pretending to offer a comprehensive analysis, this chapter focused on a number of key aspects and highlighted the main challenges, as well as the most relevant developments, concerning the rights of victims of CBRN events. The study, first of all, pointed out the lack of a definition of what constitutes a 'victim of a CBRN event' and the consequent need to rely either on the general definition provided in the UNBPG or to look for a more accurate terminology under the surveyed legal frameworks. The inquiry revealed how all those fields, which from the outset can be regarded as not particularly victim-friendly, fail to address the issue of who can, specifically, be identified as victims. Moreover, the research also underscored that supporting victims with measures of

111 This view, which is endorsed by the present author, is arguably buttressed by Article 22(2) of the Statute, which provides both that the 'definition of a crime shall be strictly construed' and that any such 'definition shall be interpreted in favour of the person being investigated, prosecuted or convicted'. See also Zimmermann and Sener (n 107) 439.

112 Ibid 448.

assistance is, in most instances, the approach pursued in the aftermath of a CBRN event, especially under the arms control and disarmament regimes and within the existing counter-terrorism framework.[113] However, victims of violations of IEL that stem from the use or transportation of CBRN materials, have access to remedies under the relevant conventions, which are mostly provided under the framework of civil liability of the owner or operator, *ie* a private actor *or* the State itself. As discussed in Section 2, currently, there is a set of international conventions which are designed to provide compensation for damage arising from nuclear incidents. However, these conventions, including the CSC, have not been widely ratified yet[114] and the lack of widespread support makes it very difficult to envisage the creation of a global nuclear liability regime aimed at ensuring that potential victims will be compensated promptly and efficiently after a nuclear accident, regardless of where it occurs.

Ultimately, the chapter investigated the extent to which IHRL and IHL can contribute to overcoming some of the shortcomings highlighted in the previous sections, since CBRN events in peace time and in situations of armed conflict can amount to breaches of international human rights or humanitarian law. The conclusion reached is that, despite significant and diversified efforts, the road to fulfilling victims' rights in the aftermath of CBRN events is still long and, evidently, uphill. On the one hand, the adoption of ad hoc instruments can be ruled out as unrealistic, at least for the foreseeable future; however, on the other, it is absolutely appropriate to advocate for strengthening and improving the existing instruments, in order to incorporate, to the maximum degree possible, a victim-centric perspective.

Bibliography

Alamuddin A and Webb P, 'Expanding Jurisdiction over War Crimes under Article 8 of the ICC Statute' (2010) 8(5) Journal of International Criminal Justice 1219.

113 An exception to this mainstream approach is represented by the view expressed by the former Special Rapporteur on the promotion and protection of human rights and fundamental freedoms while countering terrorism, Ben Emmerson, who urged States to accept a special obligation to provide reparations to victims of terrorism. See HRC (n 75).

114 According to the International Expert Group on Nuclear Liability (INLEX), only about one half of all nuclear power plants are located in States which are contracting parties to one of the nuclear liability conventions. See INLEX, 'Civil Liability for Nuclear Damage: Advantages and Disadvantages of Joining the International Nuclear Liability Regime', <https://www.iaea.org/sites/default/files/17/11/liability-regime.pdf>.

Bantekas I and Oette L, 'Victims' Rights and Reparation' in I Bantekas and L Bette (eds), *International Human Rights Law and Practice* (CUP 2018).

Bartolini G, *Riparazione per violazione dei diritti umani e ordinamento internazionale* (Jovene 2009).

Bartolini G, 'A Universal Treaty for Disasters? Remarks on the International Law Commission's Draft Articles on the Protection of Persons in the Event of Disasters' (2017) 99(3) International Review of the Red Cross 1103.

Bartolini G, 'Il progetto di articoli della Commissione del diritto internazionale sulla "Protection of Persons in the Event of Disasters"' (2017) 100 Rivista di diritto internazionale 67.

Bellamy J, 'Civil liability for nuclear damage in countries developing nuclear new build programmes' (2019) 12(1) The Journal of World Energy Law & Business 108.

Boyle A, 'Reparation for Environmental Damage in International Law: Some Preliminary Problems' in M Bowman and A Boyle (eds), *Environmental Damage in International and Comparative Law: Problems of Definition and Valuation* (OUP 2002).

Brilmayer L, Giorgetti C and Charlton L, *International Claims Commissions: Righting Wrongs after Conflict* (Edward Elgar 2017).

Capone F, 'Remedies', in R Wolfrum (ed), *Max Planck Encyclopedia of Public International Law* (OUP 2013).

Capone F, *Reparations for Child Victims of Armed Conflict: State of the Field and Current Challenges* (Intersentia 2017).

Capone F, 'An Appraisal of the Al Mahdi Order on Reparations and Its Innovative Elements: Redress for Victims of Crimes against Cultural Heritage' (2018) 16 Journal of International Criminal Justice 645.

Damrosch L F, 'Gross and Systematic Human Rights Violations', in R Wolfrum (ed), *Max Planck Encyclopedia of Public International Law* (OUP 2013).

de Casadevante Romani C F, 'International Law of Victims' (2010) 14 Max Planck UNYB 219.

Dixon P J, 'Reparations, Assistance and the Experience of Justice: Lessons from Colombia and the Democratic Republic of the Congo' (2015) 10(1) the International Journal of Transitional Justice 88.

Docherty B, 'A Light for All Humanity: The Treaty on the Prohibition of Nuclear Weapons and the Progress of Humanitarian Disarmament' (2018) 30(2) Global Change, Peace & Security 163.

Doswald-Beck L, 'Human Rights and Nuclear Weapons' in G Nystuen, S Casey-Maslen, A Golden Bersagel (eds), *Nuclear Weapons under International Law* (CUP 2014).

Evans C, *The Right to Reparation in International Law for Victims of Armed Conflict* (CUP 2012).

Feighery T J and others (eds), *War Reparations and the UN Compensation Commission: Designing Compensation After Conflict* (OUP 2015).

Gillard E C, 'Reparation for Violations of International Humanitarian Law' (2003) 85(851) International Review of the Red Cross 529.

Hausler K, 'Indigenous Communities: from Victims to Actors of Disaster Management', in Zorzi Giustiniani and others (eds), *Routledge Handbook of Human Rights and Disasters* (Routledge 2018).

Iovane M, *La riparazione nella teoria e nella prassi dell'illecito internazionale* (Giuffrè 1990).

Kleffner J K, *Complementarity in the Rome Statute and National Criminal Jurisdictions* (OUP 2008).

McCarthy C, *Reparations and Victim Support in the International Criminal Court* (CUP 2012).

Moeckli D, 'The Emergence of Terrorism as a Distinct Category of International Law' (2008) 44 Texas International Law Journal 157.

Moffett L, 'Beyond Attribution: Responsibility of Armed Non-State Actors for Reparations in Northern Ireland, Colombia and Uganda' in N Gal-Or, C Ryngaert and M Noortmann (eds), *Responsibilities of the Non-State Actor in Armed Conflict and the Market Place: Theoretical Considerations and Empirical Findings* (Brill 2015).

Moffett L and Sandoval C, 'Tilting at Windmills: Reparations and the International Criminal Court' (2021) Leiden Journal of International Law 1.

Murphy C C, 'EU Counter-terrorism Law: What Kind of Exemplar of Transnational Law?' (2019) 21(1) Cambridge Yearbook of European Legal Studies 217.

O'Donnell D, 'International Treaties against Terrorism and the Use of Terrorism during Armed Conflict and by Armed Forces' (2006) 88(864) International Review of the Red Cross 853.

Rose C, 'An Emerging Norm: The Duty of States to Provide Reparations for Human Rights Violations by Non-State Actors' (2010) 33 Hastings Int'l & Comp. L. Rev. 307.

Ruff T A, 'The Humanitarian Impact and Implications of Nuclear Test Explosions in the Pacific Region' (2015) 97(889) International Review of the Red Cross 775.

Scovazzi T, 'State Responsibility for Environmental Harm' (2002) 12(1) Yearbook of International Environmental Law 43.

Shelton D, 'Righting Wrongs: Reparations in the Articles on State Responsibility' (2002) 96 AJIL 833.

Shelton D, 'Human Rights, Remedies', in R Wolfrum (ed), *Max Planck Encyclopedia of Public International Law* (OUP 2013).

Shelton D, *Remedies in International Human Rights Law* (OUP 2015 3rd edn).

Singh N, 'Victim Assistance under the Treaty on the Prohibition of Nuclear Weapons: An Analysis' (2020) 3(2) Journal for Peace and Nuclear Disarmament 265.

Tladi D, 'The International Law Commission's Draft Articles on the Protection of Persons in the Event of Disasters: Codification, Progressive Development or Creation of Law from Thin Air?' (2017) 16(3) Chinese Journal of International Law 425.

Zegveld L, 'Remedies for Victims of Violations of International Humanitarian Law' (2003) 85(851) International Review of the Red Cross 497.

Zimmermann A and Şener M, 'Chemical Weapons and the International Criminal Court' (2014) 108 (3) The American Journal of International Law, 436.

Concluding Remarks

Andrea Gioia

In recent years, there has been an increasing interest within the international community in the legal aspects of 'disasters', defined as events having a major humanitarian impact. Until relatively recently, international law mainly concerned itself in this respect with armed conflicts. However, while armed conflicts may be included within the current concept of disasters in view of their major humanitarian impact – indeed, the international law of armed conflict (more specifically, the *jus in bello*) is also traditionally known as 'international humanitarian law' (IHL) – there is an increasing awareness that disasters other than armed conflicts create similar humanitarian challenges. Therefore, a solid and coherent legal framework is needed for all disasters in order to prevent their occurrence, as much as possible, and to minimise their impact, should they nevertheless occur.

Thus, the resolution on humanitarian assistance adopted in 2003 by the Institute of International Law (the '2003 Bruges Resolution') defines disasters as 'calamitous events which endanger life, health, physical integrity, or the right not to be subject to cruel, inhuman or degrading treatment, or other fundamental human rights, or the essential needs of the population'. The Resolution includes within this concept: (a) events 'of natural origin (such as earthquakes, volcanic eruptions, windstorms, torrential rains, floods, landslides, droughts, fires, famine, epidemics'; (b) 'man-made disasters of technological origin (such as chemical disasters or nuclear explosions)'; or (c) disasters 'caused by armed conflicts or violence (such as international or internal armed conflicts, internal disturbances or violence, terrorist activities)'. However, despite adopting a broad definition of disasters, the actions proposed by the 2003 Bruges Resolution are more limited than those contained in the current concept of international disaster law (IDL). The Resolution focuses on 'humanitarian assistance', which is defined as 'all acts, activities and the human and material resources for the provision of goods and services of an exclusively humanitarian character, indispensable for the survival and the fulfilment of the essential needs of the victims of disasters', whereas IDL covers more than humanitarian assistance. Indeed, although the two expressions are sometimes used interchangeably, IDL is also broader than the concept of international disaster response law (IDRL) because it includes prevention of disasters and preparedness therefor, in addition to response thereto.

Therefore, the more recent Draft Articles on the Protection of Persons in the Event of Disasters, adopted by the UN International Law Commission (ILC) in 2016, which contain a broad definition of disasters similar to the one in the 2003 Bruges Resolution, are especially important in that they relate not only to 'response to disasters' but also to the 'reduction of risk' thereof. As concerns disaster response, the Draft Articles provide for a duty of States to cooperate, not only on humanitarian assistance but also with respect to coordination of international relief actions and communications, and making available personnel, equipment and goods, and scientific, medical, and technical assistance. As for disaster risk reduction, the Draft Articles provide for the duty of each State to take appropriate measures to prevent, mitigate, and prepare for disasters. However, they do in fact elaborate more on disaster response than on risk reduction.

In any event, the impression one gets from an impartial observation of the existing international legal framework on disasters is of a patchwork of legal norms, which are difficult to reconcile with the perceived need to achieve a coherent system of IDL, or even merely of IDRL. While there are undoubtedly some general principles of international law, including some of a normative character (*ie* general rules of customary law), that may also be applied to disaster prevention, preparedness and response, it still appears that most of the specific relevant rules derive from international treaties which are only binding on their respective parties. A notable exception is the complex of rules of IHL, an area in which international custom plays a comparatively much greater role, but these rules only apply to armed conflicts. Moreover, this latter observation calls for another, equally important, one: the relevant principles and rules of international law do not necessarily apply to all situations covered by the current concept of disaster and when it comes, in particular, to international treaties, these have a markedly sectoral character. For example, in the area of man-made disasters of technological origin, the international legal framework for nuclear incidents, mainly developed under the auspices of the International Atomic Energy Agency (IAEA), constitutes a comprehensive treaty framework which arguably has served, and could still serve to some extent, as a model for other areas of IDL. However, this framework can hardly be construed as embodying general customary rules that could be applied, in the absence of specific treaties, to such other areas.

Within this context, the present volume specifically explores the international legal framework governing incidents related to chemical, biological, radiological, and nuclear agents ('CBRN events'). These incidents include the use of chemical, biological and nuclear weapons by both State and non-State actors; the use of CBRN agents for smaller-scale criminal acts; industrial accidents involving the release of CBRN agents into the environment; as well as natural disasters or 'other calamities'. In this latter respect, the spread of the COVID-19 virus in 2019/2020 and the ensuing pandemic have sadly demonstrated the timeliness of such an analysis. In one of the introductory essays (Part 1), Micaela Frulli recognises that most of the rules of IDL could also be applied to incidents related to CBRN agents. At the same time, she makes the case for the need to investigate whether there is room for a better coordination of international efforts to prevent, prepare and respond to global CBRN threats and, in so doing, to adopt an 'all-hazards' approach focused on managing risks rather than simply managing 'disasters'.

The various essays devoted to prevention, preparedness, response and recovery in relation to CBRN events (Part 2) confirm, first of all, that while it may be possible to distinguish between such categories in theory, there is in practice considerable overlapping between them and that it is, therefore, difficult to analyse them separately. On the other hand, the conclusions reached in such diverse areas as terrorism, industrial accidents, and naturally occurring events (including epidemic outbreaks) confirm that, apart from a few binding UN Security Council resolutions (which relate to terrorism only and whose legitimacy has sometimes been put in doubt), it is very difficult to envisage rules of international law applicable to all CBRN events. While the 'all-hazards' approach may be useful to give a general picture of the current legal situation, a more sectoral approach cannot be avoided when it comes to a more specific analysis. Thirdly, the perception that the international legal framework for nuclear and radiological events is comparatively more developed than others is also, in my opinion, confirmed. While this should not discourage the further strengthening of that specific legal framework, more attention should be devoted to other CBRN events, in respect of which *soft law* is still paramount. In this context, the studies devoted by the Sant'Anna School team to naturally occurring events are especially interesting and timely since the ongoing COVID-19 pandemic has further demonstrated that such events can have a major disruptive effect on both human health and the world's socio-economic systems. The pandemic has also shown that the existing legal framework, though comparatively well-developed, needs further strengthening, especially as concerns prevention and implementation.

Part 3 specifically relates to international obligations applicable to CBRN weapons. The analysis by various Authors from the Universities of Florence and Turin confirms, in my opinion, that the dichotomy between, on the one hand, the apparently very restrictive approach embodied in the UN Charter rules on the use of armed force and, on the other, the very wide interpretations of those same rules put forward by some important States, casts some doubt on the effectiveness of current *jus ad bellum*, and makes the perspective of *jus in bello* more interesting and rewarding. On the other hand, when it comes to the use of CBRN weapons, IHL itself is torn between the application of some important general principles – such as, among others, the principle of discrimination, the prohibition on using weapons causing unnecessary suffering, and the prohibition on means of warfare causing widespread, long-term and severe damage to the environment – which would arguably make the use of all CBRN weapons intrinsically unlawful, and the existence of specific prohibitions on the use of certain weapons which currently only cover chemical and biological weapons. Although, as Diego Mauri points out, it is hard to think of weapons whose use in armed conflict is more likely to fail to discriminate between permissible and impermissible targets, to provoke unnecessary suffering and to cause widespread, long-term and severe damage to the environment, a clear-cut prohibition on the use of nuclear weapons binding on all States currently does not exist, nor is it likely to emerge in the foreseeable future, despite the recent entry into force of the Treaty on the Prohibition of Nuclear weapons (TPNW). The patchwork impression is further confirmed by the book's very interesting analysis of disarmament and arms control obligations, where, in contrast to the regime of *jus in bello*, nuclear weapons and, more recently, chemical weapons have been subjected to a much more stringent regime than biological weapons, especially when it comes to compliance mechanisms. Moreover, in the nuclear field, the distinction between nuclear weapons States and other States, which is sanctioned by the Treaty on the Non-Proliferation of Nuclear Weapons (NPT), is not likely to disappear anytime soon, again, despite the entry into force of the TPNW.

In Part 4, a number of 'horizontal issues' are examined, such as the role played by international human rights law (IHRL) and international environmental law (IEL). As far as IHRL is concerned, there is an analysis of the admissibility of introducing limitations on human rights in response to the risk of CBRN events (or their actual occurrence), where it is rightly argued that the invocation of general derogation clauses contained in HR treaties should be a measure of last resort and that, in most cases, ordinary limitations on specific human rights that are foreseen by the same treaties should be sufficient to strike a balance between community interests and individual rights and liberties. In addition, there is also a timely analysis of how 'positive' IHRL obligations – whereby States are required to take active steps to protect individuals against violations committed by third parties or that arise from dangerous situations – can be considered as complementary rules applicable to CBRN event prevention, preparedness, response and recovery. Similarly, as far as IEL is concerned, the point is made that CBRN event risk management would benefit from greater coordination and enhanced synergies in the interpretation and application of IEL norms to such events. Moreover, *soft law* instruments increasingly recognise the need to impose obligations on private enterprises and business actors, as well as the need to apply existing due diligence obligations of States to information and communication technologies (ICTs), in order to prevent CBRN events and mitigate their consequences.

Part 5 relates to enforcement mechanisms and remedies and focuses, on the one hand, on the criminalisation and prosecution of CBRN-related offences and, on the other, on redress mechanisms available to victims of CBRN events. From the point of view of international criminal law, although some CBRN-related offences may in fact amount to war crimes, crimes against humanity or acts of genocide, the most interesting conclusions relate, in my opinion, to CBRN-related violations not amounting to such international crimes. While the impression of fragmentation given by the existing legal framework is once again confirmed, the point is made that, in the absence of general obligations applicable regardless of the type of CBRN event or agent, recent IHRL case law aiming at a better protection of the right to life may play a role in filling the gap. This further confirms the relevance of IHRL, which, as I already pointed out, is emphasised from a more general point of view in Part 4 of the book. The same goes for obligations to provide victims of CBRN events with access to adequate remedies. Depending on the applicable legal regime, with respect to remedies, the emphasis is placed either on measures of assistance or on civil liability, but IHRL – as well as IHL in cases of armed conflict – may again play a significant role in filling existing gaps.

Last but not least, mention must also be made of the specific analyses of the distribution of powers and cooperation patterns under European Union law, conducted in various sections of the book by Federico Casolari and others from the University of Bologna team. These sections are especially interesting and also timely, in particular (once again) as regards epidemic events in light of the COVID-19 pandemic. The limits of the highly fragmented and, arguably, overly flexible EU legal framework, applicable to 'disasters' in general and to CBRN events in particular, are clearly brought to light. Only time will tell whether the current discussions and initiatives aimed at strengthening the EU disaster management framework will come to a successful conclusion.

By way of a general conclusion, I think it may be stated that it is currently difficult to envisage the rapid development of a coherent set of customary and/or treaty law rules covering all aspects of CBRN risk management. There currently seem to be no easy answers to the basic questions raised in the introductory essays, *ie* whether or not it makes sense to apply strategies adopted in other sectors to CBRN events, or whether or not it makes sense to apply strategies developed from a security or counter-terrorism perspective to other events such as natural disasters or pandemics. However, or perhaps because of this, the review and analysis of the current state of international law in this field, and the 'all-hazards' approach adopted in this book, are very interesting and useful. Indeed, when it comes to IDL, including the law relating to CBRN events, 'the teachings of the most qualified publicists of the various nations' – which, under Article 38 of the Statute of the International Court of Justice, are considered as one of the 'subsidiary means for the determination of rules of law' – still play an important role, both in trying to give, as much as possible, a complete and coherent picture of the current state of the law and in pointing the way forward for its further development.

Index

Please note that this Index only mentions international law instruments receiving extended coverage in the volume.

www.ingramcontent.com/pod-product-compliance
Lightning Source LLC
LaVergne TN
LVHW021724021026
849161LV00004BA/661

9789004507982